friend H. Ariketn
with best
wishes
Vittorio

Growth-Oriented
Adjustment Programs

Washington, DC
April 1988

Growth-Oriented Adjustment Programs

Edited by

Vittorio Corbo
Morris Goldstein
Mohsin Khan

Proceedings of a Symposium
Held in Washington, D.C.
February 25–27, 1987

International Monetary Fund
The World Bank

Library of Congress Cataloging-in-Publication Data

Growth-oriented adjustment programs.

   Volume presents the proceedings of a symposium held in Washington, D.C., Feb. 25–27, 1987.
   Bibliography: p.
   1. Economic policy—Congresses. 2. Industry and state—Congresses. 3. Economic stabilization—Congresses. I. Corbo, Vittorio. II. Goldstein, Morris, 1944–   . III. Khan, Mohsin S. IV. International Monetary Fund. V. World Bank.
HD73.G76   1987   338.9   87-21361
ISBN 0-939934-92-2

Preface

This volume presents the proceedings of a symposium on growth-oriented adjustment programs that was organized jointly by the International Monetary Fund and the World Bank and held in Washington on February 25–27, 1987. Participating in the symposium were policymakers, academics and research scholars, representatives of multilateral organizations and commercial banks, staff members of the Fund and the World Bank, and executive directors of both institutions. Their purpose was to review the design of, and scrutinize the economic rationale behind, adjustment programs supported by the Bank and the Fund, and to examine how best to help developing countries achieve balance of payments stability with sustainable economic growth.

As the proceedings show, there are no easy answers to these issues. During the symposium, discussion ranged freely over, inter alia, the scope and mix of policies designed to achieve adjustment *and* growth, reliance on market forces versus state intervention as means of achieving export-led growth and a vigorous agricultural sector, the appropriate roles of commercial banks and official creditors in providing finance to developing countries, and the case for radical changes in developing-country debt strategy versus continuation of the present strategy. These conflicts were, however, neither unexpected nor undesirable, as a full and open examination of these issues had from the beginning been the raison d'être of the symposium.

The symposium was organized by Vittorio Corbo, of the Development Research Department of the World Bank, Morris Goldstein of the Fund's Research Department, and Mohsin Khan, who was with the Bank's Development Research Department when the symposium was being planned and is now with the Fund's Research Department. David Driscoll of the Fund's External Relations Department edited the proceedings for publication.

During the symposium a number of participants, observing that adjustment is a long-term enterprise, underlined the desirability of even closer cooperation between the Fund and the World Bank so that the expertise of each institution might more effectively complement and corroborate that of the other. It is hoped that the joint organization of this symposium and the joint publication of these proceedings will be seen as a determined step in this direction.

Contents

Session 2: Country Study

Economic Stabilization and Structural Adjustment: The Case of Turkey

Comment

Round Table Discussion

Opening Remarks

Barber Conable

President
World Bank

The last five years have been critical for a large number of developing countries in terms of both current economic conditions and prospects for future growth. During the 1960s and 1970s, when trade opportunities expanded and external financing was readily available, many developing countries achieved high rates of growth. In all too many instances, however, growth occurred despite major policy and structural weaknesses. In some countries, distorted domestic prices encouraged inefficient investment decisions; in others, large fiscal deficits led to persistently high inflation and balance of payments crises—and often saddled these economies with heavy foreign debt.

These weaknesses became evident in the early 1980s, with the advent of a series of adverse developments in the international economy, including slower growth in the industrial countries, falling prices for primary commodities, rising international interest rates, and sharp reductions in the availability of external financing to developing countries.

The combined effect of these two sets of factors—ineffective policies in developing countries plus negative international economic trends—has halted and, in some cases actually eroded, development. To survive, many developing countries have had no alternative but to design and implement major reforms to restore sustainable growth. Some have made substantial progress. Others have not. The nature, the benefits and the costs of these reform programs are the subject matter of this symposium.

The promotion of structural changes that support sustainable long-term growth is important not just to developing countries—it is

3

indeed increasingly preoccupying policymakers in industrial countries as well. At present we in the development business are particularly concerned with problems and prospects in two groups of national economies whose need for restoring growth is most pressing: countries laboring under an especially heavy burden of external debt (mainly in Latin America), and countries whose recent development experience and future outlook are the least robust (mainly in sub-Saharan Africa).

While the underlying causes of the two groups' difficulties have been somewhat different, and while each group is itself far from homogenous in terms of its members' past developmental experience and current and future needs, their recent growth experience has been more or less the same. For the heavily indebted middle-income countries, average annual gross domestic product (GDP) growth dropped from a healthy 6.3 percent a year in 1965 to less than one half of 1 percent a year in 1980–86. For the lowest income countries, growth fell from 5.3 percent in 1965–80 to a negative annual average of minus 0.5 percent during 1980–86.

By facing reality and trying to adjust, some of these countries have managed to cut their current account deficits and to reestablish some of the conditions for sustainable medium-term growth. In many cases, however, investment and imports have been cut to levels where both current and future output have suffered. Not surprisingly, even after five years of adjustment and some important progress, rates of growth are still very modest. In many cases, per capita consumption remains below 1980 levels.

Meanwhile, bilateral donors and multilateral financial and development institutions, and the Bank and Fund in particular, have been heavily involved in helping these countries to plan and execute essential reform programs. Naturally, country-specific circumstances must determine the details of individual programs, and these programs must be devised by the countries themselves. Nevertheless, over the past five years we had several success stories to evaluate and learn from, and the Bank, the Fund, and our member countries have together accumulated some collective experience about some of the critical components that are common to all successful adjustment strategies.

First, in countries in which inflation and balance of payment crises are major problems it is extremely difficult to achieve adjustment with growth. Nevertheless, the stabilization effort must be undertaken within the framework of an adjustment program that permits sustainable growth. In particular, if government expenditures need to be reduced, the cuts must be selective in order to protect investments that are growth enhancing and programs that benefit the most needy.

Second, to be successful, an adjustment program must achieve appropriate macroeconomic balance and simultaneously raise the level of output obtainable from existing resources. Production in many countries is often crippled by distorted factor and commodity prices, inefficient public sector enterprises, and incentives that are biased in favor of inward-looking uncompetitive industries that hinder the emergence of an export base. Reversing these existing adverse conditions is a sine qua non of any growth-oriented adjustment effort.

Third, to finance the higher investment required to achieve sustainable growth, it is necessary both to raise domestic savings and to obtain additional resources from abroad. Foreign direct investment has been a neglected element; it can play an important role. In middle-income countries, additional foreign borrowing on commercial terms, if utilized efficiently, can stimulate growth in output and ultimately enhance these countries' capacity to service their foreign debt. The lowest income countries can't do it without concessional financing.

It takes more than the most heroic adjustment efforts of the developing countries to guarantee the emergence of new potential for growth. Appropriate complementary actions on the part of industrial countries, commercial banks, and international development and financial institutions are also essential. For example, industrial countries must adopt macroeconomic policies geared to the creation of sustainable growth with low inflation and moderate interest rates. This growth is necessary to provide a market for the exports of developing countries and to sustain a more open trading system. For the developing world, trade and growth go hand in hand. In addition, commercial banks must increase their lending in support of adjustment programs in the highly indebted countries. The only alternative for developing countries is to try to finance their investment requirements solely from domestic savings and the relatively limited funds available from international development institutions. This would require further cuts in their living standards.

Countries in sub-Saharan Africa face acute problems of structural adjustment on top of many severe long-term development problems. These countries' governments must address such fundamental issues as weak physical and human capital infrastructure, inadequate institutions, rapid rates of population growth, and depletion of natural resources. For the highly indebted countries, on the other hand, the primary long-term problem is to use their existing assets in ways which will restore creditworthiness. On the external financing side, sub-Saharan Africa is in special need of concessional assistance, while restoration of support from commercial sources is essential for the heavily indebted countries.

On the multilateral front, the establishment of the structural adjustment facility at the Fund and the successful agreement for the IDA 8 replenishment at the World Bank are encouraging developments. Beyond these, additional resources are needed to ensure that sufficient financing is available to sustain adjustment programs in countries that are making, or are willing to make, true appropriate reforms.

Clearly, strong and sustainable growth is the surest guarantee for improving life for the poorest people of our developing member countries—and comprehensive programs of adjustment are the best hope of strong and sustainable growth. Nevertheless, the international development community must recognize the painful reality that adjustment programs will result in some temporary unemployment, and in real and difficult short-term reductions in living standards—which sometimes affect the poorest segment of the population most harshly. We must therefore be ready to assist member countries in framing specific targeted programs designed to alleviate the short-term impact of adjustment programs on the poor.

Finally, it is essential that we keep in mind the fundamental point that adjustment programs, however essential, are no more than instruments in the process of fostering economic development. Thus we must make every effort to ensure that preoccupation with the means of adjustment does not overshadow our vision of the ends of long-term development objectives. In the final analysis, the very best that we can do is to be faithful stewards and facilitators in the progressive process of helping the peoples of the developing world realize their capacity for growth, in order to liberate them from the tyranny of poverty, hunger, and underdevelopment.

Michel Camdessus

Managing Director
International Monetary Fund

It is a great pleasure to welcome you to this Joint IMF-World Bank Symposium on "Growth-Oriented Adjustment Programs." I am delighted that we were able to attract such a distinguished and experienced group of participants, and I am looking forward to a stimulating exchange of ideas. I hope that all participants will feel free to speak candidly about existing or emerging policy problems and about possible solutions. Indeed, it was to assure the right atmosphere for such a frank dialogue that we decided against asking representatives from the financial press to join us.

I would put the key issue facing the symposium as follows: how can we help the developing countries to achieve balance of payments viability and a return to normal debtor-creditor relationships in a way that promotes sustainable economic growth, open and growing international trade, and international monetary cooperation? During the next days, we shall be discussing the "lessons" that seem to emerge from earlier adjustment strategies; the combination of macroeconomic and structural policies that offers the best prospect of combining adjustment with durable growth; and the roles that a healthy global environment and adequate external financing need to play in a growth-oriented adjustment strategy. I am here to benefit from your diagnoses and prescriptions. They are of critical importance for me at the beginning of my mandate in the Fund. I am here to learn from you. Nevertheless, perhaps I can at least get our discussion started by sharing a few thoughts with you on these issues.

My first point is that in analyzing the relationship between adjustment and growth, we should reject two—let us say—simplistic arguments. One is that there is an inherent conflict between adjustment and growth. The other is that growth follows automatically from adjustment. Allow me to elaborate.

Economies that suffer from rampant inflation, large budget deficits, pervasive trade restrictions, misaligned exchange rates, unrealistic interest rates, heavy external debt, and repeated bouts of capital flight just cannot and do not grow rapidly for any sustained period of time. Put in other words, you cannot maintain good growth performance by attempting to avoid adjustment. Equally, we should recognize that when adjustment is delayed to the point at which a country's reserves and creditworthiness are depleted, it is likely to involve excessive cuts in investment, in imports, and in other productive expenditures. Such chaotic or "anarchic" adjustment can mortgage future growth.

I would propose an alternative hypothesis: the extent to which adjustment is conducive to growth depends in good measure on the *quality* of adjustment. Specifically, growth can best be combined with adjustment if adjustment takes the form of increases in export capacity, in savings, and in economic efficiency, and if high-quality investment projects are allowed to survive. Look at the experience of the past four years. The indebted developing countries have achieved an enormous improvement in their current account position—their combined deficit had fallen from roughly 18 percent of exports in 1982 to about 4 percent in 1984, before rising somewhat under the pressure of falling commodity prices to almost 5 percent last year. What is noteworthy is that the countries that were best able to protect growth during this difficult adjustment period were those that maintained strong export performance, that kept domestic savings and investment rates from falling sharply, and that shared the adjustment burden between increased aggregate supply and reduced aggregate demand.

The right kind of adjustment will not, of course, take place by chance. It requires that developing countries put in place a set of macroeconomic and structural policies that encourages exporting, saving, sound investment decisions, and cost-saving techniques, and that establishes an environment of overall financial stability. It also requires that creditors assist this effort by providing adequate financing, by maintaining an open and growing market for developing country exports, and by fostering an appropriate structure of exchange rates and interest rates. The important thing is that we have the capacity collectively to *manage* the adjustment process in a way that gives growth the consideration it deserves. But the reality is that we have not yet consistently done so. Perhaps this symposium can help us identify how we can more successfully mobilize the major parties into action.

Let me now turn to my second main point: the characteristics of a successful growth-oriented adjustment program. I would lay particular stress on three features: the need for country-specific program design, for a comprehensive medium-term framework, and for popular support.

Developing countries are too diverse—in economic structure, in the size of existing debt burdens, in their relations with creditors, in political sensitivities, and in the nature of existing imbalances—to allow a "standard" policy package to be effective. In some cases, the first order of business may be fiscal strengthening paired with exchange rate action and deindexation. In other cases, the pressing need may be for trade liberalization, reform of tax systems, overhaul of public enterprises, relaxation of price controls, and financial-sector reform. And in yet others, increases in producer prices, export diversification, and efforts to unlock more concessional finance may take priority. The case-by-case approach is not a slogan. It is merely sensible program design. I know that some observers see the Fund as seeking to impose a uniform, mechanistic approach to adjustment on all its member countries. I must tell you that in my few weeks in the Fund I have searched carefully through the cupboards for such a policy straitjacket. I have not found it. And if I had found it, I would have destroyed it.

The underlying conditions for durable growth can rarely be achieved in the short run. This is especially the case where the state's role in the economy has been allowed to become overextended during a period of decades and where the structure of goods, labor, and financial markets is in need of alteration. Such structural reforms often require far-reaching preparation and take time to realize their intended effects. Yet little is to be gained from delay. Recourse to on-again, off-again demand-management programs within an outmoded and uncompetitive structure of production is hardly an attractive alternative. Wanting to grow faster is not enough. It has to be backed up by an integrated program of macroeconomic and structural policies implemented with perseverance over the medium term. I might add that poor countries, despite their difficult circumstances, cannot be exempt from such policy reforms. Indeed, it is precisely because their living standards are so low that they can least afford to tolerate weak policies. More and more, leaders in poor countries understand this and we are strongly committed to cooperate with them.

No program can succeed without the support of governments and of public opinion. Yet this support will be progressively harder to maintain the longer adjustment continues without growth. That is why the 4 percent average growth performance of the indebted countries in 1984–86 is welcome. Even so, and reflecting the slow growth of the 1981–83 period, it is striking that real per capita gross domestic product in the indebted countries as a group has risen on average by only about 1 percent a year since 1980—a far cry from the 3 percent average annual rate of increase of the 1960s and 1970s. If one uses real national income per capita as the relevant indicator, the picture is still worse. The period ahead is thus likely to be one where growth is just as necessary to sustain adjustment as adjustment is to sustain growth.

Effective policies in the developing countries—central as they are to a successful growth-oriented adjustment program—are not sufficient. This is my third point. Industrial countries can and should provide crucial support by following sound monetary and fiscal policies that are compatible with healthy, noninflationary growth of world demand, lower international interest rates, and an appropriate pattern of exchange rates; by rolling back protectionism; and by providing increased official development assistance and adequate official export credit. Clearly, it will be more difficult to make progress in reducing debt burdens if the real interest rate on debt exceeds the growth rate of developing-country exports, and if the incentives to adopt more "outward-looking" policy reforms are sapped by protectionist barriers. To work well, the adjustment process must be symmetric. We cannot have two standards of adjustment—one for industrial countries and the other for developing countries.

Banks too need to play their part. They are fully justified in asking their developing-country clients to undertake genuine policy reform so as to underpin any new net lending. This attitude on their part is much sounder than that which prevailed during the 1973–81 period when private lending expanded at an unsustainable rate. But we have to be careful not to now overdo things in the opposite direction. Major changes are taking place in the developing countries. But this progress is put at risk when there is inadequate support and understanding from creditors—to say nothing about endangering their own claims in these countries. Commercial banks cannot do the job alone. Other creditors and investors have to be brought more squarely into the action, and we must make full use of the considerable inventiveness of financial markets to design financial instruments that meet the needs of lenders and borrowers.

Finally, I come to the role of the Fund. Working in close collaboration with our colleagues in the World Bank, the Fund will continue to cooperate with countries in designing growth-oriented adjustment programs and in mobilizing the finances needed, including our own, to carry them out. I chose the word "cooperate" carefully. The Fund can help members to make better-informed decisions about the balance of payments, growth, and inflation implications of their policy choices. But the final choices must rest with the country itself. The Fund is also continuing its efforts to improve the effectiveness of multilateral surveillance, with particular emphasis on strengthening economic policy coordination among the largest industrial countries. The developing countries—no less than the industrial ones—have a vital interest in the outcome of those efforts.

Adjustment for durable growth in our membership is a central mission of the Fund. No one, I think, still challenges the precept that effective adjustment and sound finance are the allies—not the ene-mies—of growth and development. I hope that your suggestions will help us in the Fund and the Bank to adjust our own policies and procedures so as to serve better the evolving needs of our membership. After all, institutions, much like countries, cannot be static if they are to thrive. Just as countries sometimes need external expertise and support to help them adjust, we in the Bretton Woods Institutions welcome your ideas in helping us to adjust.

SESSION 1

Bank-Fund Papers

World Bank Programs for Adjustment and Growth

Constantine Michalopoulos
Director, Economic Policy Analysis and Coordination
Economics and Reasearch Staff
World Bank

The experience of developing countries in the last decade has helped dramatize the importance of macroeconomic policies for sustaining economic growth and adjusting successfully to unfavorable external shocks. The external shocks of the period showed up the structural weaknesses and the limited flexibility in many developing countries' economies—factors that frequently stemmed from their own economic policies.

Developing countries have responded with significant changes in their economic policies in the last few years. Nevertheless, in 1987, developing countries as a group clearly have not recaptured the growth momentum required to restore the per capita consumption levels of the early 1980s. Some, through the pursuit of effective policies, have by and large avoided the crises of recent years. A few, after sustaining significant declines in income and output, have been able to restore their growth momentum. In far too many others, however, the adjustment process remains incomplete. Moreover, a great deal of the adjustment that has taken place has involved severe compression of investment and imports with detrimental consequences for future growth.

Note: The author would like to thank Vittorio Corbo for his contribution in the preparation of this paper, and Susan Hume and Peter Bocock for research and editorial help, respectively. The author is also grateful for helpful comments provided by many colleagues and especially Manuel Guitián, Benjamin King, Anne Krueger, Salvatore Schiavo-Campo, Marcelo Selowsky, Ernest Stern, and Joseph Wood. The author is solely responsible for the views expressed in the paper, which are not necessarily those of the World Bank.

15

In the aftermath of the Seoul meetings of the World Bank and the International Monetary Fund in October 1985, an international consensus has evolved that restoration of growth in the developing countries requires the concerted efforts of these countries, international institutions (especially the World Bank and the Fund), bilateral donors, and commercial banks. In particular, it has been recognized that the World Bank and the Fund should play a coordinated role in helping developing countries develop policy packages to restore growth and creditworthiness (Development Committee (1986a)).

This paper attempts to answer three questions. First, what should be the main focus and content of domestic policy reform designed to promote sustainable growth in developing countries? Second, what are the implications of past experience with designing policies for adjustment and growth for future Bank programs in support of policy reform efforts in developing countries? Third, what kind of financial packages are suitable to support adjustment with growth in different country settings and what are the issues the Bank faces in putting together such packages?

In attempting to answer these questions, the paper explores the analytical underpinnings of, and developing country experience with, policy reforms aimed at adjustment and growth. It emphasizes a few policies recognizing that the details of policy prescriptions must be adapted to specific country circumstances. Next, the paper examines the experience of recent World Bank programs supporting policy reform in member countries. The lessons of this experience and the issues raised can also be helpful for designing new programs, which is the focus of this paper. But the limitations of this experience should be also recognized at the outset. The available evidence is far less comprehensive than comparable evidence on the project side. Moreover, many of these programs were introduced during periods of massive internal and external disequilibria, which in turn affected both the emphasis and the effectiveness of programs.

The last section of the paper presents conclusions and implications of the analysis for future World Bank programs. An effort is also made to identify areas where the understanding of the effects of policies is incomplete and additional analysis and research are needed.

The scope of the analysis is limited in that it does not address, except in passing, such critical issues for developing countries' growth and adjustment as developments in the international economic environment and in industrial countries' policies that affect the prospects of developing countries, the prospects for commercial bank lending and other private capital flows, the flow of official financing, nor issues of debt restructuring. The paper also does not address issues of Bank program implementation, such as the aspects of conditionality, disbursement, monitoring, and donor coordination on which program effectiveness depends. It would have been impossible to do justice to these important issues within the confines of a single paper.

The Problem of Adjustment with Growth

Structural change is the essence of development. Adjustment to changing domestic and international circumstances is a continuous challenge to all countries. At present the international community's attention and the focus of this paper are directed on the acute problems of adjustment and growth facing two specific sets of developing countries—a group of highly indebted middle-income countries with debt-servicing difficulties and the countries of sub-Saharan Africa.[1] In the former, annual gross domestic product (GDP) growth in 1981–86 averaged 0.6 percent (but -0.5 percent if Brazil is excluded). In the latter, growth over the same period was -0.4 percent. Output per capita fell over this period for both sets of countries.

The level of development, the institutional and political framework, and the constraints on structural change and growth vary from country to country. But there are some important similarities.

First, a number of countries in both groups have macroeconomic imbalances resulting in a high rate of open or suppressed inflation and unsustainable rates of domestic absorption. Macroeconomic stabilization is needed in these countries in order to restore the basis for future growth.

Second, debt burdens are heavy in both sets of countries. Servicing this debt absorbs a significant amount of domestic savings. Restoration of growth requires action to raise the productivity of existing and new capital and to increase the investment rate from current levels.

---

[1] For the purposes of this discussion the aggregates presented for the first group relate to the 17 countries identified in Development Committee (1986a). A listing of this country group is included in footnote 3 to Table 3. The sub-Saharan group includes all countries south of the Sahara, except South Africa.

Productivity, however, is often impaired by distorted factor and market prices by inefficient public sector enterprises and by a structure of incentives that has helped create inward-looking uncompetitive industries. To finance higher investment, it is necessary to raise domestic savings. But there are serious constraints on how much savings can increase. Marginal savings rates must exceed 50 percent or more in some highly indebted middle-income countries for long periods in order to service debt, make up for lower external financing, and provide a margin for additional investment. It is difficult to raise marginal savings rates, however, if per capita consumption has been stagnant or declining as it has for some time, especially in sub-Saharan Africa (Development Committee (1986a)).

Third, restoration of growth also requires a rapid expansion of exports in order to be able to transform domestic savings into the payments in foreign exchange. Additional foreign exchange earnings are needed to service their large external debt obligations—as well as to finance the higher volume of imports typically associated with increases in investment. This in turn requires a change in the composition of output in favor of trade. Such a structural shift is especially difficult in sub-Saharan African countries, which have relatively inflexible and undiversified economic structures. Moreover, the size of the structural change required has been magnified and the problems of adjustment exacerbated by a significant deterioration in the terms of trade of most primary commodity exporters.

Fourth, additional financing from abroad can help restore growth and ease the domestic savings constraint. In middle-income countries, additional foreign borrowing, if utilized efficiently, can stimulate output and domestic savings. Provided domestic savings grow faster than investment (and depending on the productivity of investment and other factors such as the level of international interest rates), net borrowing and the ratio of debt to gross national product (GNP) can decline over time, and these countries' capacity to service existing debt and maintain the momentum of growth can be restored.[2] But at present, new private capital inflows, on which these countries have traditionally depended for their finance, are severely limited (World Bank (1987)).

Additional capital flows to the low-income countries of sub-Saharan

---

[2] For details of the conditions see Selowsky and van der Tak (1986).

Africa need to be on concessional terms. Given the level of domestic savings, the existing debt burden and the productivity of the current capital stock and future investment, additional debt on commercial terms could not be serviced even if it were forthcoming, which it is not. But there are limits to the availability of new capital inflows on concessional terms, that is, Official Development Assistance (ODA), which ultimately must be obtained from developed country donors that also face budgetary constraints (Development Committee (1986b)).

Finally, implementation of macroeconomic stabilization and structural change can generate transitional costs in the form of unemployment. For example, a change in the structure of incentives is needed in order to promote a reallocation of resources more conducive to long-term growth. Productive resources are not redistributed instantaneously among alternative uses in response to changes in relative commodity and factor prices, however, and thus some temporary unemployment could result.

In addition to these general problems of structural change and growth, sub-Saharan Africa faces other long-term growth constraints. These include weak physical and human infrastructure, inadequate institutions, a rapid rate of population growth, and, until recently, severe drought that adversely affected agriculture, the mainstay of these countries' economies (World Bank (1986c)).

Adjustment would be facilitated by a supportive international environment, which in turn depends critically on actions by industrial countries (Development Committee (1986a)). Regardless of the environment, however, promoting structural change and restoring growth necessarily entails further policy reforms by the developing countries themselves. In summary, these reforms should aim to restore or maintain macroeconomic stability, raise overall efficiency and factor productivity in their economies, raise savings relative to consumption, and restructure production in favor of tradables.

Analytical Framework of Promoting Adjustment With Growth[3]

Given these domestic policy objectives, what can economic theory and past experience tell us about the kinds of policies that developing

---

[3] This section draws in part on Corbo and de Melo (1987 forthcoming) and Development Committee (1986a).

countries should pursue? This section provides a summary review
of experience on some of the key policy issues affecting structural
adjustment and growth.

Stabilization and Adjustment

Experience suggests that the presence in any country of prolonged
and significant aggregate imbalances—in the sense that the aggregate
demand for resources exceeds the amounts of resources available
internally or obtainable from abroad on appropriate terms—is inimical
to longer-term growth. Such imbalances cannot be sustained indefinitely, and the longer the imbalances persist, the greater the subsequent adjustment needed and the likely adverse impact of stabilization
on short-term output.

Macroeconomic imbalances usually manifest themselves in high
and unpredictable inflation and periodic balance of payments crises.
Significant inflation (open or repressed) is itself a source of resource
misallocation and an impediment to growth[4] (Fischer (1986), Yeager
(1981)). Inflation is inimical to raising the savings rate and to
channeling savings to productive investment. Uncertainty about
future inflation rates leads to concentration of financial transactions
in instruments with short- rather than long-term maturities, thus
reducing the availability of funds for long-term investment. High
inflation does not affect all prices and costs uniformly. At the same
time, it makes relative prices volatile and reduces their information
content for purposes of resource allocation. Finally, countries with
high inflation frequently introduce interest rate and price controls.
Interest rate controls result in negative real rates, which in turn lead
to credit rationing, distort investment decisions, and reduce the size
of the formal financial system. Price controls, on the other hand,
encourage the development of black market profiteering and rent
seeking while discouraging productive activities.

Periodic balance of payments crises result in cycles of expansion
and contraction of economic activity that constrict investment and

---

[4] What is "significant" varies from country to country and has to do in part with
historical experience that shapes future expectations and the actions of economic
agents. In Latin America, 25 percent a year may be used as a rule of thumb; but in
South East Asia half this rate may be too high.

long-term economic growth. As part of the stabilization effort, absorption must be reduced to a level compatible with the level of output plus the sustainable current account deficit. Monetary, fiscal, and exchange rate policies are the main instruments of a stabilization program. Fiscal and monetary policy have mainly absorption-reducing effects while exchange rate policy has primarily expenditure-switching effects.[5] The reduction in absorption needed to reduce inflation and to achieve a sustainable current account deficit will usually be accompanied by a reduction in the rate of growth of output. Indeed, a short-run slowdown in output growth is almost a prerequisite for successful stabilization because the success of stabilization depends on applying contractionary pressure to the economy as a whole. The slowdown in the economy will be less pronounced the greater the downward flexibility of product prices and wages and the greater the availability of external finance requiring less recourse to demand management policies.

The key issue for adjustment and growth is to find the combination of the three macroeconomic policy instruments that will, for any given level of external finance, attain stabilization objectives while also being the most supportive of future structural adjustment and the least disruptive to growth. In general, it might be more advantageous if a balanced approach is used and the burden of promoting overall adjustment is not placed on any single policy instrument. Naturally, if the overall macroeconomic imbalance can be traced to a particular cause, action to address that cause should be an important part of any stabilization package.

In recent periods, excessive absorption and inflation in developing countries have often been linked to large government budget deficits.[6] Action in reducing such deficits is usually a prerequisite to stabilization. *How* these deficits are reduced has a bearing on growth and adjustment. If the burden falls primarily on physical and social

---

[5] It should be noted, however, that fiscal and monetary policy also have secondary expenditure-switching effects through their effect on the composition of expenditure, and that devaluation policy also has secondary absorption-reducing effects through its effect on real private wealth.

[6] In some cases, however, the problem derives from a deterioration of the international environment manifested in sharply declining terms of trade; in many cases, a combination of domestic and international factors has been present.

infrastructure or essential maintenance activities, future growth will be compromised.

Moreover, if the reduction in absorption is not accompanied by a change in relative prices in favor of tradable goods, demand and output for both tradable and nontradable goods will need to be reduced. To minimize the reduction in total output needed to attain any targeted reduction in absorption, it is desirable to have a real exchange rate depreciation to engineer a shift in the composition of output (and expenditures) in favor of tradable goods (Corden (1981), Dornbusch (1980)). Such a shift is also a key objective in trade reforms designed to promote a medium-term restructuring of many developing countries' economies.

If there is neither fiscal deficit reduction nor exchange rate adjustment, the whole burden of stabilization must be borne by monetary policy, and it is more likely that long-term growth objectives will be adversely affected. This is because monetary policy will have to be so restrictive as to result in real interest rates high enough to crowd out interest-sensitive components of aggregate demand and especially private investment.

Finally, any stabilization program should avoid introducing distortions that could jeopardize successful adjustment. In particular, experience in several Latin American countries suggests that, if a country needs to reduce its anti-export bias and shift resources to tradables, real exchange rate appreciation or export taxes should not be used as a stabilization device (Corbo (1987, forthcoming)).

Structural Change and Growth

Stabilization alone does not guarantee growth. The specific components of a policy package that will induce structural change and growth will vary from country to country, depending on the country's current situation and existing policies and on the international environment and its future prospects. Recent reviews of the situation in many developing countries, however, suggest that the following policies require priority attention.

More resources can be mobilized for development by raising public savings through reductions in government expenditures or increases in revenues. Significant deficits persist in many countries, and there is considerable scope for the reduction of government expenditures without compromising economic growth and distribution objectives. Although public enterprises continue to soak up resources in several countries, public sector performance can be improved through better management, improved pricing policies, and in some cases, the privatization or closing down of inefficient public enterprises. Savings can also be introduced by better targeting of government support programs, for example, food subsidies, to the groups that truly need them.

Public savings can also be increased by broadening the tax base and improving revenue collection. In the absence of restraint on expenditures, however, efforts to generate additional government revenues might only result in the continued financing of low priority public sector activities and a reduction of private savings. On the other hand, lowering tax rates and rationalizing the tax system may improve overall incentives and promote social objectives without reducing government revenues (Development Committee (1986a, p. 19)).[7]

Private savings are stimulated by stable and predictable macroeconomic policies, particularly as they pertain to interest rate policies and inflation. Macroeconomic policies alone are frequently not sufficient, however. Raising private savings usually also requires strengthening of domestic financial institutions.

Greater economic efficiency and improved productivity of investment require the elimination of microeconomic distortions, as well as measures to improve the productivity of existing and future public sector investment. The most prevalent types of distortions are price controls, highly differentiated incentives in the trade sector, subsidized interest rates, credit rationing, and impediments to labor mobility and adjustment in the real wage. In highly regulated economies, resource allocation and productivity can be improved by removing price controls and simultaneously deregulating domestic factor markets. In addition, deregulation of financial markets (subject to appropriate banking supervision rules) improves credit allocation, thereby distributing investment more efficiently. Similarly, the elim-

---

[7] Jamaica recently instituted a comprehensive tax reform, which included the establishment of a single personal income tax rate of 33.5 percent, and a broadening of the tax base, while increasing the minimum exemption level without affecting total government revenues.

ination of labor market restrictions, which impede labor mobility, promotes more efficient allocation of labor.

Many countries have experienced low yields on the stock of public capital owing to poor investment decisions, inefficient operations, or both. Investment cutbacks undertaken by some countries have focused on specific uneconomic projects. In these cases, public investment cutbacks have clearly benefited the economy. For the most part, however, governments have not made such selective investment reductions. Completion of ongoing projects has often been justified without consideration of the project's economic merits, while aggregate public investment expenditures have declined (Choksi (1986)).

It is clear that government initiatives should also be aimed at improving the allocation of public investment. Such efforts imply a redistribution of public investment away from sectors, such as industry and agriculture, in which private investment is as (or more) efficient and toward activities that have externalities, such as human resource development and physical infrastructure. Similarly, a greater emphasis on the maintenance and rehabilitation of high-return public projects can result in significant expansion of output in many countries.

In order to stimulate a shift of resources and an increase in the supply of tradables, two sets of policy measures are important: a macroeconomic policy mix resulting in an appropriate real exchange rate, and a proper incentive structure that is neutral between production for the domestic and for the foreign market. The proper incentive structure requires, at a minimum, the elimination of the anti-export bias prevalent in many countries through liberalization and rationalization of the trade regime involving the removal of quantitative restrictions, reducing tariffs and eventually attaining relatively uniform tariffs on inputs and outputs, and lowering, and when possible, eliminating export taxes.

The experience of many developing countries has shown that a trade regime that does not discriminate between domestic and export sales not only increases exports but also encourages efficient import substitution industries. Trade liberalization results in the contraction of inefficient sectors and the expansion of new, efficient ones. Over time, a new and more efficient production structure develops that will be better suited to the international environment (Krueger and Michalopoulos (1985)). Moreover, the experience of the 1970s and early 1980s has shown that countries with trade regimes characterized by a balanced set of incentives towards exports and import-competing activities have been far more resilient to external shocks (Balassa (1984), Sachs (1985)).

The Strategy of Reform

There is broad agreement on the nature of the reform packages discussed above. Uncertainties become more prominent at the implementation stage, because implementation involves the dynamics of reform—about which less is known and which depends partly on initial conditions and partly on political considerations that vary from country to country.

Three sets of issues need to be addressed: the sequencing of the program, the speed of the reforms, and the appropriate macroeconomic policies for transition to a less distorted economy.

Sequencing of Reforms

There are two broad sequencing issues: first, the sequencing of policy measures aimed at stabilization and those that focus on structural adjustment, and second, the sequence of reforms to remove distortions when many markets are initially regulated.

There is little disagreement that structural adjustment is easier if it takes place in a stable macroeconomic environment, especially one in which inflation is under control.[8] The reasons for this stem from the links between stabilization and trade reform, which is usually a key element in promoting structural change over the medium term. On the one hand, successful stabilization depends on applying contractionary pressure to the economy as a whole; on the other hand, the rationalization of trade policies calls for contraction of highly protected import-competing activities and expansion of export-oriented activities (and efficient import-competing ones). With simultaneous application of both programs, the net contractionary pressure on highly protected import-competing activities might be so strong that it could lead to business failures and significant

---

[8] How much stabilization is needed before trade liberalization and other reform steps are taken is, however, an open question.

transitional unemployment and other costs, or generate strong opposition which undermines the liberalization effort (Mussa (1987)).

Another problem might arise because of limited downward price
flexibility. A successful trade reform is helped by a quick export
response. If product prices are relatively inflexible downward, then
the supply response of export activities will be seriously delayed and
the whole effort to rationalize the structure of incentives could be
put in jeopardy. Of course, the frequent presence of unutilized
capacity in the tradables sector may well minimize this problem in
practice.

An initial real devaluation, besides helping achieve demand management objectives, can also support the rationalization of trade
incentives needed to achieve the desired improvement in the relative
prices of exportables. For those countries that have discriminated
against exportables for a long time, an up-front improvement in the
relevant incentives may be necessary to move resources toward
exportables (Mussa (1987)). Devaluation, however, will also temporarily accelerate inflation or weaken the fight against it. In many
countries, the devaluation will also increase the cost of food imports
which raises issues about how to deal with the implications of such
increased costs for the urban poor.

In practice, the onset of a balance of payments crisis has been
viewed as a politically opportune occasion to undertake a variety of
reforms, including trade liberalization. While there are historical
examples of simultaneous achievement of stabilization and structural
adjustment involving reform of the structure of trade incentives,
pursuit of both objectives at the same time presents difficulties.[9] One
of the most extensive studies of trade liberalization reforms has
concluded that their failures have stemmed mainly from the failure
of the accompanying anti-inflationary programs (Krueger (1978)). This
conclusion, however, in no way implies that certain other aspects of
structural reform, for example, rationalization of public sector expenditures including shifts of public sector investment to support
expansion in the output of tradables, should not occur at the same
time as stabilization. Indeed, the success of stabilization efforts may
well depend on such early actions.

---

[9] The current Mexican reform program tries to accomplish both sets of objectives; it
is too soon to tell how successful it is going to be.

Economic theory offers little guidance about an optimal sequence for removing market distortions. Nevertheless, some broad conclusions can be derived from general principles that recognize that the objective of structural adjustment is to achieve a reasonable and sustainable rate of growth.

One question is the sequencing of liberalization of domestic markets relative to liberalization of economic relations with the rest of the world. Little is known on this issue or on the sequencing of domestic reforms, for example, of agricultural pricing or tax regimes.[10] Much of the analysis of sequencing has focused on liberalization of international accounts. Experience from some countries, such as Yugoslavia, suggests, however, that domestic factor market liberalization should precede other reforms, because if factor mobility is significantly impaired, the benefits of reforms in product markets cannot be realized.

With respect to international accounts, it is usually argued that the current account of the balance of payments should be liberalized first, leaving the liberalization of the capital account until much later (McKinnon (1982), Frenkel (1982 and 1983), Krueger (1984), Edwards (1984)). Two arguments have been put forward for such a sequence. First, since asset prices are determined by the present value of income streams, income streams generated by distorted prices will result in distorted asset prices and thus, trade in assets will take place at distorted prices (Krueger (1984)). For example, incremental capital inflows in an environment of trade distortions may well be channeled to inefficient, protected industries. Second, since asset markets generally adjust much faster than commodity markets, liberalization of the capital account could result in large capital movements with unwanted consequences for the real exchange rate. By the same argument, the need to improve the overall balance of payments requires that the current and capital accounts be brought into line with each other. Thus, even though the two accounts tend to respond at different speeds, the overall constraint implies that the two speeds of adjustment must be harmonized. It is much easier to achieve this by slowing down capital flows than by accelerating current account liberalization (Frenkel (1983)).

---

[10] A forthcoming World Bank comparative study on agricultural pricing will focus on some of these issues (see Krueger, Schiff, and Valdes (1987)).

This point could be extended further by arguing that, within the current account, import flows respond faster than export flows. Consequently, opening up the capital account first could jeopardize the overall process of trade liberalization by producing a sharp increase in import flows much in advance of the export expansion. Some temporary measures to accelerate the supply response of exports could therefore play a central role in a successful trade liberalization. Similarly, external financing can provide the needed cushion until exports do respond.

Speed of Reforms

The issue is how quickly particular reforms should be implemented. Should trade be liberalized quickly or over 5 or 10 years? Should price controls in agriculture be removed at a stroke or gradually? Should interest rate ceilings be lifted at once or progressively?

In approaching these and other questions of implementation, it is essential to keep in mind that structural adjustment is not an end in itself. Rather, it is a means for achieving a more satisfactory and sustainable rate of output growth by using existing resources more efficiently, by encouraging savings, and by raising the efficiency of new investment. As resource allocation depends on expectations about prices, the credibility of any reform is important. In particular, reform initiatives need to be phased in terms of realistic timetables for reaching their objectives, which may differ from one policy to another and from one country to another.

The larger the original disequilibrium and the faster the intended speed of policy implementation, the greater the transitional costs of adjustment. A reform package that ignores the pace at which adjustment to the reforms can reasonably be expected to take place (a variable that is partly determined by political circumstances) runs a serious risk of failure and undermines the credibility of future reform efforts.

The credibility of a reform package might be enhanced by including policies aimed to speed up the adjustment called for by the reforms. Indeed, from the rational expectations viewpoint, issues of coherence and credibility are important in determining the likely effect of a reform package on such variables as the size and direction of new investment and thus on the success or failure of the program (Calvo (1986a and 1986b)).

On the foreign trade side, for example, the main purpose of a liberalization and rationalization of the trade regime is to raise total factor productivity by eliminating discrimination against export-oriented industries (and efficient import-competing industries) and by reducing the variance of incentives across import-competing activities as well as helping to shift resources to tradables. The speed of liberalization must therefore depend on the speed with which resources can be expected to be reallocated to the sectors that have hitherto been discriminated against; otherwise substantial unemployment could result. Initial conditions specific to each country will determine the speed at which the redeployment of resources can take place. For example, the smaller the increment of GNP that is channeled to new investment, the slower should be the speed of trade liberalization. Similarly, the greater the extent of labor mobility and the more competitive the labor market, the more quickly can resources be reallocated, and thus the faster trade rationalization can proceed. Actual experience in several countries suggests that unemployment has increased significantly only in a few cases of trade liberalization (Papageorgiou and others (1986)).

Whatever the initial conditions, a reform undertaken within an agreed and reasonably paced timetable offers major advantages.[11] First, the required reallocation of resources will not occur unless the signal given is strong enough and in a clear enough direction to make the reform credible. Second, an unduly slow pace of reforms will delay the development of export activities and interest groups whose support for reform could help counter the antagonism toward reform of existing vested interests (Papageorgiou and others (1986)). Nevertheless, the pace of reform in trade, for example, does not necessarily imply that the same pace of reform is appropriate when dealing with, say, reform of agricultural pricing. In the latter case, a large initial change may be politically difficult to implement and would in any case need to be cushioned by the establishment of a safety net to help the urban poor whose food prices would rise.

The speed of deregulation of financial markets also needs to take

---

[11] What is a "reasonable pace" would obviously vary by country. But experience suggests that a lot can be accomplished within two to four years.

into account initial conditions. For example, if regulation has led to a substantial proportion of financial institutions' assets being held at below market rates, and if real lending rates are substantially negative, then deregulation of interest rates will create difficulties for existing financial intermediaries. In particular, if deposit and lending rates are deregulated simultaneously and new entrants are allowed into the financial system, existing banks will be forced to pay market rates, with the result that they may experience substantial capital losses. This could jeopardize the functioning of the overall financial system. A transition phase may be appropriate when lending rates can be deregulated first and deposit rates gradually thereafter. In this way, the capital losses of existing banks would be minimized; then, as existing preferential loans come to maturity, controls on deposit rates could be lifted over time. A similar problem could arise if the banking system has in its portfolio a large proportion of nonperforming loans that are being financed by depositors. If no direct action is taken to provide alternative financing for these loans, financial deregulation could jeopardize existing financial institutions.

Similar considerations apply to deregulation of controls on international capital flows. On the one hand, if deposit rates are below the free market level, rapid liberalization of capital flows will result in capital outflows that would weaken the domestic financial system. On the other hand, if domestic interest rates are free and substantially *above* international levels (when expressed in the same currency), decontrol of capital flows might result in large capital *inflows* that would create a real exchange rate appreciation, which might in turn jeopardize the success of trade liberalization efforts that might have been pursued simultaneously (Bruno (1983), Corbo and de Melo (1987)).

Macroeconomic Policies During the Adjustment Process

During a liberalization of external accounts, macroeconomic policy has to accomplish a number of complex and difficult tasks; it must simultaneously ensure an appropriate and stable real exchange rate, a low inflation rate, and a sustainable balance of payments position.

The importance of an early devaluation was noted above. Besides exchange rate policy, other elements of macroeconomic policy should also be designed to support the liberalization effort. Thus, for example, where the exchange rate is pegged according to some rule, monetary expansion should be compatible with the rule, so as to avoid a loss of confidence in it that might in turn jeopardize the success of the overall reform package.

Fiscal policy must also ensure that the fiscal deficit is compatible with the domestic credit expansion and the available external financing (Buiter (1986)). Also, the part of the deficit that is financed in the domestic capital market should not crowd out the financing of the private sector—especially in activities that need to expand. Likewise, credit policy should ensure access to credit at competitive rates for the expanding sectors, while simultaneously denying subsidized credit to previously heavily protected import-competing sectors (because its availability could slow down their adjustment). Finally, measures to introduce greater flexibility in the labor market will be needed in order to allow for a drop in the real wage in previously heavily protected sectors, or to allow the reallocation of labor toward the sectors that were previously discriminated against. Otherwise, significant unemployment will result, in turn raising the transition costs of adjustment.

World Bank Programs

Program Instruments

The World Bank has always stressed the need to use limited investable resources efficiently, the importance of identifying investment priorities in recipient countries, and the restriction of its own role to projects promising a high rate of return. It has also recognized that it is virtually impossible to have a good project in a bad policy environment and has thus consistently tried to promote appropriate pricing policies for public utilities, for instance, and later for agriculture—sectors in which considerable Bank resources were being channeled (Baum and Tolbert (1985)). Relatively less emphasis was placed, however, on efforts to support changes in the macroeconomic environment or in other economy-wide policies of developing countries.

As the events of the last decade unfolded, World Bank programs also changed. While project and sector investment activities continued to absorb the largest portion of World Bank loans and credits, new instruments were introduced such as Structural Adjustment Loans (SALs) and Sectoral Adjustment Loans (SELs) and Credits, which focused directly on supporting developing countries' programs and policies of structural reform.

There are currently five categories of Bank lending operations: Specific Investment Loans; Sector operations, which include Sector Investment and Maintenance Loans, Financial Intermediary Loans and Sector Adjustment Loans; Structural Adjustment Loans; Technical Assistance Loans; and Emergency Reconstruction Loans. In practice, the conceptual distinctions between these categories are sometimes blurred, and specific operations can combine different categories.[12]

Developing country policy issues arise in different contexts in almost all categories of loans. But the focus tends to be different in each. Specific project and sector investment loans (and also in Financial Intermediary Loans), focus on specific policies that affect the viability of the project or the entity being assisted, that is, input and output prices, lending rates to sub-borrowers, and the like. Similarly, Technical Assistance Loans focus primarily on institutional strengthening and support. By contrast, the objective of Sector Adjustment Loans is to promote the introduction and effective implementation of the sector policies necessary for sustained economic growth. Finally, Structural Adjustment Loans focus on macroeconomic policies and associated institutional changes at the country level—although they frequently emphasize reforms of special relevance to particular sectors in which adjustment is most urgently needed.[13] Thus there is a lending instrument continuum, one end of which focuses on policies and institutions that ensure the viability of a narrowly defined project, while the other is concerned with the overall macroeconomic policies and institutions of a country.

The above does not exclude addressing macroeconomic policies through specific projects. Indeed, heightened concern about the

---

[12] Prior to the introduction of structural adjustment lending in the early 1980s and in some instances thereafter, the Bank has provided a small number of program loans and credits with a similar overall policy focus.

[13] The Bank's *Operational Manual* defines structural adjustment lending as "non-project lending to support programs of policy and institutional change necessary to modify the structure of an economy so that it can maintain both its growth rate and the viability of its balance of payments in the medium term" (*Operational Manual*, Statement No.3.58, Annex II, November 1982).

Table 1. Distribution of World Bank Loans and Credits by Lending Instrument, FY 1975–86

(In percent)

Lending Instrument	1975	Average 1979–80	Average 1981–82	1983	1984	1985	1986
Specific Investment Loans	58.5	58.5	44.7	39.4	41.1	49.6	45.2
Sector Investment Loans	15.9	22.5	26.3	24.6	26.4	27.0	19.0
Financial Intermediary Loans	16.7	13.1	18.6	20.6	13.3	9.6	12.4
Sector Adjustment Loans	0.0	0.5	0.5	4.4	8.5	10.3	14.0
Program and Structural Adjustment Loans[1]	8.8	3.3	8.0	9.6	8.4	1.1	5.0
Technical Assistance Loans	0.2	0.4	1.7	1.2	2.1	1.4	1.4
Emergency Reconstruction Loans	0.0	1.2	0.2	0.2	0.3	1.0	3.1
Total [2]	100.0	100.0	100.0	100.0	100.0	100.0	100.0

Source: Planning and Budgeting Department, World Bank.

[1] Includes both Program and Structural Adjustment Loans and Credits.

[2] May not add exactly owing to rounding.

policy framework can and does substantially affect the context and focus of project operations, which are likely to continue to absorb the bulk of Bank's future lending. Moreover, under certain circumstances, it might be advantageous to promote macroeconomic policy reform through the relatively lower key instrumentality of a specific project operation. But "structural (and in its own way sectoral) adjustment lending enables the Bank to address basic issues of economic management more directly and more urgently than before" (Stern (1983, p. 91)). It is on these sectoral and structural adjustment operations and the policies they support that the rest of this section focuses.

Tables 1–3 show the growing importance of sectoral and structural adjustment lending in World Bank operations. From an annual average of under 4 percent for the FY 1979–80 period, these categories combined grew to 19 percent in 1986 (see Table 1).[14] With regard to the two sets of countries identified earlier in this paper, sector lending

---

[14] Structural Adjustment Loans are quite lumpy; thus, the percentage that they represent of total World Bank lending to a particular region or in the aggregate can vary substantially from year to year.

Table 2. Regional Distribution of World Bank Loans and Credits by Lending Instrument, FY 1975-86

(In millions of U.S. dollars and percent)

Destination	1975	Average 1979–80	Average 1981–82	1983	1984	1985	1986
East and South Africa							
Total (*in millions of U.S. dollars*)	656.5	730.4	794.4	1,129.8	1,186.6	786.0	915.9
1. Sector Adjustment	0.0	3.8	3.2	17.3	6.3	8.3	17.5
2. Program and Structural Adjustment[1]	9.1	3.8	8.9	11.6	12.2	0.0	4.9
1+2 (*percent of total*)	9.1	7.5	11.3	28.9	18.5	8.3	22.4
West Africa							
Total (*in millions of U.S. dollars*)	419.2	644.0	1,012.6	664.2	1,181.7	811.3	1,130.6
1. Sector Adjustment	0.0	0.0	0.0	6.0	29.4	12.3	4.3
2. Program and Structural Adjustment	0.0	27.2	33.6	6.0	21.2	3.4	28.4
1+2 (*percent of total*)	0.0	27.2	33.6	12.0	50.6	15.8	32.7
Europe, Middle East, and North Africa							
Total (*in millions of U.S. dollars*)	1,223.7	2,378.7	2,407.5	2,535.6	3,125.8	2,429.2	2,304.8
1. Sector Adjustment	0.0	0.0	0.0	0.0	7.7	16.5	32.5
2. Program and Structural Adjustment	5.7	7.4	14.1	22.7	12.0	0.0	0.0
1+2 (*percent of total*)	5.7	7.4	14.1	22.7	19.7	16.5	32.5

Latin America and the Carribean

Total (in millions of U.S. dollars)	1,215.0	2,474.4	3,070.6	3,459.6	3,025.6	3,698.2	4,771.2
1. Sector Adjustment	0.0	0.6	0.6	11.7	21.7	9.7	26.3
2. Program and Structural Adjustment	0.0	3.6	1.6	1.7	2.0	3.6	5.2
1+2 (percent of total)	0.0	4.3	2.3	13.5	23.6	13.4	31.5

East Asia and Pacific

Total (in millions of U.S. dollars)	951.4	2,249.3	2,540.9	3,708.6	3,302.0	3,100.6	3,565.2
1. Sector Adjustment	0.0	0.0	0.0	0.0	0.0	12.0	0.0
2. Program and Structural Adjustment	10.5	0.0	11.8	12.9	9.1	0.0	0.0
1+2 (percent of total)	10.5	0.0	11.8	12.9	9.1	12.0	0.0

South Asia

Total (in millions of U.S. dollars)	1,189.6	2,256.7	2,827.6	2,979.2	3,700.6	3,559.1	3,631.0
1. Sector Adjustment	0.0	0.0	0.9	0.0	0.0	5.0	1.9
2. Program and Structural Adjustment	24.4	2.8	5.4	3.7	4.6	0.0	5.5
1+2 (percent of total)	24.4	2.8	6.3	3.7	4.6	5.0	7.4

Source: Planning and Budgeting Department, World Bank.

[1] Includes both Program and Structural Adjustment Loans and Credits.

Table 3. Distribution of World Bank Loans and Credits by Country Group, FY 1975–86
(In millions of U.S. dollars and percent)

Destination	1975	Average 1979–80	Average 1981–82	1983	1984	1985	1986
Total lending to all countries	5,895.9	10,746.1	12,653.5	14,477.0	15,522.3	14,384.4	16,318.7
Sector Adjustment Program and Structural Adjustment Loans[1]	520.0	403.3	1,082.4	2,035.6	2,619.8	1,637.9	3,099.5
As a percent of total	8.8	3.8	8.6	14.1	16.9	11.4	19.0
Low-income countries[2]	2,051.2	3,270.2	3,965.4	4,906.4	6,164.7	5,771.5	6,046.1
Sector Adjustment Program and Structural Adjustment Loans	350.0	122.5	290.0	445.9	447.5	354.5	574.5
As a percent of total	17.1	3.8	7.3	9.1	7.3	6.1	9.5
Middle-income countries[2]	3,844.7	7,476.0	8,688.1	9,570.6	9,357.6	8,612.9	10,272.6
Sector Adjustment Program and Structural Adjustment Loans	170.0	280.8	792.4	1,589.7	2,172.3	1,283.4	2,525.0
As a percent of total	4.4	3.8	9.1	16.6	23.2	14.9	24.6

Memo items:

Highly indebted middle-income countries[3]	1,803.4	3,403.7	4,428.4	4,668.3	4,398.6	4,558.4	6,070.5
Sector Adjustment Program and Structural Adjustment Loans	0.0	98.3	231.6	1,042.8	1,396.1	745.0	2,105.0
As a percent of total	0.0	2.9	5.2	22.3	31.7	16.3	34.7
Sub-Saharan Africa[4]	1,075.7	1,374.4	1,807.0	1,794.0	2,368.3	1,597.3	2,046.5
Sector Adjustment Program and Structural Adjustment Loans	60.0	230.0	429.8	406.5	818.2	192.9	574.5
As a percent of total	5.6	16.7	23.8	22.7	34.6	12.1	28.1

Source: Planning and Budgeting Department, World Bank.

[1] Includes both Program and Structural Adjustment Loans and Credits.

[2] Countries with per capita income less than US$400 in 1987 dollars are considered low-income countries; those above that level are classified as middle-income countries.

[3] The 17 countries in this category are: Argentina, Bolivia, Brazil, Chile, Colombia, Costa Rica, Côte d'Ivoire, Ecuador, Jamaica, Mexico, Morocco, Nigeria, Peru, the Philippines, Uruguay, Venezuela, and Yugoslavia. Lending to this group is also included in that of middle-income countries.

[4] This group covers all countries south of the Sahara, except South Africa.

has grown especially fast in sub-Saharan Africa,[15] while Structural Adjustment Loans have shown the sharpest percentage increase within total commitments to the highly indebted developing countries. In the West Africa, Europe/Middle East/North Africa, and Latin America regions, the two lending instruments combined represented about one third of total commitments to each region in FY 1986. In the East Asia and Pacific and South Asia regions, on the other hand, sectoral and structural adjustment lending accounted for zero and less than 8 percent of the respective regional aggregates in FY 1986 (see Table 2).

Policy Focus of Sectoral and Structural Lending

The main purpose of Bank Sector and Structural Adjustment Loans is to facilitate the adjustment required to achieve sustainable growth and the mobilization of external financing needed to support the country's adjustment efforts. Although the ultimate objective is to achieve sustainable growth compatible with available resources (including foreign financing), this is a medium-term target. Thus, adjustment loans focus on the annual steps to be taken in support of the policy reforms needed to promote sustainable growth in the medium term. Subsequent steps are supported by additional loans of various kinds so that the implementation of a reform package is supported by a series of Bank lending operations over a period of several years (Stern (1983)).

Most aspects of macroeconomic and sector policy have been the focus of nonproject Bank lending in one country or another over this period.[16] This has been done in coordination with the Fund and in ways that supplement Fund programs (see below). While the Bank has deferred to the Fund in monetary and exchange rate policy, it has sometimes been involved in the institutional reforms pertaining to exchange rate management (as in the case of setting up foreign exchange auction systems in Nigeria and Somalia); it has also worked

---

[15] Loans to financial intermediaries are sometimes included in Sector Loans. While in some respects they contain features of other non-project lending, they are excluded here primarily because their policy focus usually tends to be narrow.

[16] This review focuses on structural and sector adjustment lending by the Bank through calendar 1985. It is based in part on the findings of a review of 15 Structural Adjustment Loans to 10 countries over the 1980–82 period (World Bank (1986b)).

closely with the Fund on matters pertaining to interest rate policy reform (as in the case of Jamaica).

Individual programs have emphasized different policy issues reflecting country priorities and objectives. But within the broad array of potential policy concerns the Bank's emphasis has been on the following interrelated areas.

i. Mobilization of domestic resources through fiscal, monetary, and credit policies. This includes support for both revenue-enhancing and expenditure-limiting measures and for efforts to restrict public sector or external borrowing or to decontrol or restructure interest rates.

ii. Improving the efficiency of resource allocation and use by the public sector. This includes support for rationalizing public sector investment, strengthening the operational efficiency of public sector and parastatal enterprises, and rationalizing public sector programs, including divestiture of public holdings in enterprises.

iii. Reform of the structure of economic incentives in order to reduce distortions, promote more efficient resource allocation, and thus create a more productive economic structure. Within this area, two sets of policy issues are receiving the greatest attention.

a. Trade regime reforms designed to reduce the bias against exports, and to lower the level and rationalize the pattern of protection. Since most protection in developing countries manifests itself in a large variance of incentives within the manufacturing sector (and between manufacturing and agriculture), such reforms usually focus on raising industrial productivity and competitiveness.[17]

b. Price system reforms designed to make prices more accurately reflect opportunity costs. These reforms usually focus on the incentives affecting production and distribution in agriculture; but energy and state enterprise pricing has also received attention.

iv. Institutional reforms supportive of adjustment with growth.[18] There is little distinction between the policy focus of Structural Adjustment Loans and Sectoral Adjustment Loans. The main difference lies in the comprehensiveness of the policy and institutional

---

[17] With some exceptions, for example, the Agricultural Sector Loan to Argentina in 1986 focused on trade reforms in that sector.

[18] The fact that the subsequent analysis will not focus significantly on institutional reform in no way detracts from the importance of such reform to the success of *all* policy reform efforts.

reform involved. Relatively few countries have prepared comprehensive and implementable adjustment programs that can be supported by SALs. On the other hand, there are certain policies, for example fiscal reform, that are best tackled through an economy-wide approach. In several cases, Sector Adjustment Loans have been used to initiate the adjustment process which, as it gains in comprehensiveness, may be supported by a SAL. In Ghana, for example, two Reconstruction Import Credits in FY 1983 and 1985 and an Export Rehabilitation Credit in 1984 were followed by a SAL in 1986. In some other cases, SELs serve to deepen the adjustment process initiated by the SALs. Examples of this include Turkey, where a series of SALs in 1980–84 was followed by an Agricultural Sector Loan in 1985, and Korea, where a Financial Sector Loan in 1985 followed the earlier SAL (World Bank (1986a)).

Summary View of Policy Reforms Under Structural Adjustment Lending

While the World Bank and member governments have conducted a long-standing policy dialogue on various economy-wide issues, the 1980s have seen policy reform emerge as the main component of an increasing number of lending operations. It is worth briefly reviewing this development for two reasons. First, it is useful to determine whether the focus and content of policy-based lending are consistent with the factors identified above as being prerequisites for restoring growth in recipient countries. Second, it is helpful to identify any lessons that may emerge for future World Bank programs, which are continuously evolving in the light of experience.

The review of policy issues in this section should not be viewed as an evaluation of the "impact" of past World Bank SALs and SELs. Such an analysis lacks a credible counterfactual, that is, it is impossible to determine what would have been the recipients' policies and performance in the absence of the programs. This is a familiar problem, which reduces most analyses to contrasting country performance after the assistance to performance before (Please (1984)). Such "before compared to after" analysis is dangerous because it assumes that countries would have made no policy changes to improve their situation in the absence of the World Bank programs, while in fact their policies may have been unsustainable, and it does not take into account changes in the international environment or other exogenous events that influence country performance. In addition, it is difficult to isolate the effect of World Bank programs from those of the Fund, which has been actively working in almost all the countries that the Bank is assisting through SALs or SELs (see below). Finally, the analysis also does not address a number of implementation issues, such as the size of SALs, tranching, the scope of conditionality and the like, all of which have a bearing on the question of program effectiveness.[19]

Perhaps the most general conclusion that can be drawn from the World Bank's experience to date is the importance of the recipient's commitment to a particular course of reform for the ultimate success of the policy package. The most successful cases of reform supported by the World Bank have involved countries (e.g., Korea and Turkey) that have adopted a series of reforms over time and stuck by them. The least successful were those where, for a variety of reasons, policies were reversed after a time and the direction and purpose of reform was confused and uncertain (Guyana, Bolivia, and Senegal in the early 1980s). Some of the main lessons of policy reform in particular areas are discussed in the Sections below.

Domestic Resource Mobilization

Past Bank involvement with resource mobilization has mainly focused on supporting government efforts to reduce budget deficits through revenue-raising or expenditure-reducing measures. Bank efforts typically supplement Fund programs in this area. In all instances Bank programs aim to strengthen public sector performance and to reduce, directly or indirectly, public sector deficits that tend to crowd out private investment and to produce financial and balance of payments disequilibria. Reforms in this area have focused on raising public agencies' revenues or reducing their expenditures by, for example, raising prices of services or establishing user fees, or eliminating or retargeting subsidies, so as to reduce public sector expenditures. In other cases, Bank efforts have focused on administrative reforms of the tax system or the introduction of new taxation.

---

[19] For a discussion of some of these issues see Berg and Batchelder (1985) and World Bank (1986b).

Deficit reduction and reform of parastatals has often required public sector employment cuts; in a period of stagnant growth, such cuts have entailed transitional costs with which governments and the Bank have had to deal.[20]

In addition to fiscal reform, resource mobilization has been pursued through efforts to improve the functioning of the financial sector and to eliminate distortions in interest rate policy. Examples of such activities include the Industrial Finance Project in Korea and the Moroccan Industrial and Trade Policy Loans. The financial systems of many developing countries have also been severely strained in the last five years by being required to handle the debts of financially ailing enterprises—sometimes in the public sector. This has prompted World Bank Sector Loans designed to support rehabilitation of the financial system in a number of countries, such as Chile and the Philippines.

Broadly speaking, the key issues that have arisen from the Bank's experience with financial market and banking sector reforms are those discussed above, that is, the need to ensure an orderly transition for banking systems saddled with a lot of nonperforming loans, sometimes of public enterprises, and the liberalization of previously controlled lending and deposit rates. Financial reforms have also been difficult in cases such as Korea where the government has used financial incentives to promote exports and offset the bias of continued domestic protection.

Improved Efficiency and Resource Use by the Public Sector

This effort has included three main components: rationalization of public investment programs, improved public sector enterprise performance, and rationalization of the size of the public sector, including divestiture of public holdings.

Since 1977, the Bank has undertaken about 50 public investment reviews. A large number of them were undertaken in conjunction with Fund programs that required or depended on them. The scope of these reviews has varied considerably—ranging from analyses

---

[20] But not all governments have faced such problems (see below).

involving only a few staff weeks to major SAL-related reviews in Turkey and Jamaica. Nevertheless, many of these reviews had common characteristics. They were crisis induced, that is, they were undertaken in the context of a need to reduce public sector spending and limit investment to available resources. They focused on big, existing operations with the potential of being large drains on the government budget, and on identifying quick-yielding projects, that is, ones which could be readily completed. As there were few resources available for new starts, relatively little attention was directed to the ranking of new projects (Husain (1986)).

Most reviews recommended changes in investment priorities. In addition to overall resource constraints, the key problem usually was that ongoing projects were not accompanied by other actions required for project viability. In some cases, especially in Africa, the reviews recommended ways of restructuring expenditures so as to permit financing of maintenance and recurrent costs. In general, the reviews have been most effective when they have been based on comprehensive Bank sectoral analyses and have actively involved member government participation (Kavalsky (1986)).

For the future, an important dimension of the Bank's role should be to strengthen (and in some cases to help create) the institutional capacity that would permit developing countries to undertake effective investment reviews as an ongoing process rather than as a form of damage control in crises. It will also be important to link such reviews to other elements of government policy: pricing policy and policies for reallocating resources toward export and efficient import-competing sectors are of special importance in this context. Finally, these investment reviews can greatly strengthen aid coordination. All too often—especially in Africa or in countries in which the internal investment review has been weak—donors have supported activities without taking into account the budgetary implications of their maintenance and recurrent costs.

Improving the financial performance of public sector enterprises has also been an objective of many SALs (e.g., for Turkey, Jamaica, Senegal). The effort has focused both on better internal management of parastatals (e.g., Jamaica) and on raising prices to reflect marginal production costs and to reduce the drain on the public budget. While there is evidence that these objectives have been achieved in some cases, the experience has been less encouraging in others. In Jamaica, for example, reductions in public sector enterprise deficits were in part substituted by higher central bank losses. In Turkey, higher prices in some state enterprises that provide inputs to other entities under monopolistic conditions have harmed export competitiveness. Meanwhile, considerable progress is being made in Africa with reforms of state enterprises involved in marketing and distributing agricultural products (e.g., Senegal).

More generally, the Bank has also been helping member countries to reassess the role of government as an owner or operator of specific public enterprises. In several cases this has led country authorities to undertake divestiture programs. Such programs have been announced by many countries—Mexico, Brazil, Costa Rica, Chile, Jamaica, the Philippines, Malaysia, and Turkey are examples—but progress has been difficult. One of the problems has been the handling of financially ailing entities. Closing them down has meant increasing unemployment during periods of crisis. Without prior rehabilitation, the sale option is unattractive. Domestic capital markets are frequently thin, and foreign acquisition is not always welcome—even if there is interest by foreign investors, which is usually not the case. The government is therefore tempted to continue to run the entity, even though it may no longer believe it is desirable or appropriate to have the entity in the public sector.

Reform of Trade Regimes

Reform of the structure of incentives affecting the production of exports and import-competing goods has been a key feature of almost all SALs and many sectoral loans. On the export side, emphasis has been placed on two sets of measures: the provision of financial incentives through tax rebates, subsidies on imported inputs to offset import controls, and preferential access to imports and credit (e.g., Turkey, Jamaica, the Philippines, and Senegal), and reform of administrative procedures and the establishment of better institutional support for exporters (e.g., Kenya, the Philippines, and Jamaica).

In most instances the competitiveness of exports was expected to be enhanced by parallel liberalization and rationalization of systems of protection for import-competing activities. For example, the SALs for Jamaica, Kenya, the Philippines, Thailand, and Turkey supported the reduction of quantitative restrictions and the lowering and liberalization of tariffs. Sectoral loans to Mexico and Colombia in FY 1983 and 1985 and to Argentina in FY 1986 have also focused on correction of the anti-export bias of incentives by promoting export rebates, import liberalization, and the like and by strengthening of the institutional base for export development.

Finally, the trade reform components of SALs and SELs were expected to be buttressed by changes in other policies that would result in a supportive real devaluation. Most of the loans referred to the maintenance of competitive exchange rates as an essential condition for the success of the loan, and monitoring of such provisions was left to the Fund.

The results of the early lending operations have been mixed. Of all the countries assisted perhaps Turkey, and more recently Chile and Ecuador, have made the most progress in reforms. The financial incentives were introduced on schedule or with small delays in most cases. Progress in improving institutional support was generally slow, however, and while most countries took some steps to rationalize the trade regime, the process was frequently halted short of the desired objectives or even reversed (World Bank (1986b)). In about half of the countries that had received a SAL before 1985, the real effective exchange rate appreciated within a year of the relevant SAL commitment.

On balance, this experience confirms the earlier conclusion that implementation of trade reforms is not very successful when it is not accompanied by other measures to assure a shift in the real exchange rate—which is needed to produce the desired shifts in incentives. Experience also suggests that future reforms ensure that export expansion programs be accompanied by import liberalization and action on the exchange rate. An early export supply response is obviously helpful to import liberalization. Until the supply response occurs, external financing can help with the influx of imports as a consequence of import liberalization. Experience, however, does *not* in our view suggest that import liberalization should be undertaken only after export reforms have increased the supply of foreign exchange. This kind of sequencing is likely to be self-defeating, since it is extremely difficult to reorient producers toward export markets as long as heavily sheltered domestic markets offer them assured profits.

Other Pricing Policies

Changes in agricultural and energy pricing were also common features of many SALs and SELs. Agricultural pricing reforms almost invariably focused on raising producer prices closer to international market price equivalents, and on cutting input and consumer subsidies (e.g., Senegal, Pakistan). Agricultural sector loans to Morocco and reconstruction credits to Ghana had a similar reform focus. The same kinds of objectives were pursued with respect to energy pricing in the SALs to the Philippines, Turkey, Kenya, and Jamaica.

Experience with these loans suggests that most of these reforms, especially those related to the energy sector, were implemented with significant benefits to the recipient. In several cases there has been evidence of increased agricultural production and improved rural incomes (e.g., Ghana, Zambia, Thailand) and of increased conservation and efficient import substitution of energy resources.

The key issue in this area is how to deal with the transition costs entailed by raising the foodstuff prices paid by politically powerful urban consumers. This issue has caused serious difficulties in at least one recent case (Zambia).

Issues Raised by World Bank Programs of Adjustment

Both internal and external reviews have raised a number of issues about World Bank SELs and SALs. We will address two basic issues here: the view that Bank programs are not based on a coherent and consistent medium-term model of adjustment with growth, partly because such a model does not exist, especially when it comes to questions about the pace and sequencing of reform (Yagci and others (1985), Heillener (1986)), and the concern that Bank adjustment programs have not taken the social costs of adjustment fully into account (Overseas Development Council (1986)).

Need for a Strengthened Analytical Framework

The analytical framework discussed in the previous section provides a good basis for the design of adjustment policies in most countries. But it falls short of providing a quantitative structure for linking inputs (policy actions) and outputs (macroeconomic performance).

The Bank uses a quantitative framework to ensure consistency in its projections of financial "requirements," but this framework has very few behavioral relationships linking proposed policy steps to future outcomes (Khan and others (1986)). Indeed, the framework has little to say about the quantitative impact of key components of policy reform (e.g., trade reform, improvements in pricing, public investment reviews, and the like) on medium-term economic performance (on which the Bank usually focuses). Thus, as suggested in the previous section, one can be more confident about the long-term outcome of policy packages than about the precise dynamic profile of results following the introduction of specific reforms.

Similarly, it is desirable to develop quantifiable indicators of progress for programs with medium- to long-term objectives. All Bank programs have contained commitments to specific monitorable actions by the recipient. These have usually involved government commitments to specific policy steps at different points over time. Until recently, however, there was little effort to use quantitative performance indicators of progress that could form a framework for monitoring the effects of policy reform. The Mexico package does contain such indicators, but experience with them has been limited.

The above should not be viewed as a criticism of past programs. The state of the art in identifying meaningful indicators of progress is underdeveloped (Genberg and Swoboda (1986)). Many reforms being pursued are of an institutional nature, and their impact is inherently difficult to measure. Measuring supply-side responses to particular measures and assessing the quantitative impact of efficiency and productivity gains is also very difficult.

Moreover, even the most sophisticated model that tries to analyze the impact of alternative policy packages on economic performance at the country level should be used with extreme caution. As the rational expectation perspective suggests, there are endogenous changes in the behavior of economic agents in response to changes in policy actions, and these changes cannot be readily captured by models built on previous experience.

The lack of an aggregate model to link policy action with economic performance should not distract the World Bank from the main task of designing programs based on the framework discussed in the previous section and the World Bank experience reviewed here. It seems clear that understanding of the optimal pace and sequencing of reforms is far less complete than understanding of the direction policy reforms need to take. It is also evident that reform strategy needs to take into account the initial conditions in an individual country, the transition costs of reform, and the country's political and social situation. There is no evidence, however, that the Bank has suggested uniformly paced or sequenced reforms in member countries. On the contrary, individual programs are tailored to individual country situations. This is not to say that misjudgments have not been made or will not be made in future. What does seem true is that past (and possible future) misjudgments are not the result of the Bank's indiscriminate application of preconceived notions of the appropriate pace or scope of reforms.

For the future, two parallel approaches are needed. First, the Bank should continue to support policy reforms. Uncertainties about the quantitative impact of specific policies and developments in the international environment mean that flexibility and willingness to adjust objectives should be a key element in all programs. Second, in parallel, additional analytical work is needed if we are to continue to strengthen our understanding of the sequencing and timing of particular policies and to improve the quantitative framework for projecting economic performance in the medium term.

Distribution Issues

A key concern raised by several reviews of Bank programs in support of adjustment and growth has been the extent to which such programs have adequately addressed issues of income distribution (Overseas Development Council (1986)). Several issues usually get mixed up in this discussion. The first is the question of whether the programs undertaken produce a short-run decline in output and incomes which is somehow excessive, e.g., whether, given the amount of financing available, alternative programs would have permitted more gradual adjustment over time and required less demand restraint which is inimical to growth. Second is the issue of whether the poor have suffered disproportionately in the adjustment process, in the sense that their incomes have fallen by more than those of other groups. A variation on this issue is the suggestion that adjustment has resulted in significant absolute declines in the levels of income of the poor and has meant that many more families' incomes fall below a "poverty" standard. Third is the issue that government policies and, in particular, patterns of reductions of government expenditures have disproportionately affected the poor.

The first question is not really about distribution but about the path of adjustment and the restoration of growth. It is, however, of central importance to the question of what happens to the absolute *level* of incomes of the poor over time. Reliable evidence about changes in the size distribution of income over time does not exist. Thus, it is difficult to say what happened to the relative income changes of different groups in developing countries over the last several years. On the other hand, it is quite clear that the absolute levels of income of the poor have declined in a large number of developing countries, including many with Bank programs. But in some countries, incomes had to be reduced because the level of overall absorption was not sustainable. Of course, if a higher amount of financing were available, less reliance could have been placed on demand restraint programs that entail reductions in output, the pace of adjustment would have been slower and supply enhancing policies would have played a greater role in the stabilization effort.

The key question about the past, however, is counterfactual. Was there an alternative policy set that could have been pursued (with the same amount of external financing) that would have resulted in higher output and income in general and hence in less hardship for the poor? It is not possible to reach general agreement on this question, and in any event the answer would tend to vary in different countries.

What about the impact on the poor of specific government adjustment supported by the Bank? The Bank's approach has been to include in its lending operations an assessment of the implications for the income of the poor of the policy reforms supported. In many instances in sub-Saharan Africa, the Bank's reviews of public expenditure programs have focused on strengthening the capacity of domestic institutions to deliver services to the poor, especially in health and education. But the Bank has eschewed specifically conditioning its SALs and SELs on distributive objectives. The fundamental rationale for this position is the premise that in general, for any given original distribution of assets, the policies that would tend to promote more efficient use of resources would also be beneficial to employment and a more equitable distribution of income.

Take trade reform, for instance. There is abundant evidence that a more outward-looking development strategy emphasizing the reduction of protection and expansion of exports would tend to benefit employment and a more equitable income distribution (Krueger (1983)).

The question of pricing reform, especially in agriculture, is more complex but the presumption is similar. Raising producer prices tends to benefit the rural sector, which in most countries (the exceptions include some countries where the distribution of land assets is unequal) tends to have lower incomes than the urban sector. There is strong evidence, for example, that the recent structural adjustment in Côte d'Ivoire has resulted in a significant shift favoring the lower income rural sector within the context of the overall adjustment effort of the last several years (Addison and Demery (1986)). The Bank's approach has also stressed the elimination of general consumer subsidies via the price mechanism and overvalued exchange rates in favor of targeted subsidy programs benefiting the poor. Experience in Sri Lanka and Jamaica, among others, suggests that such programs are both effective and economical in addressing social objectives of the urban poor.

The effects of fiscal reforms on the poor are complex. On the revenue-raising side, there is increasing evidence that the tax system is not a practical vehicle for promoting finely targeted distributional objectives except in very broad terms, for example, by excluding the lowest income groups from payment of any income taxes. On the expenditure side, the evidence of the past several years suggests that expenditure cuts have tended to fall primarily on investment and maintenance rather than on consumption expenditures; at the same time, public sector employment in several highly indebted countries in Latin America has tended to rise pari passu with employment cuts in the private sector.[21] Thus, the problem may have been that governments have tended to compromise future growth relative to current consumption. This is, of course, understandable in situations where consumption is being squeezed from already low levels. On the other hand, there is some evidence, especially from Latin America,

---

[21] Pfeffermann (1986). But this has not necessarily *helped* the very poor. It is believed— but on the basis of little concrete information—that the beneficiaries were in the "middle class."

that the pattern of government consumption expenditures has benefited primarily the middle-income urban classes and that reduction
in maintenance expenditures has adversely affected the delivery of
public services to the poor (Pfeffermann (1986)).

Finally, it is clear that many adjustment programs entail some
transitional costs, especially in employment. It is necessary to distinguish, however, between temporary employment losses resulting
from reductions in unsustainable previous levels of absorption and
losses resulting from trade or other price reforms, such as rationalizing
of public sector activities. In the latter case especially, it is important
to examine what can be done to help governments address the
problems through resettlement and training programs. Recent experience with programs assisted by the International Labor Organization (ILO) in Guinea-Bissau, Gambia, and Senegal offers examples
of what can be done to improve employment access to workers
displaced as a consequence of public sector or other adjustments
efforts (Addison and Demery (1986)).

It seems reasonable to conclude that future Bank programs in
support of adjustment and growth that emphasize policies to improve
efficiency and increase productivity would benefit the poor through
the restoration of overall growth. There is also a presumption that
such programs would have a positive effect in promoting a more
equitable distribution of income. The Bank has also designed programs
specifically aimed at poverty issues related to adjustment. Greater
attention needs to be directed to the distributional impact of public
sector consumption expenditures, however, as well as to designing
employment assistance programs that would ease the burden of
structural adjustment in the short term.

Links with Fund Programs

It is clear from the discussion in earlier sections that there are close
links between the policy concerns addressed by World Bank and
Fund programs. There are two fundamental reasons for such linkages.
Bank programs focusing on increasing aggregate supply and raising
productivity are far more likely to succeed if they are pursued in the
context of a stable macroeconomic environment promoted through a
Fund program. At the same time, the presence of a Bank program
contributes to Fund efforts to support adjustment with growth, in

that it permits the Fund to rely less on demand restraint measures in restoring external equilibrium, and thus in turn reduces the likelihood that Fund-supported programs would adversely affect growth in the short term. This comes about both because of the direct impact of Bank programs on the supply side and through the provision of financing that permits the adjustment process to be stretched out and thus to require relatively less reliance on demand management for the restoration of equilibrium.

All countries that have received a SAL either already had, or were awaiting imminent approval of, a Fund stand-by or extended arrangement. The same was true for 30 of the Bank's 35 Sector Adjustment Loans. Of the remaining five, one had a Fund monitoring arrangement, and another had a first tranche drawing. Programs in which the Fund undertakes Structural Adjustment Facility operations are based on studies of the macroeconomic framework and adjustment prospects jointly developed with the Bank.

There are extensive linkages between the activities of the two institutions in specific areas of policy reform, such as fiscal and monetary issues. The success of trade reform hinges critically on the macroeconomic environment and especially on the maintenance of an appropriate real exchange rate. Bank-supported programs in fiscal and monetary policy are also coordinated with those of the Fund. For example, the Fund may focus more on targets for cutting the overall public sector deficit while the Bank might focus on developing priorities for expenditure reductions, or improvements in the performance of public sector enterprises. In monetary matters, the Fund might focus on overall credit ceilings while the Bank might concentrate on the elimination of distortions in a specific market or help facilitate the extension of credit to priority sectors. Finally, as noted earlier, the Fund relies on the Bank to undertake public sector investment reviews that are used as inputs in Fund medium-term programs (Khan and Knight (1985)).

The policy problems of restoring growth in the medium term are far too complex and our understanding of the impact of policy on economic performance is far too incomplete for differences not to arise in the approach of the two institutions. Two illustrations of this point may be worth noting. In cases where there is a need both to reduce absorption in the short run and to stimulate growth, the Bank has tended to place greater reliance on exchange rate adjustment relative to fiscal or monetary contraction as a means of demand-side adjustment because of the potential benefit that exchange rate adjustment could have to medium-term restructuring of the economy. Similarly, there have been instances in which an urgent need to reduce fiscal deficits has resulted in Fund programs that support increased taxation in the trade sector, without parallel increases of taxation in nontradables. When such measures are not lifted quickly, they tend to run contrary to efforts to promote a more outward orientation of the economy and a shift of resources to tradables. Where such divergent views have arisen at the staff level, the two institutions have developed mechanisms designed to reconcile differing views so as to avoid presenting member countries with conflicting advice (Stern (1983), Hino (1986)).

Financial Packages

The development of suitable packages of external finance to support policy reform is the other leg on which adjustment with growth in developing countries must stand. Reforms are possible without financial support, but given the current financial situation in many developing countries, they alone cannot go far in restoring growth. Additional investment in productive activities is difficult to finance through further cuts in consumption. Indeed a recent study (Selowsky and van der Tak (1986)) showed that additional external finance in the initial years of a reform could be an essential component of a strategy designed to restore long-term growth while also maintaining per capita consumption in the interim. At the same time, care needs to be taken to ensure that financial support is not an alternative to adjustment, but rather that it is used to stretch the adjustment process out over time while permitting a modicum of short-run growth. It is hard for developing countries to persevere with necessary but politically difficult reforms without some prospects of a recovery in incomes and consumption in the near term. Finally, the financial packages need to be tailored to the circumstances of individual countries.

The Bank's experience with financial packages in support of adjustment with growth dates back to its early work in the context of consortia and consultative groups. But this experience primarily involved coordination of official flows, especially of ODA. It is only recently that the Bank has become actively involved in more comprehensive packages involving commercial bank lending as well as debt restructuring. In addition, the international situation (and especially the commercial banks' attitude toward increased exposure to developing countries) has changed. Thus, experience with the early SAL financial packages offers limited guidance for the future.

Two of the early SALs, those to Turkey and Jamaica, were quite comprehensive in their scope, but the Bank's involvement with commercial bank rescheduling and new money arrangements in the development of the packages was relatively limited. Recent experience is quite different. The Bank played a major role in the formulation of the financial packages for Nigeria and Mexico, for example; in both cases, implementation of the Bank's adjustment programs as well as the Fund's was made a condition for commercial bank funding.

At present, two broadly different types of financial package can be distinguished, each of which reflects the financial circumstances and prospects of the countries assisted and the character of their existing debt obligations. The first type is associated with middle-income developing countries, primarily in Latin America, whose outstanding debt is mostly owed to commercial banks and to a lesser extent to official export credit agencies on commercial or close-to-commercial terms. Restoration of growth and creditworthiness over time can be expected to permit these countries to rely on the private market for future capital inflows. The second type of package is suitable for low-income countries, primarily in sub-Saharan Africa, which owe proportionately more of their debt to official creditors (including the international financial institutions) and which will have to continue to rely indefinitely on concessional assistance for the bulk of their foreign capital inflows, since their capacity to service credits on commercial terms is likely to be quite limited even as they develop a significant growth momentum.

The financial packages that have been developed in support of recent adjustment programs in both middle- and low-income countries have some common features, which can be summarized as follows:

i. The financial packages are based on programs of stabilization and medium-term reform agreed with the Fund and the World Bank. In the low-income countries these programs are in turn based on joint Fund/Bank analyses of a medium-term framework agreed with the governments.

ii. The packages establish explicit linkages between restructuring of debt owed to official and commercial bank credits or the provision of new financing and comprehensive adjustment programs supported by World Bank resources.

iii. Linkages between the commitments of the Bank and those of other sources of finance are becoming more frequent. This involves joint agreements by the Bank, the Fund and other sources of financial support to disburse funds. It also involves the need to review the overall financial packages in the light of progress in the recipient country, or in the light of international developments that are likely to affect the prospects for success of the original package. Stronger links with private capital flows have sometimes taken the form of increasing cofinancing or World Bank guarantees (e.g., Chile, Mexico) when necessary to complete the financial package. Strengthened ties with official lending sources are being pursued through enhanced coordination with official donors in consultative groups, especially in the context of sub-Saharan Africa.

The Bank's role in these packages is threefold. First, it assists member governments in the design of policy reforms aimed at restoring growth. Second, it provides additional amounts of its own resources. In this connection, recent packages in middle-income countries (e.g., Mexico) have involved an increase in the future net exposure of the Bank relative to that of the commercial banks. Third, it acts as a catalyst in mobilizing additional capital flows from private and official resources. The mobilization of official resources is obviously of special importance in the context of low-income countries in sub-Saharan Africa.

While significant progress has been made in designing financial packages, several issues for further action have also arisen. A common problem for both types of package has been the overall difficulty of mobilizing additional financing. In the case of highly indebted middle-income countries, this problem basically stems from commercial banks' decisions to reduce net exposure to those countries. While packages have been funded, there have frequently been difficulties and delays in reaching agreement on the size of the commercial banks' contribution. As banks have strengthened their financial position, they have seemed increasingly reluctant to mobilize additional financing. This has been especially true in the case of smaller borrowers whose existing debt is not significant in the total portfolios of the commercial banks. Apart from the US$6 billion commitment to Mexico and a much smaller new money arrangement with Nigeria, there has been very little new commercial lending to highly indebted middle-income countries. While increasing World Bank guarantees may be appropriate in specific cases, it cannot be viewed as a substitute, because the guarantees involve additional official (rather than private) exposure.

Meanwhile, ODA commitments in sub-Saharan Africa have grown significantly. Nevertheless, World Bank estimates indicate that despite this growth and additional future commitments by bilateral donors, a further US$1.5 billion a year of bilateral concessional assistance and debt relief are needed to support developing countries' reform efforts (World Bank (1986c)).[22]

Debt restructuring has continued to play an important role in financial packages. In 1986 there were nine restructurings with commercial banks; five (for Mexico, Côte d'Ivoire, Uruguay, Dominican Republic, and the Congo) were multi-year restructuring arrangements (MYRAs). There were 18 restructuring arrangments with the Paris Club, of which those with the Côte d'Ivoire and Yugoslavia were MYRAs.

Some limitations of debt relief, even in the context of MYRAs, are emerging, however. For example, even after MYRAs are concluded and even though the terms of reschedulings are softening, massive amounts of domestic resources are needed to pay interest on outstanding debt. In some cases, these amounts are so high that the level of savings alone (e.g., without new money) is inadequate to finance essential investment in export-oriented and efficient import-competing activities. In still other cases, obligations to international institutions form such a large portion of the total that restructuring other debt offers very limited scope for relief, unless interest is also rescheduled on concessionary terms—something that has not happened yet.

When new money on commercial terms is either not forthcoming or should not be relied upon, country options are sharply limited. The only possible avenue is increased concessional lending—which itself is growing only slowly. In addition, much of the ODA resources

---

[22] While the methodology for developing such estimates is rather crude, it is difficult to avoid the conclusion that generation of growth momentum in Africa will require significant additions to current aid levels.

of bilateral donors are allocated without explicit reference to the economic policies of the recipient. An additional problem has arisen in sub-Saharan Africa, where export credit agencies of industrial countries have proposed credits for projects that promote their own exports frequently without regard to the priority these projects have in the country's investment program or even the recipient's future capacity to repay.

New ways to deal with existing debt are needed and some are emerging. The chief alternative that has emerged in 1986 is conversion of debt to equity. Costa Rica, Chile, Mexico, Brazil, and the Philippines are all using this approach in varying degrees. Others, such as Nigeria and Argentina, are considering plans for the same purpose. To date, only about US$5 billion of a total of about US$300 billion of debt to commercial banks has been converted (World Bank (1987 forthcoming)), but well conceived and managed programs of debt-equity conversion are promising vehicles for reducing servicing costs and repatriating capital, especially to middle-income countries.

Old approaches are also worth reviving. For example, developing country policies to encourage new direct private capital investment can significantly assist adjustment with growth. Such policies can be supported by international assistance through the International Finance Corporation (IFC) and the newly established Multilateral Insurance Guarantee Association (MIGA).

Finally, better coordination among official creditors, including both aid and the export credit agencies of industrial countries, is clearly essential for designing effective financial packages to promote adjustment with growth in developing countries.

Conclusions

This review of appropriate developing countries' policies for promoting adjustment and sustainable growth, and World Bank programs for supporting them, suggests the following conclusions.

i. Adjustment and growth can best be promoted in an environment of relative domestic economic stability. Significant instability, manifested in high rates of inflation, makes the already difficult task of achieving adjustment and sustainable growth almost impossible.

ii. The policy mix used to promote stabilization can have a bearing on the success of parallel or subsequent efforts to promote adjustment.

In general, a balanced use of the main instruments of macroeconomic policy for stabilization is more likely to be conducive to later efforts to promote growth than a stabilization program that relies too heavily on any one policy instrument.

iii. There is widespread agreement on the nature of the policies that developing countries need to adopt when pursuing adjustment and sustainable growth under the constraints imposed by a large external debt-servicing burden. Such policies include efforts to promote resource mobilization that will raise domestic savings and investment rates, efforts to increase the overall efficiency and productivity of the economy, and efforts to restructure production in favor of tradables. While these reforms are also likely to help alleviate poverty in the longer term, they sometimes entail short-term transitional costs for the poor.

iv. There is much less certainty on the pace and sequencing of reforms in particular situations. A lot will depend on the initial conditions in the economy, including its flexibility, the extent of the original disequilibrium, and the political and social structure of the country.

v. The review of World Bank lending operations and their policy thrust showed that the Bank has a variety of lending instruments with which it can support policy reform in member countries. Over the last six years, the Bank has increased the proportion of its total commitments represented by sectoral and structural adjustment lending in support of broad economic and sectoral policy reforms. The increase has been especially pronounced for the two sets of economies currently facing the most serious problems of adjustment and growth, that is, the countries of sub-Saharan Africa and the heavily indebted middle-income countries.

vi. Experience suggests that consistent pursuit of the kinds of policy reforms the Bank has supported in recent years will promote adjustment and growth in member countries. Given the problems facing developing countries today, the thrust of policy reforms already pursued by the Bank should be maintained. Reforms must be tailored to the circumstances in individual countries. Moreover, in the light of uncertainties about the appropriate pacing and sequencing of such reforms, it is also important to maintain maximum program flexibility. This means that country reform programs should be reviewed frequently to ensure that they are on track, and that the Bank should be prepared to support modifications in policy reform packages in the light of both domestic and international developments. Where policy reform to promote generally desirable structural change gives rise to transitional costs for the poor, the Bank needs to continue to work with governments to develop programs targeted to address the problems.

vii. The success of policy reforms supported by the Bank is intimately related to and depends on adjustment policies supported by the Fund. Given the uncertainties surrounding the appropriate policy mix for effective medium-term adjustment, differences in views on specific adjustment programs are bound to arise in individual cases both between the two institutions and between them and the developing country concerned. The key objective in such cases should be to work jointly with the developing country's authorities to develop an agreed program of reforms that can be supported by all parties.

viii. The policy reforms supported by the Bank and the Fund need to be complemented by additional flows of resources to developing countries if the objective of sustainable growth is to be achieved. While some progress has been made in developing new sources of financing for highly indebted countries and additional flows of concessional assistance for sub-Saharan Africa, still more funding is clearly needed.

ix. The policy reform programs the Bank has been supporting are based on sound analytical underpinnings. The formal quantitative model that it uses to ensure the consistency of its medium-term projections does not, however, embody a significant number of behavioral relationships on key aspects of the policy reforms it is supporting. A lot of the supply side and institutional reforms the Bank is supporting are difficult to quantify and incorporate in an aggregate econometric model. Nonetheless, additional analytical efforts are needed to enrich the basic consistency framework employed by the Bank and to develop meaningful quantitative indicators linking policy reforms to actual progress.

x. The Bank should continue to play an active role in helping coordinate concessional assistance efforts and, together with the Fund, in ensuring that total net flows of resources to individual countries—including new funds and debt relief—are adequate to support developing countries' efforts to restore sustainable growth.

References

Addison, Tony, and Lionel Demery, "Poverty Alleviation Under Structural Adjustment," unpublished, Overseas Development Institute, London, 1986.

Balassa, Bela, "Adjustment Policies in Developing Countries: A Reassessment," *World Development* (Oxford), Vol. 12 (September 1984), pp. 955–72.

Baum, Warren, and Stokes Tolbert, *Investing in Development: Lessons of World Bank Experience* (Washington: World Bank, 1985).

Berg, Elliot, and Alan Batchelder, "Structural Adjustment Lending: A Critical View," World Bank, CPD Discussion Paper No. 1985–21, Washington, 1985.

Bruno, Michael, "Real Versus Financial Openness Under Alternative Exchange Rate Regimes," in *Financial Policies and the World Capital Market: The Problem of Latin American Countries*, ed. by Pedro Aspe and others (Chicago: University of Chicago, 1983).

Buiter, William, "Macroeconomic Responses by Developing Countries to Changes in External Conditions," NBER Working Paper No. 1836 (Cambridge, Massachusetts: National Bureau of Economic Research, 1986).

Calvo, Guillermo (1986a) "Fractured Liberalism: Argentina Under Martinez de Hoz," *Economic Development and Cultural Change* (Chicago), Vol. 34 (April 1986), pp. 423–671.

———— (1986b), "Incredible Reforms," unpublished, Department of Economics, Columbia University, New York, 1986.

Choksi, Armeane, "Adjustment With Growth in the Highly Indebted Middle-Income Countries," World Bank CPD Discussion Paper No. 1986–36, Washington, 1986.

Corbo, Vittorio, "Reforms and Macroeconomic Adjustments in Chile During 1974–84," *World Development* (Oxford), Vol. 13 (August 1985), pp. 893–916.

———— , "Problems, Development Theory and Strategies of Latin America," in *The State of Development Economics*, ed. by Gustav Ranis and others (Oxford: Basil Blackwell, 1987).

———— , and Jaime de Melo, "Lessons From the Southern Cone Policy Reforms," *World Bank Research Observer* (Washington), Vol. 2 (1987 forthcoming).

Corden, W.M., *Inflation, Exchange Rates and the World Economy* (Chicago: University of Chicago Press, 1981).

Development Committee (1986a), *A Strategy for Restoration of Growth in Middle-Income Countries that Face Debt-Servicing Difficulties*, Development Committee Pamphlet No. 10 (Washington, World Bank, 1986).

———— (1986b), "ODA Flows and Prospects," Development Committee Document DC/86–15 (Washington, World Bank, September 3, 1986).

Dornbusch, Rudiger, *Open Economy Macroeconomics* (New York: Basic Books, 1980).

Edwards, Sebastian, *The Order of Liberalization of the External Sector*, Essays in International Finance, No. 156 (Princeton: Princeton University, 1984).

Fischer, Stanley, *Indexing, Inflation, and Economic Policy* (Cambridge, Massachusetts: MIT Press, 1986).

Frenkel, Jacob, "The Order of Economic Liberalization: Discussions," in *Economic Policy in a World of Change*, ed. by Karl Brunner and Allan H. Meltzer (Amsterdam: North-Holland, 1982).

————, and others, "Panel Discussion on the Southern Cone," *Staff Papers*, International Monetary Fund (Washington), Vol. 30 (March 1983), pp. 164–84.

Genberg, Hans, and Alexander Swoboda, "The Medium-Term Relationship Between Performance Indicators and Policy: A Cross-Section Approach," World Bank, Country Analysis and Projections Division Working Paper, No. 1986–2, Washington, 1986.

Heillener, Gerald, "Policy-Based Program Lending: A Look at the Bank's New Role," in *Between Two Worlds: The World Bank's Next Decade*, ed. by Richard Feinberg (New Brunswick: Transaction Books, 1986).

Hino, Hiroyuki, "IMF—World Bank Collaboration," *Finance and Development* (Washington), Vol. 23 (September 1986), pp. 10–14.

Husain, Tariq, "Efficiency of Public Sector Investment Reviews," unpublished, World Bank, Washington, 1986.

Kavalsky, Basil, "Reviewing Public Investment Programs," *Finance and Development* (Washington), Vol. 23 (March 1986), pp. 37–40.

Khan, Mohsin and Malcolm D. Knight, *Fund-Supported Adjustment Programs and Economic Growth*, IMF Occasional Paper No. 41 (Washington: International Monetary Fund, 1985).

————, Peter Montiel, and Nadeem U. Haque, "Adjustment with Growth: Relating the Analytical Approaches of the World Bank and the IMF," World Bank, Development Policy Issues Series, No. 8, Washington, 1986.

Krueger, Anne O., *Foreign Trade Regimes and Economic Development: Liberalization Attempts and Consequences* (Cambridge, Massachusetts: National Bureau of Economic Research, 1978).

————, and others, eds., *Trade and Employment in Developing Countries, Volume 3, Synthesis and Conclusions* (Chicago: University of Chicago Press, 1981).

————, "Problems of Liberalization," in *World Economic Growth*, ed. by Arnold Harberger (San Francisco: ICS Press, 1984).

————, and Constantine Michalopoulos, "Developing Country Trade Policies and the International Economic System," in *Hard Bargaining Ahead: U.S. Third World Policy and Developing Countries*, ed. by Overseas Development Council (New Brunswick: Transaction Books, 1985).

—————, Maurice Schiff, and Alberto Valdes, "A Comparative Study of the Political Economy of Agricultural Pricing Policies," World Bank, Washington, 1987 (forthcoming).

McKinnon, Ronald, "The Order of Economic Liberalization: Lessons From Chile and Argentina," in *Economic Policy in a World of Change*, ed. by Karl Brunner and Allan H. Meltzer (Amsterdam: North-Holland, 1982).

Mussa, Michael, "Macroeconomic and Trade Liberalization: Some Guidelines," *World Bank Research Observer* (Washington), Vol. 2 (January 1987), pp. 61–78.

Overseas Development Council, *Between Two Worlds: The World Bank's Next Decade* (New Brunswick: Transaction Books, 1986).

Papageorgiou, Demetris, Michael Michaely, and Armeane Choksi, "The Phasing of a Trade Liberalization Policy: Preliminary Evidence," World Bank, CPD Discussion Paper No. 1986–42, Washington, 1986.

Pfeffermann, Guy, "Public Expenditure in Latin America: Effects on Poverty," unpublished, World Bank, Washington, 1986.

Please, Stanley, "The World Bank: Lending for Structural Adjustment," in *Adjustment Crisis in the Third World*, ed. by Richard E. Feinberg and Valeriana Kalleb (New Brunswick: Transaction Books, 1984).

Sachs, Jeffrey, "External Debt and Macroeconomic Performance in Latin America and East Asia," *Brookings Papers on Economic Activity: 2* (1985), The Brookings Institution (Washington), pp. 565–73.

Selowsky, Marcelo, and Herman G. van der Tak, "The Debt Problem and Growth," *World Development* (Oxford), Vol. 14 (September 1986), pp.1107–24.

Stern, Ernest, "World Bank Financing of Structural Adjustment," in *IMF Conditionality*, ed. by John Williamson (Washington: Institute for International Economics, 1983).

World Bank (1986a), "Sector Adjustment Lending: Progress Report," unpublished paper circulated to the Executive Directors, No. R86–9, World Bank, Washington, January 24, 1986.

————— (1986b), "Structural Adjustment Lending: A First Review of Experience," Report No. 6409, World Bank, Washington, September 24, 1986.

————— (1986c), *Financing Adjustment With Growth in Sub-Saharan Africa, 1986–90* (Washington: World Bank, 1986).

————— (1987), *World Debt Tables* (Washington: World Bank, 1987).

Yagci, Fahrettin, Steven Kamin, and Vicki Rosenbaum, "Structural Adjustment Lending, An Evaluation of Program Design," World Bank, Staff Working Paper No. 735, Washington, 1985.

Yeager, L.B., *Experiences with Stopping Inflation* (Washington: American Enterprise Institute, 1981).

Adjustment and Economic Growth: Their Fundamental Complementarity

Manuel Guitián
Deputy Director
Exchange and Trade Relations Department
International Monetary Fund

The purpose of this paper is to provide an overview of the direct role of the International Monetary Fund in support of economic adjustment efforts and the consequent attainment of economic growth. To this end, the paper will address a variety of issues that revolve around the essential characteristics of the relationship between the processes of adjustment and growth. As the title of the paper indicates, the analysis will stress particularly the fundamental complementarity that binds these two processes together. This property of their relationship, of course, constitutes a basic principle underlying the approach of the Fund to the issues of adjustment and growth. In the process, the analysis will also seek to bring forth the opportunities that the complementarity between adjustment and growth opens as well as the limitations that it imposes for economic policy formulation.

This paper is concerned mainly with the adjustment policies of members seeking access to Fund resources. Therefore, its scope does not extend to an examination of other important aspects of the role of the institution in the international adjustment process. The broad dimensions of the responsibilities of the Fund in this area, including its provision of financial support, reflect the universal character of its membership as well as the ample realm of its mandate. The membership encompasses a variety of countries, developing and developed, debtor and creditor alike. The mandate includes responsibility for surveillance over member economic and financial policies

Note: The views expressed in this paper are the author's and not necessarily those of the International Monetary Fund.

as a means to foster orderly economic growth with a measure of price stability in a setting of liberal and open exchange of goods, services, and capital among countries.[1] Through the exercise of surveillance, the Fund seeks to establish in the international economy conditions that are supportive of the balance of payments adjustment efforts of individual members. Surveillance can enhance the effectiveness of those efforts and therefore, it constitutes another of the important contributions of the Fund toward the improvement of the functioning of the adjustment process. But to yield results, the implementation of surveillance requires consistency with other Fund policies in support of adjustment, including, in particular, those discussed in this paper.

The focus of the paper will be on policy issues that arise in the specific context of adjustment and growth and that appear of particular relevance from the perspective of the Fund and its relationship with members that seek use of Fund resources as well as with the membership as a whole. The examination of these issues can hardly be expected to cover the complexities of the subject in their entirety; rather, the intention is to shed light on certain critical aspects of the choices that have to be made in the economic policy decision-making process as they emerge in the context of Fund operations with members.

The plan of the paper is as follows: the analysis will first focus on the nature and characteristics of the imbalances that typically confront member country economies. Second, the paper will examine the various objectives of adjustment, their interrelationship and the implications for the Fund's operations of the priorities that members set with regard to the scope and speed of achievement of the various goals. Third, the analysis in the paper will discuss the realities of adjustment and how these are influenced by the requirements of growth. Against this background, the paper will then outline a broad framework for the design of adjustment and the attainment of growth. Such a framework will permit an examination of the broad domestic and external policy areas, as well as their interplay, that are generally involved in the formulation of an adjustment plan. Given the specific requirements of the attainment of growth as a concrete objective, this examination will widen the analysis to include among the possible

---

[1] See Article IV of the *Articles of Agreement of the International Monetary Fund*, International Monetary Fund (1978).

policy actions the need for supporting measures in concrete sectoral domains. On the basis of this framework, the paper will then discuss issues, choices and constraints that the pursuit of adjustment and growth pose for the Fund and for member countries. Finally, the paper will close with some brief remarks concerning areas where scope for further action on the part of the Fund may be warranted to strengthen the positive interaction between adjustment and growth.

Nature and Characteristics of Adjustment Need

An important element for purposes of the design of an adjustment and growth strategy is an assessment of the nature and characteristics of the imbalance that needs to be redressed. On the most general level, an actual or a potential need for adjustment may arise in a variety of manners and for a variety of reasons. It can develop because the sum total of demands for resources that develop in an economy exceeds the global amount of resources that can be made available internally and those that can be obtained from abroad on an appropriate scale and on sustainable terms. But it can also emerge on account of inefficiencies in the use of available resources or other distortions that constrain the level or the rate of expansion of aggregate supply—most likely, both of them—and therefore keep the economy operating under its capacity and below its potential rate of growth. Actual or potential aggregate imbalances that conform to this general description recur in all economies, albeit with a varying degree of frequency. For purposes of addressing such recurring imbalances, it is also important to ascertain other of their specific characteristics. This will require, for example, an assessment of the origin of the imbalances—that is, whether they are the result of external or internal factors—and of their nature—that is, whether they reflect exogenous or endogenous causes and, more important, whether they are transitory or permanent.[2]

---

[2] A more extensive discussion of these issues can be found, for example, in Manuel Guitián (1981), Bahram Nowzad (1981), and Vito Tanzi (1987). In addition to the specific features of the imbalance, the characteristics of the country's economy are important for the design of an adjustment strategy. In the context of Fund operations with members, consideration of these diverse individual country characteristics calls for a measure of flexibility which has to be balanced against the institutional requirement of uniformity of treatment. These issues, of course, are country specific and have not been pursued here because this paper focuses on the general aspects of adjustment and growth. Further discussion of these subjects, however, can be found in Manuel Guitián (1983a).

An accurate assessment of the various features of the imbalance in need of adjustment can contribute greatly to the quality of the design of the required adjustment effort. For example, the particular mix of policies will of course be influenced by whether the imbalance is the result of demand or supply factors, or by whether it reflects external or internal events, or by whether or not it is attributable to domestic policy developments. Important though these features are, they are not as critical, for purposes of policy decision making, as the evaluation of the temporary or permanent character of the imbalance, which besides affecting the policy mix, will determine the strength and pace of the adjustment effort required for its elimination.

The characteristics of the adjustment need, therefore, have clear implications for the design of the adjustment effort. In addition, an issue that needs to be kept under close examination is the correspondence that has been established over time between the development of an adjustment need and the consequent formulation and implementation of an adjustment effort (both of them *flow* concepts).[3] The extent to which need and effort are commensurate with each other in scale and timeliness will determine whether or not the imbalance in one period is being passed on to the next. These considerations interact with the distinctions outlined above concerning the characteristics of an imbalance, which, in this context, may lose some of their initial relevance. For example, a temporary imbalance which is not corrected opportunely may prove to be less transitory than it seemed originally.[4] Similarly, an exogenously created imbalance, unless corrected promptly, can give rise to endogenous developments that compound it.

This line of reasoning cannot be overstressed in present circumstances in the international economy. Instances abound in recent years of imbalances accumulated over a relatively long period of time (a *stock* concept) which have led to a distribution of liabilities and

---

[3] In the context of policies on the use of Fund resources and in particular, of the Guidelines on Conditionality, this is a key notion behind guideline No. 1 that encourages members to adopt corrective measures at an early stage of their external difficulties. See International Monetary Fund (1986a).

[4] In this argument, the concept of temporariness is to be distinguished from the notion of reversibility. A transitory *and* reversible imbalance does not generally call for policy action if resources exist (reserves) or can be found (borrowing) to finance it for the duration or if the distortions (restrictions, price, and output variations) to which it can otherwise give rise are considered acceptable.

assets across countries, the characteristics of which have exacerbated the difficulties typically associated with the adjustment process. Rapid accumulation of external debt and payments arrears have constrained the scope for economic policy management in debtor countries. It has also led to a slowdown, indeed, a virtual interruption of capital flows from creditor countries along their historically normal patterns. As a result, severe constraints have arisen for the adjustment process and the attainment of economic objectives, in particular, economic growth.

Objectives of Adjustment

Economic policies in general, and adjustment policies in particular seek a broad range of objectives of a diverse but generally interrelated nature. From the standpoint of member countries, the choice among those objectives is based not only on economic criteria but also on other considerations. Objectives that are selected mainly on economic grounds include: the achievement of a sound growth rate and the maintenance of an appropriate level of employment, a measure of domestic price and exchange rate stability, and a viable balance of payments position. Among the various economic policy goals, these are the most often mentioned in the international context because, besides their clear importance for each particular economy, they are most relevant for the interrelationship among national economies.

There are also economic policy objectives the selection of which reflects a mixture of economic and other criteria and that are of importance mainly (though by no means solely) in a domestic context. The pursuit of these objectives is based on a combination of economic, social, and political considerations and frequently responds to concerns about the equity and the distributional consequences of economic policies. Thus, besides the growth, price, and balance of payments objectives outlined above, country governments often seek the establishment of standards of welfare through the pursuit of equity-oriented goals in a diversity of domains, such as income distribution, education, and nutrition.

Clearly, the scope for the attainment of the full spectrum of such varied economic policy aims is bound inevitably by the relationship that prevails between required and available resources. The setting of priorities, therefore, involves choices with regard to the mix of objectives as well as with regard to the speed of their relative attainment and constitutes an integral part of the process of economic policy formulation and decision making. Indeed, the appropriateness of those choices can be a critical factor for the sustained implementation of economic policies, which in turn is often a necessary condition for the attainment of the objectives. Alternatively, evidence of progress in the adjustment effort, which is often measured by the appropriateness in the balance in selection of economic aims and by the record of proximity toward their attainment, can provide the strongest grounds for its sustainability.

On the part of the Fund, its broad purposes are described in the basic charter of the institution, the *Articles of Agreement*. They call for the expansion and balanced growth of world trade as a means toward the promotion and maintenance of high employment and real income levels as well as toward the development of the productive resources of all members. The institution seeks to fulfill its purposes by fostering economic and financial cooperation among member countries in a setting of exchange stability and orderly exchange arrangements and in the context of a liberal system of multilateral payments. To this end, it is well known that the Fund stands ready to make resources temporarily available to members in support of their efforts to correct maladjustments in their balance of payments. The basic aim is to shorten the duration and lessen the degree of the imbalance in the payments positions of members through the adoption of policy measures compatible with individual member interests as well as with those of the membership as a whole.[5]

In the provision of financial support to members' adjustment efforts, the Fund needs to be assured that their policies are consistent with the code of conduct embodied in the institution's charter and it must also establish adequate safeguards to ensure that the use of the resources will be temporary.[6] It is, thus, clear that the *Articles of Agreement* call upon the Fund, in a particularly direct fashion, to support members in balance of payments need that are willing to adopt corrective policies that conform to the agreed code of conduct

---

[5] See Article I of the *Articles of Agreement*, International Monetary Fund (1978).

[6] See, in particular, Article I(v) and Article V, Section 3(a) of the *Articles of Agreement*, International Monetary Fund (1978).

and that give assurances that the specific objective of balance of payments recovery will be achieved over a foreseeable period.[7]

In its financial relationship with individual members, therefore, the Fund stresses the attainment of balance of payments objectives as the domain in which the interests of each member and those of the membership as a whole intersect and coincide. Of course, this does not mean that the institution is indifferent or oblivious to the achievement of other objectives. In particular, sound rates of economic activity, employment, and growth as well as price stability are objectives shared by the Fund and its membership. From the perspective of the institution, attainment of these other policy objectives cannot but strengthen the recovery of the balance of payments and make it durable. But it must be stressed that the Fund's concern with these policy aims is based on their complementarity with the strengthening of the external payments position. Members naturally seek to attain them for this as well as for other reasons of possibly more importance domestically.

Besides the safeguard and promotion of the interests of the membership, in its financial operations with individual countries[8] the Fund aims at keeping an important measure of circumspection in its interaction with members in the area of policy formulation. Such circumspection is required to avert undue international interference in domestic policy decisions. It is manifest in the priority the institution accords to external objectives—for example, balance of payments, exchange restrictions, external payments arrears—and the latitude its policies allow members to retain with regard to other domestic economic objectives—e.g., growth, price stability. The observance of what might be termed a principle of political neutrality is required

---

[7] The Fund makes resources available to members through a variety of instruments, including stand-by and extended arrangements. For a discussion of those instruments, see Joseph Gold (1980) and Manuel Guitián (1981). In 1986, the Fund established a Structural Adjustment Facility to provide concessional assistance to low-income countries with protracted balance of payments problems. See International Monetary Fund (1986a).

[8] As noted at the outset, the Fund supports adjustment directly through provision of financial resources and of policy advice in the context of annual consultations with individual members as well as through the promotion of a stable and favorable environment by the exercise of surveillance. In addition, the Fund carries out a number of other tasks in the financing sphere, including the provision of direct liquidity through SDR allocations and of temporary financing under the Compensatory Financing and Buffer Stock Financing Facilities.

to an even larger extent with respect to domestic policy objectives that are pursued for equity, social, or political considerations.[9] The exercise of discretion on these fronts, however, is not an indication of disregard or indifference. The establishment of social or political priorities, even when they overlap with economic considerations, is part of the domain of independent national policy decision making. International circumspection, therefore, is only a reflection of respect for such independence. Noninterference, of course, does not preclude the Fund, whenever necessary, from assessing the claims that domestic priorities put on available resources and from pointing out their economic implications and in particular any resulting balance of payments pressures.

Realities of Adjustment and Requirements of Growth

As made abundantly clear by developments in the international economy in recent years, a feature of the international adjustment process that cannot be overstressed is that external payments imbalances can prevail only for as long as they can be financed.[10] Thereafter, adjustment will occur, and claims on resources will be confined to those that are domestically available, whether or not specific policy actions are undertaken. Consequently, a key reality to keep in mind when confronting an external imbalance is that the issue is not whether it will be adjusted, because it will be, but rather, how it will be adjusted, efficiently or otherwise.

Another important reality that warrants attention in this general context concerns the relationship between adjustment and financing[11] and its implications for the design of a strategy to redress an external payments imbalance. The issues that arise in this regard involve intertemporal trade-offs and serve to illustrate the connection between a flow (initial) imbalance with a stock (accumulated) disequilibrium that was mentioned earlier. Financing and adjustment can substitute

---

[9] For an ample discussion of these issues, see C. David Finch (1983).

[10] The norm used in this paper to measure an external payments imbalance is whether it requires foreign financing on a scale and on terms incompatible with the economy's growth and development prospects and therefore, unsustainable. See in this context, Manuel Guitián (1983a).

[11] For a recent general discussion of the subject of adjustment and financing and the role of the Fund, see Peter B. Kenen (1986).

for or complement one another as an external imbalance develops. The possibility of relying on foreign borrowing or on international reserve use (financing) rather than on policy action (adjustment) is a course of action that, as noted above, can only be pursued temporarily. Such a strategy basically transfers and adds the imbalances from one period to the next until the cumulative adjustment need surfaces abruptly, often when no more financing is available and the scope for the incurrence of payments arrears is exhausted. At that moment, the burden of adjustment is to correct the existing flow imbalance that remains together with previous imbalances that were allowed by means of the accumulation of external liabilities on unsustainable scale and terms.

But financing can instead be used in conjunction with adjustment policies to tide the economy over the period required for the policies to yield their results. The mix of adjustment and financing required by this alternative strategy can vary depending on the strength of the policies and the speed with which they are adopted. Other things equal, the stronger the policy measures are, and the faster their implementation is, the lesser will be the associated need for financing.[12]

The characteristics of the particular blend of adjustment and financing are among the factors that influence the specific constellation of objectives achieved over time in the process of adjustment. For example, the particular path of the balance of payments during the period of adjustment and beyond will be affected, among other things, by the amount and terms of the financing that has been used in the process. The larger the magnitude of financing and the harder its terms, the higher will be the claims placed on future resources, and therefore the stronger will have to be the balance of payments results to be attained by policy action.[13]

This line of reasoning leads directly into the relationship between adjustment, financing and policy objectives, and in particular, eco-

---

[12] A point that may be advanced here is that the adoption and sustained pursuit of adjustment measures not only reduce the *need* for resources but they are also instrumental in raising their *availability*. This argument is elaborated further in later sections of the paper.

[13] These considerations are related to the question of the relative merits of a gradual versus a rapid adjustment effort which revolve around the choice between current and future absorption levels in the economy.

nomic growth. Emphasis on economic growth in the adjustment process does not run counter to the objective of balance of payments viability. It is important, however, to stress that although normally the attainment of both objectives goes hand in hand, whenever the imbalances to be corrected have led to or were associated with unsustainable growth rates in the economy, the restoration of growth to a sustained, even though lower, path represents an element of the solution rather than being a manifestation of a problem.[14]

It is conceivable that for a given amount of external and internal resources, concentration on achieving growth will constrain the range of the policy mixes that otherwise would be compatible with a viable balance of payments. To an extent, such constraints may reflect trade-offs between growth and other domestic policy objectives (particularly those of a distributional character) more than trade-offs between growth and balance of payments outcomes per se.

When correction of a balance of payments imbalance is to be undertaken, growth considerations are also raised to influence the choice of the mix between adjustment and financing. In this context, it is often argued that a bias in favor of financing is appropriate whenever growth objectives are part of the policy strategy. As developed more fully later, however, the issue at stake here tends to revolve more frequently around the efficiency of resource use than around the amount of resources. If efficiency requirements are met, the choice of the adjustment financing mix has to be guided by the relationship on the margin, between the rate of return and the cost of the foreign resources. Use of foreign financing beyond the point where their yield covers their cost would not be advisable either from the perspective of growth or the balance of payments. Another way in which this argument can be put is the following: the more foreign financing is resorted to, the more resources will have to be devoted in the future to its servicing. Consequently, unless the growth associated with such financing reflects its efficient use, it will not be sustained. Indeed, growth in the future may have been mortgaged if financing was undertaken in excess of the economy's absorptive and productive capacities.

---

[14] For discussions of the impact on growth of a variety of economic policy measures, see, for example, Mohsin S. Khan and Malcolm D. Knight (1985) and Mohsin S. Khan (1986).

Broad Framework for Adjustment and Growth

Programs of adjustment are typically required to bring aggregate demand in an economy in line with its productive capacity or, for a given global demand, to bring such productive capacity to its potential level.[15] Among their various goals, the programs include a strengthening of the balance of payments, a measure of price stability, and an improvement in growth performance. It is important to stress, at the outset, that in exact parallel with adjustment, the attainment of a sound rate of growth depends on two critical factors: the *amount* of resources available to an economy; and the *efficiency* with which it uses those resources. Consequently, adjustment programs contain an important array of policies and measures that besides restoring balance to the economy, are aimed at the mobilization and efficient use of resources, and in particular at an increase in savings and, as a result, in the potential for investment.

Policies of adjustment can be classified in accordance with a variety of criteria, but such classifications are rarely clearcut because sectors and economies are interdependent and therefore the effects of policy actions are pervasive. It is useful nevertheless to group the various policy measures according to the variables on which they exert their strongest (though not their only) impact. From this standpoint, policies and measures that influence in a relatively straightforward manner the level and composition of aggregate demand are often distinguished from policies and measures that seek to affect directly the rate and structure of production in the economy. The underlying rationale of the distinction is that among the variety of factors behind the emergence of a global imbalance in an economy, there is frequently an unsustainable expansion in aggregate demand and expenditure, and consequently, its elimination will entail a reduction in the level or the rate of growth of demand. At the early stages of the process, it is not always easy to provide an unambiguous diagnosis that such an expansion in demand is an indication of a developing imbalance that requires correction. This is particularly the case when the combination of its effects gives grounds for diverse, if not conflicting, assessments. In specific terms, incipient increases in global demand

---

[15] The discussion in this section, and in the paper in general, refers specifically to policies typically supported by the Fund, but the analysis is of a general character and it applies to any given economy confronting an imbalance.

and expenditure can—and often do—give rise to developments in certain areas (e.g., employment, output) that are generally perceived as favorable. These perceptions are not always sufficiently tempered by concurrent developments in other domains (e.g., prices, balance of payments) even though these rarely can be described as positive.

There is a variety of reasons why reactions may be biased in favor of the areas with favorable effects. To begin with, pressures on domestic prices and the balance of payments may not manifest themselves immediately, as some of the effects of the expansion in demand can be masked by borrowing abroad or by utilization of international reserves or both. Even where the resulting increases in external debt and declines in foreign assets are viewed with a measure of concern, these developments may be considered at the time to be a reasonable price to pay for the positive events elsewhere in the economy. As the process develops, however, the scope for increases in external debt and declines in international reserves becomes progressively limited. At this point, the adverse price and balance of payments performance becomes increasingly evident, often at a time when the initially positive developments in the employment and output fields either begin to falter or have already disappeared.

Amount of Resources and Macroeconomic Balance

For these reasons, a key function of economic management is to keep the level and the rate of growth of aggregate demand in a sound relationship with the level and growth prospects of the economy's productive capacity. For a given level of such capacity and a given structure of relative prices and costs (including exchange rates and interest rates), this will entail the prevalence of domestic financial policies that are consistent with macroeconomic balance in the economy. This is a first broad area of interest in the context of the relationship between the Fund and its members.

Investigation of the sources of expansion in aggregate demand frequently indicates that they are directly associated with imbalances in the fiscal accounts or more broadly in the public sector finances. Such imbalances, not surprisingly, are typically the outcome of the pursuit of objectives requiring levels of public sector expenditure that exceed the sector's willingness or ability to raise and collect revenues.

The correction of imbalances that originate in the public sector finances encompasses a variety of policy actions that constitute what may be labeled the *fiscal aspect of macroeconomic management*. All of these actions ultimately consist of measures that specifically seek to curtail fiscal spending or to raise additional fiscal revenues in order to bring the resulting public sector balance to a sustainable position. The particular mix of measures chosen to correct a fiscal disequilibrium will, of course, influence the general performance of the rest of the economy. For example, the implications for the private economy will vary depending on whether the fiscal strategy focuses on measures to control outlays or whether it stresses instead revenue-raising actions. At a first approximation, an approach based on reduction of public sector spending seeks to restore balance in the economy by directly lowering the participation or weight of the public sector in aggregate demand. In contrast, the balance that would obtain from an approach based instead on raising domestic fiscal revenues would tend to be accompanied, other things equal, by a reduction in private demand. The consequences across the economy of different fiscal policy mixes are therefore diverse, but they also vary over time as they influence differently the incentives and signals they provide for economic decisions.[16] Not only do fiscal policy packages differ in impact; they also differ in the certainty and speed with which they yield results. For example, an action to curtail spending and an action to raise revenue do not carry necessarily the same probability with regard to the magnitude and the timing of their respective results. Among other reasons, this is because the scope for a government to control its spending generally exceeds its ability to ensure that its receipts will rise.

There is, of course, a close relationship between fiscal policies— interpreted, as already noted, to mean actions that influence the flows of public sector outlays and revenues, and the broader sphere of financial policies, that is, those related to developments in credit, money and borrowing flows in an economy. In a domestic context, this relationship has been investigated extensively, among other things, to establish the relative role of fiscal and monetary policies in macroeconomic management.[17] Difficulties have been encountered

---

[16] For a general discussion of fiscal policy issues in the adjustment process, see Vito Tanzi and Mario Blejer (1984).

[17] For a discussion of this subject in the context of an open economy, see Jacob A. Frenkel and Michael L. Mussa (1981).

in making an unambiguous distinction between them if only because public sector spending or revenue measures—fiscal policy—influence strongly the public sector borrowing requirement in general and its need for domestic bank financing in particular—monetary policy.[18]

These considerations underscore that the maintenance of aggregate demand on a sustainable path calls for a measure of control over the flows of domestic financing and specifically over the rates of monetary and domestic credit expansion. These constitute what might be called the *monetary aspect of macroeconomic management* and stress as a key element the relationship that exists between the rate of domestic credit expansion and money supply increases, on the one hand, and among these and the levels of aggregate demand and expenditure, on the other. The other element to underscore in this general context is the important and well-established relationship that prevails under most circumstances between the demand for money balances and the level of global income in an economy. The combination of these two elements serves to bring to the surface the notion that, under most circumstances, a discrepancy between the supply and demand for money (an imbalance in the money market) has as a counterpart an imbalance between expenditure and income (an imbalance in the market for goods and services).[19] Therefore, the process of restoring a sound relationship between expenditure and income will also entail keeping domestic credit expansion in an appropriate balance with the prospective path of desired money holdings in the economy. Generally, although they can be influenced by policy actions, the behavior of these holdings is determined by the public.[20] Consequently, policy formulation in this area focuses mainly on the rate of domestic credit expansion to ensure that sustained balance prevails

---

[18] For a recent discussion of this subject, see Mohsin S. Khan (1986).

[19] The argument abstracts from the existence of borrowing and capital movements, an assumption that does not affect the analysis at this level. A fuller treatment of these issues can be found in the collection of articles in Jacob A. Frenkel and Harry G. Johnson (1976) and in International Monetary Fund (1977).

[20] Strictly speaking, the public determines its real money holdings, which can vary with changes in the price level or in the nominal quantity of money or both. In a closed economy, money market imbalances lead fundamentally to price level variations while in an open economy they lead to a combination of these with exchange rate and balance of payments changes; by means of the latter, the nominal quantity of money in the economy changes. See in this context, Manuel Guitián (1973) and Peter M. Keller (1980).

or is brought to the money market, in the sense that it is not bought at the expense of the balance of payments (e.g., international reserve losses, excessive foreign borrowing) or of price and exchange rate stability.

These general considerations provide the rationale for the particular importance attached to domestic credit expansion as a policy instrument in the context of Fund policies.[21] From the specific perspective of the Fund, this is perhaps best explained by stressing the close relationship that exists between this policy variable and the balance of payments. Under most circumstances, such relationship is relatively more direct that the one between monetary expansion and the external accounts, as made evident by the possibility of coexistence of a given stock of money with markedly different balance of payments outcomes. Given the need to protect the temporariness of the use of Fund resources, it is imperative that policy be formulated in a manner that does not permit, even over the limited periods in which they can occur, trade-offs among economic policy objectives that endanger balance of payments prospects and weaken international reserve positions, as would be the case if inflation or growth targets were to be pursued at the expense of international reserve losses.

Consistency in macroeconomic management requires that its fiscal and monetary aspects be complemented by supportive foreign borrowing policies—the *external debt aspect of macroeconomic management*.[22] The macroeconomic implications of external debt management policies derive from the direct influence that they can exert on the expenditure-income flow and from the substitutability that exists between foreign and domestic credit. In general, given an economy's productive and absorptive capacities, there is a level of aggregate demand and expenditure that is consistent with sustained growth, price stability and a viable, and therefore, sustainable, balance of payments position. In effect, the key aspects of macroeconomic management include monitoring the global (e.g., foreign and domestic) flow of financial resources available to the economy to ensure

---

[21] Further discussion of this issue can be found in Manuel Guitián (1973 and 1985b) and in William H. L. Day (1979).

[22] A general discussion of external debt management issues can be found in Claudio M. Loser (1977), K. Burke Dillon and David Lipton (1985), Vito Tanzi (1985), and Manuel Guitián (1987).

its compatibility with a pattern of expenditure and income that can be sustained.

From a different vantage point, the relationship between domestic financial and external debt policies also manifests itself in the latter's influence on international reserve and overall balance of payments developments as well as on the inflation and growth fronts. Put in a nutshell, in the presence of an imbalance (as defined earlier in the paper), foreign borrowing can make it temporarily possible for domestic demand and the rate of growth to reach levels beyond those that the economy can sustain. In these circumstances, the accumulation of external debt has in effect substituted for the price pressures and the international reserve losses that would have surfaced in its absence.

Efficiency in Resource Use and Economic Incentives

Until now, the discussion of macroeconomic management has proceeded on the assumption that the economy's productive capacity and the structure of relative prices and costs were given. Therefore it concentrated on key macroeconomic policies where attention has to focus to ensure that aggregate demand is kept in line with the economy's productive and external debt-carrying capacity at the prevailing relative cost-price structure. But the economy's productive potential and its capacity to service debt are influenced directly by macroeconomic policy actions as well as indirectly via their impact on relative prices and costs.

In general, the borrowing process transfers command over resources from surplus to deficit sectors or economies. In a closed economy context, with a given resource and technology endowment, output and growth will depend on the economy's propensity to save and the efficiency of its investment. The domestic borrowing process, by channeling resources from savers to investors, helps the economy with its given resource base to attain its potential level and rate of growth of production. An open economy, in contrast, has an additional source of resources, the use of foreign savings, for which the accumulation of external debt provides an important channel. Thus, aside from its already discussed macroeconomic impact, foreign borrowing adds directly to the resources available to the economy. If utilized efficiently, such borrowing can allow the economy not only to reach higher expenditure levels as noted above, but also to grow at higher sustained rates than otherwise.

These considerations highlight the link that exists, via the current account of the balance of payments, between domestic macroeconomic management, external debt policies, the saving-investment process, and the long-run evolution of the economy. They also make clear that a medium-term horizon is required for the formulation and assessment of policies, and this is also the appropriate timeframe for the achievement of objectives like growth and external payments viability.

A sustained adjustment effort, particularly where growth is an especially important objective in addition to the balance of payments, requires that macroeconomic balance be attained in a setting of appropriate incentives and signals to guide decisions to allocate and use resources efficiently in the economy. The adequacy of structure of relative prices and costs is critical in this regard. Imbalances, especially when they are allowed to persist, often result in relative price-cost misalignments both among sectors in the economy and between the economy as a whole and the rest of the world. In these circumstances, the conduct of macroeconomic policy in the various areas already discussed often needs to be supported by suitable adjustments in key prices and costs for progress in the attainment of macroeconomic balance to be durable.

This is one of the domains of economic policy where macroeconomic management blends with structural adjustment and the scope for action is indeed ample. In the realm of fiscal policy, particularly in the area of expenditure management, a key issue relates to the efficiency and composition of spending. The durability of an effort to control demand and public sector expenditure will depend, inter alia, on the curtailment of unproductive spending and in particular, on the protection of productive investment outlays. In the area of fiscal revenues, improvements in the structure of tax rates can also contribute to enhance productivity in the economy, thus underpinning the quality of global fiscal management.[23] Other possible supporting actions of equivalent importance encompass the broad realm of public sector enterprise pricing policy, including sectoral producer and consumer prices and the related question of subsidies. More

---

[23] For an extensive discussion of these issues, see Vito Tanzi (1987).

generally, the maintenance of an appropriate structure of relative prices is required to promote efficiency in the allocation and use of resources among sectors in the economy. At times, for reasons often associated with distributional aims, prices of goods and services of importance from an economywide standpoint are allowed to become unrealistic, despite adverse allocative and financial consequences. In those circumstances, a critical element for adjustment will be the restoration of adequate prices relativities.[24]

In the sphere of monetary and credit policies, these must lead to appropriate domestic interest rates, which are critical to ensure efficiency in the allocation and use of financial resources in the economy. Consequently, they are also of primary importance for growth and balance of payments viability. On a general level, these objectives call for domestic interest rates that help mobilize domestic savings, that is, interest rates that are appropriate in real terms. They also call for those interest rates to be competitive internationally so as to retain savings internally and encourage foreign capital inflows.[25] This is yet another perspective from which the policies required for purposes of growth and the balance of payments coincide, although it may be pointed out that examples abound where interest rates have been kept uneconomically low, even negative in real terms, on the grounds that high interest rates adversely affect investment and growth.

Another area the importance of which for growth and external payments viability cannot be overstressed concerns exchange rates and competitiveness. Persistent imbalances in an economy typically result in patterns and movements of domestic prices and costs that diverge significantly from those that prevail abroad. Resource allocation is distorted and competitiveness is impaired in the process and so are the growth and balance of payments performance of the economy.[26] In these circumstances, exchange rate adjustments or flexibility in exchange rate management, or both, supported by

---

[24] On the subject of the role of economy-wide prices in adjustment, see Claudio M. Loser (1984); see also Rudiger Dornbusch (1985).

[25] Interest rate policies are discussed in some detail in International Monetary Fund (1983).

[26] For a discussion of the relationship between the exchange rate and financial policies as well as their implications for growth and the balance of payments, see Manuel Guitián (1976 and 1985b); see also, G. G. Johnson (1985), Rudiger Dornbusch (1986), and Morris Goldstein (1986).

appropriate macroeconomic policies, can be crucial to restore competitiveness and balance to the economy by helping to bring factor prices, including wages, and absorption, particularly consumption, to realistic levels. In broad terms, the usefulness of exchange rate adjustments and more generally of exchange rate policy lies in their widespread effects on the economy. When competitiveness has been eroded and balance of payments pressures prevail, exchange rate action helps to shift demand from international goods to domestic goods. In the process, it also causes variations in the real value of nominal assets and as a result influences the level or rate of growth of global demand and expenditure. Therefore exchange rate policy contributes to balance the external accounts directly by containing domestic absorption and indirectly by improving resource allocation between the internal and external sectors.

But in order to improve incentives and yield results, macroeconomic policies, as well as domestic price and cost adjustments, need to be supported by the opening up of the economy. The efficiency of pricing signals in imparting information among sectors and among economies concerning their respective relative resource scarcities and demand patterns can be seriously impaired by the presence of restrictions and controls. Therefore another important and desirable component of an adjustment strategy is the liberalization of exchange and trade regimes to ensure that economic incentives and pricing signals fulfill their functions.

Specific Sectoral Measures

The attainment and maintenance of an economy's growth potential often call for other specific actions to eliminate inefficiencies in the economy as a whole or in concrete sectors within the economy. These sectoral policy domains are of particular importance in the context of structural adjustment. The liberalization of trade and exchange restrictions already noted constitutes a necessary complement to policy measures in the macroeconomic and pricing spheres for the attainment of sustained growth and balance of payments viability. From a logical perspective, an adequate adjustment effort would include among its various aims the elimination of restrictions maintained for balance of payments reasons because absence of the need for such restrictions is one of the characteristics of external viability.

Besides the external sector, there are other domains for action of a specific character that include the following: the public sector enterprises where issues of efficiency typically arise in connection with pricing, employment, investment, and financial management decisions; domestic financial sector reform, where the issues to be resolved can span from the viability of the sector to its ability and efficiency in mobilizing savings; labor market conditions, where the issues often include, besides the appropriateness of wage rates, rigidities in sectoral mobility and the realism of labor legislation; and capital markets, their adequacy and accessibility, including prospects to foster direct investment flows.[27] In this context, the importance of open capital markets in creditor and debtor countries alike cannot be overstressed because it is critical for the restoration and maintenance of balance in the structure and level of capital movements.

The measures most closely related to the broad policy areas discussed earlier are those in connection with the liberalization of exchange regimes, which fall within the direct competence and responsibility of the Fund, and of trade systems, where the Fund shares its interest with the General Agreement on Tariffs and Trade (GATT) and the World Bank.[28] Through its regular consultation as well as its technical assistance mission work with member countries, the Fund has been actively involved in the process of reform of specific economic sectors. These activities have included the development of central banking and money market institutions; the improvement of exchange market arrangements; and the establishment of adequate institutional machinery for coordination of policy decision making as well as for monitoring economic performance, particularly in the fiscal and external debt management areas. A number of these activities fall within the domain of common interest to the Fund and the Bank and the two institutions collaborate closely in the exercise of their respective roles in these areas.[29] The issues

---

[27] On the specific subject of foreign private investment flows, see International Monetary Fund (1985).

[28] A brief discussion of these institutional relationships can be found in Manuel Guitián (1985a). For an examination of the World Bank financing of structural adjustment, see Ernest Stern (1983).

[29] Issues of Fund-Bank collaboration, important though they are, fall outside the scope of this paper. For treatments of this subject, see Joseph Gold (1981–82), P. R. Narvekar (1983), and Hiroyuki Hino (1986).

that arise in connection with such institutional reforms are not generally perceived as an integral part of the broad realm of global economic management, but they can be critical for the efficient operation of the economy and therefore are important in the context of the design of a growth-oriented adjustment strategy.

Issues in the Context of Adjustment and Growth

A major aspect of the role of the Fund in adjustment consists of the provision of resources to members that are not only in need of balance of payments support but also willing to undertake policies appropriate to correct their external imbalance. As has been often remarked, the policies and conditions attached to the assistance provided by the Fund have helped to catalyze financial resources from other sources. From this standpoint, it can be said that the Fund helps to oversee the distribution of capital flows among member countries so that it contributes to the effectiveness of adjustment and thus proves beneficial to each member and the membership as a whole.[30] On this front, the institution's approach underscores that from an economic perspective, key determinants of the flow of capital include the prospects concerning its rate of return and the probability of its continued service. Only on this basis can sustainability of capital flows be postulated. Consequently, policies in borrowing countries have to provide assurances with regard to the return and servicing of capital flows in order to attract external savings on a sustained basis. In recent years, the movement of capital across countries has been severely curtailed. In the circumstances, the Fund has had to develop increasingly active procedures in an attempt to ensure that external assistance in support of adjustment efforts actually flows on the required scale. These procedures were built around members' financial arrangements with the Fund. Besides being the main vehicles for the provision of Fund resources, these arrangements became the pivot around which the institution organized its efforts to elicit support from major creditor countries and from main sources of private capital, including in particular, the commercial banks. In this manner, at a time when capital movements had virtually ceased, the

---

[30] See C. David Finch (1983) where this particular dimension of the role of the Fund in adjustment has been stressed.

Fund played an increasingly important role as a catalyst for capital flows to strengthen adjustment.[31] An important factor, therefore, for purposes of adjustment and growth in borrowing countries will be the continued ability of the Fund to muster external resources as well as to elicit responsible actions on the part of creditors and capital exporting countries to allow capital to flow efficiently.

The temporariness in the use of Fund resources prescribed by the *Articles of Agreement* constitutes a specific form of recognition that balance of payments problems have to be corrected to permit, at a minimum, timely repayment of the resources drawn from the institution. The elimination of the external imbalance will require actions to reduce the excess of absorption over production of resources supplemented in most circumstances by measures to induce a re-allocation of those resources in order to ease the foreign exchange constraint and also to increase output. The general characteristics of the main policies that will be necessary to these ends have already been discussed. But the scope and variety of possible policy packages is ample and therefore choices have to be made which, in turn, give rise to a number of issues.

From the standpoint of the member country, key decisions are required with regard to the specific mix and strength of the policies to be pursued. These decisions bear importantly on the time horizon over which the adjustment is to be made and on the constellation of objectives to be pursued, besides those related to the balance of payments. In general, the availability of choices on these various fronts is constrained by the resources that are likely to be available during the period of policy implementation. Typically, the longer the imbalance has been allowed to prevail, and therefore, the larger its magnitude has become, the tighter the constraint is and as a result, the more limited are the possible courses of action. Therefore a critical factor to take into account in the process of policy formulation is resource availability.

Given the resource constraint, emphasis in the selection of the policy mix must be placed on efficiency in resource use. This is possibly the most crucial consideration from the standpoint of policy

---

[31] Besides devising procedures to unlock capital flows, the Fund also adapted its policies on access to its own resources, including the continuation of the enlarged access policy. For an examination of these topics, see Manuel Guitián (1985a and 1987).

selection, because it can help release the resource constraint directly by eliminating inefficiencies and indirectly by stimulating resource mobilization both internally and externally. Thus, although resource availability can pose a constraint on policy choices, the quality of those policies can influence the availability of resources and therefore ease the constraint.

Besides available resources, another factor that typically influences the policy formulation process is the combination of objectives that are pursued. One of the reasons for such influence is the perception of the existence of trade-offs among policy objectives. Arguments abound to the effect that growth in an open economy is subject to a foreign exchange constraint.[32] These arguments highlight the possibilities of conflict between growth and the balance of payments. Trade-offs are also often perceived between inflation and growth as well as between inflation and the balance of payments. There is a limit, however, to the lid that can be put on inflation by incurring balance of payments deficits, as there is to the growth in demand that can be fostered either by inflationary means, by excessive external borrowing, or by international reserve losses. Despite these considerations, the perception of such trade-offs often influences the choice and mix of policies.

The fundamental point that needs to be underlined is that trade-offs among policy objectives are more apparent than real. Under most circumstances, the only trade-offs that exist are intertemporal and these depend on the scope that is available for allocating policy decisions over time. It is clearly possible for a limited period—and examples abound to this effect—for an economy to grow at an unsustainable rate and maintain a measure of price stability at the expense of deficits in the current account and the overall balance of payments. But this possibility is only a reflection of the choice that can be made between growth today versus growth tomorrow and of the trade-off of price stability today for inflation tomorrow.

A broader set of considerations apply to the relationship of growth, price, and balance of payments objectives to other aims simulta-

---

[32] A similar argument can of course be made in a closed economy to the effect that growth is subject to a domestic resource constraint. In this context, the argument underscores directly the importance of efficiency for the attainment of growth. As noted earlier, the opening of the economy, if efficiency prevails, can allow it to sustain a higher growth rate than otherwise.

neously sought on account of a combination of economic, social, and political factors. These aims reflect, among other aspects, equity standards and focus particularly on the distributional effects of economic policy actions.[33] From the vantage point of economic efficiency, the scope for trade-offs between these two sets of objectives is limited. In the context of a relatively open environment, social and political aims can rarely be pursued, on a sustained basis, at the expense of the efficient operation of the economy. In this context, it is generally futile to argue that there can be a sustained conflict between the criterion of economic efficiency and equity considerations; on the contrary, it is inefficiency and waste that run counter to equity.

These considerations, however, do not go as far as saying that economic objectives can be pursued without regard being paid to social and political aims. On the contrary, awareness and sensitivity toward these latter aims are essential to govern effectively and they can enhance a government's ability to carry out the necessary economic measures and reforms. The important question here is not that social and political considerations are to be altogether disregarded; the critical issue is rather to prevent the regard for such considerations from running counter to the requirements of efficiency in the use of scarce resources. In general, there can hardly be any question that the pursuit of goals for equity, social, or political reasons influences the performance of the economy. In general, the attainment of such goals places a claim on available resources, which therefore, become unavailable for other purposes. In this sense, trade-offs do exist between policy objectives, but as long as efficiency in resource use is not impaired and as long as choices conform to the economy's preferences, conflicts need not arise.

These relationships between policy objectives and the criteria for their selection are but aspects of a broader link that binds the political environment with economic policy implementation. The latter two are interdependent and interact in numerous ways. In general, a stable political environment is essential for the effective and sustained implementation of economic policies required in most circumstances to bring an adjustment effort to fruition.

---

[33] A discussion of distributional issues in the context of adjustment policies can be found in Omotunde Johnson and Joanne Salop (1980) and in International Monetary Fund (1986b).

A specific area that often arises in the context of discussions between the Fund and its members can be used to illustrate some of these issues and choices. It concerns the relative role of the public and private sectors in the economy. In the discussion of global imbalances in an economy earlier on, it was noted that the factors behind their emergence frequently included pressures coming from the public sector finances. Such pressures tend to arise from the pursuit by the public sector of a variety of aims requiring resources in excess of those the economy (or the rest of the world, for that matter) is willing to provide. The process of redressing the imbalance may entail decisions to abandon or postpone some of the aims on the part of the public sector (e.g., a reduction in its claims on resources) or decisions to raise additional revenues (e.g., an increase in the resources available to the sector) or both. As already argued, the nature and mix of those decisions will influence the performance of the economy in terms of growth, price, and balance of payments performance. Their sustainability, however, will depend on the accuracy with which they reflect preferences in the economy with regard to the priority being given to the various policy objectives as well as on the efficiency that they display to attain those objectives.

From the standpoint of the Fund, its options must conform to the code of conduct laid out in the *Articles of Agreement*. This code eschews certain courses of action as means of dealing with balance of payments problems (e.g., exchange restrictions, discriminatory practices). Instead, it advocates policy courses that lead to openness in the economies of members and to their progressive integration in the international economic system. There is a clear mandate for the institution in this code of conduct with regard to balance of payments and exchange matters which it must observe in the exercise of its role in the adjustment process.

Despite the interdependence among economic policies and their objectives, the mandate of the Fund focuses mainly on external objectives, in particular on balance of payments viability. To the extent that other economic objectives contribute to balance of payments viability (e.g., price stability, growth), however, the Fund argues forcefully for the adoption of policies to promote their achievement. Indeed, a key message of the argument made earlier has been that there are no sustained trade-offs between the attainment of these objectives and balance of payments recovery.

While the mandate of the Fund does not extend to policies and objectives that reflect mainly social or political considerations, the *Articles of Agreement* enjoin the institution to pay due regard to them in connection with its exercise of surveillance over exchange rate arrangements.[34] Therefore, the institution has striven to abide by this prescription in its relationship with members. In particular, it has sought to observe a principle of political neutrality and to minimize the degree of its participation in domestic policy decision making.[35] Observance of this broad principle not only has kept the Fund from entering into areas that require judgment of social or political priorities; it has also led the institution to seek that they are generally taken into account and that, in its negotiations with members, policy discussions and understandings be cast in terms of aggregate variables to keep its distance from specific decisions required for policy implementation.

An essential consideration behind this institutional principle of political neutrality has been the need to maintain an acceptable balance between the protection of the interests of an individual member and the safeguard of the interests of the membership as a whole. By distancing itself from specific economic policy decisions, the Fund acknowledges a member's independence in policy decision making. In turn, the institution's emphasis on the external objectives and consequences of members' economic policies helps protect the membership's collective interests and is based on a broad consensus among members that those are subjects of legitimate international concern. Were the Fund to widen its focus to include, besides the external area, domains with respect to which the grounds for international concern are less firm, the general acceptance of the priority that the Fund accords to external objectives would be less assured, if not contested.

---

[34] See Article IV, Section 3(b) of the *Articles of Agreement*, International Monetary Fund (1978). In the area of adjustment policies, a similar principle is contained in guideline No. 4 of the Guidelines of Conditionality, which draws attention to the domestic political and social aims of members as well as to their economic priorities. See International Monetary Fund (1986a).

[35] As already noted, in the context of policies on the use of Fund resources, these concerns are reflected in the Guidelines on Conditionality, most particularly, in the already cited guideline No. 4 and in guideline No. 9, which deals with the number and content of policy instruments (performance criteria) in Fund arrangements. See International Monetary Fund (1986a).

Concluding Remarks

The thrust of argumentation in this paper has stressed the fundamental complementarity between adjustment and growth. Indeed, by removing distortions and impediments to efficiency, adjustment is necessary for the attainment of sound growth. In the presence of imbalances, the choice that policymakers confront is adjustment *now* versus often harder adjustment *later*. The notion that adjustment is inimical to growth only serves to conceal that without adjustment, growth today is at the expense of often significantly less growth tomorrow.

These points bear importantly on the role of the Fund in the promotion of growth-oriented adjustment. Its support of policies to restore viability to balance of payments, therefore, represents also support for growth on two counts: first, because those policies typically promote efficiency in resource use, and second, because the direct financial support from the Fund as well as the assistance from other sources that the institution catalyzes in effect add, often significantly, to the resources at the disposal of member countries undertaking adjustment.

The Fund has refrained from entering into policy decisions that would take the institution toward areas outside its mandate. It has also refrained from seeking understandings on policies and objectives calling for judgments that fall in the social and political sphere and therefore belong with the national authorities. Even in those policy domains that are clearly linked to balance of payments objectives, the Fund has sought to reach understandings with members that could be formulated in terms of global instruments, thereby providing member authorities with ample choices on the specific ways of observing those understandings. In its choice of aggregate policy instruments, however, the Fund has aimed to select those that focus attention on the decisions that need to be made. In general, the combination of possible decisions is varied and the choice of the one to be adopted is left to the member.

Over time, a delicate system of checks and balances has been developed to guide the financial operations of the Fund with its members. These checks and balances are derived from the direct link established in Fund arrangements with member countries between performance under a quantitative economic policy program and the actual disbursement of Fund resources. Normally, the program is designed in terms of only those policy instruments necessary to provide an assurance of the achievement of its objectives. The number of instruments is typically limited, which thus provides the member with broad scope to select and undertake its own policy actions. In turn, the likely attainment of the program's objectives, which include balance of payments recovery, tends to preserve the revolving nature of Fund resources. Therefore, this system of checks and balances contributes to safeguarding the monetary character of the institution as well as protecting the member's independence in policy decision making. The ability of the Fund and this system of checks and balances to promote adjustment and growth to a large extent depends on its accuracy in outlining the choices available and the constraints that confront policy decision makers.

From the viewpoint of the Fund, there are a number of issues that warrant consideration for purposes of the promotion of growth-oriented adjustment in current circumstances. There is scope within the system of checks and balances for seeking that more progress in dismantling exchange and other restrictions maintained for balance of payments reasons be made by members during the process of adjustment. Indeed, as noted earlier, the continued prevalence of such impediments not only tends to impair efficiency and growth but consequently it also casts a heavy shadow over external payments viability. This is, therefore, an area where strengthened efforts to speed up liberalization and economic openness can contribute significantly to both the adjustment and growth processes.

Another related issue worthy of particular attention concerns the rising incidence of external payments arrears. Decisive action toward an orderly settlement of those arrears with a view to eliminating them within an appropriate period of time also appears called for in the context of adjustment, particularly in present circumstances in the international economy. Arrears typically result in both higher costs and in curtailment of normal trade financing flows. In addition, in common with restrictive practices, arrears generally contribute to the reluctance of capital movements, and given the environment that prevails currently in international capital markets, their continued presence cannot but compound such reluctance.

With regard to capital flows, their contribution to ease the adjustment process and to foster growth across the international system has long been recognized. Nevertheless, at present international capital movements have yet to resume their historical pattern, with regard both to their level and their composition. Indeed, the resumption of capital flows on their normal scale is proving to be a particularly protracted process. Progress has been made in the last few years toward restoring a measure of normality, but it has been limited and severe problems remain in this area. Continued efforts to find solutions to the payments difficulties confronting many countries yet will be required, including, where appropriate, external assistance in amounts and on terms consistent with the nature and magnitude of the required internal adjustment effort. But such efforts will need to be accompanied by an increasing commitment of all members, creditors and debtors alike, to the adoption of consistent and mutually supporting adjustment measures in order to lay the grounds for a timely and sustained resumption of international capital flows.

References

Day, William H. L., "Domestic Credit and Money Ceilings Under Alternative Exchange Rate Regimes," *Staff Papers*, International Monetary Fund (Washington), Vol. 26 (September 1979), pp. 490–512.

Dillon, K. Burke, and David Lipton, "External Debt and Economic Management: The Role of the International Monetary Fund," in *External Debt Management*, ed. by Hassanali Mehran (Washington: International Monetary Fund, 1985).

Dornbusch, Rudiger, "Exchange Rates and Prices," NBER Working Paper No. 1769 (Cambridge, Massachusetts: National Bureau of Economic Research, December 1985).

————, "Exchange Rate Economics: 1986," NBER Working Paper No. 2071 (Cambridge, Massachusetts: National Bureau of Economic Research, November 1986).

Finch, C. David, "Adjustment Policies and Conditionality," in *IMF Conditionality*, ed. by John Williamson (Washington: Institute for International Economics, 1983).

Frenkel, Jacob A., and Harry G. Johnson, eds., *The Monetary Approach to the Balance of Payments* (London: Allen and Unwin, 1976).

————, and Michael L. Mussa, "Monetary and Fiscal Policies in an Open Economy," *American Economic Review* (Nashville), Vol. 71 (May 1981), pp. 253–58.

Gold, Joseph, *Financial Assistance by the International Monetary Fund: Law and Practice*, IMF Pamphlet Series No. 27, second edition (Washington: International Monetary Fund, 1980).

————— , "The Relationship Between the International Monetary Fund and the World Bank," *Creighton Law Review* (Creighton), Vol. 15, No. 2, (1981–82), pp. 499–521.

Goldstein, Morris, *The Global Effects of Fund-Supported Adjustment Programs*, IMF Occasional Paper No. 42 (Washington: International Monetary Fund, March 1986).

Guitián, Manuel, "Credit Versus Money as an Instrument of Control," *Staff Papers*, International Monetary Fund (Washington), Vol. 20 (November 1973), pp. 785–800.

————— , "The Effects of Changes in the Exchange Rate on Output, Prices and the Balance of Payments," *Journal of International Economics* (Amsterdam), Vol. 6 (February 1976), pp. 65–74.

————— , *Fund Conditionality: Evolution of Principles and Practices*, IMF Pamphlet Series No. 38 (Washington: International Monetary Fund, 1981).

—————(1983a), "Fund Programs for Economic Adjustment," in *The Fund and China in the International Monetary System*, ed. by A.W. Hooke (Washington: International Monetary Fund, 1983), pp. 96–114.

—————(1983b), "International Financial Crisis or the Revolt Against Economic Interdependence," unpublished paper presented at a Seminar on Iberoamerica, International Financial Crisis and Prospects for the World Economy, La Granda-Santander, Spain, August 29–September 2, 1983.

—————(1985a), "Adjustment and Interdependence: The Challenge to Conditionality," in *Adjustment and Growth in the Current World Environment*, ed. by J. da Silva Lopes (Washington: International Monetary Fund (in Portuguese), 1985), pp. 57–83.

—————(1985b), "The Design of Adjustment and Conditionality—The Role of Exchange Rate and Monetary Policies," unpublished manuscript, International Monetary Fund, Washington, December 1985.

————— , "External Debt Management and the International Monetary Fund," in *Issues in North American Trade and Finance*, ed. by R. Tremblay (North American Economics and Finance Association, 4th International Congress, Montreal), Vol. 4 (January 1987), pp. 5–10.

Hino, Hiroyuki, "IMF-World Bank Collaboration," *Finance and Development* (Washington), Vol. 23 (September 1986), pp. 10–14.

Hooke, A. W., ed., *The Fund and China in the International Monetary System* (Washington: International Monetary Fund, 1983).

International Monetary Fund, *The Monetary Approach to the Balance of Payments* (Washington: International Monetary Fund, 1977).

————— , *Articles of Agreement* (Washington: International Monetary Fund, 1978).

————— , *Interest Rate Policies in Developing Countries*, IMF Occasional Paper No. 22 (Washington: International Monetary Fund, October 1983).

————— , *Foreign Private Investment in Developing Countries*, IMF Occasional Paper No. 33 (Washington: International Monetary Fund, January 1985).

—————(1986a), *Selected Decisions of the International Monetary Fund and Selected Documents*, Twelfth Edition (Washington: International Monetary Fund, 1986).

—————(1986b), *Fund-Supported Programs, Fiscal Policy, and Income Distribution*, IMF Occasional Paper No. 46 (Washington: International Monetary Fund, September 1986).

Johnson, G. G., *Formulation of Exchange Rate Policies in Adjustment Programs*, IMF Occasional Paper No. 36 (Washington: International Monetary Fund, September 1985).

Johnson, Omotunde, and Joanne Salop, "Distributional Aspects of Stabilization Programs in Developing Countries," *Staff Papers*, International Monetary Fund (Washington), Vol. 27 (March 1980), pp. 1–23.

Keller, Peter M., "Implications of Credit Policies for Output and the Balance of Payments," *Staff Papers*, International Monetary Fund (Washington), Vol. 27 (September 1980), pp. 451–77.

Kenen, Peter B., *Financing, Adjustment and the International Monetary Fund*, Studies in International Economics (Washington: Brookings Institution, 1986).

Khan, Mohsin S., "Stabilization and Economic Growth in Developing Countries," Report No. DRD 206, Development Research Center, World Bank, Washington, November 1986.

————— , and Malcolm D. Knight, *Fund-Supported Adjustment Programs and Economic Growth*, IMF Occasional Paper No. 41 (Washington: International Monetary Fund, November 1985).

Loser, Claudio M., "External Debt Management and Balance of Payments Policies," *Staff Papers*, International Monetary Fund (Washington), Vol. 24 (March 1977), pp. 168–92.

————— , "The Role of Economy-Wide Prices in the Adjustment Process," in *Adjustment, Conditionality, and International Financing*, ed. by Joaquin Muns (Washington: International Monetary Fund, 1984).

Mehran, Hassanali, ed., *External Debt Management* (Washington: International Monetary Fund, 1985).

Muns, Joaquin, ed., *Adjustment, Conditionality, and International Financing* (Washington: International Monetary Fund, 1984).

Narvekar, P. R., "Collaboration Between the Fund and the World Bank," in

The Fund and China in the International Monetary System, ed. by A.W. Hooke (Washington: International Monetary Fund, 1983).

Nowzad, Bahram, The IMF and Its Critics, Essays in International Finance, No. 146 (Princeton: Princeton University, 1981).

Stern, Ernest, "World Bank Financing of Structural Adjustment," in IMF Conditionality, ed. by John Williamson (Washington: Institute for International Economics, 1983).

Tanzi, Vito, "Fiscal Management and External Debt Problems," in External Debt Management, ed. by Hassanali Mehran (Washington: International Monetary Fund, 1985).

————, "Fiscal Policy, Growth, and the Design of Stabilization Programs," unpublished manuscript, International Monetary Fund, Washington, January 1987.

————, and Mario Blejer, "Fiscal Deficits and Balance of Payments Disequilibrium in IMF Adjustment Programs," in Adjustment, Conditionality, and International Financing, ed. by Joaquin Muns (Washington: International Monetary Fund, 1984).

Williamson, John, ed., IMF Conditionality (Washington: Institute for International Economics, 1983).

Discussion

Y.C. Park

President
Korea Development Institute

I agree with practically all of Mr. Michalopoulos's conclusions. Nevertheless, let me raise a few questions, not necessarily directed to the author but to the audience in general.

It seems to me that the major thrust of the paper is that if you liberalize the economy, you will be all right. That is, if you liberalize your commodity markets, trade regime, and financial markets, then that sort of liberalization policy will facilitate adjustment with reasonable economic growth. If this argument is valid—and in fact this argument has been made on many many occasions—then why aren't we doing it? Why haven't many countries embarked on economic liberalization?

I have several answers and three observations on the lack of liberalization we observe throughout the developing as well as in many developed countries. First, the international environment is not right. If these developing countries are going to produce more exportables, then some countries must be willing to import them. And, as we all know, most countries are turning to protectionism. Given that environment, it is hard to recommend that developing countries liberalize anything. Second, economic liberalization, whether it is liberalization of a trade regime or factor markets, could cause considerable macroeconomic instability, as we have found in many instances even when inflation is brought under control. In that case, policymakers will have to take into consideration the trade-off between liberalization, the macroeconomic gains you could obtain from liberalization, and macroeconomic instability. When you add these things up, it is very hard to decide which is the right direction for economic policies.

Mr. Michalopoulos emphasized that before you embark on liberalization you must stabilize your economy. But in many cases, experience shows that in order to stabilize the economy, to reduce the rate of inflation, or to reduce the size of a current account deficit, you have to install all kinds of control mechanisms, wage price control, interest rate control, credit allocation, restrictions on capital movements, and so on. By the time you install all these controls and succeed in stabilizing your economy, you will find so many vested interest groups in your economy opposed to liberalization that you have to start dismantling all these control mechanisms to liberalize the economy. At that point you are not quite sure if you are going to destabilize your economy once again.

Given these problems, in actual policymaking it is difficult to liberalize simply because economic theory advises it. Some countries have been successful in liberalizing their economies and as a consequence have been successful in adjusting without hurting economic growth. The Korean experience has been heralded in many places as the prime example of a successful case of adjustments through liberalization. In the case of Korea at least it is not clear whether liberalization is the result of good economic performance or vice versa.

The sequencing of liberalization is again a controversial point. Here everybody agrees that the current capital account of the balance of payments should not be liberalized under any circumstances in developing countries. Should you liberalize domestic factor markets and commodity markets? And if so, which one first? I think on this issue it doesn't matter which one you liberalize first. You will have problems any way. So the best policy is to choose the one that is most convenient and practical to liberalize first. In the case of Korea, I think we find it much more effective to liberalize the trade regime and domestic trade, and then use finance to allocate resources to those sectors in which efficiency is likely to be high. In this case the liberalization of finance is likely to be postponed for some time since at the initial stage of liberalization you are using finance as an instrument to reallocate resources.

I myself have worked on this problem in developing countries for a long time, and I still don't understand the role of finance in the context of developing countries. In some of the most successful East Asian countries, the financial system is not notably liberalized.

In the 1970s Fund and Bank missions came to Korea and they said we had to liberalize finance, otherwise we would be in trouble. We have heard the same message throughout the last 15 years. And even last year we heard the same message, that unless you liberalize your finance you will be in trouble in a year or two. I am not so sure.

On Bank operations I have not much to say, but I agree with this greater focus on program lending, away from project financing. Finally, people are talking about the need for more effective and closer cooperation between the World Bank and the Fund. I think it is a very good beginning, as this conference shows.

And finally, I would make one comment related to the Bank's operation. I would want the World Bank to have a little more understanding and be more careful about designing financial packages. I don't think packages should be aimed at forcing countries to follow liberalization policies or, for that matter, any policies that the Bank would like to pursue in developing countries. Instead, once again, based on my experience as an economist living in Korea, it is neither desirable nor really feasible to use the leverage of potential loans from the World Bank to force the policymakers of receiving countries to accept the World Bank policies as they are presented.

The alternative is to encourage governments to develop programs themselves, as we have done, in fact, not very successfully. But we have taken many liberalization measures not because the World Bank asked us to, but because we needed to liberalize the trade regime.

In these circumstances, that is, when policymakers are very much determined and committed to a policy, whether it is liberalization or something else, then World Bank financial assistance can be very, very effective.

John Williamson

Senior Fellow
Institute for International Economics

The paper of Mr. Michalopoulos provides an authoritative exposition of most of the policies that the Bank has been advocating and the mechanisms it had been using to promote adjustment with growth. In this process, the Bank has acquired much wisdom, but I shall largely concentrate in my comment on the points in which this good sense is either inadequately presented in the paper or absent in the Bank's practice.

I have one major complaint with the analysis, which also applies to Mr. Guitián's paper. Neither focuses on what most of the clients of the Bretton Woods Institutions regard as the central impediment to their restoration of growth, namely the existence of a foreign exchange constraint. I concede that in some countries the need to stabilize inflation may be even more urgent. And I agree that the practice of both the Fund and Bank is less misguided than the neglect of the topic in these two papers might suggest. Nevertheless, I fear that the lack of focus on the foreign exchange constraint impedes understanding of appropriate policies for growth-oriented adjustment and jeopardizes relations with many members.

Mr. Michalopoulos certainly worries about adequate access to external finance, but he fails to emphasize the importance of the issues by basing his analysis on "resources available internally or obtainable from abroad," with no hint that the shadow price of foreign resources may under certain circumstances vastly exceed that of domestic resources. The concept of a foreign exchange constraint is indeed recognized by Mr. Guitián, but only to be questioned:

> Arguments abound to the effect that growth in an open economy is subject to a foreign exchange constraint . . . However, there is a limit . . . to the growth in demand that can be fostered . . . by excessive external borrowing . . . the fundamental point . . . is that trade-offs among policy objectives are more apparent than real. Under most circumstances, the only trade-offs that exist are intertemporal . . . It is clearly possible for a limited period . . . for an economy to grow at an unsustainable rate . . . at the expense of deficits in the current account . . . But this possibility is only a reflection of the choice that can be made between growth today versus growth tomorrow. . . .

Mr. Guitián makes similar claims with respect to inflation, and I basically agree with him in that context. But the notion that there is no meaningful concept of a foreign exchange constraint, except in the sense of an intertemporal constraint, is incorrect.

The next section of my comment constructs a simple model that provides a direct refutation of Mr. Guitián's claim and a support for Mr. Michalopoulos's contrary position that "additional external finance in the initial years of a reform could be an essential component of a strategy designed to restore long-term growth while also maintaining per capita consumption in the interim." Those who do not believe that this position needs substantiation by a formal model may prefer to skip to the following section.

Consider a particularly simple version of the two-gap model that has traditionally formed the basis of Bank policy analysis. This economy produces only oranges, in a quantity Y up to a limit determined by the stock K of orange trees according to an input-output coefficient α:

$$Y \leqq \alpha K.$$

In order to transport oranges to market, the economy needs to use imported fuel equal to βY (measured in terms of exported oranges), where β is an input-output coefficient divided by the terms of trade (liters of fuel that can be bought with the frozen orange juice produced by a bushel of oranges). Oranges can be exported only in the form of frozen orange juice, and exports are therefore limited by the installed capacity Z of orange pulping and freezing equipment:

$$X \leqq \gamma Z$$

(as well as $X \leqq Y$).

The equipment Z has to be imported, so that the import equation is:

$$M = \beta Y + \triangle Z.$$

The balance of payments equation is:

$$\triangle R = X - M + B - \delta D$$

where $\triangle R$ = change in reserves, B = new external borrowing, δ = the rate of interest plus amortization (and hence $\triangle D = B - aD$, where a is the amortization rate).

To make this into a two-gap model one would also need to allow for the possibility of increasing K through investment, but for the purpose of studying the role of the foreign exchange constraint we simplify by turning it into a one-gap model.

Suppose that this economy is initially at full capacity output ($Y = \alpha K$), in balance of payments equilibrium with export capacity fully utilized ($X = \gamma Z$) and constant debt ($aD = B$) and export capacity ($\triangle Z = 0$). It is then struck at time $t = 1$ by a deterioration in the terms of trade (an increase in β) and/or an increase in debt service δ caused by higher interest rates, the total size of the shock being S.

In consequence,

$$\alpha \beta K + \delta D > \gamma Z + aD,$$

that is the balance of payments is in deficit unless borrowing B increases or income Y declines.

In this simple model, adjustment with growth does not actually involve growth but simply the avoidance of recession, that is, a decline in the output of oranges. It is achieved by running down reserves or borrowing enough to pay the extra cost of importing the fuel needed to market the full crop of this year's oranges, plus buying enough investment goods Z to permit additional exports to restore payments equilibrium by the next period. In the new equilibrium, consumption of oranges will decline by the amount needed to be diverted into exports to maintain payments equilibrium.

If adjustment with growth is infeasible owing to a foreign exchange constraint, that is, inadequate reserves and an inability to borrow more, the economy faces two alternatives. The first is permanent recession: cut output by S/β, enough to reduce imports of fuel to the point at which the balance of payments again balances with $\triangle D = \triangle Z = 0$. The second policy ("austerity") involves an even sharper cutback in current consumption so as to further reduce imports of fuel and use the resulting savings to import the investment goods Z needed to increase exports of frozen orange juice. Note that this model permits expenditure switching in order to ease the foreign exchange constraint in the long run, so that it is not subject to the standard criticism that the rigid ratios of the two-gap model preclude adjustment by assumption. Indeed, once adjustment is complete, there is no foreign exchange constraint, and consumption is simply limited by resources (the stock of orange trees).

The welfare consequences of these strategies can be compared by calculating the consumption losses that they impose on the economy. In order to simplify the comparisons I shall concentrate on one particular case, in which both the austerity and adjustment-with-growth strategies involve installing all the additional equipment needed in period t_1 and when the debt incurred under the adjustment-with-growth strategy is completely repaid, with interest, at time t_2. It is evident that the requirement that debt be paid off in one period biases the comparison against adjustment-with-growth: a presumptively superior strategy permitted by slow repayment is to invest slightly more in t_1 and avoid any recession, either at t_2 or thereafter.

Permanent recession imposes a cutback in consumption of S/β for the indefinite future, unless and until the shock S is reversed.

Austerity also involves a consumption loss of S/β at t_1. Consumption must also be cut back, by an additional S/γ at t_1. Thereafter consumption can rise, to a steady-state level S below its pre-shock level.

Adjustment with growth maintains consumption unchanged in t_1. It then falls in t_2 by S (the steady-state fall in consumption needed to release resources for the more expensive imports), plus $(1 + i)S/\gamma$ (to repay with interest the debt incurred at t_1 to buy the needed juice-making equipment), plus $(1 + i)\beta S$ (to repay with interest the debt incurred to avoid recession at t_1). From t_3 onwards, consumption again rises to a level S below the pre-shock level.

Adjustment with growth certainly involves less consumption loss than permanent recession in every period except possibly t_2. The condition for the consumption loss in that period to be less is

$1/\beta > (1 + i)(1/\gamma + \beta)$,

a very weak condition considering that β is a fraction, typically perhaps 0.2, i is likely to be an even smaller fraction, and γ is likely to be substantially larger than β. Only if γ were very small, implying that the cost of raising exports through investment was extremely high, is it conceivable that permanent recession could be a sensible choice of strategy.

The undiscounted consumption loss involved in austerity is greater than that under adjustment with growth if

$1/\beta + 1/\gamma > (1 + i)(1/\gamma + \beta)$.

This condition is even weaker than that above for adjustment with growth to dominate permanent recession in period 2. (Note that the introduction of discounting would further tilt the balance in favor of adjustment with growth.)

This example demonstrates that, contrary to Mr. Guitián's claim, circumstances can arise in which a foreign exchange constraint imposes a deadweight loss upon the economy rather than an intertemporal trade-off. Moreover, these circumstances are not far fetched. Most Latin Americans believe that they are operating under precisely such a constraint and that their adjustment is being made unnecessarily painful and lengthy as a result. If the Fund cannot recognize this, it is not surprising that it has a bad image in so many of its member countries.

It is of course an interesting question as to why countries with the socially profitable investment opportunities hypothesized in the above model should have difficulty in borrowing. At least partial explanations are provided by the existence of a debt overhang and the limited credibility of governmental promises to honor debts in a world of sovereign states. This latter factor is especially relevant in sub-Saharan Africa, where the time-scale needed to reap increased foreign exchange receipts from additional investment is so long as to create an overwhelming presumption that repudiation would at some stage appear rational if borrowing were on commercial terms. (This lack of credibility, plus concern with distributional issues, and not low investment profitability, provide the intellectual justification for concessional aid to poor countries.)

Whatever the explanation, the fact that most priority clients of the Bretton Woods Institutions are suffering from a foreign exchange constraint seems clear. Indeed, about the only client of the Bank that is currently facing the opposite dilemma to which Mr. Michalopoulos pays so much attention, of wondering whether to liberalize the capital account before the current account and risk being flooded with a capital inflow, is Korea.

The policy priority in a country facing a foreign exchange constraint is to raise the capacity to import. As the model of the orange-growing economy formalizes, additional imports are needed to restore full capacity operation of the economy (in the real world, this is important not just for the additional consumption it permits, but also because it raises the incentive to invest), as well as to provide the ability to invest. One set of benefits of an outward-oriented strategy is its ability to generate the exports that will break the foreign exchange constraint and allow the country to exploit its domestic resources to the full. These macroeconomic benefits of outward orientation are of course supplemented by the microeconomic benefits of more efficient resource use—of production according to comparative advantage, of ability to exploit economies of scale, and of maintenance of a competitive spur. Adjustment with growth requires that countries get both their macroeconomic strategies and their microeconomic incentives right at the same time.

Unfortunately only the microeconomic benefits seem to receive any attention in current Bank analysis (unlike that of an earlier generation, which perhaps made the opposite error), including the papers prepared for this conference. In the long run this does not matter much, since outward orientation will bring both sets of benefits simultaneously. But in one important short-run respect the difference is crucial: namely, with regard to insistence on early import liberalization in a program of structural adjustment. Mr. Michalopoulos appears to reflect current Bank policy accurately when he calls for ". . . export expansion programs [to] be accompanied by significant import liberalization. . . . Experience does *not* in our view suggest that import liberalization should be undertaken only after export reforms have increased the supply of foreign exchange." The nature of this experience is not described, but certainly the rationale he provides for early import liberalization—that "it is extremely difficult to reorient domestic producers toward export markets as long as heavily-sheltered domestic markets offer them sizeable assured profits"—seems to assume full capacity operation of the economy, an assumption that is by definition unsatisfied when the foreign exchange constraint is binding. Resources do not have to be squeezed out of import-competing sectors in order to permit additional output of exports as long as there are idle domestic resources. The export industries may need imported inputs—but these will be less available, not more available, if import-competing industries are forced into bankruptcy by import liberalization, except in the extreme case in which the foreign exchange cost of imported inputs exceeds the cost of the imported final goods.

As I see it, the right model is the one that, broadly speaking, Europe followed during the Marshall Plan. First, liberalize imports of critical inputs, especially of inputs needed for tradable production. Second, devalue to the point needed to gain (and maintain) a competitive exchange rate. Third, borrow anything that may be needed to restore (and maintain) full capacity operation of the economy as soon as possible. Fourth, advertise your intention to liberalize imports as circumstances permit, in order to ward off investments in uneconomic import-competing industries, and bind your promises by making international commitments so as to secure credibility of your advertised intentions with incipient local vested interests. (There is a vitally important potential role for the Bank here.) Fifth, once the economy is operating at full capacity, use payments improvements to liberalize imports across the board. When you have finished liberalizing imports, start thinking of liberalizing the capital account or appreciating the currency.

With the important exception of the priority to be accorded to import liberalization, most of Mr. Michalopoulos's advice as to the desirable content of adjustment programs is well taken. Public sector reforms, prices that reflect opportunity costs, subsidies that are targeted on the poor, institutional reforms—these are all areas in which the Bank's record is honorable. I did, however, miss any similar emphasis on education. After all, if the first lesson of Korea's success is the benefit of outward orientation, surely the second lesson is the value of massive investment in human capital at an early stage of the development effort. And perhaps the third lesson is the benefit of a well-executed land reform, which appears to be a neglected subject in the Bank today. While noting sins of omission, Mr. Michalopoulos fails to acknowledge the critical importance of sensitivity to environmental issues that is increasingly recognized in at least some parts of the Bank.

I conclude by reverting to the simple model introduced earlier, which for all its simplicity (or perhaps because of that simplicity) seems to me to offer an analytical framework for identifying some of the prerequisites for designing programs for growth-oriented adjustment. That model suggests that a key requirement for securing adjustment with growth is to combine the incentive to increase the supply of tradables (to invest in Z) with the finance to permit such investment without unnecessarily curtailing consumption. That diagnosis points to some critical political questions that confront the Bank. Should it bribe countries whose governments do not really believe in them to undertake policies that the Bank believes would promote investment in Z by offering loans with lots of detailed strings? Or should it wait till a government appears that shares its convictions about the desirable policy stance, and then give it the money to have a decent chance of succeeding? Can it increase the supply of such "enlightened" governments worthy of extensive support by policy dialog? But these are topics for another paper.

Michael Bruno

Governor
Central Bank of Israel

Among many issues, I should like to discuss for a moment how one looks at policy problems from the viewpoint of individual country experience. Usually problems arise because existing ways of handling policy have become inadequate, and then it is necessary to adjust one's way of thinking about them. My reading of both Fund and World Bank practice over the years is that both institutions have attempted to adjust the way issues are tackled. My own experience suggests that Fund missions exhibit a much more eclectic approach than is shown in official policy documents and declarations.

The problem I had with Mr. Guitián's paper is its defence of a certain orthodox position, which I would hope is not a definitive summary of what I would like to consider the Fund view. I have always had the highest regard for Mr. Guitián's many contributions to the Fund's work, but if I may sound somewhat critical, I had some difficulty with the emphasis of the present paper. I failed to find in the paper what I would regard as sufficient emphasis on the trade-offs between adjustment and growth.

I agree that, when a country is fundamentally out of balance, it has to, for example, remove the sources of high inflation first before it can hope to start growing. But there I would stop. How it adjusts is important, because adjustment depends, first of all, on the nature of the imbalance and will have a bearing on future growth prospects.

To my mind Mr. Guitián's paper overemphasizes demand management in short-term adjustment, although it is obvious that internal and external disequilibria have to be cured by using a mix of fiscal, monetary, and exchange rate policies. These are important tools, but it is important also to look at the source of disequilibrium that may affect both the mix and the choice of policies.

The underlying assumption of the macroeconomic model that puts all the emphasis on demand management is that in the short run prices and wages adjust, there is lack of friction, and there is full market clearing. All of these assumptions may be true for the long run, but they don't necessarily hold in the short run.

I would like to give two examples that bear this out. One is the experience of the 1970s in which the source of the imbalance in many cases was on the supply side, raw material prices were rising, wages were rigid, real interest rates were high, and long-term investment was down. Demand management by itself could not solve these problems. Moreover, demand managment may also have supply management effects which run counter to structural change and growth.

Fiscal adjustment, I think all will agree, is a necessary part of the adjustment process. What kind of fiscal adjustment, I mean what particular mix, will have an effect on the supply side? For example, typically in the 1970s, if fiscal adjustment included raising wage taxes, that ran against what it was desirable to achieve on the supply side, since it worsened labor costs. Likewise, cutting investment in infrastructure is a way of solving the short-term fiscal imbalance, but it harms long-run investment prospects. Much depends, of course, on how you define a deficit. If you define it to include investment expenditure, then by definition cutting investment is a way of adjusting your budget. But it will harm growth prospects. There is always a trade-off involved that cannot be ignored.

I might also note parenthetically that there are other policy tools not mentioned in the paper, such as the use of incomes policy and tripartite agreements between trade unions, employers, and government to keep wages and prices from rising.

The second example is the more recent experience of high inflation countries. In this regard I can mention my own country's experience. In the debate there are two extreme views, neither of which is valid. One takes the orthodox view that if there is an imbalance—and high inflation is always caused by basic fiscal deficit, and there's no argument about that—one must cut the deficit, restrict money, and the rest will take care of itself. That is one polar view.

The other polar view, called the structuralist view, maintains that the budget doesn't matter. All you have to do is to freeze prices and wages. The exchange rate will be quickly brought in line. Inflation is mainly a bubble that the wage and price freeze will burst. That view, of course, is invalid. Examples abound in which either one of these polar approaches would have produced either disaster or something close to it.

So the answer is you need both. If you say you need both, then you have to do certain unconventional things, such as using price controls or pegging the exchange rate. Under certain circumstances you want to peg the exchange rate because the foreign exchange that comes as a capital reflow will help you solve the balance of payments problem even if the current account may worsen for a short time.

Now I would also like to warn against the use of such unconventional methods to justify anything. You can justify any fiscal excesses or distorted price levels by appealing to such arguments. I am not making a plea for any unconventional thinking of that sort.

I have two final points. One has already been made by the Managing Director. It is to try to refrain from having one set solution that is applicable to all countries under all circumstances. We know that the choice of exchange rate regime, whether it is pegged, crawling, or floating is not independent of the structure of markets in an economy. If you have a certain type of labor market you don't want to use the crawling peg. Or if your financial markets are not developed, you don't want to use a certain type of float. It is important to bear this in mind. But more important is to try to see whether governments that one deals with are motivated to set their own house in order.

The second point has to do with the time horizon. In at least one place in the paper the statement is made that the trade-off between the balance of payments and inflation and the balance of payments and growth should not allow one to even move one inch from keeping foreign exchange balanced at all times. That is a statement which I am sure the author did not really mean, judging by his oral presentation. But it is written in the paper. Financial adjustment, like the response to high inflation that I mentioned, can be achieved within a short time. But real adjustment includes structural reform and is a prolonged process, requiring a policy formulation with a medium-term and a long-term framework. That is where Fund short-term programs can help: as part of an overall short-, medium-, and long-term plan. I can only finish with that.

Gerald K. Helleiner
Professor of Economics
University of Toronto

The Managing Director's opening address offers hope for fresh Fund approaches in the new search for growth-oriented adjustment programs. Mr. Guitián's paper, on the other hand, has a certain Bourbon flavor. (The Bourbons were the ones who learned nothing and forgot nothing.) It stands in contrast to Mr. Michalopoulos's paper from the Bank, which addresses such issues for the prospects for adjustment with growth as the current adequacy of resource flows, the Bank's own prior experience with related programs, professional limitations in respect of medium-term sequencing and dynamics, equity, poverty, and the political problems of transitional states, the likelihood of negative growth during stabilization efforts, and the need for country specificity of approaches. One can quarrel with many of the elements of the Bank paper but it deals with the real problems, including those relating to the design of appropriate policy packages, of recovery and balance of payments adjustment in Latin America and sub-Saharan Africa, the problems that have brought us to this conference.

Mr. Guitián argues, at length, that short-term stability—how much is unclear—is helpful to growth. Was this ever or is it now at issue? The sum of his advice appears to be "Do everything and do it as soon as possible." This is of dubious value as a contribution to current debate over the construction of growth-oriented adjustment programs.

Let me group my comments on the paper under three headings: the international context, the overall analytical approach and related conditionality issues, and the question of adjustment and growth through external liberalization.

But first permit me to make a parenthetical comment on the conference as a whole—perhaps an obvious one but one which I believe is important. The majority of the Fund's current programs are with low-income countries, most of them in sub-Saharan Africa. It is there that the most intractable problems of adjustment and of growth are found—and where the Fund's recent record has been particularly bleak. There are brief references to these countries here and there in the papers for this conference, but they deal mainly with middle-income countries. The problems of Turkey and middle-income Latin America are qualitatively different from those of low-income Africa. Perhaps another conference is required for addressing low-income countries' problems—including the optimal means of writing down debt to official creditors that cannot and should not now be serviced.

International Context

Severely underplayed, if not quite totally missing from Mr. Guitián's paper, is an appreciation of the international context within which adjustment efforts in debtor countries now must take place. The Fund's emphasis upon domestic monetary and fiscal policy, and the efficiency of resource use is, as always, praiseworthy. But this paper's one-sided approach to the adjustment problem—focusing upon "the adjustment problems of members seeking access to Fund resources"—, implies the very asymmetry of approaches and adjustment processes that Mr. Camdessus warned us against. The rate of global growth, the monetary-fiscal policy mix in the United States and elsewhere, the state of world primary commodity markets, OECD protectionism, policies with respect to capital exports from major surplus countries, and the treatment of the external debt cannot sensibly be assumed "given." The Fund's own global projections underline their importance to balance of payments and growth prospects in the developing countries. Constructive approaches to them are fundamental to the formulation of symmetric and sensible overall adjustment policies.

Mr. Guitián even argues that the issue of the appropriate extent of external financing for growth-oriented "adjustment" tends to revolve more frequently around the efficiency of resource use than around the amount of resources. When most of the members in question are suffering from severe foreign exchange scarcity and liquidity squeezes, this is a remarkable and unlikely proposition for which one would like to see some evidence. There is plenty of evidence to the contrary.

Mr. Guitián's "blind spot" on the international context extends to his treatment of the sources of the relevant member countries' current problems. The Michalopoulos paper notes in its opening sentence the fact of unfavorable external shocks (the most severe such shocks for most developing countries in 50 years) and the need to adjust to them. The Guitián paper, on the other hand, is still couched in terms of overexpansion of domestic demand and the frequent difficulty of ascertaining soon enough whether it exists. The size of shock surely has something to do with the capacity to adjust promptly to it—but Mr. Guitián offers only admonitions not to let problems accumulate and to keep efforts synchronous with adjustment need.

In this context, he returns to the traditional distinction between "temporary" and "permanent" shocks as an important element in appropriate policy design. But does anyone now think that we have a traditional Fund-style "temporary" problem in Latin America and Africa? Rather, there is now a need to elasticize the concept of "temporariness" for countries with prolonged use of Fund resources, not to speak of the growing number of African countries that, barring new approaches, will also become "ineligible" over the next few years. The time horizon for "temporariness" was, after all, always an arbitrary one—determined by the Fund's own self-created lending rules rather than by any objective reality. What Mr. Guitián calls "historically normal" (he refers to capital flows but the proposition is a general one) is equally arbitrary.

In his conclusion, Mr. Guitián does address some of the external issues, but he does so in a very odd manner wholly different from the forthright comment of the Michalopoulos paper which says outright that "reforms . . . without financial support . . . alone cannot go far in restoring growth," "still more funding is clearly needed," and explicitly recommends "debt relief." Mr. Guitián calls for "decisive action to eliminate [external arrears] within an appropriate period of time." He appears to mean that they should be paid off. How this is to be achieved in the current context, and with what assistance, is not addressed. He then concludes with some general comments on external capital that are difficult to interpret: ". . . at present international capital movements have yet to resume their historical patterns . . . severe problems remain in this area . . . Continued efforts . . . will be required, including, where appropriate, external assistance in amounts and on terms consistent with the nature and magnitude of the required internal adjustment effort."

What this means in terms of Fund positions on the need for external resources for adjustment is less than clear.

Nothing is said in this paper about the many elements of Fund practice that might be expected to have some influence on external constraints, where they exist, for example, overall Fund net lending, SDR issues, the duration over which Fund loans can and should revolve, contingency arrangements in performance targeting, necessary external financing commitments, the degree of front-ending on lending, the degree of conditionality in overall lending, and a Fund role in the resolution of debt problems.

Overall Analytical Approach and Conditionality

Mr. Guitián does not distinguish between stabilization and adjustment, as do Mr. Michalopoulos and most of those development economists who seek analytical clarity. This reflects the Fund's traditionally very aggregative (not to say primitive) approach to supply-side issues. For Mr. Guitián and the Fund, adjustment is a matter of getting aggregate demand back into balance with aggregate supply, with primary emphasis upon the achievement of external balance. "Structural" issues do not arise in this formulation of the current problem. Yet it is structural change—in the sense of increasing the role of tradables in the structure of overall production to overcome a foreign exchange constraint—that is of the essence of what most others describe as "adjustment." For Mr. Guitián, stabilization and adjustment are all one—and make for a substantial package.

Balance of payments objectives aside, Mr. Guitián's stated adjustment objectives—"sound" growth rate, "appropriate" level of employment, "a measure of domestic price and exchange rate stability"—are so vague as to be nonoperational. This is not criticism. It is simply to make the point that his stated "economic" objectives are no more precise or generalizable than the many "noneconomic" ones he mentions (and leaves for domestic policymakers).

One can plausibly argue that the details of stabilization and adjustment packages are not the business of the Fund or the Bank, and that all that matters is results—results in this instance relating to the early restoration of external balance (preferably with internal balance, political as well as economic, at the same time). Mr. Guitián seems to lean towards such an approach for the Fund. Certainly his paper is far less forthcoming with its recommendations than the Bank paper is. Why the Fund should not participate in the analysis of transitional costs, poverty effects, sequencing, and the like, however, is not immediately obvious. It is striking that Mr. Guitián's Fund is prepared to advise on the economic and balance of payments implications of "domestic priorities" but does not offer alternative policy packages, including ones with characteristics on which the international community has views, such as those protective of child welfare, from which these priorities may be chosen. Is the Fund professional staff really so limited in its abilities or proclivities?

Mr. Michalopoulos and the World Bank appear to be ready not only for more detailed analysis but also for greater intrusion into internal policy matters than Mr. Guitián and the Fund. Such a Fund-Bank distinction regarding the degree of respect for national sovereignty would seem to make little overall political or economic sense.

But is it a real distinction? I think not. The Fund does not even target the relevant variables (balance of payments ones) in its purportedly hands-off approach. Its concentration on and targeting of particular monetary variables already involves the taking of a position on controversial domestic issues. Mr. Guitián's approach to the stabilization (cum adjustment) question is unrepentantly monetary. He relies upon "the important and well-established relationship that prevails under most circumstances between the demand for money balances and the level of global income in an economy." This approach is subject to all the usual objections—short-run unpredictability, definitional problems with money, unrealistic assumptions about price and wage flexibility and the stability of real income, and misplaced concreteness with respect to the sources of overall imbalance. To each his own. Mr. Michalopoulos's plea for a balanced approach to the use of available policy instruments is apposite in this regard. But let me not dwell on these familiar disputes.

Fund missions also express views on all manner of pricing and other issues. So indeed does Mr. Guitián, while trying to remain as technocratic as possible, on such matters as the role of government and the desirability of overall openness.

If the Fund were to be as restrained as Mr. Guitián says it should be and, in particular, were to use balance of payments indicators for performance targeting, there would be grounds for urging parallel respect for sovereignty on the part of a currently more aggressive World Bank. In the real world, however, one must instead lament the fact that his paper addresses so few of the issues of growth-oriented stabilization and adjustment, thus leaving them, willy nilly, entirely to the Bank. As far as adjustment and growth policies are concerned, Mr. Guitián appears to opt out of all the interesting debates.

Beyond the search for stability and efficiency there are real policy choices relating to the structure and pace of change, and distributional and humanitarian objectives. Mr. Michalopoulos's paper is properly humble about our knowledge of the dynamics of adjustment processes. Mr. Guitián seems to imply that these are matters of domestic sovereignty and therefore beyond debate. The Fund circumspection Mr. Guitián describes and praises leaves the Fund apparently uninterested in growth, poverty, unemployment, development strategies, or political sustainability. This is both unfortunate and unrealistic. The appropriate degree of Fund intrusion into domestic policy matters remains a separate—and major—issue.

Adjustment and Growth Through External Liberalization

The Guitián approach to efficiency and thus structural adjustment relies upon establishing the correct "relative prices and costs." He ignores the problems of differing short- and long-run supply elasticities in different sectors, of financing the investments that would make for larger supply responses, and of transitional costs.

Mr. Guitián's enthusiasm for "opening up of the economy"— apparently for both capital and goods flows—is especially strong. (The capital proposition is particularly dubious.) The "liberalization of trade and exchange restrictions . . . constitutes a *necessary* (my italics) complement to policy measures in the macroeconomic and pricing spheres for the attainment of sustained growth and balance of payments viability." This will come as a surprise to Japan, Korea, Brazil, India, and many other countries. In his conclusion he suggests "strengthened efforts to speed up liberalization and economic openness (to) . . . contribute significantly to both the adjustment and growth processes." He has nothing to say about any "transitional costs" it might entail, about the recent record of countries that attempted to do this, whether the "success" cases really did, about its political feasiblity, or indeed any of the likely detailed effects discussed in an extensive and somewhat inconclusive literature.

More directed interventions have often been and may well in future be more efficient than the blunt instruments of restrained aggregative demand and simple reliance upon the market. Restructuring production towards tradables and protecting the welfare of the poorest (or of powerful political groups) may be better obtained by targeted incentives, credit allocation, subsidies, and investment. If effectively targeted on fast-responding sectors, especially exportables, the need for demand restraint may be eased.

Nor is his report to the Fund mandate on these matters convincing. It is true that the Fund promotes a "code" of liberal international economic conduct. But Mr. Guitián protests rather too much about the Fund's inability to deviate from it. Clearly, deviations have been made in the case of centrally planned and innumerable hard-pressed developing countries. More fundamentally, there is nothing in the Fund's Article I that requires or implicitly recommends that when imports must be restrained for balance of payments reasons this should be achieved via domestic deflation rather than import barriers.

Policy ought to be based upon the economic and political costs of the alternatives.

The Fund has always made a point of saying that it is not an aid agency. If this paper represents current thinking in the Fund it is unlikely to be a growth agency either. Mr. Guitián's prime approach is the traditional one of demand management over the short term with main reliance on domestic credit control. His assessment of other issues is too cautious and too simple to be very helpful. If the Fund chooses to play a purely monetary role, it can assuredly do so. This role can be important. But current efforts to design growth-oriented adjustment programs for Africa and Latin America demand more. One must hope that the Fund will join the effort.

Comment

Marcel Massé
Executive Director
International Monetary Fund

I do not disagree basically with the papers as written, since they appeal to economic logic and so make sense although they may be a bit repetitive. Their main problem is one I encountered many times when I was with the Canadian International Development Association: that is, I feel that the presentation represents a disembodied model. In reality, in order to judge policies we must have in mind a much more integrated decisionmaking model. The model seems disembodied because in order to judge, for instance, whether the public sector should be smaller or larger in any country (as we all know instinctively, and those who have worked in developing countries know by experience) one has to look at what the precise situation is in that country, what its culture is, what the relationships are between the various ethnic groups, what the level of education is, and so on.

In that sense, any prescription from a theoretical model must become "embodied" to make sense. For instance, I once asked an expert who had worked for years on Jamaica, with both the Fund and the Bank, why that country had so much difficulty to start back on a growth path, notwithstanding the help of Fund program after Fund program. His reply was that everything flowed from the fact that the price of bauxite had gone down, seemingly for good. As a result, he said, Jamaica had gone from wealth to poverty, and the population had to accept that they were now not a middle-income country but a lower-income country. This reality had to be reflected in their economic behavior. Well, this may well be true, but it is not what the Jamaicans themselves think; and as long as they continue to think that way, they will not adopt the policies recommended by the theoretical model.

In fact I think that the first question to be asked should concern the political and social constraints in that country and the measures that it is possible to implement given the cultural environment. By culture I mean all the elements that affect the behavior of the various decisionmakers. So, Mr. Chairman, I would conclude that the models are important but they should not be the ultimate guide in forming our views of what policies should be taken.

To take the analogy of a father, I would say that the papers show that growth is the reward of discipline and abstinence and that there is no "alternative path to development." You have to reduce consumption in order to increase investment and growth. Here Benjamin Spock is wrong, and the authoritarian father is right!

As they follow that pattern, of course, the Fund and very soon the Bank become the hated enforcers they are in a number of countries. But they believe that they are right, and that, if they have enough leverage, the countries will ultimately develop satisfactorily.

I think that the role of the Fund and the Bank as enforcers has to be modified. It has to be modified by people who would have a much better understanding of why the decisionmakers in the developing countries want to adopt decisions that from the point of view of the Fund or the Bank do not seem rational.

For instance, in terms of the adjustment period, Mr. Guitián is, I think, right when he says that the choice between adjustment and growth is really an intertemporal choice. My experience tends to confirm that this choice is better left to those who know what trade-off is acceptable locally.

Given the political constraints in most countries, however, the next most important determinant of the success of an adjustment period is probably the amount of foreign financing available to make the transition smoother and easier. Here I can only make a plea that the industrial countries examine carefully the consequences, on themselves as well as on the developing countries, of continuing the present trend towards decreasing the net financing available.

As a last point, too much attention to the doctrine of sovereignty has, I think, prevented us from agreeing that many difficulties experienced by developing countries originate in the policies of the industrial countries: at some point compensation will have to be paid, either through the nonpayment of some part of the international debt, or through an increase in bilateral and multilateral transfers from the industrial countries.

SESSION 2

Country Study

Economic Stabilization and Structural Adjustment: The Case of Turkey

Rusdu Saracoglu
Deputy Governor
Central Bank of the Republic of Turkey

The Fund symposium on growth-oriented adjustment policies is very timely given recent economic developments throughout the world and, in particular, the problems faced by a number of developing countries. Inevitably the pressures on heavily indebted countries that face continuing imbalances, both domestic and external, force such countries to seek assistance from competent international organizations such as the International Monetary Fund and the World Bank. It is therefore quite appropriate that this symposium was organized under the joint sponsorship of the two most highly regarded international financial organizations of the world. I am confident that the proceedings will add to our understanding of the issues and assist policymakers as well as the staff of the two institutions in preparing future adjustment programs.

Let me also express my sincere appreciation that Turkey was chosen as a case worth studying. It has always been our belief that Turkey's experience since 1980 with adjustment and stabilization policies merits careful analysis by scholars as well as policymakers of other countries. We believe that the lessons that we have learned from our experience, whether positive or negative, should be publicly available. I must add here that we feel that much of what we have to offer constitutes a positive lesson.

Adjustment policies together with a set of major reforms has been a continuous process since 1980 albeit with varying intensity. Our efforts, policies, structural reforms, successes, and setbacks together with economic performance under the program are detailed in various Fund-Bank documents. It would be impossible to condense that history into a brief presentation. Consequently in my presentation today I intend to concentrate on a limited number of policies and structural reforms that are of major significance and lie at the heart of our adjustment strategy. Often these policies were considered impossible to implement. They were meant to change, in a fundamental way, the orientation of the economy and the growth strategy pursued for many decades. In concentrating on a few policies, I hope to bring them into sharper focus for discussion here.

In my presentation, I will first give some background information in order to put Turkey's adjustment strategy into a historical context. It is essential that the participants appreciate the economic philosophy prevailing in Turkey at the time, the economic developments leading to a crisis, and the political turmoil that existed in the country when the adjustment program was initiated. Following this background, I will discuss in two separate sections economic stabilization policies and structural adjustment policies. I feel that discussing the two sets of policies in separate sections will facilitate understanding, even though both sets of measures were taken more or less contemporaneously and implemented in a mutually supporting manner. The discussion of policies is followed by an admittedly sketchy presentation of economic performance under the program, highlighting successes as well as weaknesses that were, or need to be, corrected. Finally, I present some conclusions that may be of value in designing adjustment programs, incorporating structural reforms aimed at enhancing productivity and long-term sustainable rates of growth.

Background

Since the formation of the Republic of Turkey in 1923, the Government has always played a significant role in economic activity. Following decades of wars with foreigners and unfortunate experiences with foreign powers that led to the War of Independence, Turks have had for a long time maintained strong feelings of mistrust toward foreigners, particularly toward Europeans, and economic policies associated with them.

Although the founding fathers tried to experiment with liberal economic policies immediately after the formation of the Republic, the experiment was short-lived owing, in part, to international economic developments leading to the Great Depression. The Turkish

Government reacted to these developments by discontinuing liberal economic policies and instituting protectionist policies. Initially, the protectionist policies were viewed as temporary measures designed to isolate Turkey from the harmful impact of the Great Depression and trade cycles. Nevertheless, these protectionist policies proved to be more in accord with the general philosophy of the Turkish administration, and the temporary measures gained permanence. It is worth noting, for example, that a temporary law on the Protection of the Value of the Turkish currency passed in 1930 for three years is still in effect, and over the decades it was used by successive governments to institute protectionist policies, to restrict or regulate domestic and external trade, to restrict external payments, and in general to interfere in and to control the economy, at times with a very heavy hand.

Under protectionist economic policies, the state was assigned to play the role of the locomotive of the economy. The Government created economic enterprises to solve critical supply problems and to accelerate industrialization. Initially few in number and operating in critical sectors, these economic enterprises proliferated rapidly and accounted for a major share of the domestic production. With the advent of economic planning in the 1960s the State Economic Enterprises (SEEs) gained even more prominence as vehicles of industrialization and accelerated capital formation in Turkey. Import substitution was a major objective of the economic policy and was adopted, with some political overtones, in order to assure the "economic independence" of Turkey.

All instruments of economic policy were used in support of import substitution. The trade regime was rendered excessively restrictive through licensing requirements, quotas, tariffs, and other levies. The payments regime was also extremely restrictive with surrender requirements on external receipts, foreign exchange allocation schemes, and excessively voluminous and complex foreign exchange regulations. The financial system was repressed and highly regulated in order to assure financial support for import substitution activities. Nevertheless, through these policies the SEEs were able to deliver what was expected of them, and Turkey was able to maintain moderately high growth rates throughout much of the 1960s and early 1970s, notwithstanding a balance of payments crisis in 1969, which resulted in even more tightening of the trade regime.

In the wake of the first round of oil price increases, the Turkish economy remained healthy despite some underlying weaknesses. During 1968–73, real GNP increased at a rate of about 7 percent a year. The current account of the balance of payments improved steadily and recorded a surplus for three years in a row during 1971–73. The current account improvement took place despite the worsening of the trade balance. Extremely buoyant workers' remittances played a crucial role in financing the trade deficit. The improvements in the current account combined with continuing surplus in the capital account led to a rapid accumulation of foreign exchange reserves. By the end of 1973, Turkey's gross international reserves stood at $2 billion, which was equivalent to more than 12 months of imports. External indebtedness of the country remained low. At the end of 1973, the total external debt, excluding Fund purchases, was under $3 billion, of which only 8 percent was short term. Moreover, the debt-service ratio, as measured conventionally, was as low as 5 percent.

On the monetary side during 1968–73, both reserve money and M2 expanded at an annual rate of about 25 percent. The rate of inflation, however, averaged only 13 percent owing chiefly to GNP growth (7 percent) and the continuing monetization of the economy (3.5 percent). Public sector finances remained the weakest aspect of the financial environment. Revenues, with a tax burden of 15 percent of GNP, were inadequate to cover expenditures and therefore the public sector ran sizable deficits, forcing governments to resort to Central Bank financing.

In 1974, oil price increases and the consequent acceleration of the rate of inflation in industrial countries led to a sharp and sudden deterioration of the terms of trade for Turkey. While the value of Turkish imports increased rapidly owing to terms-of-trade effect, the onset of recession in industrial countries coupled with the lack of domestic reorientation policies led to a stagnation of exports. The current account of the balance of payments recorded ever-increasing deficits which climbed to over $3 billion by 1977. In tandem with current account deficits, external indebtedness rose rapidly and stood at over $11 billion in 1977, 54 percent of which was short-term debt. These short-term obligations were obtained mainly under a convertible Turkish lira deposit scheme whereby the Central Bank guaranteed the exchange rate.

Although the deterioration of the economic environment originated in the external sector, failure to adopt adjustment policies on time contributed significantly to this deterioration. Particularly important in this respect were the continuation of import substitution policies, which necessitated an overvalued exchange rate of the Turkish lira, and the continuation of the aggressive public investment program, which led to a worsening of the public sector finances. The deficit of the public sector rose to 6 percent of GNP by 1977. Part of the public sector deficits were financed through domestic borrowing. In an attempt to keep the cost of servicing the public debt low, interest rates were kept depressed, and with accelerating inflation, real interest rates became negative. The delay in policy adaptation to meet emerging external difficulties was partly a consequence of the political situation in which no political party had a majority in the parliament and the Government was run by a succession of coalitions.

An attempt to redress the deteriorating economic situation was made starting in late 1977. A number of measures, designed to improve the balance of payments, were implemented and Turkey entered into negotiations with the Fund and foreign creditors. As a result of these negotiations, a stabilization program was developed that formed the basis of a two-year stand-by arrangement that went into effect in April 1978. Nevertheless the program proved to be inadequate to the severity of the economic crisis. Although some improvement took place in the current account, it was achieved by a drastic curtailment of imports and only a minor increase in exports. Moreover, the public sector finances continued to deteriorate mostly owing to a sharp rise in the operating losses of the SEEs.

There were also disappointments in our negotiations with foreign creditors. After entering into a stand-by arrangement with the Fund, the Turkish Government entered into debt rescheduling negotiations with commercial banks and the member countries of the OECD consortium for Turkey. Although the Turkish side tried to convince creditors to accept a maturity structure of ten years, they met with strong resistance. Finally an agreement was reached with maturities ranging from five to eight years and a new money facility of $407 million. However, the effectiveness of the loan commitments of the OECD countries was limited owing to the imposition of special conditions on the utilization of credits.

By the end of 1979 Turkey was in the midst of a severe foreign exchange crisis. The country was unable to import even essential items, such as crude oil. Inflation had accelerated, and unemployment was widespread and increasing. Moreover, there was political turmoil, partly because of economic difficulties and partly because of foreign subversion. During the years in which the crisis was in the making (1974–79), the growth of GNP had declined to an average of 4.4 percent. Public sector deficit expanded rapidly from under 2 percent of GNP in 1974 to over 8 percent in 1979 and averaged 4.5 percent during 1974–79. The Government financed these deficits increasingly through the Central Bank. Reserve money increased at an average annual rate of 40 percent, outstripping the increase in M2 which averaged 36 percent. The rate of inflation followed a similar course, averaging 34 percent a year during 1974–79. Moreover, interest rates became substantially negative in real terms because they were not adjusted to changing conditions. Monetization of the economy was reversed, and a demonetization process took hold during the approach of the crisis.

The inflationary environment also resulted in progressively excessive wage settlements. It was not uncommon for collective bargaining processes to result in wage and benefit increases in excess of 100 percent. These wage increases further deteriorated the SEE finances, which were then reflected as increases in the public sector borrowing requirement. The competitiveness of exports eroded further.

Thus, Turkey faced the second round of oil price increases with an extremely weak economy, a grossly overvalued exchange rate, virtually no foreign exchange reserves, highly negative real interest rates, a very high rate of inflation, widespread unemployment, stagnant output, political turmoil, and an external debt in excess of $13.5 billion, more than a quarter of which was short term.

Economic Stabilization

Faced with the most severe economic crisis in the history of the Turkish Republic, the Government finally became convinced of the need to undertake fundamental reforms that would alter the structure of the Turkish economy. On January 24, 1980 the Government initiated a major change in the orientation of economic policy and introduced a comprehensive set of economic stabilization and structural adjustment measures. Simultaneously the Government entered into negotiations with the Fund on the one hand and official and private creditors on the other. Negotiations with the Fund resulted in a three-year stand-by arrangement in June 1980. Later in 1980, the stand-by arrangement with the Fund, and more important, the strength of the underlying economic program, helped to convince the OECD governments to reschedule for ten years principal and interest payments falling due between 1980–83. Eventually, in 1981, commercial banks agreed to extend maturities of the rescheduled bank debts from seven to ten years.

The program was based on principles of a free market economy. Import substitution was discarded as the basic strategy for economic growth. Instead the Government adopted an outward-oriented growth strategy based on export promotion. With the change in economic philosophy came additional measures regarding the role of the exchange rate and the interest rate as tools of economic policy. The economic function of the SEEs was reevaluated together with their pricing policies. However, the most urgent task facing the Government was the stabilization of the economy; a task that was accomplished in a relatively short period of time because the Government made efficient use of every policy instrument at its disposal. Particularly important in this regard was the efficient and flexible utilization of the exchange rate and interest rate in a mutually supporting manner.

Until January 24, 1980 utilization of the exchange rate as a flexible instrument of economic policy was impossible owing to the politically sensitive nature of this instrument. Every devaluation in Turkey had created political problems for the Government. Consequently governments were reluctant to take appropriate action on the exchange rate until the excessive overvaluation of the domestic currency and the ensuing balance of payments problems forced them to act. Naturally excessive overvaluation necessitated a larger devaluation, which would compound the political problem of the Government. After January 24, 1980 the Government, in an attempt to maintain external competitiveness and depoliticize the exchange rate, began to undertake devaluations more frequently and by smaller amounts. The frequency of these mini-devaluations were increased continuously until May 1981 when the Central Bank started to adjust the exchange rate daily.

Throughout the program the exchange rate has been used and is being used as a central stabilization instrument. It was used, on the one hand, to restrict domestic demand and thus take the pressure off the prices. On the other hand it was used to change relative prices and thereby encourage a shift in production away from the domestic market towards exports. Indeed, the flexible exchange rate policy that was adopted and the ensuing gradual real depreciation of the Turkish lira provided the greatest incentive for Turkish exporters while at the same time helping to contain imports.

Since January 1980 the Turkish lira depreciated continuously against major currencies in order to offset relative price developments and to maintain the competitiveness of Turkish exports. Real effective exchange rate depreciated by about 30 percent in 1980, 15 percent in 1981, 12 percent in 1982, 1 percent in 1983 and 1984, 6 percent in 1985, and 12 percent in 1986. Notwithstanding this continuous depreciation, real effective exchange rate displayed wide swings in the short run owing to fluctuations in international financial markets and, at times, owing to concern for its inflationary consequences.

The second instrument that was used effectively for stabilization purposes was the interest rate. Until June 1980, deposit rates and, to a large extent, lending rates of the banking system were determined directly by the Central Bank. During the 1970s only modest increases were granted, and with the acceleration of inflation rates, they became increasingly negative in real terms. The velocity of circulation increased, and the role of the banking system in financial intermediation began to be undermined with the emergence of non-bank financial institutions not subject to interest-rate regulations. In response to these developments and in particular to arrest the increase in the velocity of circulation, interest rates were liberalized in July 1980. Initially the banks decided to act in unison through a "gentlemen's agreement" and limit the increase in interest rates. However, the competitive pressures from within the banking system and from other sources led to sharp increases in deposit rates by January 1981.

Increase in interest rates led to a very sharp increase in the demand for money and consequently reduced the pressure on prices to increase. More important, the increase in the demand for money allowed a sharp increase in bank credit necessary to finance increased economic activity and exports, without rekindling inflationary pressures. During 1981–82, broad money and quasi-monetary aggregates increased rapidly while at the same time the rate of inflation came

down significantly. Monetization of the economy and financial deepening had started once again.

Following the liberalization of interest rates there was a massive
flow of funds to the banking sector. Realistic interest rate policy
combined with the realistic exchange rate policy brought the outflow
of capital to a halt and reversed the flow. The Government felt that
owing to the volatile nature of capital flows and the revealed inability
of governments to prevent such flows through regulation, it was best
to provide an environment of confidence and to assure a rate of
return for such funds that is sufficiently high in view of international
interest rates and the perceived element of risk.

Although interest rate policy played a major role in the stabilization
of the economy and was perhaps the single most important factor in
lowering the rate of inflation, the system of free interest rates did
not work perfectly. There was competition for deposits and real
interest rates climbed to excessively high levels on both deposits and
credits, exacerbating financial difficulties of many firms. Banks were
forced to roll over their credits and capitalize interest payments. In
mid-1982, there was a financial crisis in which a number of non-bank
financial intermediaries went bankrupt. These events forced the
Government to reconsider its interest rate policy, and it was decided
to bring the rates under control once again.

Another problem created by interest rate liberalization was the fact
that it made the conduct of monetary policy very difficult. From the
start of the program, monetary policy was assigned a prominent role
in stabilizing the economy. Monetary policy was conducted through
quantitative limits on Central Bank credit derived from broad money
targets. These targets and limits on Central Bank credit constituted
the performance criteria under the stand-by arrangement with the
Fund. With the liberalization of interest rates, the reserve money
multiplier tended to increase over and beyond what was projected
owing to a shift from currency to deposits and increased efficiency
in the utilization of reserves by commercial banks, thus leading to
monetary growth in excess of programmed rates.

In evaluating the Turkish adjustment program it is necessary to
take into account the prevailing external environment. In 1980 oil
prices more than doubled, resulting in a severe deterioration in the
terms of trade. At the same time interest rates in the international
financial markets reached unprecedented highs. The unfavorable

economic environment in industrial countries and the significant deceleration in the volume of world trade during 1980–82 rendered an export-based growth strategy much more difficult to implement. Turkey was able to expand its exports rapidly partly because of appropriate policies and partly because of its proximity to the Middle East markets. Since 1983, however, the economic recovery in industrial countries and a more favorable economic environment have not been reflected in the export performances of Turkey. In this regard I would like to bring to your attention the fact that, in response to the success of our export drive, several European countries and more recently the United States have imposed quantitative restrictions on imports from Turkey, particularly on those commodities where we are internationally competitive. The impact of these restrictions on Turkish exports is significant.

I mentioned earlier that on the strength of the underlying economic program Turkey was able to convince the OECD governments to reschedule its debt. Naturally, regardless of how strong the program was, our adjustment efforts would not have been successful without the necessary balance of payments financing. Both the Fund and the Bank provided very sizable assistance to Turkey in support of our program. The Fund approved a three-year stand-by arrangement in the amount of SDR 1,250 million in June 1980. It was followed by two one-year arrangements in 1983 and 1984, both in the amount of SDR 225 million. The Bank on the other hand provided $1,600 million through five structural adjustment loans (SALs) during 1980–85 in support of wide-ranging structural reforms, from rationalization of industrial production to public finance and from external debt management systems to financial sector restructuring. In addition to SALs the Bank also had a very large project lending program in place. Finally, both the Bank and the Fund staff had a significant impact on the details of our policies and related technical matters.

In addition to balance of payments loans from the Fund and the Bank, Turkey received assistance in the form of debt relief and debt rescheduling from the OECD consortium and private creditors. Under the OECD agreement $3 billion of principal and interest was rescheduled and subjected to bonification. Soon this was followed by the rescheduling of commercial claims under similar conditions.

With regard to commercial claims I would like to briefly touch upon a specific measure that turned out to be highly successful and innovative. In rescheduling of our external debt, negotiations regarding the nonguaranteed trade arrears proved to be most difficult to resolve. Finally it was agreed that we give these creditors the option of receiving the amounts due to them in Turkish liras, instead of foreign exchange, at a much more accelerated pace, which then they could convert into investments in Turkey. Many of our creditors found the option attractive and chose to take advantage of it. Out of a total $1,215 million debt $900 million was paid in Turkish liras of which $300 million was used for capital investment, $200 million was used for prefinancing of exports, and $400 million was used as domestic credit for Turkish importers.

Overall Turkey received over $6 billion in debt relief which was crucial in reducing the need for foreign exchange at the start of stabilization and provided a much needed breathing space for the economy.

Structural Adjustment

The 1980 adjustment program aimed to achieve both the immediate goal of stabilizing the economy and the long-term objective of restructuring the economy to assure steady growth under the principles of free market economy. To accomplish the latter the Government, over the years, undertook a number of reforms with major implications for economic management and the structure of the economy. Areas that were subject to major reforms included general pricing policies, trade policies, foreign exchange policies, fiscal reforms, and financial sector reforms.

As the most important aspect of the 1980 stabilization package was a greater reliance on market mechanism, it was only natural for this principle to be applied in the determination of key economic prices, including commodity prices, interest rates, wages, and exchange rates.

Almost all price controls on various commodity prices were removed through the abolition of the Price Control Commission, and the determination of private sector commodity prices was liberalized. The main purpose of the move was to prevent the misallocation of resources owing to distortions and to eliminate the black market that emerged as a result of serious commodity shortages, especially after 1978. More important, the new economic policy involved a significant adjustment of the public sector prices (ranging from 100 percent to 400 percent), and the number of subsidized basic commodities subject to price controls was reduced drastically. SEEs producing non-basic commodities were instructed to set their prices on commercial principles. The new pricing policy allowed SEEs to reduce their operating losses and therefore relieved pressure from the budget.

The new pricing policies, particularly of SEE products, necessitated an overhaul of the SEE operations in order to restructure and streamline these enterprises to become productive and profitable ventures. New measures taken under the program opened SEEs to competition and at the same time freed their managers to adopt pricing policies based on commercial principles. To solve their inherited structural problems, however, a major reform was necessary. The managers were allowed to pursue an independent strategy in administrative, financial, and operational matters and were given flexibility in determining wages and salaries. Decisions regarding investment expenditures were constrained by their ability to finance these expenditures. Personnel expenditures were reduced by restricting new positions, a political impossibility in the past. New personnel can be hired, however, on a contractual basis, allowing SEEs to compete for skilled people with the private sector.

An important new element of the SEE reform package is the Government's intention of a partial privatization of selected SEEs. The privatization policy involves the transfer of the selected SEEs to the Public Participation Fund which would restructure them and subsequently offer their shares to the public.

There was also a major reform of agricultural pricing policies. Price controls on agricultural products, with few exceptions, were gradually lifted and most goods were eventually taken off the controlled list and prices of those few items that were kept controlled were determined by taking into consideration factors such as the world prices, input prices, stability of products' prices and producers' income, domestic inflation, etc. In determining the support prices for exportable products, world prices play a key role, while domestic demand and relative productivity factors are significant for products that are domestically consumed. The subsidies to agricultural input prices have been gradually reduced as well. In this new agricultural pricing policy, the major consideration was to reduce the burden on the government budget and to finance these purchases from sources other than the Central Bank.

These reforms improved the financial position of SEEs significantly. Their expenditures rose less than their revenues which rendered substantial profits for the first time in a long while. The borrowing requirement of SEEs fell in proportion to GNP, and the share of Central Bank borrowing and budgetary transfers fell significantly although their foreign and other domestic borrowing increased in the last few years.

A second area of reform, that of trade policies, can be described concisely and precisely as the liberalization of exports and imports. The move was extremely significant in view of Turkey's historical experience with an excessively restrictive trade regime. As the adjustment program placed a major emphasis on export promotion, policies that were necessary to promote exports were implemented rapidly. Initially, in order to give momentum to export activities, a number of incentives, in addition to realistic exchange rate policy, were offered to exporters. Exporters were given generous tax rebates and had access to preferential credit through the Central Bank. The Central Bank also extended credit to export supporting activities and export-related investments. Moreover, exporters were allowed to import raw materials and semi-finished products without customs duties.

As export activity gained momentum in 1981, the Government gave additional incentives for exports of industrial goods and, in order to boost exports in general, provided further tax rebates. In response to incentive schemes, exports increased rapidly through 1982 but stagnated in 1983 owing to slippages in policies. Starting in 1984, the newly elected government decided to shift the emphasis on export promotion away from direct subsidies and toward a more aggressive utilization of exchange rate policy. Tax rebates were gradually lowered, and the Central Bank discontinued the preferential export credit facility in January 1985 and recently replaced it with an alternative facility in which the interest rate is no longer subsidized but is lower than the commercial bank rates.

Policies aimed at export promotion were effective not only in increasing the volume of exports but also in shifting its composition toward manufactured goods. The share of manufactured goods rose from 35 percent in 1980 to 75 percent in 1985. There was also a diversification of markets. Although Turkish exports to traditional markets, such as Europe, expanded somewhat, the major market penetration was achieved in the Middle East and North Africa.

On the import side, adjustment policies aimed at a less restrictive import regime by permitting a much larger number of items that can be legally imported. Competition from the flow of imports was expected to reduce oligopolistic and monopolistic tendencies, especially in small domestic markets. In the first year of the program, import guarantee deposit rates were reduced. Around 100 items were transferred from the liberalization list II to the less restrictive liberalization list I and stamp duty charges on imports were reduced from a maximum of 25 percent to 1 percent.

In January 1981, global quotas were abolished and goods subject to quotas were transferred to liberalization lists. Liberalization policy continued in 1982 with the transfer of 200 more items from list II to list I. Also, some items were transferred to a new list called the fund list. Starting in 1983, all import transactions were required to be in convertible foreign currencies and the import guarantee deposit rates were lowered again from 20 percent to 15 percent for importers and from 10 percent to 7.5 percent for industrialists.

It must be emphasized, however, that notwithstanding this gradual liberalization, the operational principle remained of a positive list under which, if an item was not on the list, its importation was prohibited.

The major move for import liberalization came in 1984. The newly elected government changed the operational principle to one of a negative list under which, if an item was not on the prohibited list, it could be imported. The 1984 import regime classified imports under the prohibited list, imports subject to approval or license, liberalization list, or fund list.

A comparison of the 1984 import program with that of 1983 reveals the dramatic effect of the policy change. The number of liberalized items increased from 1,000 to 2,500 in one year; the prohibited list shrank from 1,800 items to 459. The approval list (former liberalization list II) was reduced from 1,300 items to 1,000. The number of items contained in the fund list increased from 40 to 100, some of which were consumption goods included in the list in order to prevent price increases because of supply bottlenecks. In May 1985 goods that were formerly included in the prohibited list were transferred to the license list, excluding narcotics, weapons, and related goods.

Another significant aspect of the 1984 import regime was the reduction in tariffs and other levies on imports.

Since December 5, 1985, the right to import from countries where foreign trade is state controlled was extended to companies holding investment certificates in addition to public institutions and export trading companies (with exports exceeding $50 million over the year).

Hence, under this program substantial liberalization of imports was achieved. Although this led, inevitably, to a higher import bill, economic benefits resulting from a more liberal trade regime easily justified the move. Particularly, since 1984, Turkish producers faced with foreign competition took measures to rationalize and streamline their operations and they increased the quality of their products markedly.

As I indicated earlier, the monetary policy was assigned a pivotal role in the stabilization program. During the implementation stage the fragility and the results of decades of financial repression of the Turkish financial markets became painfully clear. Negative real rates, credit rationing, lack of competition, excessively high intermediation costs, and lack of diversity of financial institutions and instruments were all part of the scene. Financial markets were almost completely dominated by commercial banks with high concentration. They were protected and accustomed to non-price competition.

The need for financial reforms became immediate when the financial system was severely shocked by the widespread failures of brokerage firms, which adversely affected the liquidity position and the health of the entire banking system. In 1982 the transition to positive real interest rates proved to be harder than expected for Turkish financial markets.

Financial reform had two objectives. First, it was necessary to develop adequate instruments of the monetary policy and to improve the effectiveness of the existing ones. Second, the allocational and the operational efficiency of the money and capital markets needed to be drastically improved.

Earlier I pointed out the difficulties we had in controlling monetary aggregates. Bank credits have been historically controlled by controlling the size and composition of assets of the banking system. New policies, however, were directed to exercise monetary control through the liabilities of banks. With this new philosophy in mind the Central Bank initiated changes in the management of required reserves and liquidity of commercial banks. Reserve ratios were already unified and simplified in 1983. A complex and tiered system of reserve ratios for preferential credits was either abolished or streamlined, and compliance periods were reduced. Access to the discount window was restricted, and the scope of preferential credit facilities was narrowed.

In April 1986 the Central Bank, as part of its program of extending the instruments of monetary policy, organized an interbank market, which operates like the U.S. Federal Funds market and which conducted the first open market operations in February 1987.

A new banking law was enacted with extended provisions on capital requirement, contingency reserves for problem loans, a new deposit insurance scheme, unified accounting and reporting standards, and a requirement for external auditing. The Central Bank instituted a new bank supervision system. All these innovations are expected to make the banking sector financially healthier and also more resilient in the conduct of monetary policy. In order to improve efficiency and competition in the banking sector, foreign commercial banks were allowed to enter the market.

After the collapse of the brokerage firms, known as the bankers' crisis in Turkey, there was a need to reinstate confidence in financial markets. Furthermore, in order to provide risk capital and long-term funds for the financially weakened Turkish industry, capital markets needed to be developed. The Capital Markets Board, established in 1981, assumed the responsibility of safeguarding the capital markets. After a slow start and despite the high and variable rate, corporations have made increasing use of the corporate bond market, indicating that the crisis of confidence is over and that the capital markets will eventually be able to channel long-term funds to Turkish industry and bring a healthy competition to the banking sector. In order to foster further development of equity markets, the Istanbul Stock Exchange was reorganized as a modern stock exchange, and it has already completed its first successful year of operation.

New and successful financial instruments have been introduced both in money and capital markets. Revenue participation bonds by the Public Housing and Public Participation Fund have been well received by savers. Financial deepening continued with the successful introduction of weekly auctions of Treasury securities with various maturities in money markets. The commercial paper market is expected to be a widely used tool of the money markets soon, as the regulatory framework has been recently completed and approved.

Although the developments in new institutions and instruments in Turkish financial markets are modest in comparison with those in developed markets, they are indeed impressive when one remembers that we reached this stage from a brink of a financial collapse only five years ago. It appears now that the financial industry in Turkey is poised to be the fastest growing sector of the economy.

As most sections of the Turkish economy were undergoing a thorough structural change, the country's tax system had to be improved. Rising inflation rates caused a serious bracket creep for wage earners, who constituted about two thirds of the personal income taxpayers. Increased marginal tax rates adversely affected the work and saving habits of wage earners. Antiquated and weak tax collection administration further exacerbated the problems as tax collections were delayed and tax evasion became a common practice. In order to improve the equity and efficiency of the tax system, authorities launched a major tax reform as a part of the comprehensive structural adjustment program in 1981.

The most important feature of the 1981 income tax reform was the adjustments in the tax brackets for corporations and individuals. Personal income tax brackets were initially adjusted upward, and marginal rates were restructured, providing for a gradual reduction of all rates over the next four years. Corporate income tax was unified. New taxes were introduced to broaden the revenue base.

The Government introduced tax rebates to individuals whose wages and salaries are subject to withholding tax. The purpose was to provide a partial offset to the increased tax rates and to induce compliance among business taxpayers through collection of receipts by wage earners to qualify for tax rebates.

In January 1985 Turkey instituted by far the most comprehensive tax reform in Turkish history in an attempt to broaden the tax base and introduced a 10 percent value-added tax (VAT). The VAT substituted for various production taxes and other duties that had been imposed at various rates on certain groups of commodities and services. The implementation of VAT has been very successful even though there were some operational problems at the outset, as expected. Proceeds from the VAT far exceeded expectations both in 1985 and 1986.

Economic Performance Under the Program

The economic program has resulted in a remarkable improvement in the economic situation in Turkey. The most striking feature of the recovery has been the dramatic growth of exports of goods and services. The rapid growth of exports has been indeed at the heart of the outward-looking, export-led growth strategy adopted since 1980. The value of the merchandise exports jumped by 173 percent from $2.9 billion in 1980 to almost $8 billion in 1985. As a percentage of GNP, exports rose steadily from an average of roughly 4 percent between 1975–80 to over 15 percent. A realistic exchange rate policy, with the ensuing gradual depreciation of the Turkish lira, has been the major cause of this favorable outcome.

The performance of Turkish exports becomes even more notable if the slowdown in world trade during the 1980s is considered. Under the unfavorable conditions of economic recession and the protectionist barriers, particularly in the industrial world, Turkey initiated a dynamic trade policy and penetrated successfully into the Middle Eastern and North African markets. The share of these countries in total Turkish merchandise exports rose from 23 percent in 1980 to 42 percent in 1985. Within this group Iran and Iraq have shown the sharpest growth.

In addition to the increase in the total volume of exports, there was also a major change in the commodity composition of exports in favor of industrial goods. Although the share of industrial exports continually increased over the last twenty years, the growth in industrial exports has been far more pronounced since 1980. By the end of 1985 industrial products accounted for 75 percent of the total exports while they constituted only 35 percent in 1980. Perhaps more encouraging was the significant growth in exports of capital goods as well.

Nevertheless, 1986, like 1983, appears to have been a year of interruption in the advances scored in exports during the last six years. For the ten months to October 1986, exports were 8.5 percent lower than in the corresponding period of 1985. This fall was mainly the result of the decline in oil revenues in some Middle Eastern countries but also of buoyant domestic demand. The resumption of export growth in coming years seems to be closely tied to the economic recovery in the OECD countries as well as to the impact of recent policy measures planned to be implemented in 1987 to boost exports, such as the export credit and insurance system.

In addition to efforts to increase exports, Turkey has fundamentally altered and liberalized her import regime, particularly since January 1984, with a view to opening up the economy to international competition. With the exception of a slight decline in 1982, Turkey's imports of merchandise increased throughout the period, though at a lower rate than her exports. These increases in imports provided the necessary inputs to the industrial modernization of the country. The rapid decline in oil prices during 1986 has contributed to a lessening of the growth of the import bill of Turkey. The figure for the first ten months of 1986 has shown an increase in imports of only 0.7 percent compared with the corresponding period of 1985. Much of the decline in the oil bill was compensated by increased imports of capital goods, reflecting an estimated 8 percent growth of the economy.

Improvements in the external performance led to a restoration in the creditworthiness of the country. Project related borrowing and trade credits expanded substantially since 1982, as well as syndicated medium-term balance of payments support loans.

An attempt has been made to raise the international competitiveness of the economy over the longer term by encouraging the inflow of foreign investment. To this end a number of measures have been introduced. However, direct investment inflows have not yet shown a significant expansion. Almost half the increase in direct foreign investment during the period was related to the option scheme presented to foreign creditors, as earlier discussed.

Regarding economic growth, for the 25 years from 1954 through 1978 Turkey enjoyed positive rates of growth every year. The years 1979 and 1980 were the first successive years of decline in GNP. Improvement in external performance after 1980 contributed to the resumption of growth albeit at moderate rates compared with the early 1970s. However, the growth in output in Turkey after 1980 was at much higher levels than that of comparable developing countries, averaging 4.5 percent during 1981–86 and over 6 percent since 1984.

One of the major objectives of the adjustment program was to reduce the rate of inflation, which had peaked at over 100 percent in 1980. In response to appropriate policies, the rate of inflation started to decline in the second half of 1980 and continued to decline through early 1983. Some slippages in policy during 1983, particularly in fiscal and monetary policies, fueled inflation once again, and prices increased at an accelerated rate through 1984, although in 1985 the deceleration started once again. The rate of inflation continued to decline throughout 1985–86 and by the end of 1986 stood at 25

percent; substantially below that of 1984 but still too high by international standards. In fact, throughout the program inflation proved
to be the most difficult issue to deal with because a rapid decline in
inflation necessitates a fiscal stance often considered to be too harsh
by the governments. When the fiscal stance is not appropriately tight,
undue pressures on monetary policy are exerted and Central Banks
can withstand such pressures with only a limited success.

Conclusions

First and foremost I would like to stress the fact that it is possible,
in a relatively short time, to change the orientation of an economy
from one that is severely repressed and restricted to one that is
moderately liberalized and operating on the basis of free market
principles. The economic stabilization measures and structural reforms undertaken in Turkey since 1980 indicate that with appropriately timed and mutually supporting policies, an economy can be
transformed into a state of equilibrium. Our experience suggests that
the task is not easy, and a lot of experimentation may be necessary.
It is also essential that the policymakers be pragmatic and creative in
proposing solutions to existing problems and be courageous in
undertaking the necessary measures.

Although each country will necessarily decide on the appropriate
instruments in overcoming various economic difficulties, I must stress
two policy instruments that played a crucial role in Turkish stabilization and adjustment: the exchange rate and the interest rate. We
are convinced that the appropriate and prudent use of these two
policy instruments is absolutely necessary in any "growth-oriented
adjustment strategy." Equally important are policies aimed at containing domestic demand and enhancing supply, particularly the
supply of tradables.

The commitment and the determination of the political authority
to carry through the adjustment program is also an essential ingredient
in the success of any program. It was fortunate that Turkey had
governments with the political will necessary to implement and carry
out the stabilization measures and to reorient the economy on the
basis of free market principles. The confidence of the public in
economic leadership made the adjustment process acceptable although it was made clear by the authorities that results might not be
quickly forthcoming.

Another factor that needs to be mentioned is the importance of the availability of, and easy access to, new export markets. In this regard, it is unfortunate that some countries, while they preach an outward-looking adjustment strategy for developing countries, also erect barriers to exports of developing countries. I believe that these countries could be of great assistance to adjustment efforts by assuring an easier access to their domestic markets by developing countries.

Finally, I would like to mention that prompt and sufficient assistance in the form of debt relief, as well as fresh financing, is essential for the success of any adjustment effort. In this regard multilateral institutions like the Fund and the Bank play an extremely important role both as providers of funds and as catalysts in assuring finance from commercial banks. Nevertheless, commercial banks should also assist in the adjustment efforts of developing countries by at least not reducing their exposure and, when the strength of the adjustment effort merits it, by increasing their exposure as a matter of supporting the adjustment effort; and not because the country in question happens to be a special case!

Discussion

Ahmed Abdallah
Executive Director
International Monetary Fund

I must begin by expressing my appreciation for the study which has been presented by Dr. Rusdu Saracoglu, Deputy Governor of the Central Bank of the Republic of Turkey. The paper is mainly descriptive, clear, and comprehensive. For additional background and analysis, I have consulted a study by Mr. George Kopits (a member of Fund staff) published as *Structural Reform, Stabilization, and Growth in Turkey*, IMF Occasional Paper No. 52 (Washington: International Monetary Fund, 1987), which was presented at a Fund-sponsored seminar that was held in June. I found Mr. Kopits's paper, as well as other internal staff papers on Turkey that I have also consulted, most enlightening.

Recent adjustment efforts in Turkey go back to early 1979 when the authorities adopted fairly tough demand-management policies, which included a devaluation of 23 percent in that year and another devaluation of 44 percent in 1979. The Fund supported these policies through two annual stand-by arrangements, and early in 1979 the major Western nations pledged $1 billion in special economic assistance to Turkey. By June 1980, when Turkey entered into a three-year stand-by arrangement with the Fund, the imbalances in the economy as well as its structural constraints had been under attack for some three years.

Real GNP had fallen by 1 percent in 1979 (the first time for over two decades) and was to fall again by another 1 percent in 1980. Despite a devaluation of 23 percent effected at the beginning of 1980, the current account of the balance of payments recorded a deficit of $3.4 billion or 5.8 percent of GNP owing largely to a doubling of oil prices. Central government expenditure stood at 24.2 percent of GNP, the fiscal deficit at 5.3 percent of GNP, and inflation at 104 percent. State economic enterprises were a major drain on the central budget as they continued to provide goods and services at highly subsidized prices. Terms of trade had deteriorated by 20 percent by the end of 1980 and were to deteriorate further by 10 percent by 1985.

In addition to stand-by arrangements with the Fund, Turkey also embarked on a structural adjustment program with the World Bank. The main purpose of the programs of the two Bretton Woods Institutions as well as of the many bilateral donors that supported Turkey's adjustment efforts was to restore "market signals as a principal guide to economic policy decisions." In more specific terms, the purpose was to bring Turkey toward balance of payments viability over the medium term, remove the various imbalances in its economy, and put the country on the path toward self-sustaining growth.

As a result of various energetic measures, Turkey was able to make an impressive turnaround in 1981. Real GNP grew by more than 4 percent, inflation fell to 42 percent, the national savings rate increased by 3 percentage points to 18.6 percent of GNP, and the current account deficit was reduced to $0.9 billion as exports more than doubled. Similar progress continued to be made in subsequent years, but the most remarkable transformation occurred in sharply raising exports of nonagricultural products. In 1980 agricultural commodities accounted for 58 percent of export value, while industrial products stood at 21 percent. By 1985 industrial products had more than trebled to 77 percent of export value.

Another indicator of positive change is that in 1985 the current account deficit stood at $1 billion or less than 2 percent of GNP as against 5.8 percent in 1980. There was also good improvement in the fiscal position brought about through a combination of tax reform and revenue enhancement measures. But the main burden of fiscal adjustment was borne by expenditure cutbacks at the rate of 1 percent a year, as a result of which in 1985 total central government expenditure stood at 19.2 percent of GNP as against 24.2 percent in 1980.

There can be no doubt therefore that during the 1980–85 period Turkey made impressive gains in improving its current account of the balance of payments, in reducing its fiscal deficits, in raising its rate of growth above the average for non-oil developing countries and in other areas as well. Can it be viewed as a model for others to follow in comparable circumstances?

My own conclusion is that the case of Turkey is exceptional because of the very magnitude of external resources injected into the country to bring about its turnaround. During 1980–85, the Fund, the World Bank, and concessional bilateral donors injected a total of $5.1 billion into the country. Second, Turkey was granted debt relief by official creditors and commercial lenders (both medium- and short-term) to the tune of $6.5 billion. As part of this massive financing effort, Turkey, despite the eruption of the debt crisis in August 1982, was able to raise commercial loans for balance of payments support on a spontaneous basis in an amount of $1 billion over the period 1983–85.

It is clear, therefore, that these massive capital inflows virtually ensured the success of the adjustment effort. It means that the scale of adjustment did not have to be compressed over a very short time frame as was the case in other heavily indebted or low-income countries.

Yet, despite these capital inflows, adjustment was neither plain sailing nor uninterrupted. In 1983, for instance, the Turkish economy suffered a reversal with real GNP falling by 1.3 percent, and the current account deficit rose by $1 billion owing to a decline in agricultural output and a fall in export earnings. Fortunately, this setback was overcome in 1984 when real GNP grew by 6 percent and the external current account was reduced to less than 2 percent of GNP. At this moment, we do not fully know the precise performance of the Turkish economy in 1986 but there are indications that it was mixed. If this should turn out to be so, Turkey's adjustment progress could be said to be still fragile in line with general performance of other developing countries.

My other reasons for considering Turkey's case as exceptional is its special geopolitical position and its membership in the North Atlantic Treaty Organization (NATO). It also has special historical and religious ties with the countries of the Middle East to which it sold a major part of its fast-growing nontraditional exports and also found a ready market for its expanding service sector. Turkey is also among about half a dozen countries, a substantial portion of whose labor force is employed outside its borders from whom regular remittances constitute a valuable source of foreign exchange but also complicate macroeconomic management.

Turkey, in order to strengthen its balance of payments, took special measures to attract the savings of its nonresident nationals. All were allowed to open foreign currency deposit accounts with Turkish banks, and interest was paid on these accounts in foreign exchange and at higher rates than those prevailing in the Euromarket. Reserves for these deposits that commercial banks are obliged to hold with the Central Bank are interest earning as against reserves for local currency, which earn no interest. Residents who can prove a source of foreign exchange earnings may also open deposit accounts in foreign currency. While these deposits clearly provide a useful source of foreign exchange, there is no doubt that they are highly volatile and have serious implications for the financial system.

Having made these critical remarks, let me hasten to endorse some basic statements proposed by Dr. Saracoglu. He says "throughout the program inflation proved to be the most difficult issue to deal with because a rapid decline in inflation necessitates a fiscal stance often considered to be too high by governments." Second, he lays stress on "two policy instruments that played a crucial role in the case of Turkish stabilization and adjustment effort: the exchange rate and the interest rate." I concur with both.

Finally, let me say it would have been most helpful if an example had been presented to the symposium of the responsiveness of low-income countries to the application of exchange rates, reform of public enterprises, market-determined interest rates, and other supply-side measures. What capacity do such countries have to respond to traditional instruments of adjustment, and how does one reduce their structural fragility? The case of Turkey shows that despite several years of adjustment, the economy has yet to attain durable self-sustaining growth. I wish it well.

Juergen B. Donges

Vice President
Kiel Institute of World Economics

Dr. Saracoglu gives a good presentation of a country which, having become over-indebted during the 1970s and falling virtually into bankruptcy in 1978, mended its ways afterwards, achieving remarkable economic growth, export expansion, and decelerating inflation.

On the basis of this performance international creditworthiness was restored. Hence, Turkey has been properly chosen for the concerns of this symposium, though there is always a tendency, in some quarters, to downplay a success story on the ground that it is a unique case (economically, socially, culturally, institutionally, historically, geopolitically), and therefore that this case is unrepresentative of what has been done. In a sense, all countries are special. But I think that lessons from the Turkish experience are equally valid for Latin American debtor countries.

Turkey is an interesting counter-example to these countries. The key difference seems to be that Turkey, unlike the debt-ridden Latin American countries, made a major effort not only to curb rampant inflation, but also to break with its long tradition of autarky and etatism, which had deeply distorted cost and price structures and undermined working habits in the population. It is often argued that Turkey was in a much better situation to embark upon reforms than Latin America because it enjoyed sizeable capital inflows and therefore could continue to run a balance of payments deficit on current account (though at a smaller magnitude as a percentage of GDP than prior to the reforms). This may be true, but one could also reckon that Turkey received such external support in exhange for the government's determination to attack the sources of the economic crisis rather than for just dealing with its symptoms.

It should be recalled that Turkey's external debt crisis broke out at a time when four of the international macroeconomic causes that are generally emphasized to explain the outburst of the Latin American debt crisis in the early 1980s were not yet at work. The rates of real interest had not increased (they were negative), the world economy was not in a recession (there was a boom), the U.S. dollar was not appreciating (it was depreciating), nor had OPEC caused the second oil price hike (in real terms the oil price remained more or less constant after the first explosion in 1973–74). Thus, Turkey's debt problem was not so much exogenously determined as self-inflicted; that is, it was the consequence of ill-conceived economic policies over the decades. The manifestation of this is familiar (typical also for many Latin American countries): large budget deficits along with runaway inflation; a chronic overvaluation of the domestic currency along with an incessant capital flight; a remarkable growth of public enterprises along with a low productivity of investment in the

economy; and excessive import substitution sheltered by high protection along with limited export activity.

When an economic crisis is largely self-inflicted, logic demands
that the way out of the impasse has to be effected by the national
government in the first place. The international environment, of
course, also matters, as does the size of financial assistance received
from the Fund, the World Bank, foreign-country donors, and commercial banks. But the main responsibility lies with the home
government. Turkey's experience strongly buttresses this proposition:
exchange rate policy has become more rational; a reasonably outward-
looking approach was adopted with regard to trade; interest rates
now reflect better the relative scarcity of capital; many commodity
price controls have been removed; the tax system has been made to
yield higher revenues; and the budget deficit as a percent of GNP
has been substantially reduced. Though external circumstances were
also adverse for this country and not just for Latin America during
the 1980s, notable progress was made. Turkey has not become a free-
market economy, but, on the whole, the Turkish economy now
operates under an unprecedented structure of market-determined
incentives. Hence, the achievement of self-sustaining growth is a real
possibility provided reforms are carried on over time.

The intriguing question is how the reorientation of domestic
economic policies could happen in Turkey (while it seems so difficult
to accomplish in the heavily indebted Latin American countries).
After all, the reforms were bound to cause a redistribution of incomes
and opportunities. Received theories of the political economy would
tell us that it would pay for the main beneficiaries of the previous
policy regime (such as the least competitive import-substituting
industries, the urban labour aristocracy, the domestic banks, and the
bureaucrats issuing power through controls) to invest into policy
continuity. In Turkey, as elsewhere, there was (and still is) opposition
to the new economic course. The best known example, mentioned
in passing in Dr. Saracoglu's paper, refers to the country's private
and public banks: they colluded to fix interest rates in defiance of
the government's freeing of those rates in late 1980, thereby contributing to the deep domestic financial crisis of summer 1982. Since
then, interest rates have been controlled administratively once again
(though at positive levels in real terms).

A reasonable explanation for the relative success in keeping most special-interest opponents of liberalization at bay may be two handed. On the one hand, the traumatic economic crisis at the end of the 1970s made it clear to the Turks at large that continuation of bad economic policies would end up in an overall disaster and that a "muddling-through" approach, as so often applied in the 1950s and 1960s, was no longer a viable solution. On the other hand, the government made a strong political commitment to the shift in economic policies and pursued its objectives with determination, aiming at both changing the expectations of economic agents and eliciting financial support from abroad. As rapid successes could be shown (the rates of inflation went down, exports expanded fast, and per capita income increased, while unavoidable cost of unemployment could be kept within limits), the reform package was regarded by the public as sensible and realistic. Both conditions are necessary in order to bring about economic policy change. A comparison with Latin American countries would no doubt reveal that, at best, only the first condition (the public awareness of an imminent economic collapse) was fulfilled on the southern continent, but not the second condition (political determination).

Having said this, I would like to point out that Turkey is still only half way down the road to a full restructuring of the economy. At the end of his paper, Dr. Saracoglu made some vague remarks in this sense, but the most pressing issues that have to be tackled domestically could have been mentioned more explicitly. Six areas for further policy action come immediately into mind. To begin with, the rate of inflation is still high (currently at about 30 percent), so that coordinated monetary and fiscal policies to reduce that inflation further are indispensable. Second, import tariffs will have to be overhauled with a view to lowering them and reducing their inter-sectoral dispersion (the paper unfortunately does not provide updated evidence on nominal and effective rates of protection). Third, the newly created free-trade zones (in Adana, Antalya, Izmir, and Merzin) must soon prove their viability and effectiveness or be closed down. Fourth, the public sector enterprises will have to become more efficient and some of them could perhaps be privatized. Fifth, the remaining domestic capital market imperfections have to be urgently eliminated, if more domestic financial resources are to be mobilized and the allocation of savings is to become more productive. And last but not least, the conditions for greater private foreign investment inflows should be improved, which might require also a more receptive attitude of the Turkish authorities.

Domestic adjustment policies along these lines should receive adequate support from abroad by two means. One possibility is for the World Bank and other multilateral institutions, as well as bilateral donors, to provide financial and technical assistance. Technical assistance could be of great help in achieving an effective implementation of the various measures; injections of funds would strengthen domestic investment, support the balance of payments, and provide credibility to the adjustment programs. The other means is for the industrial countries to keep their markets open for foreign suppliers (from Turkey and elsewhere), rather than succumbing to the protectionist temptation. Dr. Saracoglu rightly worries about this latter danger. After all, without adequate access to large markets, a debtor country is bound to face serious difficulties in earning foreign exchange to service the interest payments on its external debt, and without a reasonable degree of certainty about the openness of foreign markets, both policymakers and investors will lose faith in being able to reap the benefits attributable to outward-oriented economic development.

Comment

Hélène Ploix

Executive Director
International Monetary Fund

There are two issues that I think are worth discussing. I might take as the theme of my remarks "Les peuples heureux n'ont pas d'histoire," which could be loosely translated as "Happy matters do not need to be discussed."

The first is the sustainability of the economic stabilization and structural adjustment in Turkey. This is a challenge facing Turkey. Here I would like to raise the question of what is going to happen tomorrow, in particular when we note that Turkey is still experiencing a high rate of inflation, a decline in employment, and some decline in workers' real income (at least minimum salary). Furthermore, the dramatic growth of exports of goods and services was made possible first by the measures taken but also by the prior existence of an industrial sector and by the development of the Middle Eastern markets.

Concerned by the prospects for the Turkish case and considering that exports dropped by 8 percent last year, I wonder whether, had there been more open policies, the development process would have gone further and whether the allocation of resources to more productive activities has taken place as it should.

The second issue that I would like to raise is the existence in Turkey of specific and exceptionally favorable conditions at the outset of the stabilization and adjustment program. I wonder which role they played and how much this makes a difference in other cases. These favorable conditions are, among others, the very large amount of workers' remittances that responded fairly well to the government investment incentives scheme, the market potential offered by Iran and Iraq, and perhaps also the domestic political stability that contrasted to the political situation and the lack of confidence in the 1970s.

What about the countries that do not experience such favorable circumstances? Does Turkey represent an appropriate model?

SESSION 3

Macroeconomic Policies
for Economic Growth

Economic Growth and Economic Policy

Stanley Fischer

Professor of Economics
Massachusetts Institute of Technology

Economic growth has been high on the agenda of developing countries for at least four decades, and on the agenda of economics for centuries. The variety of theories of growth attests to the absence of a simple assured route to success. The variety of experiences of growth both offers a potentially fertile field for empirical generalizations and suggests the need for growth strategies that adjust to the structures of individual economies.

The growth performance of 68 developing economies in Africa, Asia, and Latin America in the last two decades is summarized in Table 1.[1] The striking fact is the disparity of performance between Asia and the other two continents.[2] Not only is the mean growth rate in Asia highest in each period; in addition there is only a small decline in the mean growth rate between decades, and in neither period is there a significant number of countries with negative per

---

Note: I am indebted to Eliana Cardoso, Jacob Frenkel, and Gerald Helleiner for comments, Takeo Hoshi for research assistance, and the National Science Foundation for research support.

[1] Blades (1980), examining gross national product (GNP) data for sub-Saharan Africa, estimates that annual growth rates have a margin of error of $+/-$ 3 percent. Whether these errors are significantly lower for decadal average growth rates depends on their serial correlation. Blade's account suggests the errors would be positively correlated over time, but possible levels of correlation are difficult to infer.

[2] Weighted average decadal growth rates of total rather than per capita GNP, taken from *International Financial Statistics* (International Monetary Fund) paint a different picture. Western Hemisphere growth of 5.7 percent and 5.9 percent in the sixties and seventies exceeds the corresponding 4.5 percent and 5.1 percent in Asia; African growth for those two periods was 4.8 percent and 3.8 percent, respectively. Asian performance is significantly superior for the few years for which there are data for the 1980s.

Table 1.   Growth of Per Capita GDP, 1965–84[1]
(In annual percent)

	Africa[2]		Asia[3]		Latin America[4]	
	1965–73	1973–84	1965–73	1973–84	1965–73	1973–84
Mean	2.1	0.5	4.1	3.6	2.8	0.3
Percentage of countries with growth rates:						
Below −2 percent	6	21	0	0	0	25
−2 to 0	9	21	7	7	0	15
0 to 2	42	27	13	13	45	40
2 to 4	24	18	27	27	25	15
4 to 6	9	9	27	40	25	5
Above 6 percent	9	3	27	13	5	0

Source: World Bank, *World Development Report 1986*.

[1] African data are based on 33 countries; Asia on 15, including China and India; Latin America on 20 countries. Countries are drawn from the low-, middle-, and upper-middle income categories. Mean growth rate is unweighted mean of countries in the group.

[2] Ethiopia, Mali, Zaïre, Burkina Faso, Malawi, Niger, Tanzania, Burundi, Uganda, Togo, Central African Republic, Benin, Rwanda, Kenya, Sierra Leone, Guinea, Ghana, Sudan, Senegal, Mauritania, Liberia, Zambia, Lesotho, Côte d'Ivoire, Morocco, Egypt, Nigeria, Zimbabwe, Cameroon, Botswana, Congo, Tunisia, and South Africa.

[3] Bangladesh, Nepal, Burma, India, China, Sri Lanka, Pakistan, Indonesia, Philippines, Papua New Guinea, Thailand, Syria, Malaysia, Korea, Hong Kong, and Singapore.

[4] Haiti, Bolivia, Honduras, El Salvador, Nicaragua, Dominican Republic, Peru, Ecuador, Jamaica, Guatemala, Costa Rica, Paraguay, Colombia, Chile, Brazil, Panama, Uruguay, Mexico, Argentina, and Venezuela.

capita gross domestic product (GDP) growth in Asia. The difficulties of the period 1973–84 for Africa and Latin America are clearly visible in the fact that 40 percent of the countries in both groups had negative growth of per capita GDP from 1973 to 1984. Growth rates of per capita GDP in the two periods were positively correlated within each group, highest for Asia and lowest for Africa.[3] The implication is that success was more permanent in Asia than in Africa.

Table 1 demonstrates not only the differences among groups, but also a range of experiences within each group. Some of the differences are directly traceable to oil or to other special circumstances, but they reinforce the point that growth strategies and models of adjustment will have to be tailored to fit individual countries.

---

[3] The correlations (R^2) for Africa, Asia, and Latin America are 0.05, 0.41, and 0.16, respectively.

The purpose of this paper is to review facts and theories of long-run growth, development strategies, and the adjustment and growth problems facing many developing countries. I conclude with lessons of policy in developing countries.

Long-Run Growth

Growth rates in the industrial economies over long periods are modest by comparison with the recent Asian experience. Angus Maddison (1982) estimates growth rates of per capita GDP since 1700 of 1 percent a year or less for France, the Netherlands (the world leader in 1700), and the United Kingdom. Performance for ten industrial economies since 1870 is summarized in Table 2. Japan's 2.7 percent is the most rapid rate of growth of per capita GDP in that period; no country shows aggregate growth in excess of 4 percent.

Kuznets (1959), summarizing his fundamental research by describing "modern economic growth as the adoption of the industrial system" (p. 110), develops the implications—that modern growth requires minimum levels of skill and literacy on the part of the population, a shift from personal or family organizations to larger scale units, the creation of transportation and communication infrastructure before the division of labor within the country can become a reality, and that growth is accompanied by urbanization as the labor force shifts away from agriculture, changes in demographics,

Table 2.   Growth of GDP and GDP Per Capita, 1870–1985
(In annual percent)

Country	GDP Per Capita	Aggregate GDP
Australia	1.1	3.1
Canada	1.9	3.6
France	1.9	2.2
Germany, Fed. Rep. of	2.0	2.4
Italy	1.6	2.3
Japan	2.7	3.8
Netherlands	1.5	2.7
Sweden	2.3	2.9
United Kingdom	1.3	1.8
United States	1.8	3.5

Source: Maddison (1982), updated from International Monetary Fund, *International Financial Statistics*, various issues.

and changes in social values. He emphasizes too the disparities among national growth processes: "the observable cases of modern economic growth are best viewed as combinations of the industrial system (including its minimum social concomitants) with the distinctive initial structure of each country" (p. 113). Theory has the task, though, of developing principles or classifications that make it possible to describe the growth process more generally than to treat each national experience as an historical accident.

Descriptions of the growth process in the industrial economies stress industrialization, or in Maddison's (1982, p. 17) more encompassing term, the scientific-technical revolution. Growth proceeds as labor shifts from low-productivity agriculture to high-productivity manufacturing, and to services, but with productivity growth in agriculture often exceeding that in the rest of the economy. Chenery and Syrquin (1975) characterize the transition to development not only by a shift to manufacturing from primary production, but also at a later stage by an increase in the share of manufactured exports in GNP.

Modern analyses of growth are supply oriented, starting from the production function. In the neoclassical framework (Solow (1956, 1957), Denison (1974)) growth is accounted for by the accumulation of capital and labor, and by technical progress.[4] Two important empirical results derived in this framework are the major role of technical progress in explaining the growth of per capita output, and the relatively small share of growth attributed to capital accumulation.

Denison's calculations for the United States, presented in Table 3, show advances in knowledge accounting for more than half the growth of output per employee over the period 1929–82.[5] Despite the importance of technical change, its sources and the role of policy in promoting technical progress are difficult to quantify. Maddison (1982, Chapter 3) cites the "institutionalization of innovation" as a cause of both a more even pace of technical progress in modern economies and more rapid technical advance. He notes encouragingly

---

[4] Inputs of raw materials are usually ignored in the basic framework, though they could easily be included. Of course discoveries of raw materials and changes in their prices have often had major effects on growth.

[5] Denison warns that these results should not necessarily be regarded as typical, since patterns differ across countries. See, for instance, Denison (1967) for an analysis contrasting post-World War II European growth with that in the United States.

Table 3. Sources of Growth of U.S. National Income, 1929–82
(In percent)

	Total	Per Person Employed
Growth rate	2.9	1.5
Percent of growth attributed to:		
Labor input except education	32	12
Education per worker	14	27
Capital	19	20
Advances in knowledge	28	55
Improved resource allocation	8	16
Economies of scale	9	18
Other	− 11	− 24

Source: Denison (1985), p.30.

that a productivity slowdown of the type seen since 1973 has occurred before, and that it is not necessarily permanent.[6]

In international comparisons, productivity growth (roughly corresponding to Denison's advances in knowledge) accounts for more than half of Southeast Asian growth, and relatively little of Latin American growth, for periods from 1955 to 1973. De Melo (1985) reports the results of studies of productivity growth in five Southeast Asian countries, five industrial market economies, and five Latin American countries. Productivity growth accounts for 46–64 percent of total growth in Southeast Asia, for 30–55 percent in the industrial market economies, and for 12–34 percent in Latin America. The capital stock increased more rapidly in Southeast Asia than in Latin America.

Growth of capital accounts in Table 2 for 20 percent of the U.S. growth rate, or 0.3 percent a year of growth, over the 1929–82 period. The resolution of the puzzle of the relatively small contribution of capital starts from the relationship between the rate of growth of capital per worker and the rate of growth of output per worker, which depends on the share of capital in total output. The relationship is that a 1 percent annual rate of growth of capital per worker adds a fraction of 1 percent, equal to the share of capital in output, to the

---

[6] Romer (1987) shows that productivity growth in the United States since 1840 is negatively serially correlated over decades: a decade of lower than average productivity growth tends to be followed by a catch-up of higher than average growth.

growth of output per worker. In the United States over the period
1929–82 capital per worker increased at an annual rate of about 1.2
percent. The share of capital in output is about a quarter. One quarter
of 1.2 percent is the 0.3 percent a year contribution of capital
accumulation per worker to the growth of output per worker in
Table 2.[7]

A slightly different perspective comes from consideration of the
rate of return to capital, usually estimated in the range of 10–15
percent a year. Using for convenience an estimate of 12.5 percent,
an increase in the share of investment in GNP by 1 percent raises
the level of GNP by 0.125 percent, temporarily adding 0.125 percent
to the growth rate. It would thus take a massive increase in net
investment of 8 percent of GNP to raise the growth rate of GNP from
the supply side by 1 percent within a period of three to four years.
If productive projects can be found, investment programs of the pre-
World War II Soviet type can contribute significantly to increasing
the growth rate of potential output. But, within the constant returns
neoclassical framework, an increase in the share of investment in
GNP raises the level of GNP permanently but the growth rate only
temporarily.

Kendrick (1980), Maddison (1982), and others have argued that the
growth accounting framework of Denison significantly underesti-
mates the role of capital in growth. Kendrick develops a more inclusive
concept of capital that includes government capital,[8] and intangible
capital, including research and development, education and training,
and health and safety. About half of GNP is investment by this
definition. By Kendrick's calculations, capital accounts for 70 percent
of U.S. growth over the 1929–69 period.

Returning to the narrower definition, the role of capital in growth
would be understated by Denison if it is the vehicle for the embodiment of new technology in production. Further, to the extent that

---

[7] Denoting output as Y, labor input as L, and capital as K, and with the constant
returns to scale production function $Y = F(K,L)$, per worker output is $(Y/L) = f(K/L)$,
with $f'(\ )$ equal to the marginal product of capital. Then denoting the growth rate of
output per worker by $g_{Y/L}$, and that of capital per worker by $g_{K/L}$:

$$g_{Y/L} = (f'(\ )K/Y) \cdot g_{K/L}$$

With capital receiving its marginal product, $(f'(\ )K/Y)$ is the share of capital in output.

[8] Denison uses the national income accounts which attribute no rental return to
government capital, thereby understating the share of capital in output.

Table 4.   Investment Share and the Growth Rate of GDP, 1965–84[1]

	Industrial market economies	Africa	Asia	Latin America
Coefficient	0.15	0.22	0.03	0.08
	(0.04)	(0.12)	(0.29)	(0.09)

Source: International Monetary Fund, International Financial Statistics, various issues.
[1] This is the result of a regression of the growth rate of GNP or GDP over the period 1965–84 on the average investment share during that period, run separately for different groups of countries. The coefficient is that on the investment share, its standard error in parentheses.

technical progress is embodied in capital, an increase in the investment rate raises the level of output more than indicated in the preceding discussion.[9] Despite the plausibility of the embodiment hypothesis, it has been difficult to find decisive measures of the extent to which increases in productivity have been the result of new technologies embodied in new investment goods.[10]

The embodiment hypothesis would explain the positive cross-sectional relationship between the growth rate of GNP and the share of investment in GNP that is shown in Table 4. The relationship is particularly strong for the developed economies. Probably coincidentally, the coefficient on the investment share in the regression for the industrial market economies is close to standard estimates of the return to capital.

Denison attributes a slightly larger share of the growth of U.S. output per worker to increased education than to capital accumulation. The Denison calculations start from a labor input series in which weights were assigned to workers with differing levels of education.[11] The weights are based on earnings by educational level, adjusting as far as possible for differences in ability correlated with education.

---

[9] In illustrative calculations, Solow (1960) assumes technical progress at the rate of 3 percent a year, and a share of capital equal to 0.3. A doubling of the rate of investment from 10 percent to 20 percent of GNP raises the level of GNP by 14 percent within a decade if technical progress is disembodied and by 26 percent if it is embodied.

[10] Denison (1964) argues that the question of whether technical progress is embodied is of little practical significance in assessing the sources of growth in the United States. His argument is that within the range of historical experience of the U.S. changes in the age of capital goods—which is how embodiment affects the role of capital—have been relatively small.

[11] Appendix I of Denison (1974) contains a full description.

Estimates of the returns to education in the United States are similar to those for physical capital, with the possibility that social returns may be higher.[12]

Despite a long tradition emphasizing increasing returns to scale in the growth process, their role has been difficult to pin down. Denison emphasizes the potential unreliability of his own calculations. Paul Romer (1986) argues that certain features of the growth process, such as apparently secularly increasing rates of growth, are more consistent with increasing than constant returns. Romer uses a one-sector production function.

Another approach focuses on what are sometimes called economies of agglomeration, or synergy. The notion is that coordinated expansion of many industries is more likely to be self-sustaining than more gradual processes. Suggestive descriptions of the early industrialization process point in the same direction:

> . . .change begat change. . . A cheap supply of coal proved a godsend to the iron industry, which was stifling for lack of fuel. In the meantime, the invention and diffusion of machinery in the textile manufacture and other industries created a new demand for energy, hence for coal and steam engines; and these engines, and the machines themselves, had a voracious appetite for iron, which called for further coal and power . . . (Landes (1969, pp. 2–3)).

Rostow's (1960) takeoff into economic growth has a similar emphasis.

It is quite likely that economies of scale of this type are more important at early stages of development than in a large developed economy. Economies of scale may thus be more significant in the growth process in smaller less-developed economies than in the United States. It is in this context that access to export markets can become a significant source of increased growth.[13] The expansion of international trade is given an important role in promoting growth in the periods 1820–1913 and 1950–73 by Maddison (1982, Chapter 3), though the contribution cannot be quantified.

The neoclassical analysis of growth places little emphasis on the role of government policy. Within that supply-side framework,

---

[12] Kendrick (1980, p. 98) estimates rates of return to human capital between 10.1 percent and 12.8 percent from 1929 to 1973.

[13] Srinivasan (1986) finds little evidence that small economies perform systematically less well than larger units, attributing the result to international trade.

investment incentives and educational spending could each contribute to raising the level of output; so too can government spending on infrastructure.

The political economy hypothesis that small governments are best for growth receives at best mixed support from the data. Dervis and Petri (1987) show that the share of government spending in GNP is smaller than average for the most rapidly growing middle income countries. Ram (1986) in a cross-section of 110 countries finds a positive partial correlation between the growth rate of GNP and the growth rate of government spending. Less formally, important counterexamples to the view that small governments are best for growth abound: although Japan has relatively low government spending, government plays an active role in coordinating economic strategies and in protecting domestic markets. Government spending in Germany is high. Government intervention in another of Europe's growth successes, France, has been pervasive. The raw correlation between the share of government in GNP and the growth rate for the industrial market economies is in fact slightly negative; in the developing countries it is weakly negative in Asia and Latin America and positive in Africa.

The role of demand factors in growth has received less quantitative attention, though steady and rapid expansion of markets is often informally cited as an important stimulant to growth. The econometric evidence for the United States implies that expanding demand is a more important factor explaining investment than the cost of capital (Clark (1979)). Expanding international markets likewise serve as an investment-stimulating source of demand.[14] The relation between macroeconomic policy and expanding markets is, however, complicated. In the short run, monetary and fiscal expansion serve to increase demand and stimulate demand-led growth, but once the economy nears full employment, the task of demand management becomes more difficult and supply factors become dominant. However difficult the task of demand management at full employment, there is no doubt that restrictive aggregate demand policies retard growth.

---

[14] Before the 1950s the conventional wisdom for developing countries emphasized the development of primary exports as an engine of growth, encouraging the growth of complementary domestic industries.

Convergence Hypothesis

The modest long-term rates of growth of the industrial economies and lessons learned from that growth are not necessarily relevant to the developing economies. The prime reason is that those countries are far from the technological frontiers; technical progress could play a significant role in their future growth without any major technological breakthroughs taking place.[15]

The convergence hypothesis asserts that countries that lag behind will catch up to the high income countries. The notion is consistent with the neoclassical approach with constant returns to scale and access (perhaps only gradually) to the same technologies around the world. A quick look at the evidence is not supportive of the hypothesis. Except for Japan, most of the countries currently in the ranks of the industrial market economies have been among the high income countries for at least a century. To be sure, some (including Argentina and Uruguay) have dropped out of the top ranks, relative positions shift, and some of the countries listed as upper middle income have per capita incomes above those of the lowest industrial market economies.[16] But the overall picture is not one of rapid change.

Baumol (1986) finds convergence within Maddison's group of sixteen industrial economies.[17] When the sample is extended to 72 countries for which Summers and Heston have provided GNP data and 1950–80 growth rates, there is no convergence except among the highest income countries and within the centrally planned economy group. Nor is there convergence within the three groups, Africa, Asia, and Latin America, over the period 1965–84: in all three cases the correlation between the growth rate of GDP per capita and the initial level of income is positive, though it is almost zero for Latin America.[18]

---

[15] Of course, modifications of technologies may be needed to adapt them to local conditions.

[16] In *World Development Report 1986* four small upper middle-income countries (Israel, Hong Kong, Trinidad and Tobago, and Singapore) could, by the income criterion, make it into the next rank.

[17] Baumol, noting the criticism by Paul Romer (1986) that examination of the growth records of the successful countries biases the results by choosing countries that end up within a particular range of incomes, states that the tendency to convergence remains when the data for wealthy countries in 1950 are examined for convergence over the next three decades. The convergence hypothesis implies a negative correlation between the growth rate of income and the initial level of income.

[18] The correlations (R) are for Africa 0.35; for Asia 0.62; and for Latin America 0.08.

Rostow (1979) offers another version of the convergence hypothesis in which growth rates are low in the lowest income groups, then accelerate as income rises, and eventually decelerate. The argument is based on his well-known *Stages of Economic Growth*, and on empirical results by Chenery and Syrquin (1975), and with shorter-run data by Kristensen (1974).

At most, the convergence hypothesis could demonstrate a tendency to eventual catch-up by the developing countries. Even so catching up would take a very long time. The low-income countries would have to grow 3.9 percent per capita a year faster than the industrial market economies to catch up within a century.[19] Such growth is certainly not to be expected. However, the evidence for the convergence hypothesis is weak. And, as the Argentinian and Uruguayan, and in the longer run, Spanish and U.K. examples show, getting to the top is no guarantee of staying there.

The most important lesson of the historical record is the power of compound interest. The extraordinary progress of the developed economies over the last century was brought about with growth rates that look modest to those used to the 1950–70 data. The implication is that small differences in growth rates—for instance those brought about by changes in the share of investment in GNP of 2–3 percent—can have important long-run impacts on living standards.

Small changes in growth rates matter a great deal in the long run, and generally policy is likely at best to make small changes in growth rates. Work on the stages of economic growth nonetheless holds out hope for developing countries. Several economies have experienced a period of very rapid growth, associated with industrialization or raw material booms. Since 1950, output has grown at rates near 10 percent for a decade or more in some Latin American, Middle Eastern, and Southeast Asian countries. Such growth rates cannot be sustained for very long, for countries at the frontier are unlikely to grow much more rapidly than their historical average rates in Table 1 over prolonged periods. But there is precedent for developing countries to move, for a time, rapidly toward the frontier.

---

[19] The calculation is based on per capita GDP estimates for 1984 of $260 in the low-income economies and $11,430 in the industrial market economies from the *World Development Report 1986*. Of course the reported GDP data are not good measures of relative real incomes. The statement in the text is nonetheless accurate as a description of required rates of growth of measured GDP.

Strategies of Development

The neoclassical supply-side analysis of growth does not emphasize the role of economic policy. Nor does it provide signposts to rapid development, except perhaps in cases of Soviet-style industrialization through massive capital accumulation.

Two basic approaches to growth policy can be detected. One, coming down from Adam Smith, is laissez-faire, seeing growth policy as consisting mainly of reducing governmental impediments to growth. The other is more technocratic, looking to government policy to direct economic development in particular directions.

In the absence of guidance from theory, strategies for growth developed in the post-World War II period have seized on particular aspects of the structures of developing economies or of the growth process as the keys to rapid growth.[20] Aside from the laissez-faire strategy of relying on the market, development strategies have focused on the most obvious characteristic of growth spurts, industrialization. They differ according to the methods used to encourage the development of industry.

Import substitution was the first such strategy. Developed in the late 1940s and early 1950s, the analysis of the problem of the developing economies started from their international role as suppliers of raw materials and agricultural products. The terms of trade had and would turn against these goods. Industrialization would not only bring rapid productivity growth but also reduce vulnerability to the swings and trends of primary product prices. The strategy was to develop industry to replace manufactured imports and to reduce reliance on primary exports. It emphasized the development of the internal market rather than exports as the source of demand for the products of the new industries. Domestic industry could be protected by high tariffs, and domestic agriculture, where supply was thought to be inelastic, could be taxed.

Despite rapid growth in the 1950s and 1960s, particularly of industrial output, several Latin American countries ran into difficulties—in the form of external and sectoral imbalances and on the fiscal front, leading to inflation.

---

[20] I draw here on interesting papers by Fishlow (1985) and Corbo (1986) describing in some depth Latin American development thinking and growth policies.

Fishlow (1985), reviewing Latin American experience, argues that import substitution paradoxically increased foreign exchange vulnerability. The anti-export bias of the policy reduced the growth rate of exports. Reductions in marginal imports made the remaining imports even more crucial; further, the increasing sophistication of domestic manufactures increased the demand for imported inputs. Increasing current account deficits in the late fifties were solved in part by direct foreign investment, which meant increased rather than reduced dependence on the outside world.[21]

Although the import substitution strategy was developed in the Latin American context, the development strategies followed in much of Africa and Asia were similar.[22] The difficulties that resulted on all three continents are not an inevitable consequence of an industrialization strategy. Rather they result from the emphasis on import substitution at the expense of the development of the primary sector and of exports.

Balance of payments difficulties and inflation in Latin America produced several reactions pointing in different directions: that the import substitution strategy should be pursued on a larger scale through a Latin American free trade area; that increased official capital inflows could solve both the government budget and foreign exchange problems; and that structural reform reducing foreign dependence and increasing the role of the state was needed. The free trade area solution brings the hard-to-quantify benefit of expanding markets that growth analysts have long emphasized. Nevertheless, the proposal has repeatedly failed to leave the ground, despite recent stirrings between Brazil and Argentina. Increased aid appeared for a while in the late fifties and early sixties, but was not a permanent solution. The third approach, closing the economy off further, was not attempted. In Africa, where the problems appeared later, aid inflows did increase, but fell far short of amounts required to maintain living standards.

The import substitution strategy is widely regarded as a failure, but manufacturing output in fact grew rapidly, on average 6 percent

---

[21] Corbo (1986) develops this argument in detail.

[22] Of course, not all countries followed the same strategies. In Asia, India and China both pursued import substitution for long periods.

a year, in Latin America in the 1950s and 1960s.[23] Development thinking and strategy in the 1960s continued to emphasize industrialization, but with greater attention to constraints.

From Repressed Economies to Liberalization

The standard World Bank two-gap model developed during this period[24] focuses on the saving-investment balance and the foreign exchange constraints, both of which gaps can be closed through foreign capital inflows. Development strategies based on these models emphasized the flow of foreign resources to the developing countries, and capital inputs needed to generate planned outputs.

The models were generally criticized for assuming credit rationing in the international capital markets, and for ignoring substitution possibilities, and thus underestimating the equilibrating role of relative prices. Nonetheless, the two gaps plus the government budget constraint have to be at the center of any realistic economic model.

The 1970s saw the development of *international monetarism* as an explanation of both inflation and the balance of payments. The basic model had long been in use at the Fund for financial programing.[25] Based on the simple accounting identity that the balance of payments deficit is equal to the change in international reserves, in turn equal to the growth of the money supply minus domestic credit creation, the analysis suggests that the rate of domestic credit creation is the key to controlling the balance of payments at a given exchange rate. As it is often put, the balance of payments is a monetary phenomenon. Since inflation is also a monetary phenomenon, the international monetarist approach appeared to offer a route both to stabilization of inflation and balance of payments equilibrium.

The identities from which Fund financial programing begin are correct, but it takes a subsidiary set of assumptions on the flexibility

---

[23] This compares with GDP growth averaging 4.8 percent a year. Data are from Corbo (1986).

[24] Khan, Montiel, and Haque (1986) provide a simple exposition of this approach. Chenery and Strout (1966) is one of the classic references.

[25] See Khan, Montiel, and Haque (1986) for an exposition, Polak (1957) for a highly influential paper, and Frenkel and Johnson (1976) for the Chicago contributions to the approach.

of prices and wages and the credibility of policy to reach international monetarist conclusions. As failed Southern Cone stabilization attempts based on preannounced paths for the exchange rate show, analysis of stabilization and exchange rate problems has to deal with the inflexibility of wages and expectations, and the effects of capital flows on exchange rates.

Consistent with domestic monetarism of the old Chicago school, international monetarism did not pay particular attention to growth policies. It relied on non-interventionist microeconomic policies combined with macroeconomic stability to allow markets to produce the right allocation of resources, both at a moment of time and intertemporally.

But markets in the developing countries are heavily distorted, with agricultural prices out of line with world prices, many financial markets thin or nonexistent, exchange rates overvalued, capital controls in place, tariffs high, and subsidies ubiquitous. The financial repression view of the development problem, associated with the work of Shaw and McKinnon[26] in the Republic of Korea, argued that simple domestic capital market changes could unleash powerful forces for development. Deregulated interest rates would stimulate saving, helping reduce domestic absorption and strengthening the balance of payments, and make for more efficient investment decisions. The extraordinary growth of Korea, where real GDP doubled in the years 1967–73 and then grew another 70 percent in the next six years, lent support to the strategy, even though it has been difficult to find direct evidence of interest rate effects on saving.[27]

Liberalization and Export Promotion

The *liberalization* strategy developed in the mid-1970s, and still prominently associated with the World Bank, moves beyond financial repression to advocate the eventual removal of all the major economic distortions in developing countries. Liberalization, unlike industrialization, provides a clear policy agenda. Of course, the aim of the policies is largely to remove the consequences of past mistakes, and in that sense the long-run growth strategy is laissez-faire, not

---

[26] McKinnon (1973) is particularly influential.

[27] See Giovannini (1985) for a careful study.

interventionist. But there are enough distortions to keep policymakers busy removing them for the foreseeable future.

Krueger, perhaps the leading exponent and analyst of the liberalization strategy, puts the case simply (1986, p. 15):

> The highly successful developing countries have generally had liberalized trade and payments regimes, which in turn have been feasible only with relatively liberal domestic economic policies.

As she notes, it is important to concentrate on the major distortions, for every economy exhibits countless minor infractions, such as rent controls. Most developed economies are also guilty of significant distortions in agriculture, but the relative loss of efficiency from such distortions is smaller in the industrial economies where agriculture accounts for only a few percent of GNP.

Analysis of the liberalization strategy has concentrated on the foreign exchange markets, for both current account and capital transactions, the labor market, the market for agricultural commodities, the domestic financial markets, and the efficiency and possible privatization of government enterprises. Advocates of liberalization have been cautious about the order of liberalization and the coordination of liberalization with macroeconomic stabilization policies. A related issue is that of gradualism in the implementation of liberalization versus shock treatment.

The theoretical case for liberalization is that the removal of all distortions will improve the allocation of resources after the economy has fully adjusted,[28] and provided the distribution of income has not worsened. The question of the right order in which to liberalize arises because the removal of a distortion in an economy in which there are many other distortions may worsen rather than improve the allocation of resources. For instance, if agriculture is taxed but imported agricultural inputs subsidized, removal of the subsidy alone may not be a good idea.

More concretely, consider the example of the order of liberalization of the balance of payments. There are issues of how to liberalize the current account, for instance, whether to start by replacing quantitative restrictions with an equivalent set of tariffs, which are then reduced, or whether gradually to reduce quantitative restrictions. But

---

[28] Mussa (1986) presents guidelines on trade liberalization.

the most important issue is how rapidly to liberalize the capital account.

Liberalization of the capital account means that macroeconomic policy has to deal with the potentially powerful effects of capital flows on the exchange rate and domestic inflation in addition to the changes that need to be made as the current account is liberalized. It may also encourage capital flight, as domestic residents wait skeptically for the remainder of the liberalization policy to go into place. The experiences of Israel and the major Latin American countries in the late seventies attest to the power of international capital movements. An earlier example also illustrates the dangers of premature capital account liberalization. As a condition for a postwar loan, the United States in 1946 required Britain to make sterling convertible within a year. Convertibility, implemented in 1947, lasted only seven weeks as the proceeds of the loan (equal to more than 1 percent of U.S. GNP) were rapidly being exhausted.[29]

Capital flight aside, the effects of capital account liberalization are uncertain because the pace of international portfolio diversification is hard to predict. Optimal portfolios in small open economies should probably have a large share of foreign assets; correspondingly portfolios in large numbers should include some assets of small foreign economies. Eventually diversifications will be balanced, but flows during the adjustment period could be predominantly in one direction with major impacts on the exchange rate of the small economy. It is widely and appropriately agreed that capital account liberalization should be virtually the last step in a liberalization program—incidentally one that some successful European countries have not yet implemented.[30]

Many of the economies in which liberalization is needed suffer from high inflation and balance of payments problems. There is accordingly an issue of whether to try to straighten out the macroeconomic mess first and then attend to microeconomic problems, to

---

[29] Kindleberger (1984, pp. 430–32) discusses this episode. The loan was for $3.75 billion; U.S. GNP was $235 billion in 1947.

[30] Edwards' (1986) analysis suggests that starting with the current account is more prudent. McKinnon's discussion of this paper contains an interesting review of developments in the Republic of Korea after the reforms of 1964–65, where a massive and unexpected capital inflow touched off an inflationary process. Lal's discussion of the Edwards paper shows that agreement on the issue is not complete.

attempt all the changes simultaneously, or to attempt a judicious blend by implementing some of the microeconomic reforms simultaneously with the macroeconomic. Because the private sector cannot respond well to price signals when there is macroeconomic disequilibrium, it is essential that macroeconomic stabilization be undertaken at the beginning of any program. Some microeconomic distortions, such as subsidies, may have major budgetary impacts, and it is therefore desirable that they be removed simultaneously with the macroeconomic stabilization. But no economic management team in any country has the capacity to attend to all serious structural distortions at the same time. Thus only selected microeconomic changes—preferably those with serious budgetary implications— should be attempted at the time of the macroeconomic stabilization.

The choice between gradualism and shock treatment turns on both economic and political economy considerations. A comprehensive immediate reform program has the advantage that, if successful, it takes the economy directly to a more efficient allocation of resources. Any staged program runs the risk of worsening the allocation of resources in the interim. However, when it is costly to reallocate resources, typically because unemployment rises in the transition, a policy that is announced beforehand and implemented gradually may be preferable. For instance, a gradual program of import liberalization gives existing producers time to plan the adjustments in their production plans.

The political economy argument revolves around the pressures that affected interests will bring on policymakers. Depending on the form of the government, those pressures may also be directed from individual ministries to the economic policymakers. Shock treatment puts the initiative in the hands of the policymakers whereas preannounced future policy changes give interest groups the time necessary to exert effective pressure.[31] Although technocrats think of interest groups as an obstacle to desirable policy changes, they may also prevent foolish policy changes; shock attacks should only be implemented after the changes have been thought and calculated through with extreme care. Political economy considerations are also relevant to the choice between piecemeal and gradual reform: comprehensive

---

[31] Mussa (1987) argues that too rapid an implementation of trade liberalization will increase the pressures brought by affected groups.

programs have the advantage that interest group pressures will offset each other.[32]

How adequate is the liberalization agenda for growth? There is no question that it points to serious distortions that inhibit efficient production in most countries. There is no question that most of the distortions should be removed, many of them quickly. But there remains the question of whether the liberalization agenda is to be enhanced by a more positive vision of government policy.

One such vision, inherent in liberalization, is the *outward-looking strategy*, of which Balassa (1982) is a prominent exponent. The strategy is to align domestic with international prices and to encourage both exports and imports by setting a realistic exchange rate and removing import restrictions. The attraction of the strategy is the success of the East Asian countries, whose rapid growth has been accompanied by even more rapid growth of their international trade, and the success of Turkey since 1980.

Closely related is a strategy of *export promotion*, which relies on an alternative interpretation of the Southeast Asian experience. Japan, the Taiwan Province of China, and the Republic of Korea certainly do not have an anti-agriculture bias, and at some stage each liberalized by reducing protection of imported inputs. But they aggressively encouraged exports, both by setting undervalued exchange rates and by protecting domestic manufacturing industry from foreign competition. Their strategy has been much closer to a combination of import substitution and export promotion than pure liberalization: they rely on the international economy, they have relatively few distortions, but their governments are far from a laissez-faire philosophy and policies.

Of course, the success of outward-looking or export-promotion strategies depends heavily on the continued growth of the world economy and international trade. The strategy is thus vulnerable to the effects of policies in the industrial countries. That vulnerability has led to calls for international surveillance of the developed economies. Understandable as the impulse is, and although policies in developed countries could stand improvement, effective surveillance of this type is unlikely.

---

[32] When accused of voting in his private interest in the House of Commons, David Ricardo is reputed to have replied that he had so many interests he did not know which way he came out on the issue.

The broad strategic approaches reviewed in this section provide only background and general guidance to growth policy in developing countries. Liberalization, carefully carried out, will certainly have to be a major part of a growth strategy in most developing countries. It is also true that a major part of the government's task is to avoid making big policy mistakes. But there is no pure laissez-faire policy. Government policy is bound to affect growth, at a minimum in the provision of physical and social infrastructure, more actively in encouraging investment at the least by avoiding excessive budget deficits that soak up saving, and beyond that, through exchange rate and export promotion policies.[33]

Economic Structures and Models

Broad guidelines are useful, but the effects of alternative adjustment and growth strategies have to be examined for each economy individually. In this section I first discuss common problems facing different groups of countries and then briefly advocate the use of economic models in economic policymaking, for both national governments and international institutions.

Both the heavily indebted and the primary producing countries face particular difficulties in the present world economy—and those which are both have an even harder task. Among the debtors it is convenient to separate countries into African and Latin American, equivalently those whose debts are primarily to official and private lenders, respectively, and to a significant extent, those which are low income and middle income, or less and more industrial.

The debt problem dogs economic policymaking in the debtor countries. The debtors face a choice among accepting and attempting to adjust to their current debt burdens and levels of net capital flows, treating the current difficulties as temporary and attempting, if necessary by arrears, to obtain more financing, and trying to reduce the debt burden through negotiation with creditors. Whether debtor

---

[33] The four-part growth strategy recently recommended by Balassa, Bueno, Kuczynski, and Simonsen (1986) for Latin America shares much of the emphasis of this section. It includes an outward orientation of economic policy, with emphasis on export promotion and efficient import substitution, attempts to improve saving and its allocation (meaning reductions in government deficits), a reduced role for government in direct production, and open markets by the developed countries.

governments have the internal political strength to enforce the radical reductions in living standards that the first strategy requires in several countries is not known. The miracle so far is that the debt crisis has seen a movement toward rather than away from democracy.

Unless the debtor countries themselves, the international institutions, and responsible governments bring pressure for a longer-term solution than the constant renegotiating that has been the pattern of the last five years, adjustment strategies will be difficult to map out. A similar strategic problem faces the creditor banks and the debtor countries: to the extent either makes a serious adjustment effort—in the banks' case the creation of loss reserves, on the debtors' side, macroeconomic adjustment—it weakens its case at the next bargaining session. One way or the other, it is important to resolve the uncertainties over the treatment of the existing international debts.

Whatever the treatment of the existing debts, one lesson of the current crisis will ease the task of policymaking. It is now clear that floating rate bank lending should be avoided for anything other than short-term balance of payments financing. Capital inflows can certainly contribute to development, but they should take the form of direct investment, or equity investment, or long-term official capital. Here the role of the international organizations comes to the fore: they will be more important sources of external development finance than they were in the 1970s.

The debtor countries cannot in the next few years look forward to any significant private inflows of funds and will have to plan their growth and adjustment strategies accordingly, with details of course differing from country to country. This is easily said, but the burden on low-income debtors, particularly in primary exporting sub-Saharan African countries with low-income levels, is severe. Their hope must be for a recovery of commodity prices; their strategies will have to be based on the assumption that those prices will rise little in the next few years. These are the countries where the removal of remaining domestic distortions, especially between agriculture and urban economies, may be extremely important, and where positive policies to increase agricultural output with the aim of attaining food security are possible.[34] They are also the countries where official aid

---

[34] Lele (1986) and Loxley (1986) discuss adjustment in Africa with special attention to agriculture.

and the policies of the international organizations can have a large effect and where improved weather has already helped.

The problem for most countries is to make needed short-run macroeconomic adjustments while both macroeconomic policy and longer-run supply-side policies encourage growth.[35] The short-run macro adjustments have to focus on the basics: the government budget, the balance of payments and the exchange rate, wages, and monetary policy. Both the balance of payments and the need for investment suggest tight budgets, with the exception that productive government investment spending should not usually be cut back. There is likely here to be a tradeoff between growth and the distribution of income, as governments may have to cut back on subsidies and transfer payments as a major part of a budget balancing strategy.

The wage problem, or more generally the problem of adapting the standard of living to reduced resource availability, is a key to both current account and inflation adjustment. Generally, the adjustments will imply an initial cut in real wages, followed by later increases as productivity rises. If there is indexing of wages, it will be necessary to adjust the base wage downwards. Incomes policy may take its place here as a means of reducing adjustment costs to the new structure of supply and demand.[36]

The problem of adjusting without causing a recession is difficult, but a successful devaluation that begins to shift resources into exports, the use of incomes policy, the avoidance of excessively high interest rates and continued government investment spending can help. Fund adjustment programs that recognize the effects of inflation on the government budget, and that recognize government investment[37] as a source of growth will require less rigorous and more believable budget adjustments than was the norm in the past.[38]

---

[35] Pfeffermann and Jaspersen (1986) provide a careful analysis of the problem of adjustment with growth in Latin America, emphasizing export growth.

[36] Reductions in payroll taxes or temporary wage subsidies can ease the burden on the wage earner. But the budgetary implications of such policies have to be considered.

[37] Of course, there are many examples of wasteful government investment projects. But there are also in all countries many positive return projects. The international organizations in discussing growth with adjustment strategies may have to examine the details of proposed government investment programs.

[38] Aghevli and Marquez-Ruarte (1985) describe the successful Korean adjustment program in 1980–84, which followed reasonably orthodox procedures including a devaluation, and some, but relatively little, fiscal tightening.

To the extent that countries are also attempting to adjust from high inflation, they can look to the Argentinian, Israeli, and Brazilian stabilizations of 1985–86 for lessons. The primary lessons are that it is possible to disinflate without causing a recession—and, at least as important, that monetary and fiscal policy and wages have to be consistent with the new non-inflationary equilibrium.

At a general level, the long-run growth policies are to encourage investment in both physical and human capital, to remove distortions by liberalizing, to secure the economy's agricultural base, and to encourage the development of industry in part through export promotion. Details, which are all that matter, have to be left to a careful analysis of the structure of each economy.

Such analyses draw on explicit or implicit economic models. Both the Fund and the World Bank in their consultative and lending roles have developed models for individual countries and groups of countries.[39] The models need to be developed further for use in policy analysis, both by the international institutions and the countries themselves. The alternative to using models is to rely on general principles—for instance, that so long as policy is sound, market adjustment will produce satisfactory economic performance. The latter principle is right in the long run, but it is nonetheless advisable to use explicit models to try to anticipate difficulties that may arise in the adjustment process.[40]

The likelihood that the economy will achieve targets derived using models is of course slight. Policy mistakes or other shocks will produce deviations of outcomes from target levels. But the models enforce discipline on the analysis of adjustment, ensure the consistency of policy measures, and provide a framework in which the prospects of meeting balance of payments and growth targets can be coherently discussed. The target paths derived using models provide

---

[39] See Khan, Montiel, and Haque (1986) for the structure of these models. Taylor (1986) provides a taxonomy of stabilization and growth models.

[40] In Fischer (1986) I suggest that until a consistent model incorporating both real and financial sides of the economy is developed, two models can be used in economic policymaking. The first is a medium-term (four- or five-year) real model that produces paths of real activity consistent with the paths of the trade account and budget that are needed over the next four to five years. The second would be a shorter-term model incorporating the balance of payments-debt constraint, the government budget constraint, a description of the assets markets, wage and price formation, and monetary and fiscal variables linking government decisions to the required paths. Such models already exist and are widely used in the international institutions.

a baseline from which to judge events and to justify deviations that will inevitably be needed.

Lessons for Policymakers

The previous sections have summarized the conclusions of studies of long-run economic growth, discussed alternative growth strategies, and touched on the problems of adjustment and growth that now confront primarily African and Latin American countries. In adjusting and mapping out strategies, countries need to use models that connect their targets with their policies.

The approach suggested by this paper is eclectic—the fundamental reliance is on markets, but government policies make a difference for good or ill. But, as has been emphasized, success or failure depends on the details as they are developed for each country. There policy economists, both internal and external, can play an important role.

Keynes hoped economists would eventually attain the humble status of the dentist. The development economist active in policy-making is more like a doctor, called on to diagnose diseases and prescribe cures (always aware that the medicine may not be taken, and if taken may have unexpected side effects) for illness and sometimes to produce good health. Although the modern doctor is an impressive technician, many prefer the old-fashioned GP, whose experience and intuition more than compensate for the latest in technique.

Harberger (1984) has summarized the pragmatic lessons professionals have learned from studying and advising on economic policy in developing countries—and most apply also to developed countries. Here are the most important of his lessons:

1. Keep budgets under adequate control. Absolute balance may be impossible, but there is not much room for deficits.

2. Take advantage of international trade.

3. If tariffs are used, keep effective tariff rates reasonably uniform. If tariffs become excessive, use export incentives.

4. Use price and wage controls sparingly if at all.

5. It is rare that quotas, licenses, and quantitative restrictions are justified. They are inefficient and breed corruption.

6. Adopt a technical view of public enterprises. The right criterion is the efficient operation of the enterprise.

The missing, most important, commandment is:

7. Don't let the exchange rate become overvalued.

This list is evidence not only of what should be done, but also of what often is done. The domestic distortions and problems that new policies have to cure were usually introduced within the same political system that now has to be reformed. This is not the place to expand on the political economy of reform,[41] except to note that the outcome of policy packages depends not only on the economics but also on the political equilibrium.

There are two reasons for hope. One is that deep-rooted distortions are most likely to be eliminated at times of deep crisis. The other is that well-designed conditionality of outside lending can provide incentives for the adoption of better policies.

References

Aghevli, Bijan B., and Jorge Marquez-Ruarte, *A Case of Successful Adjustment: Korea's Experience During 1980–84*, IMF Occasional Paper No. 39 (Washington: International Monetary Fund, 1985).

Balassa, Bela, and others, *Development Strategies in Semi-Industrial Economies* (Baltimore: Johns Hopkins Press, 1982).

_____ , and others, *Toward Renewed Economic Growth in Latin America* (Washington: Institute for International Economics, 1986).

Baumol, William J., "Productivity Growth, Convergence, and Welfare," *American Economic Review* (Nashville), Vol. 76 (December 1986), pp. 1072–85.

Blades, D.W., "What Do We Know About Levels and Growth of Output in Developing Countries? A Critical Analysis with Special Reference to Africa," in *Economic Growth and Resources*, Vol. 2, ed. by R.C.O. Matthews (New York: St. Martin's Press, 1980).

Chenery, Hollis, and Allan M. Strout, "Foreign Assistance and Economic Development," *American Economic Review* (Nashville), Vol. 56 (September 1966), pp. 679–733.

_____ , and Moises Syrquin, *Patterns of Development, 1950–1970* (New York: Oxford University Press, 1975).

Clark, Peter, "Investment in the 1970s: Theory, Performance, and Predictions," *Brookings Papers on Economic Activity: 1* (Washington, 1979), pp. 73–113.

Corbo, Vittorio, "International Prices, Wages and Inflation in an Open Economy: A Chilean Model," *Review of Economics and Statistics* (Cambridge), Vol. 67 (November 1985), pp. 564–73.

---

[41] Krueger (1986) examines the political forces that create the need for liberalization.

_____ , "Problems, Development Theory and Strategies of Latin America," World Bank Discussion Paper, DRD190 (September 1986).

De Melo, Jaime, "Sources of Growth and Structural Change in the Republic of Korea and Taiwan: Some Comparisons," in *Export-Oriented Development Strategies*, ed. by Vittorio Corbo and others (Boulder: Westview Press, 1985).

Denison, Edward F., "The Unimportance of the Embodied Question," *American Economic Review* (Nashville), Vol. 54 (March 1964), pp. 90–94.

_____ , *Why Growth Rates Differ* (Washington: Brookings Institution, 1967).

_____ , *Accounting for United States Economic Growth* (Washington: Brookings Institution, 1974).

_____ , *Trends in American Economic Growth, 1929–1982* (Washington: Brookings Institution, 1982).

Dervis, Kemal, and Peter Petri, "The Macroeconomics of Successful Development: What are the Lessons?" *NBER Macroeconomics Annual* (Cambridge, Massachusetts: MIT Press, 1987).

Edwards, Sebastian, "The Order of Liberalization of the Current and Capital Accounts of the Balance of Payments," in *Economic Liberalization in Developing Countries*, ed. by Armeane M. Choksi and Demetris Papageorgiou (New York: Basil Blackwell, 1986).

Fischer, Stanley, "Issues in Medium-Term Macroeconomic Adjustment," *World Bank Research Observer* (Washington), Vol. 1 (July 1986), pp. 163–82.

Fishlow, Albert, "The State of Latin American Economics," in *Report on Economic and Social Progress in Latin America*, ed. by Inter-American Development Bank (Washington: IADB, 1985).

Frenkel, Jacob A., and Harry G. Johnson, *The Monetary Approach to the Balance of Payments* (London: Allen and Unwin, 1976).

Giovannini, Alberto, "Saving and the Real Interest Rate in LDCs," *Journal of Development Economics* (Amsterdam), Vol. 18 (August 1985), pp. 197–217.

Harberger, Arnold C., "Economic Policy and Economic Growth," in *World Economic Growth*, ed. by A.C. Harberger (San Francisco: Institute for Contemporary Studies, 1984).

Kendrick, John W., "Total Investment, Capital, and Economic Growth," in *Economic Growth and Resources*, Vol. 2, ed. by R.C.O. Matthews (New York: St. Martin's Press, 1980).

Khan, Mohsin, Peter Montiel, and Nadeem U. Haque, "Adjustment with Growth: Relating the Analytical Approaches of the World Bank and the IMF," World Bank Discussion Paper, VPERS8 (October 1986).

Kindleberger, Charles P., *A Financial History of Western Europe* (London: Allen and Unwin, 1984).

Kristensen, Thorkil, *Development in Rich and Poor Countries* (New York: Praeger, 1974).

Krueger, Anne O., "Problems of Liberalization," in *Economic Liberalization in Developing Countries*, ed. by Armeane M. Choksi and Demetris Papageorgiou (New York: Basil Blackwell, 1986).

Kuznets, Simon, *Economic Growth* (New York: Free Press, 1959).

Landes, David, *The Unbound Prometheus* (Cambridge: Cambridge University Press, 1969).

Lele, Uma, "Comparative Advantage and Structural Transformation: A Review of Africa's Economic Development Experience," World Bank Discussion Paper, DRD174 (March 1986).

Loxley, John, "Alternative Approaches to Stabilization in Africa," in *Africa and the International Monetary Fund*, ed. by Gerald K. Helleiner (Washington: International Monetary Fund, 1986).

Maddison, Angus, *Phases of Capitalist Development* (New York: Oxford University Press, 1982).

McKinnon, Ronald J., *Money and Capital in Economic Development* (Washington: Brookings Institution, 1973).

Mussa, Michael, "The Adjustment Process and the Timing of Trade Liberalization," in *Economic Liberalization in Developing Countries*, ed. by Armeane Choksi and Demetris Papageorgiou (New York: Basil Blackwell, 1986).

————, "Macroeconomic Policy and Trade Liberalization: Some Guidelines," *World Bank Research Observer* (Washington), Vol. 2 (January 1987), pp. 61–78.

Pfeffermann, Guy, and F. Jaspersen, "Adjustment with Growth in Latin America," unpublished, World Bank (Washington), March 1986.

Polak, Jacques J., "Monetary Analysis of Income Formation and Payments Problems," *Staff Papers*, International Monetary Fund (Washington), Vol. 5 (November 1957), pp. 1–50.

Ram, Rati, "Government Size and Economic Growth: A New Framework and Some Evidence from Cross-Section and Time-Series Data," *American Economic Review* (Nashville), Vol. 76 (March 1986), pp. 191–203.

Romer, Paul M., "Increasing Returns and Long-Run Growth," *Journal of Political Economy* (Chicago), Vol. 94 (October 1986), pp. 1002–37.

————, "Puzzles in Explaining Long-Run Growth," in *NBER Macroeconomics Annual* (Cambridge, Massachusetts: MIT Press, 1987).

Rostow, W.W., *The Stages of Economic Growth* (Cambridge: Cambridge University Press, 1960).

————, *Why the Poor Get Richer and the Rich Slow Down* (Austin: University of Texas Press, 1979).

Solow, Robert M., "A Contribution to the Theory of Economic Growth," *Quarterly Journal of Economics* (Cambridge), Vol. 70 (February 1956), pp. 65–94.

————, "Technical Change and the Aggregate Production Function,"

Review of Economics and Statistics (Cambridge), Vol. 39 (August 1957), pp. 312–20.

_____ , "Investment and Technical Progress," in *Mathematical Methods in the Social Sciences 1959*, ed. by K.J. Arrow, S. Karlin, and P. Suppes (Stanford: Stanford University Press, 1960).

Srinivasan, T.N., "The Costs and Benefits of Being a Small, Remote, Island, Landlocked, or Ministate Economy," *World Bank Research Observer* (Washington), Vol. 1 (July 1986), pp. 205–14.

Taylor, Lance, "Stabilization and Growth in Developing Countries: How Sensible People Stand," unpublished, Massachusetts Institute of Technology, 1986.

Adjustment in Latin America, 1981–86

Andrés Bianchi
Director, Economic Development Division
Economic Commission for Latin America and the Caribbean

Latin America is entering the sixth year of an adjustment process, whose end is not yet in sight notwithstanding the fact that the process has entailed the costliest recession since the Great Depression and strong efforts in most countries to restructure policy. Although 1986 showed some improvement in domestic economic activity and control over inflation, their sustainability is unfortunately in doubt because of a simultaneous deterioration in external accounts. Given the duration and severity of the crisis, adjustment is no longer feasible except when accompanied by growth. Nonetheless, with the rebound in the current account deficit in 1986 and the reluctance of private creditors to renew voluntary lending, the financing of an expansive growth-oriented adjustment would not seem forthcoming. Therefore, new, bolder, and more comprehensive initiatives may have to be introduced in order to achieve adjustment with growth.

The Adjustment Process

Origins of the Crisis and Need for Adjustment

Latin America's debt crisis exploded in August 1982 when, as a result of Mexico's debt moratorium, banks cut back lending abruptly

Note: Robert Devlin and Joseph Ramos of the Economic Commission for Latin America and the Caribbean (ECLAC) are, with Andrés Bianchi, co-authors of this address, which was delivered at the symposium by Mr. Bianchi.

and forced the region virtually to close its current account deficit of $40 billion (equivalent to about 35 percent of its exports of goods and services and some 6 percent of gross domestic product (GDP)) in but two years.

Nevertheless, at least in the oil importing countries of the region, the need to adjust originated earlier. It was set off by the oil price hike of 1979 and subsequent reaction by the OECD. The simultaneous pursuit of anti-inflationary policies in the industrial countries, coupled with the decision to target money growth rather than interest rates in most OECD economies, induced a prolonged recession in the North, together with unusually high real interest rates.

Oil importing developing countries were thus faced with huge and simultaneous increases in both their oil import bills and interest payments, just when the contraction in international trade lowered the prices and the demand for their primary commodity exports. Judging the crisis to be cyclical and consequently temporary, nearly all these countries borrowed heavily to finance their rising current account deficits, most, largely to maintain consumption. A few, Brazil for example, invested to increase export capacity and to substitute imports. Others, especially in the Southern Cone, also borrowed to acquire imports in an attempt to reduce inflation, but this led to ever more overvalued exchange rates.

Oil exporters, buttressed by independent forecasts of continuously rising energy prices, also borrowed heavily to expand production and to raise public and private consumption to a level consonant with their higher expected permanent income.

Since banks were once again awash in liquidity, they attempted to recycle petrodollars as quickly and easily as they had done after 1973. In merely two years, 1980–81, the region's external debt rose some $100 billion to nearly $290 billion, most financed by commercial banks. Banks sharply increased lending, apparently unconcerned that by 1979 debt/export ratios were much higher than in 1973 (2.1 vs. 1.4). Moreover, banks overlent to borrowers with conflicting interpretations of the shocks (losers considering them transitory; gainers, permanent) and hence with mutually incompatible rationales for borrowing. Thus the debt crisis grew out of imprudent lending as well as imprudent spending.

Difficult though it was in 1979 to foresee the magnitude and duration of the OECD recession, the exceptional rise in international interest rates, or the length and depth of the depression in the prices of basic commodities (except oil), it was even more difficult to predict the coincidence of these three events. Had real interest rates remained at, or soon returned to, their historic levels (2 percent), and had prices of basic commodity exports (exclusive of oil) maintained their long-term (1950–70) values in real terms, the external crisis would have been relatively mild and the region would have been in current account surplus (in theory able to reduce debt) from 1983 onwards (Table 1). Unfortunately the protracted crisis rendered permanent the damage caused by presumably cyclical factors.

This unstable state of affairs came to a close in 1982, when the prolonged recession in the OECD and the Mexican debt moratorium made banks fearful of their exposure in Latin America and led them to curtail their lending. Because of this abrupt fall in net capital inflow, Latin America could no longer finance current account deficits of the colossal magnitude it had run in 1981–82, or even of the modest extent recorded in 1977–79. Adjustment became mandatory in nearly every country.

Table 1.   Effect of Deterioration of Unit Prices of Non-Petroleum Exports and of Rise in International Interest Rates on Latin America's Current Account Balance

(In billions of U.S. dollars)

	Deficit in Current Account Arising from			Counterfactual Current Account Balance Without Deterioration in Export Prices or Rise in Interest Rates
	Export prices (excluding oil) below 1950–70 average in real terms	LIBOR above historic rate (2 percent) in real terms	Actual Current Account Balance	
	(1)	(2)	(3)	(4) = (3) − (1) − (2)
1981	4.7	5.4	− 40.5	− 30.4
1982	9.8	7.5	− 40.6	− 23.3
1983	12.8	6.8	− 7.4	12.2
1984	10.8	8.6	− 0.2	19.2
1985	11.7	5.0	− 4.0	12.7
1986	8.5	7.0	− 14.2	1.3

Source: Calculated on the basis of ECLAC's balance of payments series.

Phases of the Adjustment Process

From the beginning the adjustment process had to be carried out under unfavorable external conditions. International interest rates reached an all-time maximum in 1981 and in real terms remained until 1985 at the highest level for half a century. The prolonged recession in the OECD countries slowed international trade and contributed to the sharp decline in the prices of primary products, setting off a continuous deterioration in Latin America's terms of trade.

Moreover, since mid-1982, voluntary lending by the international commercial banks disappeared altogether, thus reversing the steep and sustained upward trend of 1970–81. Because of this shift and despite Fund-led efforts to organize rescue packages, net capital inflow to Latin America plunged from $37.5 billion in 1981 to $3.2 billion in 1983 and fluctuated around $6.5 billion in the three following years.

Such a radical drop in external financing would have been difficult to handle in the best of circumstances. In this instance, however, its negative effects were compounded by a sizeable increase in factor payments and in some countries by large capital flight. In fact, after rising by 40 percent to a record level of nearly $39 billion in 1982, net payments of interest and profits hovered around $35 billion thereafter, double their average level in the four years preceding the crisis.

The increase in factor payments and the near cessation of net capital inflow led in turn to a dramatic reversal in the external transfer of resources. In effect, after receiving net resources from abroad amounting to an annual average of $13 billion in 1978–81, Latin America was forced to transfer to the rest of the world more than $26 billion a year during 1982–86. Hence, while in 1978–81 capital flows covered amortization and interest payments and added to the region's import capacity the equivalent of 18 percent of the value of exports, in 1982–86 the net transfer of resources subtracted from the import capacity an amount equivalent to 25 percent of the region's exports. This shift was equivalent to the effect of a 36 percent fall in the terms of trade. Thus, since 1982, rather than serving to cope with external disequilibrium, procyclical private capital flows aggravated the crisis and constituted an additional factor to which the region had to adjust.

Phase I: Recessionary Adjustment (1982–83)

Because of this unfavorable external environment, Latin American countries were forced to adjust quickly. Notwithstanding higher interest payments, the region's current account deficit was cut from over $40 billion in 1981–82 to less than $0.2 billion in 1984. The current account disequilibrium was virtually eliminated by a turnaround in the trade balance, which, after recording a deficit of nearly $2 billion in 1981, marked up a surplus of over $39 billion in 1984 (Table 2).

Nevertheless, because of the way in which it was achieved, the closing of the current account deficit entailed large costs in terms of output, investment, employment, and living standards. Owing to Latin America's heavy dependence on primary products for its export earnings and the fall in the international prices of most commodities, the value of the region's merchandise exports, after declining in 1982 and 1983, barely recovered in 1984 the level obtained before the crisis, in spite of a 20 percent expansion of their volume between 1981 and 1984. Hence, the burden of correcting the external imbalance had to be shouldered by imports, which plunged from $98 billion in 1981 to $56 billion in 1983 and stabilized at less than $60 billion in 1984–86.

Of course, this cutback in the value of imports reflected in part the excessive level that these had reached in 1981, at the height of the period of easy, overabundant, external financing. Nevertheless, the contraction in the volume of imports (35 percent in 1982–83) went well beyond the "fat" in the pre-crisis import bills (luxury consumer goods, military hardware, and less urgent capital goods), so requiring sharp cutbacks in the imports of indispensable intermediate inputs, as well.

Consequently, despite the rapid pace of import substitution— which manifested itself partly in the plummeting of the import coefficient to its lowest level in 40 years—the reduction in the availability of imports had strong recessionary effects. In 1982 and again in 1983, the region's GDP fell for the first time in the postwar period while fixed investment, contracting by 30 percent, failed to

Table 2.   Latin America: Main Economic Indicators, 1980–86

	1980	1981	1982	1983	1984	1985	1986
				Indices (1980 = 100)			
Gross domestic product	100.0	100.5	99.0	96.6	99.8	102.4	105.9
Per capita gross domestic product	100.0	98.1	94.5	90.1	90.9	91.3	92.4
Per capita national income	100.0	96.5	89.8	85.6	86.7	86.7	...
Terms of trade	100.0	94.0	85.2	85.6	90.1	85.6	78.1
Exports of goods							
Value	100.0	107.6	98.1	98.2	109.6	103.1	87.8
Volume	100.0	108.5	110.2	119.8	130.6	130.6	127.3
Purchasing power of exports of goods	100.0	101.9	94.2	104.6	118.5	112.8	101.9
Imports of goods							
Value	100.0	108.1	86.6	61.9	64.4	64.6	66.2
Volume	100.0	102.6	83.4	65.5	70.7	71.7	76.7
				Growth Rates			
Gross domestic product	5.3	0.5	−1.4	−2.4	3.2	2.7	3.4
Per capita gross domestic product	2.8	−1.9	−3.7	−4.7	0.9	0.4	1.2
Per capita national income	3.6	−3.5	−6.9	−5.1	1.4	0.0	...
Consumer prices	56.1	57.6	84.8	131.1	185.2	275.3	69.1

Current value of exports of goods	32.2	7.6	-8.8	0.1	11.7	-5.9	-14.8
Current value of imports of goods	34.9	8.1	-19.8	-28.5	4.0	0.3	2.4
Terms of trade	4.3	-5.8	-9.0	1.1	6.5	-5.0	-8.7
Purchasing power of exports of goods	10.3	1.9	-7.6	10.1	13.3	-4.8	-9.7

Billions of Dollars

Current account balance	-28.3	-40.3	-41.0	-7.6	-0.2	-4.0	-14.2
Merchandise trade balance	-1.3	-1.9	9.1	31.5	39.4	33.5	18.4
Exports	89.1	95.9	87.4	87.5	97.7	92.0	78.3
Imports	90.4	97.6	78.3	55.0	58.3	58.5	59.9
Factor payments	17.9	27.2	38.7	34.3	36.2	35.3	30.7
Capital account balance	29.4	37.5	20.0	3.2	9.2	2.4	8.6
Global balance	1.4	-2.8	-21.0	-4.4	9.0	-1.6	-5.6
Net transfer of resources	11.5	10.4	-18.7	-31.2	-27.0	-32.9	-22.1
Gross external debt	230.4	287.8	330.7	350.8	366.9	373.2	382.1

Percentages

Current account deficit/total exports	26.0	34.7	39.8	7.4	0.2	3.7	15.7
Net transfer of resources/total exports	10.7	9.0	-18.1	-30.5	-23.7	-30.2	-23.2
Interest payments/total exports	20.2	28.0	41.0	36.0	35.6	35.2	35.1
External debt/total exports	214	248	321	343	322	342	401

Source: ECLAC, on the basis of official data.

meet even replacement needs in several countries. By 1983, output per capita was fully 10 percent lower than in 1980 and had fallen back to the 1976 level. Moreover, because of the deterioration in the terms of trade and the increase in factor payments, the reduction in national income per head—by far a better indicator of economic well-being than GDP per capita—was even larger (14 percent).

Phase II: Adjustment with Partial Recovery (1984–85)

The recessionary nature of the adjustment process seemed to change in 1984, however, as the downward trend of economic activity was interrupted. In effect, favored by the acceleration of world trade, and in particular by the increase in U.S. imports, and stimulated by higher real effective exchange rates, exports rose almost 12 percent. This and a partial recovery of net capital inflows made it possible for imports to increase moderately, thus facilitating the first rise in GDP per capita since 1980. At the same time, the region's current account deficit virtually disappeared, primarily as a result of improvements in the external accounts of Brazil (which eliminated the current account deficit of $16 billion it had recorded in 1982), Mexico (where a current account surplus of over $4 billion replaced the $14 billion deficit registered in 1981), and Venezuela (which, after incurring a $4.2 billion deficit in 1982, ran a $5.4 billion surplus in 1984), and the sharp reductions of external imbalance in Argentina, Chile, Ecuador, Peru, and Uruguay, all of which had by 1984 cut their 1981–82 current account deficits by at least 50 percent.

That in 1984 Mexico and Brazil—the most indebted countries in the region—and Venezuela—the fourth largest debtor—covered their interest payments with their respective trade surpluses and that Argentina, Ecuador, and Peru generated trade surpluses that financed nearly 60 percent of interest payments, together with improvements in the debt renegotiation mechanisms, prompted optimistic assessments in some circles about the prospects for adjustment. In this view, that the huge external imbalance had been closed in the brief span of two years, seemed to open the way in several countries for the resumption of growth, external equilibrium, and, in some cases, renewed access to voluntary lending by the banks.

Phase III: Frustration of Expansive Adjustment (1986–?)

These expectations were, however, short lived. By mid-1985, Mexico—the "model adjuster"—was facing severe balance of payments difficulties primarily because of having let its currency again become dangerously overvalued, with the consequent need to devalue. At the same time, Latin America's terms of trade fell once more, thus continuing the downward trend only briefly interrupted in 1984. Moreover, in December oil prices began their precipitous dive.

Because of this massive external shock, and despite the relief brought about by the decline in international interest rates, the balance of payments position of the oil-exporters changed markedly. By the end of 1986, their combined current account surplus of $8.6 billion in 1984 had been replaced by a deficit of about $7.5 billion, and their trade surpluses financed only one fourth of their interest payments instead of all of them as in 1983–85 (Table 3).

The trend toward a sounder external position was also reversed in

Table 3.   Latin America: Relationship Between the Trade Balance and Total Interest Payments, 1980–86[1]
(In percent)

	1980	1981	1982	1983	1984	1985	1986[2]
Latin America	**−46.9**	**−39.0**	**−3.0**	**74.8**	**88.7**	**80.0**	**46.2**
Latin America without Brazil	−28.9	−50.1	5.5	88.8	84.5	72.8	27.4
Oil exporting countries[3]	39.6	−14.5	19.4	139.3	126.8	99.6	25.6
Non-oil exporting countries[4]	−106.8	−56.5	−21.2	23.6	58.0	64.9	60.4
Argentina	−146.7	−19.7	54.1	63.9	58.0	84.8	48.8
Brazil	−79.6	−16.3	−22.3	39.7	99.1	97.0	88.0
Colombia	−20.0	−184.2	−197.8	−194.9	−16.2	−26.6	76.6
Costa Rica	−212.5	−38.6	18.1	−4.3	−5.0	−28.5	6.5
Chile	−91.6	−167.0	−16.5	35.0	−6.5	26.2	31.2
Ecuador	−11.1	−29.6	−25.0	101.7	69.1	98.2	20.0
Mexico	−40.6	−55.6	50.9	40.9	118.8	89.8	43.0
Peru	102.7	−89.6	−72.5	3.5	62.1	86.4	−19.5
Uruguay	−367.9	−180.5	−14.0	62.0	49.7	54.7	100.0
Venezuela	300.0	144.3	−56.2	196.9	205.0	136.7	−0.9

Source: ECLAC, on the basis of official figures.
[1] Trade balance in goods and services.
[2] Preliminary figures.
[3] Includes Bolivia, Ecuador, Mexico, Peru, and Venezuela.
[4] Includes Argentina, Brazil, Colombia, Costa Rica, Chile, El Salvador, Guatemala, Haiti, Honduras, Nicaragua, Paraguay, Dominican Republic, and Uruguay.

1986 in Argentina—both because of a fall in the terms of trade and a large increase in imports—and, surprisingly, in Brazil. In this latter country—which in the two previous years had succeeded in combining rapid economic growth with near equilibrium in its current account, thanks to the expansion and diversification of exports and substitution of imports—the trade surplus virtually vanished in the last quarter of 1986 as a result of the large increase of domestic demand unleashed by the Plan Cruzado. Hence, in spite of positive external shocks in the form of lower oil prices and lower interest rates, both the current account and the overall balance of payments closed with deficits in 1986.

Among the highly indebted countries of the region, only Chile, because of the fast expansion of non-copper exports and import substitution in agriculture and manufacturing, Uruguay, thanks to the recovery of exports, which benefited from the huge increase of Brazilian imports, and Colombia, whose exports rose nearly 50 percent as a result of high coffee prices, the growth of exports of coal and petroleum (made possible by the coming on stream of investments undertaken in previous years) and expansion of manufactured exports (under the stimulus of a high real effective exchange rate), were able in 1986 to record advances along the path of adjustment with growth that seemed to be open in 1984.

Nevertheless, because of the worsened external situation, in 1986 debt indicators in most countries deteriorated. Debt-to-export ratios shot up 17 percent, rising, on the average, even in oil importing countries, so that they reached a new historic maximum of 4 to 1 for the region as a whole. Hence, after five years of adjustment, debt-to-export ratios were 60 percent higher than in 1981—when they had already surpassed critical thresholds—and interest-payments-to-export ratios were 20 percent higher, notwithstanding the fact that the London Interbank Offered Rate (LIBOR) fell by over 50 percent between these years.

Domestic Policy Response

Adjustment requires expenditure reduction, expenditure switching, and structural transformation. No longer having financing to support transformation, adjustment necessarily fell on the first two, usually under the aegis of Fund agreements. Generally speaking, demand was restrained through the reduction of both fiscal expenditure and real wages. Interest rates were raised to discourage consumption and promote savings. Exchange rates were increased to promote exports and discourage imports. Commercial policy (tariffs and export incentives) tended to be modified in this same direction.

Real effective exchange rates have been raised throughout the region, with increases reaching over 50 percent relative to the trough of the crisis in Argentina, Chile, Colombia, Ecuador, Mexico, and Uruguay, though these higher rates were not maintained consistently (especially in Mexico). Indeed the crisis often gave rise to multiple exchange rates: one for traditional exports and preferential imports, another (sometimes free) for other trade flows, and yet a third for debt-service payments, in addition to a free market or parallel rate. Such a phenomenon ocurred even in countries characterized in the past by single, often times fixed, rates (e.g., Ecuador, Mexico, and Venezuela) and indeed for a time also affected countries with a neo-conservative bent (e.g., Argentina in 1981 and Chile in 1982).

Commercial policy was widely used as well to discourage imports and encourage exports, especially during 1982–84. Tariffs and import surcharges were raised or foreign exchange for travel reduced, in Brazil, Costa Rica, and Peru, among others, while tighter quotas (or bans) were placed on imports at least for a time in most countries of the region. Even in Chile, tariffs were raised from 10 percent to 35 percent before they were finally left at 20 percent; in addition, surcharges were imposed on some manufactured imports and large implicit tariffs were established on imports of wheat, sugar beet, and oil seeds, through the policy of agricultural support prices. Nevertheless, to the extent that the exchange rate has been raised, the pressure to increase tariffs has abated in most countries. Thus, since 1985 many of the restrictive measures placed on imports after 1982 have been relaxed.

Export incentives, especially for nontraditional products, be they in the form of tax rebates, tax credits, subsidized interest rates for export financing, or duty-free zone arrangements have been implemented in Brazil, Colombia, Mexico, Chile, Peru, and Uruguay. Yet, except for Brazil, these have not been as important in trade policy as increased import restrictions. Nevertheless, most export incentives established during the crisis remain in place.

As for policies to restrain demand, fiscal expenditures tended to fall in real terms throughout the region, especially between 1982 and 1984. Real expenditures were cut 20 percent or more in Argentina (1982–85), Ecuador (1982–83), Mexico (1983–84), Uruguay (1982–84), and Venezuela (1982–83); smaller but sizeable cuts were also registered in Brazil, Chile, and Peru. Only Colombia, which really did not face a debt crisis and had accumulated large international reserves during the coffee bonanza of the mid-1970s, continued to increase real fiscal outlays until 1984.

As could be expected, the heaviest reductions were made in capital expenditures, closely followed by declines in public sector wages. Other current expenditures proved difficult to cut; indeed interest payments rose throughout the period. Though emphasis was placed on reducing investment in machinery (to save scarce foreign exchange), public investment in construction also fell, thus reducing domestic output (and in this case with a low, direct, import component). In fact, construction has been the activity most seriously affected (falling almost 20 percent between 1981 and 1984). Moreover, in the three countries (Argentina, Uruguay, and Venezuela) where construction has been most depressed (operating in 1986 at some 50–60 percent of 1980 levels), total GDP in 1986 was still well below 1980 levels, whereas in the rest of the region it had surpassed that level by 1985–86.

Cuts in fiscal expenditures were not matched by like reductions in fiscal deficits. For fiscal revenues are sensitive to the economic cycle, and, as already noted, until 1983 adjustment tended to be recessive. For example, Peru's deficit rose from 4 to 5 percent of GDP between 1982 and 1984, despite a 9 percent cut in real expenditures, because revenues fell 14 percent as total output declined 7 percent. Much the same occurred in Argentina and Chile in 1982 and in Uruguay in 1984. In such circumstances, larger deficits were a sign not of increased excess demand, as is normally presumed, but of a demand-deficient recession.

Conversely, success in lowering fiscal deficits during adjustment was associated not only with cuts in expenditures but with the ability to maintain or even raise fiscal revenues. The most dramatic reductions in the weight of public deficits in GDP were achieved in Argentina (8½ points in 1985), Bolivia (10 points in 1986), Ecuador (6 points in 1982–85), and Mexico (9 points in 1983), countries that in those periods succeeded in raising government revenues. In particular, fiscal revenues rose in countries which dramatically reduced inflation (Argentina and Bolivia) because, as inflation declined, the loss in real revenues owing to the lag in collecting taxes fell. Elsewhere revenues rose because efforts were made to increase general tax rates (e.g., Mexico raised the value-added tax in 1983 from 10 to 15 percent for all but necessities), to reduce tax evasion, and to adjust public sector prices. In this latter regard, the rise of public utility rates and of the prices of goods produced by state enterprises in Mexico in 1983 and in Argentina just before the start of the Austral Plan made important contributions to the reduction of the government deficit. Even more noteworthy were energy prices in Bolivia: as part of the 1985–86 stabilization program, special taxes were placed on these products, so that revenues arising from them came to constitute over half of fiscal income and over 5 percent of GDP.

Wage policy too was an important component of expenditure-reducing adjustment packages in most of the region. Except for Argentina's short-lived effort to raise real wages in 1983–84, which finally gave way to runaway inflation in 1985, Brazil's policy of increasing real wages in 1985–1986, and Colombia, where wages went on increasing until 1984, in the rest of the heavily indebted countries of the region real wages fell during the crisis (Table 4). Worse yet, in Ecuador, Mexico, Peru, and Uruguay through 1985, this decline far exceeded the fall both in per capita national income and output, suggesting that up to that year adjustment in these cases was unnecessarily regressive as well as costly. Finally, credit tended to be tightened, and interest rates were raised during the adjustment program. While negative real interest rates characterized much of the region before the crisis, real interest rates are now positive, and oftentimes excessively so. For example, real rates of over 5 percent a month have been observed in Argentina, Bolivia, and Brazil, and for considerable periods of time.

The objective of all of these policies was to shift output to tradables, and expenditures to nontradables, as well as to contain capital flight. While, as already noted, these policies succeeded in virtually eliminating the region's current account deficit by 1984, they did so, not so much because output shifted, but because expenditure fell, compressing imports and stunting growth. It is not that switching policies failed to increase exports. In fact, export volumes increased 27 percent in the region since 1980 (and 34 percent for non-oil exporters) despite

Table 4.   Latin America: Evolution of Real Wages, 1981–85[1]
(Percentage variation)

	1981	1982	1983	1984	1985	Cumulative Variation During	
						Present crisis[2]	Former decade
Argentina	− 10.6	− 10.4	25.5	26.4	− 15.2	7.8	− 6.9
Brazil	8.5	12.1	− 7.3	− 6.7	7.1	12.6	55.5
Colombia	1.4	3.4	5.2	7.4	− 2.9	13.4	− 0.6
Costa Rica	− 11.7	− 19.8	10.9	7.8	8.9	− 7.8	31.6
Chile	9.1	− 0.4	− 10.6	0.3	− 4.5	− 14.8	− 0.8
Ecuador	− 13.8	− 11.9	− 16.2	− 1.3	− 3.2	− 39.2	15.2
Mexico	3.6	0.8	− 22.7	− 6.2	1.2	− 26.1	15.4
Peru	− 1.7	2.3	− 16.8	− 15.2	− 15.3	− 38.9	− 13.9
Uruguay	7.5	− 0.3	− 20.7	− 9.2	14.1	− 18.1	− 50.2

Source: ECLAC, on the basis of official information.

[1] Average real wages in urban activities (Costa Rica, Chile, and Uruguay) or in industry (Argentina, Brazil, Colombia, Mexico, and Peru). Real minimum wages in urban area for Ecuador.

[2] Since the crisis did not begin simultaneously in all the countries included, cumulative variations have been calculated over different periods in order to reflect the impact of adjustment on real wages more accurately. Figures in this column thus show the variation registered between 1980 and 1985 for Argentina, Brazil, Costa Rica, and Ecuador; and between 1981 and 1985 for Colombia, Chile, Mexico, Peru, and Uruguay.

the world recession and the difficulties of increasing exports for countries so heavily dependent on basic commodities. Yet the fall in the unit value of exports in that period (20 percent for non-oil exporters, 45 percent for oil exporters) wiped out for the latter and virtually wiped out for the former the effects of the increased volume of exports achieved in this period.

The speed with which switching policies in fact succeeds in reallocating resources to tradables depends not only on correct price signals but on the volume of investment. While the *proportion* of investment allocated to tradables probably rose, the *amount* of investment in tradables may in fact have grown not much, for overall investment fell by almost one-third in 1983–85 compared with 1980. This decline in investment took place although domestic savings held up and indeed rose as a percentage of gross domestic income, notwithstanding the simultaneous fall in per capita income. Higher savings failed to materialize in greater investment because of increased interest payments and the reversal in the net transfer of resources. While the share of savings in gross domestic income rose from 22 percent in 1980 to 23 percent in 1985, the investment coefficient in the same period fell from 24 percent to 16 percent.

Significant structural transformation of output was largely limited to Brazil and Colombia. Colombia was able to maintain, indeed raise, the investment coefficient until 1983 and by 1985–86 was deriving foreign exchange from the coming on line of investments in oil, coal, and nickel. Brazil for its part invested heavily in the second half of the 1970s, while financing was available, in petroleum, energy substitution (cane alcohol), chemicals, heavy metals, and fertilizers, which allowed it to substitute energy imports and increase exports after 1981. Thus structural transformation in the case of Brazil began to take place with the investment program designed after the oil crisis of 1973.

Once outside financing dried up and interest payments rose, however, investment was called on to bear the brunt of adjustment in most countries, thus slowing structural transformation. Nevertheless, most countries did not shirk from checking consumption in order to try to raise savings. In fact, consumption per capita in the region fell almost 10 percent on the average during the crisis, often cutting into critical expenditures on health, education, and nutrition.

In short, despite the efforts to increase exports (not simply to compress imports), to check consumption and raise savings (not simply to cut investment), and to reduce expenditures (but not output), adjustment was largely achieved at the expense of growth. This outcome resulted not from the absence of switching policies, but because, given the magnitude of the needed turnaround in the trade balance, the brief time span available to effect it, and the unfavorable evolution of the world economy, the principal short-run effect of switching policies centered on demand, for the contractive income effect of switching policies swamped the expansionary substitution effect, thus accentuating rather than mitigating the recessive impact of expenditure-reducing policies.

Consequently, adjustment, which necessarily entails lowering the level or the rate of growth of domestic absorption, unnecessarily cut economic growth as well, with per capita output in 1986 for the region as a whole still 8 percent below 1980 levels, likely making this a lost decade for most of the countries. What is worse, given the deterioration in the region's external position in 1986 and its heavy debt burden, adjustment has proven to be not only costly and inefficient, but indeed is far from complete.

Why Has Adjustment Been so Costly and Protracted?

The costs of adjustment depend on the structure of the economy and its capacity to respond, on the effectiveness of policy, and on the international context in which adjustment is effected. These factors, together with the exceptional size of the initial external imbalance, contributed to the severity and duration of the adjustment process.

Weak Initial Position

Four features characterized the bulk of the region's economies at the onset of the crisis, which both magnified the shock and limited the speed and effectiveness of response (Table 5).

The first was a high level of debt. In fact, the debt-led growth strategy pursued in the region between 1970 and 1981 raised the debt-to-export ratio from 1.4 in 1973 to 2.5 in 1981 (as opposed to 1.0 in the Republic of Korea); moreover interest payments in 1981 amounted to 27 percent of exports (tripling their percentage in 1973). Hence, in 1981 the region was far more vulnerable to interest rate hikes than were other countries or than it was itself at the beginning of the 1970s. Moreover, precisely because indebtedness was reaching precarious limits, countries were unable to draw on capital inflows to compensate deteriorations in trade flows as they did after the 1973 oil crisis.

The second feature was the high proportion of debt at floating interest rates. In 1970–81, commercial banks lent heavily to Latin America, so that by 1981 not only was the region's level of debt dangerously high, but some two thirds of it was at floating interest rates. This again contrasts with Asia in general (12 percent) and the Republic of Korea in particular (33 percent) as well as to the region itself in 1970 (less than 25 percent).

A third feature in most countries was the low levels of exports relative to GDP. Despite a fairly strong export push in the 1970s, when the value of exports grew 20 percent a year and the *quantum*

Table 5. Indices of Financial Vulnerability and Trade Flexibility at the Onset of the Crisis (1980–81): Selected Latin American and Asian Countries
(In percent)

	Financial Vulnerability		Trade Flexibility		
	Percent of debt at floating rates	Interest payments to exports	Exports to GDP	Exports to tradables[1]	Basic commodity exports[2] to total exports
Latin America	**64.5**	**28.0**	**13**	**27**	**76**
Argentina	58.3	15.1	7	15	79
Brazil	64.3	28.3	9	19	60
Colombia	39.2[3]	16.3	15	26	76
Costa Rica	49.3	12.6	35	71	67
Chile	58.2[3]	28.2	20	47	85
Ecuador	50.5[3]	21.3	23	45	97
Mexico	73.0	19.0	14	30	61
Peru	28.0[3]	19.8	21	40	84
Uruguay	33.5[3]	12.0	12	29	66
Venezuela	81.4[3]	10.4	32	62	98
Asia					
Republic of Korea	33.3	6.2	38	67	10
Taiwan, Province of China	. . .	<5.0	52	. . .	14

Source: ECLAC, *Preliminary Balance of the Latin American Economy 1986* (December 1986); World Bank, *World Development Report*, various years; and G. Ranis, "East Asia and Latin America: Contrasts in the Political Economy of Development Policy Change" (unpublished, May 1986); and J. Fei, G. Ranis, and S. Kuo, *Growth with Equity: the Taiwan Case* (World Bank, 1979).

[1] Agriculture, mining, and manufacturing.
[2] Fuels, minerals, metals, and other agricultural commodities.
[3] 1980–82.

of manufactures grew 15 percent a year, exports averaged 13 percent of GDP in 1979, and in few countries did they exceed 20 percent (as opposed to the Republic of Korea's 38 percent or the Taiwan Province of China's 52 percent). To be sure, this was a reflection not of a God-given fact, but of the policy option to pursue a largely inward oriented, import substituting development strategy during most of the post-World War II period. For this reason, exports made up a low proportion of tradables in Latin America, accounting for just one fourth of all tradables. So, at the beginning of the 1980s the region in fact possessed a very low export (and import) base from which to adjust trade flows (either by further import substitution or by export expansion) to external shocks.

Finally, a fourth crucial characteristic was the high dependence (over 75 percent) on the export of relatively few primary commodities. On the one hand, this led to fluctuations in the terms of trade; on the other, because such goods are relatively inelastic both in supply and demand, it provided a restricted margin for adjustment through export expansion. This contrasts with the Republic of Korea and the Taiwan Province of China, where 80 to 90 percent of their exports was represented by manufactures with far higher price and income elasticities.

The first three problems were largely determined by policy, whereas the latter also reflected Latin America's rich natural endowment of resources. Yet, whatever the cause, these four factors heavily con-ditioned the region's adjustment process. Thus, unlike what hap-pened after the 1973 crisis, when the region was able to compensate this export structure by drawing on capital inflows until the OECD's recession was over and the quantum and value of its exports picked up, at the beginning of the 1980s this latter route would be severely limited because of the region's already heavy debt and exposure in the banking system. Indeed since real interest rates shot up and bank lending eventually collapsed, capital inflows soon ceased to be a variable that could ease trade adjustment, and became a variable to which the region had to adjust further.

Nor was the region able to pursue on its export base an expansive adjustment as did the Republic of Korea. Since export expansion must come largely from manufactured exports, and since these accounted for only one fourth of exports and less than 5 percent of GDP (as opposed to 85 percent of exports and 45 percent of GDP in both the Republic of Korea and the Taiwan Province of China), no reasonable short-run growth of nontraditional exports could correct the external imbalance that the region was forced to eliminate. Thus, in the brief time frame available, adjustment could hardly be expansive, but had to be based largely on recession-inducing import compression.

Policy Shortcomings

However limited the freedom of policy response, once the crisis set in, there was still room for maneuver. Obviously, then, some of the variations in the costs of the crisis can be attributed to the differing policy responses. While, in general, domestic policies moved in the right direction, in many instances response has been sluggish, shortsighted, incoherent, or lacking in continuity.

The single most serious error in policy in most oil importing countries of the region (with the important exception of Brazil) was the decision to use the strong capital inflows of 1979–81 to postpone rather than to facilitate adjustment. Rather than augmenting investment, the bulk of such inflows went to maintain, or even raise, consumption, and, in some countries, facilitate capital flight. Unfortunately much of the investment was, in fact, poorly allocated, at least in part because relative prices were distorted owing to exchange rate policies aimed at combating inflation rather than maintaining external equilibrium.

In the same vein, Chile's persistence in maintaining its fixed exchange rate well into 1982, in hope of achieving a real exchange depreciation through a reduction in absolute prices and wages, is a prime example of policy sluggishness or obstinacy in the face of facts. This policy, which was followed closely by Uruguay, no doubt helps explain the severity of the ensuing recession in both these countries in 1982 (-13 percent and -10 percent growth rates, respectively). So too, if to a lesser extent, was the failure of most oil exporters to set domestic energy prices at international levels. Venezuela was by far the most laggard in this regard, with gasoline retailing for less than 5 cents a liter as late as 1985 when the international price was five times that. Not only did this policy foment excessive domestic consumption, but it also reduced fiscal income.

Policy instability has also prolonged, if not accentuated, the crisis.

National currencies have been devalued to raise real effective exchange rates throughout most of the region. Yet movements have often been extremely erratic, with cycles of overshooting and undershooting, making it difficult for would-be exporters to determine whether in fact there is any but a momentary advantage in exporting, and consequently effectively discouraging them from incurring the costs of penetrating and developing markets. Mexico's exchange policy probably is the most notable example of such policy discontinuity: the real effective exchange rate doubled between the end of 1981 and the end of 1982; then it was allowed to fall steadily through mid-1985, almost reaching its 1981 trough once again, before it was pushed up 30 percent. Such a roller coaster exchange policy could hardly serve as a useful signal to exporters. While Venezuela's exchange rate has fluctuated less extremely, it has unfortunately allowed the real effective exchange rate to continue to fall in the face of the fall in energy prices in 1986.

Another variant of policy instability is given by the frequency of changes in exchange rate regimes in Chile in 1982. The year began with a fixed exchange rate; adjustment was to take place through price declines. In mid-year, however, this policy was reversed. The exchange rate was raised 18 percent and a further monthly devaluation of 0.8 percent was pre-announced. Two months later, a third regime was enacted—a free float (to save reserves). Within a month, this became a dirty float (scarce reserves again being used to control the exchange rate), while a preferential rate was set for service of the foreign debt. One month later, a formally controlled, crawling peg was reestablished (after a further devaluation). Thus five exchange regimes were experimented within less than six months.

Wages and interest rates have been subject to fluctuations of almost equal severity. For example, real wages fell 20 percent in Argentina between 1980 and 1982, grew 59 percent in the next two years, and then fell again 15 percent in 1985. Given such behavior, employers are simply apt to hire in accordance with expected labor costs, rendering employment inelastic to any but the sharpest variations in ongoing wages. These thus cease to serve their allocative role in the economy, which simply confirms the acute zero-sum conflict mentality prevailing in many countries and renders efficiency considerations marginal in the face of distributive concerns. As for interest rates, although negative real rates tend to misallocate investment, unduly high real rates (which in Argentina and Bolivia have reached 5 percent a month) simply choke it off.

Adjustment policy has not only been sluggish, shortsighted, and unstable; at times it has been inconsistent. An example of this is Brazil's policy during 1986. Though the Cruzado Plan was conceptually well designed in its insistence on the feasibility of ridding the economy of the inertial component of inflation without recession, it was mistaken in two issues: (1) as a matter of empirical fact, the government's operational deficit was not zero (as the Plan's authors apparently thought to be the case); hence there was a disequilibrium component of inflation to be attacked along with the inertial one; and (2) in its assessment that to avoid the risk of recession, an 8 percent real wage increase should also be decreed at the onset of the Plan. The result is well known: an extraordinary boom, which led to scarcities and repressed inflation on the domestic front at the expense of external disequilibria and the resurgence of inflation at the end of the year. In fact, the trade surplus fell from an enormous $1 billion a month in the first nine months of 1986 (sufficient to cover interest payments) to about $180 million a month in the last quarter, while consumer prices rose over 7 percent in December and were expected to increase at an even faster pace in January and February. Thus Brazil will need to adjust and fight accelerating inflation in 1987 as well as seek out new money from the banks.

Important components of adjustment policy have at times been in error as well. In Mexico, the growth in nominal wages was curtailed between 1982 and 1985 in an attempt to bring down inflation, and yet to little avail. Inflation rebounded to 100 percent in 1986 (never having gone below 60 percent), whereas real wages have, in fact, been cut 26 percent. Since this is double the fall in per capita national income, it implies that the failed attempt to lower inflation led to an unnecessary, not to mention regressive, sacrifice of wages, which was only partially offset by the apparent rise in modern sector employment.

Finally, inflationary escalation occurred with the crisis. The region has long been characterized by high inflation. Yet with the crisis, average inflation quintupled from 55 percent a year in 1979–81 to 275 percent in 1985 (before stabilization programs again lowered it to 70 percent in 1986). Indeed, in the course of the crisis seven countries experienced triple digit inflation (and Bolivia over 20,000 percent in August 1985). Moreover, this inflationary escalation beset several countries heretofore characterized by relatively low inflation (e.g., Costa Rica, in which it exceeded 100 percent in mid-1983; Ecuador, in which it exceeded 50 percent in 1983; Mexico, in which it reached 100 percent in early 1983 and again in 1986; Nicaragua, in which it exceeded 750 percent in 1986; and Peru, in which it exceeded 150 percent in 1985). It is not easy to control domestic inflation in the face of a sharp hike in oil prices, and certainly the magnitude of the adjustment required placed a demand on fiscal resources well beyond its proven capacity to satisfy in the short run (since fiscal deficits were already of the same order of magnitude). It is even less easy if adjustment has to be effected in the face of already high and persistent inflation, in economies characterized by widespread indexing. Hence, it is understandable that inflation has accelerated. That the magnitude of that acceleration often bore little relation to the size of the external (and fiscal) shock denotes serious failings in policy design and implementation.

Unfavorable External Environment

Nevertheless, the high costs of adjustment have been not so much the consequence of ill-designed or badly applied domestic economic policies, but, in most cases reflect the exceptionally adverse external environment under which the adjustment process had to be carried out. In fact, during the 1980s the region has faced a uniquely grave external crisis in both trade and external finance, involving not only cyclical but also structural elements. Moreover, the negative consequences of the crisis have been compounded by the acute instability and unpredictability of world economic trends.

Managing adjustment has undoubtedly been rendered more difficult because of these erratic features in the world economy. The first rise in Organization of Petroleum Exporting Countries (OPEC) prices was generally viewed as temporary but proved to be more permanent than originally thought, while the second price hike, which was generally viewed as permanent, turned out to be a temporary change. Similarly, over the last six years the dollar has soared and tumbled. So too, nominal international interest rates, after skyrocketing at the turn of the decade, began their downward course in 1982, but not before an unexpected and worrisome rise in 1984. In addition, they remained persistently high in real terms even after an extended period of world price stability. Meanwhile, recovery from the world recession in 1981–82 has been slow and uncertain. The forecasts announcing the beginning of a strong recovery in the OECD in 1983–84 did not materialize. Moreover, in subsequent years industrial countries' annual performance has disappointed and frequently required downward revisions of world growth projections. And, of course, still looming large is the question of how quickly the United States, Germany, and Japan will adjust to their respective trade deficits and surpluses.

In any event, the effects of adjustment policies have been limited and their costs have been increased by the insufficiency and burdensome terms of external finance as well as by the adverse trading conditions that most Latin American countries have had to face since 1981.

The Pro-Cyclical Retreat of Creditors

As already noted, since mid-1982 net capital inflow to Latin America has declined, largely as a result of the withdrawal of private banks, the region's principal creditors. Because of its size and suddenness, this pro-cyclical retreat of the banks was scarcely offset by the rise of net loans extended by the international and national public financial agencies. In fact, during 1982–85 total external finance fell far short of even the transitory components of the current account deficits. Far from acting as a countercyclical force facilitating a gradual and efficient correction of external imbalances, external financing (or rather underfinancing) forced Latin America to "overadjust." Moreover, in some countries, and especially in Argentina, Mexico, and Venezuela, what financing became available was sometimes negated by the flight of private domestic capital to northern financial centers.

The adjustment process was handicapped not only by the scarcity of external financing but also by its high costs. When Latin America began to adjust, international interest rates were at record levels and acted simultaneously as a factor in the need to adjust as well as in the costliness of the process. LIBOR peaked at 16.5 percent in 1981, averaged 10.7 percent in 1982–85, and declined to an average of 6.7 percent in 1986, hovering around 6 percent at year-end—its lowest level since 1977. In spite of this downward trend in nominal rates, real rates remained persistently high. The real LIBOR measured by the industrial countries' rate of inflation averaged 5 percent in 1982–86, which compares unfavorably with a real rate of zero in the 1970s and a long term historical rate of around 2 percent.

But this tells only part of the story. The burden of interest payments depends too on the dollar value of the debtors' exports. Since Latin America's exports suffered generally declining prices during the adjustment period, the annual average real interest rate from their perspective was an extraordinarily high 17 percent for the period 1982–86. This compares with an average of −4 percent during 1971–80, when most of the region's foreign debt was contracted (Table 6). That the real weight of interest payments remained burdensome throughout the adjustment process is seen in Table 7.

Table 6.   International Rates of Interest, Nominal and Real, 1970–86
(In percent)

| | Nominal LIBOR[1] (1) | Percentage Variation in | | Real LIBOR (1) / (2) (4) | Real LIBOR (1) / (3) (5) |
		Consumer prices industrial countries (2)	Unit price of exports of Latin America (3)		
1970	8.47	5.6	8.1	2.7	0.3
1971	6.79	5.2	1.9	1.5	4.8
1972	5.41	4.7	9.2	0.7	−3.5
1973	9.31	7.7	33.0	1.5	−17.8
1974	11.20	13.3	57.5	−1.9	−29.4
1975	7.61	11.1	−5.7	−3.1	14.1
1976	6.12	8.3	8.1	−2.0	−1.8
1977	6.42	8.4	10.6	−1.8	−3.8
1978	8.33	7.2	−3.7	1.1	12.5
1979	11.99	9.2	21.0	2.6	−7.4
1980	14.15	11.2	21.2	2.0	−5.8
1981	16.52	9.9	−2.8	6.0	19.9
1982	13.25	7.5	−11.2	5.3	27.5
1983	9.79	5.0	−6.5	4.6	17.4
1984	11.20	4.8	2.6	6.1	8.4
1985	8.64	4.2	0.6	4.3	9.3
1986	6.71	1.8	−12.7	4.8	22.2

Source: ECLAC, on the basis of data in Morgan Guaranty Trust, World Financial Markets, and International Monetary Fund, International Financial Statistics, various issues.
[1] 180 days.

Table 7. Latin America: Ratio of Total Interest Payments to Exports of Goods and Services, 1978–86[1]
(In percent)

Country	1978	1979	1980	1981	1982	1983	1984	1985	1986[2]
Latin America	**15.7**	**17.6**	**20.2**	**28.0**	**41.0**	**36.0**	**35.6**	**35.2**	**35.1**
Oil exporting countries[3]	16.1	15.7	16.6	22.6	35.6	31.4	32.5	32.3	36.5
Non-oil exporting countries[4]	15.5	19.3	23.7	33.6	46.7	40.7	38.7	37.9	34.2
Argentina	9.6	12.8	22.0	35.5	53.6	58.4	57.6	51.1	51.8
Brazil	24.5	31.5	34.1	40.4	57.1	43.5	39.7	40.0	37.7
Colombia	7.5	9.9	11.8	21.9	25.9	26.7	22.8	26.3	18.6
Costa Rica	9.9	12.8	18.0	28.0	36.1	33.0	26.6	27.3	22.7
Chile	16.9	16.5	19.3	38.8	49.5	38.9	48.0	43.5	39.2
Ecuador	10.4	13.6	18.3	24.3	30.0	27.4	30.7	27.0	32.2
Mexico	24.0	24.5	23.3	29.0	47.3	37.5	39.0	36.0	40.0
Peru	21.2	15.5	16.0	24.1	25.1	29.8	33.2	30.0	27.3
Uruguay	10.4	9.0	11.0	12.9	22.4	24.8	34.8	34.2	23.8
Venezuela	7.2	6.9	8.1	12.7	21.0	21.6	20.1	26.3	33.3

Source: 1978–1986: ECLAC, on the basis of official data.

[1] Interest payments include those on the short-term debt.

[2] Preliminary estimates subject to revision.

[3] Includes Bolivia, Ecuador, Mexico, Peru, and Venezuela.

[4] Includes Argentina, Brazil, Colombia, Costa Rica, Chile, El Salvador, Guatemala, Haiti, Honduras, Nicaragua, Paraguay, Dominican Republic, and Uruguay.

Notwithstanding lower nominal interest rates, since 1983 there has not been much change in the coefficient of interest payments to exports in the region, which has been stuck at around 35 percent and is, of course, higher in the most heavily indebted countries.

Private banks aggravated the problem of the cost of credit by jacking up their spreads and commissions and shortening amortization periods on rescheduled debt and fresh credit during the first round of the rescheduling exercises. It has been estimated that the negotiated cost of credit (based on spreads, amortization period, and commissions) rose in most debtor countries by between 100 and 250 percent.[1]

It is true that in subsequent rounds of rescheduling the private creditors have reduced the negotiated cost of credit in response to criticism at home and to the stiffer bargaining positions of the debtors. Concessions have included multi-year reschedulings, lower spreads, longer amortization periods, and the foregoing of commissions. By the third round in 1984–85, the negotiated terms were almost the same as those that countries were contracting before the crisis. Nevertheless, while these concessions have been welcome and helpful, they arrived late in the adjustment process and in general still lag behind the reality confronting borrowers. While the banks made important concessions, they kept the negotiated terms at commercial levels even though a number of problem borrowers were in need of noncommercial repayment terms.

Because of the abrupt fall in net capital inflow and the simultaneous rise in interest payments, Latin America has since 1982 been experiencing a protracted transfer of resources to its creditors that is nonvoluntary, premature with respect to its stage of development, and large by any measure. In fact, in the last five years this transfer is estimated to be equivalent on average to roughly 4 percent of the region's GDP and 25 percent of its export earnings. Moreover, the cumulative outward transfer in this period ($132 billion) nearly doubled the cumulative inward transfer during the previous six years (Table 8).

Latin America's outward transfer also compares unfavorably with historically famous transfer cases, such as the war reparations effected

---

[1] See ECLAC, *External Debt in Latin America* (Boulder, Colorado: Lynne Rienner Publishers, 1985), Table 15.

**Table 8.   Latin America: Net Inflow of Capital and Transfer of Resources,
1973–86**
(In billions of U.S. dollars and percent)

Year	Net Inflow of Capital (1)	Net Payments of Profits and Interests (2)	Transfers of Resources (3) = (1) − (2) (3)	Exports of Goods and Services (4)	Transfers of Resources/ Exports of Goods and Services[1] (5) = (3)/(4) (5)
1973	7.9	4.2	3.7	28.9	12.8
1974	11.4	5.0	6.4	43.6	14.7
1975	14.3	5.6	8.7	41.1	21.2
1976	17.9	6.8	11.1	47.3	23.5
1977	17.2	8.2	9.0	55.9	16.1
1978	26.2	10.2	16.0	61.3	26.1
1979	29.1	13.6	15.5	82.0	18.9
1980	29.4	17.9	11.5	107.6	10.7
1981	37.5	27.1	10.4	116.1	9.0
1982	20.0	38.7	− 18.7	103.2	− 18.1
1983	3.2	34.3	− 31.2	102.4	− 30.5
1984	9.2	36.2	− 27.0	114.1	− 23.7
1985	2.4	35.3	− 32.9	109.0	− 30.2
1986[2]	8.6	30.7	− 22.1	95.2	− 23.2

Source: 1973–85: ECLAC, on the basis of data supplied by the International Monetary
Fund. 1986: ECLAC, on the basis of official figures.

[1] Percentages.

[2] Preliminary estimates subject to revision.

by France in the 1870s after the Franco-Prussian War and Germany's
payments to the victorious nations after World War I. In fact, the
weight of Latin America's financial transfers to its creditors in terms
of the debtor nations' income and exports is almost twice that of
Germany's and is roughly comparable to that of France (Table 9).
More pertinent are the still more adverse results that emerge from
comparing the real effective burden represented by the transfer of
resources currently being effected by Latin America and those can-
celed out by Germany and France in the past. To gain an idea of this
burden, it is necessary to consider to what extent a transfer is
facilitated by financial resources coming from other sources. For
instance, Germany received loans and other foreign capital in excess
of its war reparations through most of 1925–28; hence, its reparations
exceeded those capital flows only during 1929–32. Consequently, in

**Table 9.   Latin America's Registered Net Outward Transfer of Financial
Resources Compared with War Reparations of France and Germany[1]**
(In percent)

	Transfer/ GDP[2]	Transfer/ Exports[3]	Transfer/ Domestic Savings
France, 1872–75[4]	5.6	30.0	. . .
Germany, 1925–32[5]	2.5	13.4	. . .
Latin America, 1982–85[6]	**4.2**	**25.7**	**18.7**
Argentina	6.0	41.4	31.0
Brazil	2.9	24.2	13.7
Colombia	−0.3	−2.8	−1.8
Costa Rica	−0.3	−1.2	−1.7
Chile	3.3	14.2	18.6
Ecuador	4.5	19.6	16.9
Mexico	7.9	42.1	28.5
Peru	0.8	4.6	3.2
Uruguay	5.3	20.8	30.6
Venezuela	9.3	33.6	34.2

Sources: Germany and France: calculated from data in Fritz Machlup, *International Payments, Debt and Gold* (New York: New York University Press, 1976); and Helmut Reisen, "The Latin American Transfer Problem in Historical Perspective," in OECD, *Latin America and the Caribbean and the OECD* (Paris: OECD, 1986). Latin America: Estimated on the basis of ECLAC's balance of payments and national income data series.

[1] In view of the dates of the German and French cases, data should be viewed with appropriate caution and taken as estimates of rough orders of magnitude.

[2] The denominator is national income in the case of Germany and France and GDP in the case of Latin America. Note that GDP is larger than national income for debtor nations.

[3] Presumably goods for France and Germany. Goods and services for Latin America.

[4] War reparations of F5,000 million as part of the 1871 peace treaty of Frankfurt, which ended the Franco-Prussian War.

[5] War reparations to victorious nations of RM10,720 million in currency and payments in kind as formulated in the 1919 Treaty of Versailles.

[6] Net inflow of capital less net payments of profits and interests.

order to facilitate the transfer, Germany did not have to generate a trade surplus until 1929. France, on the other hand, ran a surplus throughout 1872–75, while Latin America has had a trade surplus since the outbreak of the crisis in 1982. The trade surplus in Latin America, however, has been roughly double the magnitude of that registered in France and Germany, whether measured as a percentage of income or of exports (Table 10).

Because of both its size and protracted nature, the outward transfer of resources has inhibited growth-oriented structural adjustment. In the first place, except in Colombia, Costa Rica, and Peru, the transfer

Table 10. Accumulated Trade Surplus of Germany, France, and Latin
America During Periods of Nonvoluntary Transfers[1]
(In percent)

	As Percent of Income[2]		As Percent of Exports[3]	
	Trade surplus in goods	Trade surplus in goods and services	Trade surplus in goods	Trade surplus in goods and services
France, 1872–75	2.3	. . .	12.3	. . .
Germany, 1925–28	—	—	—	—
1929–32	2.5	. . .	13.8	. . .
Latin America, 1982–85	**4.3**	**3.5**	**31.1**	**21.4**
Argentina	5.9	5.6	48.0	38.1
Brazil	3.7	2.7	34.6	22.9
Colombia	− 2.8	− 3.6	− 25.0	− 25.7
Costa Rica	− 0.4	− 0.3	− 1.5	0.7
Chile	2.6	0.8	14.3	3.7
Ecuador	6.6	4.5	32.2	19.7
Mexico	7.0	7.3	46.8	39.3
Peru	2.3	1.2	15.8	6.8
Uruguay	4.6	2.9	23.7	11.4
Venezuela	11.2	7.2	43.3	26.0

Sources: Germany and France: Calculated from data in Fritz Machlup, *International Payments, Debt and Gold* (New York: New York University Press, 1976); and Helmut Reisen, "The Latin American Transfer Problem in Historical Perspective," in OECD, *Latin America and the Caribbean and the OECD* (Paris: OECD, 1986), pp. 148–154. Latin America: Estimated on the basis of ECLAC's balance of payments and national income data series.

[1] In view of the dates of the German and French cases, data should be viewed with appropriate caution and taken as estimates of rough orders of magnitude.

[2] In the case of Germany and France the denominator is national income and in the case of Latin America it is GDP. For a debtor nation GDP is normally higher than national income.

[3] In the first column exports are measured in goods and in the second column in goods and services.

has siphoned off large proportions of domestic saving needed to stimulate the growth and transformation of the economy. Indeed, as already mentioned, the reversal in the direction of the transfer of resources largely explains the growing gap that has emerged in recent years in most countries of the region between a stable or rising domestic savings effort and a falling investment coefficient. Second, this transfer of resources has restricted the capacity to import, which fell abruptly in 1982 and has represented since then the most binding constraint on economic growth in virtually all Latin American countries. Third, in some countries the transfer of resources has contributed to accelerate inflation. This is because most debt is by now guaranteed by the state, either because it was originally contracted by public agencies or because in the successive negotiation rounds governments were pressured by the banks to provide *ex-post* guarantees of private debts that the banks had originally not requested but for which they had charged appropriately higher premiums. Most of the transfer has consequently had to come directly or indirectly out of government budgets. As Helmut Reisen has shown, this "budgetary phase" of the transfer process was generally not resolved during the 1982–85 adjustment. In his view, because of the budgetary burden involved, governments found it impossible to enforce fully the required restrictive fiscal and credit policy.[2] Deficits resulting from the transfer burden and other factors had hence to be financed by borrowing from the domestic banking system, which led to inflationary consequences.

Adverse Trading Conditions

The costs of adjustment have also been high because the process had to be carried out during a period of sluggish growth in the industrial economies and in world trade. With the exception of 1984, economic growth in the industrial countries during 1982–86 was well below the average annual rate of 3.5 percent registered in 1968–77. The same was true for the volume of world trade, whose growth was considerably below the 8 percent annual average mark registered over 1968–77. Moreover, the strong growth of world trade volume (8.6 percent) recorded in 1984 was disproportionally reliant on the robust expansion of the U.S. economy, which, after its 1982 slump, was the only major industrial country to grow at a rate equal to, or greater than, its 1966–78 average.

Under these circumstances, a significant part of the benefits that could be expected from the expansion of the volume of Latin America's exports were in fact offset by the fall in export prices. The figures in

---

[2] Helmut Reisen, "The Latin American Transfer Problem in Historical Perspective," *Latin America and the Caribbean and the OECD* (Paris: OECD Development Centre, 1986), p. 151–52.

the first column of Table 11 confirm this for nearly all the countries of the region, as the increase in the value of exports over 1982–86 was but a fraction of the rise in export volume. As might be expected, the most severe cases occurred among the oil exporting countries, but non-oil exporters, such as Argentina, Chile, and Uruguay, also had part of their export effort frustrated by declining world prices for their goods. Brazil, which is less dependent on exports of primary products, suffered somewhat less. Only Costa Rica and Colombia escaped running the treadmill of falling prices, mostly because of high prices for coffee in 1986.

The second column of Table 11 shows that for the majority of non-oil exporting countries real devaluations during 1982–86 were associated with a more than proportional movement in export *volume*. Nevertheless, the corresponding relation for export *value* was positive only in Colombia and Costa Rica.

Over the period 1982–85 the loss of income because of the deterioration in the terms of trade was equivalent to nearly three quarters of the region's bill for net interest payments. Indeed for Costa Rica and Chile the loss of income stemming from the fall in the terms of trade was equal roughly to the value of net interest payments, and for Uruguay it was substantially greater.

Finally, the negative effects of the evolution of world trade over this period can be seen by analyzing what would have happened if export prices had held their ground while the countries increased the volume of their exports in order to carry out an expansive adjustment. The figures in the last two columns of Table 11 are instructive. Valuing 1986 exports with 1980 export prices shows the fall in the net interest payments/export coefficient in comparison with its actual 1986 level. Indeed, had export prices remained stable, the region's coefficient would be 24 percent instead of 35 percent. All countries except Colombia and Costa Rica show important declines in their respective coefficients. Moreover, some countries, such as Ecuador, Peru, and Uruguay, would have recorded what might be termed acceptable coefficients and Venezuela's would have turned out to be a remarkably low 9 percent.

Adjustment With Growth: Prospects and Requirements

While the region as a whole is in difficult straits, the situation differs significantly among countries. By 1986 Colombia no longer

Table 11. Latin America: Selected Trade Indicators
(Coefficients)

| | Variations in 1982–86 in | | | 1982–85 | 1986 | |
| | | X Volume | X Value | Effect of change in the terms of trade | Net interest payments | Net interest payments |
	X Value X Volume	Real effective exchange rate	Real effective exchange rate	Net interest payments	X in current prices	X in 1980 prices
Latin America	**70.4**	...	...	**−72.6**	**35.1**	**24.2**
Oil exporting countries	53.9	...	...	−63.6	36.1	19.9
Non-oil exporting countries	85.5	...	...	−78.9	34.5	27.6
Argentina	68.5	77.9	54.1	−78.0	58.6	37.2
Brazil	86.7	111.7	97.4	−69.0	36.7	29.8
Colombia	118.1	111.5	131.9	−37.1	19.3	20.2
Costa Rica	106.7	113.6	134.5	−99.4	25.0	24.0
Chile	74.2	88.1	66.6	−93.6	39.4	25.2
Ecuador	55.1	93.0	51.2	−65.5	36.0	19.4
Mexico	61.6	74.3	41.8	−74.9	47.5	26.6
Peru	67.2	116.4	77.9	−69.7	31.3	21.0
Uruguay	78.0	77.8	60.5	−122.1	27.4	20.3
Venezuela	47.6	94.5	45.0	−4.1	18.4	9.2

Source: Calculated from data in the balance of payments series prepared by ECLAC.

had a debt problem, if it ever had one; its ratios of debt to exports (2.0) and interest to GDP (3.0 percent) were below regional averages for 1980, before the crisis emerged, and its trade surplus allowed it to meet almost 80 percent of its interest payments (Table 12). While Brazil's current account deficit increased at the end of 1986, it did so because of excessively expansive domestic policies. Thus correction of this imbalance "merely" requires redressing previous policy errors, which, needless to say, will be no easy task.

More complex, however, is the situation of Costa Rica, Chile, Uruguay, and Argentina, whose debt burdens—as measured by interest payments to GDP—are among the highest in the region (9.1 percent, 8.4 percent, 6.5 percent, and 6.5 percent, respectively). Though the first three reduced their external disequilibrium in 1986, their high level of debt nevertheless implies the need for long-enduring, and, except for Uruguay, even further adjustment. While Peru's debt burden is lower than average for the region (its interest

Table 12. Debt Burden, Domestic Effort, and Effort or Financing Still Required as of 1986[1]
(In percent)

	(1) Debt Burden i/GDP[2] (1)	(2) Domestic Effort TS/GDP[3] (2)	(3) Effort to Be Made and/or Further Financing Needed (3) = (1) − (2)
Latin America	5.3	2.3	3.0
Argentina	6.5	3.2	3.3
Brazil	4.0	3.2	0.8
Colombia	3.0	2.3	0.7
Costa Rica	9.1	2.4	6.7
Chile	8.4	2.6	5.8
Ecuador	5.8	1.2	4.6
Mexico	5.7	2.5	3.2
Peru	3.9	−0.6	4.5
Uruguay	6.5	6.5	0.0
Venezuela	5.3	−0.1	5.4

Source: Estimated on the basis of ECLAC's balance of payments and national accounts series.

[1] Preliminary estimates.

[2] i/GDP = net interest payments on foreign debt as a percentage of gross domestic product.

[3] TS/GDP = trade surplus in goods and services as a percentage of gross domestic product.

payments are just under 4 percent of GDP), its trade surplus disappeared in 1986, in part because of a deterioration in the prices of its exports, in part because of its domestic demand-driven expansion. Finally, the major oil exporters (Mexico, Ecuador, and Venezuela), face the stark prospects of adjustment on top of adjustment. Given their high debt burden, this process would seem to be manageable only if oil prices stabilize in the medium run at levels well above those prevailing in 1986.

Nevertheless, despite these differences, the basic problem is similar. Put in a nutshell, interest payments on debt amount to 5.3 percent of GDP, notwithstanding the fall in interest rates in 1986, whereas the trade surplus amounts to 2.3 percent of GDP despite the efforts of recent years. This implies that, were the terms of trade not to improve and were the region unable to attract fresh money, the meeting of interest payments would require an *additional* effort to improve the trade balance *larger* than that which has already taken place in the past five years in all countries except Brazil, Colombia, and Uruguay (Table 12). Since this effort has driven per capita income below 1980 levels in all countries except Brazil, Colombia, and Panama, small wonder that adjustment weariness has set in.

Recessionary adjustment is therefore no longer feasible, politically or socially. In fact, adjustment is acceptable only if it is subject to a minimum growth in output and consumption. This means that while, under recessionary adjustment, debt service was the prime recipient of foreign exchange and growth a residual, in expansive adjustment, the first priority for scarce foreign exchange is to meet the import requirements for minimum acceptable growth and debt service is the residual. In other words, while recessionary adjustment placed the onus of costs on debtors, expansive adjustment shifts part of the costs to creditors. Not only does expansive adjustment redress the heretofore exclusively one-sided nature of adjustment costs between creditors and debtors, but it also redresses the skewed absorption of these costs in creditor nations between its productive and financial sectors, that is to say, between OECD exporters and bankers, for the reduced sales to the region by the former largely account for the trade surpluses needed to meet interest payments to the latter.

At first sight, this reordering of priorities may not seem pleasing to banks or developed countries. Yet a moment's reflection should suffice to show that this more symmetrical approach is the only nonconfrontational way to solve the debt crisis and to carry on the adjustment process.

Ultimately there are only two ways of servicing the debt of the developing countries: either through fewer OECD exports or through more developing country exports. The first is the approach that has prevailed so far: the banks gain, developed countries' growth and exports suffer, and development is hamstrung. Moreover, the international financial system is jeopardized because, the longer debtors are forced to stagnate, the stronger the temptation to adopt unilateral solutions. Only in the second approach in which banks are paid from the growth of developing country exports and not from further import compression (at the expense of OECD exports) can all gain.

This second approach requires the concurrence of the key participants—private creditor banks, debtors, international financial institutions, and the governments of developing countries and of the OECD—in recognizing that the debt problem is systemic, and not merely one specific to, or brought on by, individual creditors or debtors. This is what the region means by a "political" solution to the debt problem.

To be sure, the strategy of growing out of the debt problem requires structural adjustment. Domestic policies need be pursued both to mobilize currently idle resources as well as to restructure production from nontradables to exports and imports substitutes. Yet expansive adjustment also requires adequate financing to provide the needed time for such transformation to take effect. Thus structural adjustment is the counterpart to adequate financing.

Domestic Requirements

In the long run, to grow out of the debt problem requires a structural transformation of the economy in at least two senses: the growth strategy needs to be outward oriented and largely based on domestic efforts to raise savings and productivity. Hence, foreign exchange, the savings/investment process and efficiency-raising innovations will be the key bottlenecks to growth and the central focus of policy attention.

Outward-oriented growth means that investment in the production of tradables must increase to expand and diversify exports and to augment the region's capacity to substitute imports. This involves not only raising and maintaining the incentives for saving or generating additional foreign exchange (i.e., a high and stable real effective exchange rate), but also equalizing on the margin and over time the incentives or costs of saving additional foreign exchange through import substitution or generating it through export expansion. Given the bias of the past strategy of import substitution in favor of production for home markets, presumably such an equalization of incentives will give rise to the expansion and diversification of exports far more than to further import substitution. Thus growth is likely to be not only outward oriented but also more export led and based especially on the expansion of manufactures and other nontraditional exports.

Given the debt burden and the likely insufficiency of voluntary capital inflows in the immediate future, this upsurge of investment in tradables will have to be based largely, if not exclusively, on domestic savings. Still, given the need to recover consumption levels, savings cannot be expected to do the job alone. Rather the productivity of investment and the overall efficiency of the economy will have to rise. Fortunately, the high incremental capital output ratios of investments in the 1970s suggest that there would be ample room for improvement in this regard.

In much the same vein, austerity implies not that distributive concerns be sacrificed, but that what efforts are made be focused on the needy lower 25 percent of the population. For not only are these groups living in abject poverty, but they receive only 4 percent of GDP. Hence, even modest redistributive efforts (say 2 percent of GDP), which spread over the bulk of the population (say the lower 80 percent which receive 50 percent of GDP) amount to very little, if focused on the lowest 25 percent, could eliminate extreme poverty, raising the income of this group 50 percent.

Finally, the experience of the past 15 years suggests that it would be imprudent to organize economic structures in the expectation of a smooth and steady evolution of the international economy. Rather, strong fluctuations in the terms of trade, in real interest rates, in the value of the U.S. dollar, and in the relative prices of basic commodities may be the rule rather than the exception. This not only heightens the importance of macroeconomic policy in establishing and maintaining basic internal, external, and distributive equilibria, but it implies the further need to bias policy planning and economic structures in favor of flexibility.

It is likely that there will be agreement on the importance of a less inward-oriented, more export-led growth, of greater domestic savings, of a more focused distributive effort, of improved productivity and efficiency, and of the need for a firmer, more coherent, and stable macroeconomic policy. Disagreements, however, are likely to emerge as to the means.

Thus, most will agree on the critical importance of a high and stable real exchange rate in promoting exports and efficient import substitution. But commercial policy? To be sure, tariff "policy" in the region has been more the result of the principle "to each activity the protection it needs," that is, protection at any social cost, rather than the attempt to redress divergences between social and private costs associated with, say, infant industries, technological externalities, or labor market distortions. Yet more than their elimination, this implies that tariffs should be lowered to levels proportionate to social (and not private) need and, where justified, should be rationalized among sectors so as to tend to equalize effective protection.

Moreover, to the extent that the arguments to protect a sector are socially valid, they justify equivalent incentives for production to all markets, external as well as domestic—all the more so if there are economies of scale. Put differently, unlike as was done in the past when incentives were provided only for production for domestic markets (at the resulting expense of exports, especially nontraditional ones), in the future these ought to be extended to production for international markets as well.

Nor does it suffice to do away with all tariffs and export incentives and replace these with a higher exchange rate. This would, in fact, be correct were all sectors deserving of equal amounts of protection and export incentives. Yet this would be an extreme case. More likely, important divergences between social and private benefits[3] will occur

---

[3] We say *important* divergences for it would be an administrative nightmare to try to compensate all theoretically conceivable divergences; much as it would be a gross oversimplification to disregard all such divergences, as do neoconservative policy-makers for the sake of administrative simplicity, and put policy on "automatic pilot," as if all such divergences were trivial or nonexistent.

in only some sectors and are likely to vary in degree and over time. At one and the same time new activities may be receiving tariff protection, import substituting activities that are coming of age will be increasingly receiving only export incentives, and fully mature activities will be receiving no special incentives at all.

A second critical bottleneck is the savings-investment process. Experience has clearly demonstrated the drawbacks of negative real interest rates, if not as to the amount of savings, certainly as regards the poor quality of investment: oversized plants, excessively capital-intensive technologies, investment determined by easy access to capital rather than by rate of return, and so forth. Yet excessively high real interest rates have proven to be equally disastrous, leading more to the pursuit of ephemeral quasi-rents (through financial speculation) than to investment in productive activities. The former are normally the result of long-term intervention in capital markets, the latter of financial market liberalization in the throes of disequilibrium often arising out of adjustment or stabilization programs. Hence, a case can be made to move towards liberalization through transitorily controlled rates, keeping these positive, but not much above real international rates.[4]

In fact, liberalization would seem to be but one, and certainly not the most critical, aspect of improved capital markets. More important is the need: (1) to correct capital-market segmentation between size of firms and types of credits. That large firms enjoy easy access to capital, while small and medium-size firms have little or no such access, biases lending "backwards" to firms with guarantees rather than "forward" to firms with high prospective rates of return. Segmentation between types of credit biases lending towards new equipment, which normally enjoys ample supplier credits at relatively low international interest rates, and away from used equipment and working capital, where financing, when available, is at high interest rates; and (2) to compensate for the absence of critical sections of

---

[4] For a few months high real interest rates may be needed to help stem capital flight in the midst of an adjustment or stabilization program, while expectations adjust. Yet, if real interest rates need be very high for long, it is a signal that the exchange rate in particular and macroeconomic policy in general, are in doubt. High interest rates are simply no substitute for credible macroeconomic policy.

capital markets, the most obvious being the lack of fluid, long-term capital markets.

Increased savings would seem to be more sensitive to appropriate fiscal policy than to higher (though certainly positive) real interest rates. Given the squeeze on consumption of the past five years, efforts should especially focus on channeling to savings far higher proportions of the new income generated in the recovery phase, be it that deriving from greater exports, improved terms of trade, or lower international interest rates. This implies a "carrot and stick" policy: increases in marginal tax rates, especially on increased consumption, and special incentives for savings.

Finally, the restoration and preservation of basic macroeconomic equilibria implies not only the reduction in the current account deficit (external equilibrium) but the reduction in the unemployment of labor and in the generally widespread levels of underutilized capacity (internal and distributive equilibria). Though the simultaneous achievement of the three is a difficult task, it is the only way open to *maintain* any of those equilibria in the long run. For the achievement of the one at the expense of another is but transitory and hence ultimately self-defeating.

Since adjustment in the region has been largely recessive, this establishes a prima facie case for short-run policy to be biased in favor of utilizing currently underutilized productive capacity, while the longer run effects of policy on investment take hold. Ordinary aggregate demand policies will not do, however, for these will soon run up against the dearth of foreign exchange to purchase needed intermediate inputs. It is essential for expansive adjustment that a significant part of the output obtained from this increased capacity utilization be for export, not necessarily 100 percent, but enough to generate the foreign exchange required to direct the rest of unused capacity for domestic use, in both import substitution and the production of socially needed nontradables (e.g., housing).

To do this, an appropriate rule of thumb is to equalize the short-run marginal costs of generating or saving foreign exchange through expenditure-switching or expenditure-reduction policies. Since it can be foreseen that expenditure-reduction policies will operate far more quickly than switching policies, heavy and selective switching policies would be called for in the short run. These incentives should, however, be transitory, set in accordance with the degree of currently unused capacity and limited only to those products with the highest short-term output elasticity to price and those with the best chances of achieving long-term international competitiveness.[5]

In brief, the experience of recent years suggests two types of pitfalls: those deriving from pervasive intervention and a virtual disregard of the market and those deriving from overly rapid liberalization and an excessive reliance on the market. At the risk of oversimplification, our analysis suggests the merits of intervention in the short run (while macroeconomic relations are in disequilibrium) and increased reliance on the price system and a few, simple *rules* of intervention for the long run (once the economy is closer to basic equilibrium). Intervention in the latter case should be largely limited to attacking the two critical bottlenecks (foreign exchange and the savings-investment process) and to achieving distributive objectives.

More generally, we would emphasize the need for sectoral, not just across-the-board, policy and for selective, and not just general, policy instruments. We would also insist, however, on the need for an outward-oriented development strategy, export promotion being the natural follow-up to the industrial base created by import sub-stitution. Thus, while industrialization based on import substitution was at the heart of regional policy in the past, the reorientation of this established industrial base toward an export-oriented industrial-ization would seem to be the direction of the future for many countries. This would suggest the virtues of combining orthodox goals and instruments (export orientation and devaluation) with their structural counterparts (industrialization and carefully chosen selec-tive incentives).

For those who see the essential policy issue as between more intervention or more markets, such an "unholy alliance" would appear to be a contradiction in terms. For those who see the challenge

---

[5] Once again, the temporary and selective use of such instruments permits incentives to be tailored to those export- and import-substituting activities with the fastest response in the short run, as opposed to an across-the-board instrument such as an even greater devaluation. Selective instruments have the further advantage of having a lesser impact on costs and expectations, and hence on inflation, than a devaluation. Finally, precisely because these selective instruments should be temporary, the exchange rate can be set for long-run equilibrium, thus rendering a clearer and stabler signal to producers as to the objective of policy. Obviously, once the effect of regular switching policies (devaluation) on investment takes hold, these transitory super-switching incentives should be phased out.

as to how to achieve *better* intervention and *better* markets, this proposal may ring true, as the essence of balance and common sense.

External Requirements

However effective the design and implementation of domestic adjustment policies may be their efficacy is in fact today heavily conditioned by external events. For one, growth-oriented adjustment relies critically on the expansion and diversification of exports. While this certainly depends on domestic economic decisions, especially exchange and commercial policy, it will be easier or more difficult as the expansion of international trade becomes brisk or sluggish and the currently depressed basic commodity prices rebound or continue to fall. Not much can be done to reverse depressed demand resulting from structural or technological changes. Yet, much of the sluggish demand for Latin America's exports is a result of weak OECD growth, policy-induced artificial surpluses in agricultural commodities, and increased protection generally.

There are sectoral interests which OECD authorities must take into account in formulating policies. Nevertheless, these policies must clearly be reconciled with the basic accounting identity that interest payments from debtor countries require equivalent trade deficits in creditor countries or corresponding capital inflows to debtors. If creditors want interest repayment and low capital flows, they must run high trade deficits (hopefully through increased imports from debtors, rather than through reduced exports to them). Alternatively, if creditors want protection and trade surpluses they need to promote capital flows to debtors or else to assume the consequences of debt moratoria. In short, creditor countries can have trade surpluses, or receive full interest repayment or extend no new net loans. What is impossible for them is to have all three simultaneously. Hence, the improvement and harmonization of their macroeconomic, sectoral, trade, and financial policies is not simply a matter of international "do goodism" but a basic condition for economic equilibria in the center's *own* external accounts.

Expansionary adjustment also requires time and resources. For the speed with which exports expand and efficient import substitution takes place depends not only on correct relative prices but on the amount of resources actually available for investment. So long as the region must transfer the equivalent of 25 percent of its savings for these purposes, such investment can hardly be forthcoming in the appropriate amounts to permit significant trade surpluses and a rapid and sustained rate of economic growth. Hence, if expansionary structural adjustment is to take place, the region's net outward transfer of resources need be sharply reduced.

This can be achieved through lower international interest rates and the return of flight capital, or increased net lending, or debt forgiveness. Given the severity and duration of the crisis, it is likely that in many cases solutions will require most of the above.

Lowering Interest Rates

During the past four years net interest remittances have absorbed around 35 percent of the total value of the region's exports, which is double the percentage they represented before the crisis. Hence, ceteris paribus, if these payments are reduced, it would be possible to raise imports without producing any increase in the deficit on current account. Furthermore, if the decline in interest payments was the result of a drop in international interest rates, the reduction in the transfer of resources could be achieved with less pressure on bank profits, and the ensuing recovery of the economy could be achieved without expanding the external debt. It would therefore have the additional advantage of not jeopardizing future import capacity. In other words, the reduction of international base rates constitutes the less conflictive solution to the debt problem.

Hence, it is important that the recent fall in international interest rates be maintained and strenghthened. Yet such a decline, welcome as it is, should not be overrated, for the decline that took place in 1985–86 was in nominal interest rates while real rates fell much less. What is required is that real interest rates decline; only if nominal interest rates fall more than inflation will total interest payments decline in relation to the region's capacity to pay them (which depends on exports, whose value tends to rise and fall with world inflation). In contrast, as long as real interest rates persistently remain higher than the growth rate of output, and nominal interest rates remain higher than the growth rate of export earnings, there is a progressive risk that debtor countries will drift into insolvency.

The reduction of interest rates depends ultimately on neither debtors nor creditors but on the policies of the principal industrial countries. This is an example—possibly the example par excellence—of why a satisfactory resolution of the debt crisis cannot be found within the limited confines of debtors and creditors but depends strongly on the public policy of industrial countries as well. Thus industrial countries must more decisively tackle their own internal adjustment problems, because without it the world-wide adjustment process is asymmetric and places an unnecessary burden on the developing country debtors.

Reversing Capital Flight

As mentioned earlier, the region, and especially some countries, have experienced a large amount of capital flight. This is reflected in the fact that toward the end of 1985, Latin American residents had $83 billion deposited in the international banking system, more than 2.5 times the level of the region's official gross international reserves. The reduction of the outward transfer of resources and a growth-oriented adjustment process would clearly be facilitated if most of this capital began to return to the region. This, of course, would be another nonconflictive way of reducing the debt problem and easing the adjustment process.

Both the outflow of this capital and its return depend heavily on the macroeconomic policy and political conditions in the debtor countries. For a return to be effected, good macropolicy must be sustained and rates of return must rise on productive investments. There also must be political stability and guarantees for the security of private capital. That this is a possible and not just a theoretical option is demonstrated by the fact that some countries, such as Mexico, Chile, and Uruguay, were able to stop the capital outflow and even partially reverse it in 1986. It is unlikely, however, that in most countries the amounts will be very large, at least until this critical juncture of the debt crisis be over, given flight capital's tendency to be first out, last in.

Increasing Net Lending

An alternative and complement to lower interest rates and the return of flight capital is more lending. The less interest rates fall for the debtor countries, the more new lending is required from the creditors to reduce the outward financial transfer and support dynamic and socially efficient adjustment.

At the outset of 1986 there was a surprising consensus about what constituted a conservative estimate of Latin America's financing needs to support a growth-oriented adjustment process: roughly $20 billion a year for annual growth rates of 4–5 percent a year.[6] This compares with actual net capital inflows of $2 billion in 1985 and $9 billion in 1986.

As already mentioned, private banks have demonstrated in recent years a great reluctance to lend to Latin America. More concerted nonvoluntary lending to Latin America is unattractive for many banks since they want to further reduce their asset/capital ratios in the region. Moreover the banks' ability to resist new lending has been enhanced by loan writeoffs and growth of loan-loss reserves. That resistance can be especially strong in European institutions which are often obliged to set aside new reserves for any additional dollar lent. This situation will put increased pressure on public lenders, which so far do not have adequate resources to fill the perspective gap.

Nevertheless, to the degree that the debtor country has the necessary underlying economic conditions to support its commercial debt—or merits the benefit of the doubt—a violent pull-back of new lending by the banks constitutes a certain degree of myopia on the part of private markets. This is where public policy in the OECD can legitimately employ strong moral suasion to "encourage" private lenders to stay in the game and support the financing of a dynamic adjustment process with new loans. The required financing can come about directly by the authorization of new credits or indirectly through the semi-automatic capping of interest rates (which, of course, should be commercial) and the rescheduling of amortization. The amount of financing required from the banks will vary in individual cases, but

---

[6] The $20 billion figure was cited in early 1986 in separate reports of the World Bank, ECLAC, and the Inter-American Dialogue. The ECLAC report, however, did not take into account the net effect of the sharp fall in petroleum prices in early 1986. The timing of the two other reports suggests that they could not incorporate this effect either. Since Latin America is a net petroleum exporter, annual financing requirement may in fact be higher than $20 billion. See ECLAC, *The Problem of External Debt: Gestation, Development, Crisis, and Prospects* (Santiago, Chile: January 1986); Inter-American Dialogue, *Rebuilding Cooperation in the Americas* (Washington: April 1986) and David Knox, "Address at the Bankers Club," Tokyo, February 20, 1986.

creditors would have to commit themselves to an annual financial transfer that subordinates itself to the requirements of a growth-oriented adjustment program, as banks themselves have in fact accepted in the recent Mexican package, for which new finance adjusts itself to the need to support a 3–4 percent rate of economic growth in that country.

Debt Forgiveness

While new lending to the borrowers in whatever form is perhaps better than no finance at all, commercial reschedulings and new loan packages are not technically appropriate for all of them. There are countries where the debt overhang is large either because of the past willingness of lenders and borrowers to create debt largely for purposes which had little prospect of generating a commercial return or because of possibly permanent adverse shifts in the debtors' terms of trade. In either case the country's economic structure needs a thorough and time-consuming overhaul before internal rates of return will be high enough to support a commercial interest rate. Consequently, for these countries, adjustment promises to be unusually protracted and the prospects of regaining autonomous access to private credit markets in the foreseeable future are remote. They are analogous to an insolvent commercial borrower and some form of noncommercial debt relief, with hidden or explicit debt forgiveness, is appropriate.

The market already admits to the problem because as soon as Latin American paper is subject to competitive trade, an automatic discount materializes. Although the secondary trading market is thin, and its valuation of paper may not be entirely reliable, any discount above a third of face value is suggestive of a problem loan. For these countries, continuing insistence on commercial returns for loans of noncommercial value only burdens the adjustment process and leaves open the prospects of permanently high and rising debt/export and debt/GDP coefficients in the debtor country. It also involves wishful accounting in the banks and undermines the strength of the home country banking system.

The form debt forgiveness takes—noncommercial interest rates or partial cancellation of principal—would vary from country to country and ideally should be done as painlessly as possible for banks. Yet it is clear at this stage, after five years of adjustment, that countries with very severe and protracted additional adjustment problems will need some form of debt forgiveness.

Of course, debt forgiveness represents a cost for the creditors. Nevertheless, this organized and predictable financial cost must be weighed against other costs, such as loss of export markets and jobs in the creditor countries, as well as the potential and unpredictable financial costs deriving from the risk of disorderly defaults by the debtor countries.

While banks do write down loans (as many have done to date) or even write them fully off, there is no incentive for them to forgive debt. Hence, the menace of the debt crisis continues. The problem then is how to translate the costs of debt writeoffs to banks into equivalent benefits for debtors. Since the debt problem is by now systemic, and the object of OECD governments should be, at least, to minimize the disruption to the international financial systems of spasmodic moratoria on the part of problem debtor nations, creditor governments should now act to minimize this eventuality and push for concerted debt forgiveness. Certainly there are precedents for this. Debt forgiveness by banks, often with their governments' help and cost sharing, is frequently practiced in the domestic markets of the creditors. Recently there have been a number of measures introduced providing debt forgiveness on problem farm loans, with the appropriate accounting flexibility for the lenders. Why not practice internationally principles that already are considered appropriate for systemic debt problems at home?

Conclusions

By and large, most countries of the region reacted to the post-1979 crisis initially by putting off domestic adjustment and then overadjusting. The first was ineffective; the latter inefficient. The former, because domestic policies failed to adjust while financing was available, achieved short-term growth at the expense of worsened external disequilibria; the latter, because financing collapsed. Thus, though domestic policies were adjusted, the improvement in external accounts was obtained at the expense of economic growth.

Efficient adjustment requires better domestic policies together with adequate financing. The first assures its permanence, the latter wins valuable time for the needed structural transformations to take hold. Efficient adjustment requires not only expenditure reduction and import compression—which can be as sharp as desired—but also a reallocation of real resources from nontradables to exports and import substitution—which is necessarily a slower process. In short, there is no such thing as an efficient *shock* adjustment program.

In any case, the dramatic improvement in external accounts achieved by 1984 at the expense of costly reductions in output, employment, and wages was seriously set back in 1986, in large part because of the fall in the prices of oil and other basic commodities. Hence, debt indicators deteriorated in most countries of the region, implying the need for more prolonged, if not more pronounced, adjustment. In addition, because of the length and severity of the crisis, adjustment weariness has set in among debtors and debt fatigue among creditors. The former are unable to postpone growth any longer; the latter want to supply little, if any, new money.

In the face of such an impasse, a scenario which could ultimately lead to spasmodic moratoria, which would jeopardize not just particular creditors and debtors but the international financial and open trading system as well, cannot be discounted. To break this impasse and reconcile growth and creditworthiness, concerted action by all parties involved is now essential. Debtor countries—which up to the present have shouldered a disproportionate amount of the burden of adjustment—must persist in their efforts to restructure their economies. In return, and to make this process both economically efficient and politically viable, private creditors, their governments, and official lenders must provide finance far above present levels, thus restoring symmetry to the adjustment process.

In some ways this resembles the Baker Initiative, but with important differences. On the one hand, the content of adjustment that we have outlined is more selective in the use of policy instruments, more pragmatic with regard to the role of state intervention, and more directly concerned about social questions of equity. On the other, we stress that while commercial solutions are acceptable for some problem borrowers, some degree of debt forgiveness is unavoidable for others.

Discussion

Jacob A. Frenkel

Director, Research Department
International Monetary Fund

Mr. Fischer has provided us with a comprehensive and illuminating paper on economic growth and economic policy. With characteristic clarity and economy he presents a balanced summary of the literature on the determinants of long-run growth in developing countries, discusses the pros and cons of alternative growth strategies, identifies key problems of adjustment and growth facing indebted countries, and draws together the main lessons for economic policy.

To set the stage for my discussion it is worth recalling some of the implications of Mr. Fischer's analysis. First, our concrete knowledge of the fundamental sources of growth is still meager. Indeed, using the traditional framework of growth accounting, Mr. Fischer shows that about 50 percent of per capita growth cannot be attributed to conventional sources like changes in the quantities of factors of production (labor and capital), education, economies of scale, and improved resource allocation. The unknown residual is typically referred to as "technological progress" or "advance in knowledge." In view of our limited understanding of the factors governing the growth process, a certain amount of humility is clearly warranted. It follows that programs that aim at growth should be designed with sufficient flexibility so as to correspond to our limited knowledge.

Second, while investment in capital formation contributes to the growth process, its quantitative contribution is rather limited.

Third, while small changes in growth rates have little effect in the short run, their cumulative effect may be very significant for the long run. Mr. Fischer characterizes this fact as "the great power of compounding." The implications of this observation are profound. Programs, even those aimed at short-term crisis management, must be designed with a long-term perspective. Indeed, there are no short cuts. A runner planning for a successful long-distance race must follow a steady, feasible, and sustainable pace; unsustainable accelerations in mid-course may yield illusory short-term gains but at the cost of jeopardizing the successful completion of the race.

Fourth, and on a bit more pessimistic note, even the long-run effects of a steady rise in the growth rate are somewhat limited: the low-income countries would have to grow (in per capita terms) 3.9 percent a year faster than the industrial market economies to catch up within a century. Such a growth rate is clearly unlikely, and therefore a complete convergence of the economic positions of developing and industrial countries is unlikely to take place. The fifth fact to which Mr. Fischer draws our attention is that most success stories involve outward orientation of policies, although the role of government varies in implementing these policies.

The main theme emerging from Mr. Fischer's analysis is that the analysis of economic growth and economic policies is highly complex, that economic growth involves hard policy decisions, and that one should not expect immediate results. Simply stated, there is no quick fix.

In discussing the implementation of policies, Mr. Fischer recommends a balanced approach to the design of programs; I certainly agree with his general line of reasoning. Perhaps I can best contribute by expanding on some of the issues that emerge from Mr. Fischer's analysis. The first concerns the question of gradualism versus drastic measures. The advantages and disadvantages of each one of the two extremes are well known. It seems, however, that the desirable solution to the problem of the choice between gradualism and drastic measures should be a plan that incorporates the best elements of each option. Such a balanced solution could be obtained through a pre-announcement of a feasible path for the policy instruments. Thus, if stabilization involves a cut in government spending, a reduction in the rate of monetary growth, and the like, a gradual reduction coupled with pre-announcement of the entire path is likely to avoid the undesirable consequences of immediate drastic cuts, while, at the same time, the feasibility and the consistency of the plan is likely to indicate the government's long-term commitment, and thereby enhance the plan's credibility and promote stabilizing expectations.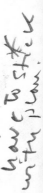

A second area where a balanced view is called for involves the choice between an analysis that is based entirely on formal models and an analysis that is based entirely on informal judgment. Since structural parameters are unlikely to remain constant in the face of large policy changes, it is clearly unwise to follow mechanically the predictions of rigid models. On the other hand, models may be very useful in disciplining what might otherwise be an unstructured analysis by providing consistency checks. Informal judgment can aid and can be aided by formal models.

A third area involves the relation between adjustment and growth. In this context several points are noteworthy. The first concerns timing: should adjustment policies precede growth policies, or vice versa? I believe that the correct answer is neither of the above. Growth policies cannot be effective if implemented in a highly distorted economy that needs adjustment. By the same token, adjustment policies will not be sustainable unless implemented in an environment of growth. The two sets of policies should not be viewed as alternatives, but rather as complements to each other. They must be implemented in a balanced fashion; they must be implemented simultaneously. The second point involves the quality of adjustment and growth. There is a "good adjustment" and there is a "bad adjustment"; there is a "good growth" and there is a "bad growth." An analysis that distinguishes the good patterns of adjustment and growth from their bad counterparts must focus on the commodity composition of aggregate demand and aggregate output. Aggregate measures of demand and output levels are not "sufficient statistics" for this purpose.

The third point relates to the composition of government revenue and outlays. One of Mr. Fischer's policy lessons is: "Keep budget deficits under adequate control. Absolute balance may be impossible; but there is not much room for deficits." Very sensible advice. But I think that if we are to embed sound fiscal policy within a program that has growth, current account, inflation, and perhaps even income distribution objectives, it makes a big difference not only if the country reduces its fiscal deficit but also how it does so. Let me elaborate.

If a country wants to improve its current account or to effect a change in its exchange rate, it matters a lot whether it reduces the deficit by cutting expenditures or by raising taxes, or by cutting expenditure on tradable goods versus nontradables. Similarly, the growth implications of fiscal consolidation will be different depending

on whether higher taxes fall mainly on consumption or on investment,
or on whether these taxes promote or impede work effort. Likewise,
the success of efforts to protect the most vulnerable groups in an
economy will not be indifferent to whether cuts in expenditure take
the form of decreases in defense spending or reductions in health
and nutrition expenditures. In short, one cannot draw useful predictions about the impact of fiscal policy without being quite specific
about the structure of expenditure and revenue measures.

A fourth area involves the balance between short-run and long-
run considerations. To begin with, it is important to emphasize that
a sharp dichotomy between the two is unhelpful and may result in
fundamental errors. A sensible model of economic behavior must
recognize that the short-run effects of policies depend on the degree
to which the policies are perceived as being sustainable in the longer
run. Furthermore, decisions on whether to implement short-run
policies must hinge on their longer-run consequences. This interdependence between the short and the long runs implies that it makes
little economic sense to argue that the International Monetary Fund
should be concerned only with short-run considerations involving
short-run balance of payments adjustments, whereas the World Bank
should be concerned only with long-run considerations involving
long-run growth. A proper analysis of the short run must recognize
the long-run consequences, and a proper analysis of the long run
must recognize that the path involves a succession of short-run
policies. This logical overlap of interest provides the intellectual
rationale for enhanced Bank-Fund cooperation.

A fifth area involves the balance and interaction between growth
and external finance. In general, the specification of programs and
the length of the time horizon that is incorporated into the program
design depend on the amount of available external finance. There is,
however, the difficulty of circular reasoning since the amount of
available external finance depends itself, in some measure, on the
particular elements in the program and on the length of the time
horizon assumed in the program design. A proper balance must
allow for these two interacting factors.

A sixth area in which a delicate balance must be found is between
the case-by-case approach and the general approach. The virtues of
the former approach are well known. It recognizes that countries
differ from each other in customs and conventions, in political

systems, in socioeconomic structures, in economic organization, in circumstances, and the like. On the other hand, one must recognize that a strong case can be made in favor of consistency and of a general application of common basic principles. Accordingly, a midway course between the two extremes would acknowledge that a properly functioning system needs some general rules, but at the same time these rules must allow for the prevailing large diversities among member countries. The recognition of such diversity would facilitate the adoption of policy measures tailored to the circumstances and needs of a given country without the paralyzing concern that such necessary measures create dangerous precedents that must be generalized and applied in all other cases and under all other circumstances.

A seventh area of prime importance relates to the policy lessons drawn from the inflationary experience. I agree with Mr. Fischer's dictum that in promoting growth policy one needs to make sure that inflationary pressures do not get out of line. The key question is how to bring inflation down without significantly damaging growth. The issue is perhaps of particular interest when the inflation rate is high and long-lived and when labor, goods, and financial markets have adapted to "living with inflation" via various indexation mechanisms.

One option is to rely more heavily on wage and price controls to deal with the "inertial" nature of inflation, while simultaneously de-indexing. The worry, of course, is that the longer these controls stay in force, the more they distort market signals and lead to serious misallocation of resources. On the other hand, high and variable inflation rates also cloud the information content of the price system so that, at least initially, the resource-misallocation cost of controls may be limited. The other danger is that the initial success of the controls in reducing inflation may lead to a weakening of monetary and fiscal discipline, the results of which can become readily apparent during the "re-entry period" when the authorities move to gradually relax the price and wage controls. Yet another concern is to see that increases in the demand for money induced by greatly reduced inflationary expectations do not lead to dramatic rises in real interest rates—a consideration that argues against excessively restrictive monetary policy. In the end, I fully support Mr. Fischer's conclusion: "Use price and wage controls sparingly if at all."

A second general option is to stick closer to orthodox stabilization measures to combat inflation but to adopt a gradualist approach that produces a smooth adjustment path so as to minimize any employment losses. While, as indicated earlier, the choice of shock treatment versus gradualism has many dimensions, the political one will often be decisive. It may not be possible to sustain gradualist policies over a long period. In this sense, a sharp cut in real wages followed by a gradual rise may be more manageable than a steady decline over several years. Equally, the temptation to put off painful measures until the future carries the risk that politicians will not do what they pledged when the time comes. Concerning the lessons from the recent experience with heterodox stabilization programs (Argentina, Brazil, and Israel), my impression is that there is no substitute for orthodox measures. Heterodox programs that do not include significant orthodox components—budgetary consolidation and real wage restraint—do not seem to succeed owing to lack of credibility. Once the key orthodox measures are implemented, the heterodox aspects of the programs may provide some of the tranquil environment necessary for the breaking of vicious circles. I should note that these impressions are tentative since (at least for some of the programs) the jury is still out.

Another issue for inflation control concerns the role of exchange rate policy. Here, one has to guard against the danger that real exchange rate rules—put in place to avoid slippages in competitiveness and to underpin improvements in the current account—do not destabilize the price level. If inflation is to be controlled over the long term, experience shows that it is helpful to have some nominal anchor for monetary policy. I couldn't agree more with what Mr. Fischer regards as the most important lesson: don't allow the exchange rate to result in an overvalued currency—but we also should recognize that fixation with the current account can play havoc with other objectives of programs if exchange rate management is too mechanical. In this context, I should note that the real exchange rate is one out of three critical indicators that should not be allowed to get out of line. The other two are the real rate of interest and the real wage. An economy for which any one of these three indicators is out of line is likely to be heading for difficulties.

The final issue on which I wish to comment concerns Mr. Fischer's question of the proper order of economic liberalization measures. What markets should be liberalized first and what should be the proper sequencing? To begin with, it is worth noting that the question of the optimal process of economic liberalization involves one of the most difficult aspects of the theory of economic policy, namely, the transition toward equilibrium. The prescription of economic theory is very clear when applied to "first-best" situations. Economic theory, however, is much more reserved when it comes to evaluation and comparison of distorted situations. The evaluation of alternative strategies for economic liberalization involves making comparisons among various distorted situations that characterize alternative paths an economy may adopt in its approach to undistorted, first-best equilibrium. Consequently, views about the "proper" sequencing of liberalization measures should be put forward with great care and modesty; economic theory does not provide an unambiguous answer to that important question. With these reservations in mind, some general principles may still be stated.

Consider an economy that suffers from numerous distortions in goods and capital markets and suppose that in the past many barriers to international trade in goods and capital were imposed. Suppose that the government wishes to remove the distortions and to liberalize trade in goods and capital. Under these circumstances, the general rule is that the first step in the liberalization process should be removal of domestic distortions in goods and capital markets and attainment of fiscal order, so as to reduce the heavy reliance on inflationary finance. The second step should be the liberalization of the economy's links with the rest of the world. The external liberalization should also proceed in two phases. The first phase should reduce distortions to the free flow of goods by liberalizing the balance of trade. The capital account of the balance of payments should be opened up and liberalized only in the final phase. In what follows, some arguments are offered in support of the proposed order of liberalization of the trade and the capital accounts of the balance of payments.

The key distinction between the effects of opening up the trade account and those of opening up the capital account of the balance of payments stems from the fundamental difference between goods and asset markets. As is known, the speed of adjustment in asset markets is much faster than in goods markets. Asset markets are more sensitive to expectations concerning the distant future, and new information that alters expectations is reflected in asset prices much faster than in the prices of goods and services. This intrinsic difference in the basic characteristics of goods and assets has several implications. First, since the economy under consideration has been distorted for a significant period, nobody (including economists) can be certain about the precise paths that its various sectors will follow after liberalization. Under such uncertain circumstances, prudence is called for. A program of liberalization that opens up the trade account first has the virtue of providing policymakers with an opportunity to examine the market's reaction and to correct any errors found. A program that opens up the capital account first is not likely to provide such an opportunity, since once the capital account is opened up, the initial reaction is likely to take place very quickly and the resulting capital flows are likely to be huge. Thus, although it is eventually desirable to have an open capital account, prudence calls for a gradual transition to openness so as to facilitate the required change in institutions and the economic structure. An analogy can be made between an economy recovering from a long history of distortions and an individual recovering from a heart condition and a by-pass operation. While the latter's complete recovery may well be antici-pated, nobody would recommend that he start his rehabilitation program by running a marathon race.

The implications of the different speeds of adjustment of the trade and capital accounts can be illustrated picturesquely by a carriage pulled by two horses. Suppose that one of the horses is a fast runner while the other is a slow runner. As is obvious, if the two horses run at different speeds, the carriage would turn over. To avoid a disaster, the speeds of the two horses must be equalized. This can be achieved by speeding up the slow horse or by slowing down the fast one. It stands to reason that the former solution is not sustainable while the latter can be achieved with little effort. Analogously, the overall balance of payments constraint requires that the trade and the capital accounts be brought into line with each other, and thus, even though the two accounts tend to respond at different speeds, the overall constraint implies that the two speeds of adjustment must be harmonized. It seems that such consistency could be achieved with less effort by slowing down capital flows than it could by speeding up trade flows.

Second, it is easier (and less costly to society) to reverse wrong portfolio decisions than to reverse wrong real investment decisions. This potential difference in social costs also supports the thesis that the proposed sequence of liberalization measures is the correct one. Once the authorities remove distortions in the commodity markets and open up the trade account, real investment in the economy will take place in a less distorted environment—and thus will be more consistent with long-run patterns of real investment. Portfolio investments will continue to be based on a distorted capital market as long as the capital account is not opened up. Once the capital account is liberalized, some portfolio decisions will have to be reversed, but such a reversal is not likely to be very costly. On the other hand, if the capital account is opened up first, portfolio decisions are likely to reflect more accurately the undistorted long-run conditions, but real investment decisions will still reflect a distorted environment as long as the trade account is not opened up. Owing to the distortions, the social costs of investments are likely to exceed the private costs. Such real investment decisions will have to be reversed once the trade account is liberalized. Therefore, the trade account should be liberalized before the capital account. In this context, it should be noted that distortions in the flow of goods affect both the trade account and the capital account and, by the same token, distortions in the flow of capital also affect both accounts. However, it is likely that the relative effects of each distortion on the two accounts differ; distortions in the flow of goods are likely to have a stronger effect on the trade account than on the capital account, while distortions in the flow of capital are likely to have a stronger effect on the capital account than on the trade account. This difference in the relative sensitivities of the two balance of payments accounts to the two distortions underlies the recommended order of liberalization.

Third, the cost of a distortion depends on the distortion itself and on the volume of transactions that take place in the presence of the distortion. Thus, when the trade account is opened up first, the cost of the remaining distortion (i.e., the closed capital account) is proportional to the volume of trade, which, owing to the slow adjustment of the market for goods, is likely to be relatively small. On the other hand, when the capital account is opened up first, the cost of the remaining distortion (i.e., the closed trade account) is proportional to the volume of capital flows, which, owing to the high speed of adjustment in asset markets, is likely to be very large. Thus, a comparison of the costs of distortions also supports the proposition that the trade account should be opened up first.

The removal of various distortions in the market for goods—including various taxes, subsidies, and tariffs—will yield a new equilibrium price level, a new nominal exchange rate, and a new real exchange rate. It is pertinent to note that prior to setting out on such a path, the initial conditions have to be set correctly, so as to reflect the new equilibrium exchange rate and the prices that will prevail following the removal of the distortions. In this context, it is useful to recall that several attempted liberalizations have resulted in uncontrolled inflation. These outcomes can be explained, in part, by the nature of indexation clauses. In order to avoid such failures, it is critical that the initial (once-and-for-all) changes in prices that result from the removal of subsidies and other distortions be excluded from the indices that are used for wage indexation.

As was emphasized earlier, it is essential that the liberalization program be preceded by restoration of a fiscal order that reduces the government's dependence on inflationary finance. This restoration is an especially important prerequisite to opening up the capital account. The liberalization of the capital account is likely to encourage the process of "currency substitution." This phenomenon results in an effective reduction of the "tax base" for inflationary finance. Unless the need for inflationary finance is reduced, the opening up of the capital account and the resultant shrinkage of the inflationary tax base may result in an accelerated rate of inflation as the government attempts to collect the needed revenue from a smaller tax base.

The success of the liberalization program depends crucially on expectations concerning the feasibility and credibility of the program. It is important that the various measures that are undertaken hang together in a consistent way. Trust and confidence that has been built up with great difficulty can be destroyed very easily. Therefore, it is important not to start the program until all loose ends are tied up. The economic system, through the mechanism of memory that builds itself into expectations, shows little tolerance of errors. Therefore, while a slight delay in the introduction of a program will not be fatal, the premature introduction of an inconsistent plan might be.

Mr. Fischer concludes his paper with a perceptive list of key lessons and commandments for policymakers. I would amend that list with the additional obvious but, in view of past experience, very important principle: avoid correcting a mistake by overreacting. Stated differently, do not attempt to undo a mistake by making another mistake in the opposite direction. As noted by the Austrian economist, Ludwig Von Mises, if somebody has been run over by an automobile, you do not put him back on his feet by letting the car run over him in the other direction.

S. Shahid Husain
Vice President, Operations Policy Staff
World Bank

I will be very selective and mention three basic issues about the role of governments.

First, regarding the whole question of controls and rent creation in developing countries, one of the most common causes of frustrated growth is large-scale rent creation and rent receiving that may follow from specific control and allocation decisions. While for a short period transfers implicit in subsidized exchange rates and subsidized interest rates may be justifiable in terms of creation of capital and the establishment of a technological base, there is evidence that before too long they start frustrating the whole process of growth.

Let me mention the extreme case of Nigeria, where, during ten years of the oil boom when the investment rates were 20 or 30 percent, there was no increase in GNP at all, none. Basically what happened is that the so-called investment was nothing but a way of getting hold of scarce resources to create monopolies. Clearly any process which is going to lead to adjustment and viable growth has to tackle this issue in developing countries.

The second point I want to make is that there is an inherent contradiction in any development approach that discriminates against exports and yet relies heavily on external borrowing. The sheer arithmetic of the debt cycle is such that if the mutually supportive process of borrowing, growth, and debt servicing is not to come to an abrupt end, then sooner rather than later exports and GNP have to increase faster than debt.

The only ways this eventuality can be postponed is through substantial flows of concessional assistance, which has been the case in such countries as India that have avoided this crisis, or a substantial improvement in terms of trade. That is the second issue.

The third point I want to make is that in many developing countries there has been a large expansion of government ownership and control of the directly productive sectors. This creates an inherent conflict of interest in the formulation of policies. There is evidence in Africa, Asia, and Latin America that stretching government management and finance has caused an internal impediment because of the conflict between the policy setting and the management of government enterprises in exposing particular industries to competition and to financial discipline.

A word about stabilization and adjustment. It is true that in an environment of high inflation and high expectation of inflation there has to be some priority in bringing to balance the fiscal and monetary factors. And yet if we examine what has happened in developing countries we find that most of these apparent stabilization issues have a base in institutional questions.

For example, how do you bring government expenditures into control and to balance without going deeply in the issues of the management of public enterprises or of the agricultural support-price mechanism? At this stage in the process of stabilization and development it is very difficult to distinguish between the issues of stabilization and the longer-term issues of viability of growth. In my view, they go hand in hand and have to be tackled as integral parts of a coherent and cohesive program.

A. David Knox

Vice President, Latin America and the Caribbean Regional Office
World Bank

Let me say that I found Mr. Bianchi's paper an excellent one. I thought it was lucid and balanced. And indeed I would be quite happy to stop there, but I fear that the organizers of this conference might withdraw my invitation to lunch tomorrow. So I will continue for a little bit longer.

I think in the paper and in his presentation Dr. Bianchi has made a number of excellent points, bringing out the nature of an extraordinarily prolonged and severe crisis that has beset the Latin American countries for the last five years now. And as he says, it is the result of an extraordinary combination of events, both external factors that have been extremely unfavorable for the countries, in terms of the countercyclical behavior of most of the sources of capital, and the very sharp deterioration in the terms of trade.

In addition to those external factors that have been so adverse, I think he very rightly points to the fact that the Latin American countries began this long period of crisis in an extraordinarily weak position. They began it indeed with economies weakened as a result of policies that have been followed in most of them for many years. They began it with policies that were ill-adapted to insuring sustained growth under almost any conditions.

I would just like to emphasize that because I think it is important to keep in mind that while much of our attention is devoted to how to overcome the problem of debt and the crisis produced by the problem of debt, even if there were no debt problem there would still be a need for some basic changes in the economic policies of most Latin American countries.

I think that point is brought out very clearly in Mr. Bianchi's paper.

Now what need one to do about this? Well again, I think that he emphasizes, briefly but correctly, the key elements of change, the key areas where change has to be made.

Without trying to elaborate on them, because you wouldn't allow me to even if I wanted to or even if I could, these areas are first the need to redirect those economies to make them much more outward-oriented than they have been in the past. It is, as the paper points out, an extraordinary feature of Latin America that external trade contributes a very small proportion to gross domestic product. And it is an even more extraordinary feature that within their exports something like 75 percent (I think this is the figure quoted in the paper) consists of primary products.

If I were to have one small point of disagreement with the paper, I was a little bit surprised to see this fact attributed simply to the rich resource endowment of the countries. It is true that they are richly endowed, and therefore it is easy for them to have substantial exports of primary products. But it is also paradoxical that in the countries that also have a substantial industrial base, countries in which manufacturing industry contributes a very high proportion to total domestic product, that such an industrial base is so little reflected in their external trade. And I think one of the things that clearly needs to be done, as is brought out in the paper, is to move away from this extreme dependence on primary products and to develop the manufactured exports that are certainly possible in the Latin American countries.

Mr. Bianchi went on, of course, to tell us in addition to that, the countries need to do more to promote their domestic savings. I would subscribe very much to that. And also to increase the efficiency of their investments. No one can look at the capital output ratios in Latin America over the years without being struck by the fact that these countries have unfortunately in the past made ineffective use of the capital resources at their disposal. It also means, of course, that they therefore have the capacity to get much more out of available capital.

I would subscribe also to what Mr. Bianchi had to say about the need to redirect investment to try to address some of the problems of unemployment and poverty that are so endemic to Latin America.

Again, I think he is correct in saying that one of the problems of Latin American investment has been its extremely capital intensive nature, another way of saying its higher capital output ratios. Putting it in terms of capital intensity draws attention to the fact that the investments have been so predominantly those that have contributed little to employment and have therefore contributed much to un-employment which is so severe throughout the continent today.

These are certain areas where I think change is needed and where change is possible. How to bring that about? Well, he tells us to avoid the extremes, and not to be laissez-faire on one side. I would subscribe to that. I might be a little more on the laissez-faire side than he might be. I don't know.

I was struck at one point where he argues in his paper in favor of the use of selective policies. I am never quite sure what selective policies mean but I suspect they mean that governments know which industries to promote and which commodities to push. That would be very nice, I am sure. I am a little skeptical as to whether experience shows that most governments really know how to do this. But if we can find one that can, I for one would certainly be prepared to support it. I am a little skeptical as to whether I ever will find one. But never mind.

One point, however, on which I think I would differ from him a bit is that he put, particularly in his oral presentation, a great deal of emphasis on the adverse developments of 1986. I would certainly agree, they were very adverse. Whether this really means that the clock has been rolled back, I am less certain. If you look at Mr. Bianchi's Table 3 at the end of his paper, you will see this very interestingly. I think the worsening of the external situation in 1986 had very much to do with three things: one, oil; two, the problems, particularly of Argentina, with terms of trade; and third, Brazil.

I say that with due respect, but I would also say that just as Brazil got into serious trouble in 1986 with a catastrophic decline in its trade surplus, Brazil could almost as easily get back to a substantial trade surplus.

I would also say that oil prices are not quite as catastrophically low as they were. And that there is some reason to hope that the oil countries are improving their situation.

In addition to that, I would draw attention to the fact that in the oil countries themselves (Mexico is a good illustration of this), it is encouraging to see the extraordinary development of non-petroleum exports. Mexican non-petroleum exports rose last year by something like 32 percent. And this is, I think, an indication of the kinds of changes, the kinds of potential, that exist in Latin America.

But, again, let me just conclude that I thought the paper that we were given was an excellent one and one I certainly could subscribe to in very great measure.

Arjun Sengupta

Executive Director
International Monetary Fund

Messrs. Bianchi, Devlin, and Ramos have given in their stimulating paper a graphic description of the adjustment process in Latin America during the five years ending 1986. The paper is, however, not just a historical review of the recent Latin American experience, as it also provides an assessment of the prospects for growth-oriented adjustment in that region. That assessment, which is quite detailed, forming almost one third of the paper, is most illuminating and original. It is good that this paper has been presented at this symposium, particularly because of the unconventional way it has dealt with some of the conventional questions.

The Debt Crisis and Resource Transfer

The debt crisis was precipitated, according to the authors, by an abrupt cutback in the commercial bank lending since the second half of 1982, reversing its sustained upward trend between 1970 and 1981. This forced the Latin American countries to engage in a sharp recessionary adjustment to bring down the region's current account deficit of over $40 billion in 1981–82 to less than $0.2 billion in just two years. This was done despite a high level of factor payments of interest and profit of around $35 billion a year, double their average level in the four years preceding the crisis. Closing this deficit through severe import compression was costly to output, investment, employment, and living standards. The volume of exports expanded by 20 percent between 1981 and 1984, but because of a drastic fall in the prices of primary products, the value of exports remained virtually unchanged. The Latin American GDP actually fell in 1982–83, and fixed investment contracted by 30 percent, unable to meet even the replacement needs in several countries. There was a partial recovery of GDP in 1984–85 because of the acceleration of world trade and increase in U.S. imports, and a partial recovery of capital inflows. Mexico, Brazil, and Venezuela covered their interest payments with trade surpluses, and Argentina, Ecuador, and Peru covered nearly 60 percent of such payments. But the hope that this would lead to expansionary adjustment in the region was frustrated by mid-1985 by the slackening of international activity and a fall in the terms of trade despite the decline in international interest rates. This is the scenario of crises portrayed by the authors, who also point out that after receiving net resources from abroad of $13 billion a year on the average in 1978–81, Latin America transferred to the rest of the world $26 billion a year during 1982–86. The net transfer of resources to the rest of the world totaled over $130 billion in 1982–86.

The paper shows that scarcity of external financing and high interest costs, in the context of large outward transfer of resources, have severely limited the possibilities of launching a growth-oriented, structural adjustment process in these countries. The outward resource transfer from Latin America compares unfavorably with historically famous transfer cases, such as the war reparations effected by France in the 1870s after the Franco-Prussian War and Germany's payments to victorious nations after World War I. The real weight of

Latin American interest payments was high. If the London Interbank Offered Rate (LIBOR) is deflated by the dollar value of the debtors' exports, the annual average real rate of interest was as high as 17 percent during 1982–86.

The authors note that so long as the ratio of interest payments on debt to GDP is higher than the ratio of trade surplus to GDP, the problem cannot be resolved by "recessionary" adjustment. They advocate "expansive adjustment" in which the scarce foreign exchange is used to meet the import requirements necessary for minimum acceptable growth. Such an expansive adjustment would require adequate financing to provide the needed time for structural transformation to take full effect. It is not a question of trade-off between adjustment and external financing. The two are complementary—appropriate adjustment requires adequate financing. They emphasize the need to combine orthodox approach (export orientation and devaluation) with structural policies (industrialization and carefully chosen selective incentives) together with a more focused distributive effort. Clearly there will be agreement on the policy orientations that they advocate, but disagreements would likely emerge on the details, especially regarding the details of specific incentives and discriminating interventions.

Global Implications of Adjustment

I would like to concentrate on a few issues raised here which have global implications beyond Latin America. First, the authors rightly emphasize the accounting identity that interest payments from debtor countries require equivalent trade deficits in creditor countries or corresponding capital flows to debtors. This brings out the interdependence of the countries very clearly. If the banks extend no new lending and other capital flows are reduced, creditor countries can receive full interest repayments only if they give up protectionism, generate trade deficits, and increase imports from debtors. The alternative route of generating trade deficits in the OECD countries through a reduction of exports from these countries and a corresponding reduction of imports in the debtor countries harms everybody. Even the banks, which seem to gain immediately, suffer in the long run, because of general stagnation and the likelihood of debtors falling in default.

Management of their interdependence, I am afraid, does not admit any Adam Smithian solution. Policy coordination has to be organized, as uncoordinated policies harm everybody. International institutions have a clear role to play, particularly the Fund with its mandate for international surveillance. We in developing countries have repeatedly pointed out that this surveillance function is conducted highly asymmetrically—developing deficit countries that borrow are subjected to all the rigors of policy prescriptions, but the surplus industrial creditor countries have little compulsion to adjust. This was surely not the intention of the founding fathers of the Bretton Woods institutions, and today the need for the surplus countries to adjust has become even more important in view of the debt crisis.

Policy coordination to manage the adjustment of the surplus countries depends not just on technical issues, such as the choice of indicators and appropriate policy rules, which the Fund with its technical expertise can help to resolve. It basically depends on the political will to cooperate among the major industrial countries, which also to some extent, and only to some extent, the Fund can help to generate by working out the trade-offs, the costs and benefits of different options, and their implications for the sharing of the burden of adjustment among countries.

Role of the Fund

If the Fund can perform this role, it is not difficult to imagine that the Fund can also play an effective role in mobilizing the finance that is necessary to help the debtor countries to implement policies for adjustment with growth. The Fund has in the past played the role of a catalyst, but this, as the recent experience of the Mexican package shows, has *not* yielded satisfactory results. Perhaps the Fund has to have a role in debt consolidation, and even in debt forgiveness, apart from encouraging new net financial flows. The Fund could provide bridge finance by itself or in collaboration with other multilateral institutions. The main problem in discharging this task would be constraints on the Fund's own resources and the policy of access limits, which the Fund has imposed upon itself, even when it has no immediate problem of liquidity.

I was very much encouraged by the statement of the Managing Director indicating his determination to have the Fund play a major role in the international process of adjustment with growth. Nevertheless, as the international community settles down to cope with the problems of balance of payments adjustment with growth, it becomes increasingly clear that a number of conceptual cobwebs have to be cleared, some very complex issues have to be resolved, and a number of basic institutional reforms have to be introduced. I want to touch upon some of these problems.

Balance of Payments Adjustment with Growth

First is the concept of adjustment with growth—and the problems of reconciliation of the conventional Fund approach to balance of payments adjustment with the new paradigm—not so new to many of us—that such adjustment has to take place with growth.

Take the assertion about the "fundamental complementarity between adjustment and growth," which is the title of Mr. Guitián's paper in this symposium. According to the orthodox approach to the Fund programs, it means that adjustment is necessary for growth. Sometimes it also implies that adjustment is sufficient for growth. Contrast this to the argument that for many countries, and particularly developing countries, growth is necessary for adjustment. This argument is behind all the emphasis on supply-oriented policies. If adjustment means a sustained balance of payments viability, the supply of tradable goods must increase, and that cannot happen without an increase in productive capacity and a removal of the bottlenecks stemming from specific shortages that prevent the full use of the existing capacity. Both require growth. Even the distortions caused by policies, preventing the fuller utilization of capacity can be removed effectively only if their causes are removed. One must appreciate that the causes of these policy distortions are not always the stupidity of the policymakers but are most often introduced by the need for rationing scarce resources, for reconciling multiple objectives. Such policy distortions cannot be removed without creating the conditions that would allow policymakers to correct their policies. This would essentially require expanding the availability of such resources, so that they can be more rationally allocated among compiling claims, and growth is a necessary condition for that.

The argument that growth is necessary for adjustment should not be caricatured by saying that it means that the higher the growth, the better the adjustment. Everybody recognizes the constraints on optimal growth. Appropriate adjustment cannot take place without appropriate growth, and adjustment policies that detract from growth and contract output cannot produce viable adjustment.

Demand-Management and Supply-Augmenting Policies

An implication of this is that demand-management policies alone cannot produce such adjustment in developing countries, because the balance of payments problems in these countries are rarely the result only of excess demand. Maybe in a full employment economy or in a mythical economy where all prices are fully flexible, all resources are fully mobile, and all markets are instantaneously cleared, this would work, but not in a developing country as we know. It does not mean there should be no control over demand, but it means that policies should be emphasized that stimulate the growth of supplies.

Such supply-augmenting policies take time to fructify. Even the exchange rate policy, which the Fund makes often, and sometimes rightly, the centerpiece of policy advice, takes time to yield its "switching" effects through which supply-side adjustments take place. There is a J-curve effect of exchange rate changes in developing countries, though not for the same reason as in industrial countries. There would normally be a period of time during which the deficits actually increase and would have to be financed. This is true for most supply-oriented policies. Deficits during the period these policies take to produce their effect have to be financed. The longer the period of such adjustment, the longer the period for which finance should be provided and the larger would be the amount of finance needed.

Two conclusions derive from this perception of the balance of payments problems of developing countries. First is that finance and adjustment are not substitutes, but are complements. It is no longer a question of more adjustment and less finance; it is more adjustment and more finance. Second, and for the Fund particularly important, appropriate adjustment requires longer period of finance.

Let me dwell on both points. If excess demand were the cause of payments deficit, only adjustment with demand-management policies would have been sufficient, requiring not much finance except for meeting specific shortages to remove frictions, as the demand policies usually take a short period to fructify. Since the deficits are supposed to equilibrate with the normal level of autonomous capital flows, external finance is basically needed to supplement these flows if they temporarily fall short of their normal or "trend" level. In a purely excess-demand situation, more finances would arguably tend to sustain such excess demand and so would hamper adjustment. This would not be the case, however, if the situation is not purely of excess demand. A current account imbalance, ex post, always shows up as domestic absorption exceeding domestic output; but if the corrective policy leans more toward increasing output and not so much toward decreasing absorption—at best maintaining a constraint on absorption—it would require more finances to support that policy. The normal level of capital flows would also be difficult to estimate. The level cannot be based on the projection of the past trend, because if the program succeeds in producing adjustment with growth, autonomous capital flows should also increase in the future. So the current shortfall of resources that have to be compensated by external finance to help payments equilibrium to work itself out would have to be calculated not from a normal level of capital flows based on past trends but from higher level consistent with sustained growth. We cannot avoid this problem by saying that the market would have foreseen this development and therefore would have supplied the additional capital. The market does not work this way for developing countries whose exposure to the capital market is low for a variety of factors (and not just information). More important, improved growth prospects would not materialize if appropriate growth-oriented adjustment policies are not adopted, and they cannot be adopted if adequate finance is not available. If the required finance is made available by the Fund or some other international institution, the appropriate policies can be followed in turn which would increase the inflow of external finance.

The second problem is more tricky. If the policies are basically supply oriented, they will take time to work out—the more under-developed the economy, the longer the time they usually take—and during that period the deficits have to be financed. So the financing available from the Fund cannot be for a very short period, and may have to be stretched over a number of years. The Fund seems reluctant to extend its lending period beyond 1–2 years to be repaid between 3–5 years—the normal stand-by arrangements. The Extended Financing Facility introduced in mid-70s involving disbursements over 3 years, and repayment between maximum 4–10 years has fallen into disuse, with only one such program being allowed between 1984 and 1986.

Monetary Character of the Fund and Repayment of Fund Loans

The reluctance to use this facility is based on an interpretation of "the monetary and revolving character of the institution," whose Articles provide for adopting adequate "safeguards" to allow "temporary use" of its resources by the members. It is necessary to look into this question carefully, and more academic work needs to be done to define the appropriate role of a monetary institution and the nature of a revolving fund, and differentiate it properly from a developmental institution. Peter Kenen's latest Brookings Institution volume is a major contribution in this direction. I may also refer to the paper by Sidney Dell in *World Development* to show that at the time of the Bretton Woods conference there was a strong American position, supported by Keynes, that stabilization often needed long-term finance and the international institution concerned with problems of stabilization should be prepared to offer such finance.

One would have thought that the revolving nature of a monetary institution depends on the prospect that the loans made by it are repaid with interest and that the interest should reflect the opportunity cost of its funds. If repayments are assured, and the monies actually revolve, this institution can only face temporary liquidity problems, which may arise mainly from a mismatch of flows of funds, and not from the period of repayment.

The problem really boils down to the prospects of repayment. If the adjustment programs are successful and produce a viable balance of payments outcome, there should be no problem of repayment. So the first "safeguard" for the "temporary" use should be designing the adjustment program appropriately so that the borrowers are able to repay at the right time. Even if the balance of payments adjustment results in a payments surplus but is accompanied by a contraction of output, the surplus position may not be viable and the sustained ability to repay by the country may be in question, especially if the

Fund loan is only one part of a larger liability of the country. So it is possible to argue that an adequate amount of finance is not only more likely to produce appropriate balance of payments adjustment consistent with growth, it is also more likely to ensure its repayment, and thus better protect the revolving character of the Fund than would a smaller or inadequate amount of finance.

In fact, in the original design of the Fund, its lending was not subjected to a fixed repayment schedule. It may be worthwhile to revive that flexibility in the repayment obligation to the Fund, which would normally be a fraction of a borrowing country's total external payments. Indeed, such repayment obligations may be linked to a country's ability to repay, and it may be agreed between the Fund and the borrowing member that its repayment schedule is linked with, say, a proportion of the country's export earnings, according to a projection of exports based on the past trends or used in the baseline scenario of the Fund program. If actual exports exceeded the projected exports, then this repayment could be accelerated. If exports turned out to be less than this projected level, then obligations should be automatically rescheduled or capitalized according to a predetermined formula. This would be in the spirit of helping the country to plan its policies of adjustment. If the policies are right, there is no reason why money lent would not revolve.

There is one problem in this scheme. If the adjusting country meets with an exogenous shock because of factors beyond its control, causing a fall in exports despite all its adjustment efforts, its repayments will have to be postponed. If this happens to a large number of Fund borrowers, at the same time, the Fund may suddenly encounter a liquidity problem. A provision has to be made so that the Fund can overcome this liquidity shortage.

A financial institution can of course face temporary liquidity problems. If it does, it normally borrows from other financial institutions to tide over the situation. A similar approach may be adopted for the Fund also, especially because when some of its members face deficits, some other members must be facing surpluses. This means that in a liquidity squeeze, the Fund should be automatically entitled to borrow from these surplus countries. In practice, this would mean activating the General Arrangements to Borrow (GAB) at the discretion of the Fund and not as at present dependent upon the agreement of the GAB lender.

The Fund is not a commercial bank; it is an international cooperative institution to facilitate an orderly development of the international monetary system. The benefit of this orderly development accrues to all membership, including the creditor countries, which should lend to the Fund not in the expectation of normal commercial returns but because of the value they attach to such benefit of orderly international development. If this principle is accepted, the operation of the Fund should focus on the appropriate management of the world economy to the benefit of all the participants and not on protecting the narrow commercial interest of the Fund as a financial institution.

Comment

Salvatore Zecchini

Executive Director
International Monetary Fund

Since the papers presented in this session have already been discussed in detail, I can approach the subject under examination in a broader perspective. The subject basically concerns the role that macroeconomic policies should play in reconciling external adjustment with a satisfactory rate of economic growth. The starting point is the experience of many indebted developing countries since the beginning of the 1980s together with the approach followed by the Fund so far in supporting these countries.

To understand the terms of this issue, it is essential to reflect on both the macroeconomic policies and their objectives. The policies under consideration aim at affecting macroeconomic aggregates related to the demand or expenditure side of the economy, a realm in which the Fund has exercised its competence and addressed its recommendations. The supply side, the productive sectors, the factors of production, and the structure of the markets have traditionally been at the margins of Fund conditionality and have been drawn into adjustment programs only when the expected results of macroeconomic policies failed to materialize. Several of these policies are, however, at the core of the World Bank's approach and recommendations, and where both institutions have intervened, the economies of these countries have been influenced by both macroeconomic policies and structural measures.

The objective of external adjustment lends itself to different interpretations. Adjustment may refer to the correction of a transitory excess of domestic investment over the total saving made available at home and from abroad. Adjustment may equally refer to the correction of the level of domestic demand, and particularly of imports, in the face of a prolonged worsening of the terms of trade or of the structural capacity to generate foreign exchange earnings.

In the 1980s both notions of adjustment apply to the economic and balance of payments conditions of most developing countries. As shown in the paper by Mr. Bianchi and others, in 1982–84 adjustment was pursued on the understanding that the causes of the imbalances were transitory and amendable over a short period. It should be recognized that now most of these causes appear permanent and consequently the adjustment has to be structural in nature. These causes are basically adverse shifts in the external terms of trade and the excess of real interest rates over the growth rate of real output. Today, both these factors, coupled with inadequate prospects of expansion of external demand, have made exorbitant a level of external debt, which was already high at the beginning of the 1980s. This is the result if the debt level is compared with the actual capacity of these economies to service their debt by transferring resources abroad on a net basis in the second half of the 1980s and perhaps in the 1990s. Current debt levels include a part of debt which is not in line with the present fundamentals of these economies. This part did not exist, but to a minor extent, in the light of the fundamentals of the 1970s.

The realization of this basic truth has, in turn, given rise to the discontinuation of spontaneous lending by the banking community and to the banks' insistence that the debtor enter into Fund-supported adjustment programs in the hope of rapid adjustment. This hope is unwarranted, however, as the Fund's standard approach to adjustment seems unsuitable to deal with structural adjustment. Today it is unrealistic to expect that developing economies, after the adjustments in 1982–84, can continue to transfer resources abroad on a net basis in an effort to balance their current accounts by reducing their standards of living. If the present capacity of indebted developing countries to service debt persists, their adjustment efforts can aim only at a more restricted servicing of debt that excludes the part that represents a structural excess of debt. Such structural excess over debt capacity has to be spread over many years and serviced on concessional terms, as long as the fundamental determinants of the capacity to service debt do not improve. To estimate the structural part of the debt overhang, rational indicators can be used that take into account prolonged shifts in the terms of trade, the new relationship between real rates of interest and growth, the disappointing prospects for expansion of world trade, and the degree of adjustment that can be achieved without cutting into per capita income levels.

As far as growth is concerned, Professor Fischer's paper recalls the wide variety of growth strategies ranging from laissez-faire to intervention. There is also a wide range of growth processes, most of which rely on capital accumulation, technical progress, productivity rises, and expansion of overall demand and markets. No optimal strategy for growth exists that can be applied to any country. The best approach to growth has to be predicated on the initial conditions and structural constraints of the individual country. Moreover, growth does not imply a transitory flare-up of economic activity which will soon die down, but involves raising the output level in the long term and, if possible, establishing a sustainable rate of output expansion.

Having defined the extent of the adjustment, the possibilities for growth and the appropriate macroeconomic instruments, we must look to some highly controversial basic issues. First, are macroeconomic policies appropriate for growth identical to policies appropriate for adjustment? So far the Fund has tended to consider the two sets of macro-policies as roughly identical. The Fund's philosophy, as confirmed by the paper by Mr. Guitián, holds that there is no real trade-off between adjustment and growth, defined as a sustainable increase in output and pace of economic activity. Adjustment has to take priority over growth since, once adjustment has been completed, growth will ensue more or less automatically because adjustment policies "typically promote efficiency in resource use."

This line of approach is very close to international monetarism which, as Professor Fischer has pointed out, is not concerned with

growth policies. Specifically, a combination of macroeconomic stabilization with liberalization measures is thought to be adequate to
restore growth. Hence, we often find in the Fund the simple attitude
of recommending that liberalization be accelerated and the economy
be opened to foreign competition. Undoubtedly these measures have
the advantage of quickly pointing out shortcomings in domestic
policies. Such an approach fails, however, to recognize that the
avenues to growth are multiple and the choice among them has to
be based on the structural features and constraints of an economy
and on its need to grow. In many developing countries, thin and
imperfect markets cannot perform the role that many advocate for
them. Moreover, the successful strategies pursued by Japan, Korea,
the Taiwan Province of China, and other newly industrialized countries in recent decades have been centered on export promotion and
import substitution through protection of domestic markets, and this
casts doubt about the extent to which liberalism has been applied in
these economies and has been the engine for their success.

More generally, I am of the opinion that despite some overlap the
two sets of macroeconomic policies for adjustment and growth do
not coincide. Consequently, a general case for assigning absolute
priority to adjustment policies over growth policies is not warranted.
Neither does a specific case seem warranted today to give priority to
adjustment in those countries that have already adjusted the cyclical
part of their deficit but not the part attributable to the structural debt
overhang.

The challenge that developing countries and the Fund have to face
is how to combine macroeconomic policies for adjustment with those
for growth. Any measure for adjustment necessarily involves reducing
absorption while most growth strategies imply switching production
and expenditure as well as expanding demand. To reconcile the two
objectives, the country has to select the policies which are best suited
to reduce absorption while increasing output, so as to leave some
resources for upgrading income standards. Evidently, this implies an
adequate expansion of aggregate demand since without it adjustment
and expenditure switching become extremely costly and consequently
impracticable. Success in these efforts also depends on the macroeconomic and trade policies pursued in the major world economies,
and ample room is still left for a better coordination in these fields
on a worldwide scale.

In reconciling adjustment with growth, a second basic issue comes to the fore. What relative importance has to be attached to macroeconomic and to microeconomic measures? In my opinion macroeconomic adjustment can create only the general conditions appropriate to promote fixed investment, to maximize sources of domestic savings, to preserve price stability, and to enhance external competitiveness. These measures, however, are not sufficient to generate economic growth if they are not complemented by corrections and improvements at the microeconomic level. Microeconomic intervention must focus particularly on the functioning of markets, both for production and for production factors, on the price structure and price formation, on the system of subsidies, and on the development of financial markets.

The third basic issue is whether to reduce government's intervention to a minimum or to rationalize this intervention. As Professor Fischer's contribution has shown, the issue is not of liberalization versus interventionism, but to decide the appropriate degree of liberalization or of its reciprocal, intervention. Every economy, even the most successful, has shown a measure of intervention that has been justified in principle with the need to correct market imperfections. In fact, in some countries intervention has become so pervasive as to distort the economic processes, as Mr. Bianchi's paper seems to indicate for Latin America. The optimal degree of intervention must be decided in the light of the structural and institutional characteristics of the country. Nevertheless, Mr. Bianchi's suggestion of limiting intervention to a few simple rules can be accepted as long as excessive emphasis on sectoral over general measures is avoided. In this respect, balancing macroeconomic aggregates is an inescapable condition of any economic process, whether it is directed to external adjustment or to growth.

Another basic issue a developing country has to face is whether to use a shock treatment or gradualism. Professor Fischer correctly states that the choice between the two alternatives "turns on economic and political economy considerations." (The availability of external financing is to be recalled, however.) In the adjustment programs supported by the Fund, gradualism is almost a blasphemous word. In the Fund's philosophy adjustment has to be accomplished in a limited number of years: by the time of the first repurchase, that is, 4½ years, the balance of payments position has to be such as to allow an easy servicing of all external debt. If this is not considered achievable on the basis of the authorities' intended policies, the Fund cannot support the country and, because of the Fund's catalytic role, the support of the entire financing community might be withheld. Nevertheless, in several cases it is evident that the causes of external imbalances are such as to require longer periods for their corrections. The Fund recognized this problem by introducing the Structural Adjustment Facility in 1986, but its scope is relatively limited compared with the size of the problem. A strengthening and a widening of the facility seems necessary.

There is no room for embarking on a taxonomy of macroeconomic policies that are optimal for ensuring that adjustment is compatible with economic growth. Two examples related to fiscal and exchange rate policy must suffice. On fiscal policy, it is evident that any stabilization effort has to involve a reduction of the net claims of the public sector on the resources provided by the other sectors. But not every deficit reduction measure has the same impact on output growth both in the short and long run. Hence the country has to search for expenditure or revenue measures that can encourage the growth durably. For instance, a restructuring of public expenditure or of the tax system might be required. Unfortunately, these corrections are often disregarded by the authorities, if not clearly resisted because of their political implications.

On exchange policy, exchange rate adjustment is a powerful and necessary incentive to switching output toward tradables. It has been shown, however, that for developing countries whose exports are heavily concentrated in few primary products collective depreciation of their currencies may fail to produce the expected boost to exports inasmuch as higher export volumes will be offset by lower unit values.

In conclusion, the challenge that lies ahead for the developing countries as well as for the Fund is to select among the various combinations of macroeconomic policies for external adjustment the one that is most beneficial for a continuing expansion of the economy. The result of this policy choice will not contradict the basic macro-economic identities of the Fund stabilization philosophy but will add to it the new dimension of a higher social welfare.

SESSION 4

Outward Versus Inward Policies

Outward Orientation: Trade Issues

Jagdish Bhagwati
Professor of Economics
Columbia University

This session addresses the question of outward-oriented growth. There are two aspects of the question that need to be distinguished: the wisdom of adopting a strategy of outward-oriented trade policy and the problems of transitting to this strategy if a country is not already embracing it. I shall focus mainly on the wisdom of adopting such policies since the companion paper by Professor Sachs addresses the transitional questions that raise, in many cases, issues of macroeconomic and exchange rate policy.

Components of an Outward-Oriented Trade Strategy

The question of the wisdom of an outward-oriented ("export-promoting" (EP))[1] strategy may be considered to have been settled. The strategy has been demonstrated in numerous studies to have produced not merely rapid export growth but also rapid economic growth. It has also, over the last few years, become an accepted component of conditionality from the World Bank and from some bilateral donors since conditionality generally follows the triumph of certain trends in economic thinking instead of being capricious or ideological.[2]

---

[1] Throughout this paper, outward-oriented and EP strategies will be referred to interchangeably.

[2] Aid conditionality reflected in the 1950s the dominance of the Harrod-Domar type of thinking. Since that model basically related growth to investment, with the productivity of investment (in the shape of the capital-output ratio) taken as technologically given by the composition of output, the performance of the aid recipient was measured simply by how much was done to raise the contribution of domestic savings to domestic investment. Hence, savings performance, and therefore tax effort, became

In economics, consensus is produced by sharpening differences; in politics, by obfuscating them. Much of the debate over the merits of the outward-oriented strategy is the result of different conceptions of what that strategy is; these need to be clarified if we are to illuminate the issues and convince the few skeptics of its merits.

The outward-oriented trade (or EP) strategy, as defined by international economists, has little to do with "export-led" growth or with customary decompositions (e.g., by Professor Chenery and his associates) of output growth from identities into elements attributed to "export-growth" and "import-substitution."[3] It is rather a matter of setting price incentives in such a fashion as to ensure that the home market does not become more lucrative than the foreign market.

The commonly accepted price-incentives definition of the outward-oriented trade strategy is that the effective exchange rate for the country's exports (EER_x) is less than for its imports (EER_m). These effective exchange rates measure the incentives to export and to substitute for exports, respectively.[4] For, if $EER_x < EER_m$, this implies that sale in the home market produces more revenues than sale

---

the key elements of conditionality. By now, it is well known that investment is a necessary, but not a sufficient, condition for developmental success. Conditionality has thus moved on to include questions of efficiency in use of resources, which brings into the picture the question of outward orientation, in turn. Cf. Jadish Bhagwati, *Wealth and Poverty*, Vol. 1 of *Essays in Development Economics*, ed. by Gene Grossman (Oxford: Basil Blackwell, 1985), Chapter 1.

[3] These decompositions are essentially just descriptions, and the attribution of causality and explanation based thereon (e.g., export growth "led to" so much of the output expansion), while common, is to be avoided.

[4] The EER_x, as international trade economists have long used the concept, is simply the domestic currency acquired per unit of foreign exchange earned, taking into account not just the parity but also adding subsidies and subtracting duties, and the like. Identically, EER_m is the domestic currency that must be paid, taking all pertinent duties, subsidies, and other charges into account, to acquire a unit of foreign exchange. As such, the macroeconomists' use of the phrase "effective exchange rate" is different, insofar as their usage simply deflates the parity by the domestic price level. This latter usage is basically inadequate since, in many developing countries, duties, subsidies, and other subventions and charges are important, and concentrating on the parity is not enough. For this purpose, the Bhagwati-Krueger National Bureau of Economic Research (NBER) Project defined the added concept $PLDEER$, that is, price-level-deflated EER, to get at the appropriate concept that macroeconomists should use. Cf. J. Bhagwati, *The Anatomy and Consequences of Exchange Control Regimes* (Cambridge, Massachusetts: Ballinger, 1978), and A. Krueger, *Liberalization Attempts and Consequences* (Cambridge, Massachusetts: Ballinger, 1978).

abroad, so that the price incentives are, on balance, set such that there is a "bias against exports."

Outward orientation then implies a trade-and-payments regime that ensures that this bias against exports is reversed or absent, such that EER_x is no longer below EER_m. Hence, many trade economists identify the outward-oriented, EP strategy as one that broadly ensures $EER_x \simeq EER_m$, and is therefore synonymous with "neutrality" of relative incentives for home and export sales. On the other hand, a significant excess of EER_x over EER_m may also obtain: a phenomenon described sometimes, to avoid terminological confusion, as ultra-EP strategy.[5]

A few classifications are in order, to clear up the confusions over what an EP trade strategy implies.

First, the definitions relate to average incentives. Within the EP strategy, some activities may be import substituting in the sense that their EER_m exceeds the average EER_x. The pursuit of either the EP or ultra-EP trade strategy does not preclude import substituting in selected sectors. This is, in fact, true for most of the successful Far Eastern developers. Nor does this fact render meaningless the distinction among the different trade strategies, as is sometimes contended. As I have argued elsewhere,

> We also need to remember always that the average EER_x and EER_m can and do conceal very substantial variations among different exports and among different imports. In view of this fact, I have long emphasized the need to distinguish between the questions of the degree of import substitution and the pattern of import substitution. Thus, within the broad aggregates of an EP country case, there may well be activities that are being import-substituted (i.e., their EER_m exceeds the average EER_x). Indeed there often are. But one should not jump to the erroneous conclusion that there is therefore no way to think of EP versus import substitution (IS) and that the distinction is an artificial one — any more than one would refuse to acknowledge that the Sahara is a desert, whereas Sri Lanka is not, simply because there are some oases.[6]

---

[5] Cf. J. Bhagwati, "Export Promoting Trade Strategy: Issues and Evidence," VPERS Report No. 7, World Bank, October 1986.

[6] J. Bhagwati, "Rethinking Trade Strategy," in *Development Strategies Reconsidered*, ed. by John Lewis and Valeriana Kallab (Washington: Overseas Development Council, 1986).

Second, one should not equate the EP strategy with the absence of government intervention, as is often done by proponents of IS strategy and sometimes by advocates of the EP strategy as well. It is true that a laissez-faire policy would satisfy the requirement that $EER_x \simeq EER_m$. On the other hand, this is not a necessary condition for this outcome. In fact, the Far Eastern economies (with the exception of Hong Kong) and others that have come close to the EP strategy have been characterized by considerable government activity in the economic system. Such intervention can be of great value, and almost certainly has been so, in making the EP strategy work successfully. This is because credibility of commitment on the part of governments is necessary to induce investors to take decisions that reflect the inducements offered by the policy framework. By publicly supporting the outward-oriented strategy, by even bending in some cases towards ultra-export promoting, and by gearing the credit institutions to support export activities overtly, governments in these countries appear to have established the necessary confidence that their commitment to the EP strategy is serious, thus inducing firms to undertake costly investments and programs to take advantage of the EP strategy. The laissez-faire model does not quite capture this aspect of the problem since its proponents implicitly assume that the policy of laissez-faire will be accepted at face value. But neither the establishment nor the continuation of laissez-faire is a realistic assumption since governments, except in the models of Friedman and Bakunin, fail to abstain or self-destruct; they will find invariably something, indeed much, to do. Therefore, explicit commitment to an activist, supportive role in pursuit of the EP strategy would appear to constitute a definite advantage in reaping its benefits.

Third, the incentives-defined EP strategy has to be distinguished from the traditional concept of "export-led" growth with which it is often confused. Export-led growth relates to a situation in which external growth, owing to income effects centered on a country's exports, generates income expansion attributable to direct gains from trade and indirect beneficial effects. On the other hand, it is evident that the incentives-related EP definition has nothing to do with such beneficial external phenomena. Whether the success of an EP strategy, defined in terms of freedom from bias against exports, requires the presence of a beneficial external environment is an important issue discussed below in light of the current international environment.

Fourth, the concept of EP or outward orientation relates to trade incentives (as defined by either trade policies directly or by domestic policies that influence trade or by exchange rate policies that have consequences for trade) but does not imply that the EP strategy countries must be equally outward oriented in regard to their foreign investment policies. As it happens, Hong Kong and Singapore among the four Far Eastern economies have been more favorable in their treatment of foreign investors than the great majority of the IS countries, though the historic growth of Japan, presumably as an EP country, was characterized by extremely selective control on the entry of foreign investment. Logically and empirically, the two types of outward orientation, in trade and in foreign investment, are therefore distinct phenomena, though whether one can exist efficiently without the other has been raised in the literature and is surrounded by far more controversy than the question of the desirability of an EP strategy in trade.

Finally, the pattern of incentives, defining the relative attractions of the home and foreign markets, is a result of not just trade but also exchange rate policies. An overvalued exchange rate, by making foreign exchange scarce (i.e., creating an excess demand for it at the given exchange rate) and hence allocated by administrative allotments, will lead to a scarcity premium on imports and hence to $EER_m > EER_x$, that is, to bias against exports. In fact, much of the inward-oriented or import-substituting trade strategy during the bulk of the postwar period can be attributed to the effects of overvalued exchange rates rather than to the use of tariffs to protect import-competing industries. The macroeconomic management of payments accounts in a manner that permits the avoidance of overvaluation and attendant exchange or import controls is essential to the pursuit of an outward-oriented trade strategy.

Benefits of Outward-Oriented Trade Strategy

By now, most developmental experts agree that an outward-oriented trade strategy promises economic benefits, even though this consensus emerged after considerable controversy and the eventual demonstration effect of successful countries on the outward strategy and failure of those continuously wedded to an inward course. Nonetheless, the recent return of the export pessimists, who in the

1950s provided the intellectual backbone for the IS strategy, has rekindled skepticism on the question of the desirability of outward trade orientation. This second pessimism, as I shall argue below, has an altogether different basis, in the threat of protectionist closure of access to foreign markets and will require an assessment of this threat in terms necessarily characterized by considerations of political economy. It also necessitates a brief recapitulation of what we have learnt about the sources of the EP strategy's success in promoting economic development.

Empirical Findings

Several studies, conducted as large-scale comparative projects of diverse countries, examined the question of the relationship between trade strategy and economic performance and concluded in the 1970s that the EP strategy comes out the winner.[7] In particular, the evidence on this issue is strong in the NBER project, where the EP strategy was clearly defined in terms of incentives in the way set out above and transition to it from an IS strategy via several phases was systematically discussed for ten semi-industrial countries.[8]

Other evidence relates largely to associations between growth rates of exports and growth rates of income, as in the work of Michaely (1977), who used data for 1950–73 for 41 countries, and the further extension of this type of work by Balassa (1978) and Feder (1983).[9]

Complementing this approach is the altogether different statistical formulation in Michalopoulos and Jay (1973). This study takes a different approach to the problem by using exports as an argument in estimating an economy-wide production function from aggregate

---

[7] The chief studies were directed by Little, Scitovsky, and Scott (1970) at the Organization for Economic Cooperation and Development (OECD), Balassa (1971) at the World Bank, Bhagwati (1978) and Krueger (1978) at the National Bureau of Economic Research (NBER) in the United States, and Donges (1976) at the Kiel Institute in Germany. Complementing and overlapping each other, these studies represent a massive analysis of the central question that has preoccupied development economists from the very beginning of the discipline.

[8] See the synthesis volumes by Bhagwati (1978) and Krueger (1978).

[9] Krueger's synthesis also contains similar cross-country regressions for the ten semi-industrial countries in the NBER project. See the extensive review in Lal and Rajapatirana (1986).

output and factor-use data. Using data for 39 countries, this study argued that exports are an independent input into national income.[10]

While these cross-country regressions are certainly interesting, valuable, and suggestive, they cannot be considered compelling on this issue. By contrast, the detailed country studies are indeed methodologically superior and more persuasive. And, as noted already, they do indicate the superiority of the EP strategy.

Explanatory Factors

The reasons why the IS strategy has been generally dominated by the EP strategy, and why the countries that rapidly made the transition from the former to the latter have done better, have preoccupied economists since these findings came to light.

Resource Allocation Efficiency

The first set of reasons relies on the fact that the EP strategy brings incentives for domestic resource allocation closer to international opportunity costs and hence, as international economists recognize, closer to what will generally produce efficient outcomes.[11]

This is true, not merely in the sense that there is no bias against exports and in favor of the home market (i.e., $EER_x \simeq EER_m$) under the EP strategy, whereas often the researchers have observed a substantial excess of EER_m over EER_x in the IS countries. It is also valid in the sense that the IS countries seem generally to have had a chaotic dispersion of EERs among the different activities within the

---

[10] Balassa's (1978) re-estimation of Michaely-type regressions also incorporates the Michalopoulos-Jay approach, thus combining the two methodologies under one rubric.

[11] Factors that lead to improved efficiency and hence to income improvement need not necessarily lead to sustained higher growth rates. Thus, in the Harrod-Domar model, where labor supply is slack, a once-for-all improvement in efficiency will indeed translate into a permanent higher growth rate of income, but not so in the steady state in the Solow model where the growth rate is determined by the growth rate of labor and the rate of technical change. Over the medium-run periods, however, for which the discussion in the text is couched, and for which we are explaining growth rates of over two or three decades, these subtleties are not particularly relevant. Moreover, it is important to note that, for any given growth rate, a more efficient economic regime will require less savings (and hence less blood, sweat, and tears) to sustain it than a less efficient economic regime.

broader categories of export and import-competing activities as well. That is, the degree of IS goes far and the pattern of IS reflects widely divergent incentives. By contrast, the EP strategy does better on both degree and on pattern.

The interesting further question relates to why the degree becomes outsized and the pattern also goes wrong under IS. The answer seems to lie in the way in which IS is often practiced and in the constraints that surround EP. IS could, in principle, be contained to modest excess of EER_m over EER_x, but, as I have already argued, typically IS arises in the context of overvalued exchange rates and associated exchange controls. So, there is no way in which the excess of domestic over foreign prices is being tracked by government agencies in most cases, and the excesses of EER_m over EER_x simply go unnoticed. The nontransparency is fatal. By contrast, EP typically tends to constrain itself to rough equality, and ultra-EP also seems to be moderate in practice, because policy-induced excesses of EER_x over EER_m would generally require subsidization that is constrained by budgetary problems.

In the same way, the pattern of EER_m can be terribly chaotic because exchange controls and quota restrictions on trade will typically generate differential premia and hence differential degrees of implied protection of thousands of import-competing activities, all of which are simply the side consequence of the administrative decisions on exchange allocations. By contrast, the EP strategy will rely more on unifying exchange rates that avoid these problems and, when relying on export subsidization, will be handled both with necessary transparency and with budgetary constraints that would then prevent IS-type spectacular dispersions in resulting $EERs$.

Directly Unproductive Profit-Seeking (DUP) and Rent-Seeking Activities

Yet another important aspect of the difference between EP and IS strategies, once we recognize that IS regimes have typically arisen in the context of exchange rate overvaluation and associated controls on foreign exchange and trade, is that this kind of regime is more likely to trigger what economic theorists now call DUP (Bhagwati, 1982b) and rent-seeking activities (Krueger, 1974). These activities divert resources from productive use into unproductive but profitable activities designed to earn profits (or income) by lobbying to change policies, or by evading them, or by seeking the revenue and rents they generate.[12]

With IS policies typically conducted within the framework of quantitative allocation systems, the diversion of entrepreneurial energies and real resources into such DUP activities tends to add to the conventionally measured losses from the high degree and chaotic pattern of IS.

How important are such DUP-activity costs? Attempts have been made by several economists to estimate some aspects of these costs in developing countries. Krueger (1974), in her classic article, estimated the costs of license-seeking in Turkey, assuming that it cost one Turkish lira in real resources to chase one lira worth of premium on these licenses, producing staggering estimates of the resulting losses relative to Turkish national income! Recently, computable-general-equilibrium (CGE) practitioners, such as Dervis, de Melo, Whalley, and Robinson, have incorporated DUP activities into the corpus of their work, emerging again with noticeable estimates that exceed the conventional, small deadweight losses.[13] Nevertheless, this area of analysis is still new, and micro studies that would provide more realistic foundations to enable these economists to make reliable parametric estimates of DUP-activity costs of different kinds to work into their CGE exercises are still lacking.

There is, however, plenty of casual evidence that evasion and rent seeking (directed at licenses), among other DUP activities, are rampant in many developing countries and absorb significant resources.

Foreign Investment

If IS regimes have tended to use domestic resources inefficiently in the ways that were just outlined, the same applies to the use of foreign resources.

This is perhaps self-evident, but substantial theoretical work by Bhagwati, Brecher and Diaz-Alejandro, Uzawa, Hamada, and others has established that foreign investment that comes in over quota restrictions and tariffs—the so-called tariff-jumping investment—is

---

[12] See Bhagwati and Srinivasan (1983, Chapter 30) for a taxonomy of such activities.
[13] Cf. Dervis, de Melo, and Robinson (1981) and Grais, de Melo, and Urata (1986).

capable of placing the recipient country under conditions that seem uncannily close to the conditions in the IS countries in the postwar decades. These conditions require capital flows into capital-intensive sectors in the protected activities. It is thus plausible that, if these inflows were not actually harmful, the social returns on them were at least low compared to what they would be in the EP countries in which the inflows were not tariff jumping but rather aimed at world markets, in line with the EP strategy of the recipient countries.

In addition, one may hypothesize (Bhagwati (1978)) that, ceteris paribus, foreign investments into IS countries will be self-limiting in the long run because they are aimed at and therefore constrained by the home market. If so, and there seems to be some preliminary evidence in support of this hypothesis in econometric analysis,[14] then IS countries would have been handicapped also by the lower amount of foreign investment flows and not just by their lower social productivity compared with the EP countries.

Grey Area Dynamic Effects

While the arguments so far provide ample satisfaction to those who seek to understand why the EP strategy does so well, dissatisfaction has continued to be expressed that these are arguments of static efficiency and that "dynamic" factors, such as savings and innovations, may well be favorable under IS.

Of course, if what we are seeking to explain is the relative success of the EP countries with growth, this counter-argumentation makes little sense since, even if it were true, the favorable effects from these "grey area" sources of dynamic efficiency would have been outweighed in practice by the static-efficiency aspects. The fact remains, however, that while in the NBER project which was the only one of the major projects on trade strategy to address these questions in some fashion, the results were generally not clearcut on the issue,[15]

---

[14] See the discussion in Balasubramanian (1984) and in Bhagwati (1986a). In private communication, Mr. Balasubramanian has provided further results on this hypothesis.

[15] See, in particular, the extensive analysis of this question in the NBER synthesis volume by Bhagwati (1978) where some chapters are specifically addressed to summarizing and evaluating these kinds of arguments with the aid of the findings in the ten country studies as also extraneous evidence and argumentation on these subjects.

recent studies have generally strengthened the case for EP strategy on some issues here as well.

It is impossible to claim that IS regimes enable a country to save more or less than EP regimes. The evidence in the NBER project, for instance, went both ways.[16] Little has changed since then by way of new evidence. Nor does it seem possible to maintain in theory that EP or IS regimes are necessarily more innovative. It is possible to argue that EP regimes may lead to more competition and less sheltered markets and hence more innovation. But equally, Schumpeterian arguments suggest that the opposite might also be true.

Recent studies, however, suggest that the EP strategy encourages greater innovation. Thus, Krueger and Tuncer (1980) have examined the 18 Turkish manufacturing industries during the 1963–76 period. They found that periods of low productivity growth roughly occurred during periods when foreign exchange controls were particularly restrictive and hence the IS strategy was being accentuated. The overall rate of productivity growth was also low throughout the period during which Turkey pursued an IS strategy.

Again, in an analysis of productivity change in Korea, Turkey, Yugoslavia, and Japan, Nishimizu and Robinson (1984) argue that if growth is decomposed into that attributable to domestic demand expansion, export expansion, and import substitution, the inter-industrial variation in factor productivity growth reflects (except for Japan) the relative roles of export expansion and import substitution, the former causing a positive impact and the latter a negative one. This careful and important research is certainly suggestive, but, as the authors recognize, export expansion may have been caused by productivity change rather than the other way around, the regressions begging the issue of causality.

What about economies of scale? Theoretically, the EP success should be increased because world markets are certainly larger than just home markets, but systematic evidence is not yet available on this question. For instance, evidence is lacking to date indicating whether firms that turn to export markets are characterized by greater scale of output than those firms that do not.

On the other hand, if one assumes that economies of scale will indeed be exploited when trade expands, the cost of protection will

---

[16] See Bhagwati (1978), Chapter 8.

evidently rise significantly. Harris (1986) has recently calculated for Canada that a 3.6 percent increase in GNP could follow from the unilateral elimination of Canadian tariffs, the unusually large gain accruing thanks to economies of scale.

Finally, in the matter of X-efficiency, it is again plausible that firms under IS regimes should find themselves more frequently in sheltered and monopolistic environments than under EP regimes; in fact, a great deal of such evidence is available from the country studies in the several research projects discussed. X-efficiency therefore ought to be greater under the EP regime, although this is a notoriously grey area in which measurement has often turned out to be elusive.

Other Objectives than Growth

A final word is necessary on the superior economic performance of the EP strategy. What about other objectives?

When it became evident that the EP strategy yielded higher growth and that the static versus dynamic efficiency arguments were not persuasive and probably went in favor of the EP strategy, the IS diehards shifted ground. They took to arguing that the objective of development was not growth but the eliminating of poverty or increasing employment, and that EP might be better for growth but was worse for these other objectives. This was part of a larger argument that became fashionable during the 1970s in certain development circles: that growth had been the objective of development to date, that the objective was wrong, and that the true objective of poverty amelioration was ill-served by development efforts directed at growth. In fact, growth even harmed (in certain formulations of such critics) the poor.

Of course, in theory, economists can prove anything if they are smart enough. Conflicts among different objectives can be readily demonstrated in well-defined, suitably chosen models. What was novel, however, was the assertion that the empirical experience of the 1950s and 1960s had shown that growth did not affect poverty and that it had even harmed it. These views, however, have not stood the test of detailed scrutiny.

The evidence does not support the views that the early planners in developing countries desired growth per se, that poverty elimination was not the stated objective which was pursued by means which included as a key element the acceleration of growth rates to pull up the poor into gainful employment, and that growth on a sustained basis has not helped the poor. These orthodoxies are no longer regarded as plausible.[17]

In regard to the narrower question whether the EP strategy procures efficiency and growth but adversely affects poverty and employment, evidence has now been gathered extensively in a sequel NBER project, directed by Krueger (1982). Essentially, she and her associates document how the investment allocations under EP require the expansion of labor-intensive activities since developing country exports are typically labor intensive. Therefore, ceteris paribus, they encourage the use of labor and hence employment and hence, in countries which typically have underemployed labor, also the alleviation of poverty.

Moreover, after more than two decades of successful growth in the EP countries, especially in the four Far Eastern economies, it has become easier for economists to contemplate and comprehend the effects of compound rates and the advantages of being on rapid escalators. Even if it had been true that the EP strategy yielded currently lower employment or lower real wages, the rapid growth rates would overwhelm these disadvantages in the long run, which can be simply one generation.

Both the employment-intensive nature of EP growth in developing countries and the higher growth rates in the EP countries have provided a massive antidote to the poverty and underemployment that afflicted these countries at the start of their development process.

Second Export Pessimism: Assessing the Protectionist Threat

It is fair then to conclude that the outward-oriented strategy emerges from both theory and empirical experience as a desirable policy option for developing countries. But this option is not independent of conditions external to the developing countries. The EP strategy, in principle, makes sense only insofar as markets can be found elsewhere

---

[17] I have discussed these propositions elsewhere (Bhagwati, 1985c) at some length, drawing on a vast literature that includes important writings by Ahluwalia, Little, Srinivasan, Streeten, Bhalla, Griffin, Isenman, Bardhan, and others.

to absorb exports at prices that generally do not fall as exports rise. For, according to the oldest argument for tariffs (i.e., for a well-defined IS strategy), individual nations would otherwise find it worthwhile to impose an optimal tariff that enables the country to exercise its monopoly power in world markets.

In fact, this provided a key rationale for the adoption of the IS strategy in the 1950s, as in the writings of Nurkse and others. They thought that the markets for the exports of developing countries were getting tighter and hence these countries had to shift to inward-looking, balanced growth that largely matched domestic production to domestic consumption instead of exploiting international special-ization in production. This "first export pessimism" was thus based on an (as it turned out, unwarranted) assessment that export markets were simply not available.

By contrast, while the revival of IS sentiment today in several quarters is equally based on export pessimism, the source of it is altogether different. This, second export pessimism is based on fears of protectionism. That is, that while markets do exist and could justify an outward-oriented strategy, the markets would not be allowed by protectionist forces to be exploited effectively.

The second pessimism is founded on man-made restrictions, not on natural limits as the first pessimism was. As such, it is paradoxically less worrisome. For, what is made by man can be undone by man. If protectionism is indulged in by governments, it can in principle be contained by governments. An appropriate response by developing countries to protectionism may then be not simply to accept it as given and then to retreat into IS policies, but to engage with the developed countries in exercises such as the MTN (multilateral trade negotiations) to keep market access available. This requires developing-country governments to be interventionists and energet-ically active, not in the exercise of extensive national protection of the IS variety, but rather in sustaining and expanding the open-trading international system. The first pessimism led to balanced national growth and IS; the second pessimism leads to international engagement and diplomacy to sustain EP—unless the assessment is that the protectionist threat is unmanageable and its translation into actual protection is either already large and irreversible or imminent despite national and international efforts to maintain an open trading system.

That proviso is evidently important. Therefore, it is necessary now to assess the protectionist actuality and threat.

State of Protection

Has protection increased significantly in the last decade for instance? Here, one distinguishes between actual protection and the threat thereof.[18]

It is well known that successive tariff-cutting exercises under GATT auspices have reduced the average tariffs for the United States, the European Community, and Japan down to extremely low levels, the Tokyo Round having reduced them to levels around 4–4.5 percent for manufactures. Weighted by total imports, the eventual tariffs on semi-manufactures and manufactures average only 4.9 percent, 6.0 percent and 5.4 percent for the United States, the Economic Community, and Japan, respectively (Table 1).

While therefore the tariffs have in fact gone down, including in the last decade, to negligible levels, two qualifying observations can be made about tariff protection as it applies to developing countries.

While the developed-country nominal tariffs are low on all countries, they are higher for products of interest to the developing countries (Table 1). This, as Finger has noted, is in turn attributable partly to the fact that developing countries have traditionally not engaged in reciprocal tariff-cut bargaining that GATT works with, preferring to rely on nonreciprocal MFN-route extensions of tariff cuts to them. Altruism, in contrast to mutual exchange, in GATT's bargaining framework, has led to smaller tariff cuts than if developing countries had engaged in mutual tariff cuts.

Tariff escalation also exists on tariffs on developing country exports.[19] Value-added protection is therefore yet higher than what the nominal tariffs imply.

---

[18] There is a gray area here, however. If the Japanese auto exports are restricted, not because the United States negotiates voluntary export restraints but because even though they have lapsed (as in 1985) the Japanese voluntarily restrict them for prudential reasons lest the protectionist Congress react adversely if exports are greater, is this the exercise of actual protection or simply a result of a protectionist threat? I would opt for the latter.

[19] See Alexander Yeats's (1981) demonstration of such tariff escalation for 11 processing chains involving products such as fish, coffee, silk yarn, natural rubber, cocoa beans, raw jutes and skins, fruits, wood and oil seeds, and flour.

Table 1. Tariff Averages Before and After the Tokyo Round Agreement

	Tariffs on Total Imports												Tariffs on Imports from Developing Countries		
	Raw materials			Semi-manufactures			Finished manufactures			Semi- and finished manufactures			Semi- and finished manufactures		
	Before	After	Percent change	Before	After	Percent change	Before	After	Percent change	Before	After	Percent change	Before	After	Percent change
United States															
Weighted	0.9	0.2	77	4.5	3.0	33	8.0	5.7	29	7.0	4.9	30	11.4	8.7	24
Simple	3.3	1.8	45	10.0	6.1	39	13.0	7.0	46	11.6	6.6	43	12.0	6.7	44
European Community															
Weighted	0.2	0.2	15	5.8	4.2	27	9.7	6.9	29	8.3	6.0	28	8.9	6.7	25
Simple	1.9	1.6	16	8.9	6.2	30	9.9	7.0	29	9.4	6.6	30	8.5	5.8	32
Japan															
Weighted	1.5	0.5	67	6.6	4.6	30	12.5	6.0	52	10.0	5.4	46	10.0	6.8	32
Simple	2.5	1.4	45	9.8	6.3	36	11.6	6.4	45	10.8	6.4	41	11.0	6.7	39

Source: The Tokyo Round Multilateral Trade Negotiations, Supplementary Report by the Director General of the GATT (Geneva: GATT Secretariat, 1980), pp. 33–37.

Of greater importance, however, is the fact that the reduction in tariff levels has been accompanied, since the mid-1970s, by an offsetting rise in the incidence of NTBs (nontariff barriers). Whether, however, these barriers have increased is a complex issue since the answer basically requires, if it is to be meaningful, an examination of how restrictive they are. A tightening of a quota when import supplies have become more elastic may mean nonetheless that its restrictiveness has diminished rather than increased; and two weak restrictions may be less protective than one strong restriction. The existing attempts at estimating the worldwide growth of NTBs are unable to cope with these difficulties, much as their authors are aware of them. With the corresponding caveats in mind, therefore, the following statistics may be noted.

Finger and Olechowski (1986) have estimated that, accounting for several NTBs including quota restrictions, voluntary export restraints (VERs), variable import levies, and monitoring measures, the unweighted percent of value of imports covered by NTBs in individual countries seems to range around 17 percent in 1981 and 18 percent in 1984 for all products from all sources, and 18 percent and 19 percent respectively for products imported only from developing countries. This indicates a certain stability, though at nearly a fifth these figures are not negligible.

The UNCTAD has also estimated trade coverage ratios for NTBs, using trade weights of a fixed base year (1981). A frequency index is also calculated, with the number of trade flows subject to selected nontariff barriers expressed as the percentage share of the total number of trade flows.[20]

With regard to all NTBs covered, the UNCTAD indices (which do not of course estimate the restrictiveness of the NTBs in question)[21] show an increase during 1981 to 1986. For all nonfuel imports, both

---

[20] "The number of trade flows for each importing country is the number of national tariff lines times the number of trading partners in which imports originated at each tariff line in the base year. A trade flow subject to NTMs is counted, at the national tariff line level, every time that imports from a specific source are affected by one or more NTMs." Cf. UNCTAD, *Protectionism and Structural Adjustment*, 23 March 1987, Geneva, Part I (p. 14).

[21] Thus, even import surveillance (including *automatic* licensing) are routinely included in the ratio and index. UNCTAD does estimate the ratio and index for smaller groups of NTBs, however.

the trade coverage ratio and the frequency index increased, reflecting largely added restrictions on steel and animal and vegetable oils, while interventions in fuels (mainly in the United States) and footwear (also in Canada and Japan) diminished.[22] Bad years were 1981–82 and 1983–84; 1986 seems stable.

Not merely, however, does the increase in the UNCTAD measures conceal important elements of liberalization (as on fuels and footwear). The increase is also, when examined closely, from 19.6 percent to 22.7 percent between 1981 and 1986 for nonfuel imports. This is a far cry from the notion that massive protection broke out during the 1980s. Indeed, a detailed eye-scan of the components of UNCTAD's measures, which are an invaluable contribution to our knowledge, suggests that many, indeed an overwhelmingly large number of, import markets for industrial products are still free from NTB restraint: in absolute terms, nearly 580,000 trade flows out of almost 700,000 are free from NTBs that include a comprehensive list including (controversially) anti-dumping (AD) and countervailing (CVD) duty actions.

Trade Growth and Porous Protection

As I have already stated, the question still remains: how restrictive has the growth in NTBs been? I propose to argue that, even on this dimension, the growth of protectionism has permitted trade to grow and that one of the early virtues of NTBs may well have been their nontransparency in this regard.

Trade expansion certainly slowed down during the 1970s. But even then, world trade continued to grow faster than world increase during 1970–1984. In fact, the developing countries' exports of manufactures to the developed countries grew almost twice as fast as the exports of these countries to one another, registering during the relatively depressed 1970s an annual growth of over 8 percent. This happened in the teeth of newly proliferating NTBs and substantial macroeconomic difficulties in the OECD countries.

---

[22] Again, auto VERs were eliminated by the United States in 1985, but it is not clear whether this substantial liberalization has been interpreted as such or ignored because Japan continued prudential, voluntary restraint herself.

That exports from the developing countries continued to grow in this fashion was first highlighted by Hughes and Krueger (1984) who thought that it was a puzzle since protectionist threats had been felt to be translated into a large amount of actual protection already. This puzzle has stimulated Baldwin (1968 and 1985) into developing the interesting thesis that protection is far less effective than one thinks simply because there are many ways in which exporting countries can get around it in continuing to increase their export earnings. Baldwin states (1985):

> Consider the response of exporting firms to the imposition of tighter foreign restrictions on imports of a particular product. One immediate response will be to try to ship the product in a form which is not covered by the restriction. . . . One case involves coats with removable sleeves. By importing sleeves unattached, the rest of the coat comes in as a vest, thereby qualifying for more favorable tariff treatment. (p. 110)

> The use of substitute components is another common way of getting around import restrictions. The quotas on imports of sugar into the United States only apply to pure sugar, defined as 100 percent sucrose. Foreign exporters are avoiding the quotas by shipping sugar products consisting mainly of sucrose, but also containing a sugar substitute, for example dextrose. . . . At one time, exporters of running shoes to the United States avoided the high tariff on rubber footwear by using leather for most of the upper portion of the shoes, thereby qualifying for duty treatment as leather shoes. (p. 110)

Yoffie (1983) has also recently examined the VERs on footwear and textiles from a political scientist's perspective and found that the dynamic exporting economies such as the Republic of Korea and the Taiwan Province of China have embraced them with considerable ingenuity, much as Baldwin has documented and argued, to continue expanding their exports significantly.

There is also a more subtle factor at play here which relates to why VERs, which represent the method by which an attempt has been made to cut imports in many recent NTB actions, may have provided the mechanism by which the executives interested in maintaining freer trade despite mounting protectionism may have succeeded in keeping trade expanding. VERs are, in that view, a porous form of protection that is deliberately preferred because of this nontransparent porousness. I have argued recently (Bhagwati, 1986b) that in industries, such as footwear, two characteristics seem to hold that lend support to this porous-protection model as an explanation for why protection is ineffective. First, undifferentiated products (i.e., cheaper varieties of garments and footwear) make it easy to transship, that is, to cheat on rules of origin, passing off products of a country restricted by VERs as products of countries not covered by VERs. Second, low start-up costs and therefore small recoupment horizons apply in shifting investment and products to adjacent third countries that are not covered by VERs, so that an exporting country can get around (admittedly at some cost) the VERs by investment shunting to sources unaffected by VERs. This type of strategy allows the exporter to recover his investment costs since it is usually some time before the VERs get around to covering these alternative sources or VERs are eliminated as the political pressure subsides (as was the case with United States footwear).[23]

In both ways VERs in these types of industries can yield a closer-to-free-trade solution for the exporting countries that are afflicted by the VERs. These countries can continue to profit from their comparative advantage by effectively exploiting, legally (through investment shunting) and illegally (through transshipments), the fact that VERs leave third countries out whereas importing-country tariffs and quotas do not.[24]

Why would the protecting importing countries prefer this porous protection? Does it not imply that the market-disrupted industry fails to be protected as it would under a corresponding import trade restraint? Indeed it does. But that is precisely its attractiveness.

If executives want free trade in the national interest whereas legislatures respond to the sectoral interests—definitely the stylized description of the two-headed democracies such as exist in the United

---

[23] The investment shunting need occur only insofar as it is necessary to meet value-added rules of origin, of course, making the cost of profiting from this porousness even less than otherwise.

[24] Of course, the VERs in this instance represent only a partial and suboptimal approximation to the free trade solution which remains the desirable but infeasible alternative. Moreover, not all exporting countries are capable of the flexible and shrewd response that underlies the model of porous protection sketched above.

States and Britain—then it can be argued that executives will prefer to use a porous form of protection that, while assuring free market access, will nonetheless manage to appear as a concession to the political demands for protection from the legislature or from its constituencies.[25] Whether this game plan works over time as the porosity is increasingly perceived is an important question. In the multi-fiber agreement, the VERs have proliferated, successively closing loopholes and increasing coverage until they come to approximate comparatively non-leaky import restrictions instead. In other cases, as in footwear, they were terminated and evidently gained the freer trade-oriented executives and exporters the access that import restrictions would have denied them.

Shifting International Political Economy

While the preceding analysis suggests that protection has left significant access open for developing countries in the markets of the developed countries, and that the protection has been relatively porous often permitting trade to grow despite it, what about the future prospects? Is the threat of new protection extremely serious?

It would be foolish to disregard this threat altogether. Indeed, it is an important reality in the United States and the Economic Community today. Some of it is due to the substantial unemployment rates in the Economic Community; some of it is attributed to Eurosclerosis which, in turn, cannot be treated as exogenous to unemployment since it is evident that a growing and prosperous economy makes it easier for sectoral adjustments by, first, providing jobs for those who must exit from declining industries and, second, often making adjustment to imports possible by reducing growth of jobs rather than their absolute number in the industries losing comparative advantage. It is trivially true therefore that if macroeconomic policies can be worked out to ensure a growing world economy, protectionism will tend to ease. Bad macroeconomics and protectionism are happy bedfellows.

---

[25] This two-headed version of governments underlies the Feenstra-Bhagwati (1982) model of the efficient tariff. The argument above is also compatible with Pastor's (1983) "cry-and-sigh" syndrome thesis of U.S. tariff making and with Destler's (1986) work, which suggests that the Congress relies on the Executive to ensure open markets and to protect U.S. trade policy from the consequences of protectionist cries that the Congress must make to satisfy constituents.

Moving beyond this truism, I believe that the international political economy has changed dramatically in the last two decades to generate new and influential actors supportive of freer world trade.

A fairly common complaint on the part of analysts of the political economy has been the asymmetry of pressure groups in the tariff-making process. The beneficiaries of protection are often concentrated, whereas its victims tend to be either diffused (as is the case with final consumers) or are unable to recognize the losses they incur as when protection indirectly affects exports and hence hurts those engaged in producing exportables.[26]

Direct foreign investment (DFI) and the growing maze of globalized production have changed this equation perceptibly. When DFI is undertaken, not for tariff jumping in locally sheltered markets, but for exports to the home country or to third markets, as is increasingly the case, protectionism threatens clearly the investments so made and tends to galvanize these influential multinationals into lobbying to keep markets open.

For example, it was noticeable that when the United States semi-conductor suppliers recently gathered to discuss anti-dumping legal action against Japanese producers of memory microchips known as EPROMS (or erasable programmable read-only memories), noticeably absent were Motorola, Inc. and Texas Instruments, Inc., which produce semiconductors in Japan and expect to be shipping some back to the United States.[27]

Almost certainly a main reason why United States protectionism did not translate into a disastrous Smoot-Hawley scenario, despite high unemployment levels and the seriously overvalued dollar (in the Dutch-Disease sense) until recently, is that far fewer congressmen today have constituencies in which DFI has not created such pro-trade, anti-protectionist presence, muddying waters where protectionists would have otherwise sailed with great ease. The spider's web or spaghetti-bowl phenomenon resulting from DFI that criss-crosses the world economy has thus been a stabilizing force in favor of holding the protectionists at bay.

---

[26] See, for example, Olson (1971), Finger (1982), and Mayer (1985).

[27] See the report by Miller (1985) in the *Wall Street Journal*.

It is not just the DFI in place that provides these trade-reinforcing political pressures.[28] As I have often argued (1982a and 1986a), the response to import competition has been diluted by the possibility of using international factor mobility as a policy response. Thus, the possibility of undertaking DFI when faced with import competition also provides an alternative to a protectionist response. Since this is the capitalist response, rather than that of labor which would lose jobs abroad, the defusion of protectionist threat implied here works by breaking and hence weakening the customary alliance between both pressure groups within an industry in their protectionist lobbying, a relationship with which Magee has made us long familiar.

Interestingly, labor today seems also to have caught onto this game and is not averse to using threats of protection to induce DFI from foreign competitors instead. The United Auto Workers labor union in the United States appears to have in this way helped induce Japanese investments in the car industry. This is, in fact, quite a generic phenomenon where DFI is undertaken by the Japanese exporting firms to buy off the local pressure groups of firms or unions which can, and often do, threaten legislative pressures for tariffs to close the import markets. This type of induced DFI has been christened as quid pro quo DFI (Bhagwati, 1985c) and appears to be a growing phenomenon[29] (certainly on the part of Japanese firms), representing a new and alternative form of response to import competition than provided by old fashioned tariff-making.[30]

---

[28] Of relevance here is the work of Helleiner (1977) and others. These authors, and most recently Lavergne and Helleiner (1985), have argued that multinationals have become active agents exercising political pressure in favor of free trade. These authors have also investigated, for the United States, correlations on a cross-industry basis between multinationals and tariff changers, but without much success. Their work, however, does not extend to the potential DFI effects in favor of freer trade (through DFI becoming an alternative response to import competition) that is discussed in Bhagwati (1982b and 1986a) and in the text.

[29] In fact, MITI (Ministry of International Trade and Industry) of Japan has recently completed a survey of Japanese DFI abroad and found that a large fraction of the respondents cited reasons of the quid pro variety to explain their investment decisions. I am indebted to Professor Shishido of the International University of Japan for this reference.

[30] See the theoretical modeling of such quid pro quo DFI in Bhagwati, Brecher, Dinopoulos, and Srinivasan (1987) and in Bhagwati and Dinopoulos (1986), the former using perfectly competitive structure and the latter using monopoly and duopoly structures instead.

In short, both actual DFI (through the spider's web effect) and potential DFI (outward by domestic capital and quid pro quo, inward by foreign capital) are powerful forces influencing the political economy of tariff-making in favor of an open economy. They surely provide some counterweight to the gloom that the protectionist noises generate today.

Can All Export? The First Export Pessimism

Old worries do not always die out, they often smoulder. The fear that markets simply cannot exist for developing country exports keeps coming up; it is particularly alive and well in some diehard IS countries.

Perhaps the best exposition of this view is, however, in the work of Cline (1982), who has tried to answer the question: if the EP model is exported to all other developing countries, can the markets absorb the resulting trade volumes? Yet another question has been one revised by Arthur Lewis's (1980) contention that trade of the developing countries is in a tight embrace with growth in the developed countries, hence external growth determines what developing countries can export, hence slow OECD growth condemns them to an IS strategy.

On the latter version of the first pessimism, several analyses by Kravis (1970) and most recently and thoroughly by Goldstein and Khan (1982) and Riedel (1984), have laid this relationship to rest.[31] Indeed, the comparative and absolute export performance of the developing countries is better explained by reference to domestic incentives (or supply) than to external (or demand) conditions. Stable relationships based on foreign demand simply will not fly.

The Cline exercise, on the other hand, suffers from two different afflictions: the fallacy of composition and an unwarranted conceptual leap.

First, Cline puts all countries on a curve, duly adjusted, for the successful Asian exporters with very high ratios of trade to national income. The pursuit of an EP strategy, however, simply amounts to

---

[31] See the detailed arguments in the latter two papers which explicitly address the Lewis proposition.

the adoption of a structure of incentives which does not discriminate against exports in favor of the home market. This does not imply that the resulting increases in trade-to-income ratios will be necessarily as dramatic as in the Far Eastern cases! To infer otherwise is a non sequitur.

Second, the share of developing countries in the markets for manufactures in most developed countries has been, and continues to be, relatively small. While there are obviously variations in individual industries, in the aggregate the share of manufactured exports from developing countries in the consumption of manufactures in the developed countries runs even today at a little over 2 percent. Absorptive capacity purely in the market sense, therefore, is not prima facie a plausible source of worry.

Third, a chief lesson of the postwar experience is that policymakers who seek to forecast exports typically tend to understate export potential by understating the absorptive capacity of import markets. This comes largely from having to focus on known exports and partly from downward estimation biases when price elasticities for such exports are econometrically measured. Experience underlines the enormous capacity of wholly unforeseen markets to develop when incentives exist to make profits. Miscellaneous exports often represent the source of spectacular gains when the bias against exports, typical of IS regimes, is removed on a sustained basis.

Fourth, trade economists have increasingly appreciated the potential for intra-industry specialization as trade opportunities are provided and seized. The experience of the Economic Community, where the progressive dismantling of internal trade barriers led to increased mutual trade in similar products rather than to massive reductions in scale of output in industry groups within industrial member states, has only underlined this lesson.[32] There is no reason therefore to doubt that such intra-industry trade in manufactures among developing countries and between them and the developed countries can also develop significantly, difficult as it is to forecast with plausible numbers.

---

[32] There is a substantial empirical literature on this subject, with important contributions by Balassa, Grubel, and Lloyd. In addition, recent theoretical work by Dixit, Lancaster, Krugman, Helpman, and others has provided the analytical explanation for such intra-industry trade.

Finally, if we reckon also with the potential for intra-developing country trade (where again policies can change to permit its increase), and the possibility of opening (again by policy) new sectors, such as agriculture and services, to freer trade, then the export possibilities are even more abundant than the preceding arguments indicate.[33]

Export pessimism, if traced to market forces as in the postwar period, is then unwarranted.[34] If, however, it is traced to policies, that is, to protectionism as with the Second Export Pessimism today, then I believe that the earlier analysis in this section suggests again caution in leaping into the IS strategy based on unexplored and exaggerated fears.

Concluding Observations

My main conclusion therefore is that the appropriate policy for the developing countries is indeed to seek the advantage of outward orientation, without being overwhelmed by the renewed export pessimism. SAL and donor conditionality, where extended to such a shift in strategy for countries that are strongly inward looking, is not a matter of uninformed economic ideology, unmindful of existing economic conditions, but rather a matter of a considered evaluation of the prospects of keeping a functioning trading order with access to foreign markets. The occasional charges that such conditionality is a matter of ideology are therefore not based on a valid assessment of the donors' views and predilections.

On the other hand, it is equally imperative that the developing countries, and these very international agencies seeking to spread outward-oriented strategy today, energetically engage in diplomatic efforts to sustain the open trading order. This requires that the developing countries actively participate in the multilateral trade negotiations at Geneva, seeking the kinds of bargains and trade-offs that characterize these negotiations and have led to the immense reduction in tariff levels that were noted earlier. It also requires that

---

[33] All these arguments are effectively a rebuttal also of Dornbusch's (1986) restatement of the limited-absorptive-capacity thesis for developing country exports, which asserts that substantial terms of trade losses would follow from the simultaneous resort to EP strategy by many developing countries.

[34] See also the excellent critique of Cline's analysis offered by Ranis (1985).

the international agencies that encourage or require outward orientation also strengthen their own expertise in the analysis of protectionism, its incidence, causes, and consequences, and offer the
benefits of this expertise also to member countries who must confront
these questions at the multilateral trade negotiations and in other
areas of trade diplomacy.[35]

Postscript

The discussion of this paper and Professor Sachs's companion
contribution prompts a few observations.

The EP strategy can be pursued in alternative formats. Broadly
speaking, the anti-export bias of overvalued exchange rates can be
eliminated either by adjusting them to offset the overvaluation or by
providing export subsidies that bring EER_x into line with EER_m on
the average. In the Bhagwati-Krueger NBER project, the latter regime
was described as Phase II and the former as Phase IV in a sequencing
scenario.

Are the two methods equivalent or is one superior to the other?
Michael Bruno and I reminded Professor Sachs that, even if the
export-subsidization route is superior as he seemed to believe, it is
simply unavailable in the world of the 1980s in which countervailing
(CVD) duties and anti-dumping (AD) actions are the norm. Professor
Sachs properly responded that he was more interested in what was
theoretically good for developing countries than in what was practically feasible.

Even at the theoretical level, however, I am afraid that there are
problems with the export-subsidization route that may have been
insufficiently appreciated by its proponents. First, if you replace a 50

---

[35] For example, it is extremely important to assess the growing trend toward fair
trade in the United States and in the EC, and its implications for protectionism.
Increasingly, it is feared by many that countervailing and anti-dumping (CVD and
AD) duties and processes are captured by industries seeking protection, and that
foreign competitors are harassed by this soft-core protection. Assessing this threat is
a very important task, which also bears on what the developing countries ought to
seek at the multilateral trade negotiations. Splendid studies of this problem have been
undertaken, as it happens, in the World Bank of this issue, in research papers by
Finger and Nogues, Nam, and Messerlin. See also Bhagwati and Irwin (1987), where
these issues are discussed in a wider context.

percent devaluation by a 50 percent import duty and a 50 percent export subsidy, the two measures are equivalent in the classroom and graduate texts on trade theory. In reality, however, think of what happens in the latter alternative by imagining the incentives for evasion via faked invoicing (Bhagwati (1974, 1981)) and bribery that this will give rise to. The equivalence disappears fast in favor of devaluation in the reality of the developing countries, for sure. Second, similar considerations of political economy suggest that the export subsidization alternative is likely to be captured in many developing countries by pressure groups that will use the theme of offsetting the anti-export bias in the overvalued exchange rate regime to seek wasteful but self-serving export subsidies. This was evident in some developing countries of the set of ten studied in depth in the Bhagwati-Krueger NBER project, especially India and Israel in their Phase II trade-and-payments regimes. In fact, it was an encounter with these realities that prompted the now-burgeoning theoretical literature on rent seeking (Krueger (1974)) and directly unproductive profit seeking (DUP) (Bhagwati (1982)) activities.[36]

None of this is to deny that an export subsidy program may well be important and welfare improving. Thus, in conventional trade theory, many have argued such a case on theoretical grounds, implying that $EER_x > EER_m$, that is, an ultra-EP strategy, can be sensible under appropriate circumstances.[37] For example, there may be externalities to a firm in export markets that are not matched by similar externalities in the domestic market, as when the export markets require investment promoting a product among foreign buyers who are unacquainted with a country's capacity to export this type of good and the returns to this investment then accrue equally to other free-riding potential exporters from that country.

But a case for net export subsidization may be made also along the lines I have indicated already in the main text. It can provide convincing credibility of commitment on the part of the government

---

[36] DUP activities include rent-seeking activities designated to secure rents on quote restrictions but embrace a wider set of activities that use resources to make a profit (or income) but produce no output, directly or indirectly. For a relationship between the two concepts, see Bhagwati and Srinivasan (1983), Chapter 30, and Bhagwati (1984).

[37] Thus, see Bhagwati (1968) and a fine, recent formalization of an argument for export subsidy advanced therein by Mayer (1985).

to the maintenance of a policy framework that protects the EP strategy from random or systematic inroads in the foreseeable future, thus facilitating the investment of resources and entrepreneurial energies in exploiting foreign markets. This may well be an important, distinguishing rationale for permitting a net export subsidy by developing countries in which the role of the government is almost always more manifest, as the great historian Alexander Gerschenkron observed, and hence the assurance is correspondingly greater that a strategy will be protected from disruption in search of myriad other policy pressures and goals. In this precise sense, I do have some sympathy for the proposition that a more benign view of limited export subsidization in developing countries, even in the presence of properly functioning exchange rates, would be appropriate if only the developed countries could be so persuaded today.

This brings me to the question of the role of the government. Professor Sachs is indeed right in underlining the fact, noted in my main text as well, that the Far Eastern success stories are not proof of the merits of a laissez-faire government. Indeed, this has been long known in the extensive literature on trade-and-payments regimes. For instance, in the synthesis volume for the NBER project (Bhagwati (1978), Chapter 8), this was explicitly noted. This is not to deny that some have astonishingly believed otherwise. Thus, in the segment on Tyranny of Controls in his "Free to Choose" television series, Professor Milton Friedman characterized Japan as an example of the success of the market over government. As a member of the panel that debated him, I remarked that the visible hand in Japan may be invisible to him, but was certainly not so to the Japanese! But Professor Friedman can be forgiven perhaps for this self-indulgence toward his economic beliefs; we are all prey to this in varying degrees. After all, how can an economic miracle have occurred if the policymakers had not followed our preferred policies? Recalling that public goods have the property that I can enjoy them without depriving you of that pleasure too, I have formulated the following law: economic miracles are a public good; each economist sees in them a vindication of his pet theories.

The key question then is not whether there is governmental action in the Far Eastern economies, but rather how have these successful economies managed their intervention and strategic decisionmaking in ways that dominate those of the unsuccessful ones? This is a complex question but one to which some stylized answers can nonetheless be attempted.

An important aspect of the difference in governments in their behavior vis-à-vis the private sector seems to be that the Far Eastern economies are by and large governments that practice do's rather than don'ts (Bhagwati (1978), Chapter 8). The reverse is true of governments that have generally shown an inferior performance. The key examples are highly regulated economies, such as India, with detailed controls over what entrepreneurs can do. Is there any reason why the proscriptive governments of don'ts should tend to do worse than the prescriptive governments of do's?

There are two reasons why this might be so. First, a prescriptive government may prescribe as badly as a proscriptive government proscribes, each leading to a suboptimal outcome if you believe that such interventions tend to subtract from efficiency. But a proscriptive government will tend to stifle initiatives, whereas a prescriptive government will tend to leave open areas (outside of the presciptions) where initiatives can be still exercised. Thus, even though each government might distort allocation of existing resources equally, the proscriptive government will tend to stifle technical change and entrepreneurial activity and hence hurt growth.

Second, proscriptive governments tend to generate DUP activities by entrepreneurs seeking to avoid and evade the don'ts, thus diverting productive resources into unproductive ways of making an income. By contrast, the prescriptive governments tend to generate less such DUP activities since large areas are left open for initiatives that the do's do not touch.

Finally, governments that are proscriptive are more likely to be adversarial to private entrepreneurship, with the bureaucrats and politicians exclusively in the driving seat. Prescriptive governments, by contrast, appear to work in a symbiotic relationship with private entrepreneurs. To take two well-known illustrations of this contrast, the relationship between The Ministry of International Trade and Industry (MITI) and the Japanese firms, for instance, is intimate, whereas that in India between the planners and the private entre-preneurs has not been. The former pattern of governmental relation-ship with private entrepreneurs can have two favorable effects. First, the government thereby can take decisions informed by the micro-economic know-how that is embodied in the entrepreneurs familiar with the industry being planned for, know-how that cannot otherwise be obtained by bureaucrats. Second, the symbiosis can reinforce the credibility of commitment to a strategy that I have already mentioned as important. With MITI agreeing to a projected or planned scenario of future growth, the government can be expected to adhere to a supportive policy mode which would otherwise not be available. Where these two favorable effects obtain, they can reinforce the advantages of a prescriptive government that I set out earlier.

References

Balassa, Bela, *The Structure of Protection in Developing Countries* (Baltimore: Johns Hopkins University Press, 1971).

————, "Exports and Economic Growth: Further Evidence," *Journal of Development Economics* (Amsterdam), Vol. 5 (June 1978), pp. 181–89.

————, and Carol Balassa, "Industrial Protection in the Developed Countries," *World Economy* (Oxford), Vol. 7 (June 1984), pp. 179–96.

Balasubramanian, V.N., "Incentives and Disincentives for Foreign Direct Investment in Less Developed Countries," *Weltwirtschaftliches Archiv* (Kiel), Vol. 120 (1984), pp. 720–35.

Baldwin, Robert, *The Inefficacy of Trade Policy*, Essays in International Finance, No. 150 (Princeton: Princeton University, 1968).

————, "Ineffectiveness of Protection in Promoting Social Goals," *World Economy* (Oxford), Vol. 8 (June 1985), pp. 109–18.

Bhagwati, Jagdish, *The Theory and Practice of Commercial Policy*, Essays in International Finance, No. 8 (Princeton: Princeton University, 1968).

————, "On the Underinvoicing Imports," in *Illegal Transactions in International Trade: Theory and Measurement*, ed. by Jagdish Bhagwati (Amsterdam: North-Holland, 1974).

————, *Anatomy and Consequences of Exchange Control Regimes* (Cambridge, Massachusetts: Ballinger Publishing Company, 1978).

————, "Alternative Theories of Illegal Trade: Economic Consequences and Statistical Detection," *Weltwirtschaftliches Archiv* (Kiel), Vol. 117 (1981), pp. 409–26.

————, "Shifting Comparative Advantage, Protectionist Demands, and Policy Response," in *Import Competition and Response*, ed. by Jagdish Bhagwati (Chicago: Chicago University Press, 1982a).

————, "Directly-Unproductive, Profit-seeking (DUP) Activities," *Journal of Political Economy* (Chicago), Vol. 5 (October 1982b), pp. 988–1002.

————, "DUP Activities and Rent Seeking," *Kyklos* (Basle), Vol. 36, No. 4 (1983), pp. 634–37.

_____ , *Dependence and Interdependence*, Vol. 2 of *Essays in Development Economics*, ed. by Gene Grossman (Cambridge, Massachusetts: MIT Press, 1985a).

_____ , "Protectionism: Old Wine in New Bottles," *Journal of Policy Modeling* (New York), Vol. 7 (Spring l985b), pp. 23–33.

_____ , *Growth and Poverty*, Michigan State University Center for Advanced Study of International Development, Occasional Paper No. 5 (East Lansing: Michigan State, 1985c).

_____ , *Investing Abroad*, Esmee Fairbairn Lecture, University of Lancaster, England, 1986a.

_____ , "VERs, Quid Pro Quo Foreign Investment and VIEs: Political-Economy Theoretic Analyses," unpublished, World Bank, Washington, 1986b.

_____ , and Douglas Irwin, "The Return of the Reciprocitarians: U.S. Trade Policy Today," *World Economy* (Oxford), June 1987 (forthcoming).

_____ , and T.N. Srinivasan, "Trade Policy and Development," in *International Economic Policy: Theory and Evidence*, ed. by Rudiger Dornbusch and Jacob Frenkel (Baltimore: Johns Hopkins University Press, 1979).

_____ , and T.N. Srinivasan, *Lectures on International Trade* (Cambridge, Massachusetts: MIT Press, 1983).

_____ , Richard Brecher, and T.N. Srinivasan, "DUP Activities and Economic Theory," *European Economic Review* (Amsterdam),Vol. 24 (April 1984), pp. 291–307.

_____ , Richard Brecher, Elias Dinopoulos, and T.N. Srinivasan, "*Quid Pro Quo* Investment and Policy Intervention: A Political-Economy-Theoretic Analysis," *Journal of Development Economics* (Amsterdam), 1987 (forthcoming).

Brecher, Richard, and Carlos Diaz-Alejandro, "Tariffs, Foreign Capital and Immiserizing Growth," *Journal of International Economics* (Amsterdam), Vol. 7 (November 1977), pp. 317–22.

Cline, William, "Can the East Asian Model of Development be Generalized?" *World Development* (Oxford), Vol. 13 (February 1982), pp. 81–90.

Dervis, Kemal, Jaime de Melo, and Sherman Robinson, "A General Equilibrium Analysis of Foreign Exchange Shortages in a Developing Economy," *Economic Journal* (London), Vol. 91 (December 1981), pp. 891–906.

Desai, Padma, "Alternative Measures of Import Substitution," *Oxford Economic Papers* (London), Vol. 21 (November 1979), pp. 312–24.

Dinopoulos, Elias, and Jagdish Bhagwati, "*Quid Pro Quo* Investment and Market Structure," paper presented to the Western Economic Association Conference, San Francisco, July 1986.

Donges, Juergen, "A Comparative Study of Industrialization Policies in Fifteen Semi-Industrial Countries," *Weltwirtschafliches Archiv* (Kiel), Vol. 112 (1976), pp. 626–59.

Dornbusch, Rudiger, "Impacts on Debtor Countries of World Economic Conditions," unpublished paper presented to a Seminar on External Debt, Saving and Growth in Latin America, October 13–16, 1986.

Feder, Gershon, "On Exports and Economic Growth," *Journal of Development Economics* (Amsterdam), Vol. 12 (April 1983), pp. 59–73.

Feenstra, Robert, and Jagdish Bhagwati, *Import Competition and Response*, ed. by Jagdish Bhagwati (Chicago: Chicago University Press, 1982).

Findlay, Ronald, "Trade and Development: Theory and Asian Experience," *Asian Development Review* (Manila), Vol. 2 (1984), pp. 23–42.

Finger, J.M., "Incorporating the Gains from Trade into Policy," *World Economy* (Oxford), Vol. 5 (December 1982), pp. 367–77.

————, and Andrzej Olechowski, "Trade Carriers: Who does What to Whom," unpublished paper delivered at Kiel Institute of World Economics, Kiel, June 1986.

Goldstein, Morris, and Mohsin S. Khan, *Effects of Slowdown in Industrial Countries on Growth in Non-oil Developing Countries*, IMF Occasional Paper No. 12 (Washington: International Monetary Fund, August 1982).

Grais, Wafik, Jaime de Melo, and Shujiro Urata, "A General Equilibrium Estimate of the Effects of Reductions in Tariffs and Quantitative Restrictions in Turkey in 1978," in *General Equilibrium Trade Policy Modeling*, ed. by T.N. Srinivasan and John Whalley (Cambridge, Massachusetts: MIT Press, 1986).

Harris, Richard, "Quantitative Assessment of the Economic Impact on Canada of Sectoral Free Trade with the United States," *Canadian Journal of Economics* (Toronto), Vol. 19 (August 1986), pp. 377–94.

Helleiner, G.K., "Transnational Enterprises and the New Political Economy of United States Trade Policy," *Oxford Economic Papers* (London), Vol. 29 (March 1977), pp. 102–16.

Hufbauer, Gary, and Jeffrey Schott, *Trading for Growth: The Next Round of Trade Negotiations* (Washington: Institute for International Economics, 1985).

Hughes, Helen, and Anne Krueger, "Effects of Protection in Developed Countries on Developing Countries," in *The Structure and Evolution of Recent U.S. Trade Policy*, ed. by Robert Baldwin and Anne Krueger (Chicago: University of Chicago Press, 1984).

Kravis, Irving, "Trade as a Handmaiden of Growth: Similarities Between the Nineteenth and Twentieth Centuries," *Economic Journal* (London), Vol. 80 (December 1970), pp. 850–72.

Krueger, Anne, "The Political Economy of the Rent-Seeking Society," *American Economic Review* (Nashville), Vol. 64 (June 1974), pp. 291–303.

————, *Foreign Trade Regimes and Economic Development: Liberalization Attempts and Consequences* (Cambridge, Massachusetts: Ballinger Publishing Company, 1978).

————, "Trade Policy as an Input to Development," *American Economic Review* (Nashville), Vol. 70 (May 1980), pp. 288–92.

_____ , Trade and Employment in Developing Countries: Synthesis and Conclusions (Chicago: University of Chicago Press, 1982).

_____ , and Baran Tuncer, "Estimating Total Factor Productivity Growth in a Developing Country," World Bank, Staff Working Paper No. 422 (Washington), 1980.

Lal, Deepak, and Sarath Rajapatirana, "Trade Regimes and Economic Growth in Developing Countries," unpublished paper prepared for the Kiel Conference on Free Trade, June 1986.

Lavergne, Real, and G. K. Helleiner, "United States Transnational Corporations and the Structure of United States Trade Barriers: An Empirical Investigation," unpublished, 1985.

Lewis, W. Arthur, "The Slowing Down of the Engine of Growth," American Economic Review (Nashville), Vol. 70 (September 1980), pp. 555–64.

Little, Ian, Tibor Scitovsky, and Maurice Scott, Industry and Trade in Some Developing Countries (London: Oxford University Press, 1970).

Mayer, Wolfgang, "Infant-Export Industry Argument," Canadian Journal of Economics (Toronto), Vol. 17 (May 1984), pp. 249–69.

Michaely, Michael, "Exports and Growth: An Empirical Investigation," Journal of Development Economics (Amsterdam), Vol. 4 (March 1977), pp. 49–53.

Michalopoulos, Constantine, and Keith Jay, "Growth of Exports and Income in the Developing World: A Neoclassical View," AID Discussion Paper No. 28 (Washington), 1973.

Miller, Michael, "Big U.S. Semiconductor Makers Expected to Sue Over 'Dumping' of Japanese Chips," Wall Street Journal, October 1, 1985.

Nishimizu, Mieko, and Sherman Robinson, "Trade Policies and Productivity Change in Semi-Industrialized Countries," Journal of Development Economics (Amsterdam), Vol. 16 (October 1984), pp. 177–206.

Nurkse, Ragnar, Patterns of Trade and Development (Stockholm: Almquist and Wicksell, 1959).

Olson, Mancur, The Logic of Collective Action: Public Goods and the Theory of Groups (Cambridge, Massachusetts: Harvard University Press, 1971).

Ranis, Gustav, "Can the East Asian Model of Development be Generalized?" World Development (Oxford), Vol. 13 (April 1985), pp. 543–45.

Riedel, James, "Trade as the Engine of Growth in Developing Countries, Revisited," Economic Journal (London), Vol. 94 (March 1984), pp. 56–73.

Srinivasan, T.N., "Development Strategy: Is the Success of Outward Orientation at an End?" in Essays on Economic Progress and Welfare, ed. by S. Guhan and Manu Shroff (New Delhi: Oxford University Press, 1986).

Streeten, Paul, "A Cool Look at 'Outward-looking' Strategies for Development," World Economy (Oxford), Vol. 5 (September 1982), pp. 159–69.

Yoffie, David, Power and Protectionism (New York: Columbia University Press, 1983).

Trade and Exchange Rate Policies in Growth-Oriented Adjustment Programs

Jeffrey D. Sachs
Professor of Economics
Harvard University

The search for "growth-oriented adjustment programs" reflects a widespread malaise concerning Fund stabilization programs in countries suffering from external debt crises. After several years of poor economic performance, most of the indebted developing countries under Fund supervision have still not resumed economic growth. The political will of the debtor governments to continue with Fund adjustment programs, much less debt servicing, is clearly on the wane. The cooperative arrangements between debtors, creditors, and the Fund that have been in place for the past five years seem to be in danger of collapsing. Hence, the search is on for new policies that might enable the debtor countries to resume economic growth while continuing to service their debts.

A new orthodoxy is emerging from this search, which links recovery in the debtor countries to a shift to "outward-oriented" development strategies designed to produce export-led growth. Increased exports from the debtor countries are seen as the key to more output, more employment, and more foreign exchange to service the foreign debts. The new orthodoxy defines the policy content of outward orientation to include the following measures: trade liberalization, especially the conversion of quantitative restrictions to low, uniform tariffs; real exchange rate depreciation and unification of the exchange rate; an emphasis on the private sector as the source of growth, including the privatization of state enterprises; and a general reduction in all forms of market intervention by the government, in capital markets, factor markets, and in the overall level of government taxation and expenditure. This "liberalization package" is urged by the U.S. government as part of the Baker Plan, by many influential academicians, and by the Fund and World Bank (as exemplified by the papers by Guitián and Michalopoulos for this conference).

The perceived urgency of such liberalization policies is causing a redesign of Fund and the World Bank programs. Increasingly, the liberalization package, including the attendant exchange rate management, is viewed by both institutions as a key tool of crisis management in the debtor countries. Fund missions put ever increasing stress on the promotion of exports, mainly by urging an activist policy of exchange rate depreciation to raise export profitability. Inflation targets are downplayed in the process. This increased emphasis on exchange rate adjustment was suggested recently by data in the International Monetary Fund's Occasional Paper No. 36 on Fund exchange rate policies, which shows that while exchange rate actions were contained in only 31 percent of Fund programs during 1963–72, such actions were part of 51 percent of programs during 1973–80, and 64 percent of programs during 1981–83 (and fully 82 percent, if countries belonging to monetary unions are excluded from the sample).

With respect to the World Bank, structural adjustment loans and sectoral adjustment loans are becoming a much bigger part of World Bank business. With increasing frequency and perceived urgency, the World Bank is offering detailed blueprints for deregulation, privatization, and trade liberalization to member countries. Policy-based lending (as opposed to project lending) accounted for no less than 35 percent of World Bank lending to the heavily indebted countries in 1986, up from less than 10 percent five years ago. Additionally, the Fund and the World Bank are increasingly working in tandem to plan medium-term programs to support outward-oriented structural adjustments.

As a general matter, there is much to be said in favor of outward-oriented development strategies relative to inward-oriented development strategies. The outward-oriented developing economies of East Asia have certainly outperformed the inward-looking economies of Latin America, a conclusion which has been reached by many observers, including the present author (see Balassa (1986) and Sachs (1985), among others). It is also plausible to link much of this superior performance directly to the trade regime. But general observations such as these do not really justify the equation of outward orientation with market liberalization, nor the emphasis on liberalization as an instrument of crisis management in the debtor countries. In my view, the increasing policy emphasis on liberalization as a tool of debt crisis management is fraught with difficulties.

At the very least, the strategy can find little historical support. The success stories of East Asia, so frequently pointed to as illustrations of the benefits of export-led growth, do not demonstrate the utility of trade liberalization in the midst of a macroeconomic crisis. In the first place, Japan, the Republic of Korea, and the Taiwan Province of China did not adopt their strategies during, or in response to, macroeconomic or debt crises. These countries solved their macro-economic and financial difficulties of the late 1940s and early 1950s long before they embarked on the path of export-led growth. The real historical cases of liberalization during macroeconomic crisis are the Southern Cone countries (Argentina, Chile, and Uruguay) during the 1970s, and these episodes are well-known debacles, in part because of the conflicting requirements of stabilization and liberalization.

Moreover, the East Asian exemplars of outward orientation dem-onstrate the practical distinction between export promotion and liberalization, i.e., laissez-faire policies, a distinction which casts doubt on some of the policy advice emanating from the international institutions (see Bhagwati (1975) for an entertaining and astute discussion of similar points). In the case of Japan, for example, MITI is today world famous for its use of foreign exchange controls and administrative guidance to spur export industries, but the World Bank is apparently not recommending such activist ministries in countries seeking to promote exports! Nor is it advocating that governments pursue policies to support the formation of giant trading companies, as in Korea. The East Asian experience suggests that export promotion policies can be pursued (and maybe are best pursued) by a dirigiste government, and even in the presence of tight import controls and tight regulations in the capital markets.

The important role of the government in East Asian development does not, of course, imply that the public sector should be involved in every aspect of economic affairs. Moreover, the successes of dirigiste policies in East Asia have likely depended on the presence of a highly educated and well trained professional bureaucracy in these countries, a crucial human capital base that is currently lacking in many other developing countries. The Asian experience does suggest, however, that successful development might be helped as much by raising the quality of public sector management as by privatizing public enterprises or liberalizing markets.

From a global point of view, liberalization might be defended not as in the interest of the initiating country, but rather in the interest of the rest of the world, to the extent that trade restrictions are beggar-thy-neighbor policies. Some of the U.S. pressures for liberalization in the developing countries (e.g., Brazil, Korea, and Mexico) indeed emanate more from concerns about U.S. trading interests than from concerns about the welfare of the developing countries. To the extent that this is the real motivation for pressures for liberalization, however, it makes little sense to press poor countries in dire economic difficulties to make rapid structural changes on behalf of the rest of the world.

The current focus on liberalization is distracting attention from the more urgent needs of the debtor countries by overloading the political circuits in those countries and by misdirecting the energies and attention of the international financial community. In such countries as Argentina, Bolivia, Brazil, Mexico, and Peru, with high inflation levels and acute macroeconomic imbalances, the highest priority of the Fund and World Bank should be to return the debtor country to a position of fiscal balance and low inflation, since other policies for long-term growth require a macroeconomic foundation of stability. As there are macroeconomic and political limits to cutting budget deficits in the short run, and as these limits are especially constraining in the middle of an economic crisis, debt forgiveness and more generous foreign aid should play a large role in stabilizing the economies of a number of countries. Moreover, I shall emphasize that the attempt to stimulate exports at all costs through trade liberalizations or aggressive depreciations of the exchange rate can often undermine a stabilization program and thus postpone a reso-lution of debt crisis.

Since comparative case studies provide a good antidote to facile orthodoxy, and since the goal of this paper is to urge a bit less neoclassical orthodoxy and a bit more realism in the kinds of exchange rate and trade policies that are recommended to the middle-income debtor countries, the following section is devoted to a further discussion of the experiences of the East Asian countries. After this discussion, I turn the focus to Latin America, to take up the linkages of exchange rate policy, budget policy, and debt relief. Discussions of exchange rate management sometimes leave the impression that there is a technical fix for the exchange rate that can be divorced from budget policies, issues of income distribution, and so on. Nothing could be further from the truth, as I hope to stress.

Policy Aspects of Outward-Oriented Growth in East Asia

Let us begin with a country example. Country "X" pegged its currency to the dollar in 1950, and kept the nominal parity absolutely fixed for more than twenty years. During the first 15 years of this period (until 1964), foreign exchange was strictly rationed by a government agency, and the currency was always overvalued. Purchasing power parity calculations using home and U.S. consumer price indices show a 60 percent real appreciation in the 20-year period. A Foreign Exchange and Foreign Trade Control Law of 1949 required that exporters remit all earnings to the government within ten days, making the government the only legal source of foreign exchange, a privilege jealously guarded by the bureaucrats in charge of foreign exchange rationing. No explicit rules governed the distribution of foreign exchange. Bureaucrats allocated foreign exchange to favored sectors and clearly gave attention to particular firms that they were interested in nurturing. Government bureaucrats often retired to those firms at the end of their official careers. Rationing was so tight that private individuals were not allowed any foreign exchange for tourism abroad between 1950 and 1964.

Domestic capital markets were highly regulated and completely shut off from world capital markets. The government was the only sector with access to international borrowing and lending. Foreign direct investment was heavily circumscribed, with majority ownership by foreign firms both legally and administratively barred. During the early to mid-1950s, about a third of external funds for industrial investment originated in loans from government financial institutions, at preferential rates that varied across firms and industries. These state financial institutions remained an important source of cheap financing until the 1960s.

The country in question, as will be familiar to many, is Japan. But the description sounds like many countries in Latin America, complete with overvalued exchange rates, foreign exchange rationing, restrictions on foreign direct investment, government allocation of credit, and so on. Moreover, this policy framework was in place for much of the "rapid growth period" in Japan (conventionally dated as 1955–73), which may arguably be the most remarkable two decades of a country's economic development in world history. I begin with this example to urge on the reader a humble and inductive state of mind regarding growth-oriented adjustment. The policies of "outward orientation" in Japan, and in East Asia generally, have not been modeled on a free market approach as is frequently asserted.

Even though the real lessons of the East Asian successes are not yet understood by scholars, a brief review of the experiences of Japan, the Republic of Korea, and the Taiwan Province of China can do much to inform the current debate about growth-oriented adjustment programs. The histories of these countries demonstrate that, while not mainly free market in spirit, these governments have consistently followed certain basic precepts in the design of their economic policies. First, government budgets have generally been maintained near balance, often with large surpluses on the current account of the budget. Tight budgets have had several salutary effects. Inflation rates have been low and fairly stable, since governments in East Asia have not had to resort to the inflation tax for purposes of government finance. This has meant, among other things, that nominal exchange rates could be maintained at fairly stable levels without jeopardizing export profitability. Also, with surpluses in the current account of the budget, government savings have contributed to the rapid rate of capital accumulation in these countries. A third benefit of tight budgets has been that governments have had the resources and flexibility to use subsidies and other fiscal incentives to promote particular sectors of the economy or to offset reductions in general export profitability that might arise from an overvaluation of the nominal exchange rate.

With respect to export policy, once these economies started on the path of export-led growth in the early 1960s, the profitability of exports was jealously guarded, not through a generalized liberalization of imports, but rather through a combination of exchange rate management and fiscal incentives for exports. Incentives have generally been applied to promote exports with a natural comparative advantage (labor-intensive manufactures initially; capital-intensive manufactures later). Agriculture has not been taxed but, if anything, protected relative to industry. Nominal exchange rates have been adjusted periodically to keep real exchange rates at realistic levels (a policy which has been easier to pursue than in Latin America because of the lower inflation), and when exchange rates have become overvalued, they have been devalued or compensated for by greater export subsidies. In the three countries, exporters have enjoyed certain key fiscal incentives, especially the rebate on tariffs that they paid on imported inputs for export production, low or zero export taxes, and subsidized credits. A cardinal principle for export policy has been that the input and output prices faced by exporters should be maintained at world levels so that exporters may compete effectively with foreign firms facing similar prices and technology.

The preservation of export profitability is an orthodox policy recommendation, but much else about export promotion in Japan, the Republic of Korea, and the Taiwan Province of China deviates significantly from typical Fund–World Bank policy recommendations. This is not surprising given the absence of a liberal tradition in the histories of any of these countries. In each of the countries, policy-making on exports has started from the premise that successful export promotion requires the import of foreign technologies and the exploitation of static and dynamic scale economies, and this must take place in the context of weak and fragmented domestic capital markets. In these circumstances, purely free markets have little to recommend, and even neoclassical economics recognizes a strong potential case for government intervention, as was recently stressed by Robert Lucas (1985). The case for intervention is strongest when the adoption of new technologies involves positive externalities (e.g., through industry-wide learning curves), or when production involves significant economies of scale.

In Japan, the government role started as far back as the Meiji restoration, when state enterprises were set up as the country's first exporting firms. As Smith (1955, p. 102) notes in his classic study of the Meiji period,

> In developing modern industry the government had no choice but to act as entrepreneur, financier, and manager. Except in the silk

industry, where uniquely favorable conditions prevailed, private capital was too weak, too timid, and too inexperienced to undertake development—even with government aid which was given generously but without initial success.

Johnson (1982) details many of the features of government intervention in the years after World War II. In this period, the promotion of industry was less through direct state production than through an activist role of the government in supporting large enterprises, strengthening their bargaining position vis-à-vis foreign firms (especially in the licensing of foreign technologies and in the imports of raw materials), and preventing their acquisition by foreign firms. Until the 1960s, for example, Japan maintained strong explicit controls on foreign direct investments into the country (e.g., by requiring Japanese majority ownership of firms), and even after the formal liberalization, MITI has continued to block foreign direct investments in industries that MITI is trying to promote.

The whole nexus of Japanese policies may be seen as having the goal of fostering domestic entrepreneurs, with a sound technology base, and with a strong bargaining position vis-à-vis foreign rivals in home and foreign markets. Other policies discussed by Johnson in support of these goals include the state role in allocating credit through state banks and the Fiscal Investment and Loan Plan (which is the public sector investment budget, under the control of the Ministry of Finance), the elaborate trade promotion apparatus of MITI, the virtually total control over foreign exchange by MITI until 1964, the virtually total screening of foreign capital imports and exports by MITI and the Ministry of Finance until 1980 (despite de jure liberalization of foreign direct investment in the 1960s), and public-private forums such as the Industrial Rationalization Councils run by MITI.

The Taiwan Province of China has also pursued activist industrial policies that are most marked in the large role of state-owned enterprises in the industrial sector. It is more heavily dependent on state-owned industry than is probably any country in Latin America, with the possible exception of Venezuela. During 1978–80, for example, state-owned industry in the Taiwan Province accounted for no less than 32 percent of domestic capital formation, while the comparable shares for Argentina, Brazil, and Mexico were 19.6

percent, 22.8 percent, and 29.4 percent, respectively.[1] Outside of the state sector, the government has encouraged small and medium-size enterprises through a variety of tax incentives and regulatory policies.

Korean export policies have differed from those of the Taiwan Province of China, and have been closer to Japan's in their emphasis on fostering large-scale firms in the private sector through extensive state support. A major policy instrument has been interest rate subsidies for export firms. While many observers feel that the emphasis on state support of heavy industry was pushed too far at the end of the 1970s, government support was critical in development of several industries, particularly iron and steel, cement, fertilizers, and petroleum. As in Japan, the state has consciously fostered a few large trading firms that account for a large share of the country's international trade.

We can summarize this part of the discussion by saying that the role of government in Japan, the Republic of Korea, and the Taiwan Province of China has been large, as in Latin American, but it has been systematically different. In Table 1, some summary data show that there is also no case for calling Asia a case of "small" government versus Latin America as a case of "big" government by more standard criteria, such as tax revenues and government expenditure as a percent of GNP or the predominance of state enterprise in industrial production and domestic fixed investment.

A third fundamental aspect of government policy in Japan, the Republic of Korea, and the Taiwan Province of China has been the promotion of relatively equal income distributions, most fundamentally through policies that equalized the rural income distribution and that kept the urban rural differentials much narrower than in other developing countries. One measure of the greater income equality in these countries than in Latin America is shown in Table 2, which illustrates income shares of upper and lower quintiles. By historical accident, Japan, the Republic of Korea, and the Taiwan Province of China were all pushed to undertake fundamental land reforms in the late 1940s and early 1950s. In Japan, the impetus came from the U.S. occupation authorities, who assumed (with some

---

[1] See Floyd, R. H., and others, *Public Enterprise in Mixed Economies* (Washington: International Monetary Fund, 1984), Table 1.

**Table 1.   The State Sector in the Macroeconomy, Selected East Asian and
Latin American Countries**
(In percent of GNP)

	Government Expenditures	Government Revenues	State Enterprise Value Added[1]	State Enterprise Investment[2]
Japan	18.9	n.a.	n.a.	11.6
Republic of Korea	19.5	19.1	6.4	25.1
Taiwan Province of China	27.5	20.0	13.6	35.0
Argentina	21.6	16.5	4.8	20.7
Brazil	21.8	26.1	n.a.	22.8
Mexico	31.7	17.0	6.1[3]	27.0

Sources: Government expenditures: Japan, Korea, Argentina, Brazil, and Mexico from
World Development Report (1986), Table 26. For the Taiwan Province of China, Myers
(1986), p. 43. Data are for 1982 for all countries except the Taiwan Province of China,
for which 1981 is reported. Government revenues, same as expenditures. State enterprise
data are from Floyd, and others, (1984), Table 1, and apply for the following years: Japan,
1974–77; Korea, 1974–77; Taiwan Province of China, 1974–77; Argentina, 1976–77;
Brazil, 1980; Mexico, 1975–77.
   [1] Percent of aggregate GDP at factor cost.
   [2] Percent of total fixed investment.
   [3] Largest 22 state enterprises only.

exaggeration) that wealthy rural landlords had supported Japanese
militarism. In the Republic of Korea, the impetus came from several
sources, including the example of North Korean land reform in 1946
and the fact that many large landholdings had been held by the
Japanese, or by individuals linked to the Japanese. In the Taiwan
Province of China, land reform was carried out by the new Chinese
Nationalist government at the expense of the Taiwanese landholder
class to whom the Nationalists had no obligations or ties. As in the
Republic of Korea, the expulsion of the Japanese made the case for
land reform easier. Land reform was viewed as vital in establishing
peasant support for, or at least acquiesence in, the Nationalist rule
over the Taiwan Province of China. In all three cases, the land reform
was extensive, virtually eliminating farm tenancy, which was widespread prior to the reforms. In Japan in 1936, pure tenancy accounted
for 27 percent of farmers, while 42 percent leased some of their land
from landlords (see Allen (1965)). Almost all these farmers were
converted to individual proprietors by the reforms. In pre-reform

Table 2.   Income Shares of the Top and Bottom Quintiles in East Asia and Latin America

	Income Share of Households		Ratio
	Bottom 20 percent	Top 20 percent	Top to bottom
Argentina (1976)	4.4	50.3	11.4
Brazil (1972)	2.0	66.6	33.3
Mexico (1977)	2.9	57.7	19.9
Japan (1979)	8.7	37.5	4.3
Republic of Korea (1976)	5.7	45.3	7.9
Taiwan Province of China (1976)[1]	9.5	35.0	3.7

Sources: World Development Report, (1985), Table 28, pp. 228–29, and for Taiwan, Province of China, Myers (1986), Figure 6, p. 24.

[1] Approximate.

Korea, 49 percent of the farm households consisted entirely of tenant farmers, while 35 percent were partly tenants (Cole and Lyman (1971, p. 21)). In the Taiwan Province of China, tenancy accounted for approximately 44 percent of households before the reform but dropped to about 15 percent five years after the land reforms went into effect (Fei, Ranis, and Kuo (1979, p. 43)).

These land reforms were probably more extensive than in any other case in modern history and could be accomplished only because of the extraordinary national circumstances in each country. Not only was the land redistributed, but the land reforms represented a substantial expropriation of landlords since compensation for the land taken was in each case substantially reduced by high concurrent inflations. The landlords, without political power in U.S.-occupied Japan, the Taiwan Province of China under the Nationalists, and the Republic of Korea in wartime conditions, could not effectively mobilize political opposition.

The political and economic importance of these reforms for subsequent growth cannot be overstated. By creating a rural sector of small, independent proprietary farmers, the reforms allowed these countries to escape from a seemingly endless cycle of rural violence and instability and instead created a conservative peasantry that lent strong support to the national governments. In terms of production, the long-term effects were highly salutary, with a great boost to farmer incentives. In part, this reflects the good fortune of technology since the reforms applied mainly to paddy rice, for which plantation-style economies of scale do not exist. In fact, the conversion of tenants to proprietors probably had little direct effect on technology, since the pre-reform tenants already worked the land as individual producers.

All studies show that the land reforms directly narrowed the income distribution to a substantial extent (other factors that also contributed to income equality were the destruction of wealth by war in all three countries, the fact that much wealth was held by colonial Japanese in the Republic of Korea and the Taiwan Province of China, and the high inflations in all three countries, which wiped out the values of government bonds). The land reforms also had a pervasive long-term but indirect effect on the income distribution by shifting the political balance toward rural interests. As an interest group, farmers were strengthened significantly because a tiny class of unpopular landlords was replaced by a massive class of small and prosperous peasants, who could now voice demands on their own behalf. In all three countries, government expenditures and regulations subsequent to the reforms have acted to give positive effective protection to agriculture, and to devote a sizable fraction of government infrastructural investment to the rural sector. In the 1986 *World Development Report*, for example, the Republic of Korea is shown to give the highest degree of producer protection in wheat and rice of all the countries covered in the study (Figure 4.1, p. 64; Japan and the Taiwan Province of China are not in the sample of countries).

In Sachs (1985), I speculated that the political strength of the rural sector in East Asia could help to explain the historical willingness of the East Asian economies to make timely exchange rate depreciations, in distinction to the notorious Latin American resistance to depreciations. Relying on computable general equilibrium models and well known analytical results, I noted that exchange rate depreciations can be expected to transfer incomes from the urban to the rural sector, compared with a policy of quantity rationing of foreign exchange. In Asia, rural interests of the class of independent farmers has been influential. In Latin America after the Great Depression, the class of rural landlords has lost out to urban interests. In Asia, the effect of devaluation on income distribution will be neutral or even equalizing, since incomes of a large class of small farm proprietors will be raised. In Latin America, the effect will be to widen the income distribution, or at least will be perceived to be so by political actors, since large landholders will benefit by increased rental income, while landless peasants may well experience a fall in their real incomes. Unfortunately, the International Monetary Fund *Staff Papers* has apparently never contained in 30 years an empirical study on the actual distributional effects of devaluations.

The preceding sketch of the basic macroeconomic, trade, and industrial policies in East Asia might leave the wrong impression that economic success in the region has been fundamentally the result of particular government policies. Economists do not know enough even in principle to draw such a conclusion, and it is also clear that there have been several other factors at work. For completeness, one must mention high private sector savings rates, a low degree of labor unrest, which in the Republic of Korea and the Taiwan Province of China is partly the result of government suppression of union activity, remarkable political stability, with 30 years of one-party rule in all the countries (democratically so in Japan, of course), and extensive political, strategic, and financial support from the United States, especially in the key early phases of the high-growth period.

Finally, we should examine the critical issue of the time phasing of the policies in Japan, the Republic of Korea, and the Taiwan Province of China. There is much talk about the need for proper phasing of stabilization and liberalization, but there is less serious attention to the matter in practice. The paper by Michalopoulos states, for example, that "There is little disagreement that stabilization needs to precede structural adjustment if the latter is to succeed." But there are few cases indeed in which the World Bank has been content to let structural matters sit for a period of months, not to mention years, while waiting for stabilization to solidify. The East Asian experience does not suggest that stabilization can be completed in one year, and liberalization in the next. The proper phasing is likely to be much more extended.

In the three East Asian countries under review, the postwar period began with an initial phase of macroeconomic instability, which was followed by several years of stabilization and import substituting growth, and eventually by a turn to export-led growth in the early 1960s.[2] In Japan, hyperinflation prevailed after Japan's defeat in

---

[2] The very high inflation rates in the three economies give an indication of the extent of the initial macroeconomic imbalances. Annual inflation rates reached 334 percent in Japan in 1947, 500 percent in the Republic of Korea in 1951, and 3,400 percent in the Taiwan Province of China in 1950.

World War II until the stabilization program of 1949 (the so-called Dodge Line). From 1950 to about 1960, growth was mainly oriented toward import substitution and the building of domestic infrastructure. The export-led high growth spurt may be dated from the onset of the "Growth Doubling Plan" of 1960. In the Republic of Korea, the hyperinflation during the Korean War was not finally brought under firm control until 1957. During the 1950s, the democratic administration of Rhee Seung Man pursued a policy of import substitution financed heavily by U.S. aid. The export promotion phase first got started after the toppling of Rhee in 1960, with a devaluation in 1961, but it is usually dated to the major policy reforms undertaken by the military government of General Park Chung Hee in 1964 and 1965. The prospects of the phased withdrawal of U.S. financial assistance in the mid-1960s was a major prod to these policy changes. In the Taiwan Province of China, the hyperinflation of the Chinese Civil War was brought under control by 1951. As in the Republic of Korea, the new government pursued a policy of import substitution during most of the 1950s. The prospect of declining U.S. financial assistance was again a major spur to the shift to export promotion at the end of the 1950s. In 1958–59 the Nationalist Government introduced a devaluation and unification of the exchange rate, as well as other reforms, to initiate the phase of export-led growth.

There are three notable features of these transitions. The first is the significant time interval between economic stabilization and the beginning of export-led growth. By the early 1960s in each of the countries, the dire macroeconomic imbalances of the preceding decade were long in the past. Inflation and budget imbalances had been under control for at least five years. Economic growth was adequate, if not spectacular in the Republic of Korea and the Taiwan Province of China, and it was already truly spectacular in Japan. The governments had in hand, and in prospect, the financial means to make large infrastructural investments, to provide export subsidies or other fiscal incentives to exports when desirable, and to avoid a debilitating fiscal contraction in the near future. Of course the economies did not look as strong in prospect as they now look in retrospect, and the anticipated withdrawal of U.S. financial assistance from the Republic of Korea and the Taiwan Province of China was viewed with great anxiety, but at least the reforms were not emergency measures.

There are good conceptual reasons for believing that this phasing was important for the political and economic success of the export-led growth policies. In an unstable macroeconomic environment, investors are unlikely to begin to expand export capacity to absorb the slack from a declining import-competing sector. Moreover, the instruments of stabilization may well compete with the instruments of liberalization. Stabilization might require the confidence building measure of a stable exchange rate; liberalization might require a real exchange rate devaluation. Stabilization might require a rise in trade tax revenues; liberalization might require a cut in trade taxes or even an increase in export subsidies. Stabilization might require a cutback in public investments; liberalization might require a rise in public infrastructure investment in ports, communications, and transportation. And as Calvo (1986) has stressed, the welfare gains from a reform can be diminished, or even become losses, when the sustainability of the reform is doubted by the public, or in Calvo's terms, when it is an "incredible reform." All these problems obviously afflicted the Southern Cone stabilizations at the end of the 1970s.

The second important aspect of the transition process was the substantial levels of U.S. financial assistance provided to each of the countries. There is presently a dangerous myth that governments can work their economies out of any difficulties, no matter how severe, if only the correct policies are followed. The East Asian economies are often taken as examples where such hard work paid off. The truth, however, in the cases of Japan, the Republic of Korea, and the Taiwan Province of China, is that extensive financial and political assistance from the United States was a vital component of stabilization. (The same key stabilizing role of foreign assistance, in the form of substantial debt forgiveness, as well as foreign aid is evident in the case of Indonesia after the fall of Sukarno.) The U.S. paid for a large share of the imports and budgets of the Republic of Korea and the Taiwan Province of China for most of the 1950s, and U.S. military expenditures in Japan (the so-called special procurement funds) similarly provided enormous balance of payments support. The importance of this foreign aid is illustrated in Table 3, where we see that U.S. foreign aid to the Taiwan Province of China and the Republic of Korea financed a large share of their imports during the period, and a large share of government expenditures. (Other estimates of import shares covered by foreign aid, as in Mason and

Table 3.   U.S. Financial Assistance to The Republic of Korea and the Taiwan
Province of China, 1955–59
(In millions of U.S. dollars and percent)

	1955	1956	1957	1958	1959
Taiwan Province of China					
Total U.S. aid	90.4	97.3	96.9	93.7	86.3
Percent of Taiwanese imports	43	39	36	30	29
Republic of Korea					
Total U.S. aid	149.3	131.3	103.2	97.0	105.9
Percent of Korean imports	46	n.a.	36	30	35
Percent of Korean central					
government expenditures	68	n.a.	27	16	33

Sources: For Taiwan Province of China, Lin (1973), pp. 72–73. For the Republic of
Korea, Cole and Lyman (1971), p. 266, and International Financial Statistics Yearbook
(1985).

others (1980, pp. 165–208), in the case of the Republic of Korea, show
an even larger role for aid.) We will return later to the case for partial
debt forgiveness in the Latin American economies as a way to give
them a comparable financial fresh start.

The third aspect of timing involves the policy reforms once export-
led growth commences. In none of the countries was there a sudden
removal of tariff or quota protection for domestic industry, or indeed
anything approaching the adoption of a flat tariff of 10 to 20 percent
in the course of a five-year period (this is the policy recommendation
of Balassa and others (1986, p. 89) for Latin America, one that is
made after the inevitable bow to East Asian success). As Lin (1985,
p. 46) notes with regard to the Republic of Korea and the Taiwan
Province of China:

> In fact, systematic decontrol of imports did not occur in either
> country until the late 1960s, well after the success of their export
> promotion efforts. In the interim, trade liberalization measures
> consisted primarily of allowing imports of intermediate products
> duty-free for use in export processing and of requiring domestic
> producers of import substitutes to reduce their prices relative to
> potential imports in order for their products to remain under import
> control.

In Japan as well, the process of shifting to export-led growth got
underway only in the 1960s, and indeed it was not until 1964 that

the yen became a convertible currency in the sense of adherence to Article 8 of the Fund's Articles of Agreement. Even after Japan adopted the formal commitments to currency convertibility and to reduced tariffs, the process of liberalization has been slow. Certainly no U.S. trade official would be willing to cite Japan as a case where rapid liberalization was the instrument of export promotion!

Exchange Rate and Trade Policies for the Latin American Debtors

Overview

Viewed against the backdrop of the East Asian experience, the current policy debate over the Latin debtor countries is problematic in several ways. Too much of the policy debate in Latin America, and between the Latin American governments and the international institutions, is about market liberalization even though across-the-board liberalization is probably not the key to export promotion, and even though liberalization is unlikely to succeed in the midst of macroeconomic instability. Also, the international institutions are addressing income distributional concerns in a vague way at best, even though it is income distributional conflicts that are at the core of many of the region's problems.

For most of the Latin American countries, the most pressing problem is an ongoing fiscal crisis that erupted in the early 1980s. The crisis erupted for several reasons, including: (1) overspending in the 1970s, which left a legacy of enormous foreign and internal debts; (2) the sharp rise in world interest rates in 1980, which increased the burden of the public sector debt; (3) the cutoff in international lending to Latin American governments in 1982, which suddenly left them unable to finance fiscal deficits with foreign loans; (4) the adverse shift in the terms of trade, which depressed public sector revenues; and (5) the enormous declines in real income in the Latin countries since 1982, which have further depressed tax collections. As a result, public sector finances are under great strain in several countries. The very high inflations in Argentina, Bolivia, Brazil, Mexico, and Peru are the best reflections of the dire fiscal situation.

The foreign debt crisis in Latin America is to a large extent an aspect of this fiscal crisis. Three fourths of the foreign debt in Latin

America is a liability of public sectors. The problem of the debt is not only (or even mainly) that the various countries owe large sums to foreign creditors, but that the sums are owed by cash-strapped public sectors. In some cases, particularly Argentina, Mexico, and Venezuela, it is suspected that the country's net foreign debt position is rather modest as a percentage of national income, because the public sector's external debts are matched partially by the private sector's external assets (the cumulative capital flight of the past). According to one estimate (Dooley (1986)), by the end of 1983, cumulative capital flight accounted for 61 percent of Argentina's gross external debt, 44 percent of Mexico's debt, and 77 percent of Venezuela's. To the extent that external debts and assets balance, the relevant transfer problem is to get money from the private sector to the public sector of the debtor country, rather than to transfer income between the country and the rest of the world.

The failure to link the debt crisis and the fiscal crisis has left many observers puzzled as to why the debt crisis doesn't get better despite large trade surpluses in many of the debtor countries. Bankers expressed annoyance, for example, that despite Mexico's large trade surpluses in 1984 and 1985, the Mexican debt situation did not improve. The bankers' interpretation for Mexico (and other countries in a similar situation) was that net export surpluses were being "lost" in capital flight, so that the net exports were not reducing Mexico's debt burden. One policy prescription was to prevent the accumulation of foreign assets by Mexican exporters. But this view fundamentally misunderstands the problem. The Mexican government owes the debt, but it does not own the net exports. The fact that large trade surpluses did not relieve the debt crisis is a result of the fact that with national trade surpluses or not, the Mexican government still could not afford to service the public sector debts.

Even an export boom would have no direct bearing on the debt crisis, except to the extent that it raises national income and therefore government revenues. An export boom might improve the welfare of Mexican citizens, but it would not directly relieve the debt crisis per se. Policies to stimulate exports, through large depreciations of the real exchange rate, for example, or tariff cuts on imports, may worsen or improve the state of the budget, and if they worsen the budget deficit they may thereby worsen the debt crisis even if exports increase. A cut in tariffs will tend to worsen the budget deficit and could well intensify the debt crisis; a conversion of quantitative restrictions to tariffs will tend to reduce the budget deficit and thus ameliorate the crisis.

Liberalization measures that do not directly bear on the budget, such as a removal of quantitative restrictions, can also have important though indirect effects on the budget balance. Government makes expenditures on nontradables (e.g., public sector salaries) and tradables (e.g., interest payments on the foreign debt), while collecting income from nontradables (e.g., taxes on labor) and tradables (e.g., earnings from state enterprise exports, and from trade taxes). Shifts in the relative price of nontradables and tradables can therefore have an important bearing on the budget balance. With a large overhang of external debt, a real exchange rate depreciation (i.e., a fall in nontradables prices relative to tradables prices) will tend to worsen the budget deficit. The dollar cost of foreign debt servicing will stay the same, but the dollar value of domestic tax receipts (which arise partly from taxes on nontradables) will tend to fall. Thus, the removal of quantitative trade restrictions, by tending to cause a real depreciation, might intensify a budget deficit even if the quantitative restrictions have no direct fiscal effect. (On the other hand, in cases in which the government receives a large fraction of income from the sale of tradable goods by state enterprises, the real depreciation might help to reduce the fiscal deficit.)

My focus on budget problems does not undermine the case for more export-led growth for Latin America, but rather stresses the need for a thorough macroeconomic stabilization of the region as the first priority. The stabilization phase will require several years, and the implementation of reforms for export-led growth should be gradual during this phase. The region's long-term growth prospects will certainly be enhanced by a greater outward orientation, as stressed in Sachs (1985) among many other places, as long as it takes place in the context of macroeconomic stability. Judging from the East Asian experience, the greatest long-term gains to export-oriented growth would be a more rapid transfer of technology to the region, the exploitation of the region's comparative advantage in labor intensive manufacturing, the end of discrimination against agriculture in the region, and the benefits from important static and dynamic economies of scale achieved by producing for world markets. Another lesson from East Asia is that as the Latin American countries move toward outward orientation, they may do so with a shared role for the public and private sectors.

Nor should we be pessimistic about export growth over the longer term. It is clear that even in the hothouse environment of Latin American import substitution, many Latin American countries have been able to stimulate manufacturing exports, a point stressed by Pazos (1985–86). As an example, Brazil's dollar earnings from manufactured exports rose more than *tenfold* between 1972 and 1981, despite a heavily controlled and protected economy. Manufacturing exports rose from 21 percent of total exports to 48 percent of total exports. The key was a realistic exchange rate, attention to labor intensive manufactures, and sustained export promotion policies, but not a laissez-faire economy with a liberal import policy.

Inflation Control and Budget Deficits

Without necessary fiscal actions, no extent of exchange rate devaluations or trade liberalizations can stabilize the economies of Latin America, even if such policies stimulate exports and improve trade balances. The large inflations throughout the hemisphere are first and foremost a reflection of the continuing fiscal deficits. In the absence of fiscal correction, continuing resort to the inflation tax will be necessary, and the exchange rate will have to be devalued in line with the underlying budgetary needs for the inflation tax. If the government attempts to hold the line on a freely convertible exchange rate without correcting the fiscal situation, it will lose foreign exchange reserves. If it then institutes exchange controls and rations foreign exchange, it will suffer from a growing black market premium on foreign exchange, which will not prevent prices from rising, but which will arbitrarily squeeze exporters, to the extent that they have to relinquish foreign exchange at the official rate, or to the extent that they have to engage in costly smuggling.

Several countries have attempted to stabilize exchange rates for the purpose of ending high inflations without correcting underlying budget deficits. Such a policy for the exchange rates can be seriously harmful, and particularly pernicious, since the policy will appear to be working in its early stages, even when the public knows that it will eventually break down. The dangers can be illustrated with a simple theoretical example. Suppose that a country is relying on inflation taxation to finance a budget deficit. Inflation is proceeding at a high rate, and the exchange rate is depreciating at the same rate, with a constant real exchange rate. Let us assume that purchasing power parity holds so that by fixing the exchange rate even temporarily the inflation rate can be made to fall to the level of the world inflation rate, which we will take to be zero. The demand for real money balances is a decreasing function of the instantaneous inflation rate, and thus of the instantaneous rate of currency depreciation. Suppose finally that the currency is perfectly convertible. When the government acts to stabilize the exchange rate, it freely buys and sells foreign exchange at that rate unless and until it runs out of reserves (or hits an acceptable minimum level of reserves), at which point it allows the exchange rate to float.

If the government starts out with a positive level of reserves it will be able to peg the exchange rate for a while (during which time the reserves run out) even if the budget deficit is not brought under control. The inflation will temporarily be brought under control. Eventually, the pegged rate will collapse and the high inflation will return. The specific time pattern of reserves and inflation in such a case is especially interesting. At the time that the government begins to peg the rate, inflation drops to zero. Even though everybody in the economy understands that the program will break down (perhaps in six months or a year) when the reserves run out, they know the program will *not* break down immediately. Therefore, they choose to *increase* their holdings of real money balances in the short term, knowing that inflation will be low during the short period. They rebuild money balances by bringing in assets from abroad, fully preparing to reverse the process before the fixed rate breaks down and the inflation resumes. Thus, upon the announcement of the fixed rate, foreign exchange reserves at the central bank increase, but this is not as a sign of long-term confidence, only of very short-term confidence.

Over time, reserves will fall from their now higher level, while inflation will be zero. Eventually, reserves will fall low enough that the prudent private sector will once again begin to move its assets out of the country. This will occur before the minimum reserve level is reached. A speculative attack on the central bank will occur, even though reserves appear to be well above the minimum, and the speculative attack itself will in fact rapidly drive the reserves down to the minimal level. The pegged exchange rate collapses, leading to a renewed inflation cum depreciation. Now, however, the inflation will occur at a faster rate than originally, because the government is now deeper in net debt (it has lost foreign exchange reserves during the life of the program). It therefore needs a higher inflation tax to pay for the higher net interest servicing on its debts.

This basic story captures the essence of many episodes of pegged exchange rates in recent years. The Martinez de Hoz policies in Argentina (1978–81), the Aridor policies in Israel (1982–84), and the Cruzado Plan in Brazil (1986–87) have all harbored the misconception that exchange rate stabilization alone can eliminate a high inflation, even though the underlying fiscal deficit is not relieved. In the case of Martinez de Hoz and Aridor, inflation upon the collapse of the programs was indeed well above the initial rates, and the same may soon be true of the Cruzado Plan. The advocates of the these policies often misunderstand even in retrospect why they fail. After all, the finance minister observes that the reserves go up at the beginning (a sign of confidence!) and that inflation stabilizes (success!). And then, even when reserves appear to be adequate ("oh sure, with a little slippage"), the program collapses. The public appears to be fickle, ungrateful, and even a bit unpatriotic, for instigating a run on central bank reserves.

Even when governments have understood the need for budget cutbacks, there has been only a slow process of reconstructing the public sectors in Latin America. There are two interrelated reasons for the lack of decisive progress. First, the size of the shocks has been enormous, far larger than anything that industrial countries have had to grapple with in decades. Second, there is a powerful stalemate over income distribution in most of the Latin America countries, which prevents decisive fiscal actions. The wealthy can block higher taxes, but they cannot enforce spending cuts without provoking unrest. The situation is aggravated by the fact that the external public debt is a large part of the fiscal burden, and the will to undertake powerful actions on behalf of foreign commercial banks is understandably limited. The Fund and World Bank sometime seem oblivious to the distributional struggle, which is remarkable given the degree of unfairness and inequity that is pervasive in Latin American society.

Several Latin American countries exercised remarkable fiscal laxity during the easy money period of the 1970s. Mexico squandered an enormous increase in oil revenues with public sector deficits that reached almost 18 percent of GNP in 1982. Argentina, Bolivia, and Brazil similarly ran large and chronic budget deficits during the 1970s, which were easily financed with foreign borrowing. By 1980, the public debt levels in these countries was already extraordinary. The real fiscal crisis did not become obvious, however, until world interest rates on the public sector debt rose sharply in the early 1980s and until access to foreign loans was cut off, which occurred in most countries in 1982 (1981 for Bolivia; 1983 for Venezuela). The ferocity of the shocks has meant that even stringent adjustments since 1982 have proven insufficient given the size of the resulting fiscal crisis. I will illustrate this with a case I know well, Bolivia, which almost fell into anarchy because of its fiscal crisis (see Sachs (1987) for further details). While the Bolivian picture is extreme (inflation eventually reached 50,000 percent in 1985, before being brought under control), the underlying mechanics are indicative of Argentina, Brazil, Mexico, and Peru as well.

The Bolivian government was receiving a net foreign transfer of resources of about 5 percent of GNP during 1978–80. When world interest rates rose sharply in 1980, Bolivia entered a fiscal crisis, and new lending ceased. A succession of unstable Bolivian regimes attempted nonetheless to maintain debt servicing. With skyrocketing world interest rates and no new loans, the net resource transfer of the public sector shifted to an outflow of 5 percent of GNP. The various Bolivian governments during 1980–83 did little to reduce spending or increase taxes. Rather, they substituted seignorage (i.e., money printing) for the lost foreign borrowing. Seignorage as a percent of GNP therefore rose by almost 10 percent of GNP between 1980 and 1983, about equal to the size of the shift in net resource transfers.

Inflation naturally accelerated. A new democratic government came to power in October 1982, determined to stabilize the situation, but it was overwhelmed by the task. While the Siles government did not raise spending despite enormous social pressures from its political constituency, and indeed fought several bitter fights to cut spending, it presided over a collapse of the tax system before it really recognized it. High inflation undermined a fragile system of property taxes fixed in nominal terms, specific trade taxes, specific excise taxes, and income taxes paid with a significant lag. The Tanzi effect operated with a vengeance. Public sector prices also lagged seriously in real terms, as did nominal exchange rate devaluations. Between 1980 and the first half of 1985, government revenues as a percent of GNP fell from about 10 percent to just over 1 percent! Even though the Siles government presided over the world's worst hyperinflation in 40 years, the government should not be considered profligate or expansionary. Real cuts in government spending under Siles were certainly the largest in Bolivian modern history. The government was overwhelmed by a cumulative process in which large deficits led to high inflation, an erosion of tax collections, and a further widening of the budget deficits.

The Paz government was elected in August 1985 and ended the hyperinflation within two months. Actions on the budget and supporting actions on the exchange rate were fundamental. The exchange rate was stabilized vis-à-vis the dollar, which rapidly stabilized prices, but in contrast to the earlier theoretical example about fixing the exchange rate, the exchange rate stabilization took place in the context of deep fiscal reforms. Government expenditures were reduced by a complete moratorium on foreign debt payments, as well as by a cut in public sector pay and a virtual cessation of public investment projects. Government revenues were raised at first mainly through higher public sector prices, and later via a tax reform program, which became possible to implement once prices were stabilized.

While the budget crises are less severe in the other debtor countries, the same pattern is found. The public sectors in each of the major countries experienced a sharp turnaround from positive to negative net resource transfers from abroad between 1980 and 1983. In the cases of Argentina, Brazil, Mexico, and Peru, the governments substituted money financing for part or all of the lost borrowing. In each of the countries, the cutback in international lending contributed to a fall in real output, which together with rising inflation depressed tax revenues. By 1985, the burden of the external public debt was a very large share of the budget. This is illustrated in Table 4 for Argentina, Bolivia, and Mexico, by measuring the external debt and the interest charges on all public debt, relative to general government revenues. Interest expenses alone account for about a *third* of government revenues. (Note, however, that Bolivia has suspended interest payments to the commercial banks and has rescheduled 100

**Table 4.   Budgetary Burden of Public Debt, Selected Indicators for
Argentina, Bolivia, and Mexico**
(As proportions of total government revenues)

	Net External Debt	Interest Payments on Public Debt		
		External	Internal	Total
Argentina (1985)	255	27.3	3.1	30.4
Bolivia (1985)	1,200	28.0[1]	—	28.0
Mexico (1986)	184	15.5	17.8[2]	33.3

[1] Commercial bank debt only, which is approximately one fourth of total external debt.
[2] Inflation corrected, thus representing the real interest burden.

percent of interest payments due in 1986 to bilateral official creditors.)
In Argentina and Bolivia, the high inflation wiped out the real value
of most of the internal debt, while in Mexico, the real debt grew
rapidly, because domestic bond financing supported much of government spending during 1983–86, before the emergence of triple-
digit inflation. Through bond financing, Mexico postponed its high
inflation until recently, but now will pay with much higher inflation
rates than if it had closed its budget deficits earlier.

Debt-strapped governments have several fiscal choices concerning
the size of the deficit and the methods of financing it. Different ways
of closing budget deficits have different macroeconomic consequences, not to mention distributional consequences. Normally, it is
supposed that a cut in the budget deficit will have a contractionary
effect on the real economy in the short run, and this is probably
correct for a shift from debt financing to higher taxes or reduced
spending. When the shift is from *inflationary* finance to taxes, however,
the contractionary effect is likely to be much smaller. A rise in taxes
that allows a stabilization of prices is really a shift from one tax, the
inflation tax, to another. There is little reason why such a shift in
taxes should be contractionary. For this reason, "shock" anti-inflation
programs, involving simultaneous tax increases and sharp cuts in
inflation, need not have a major contractionary effect on the economy.
In the case the fiscal cutback involves a suspension of foreign debt
servicing, as in Bolivia and Peru, then the program might be
expansionary on balance, since the drop in the inflation tax is matched
by a decline in transfers to foreigners, rather than a rise in domestic

taxes. The private sector on balance ends up paying less "taxes" (inclusive of the inflation tax).

The postwar examples of East Asia and the histories of the Central European hyperinflations teach the limits of fiscal reform. Foreign financing has almost always been needed to help a government end a high inflation, as we already noted in the cases of Japan, the Republic of Korea, and the Taiwan Province of China. Foreign largess has similarly played a role in the Israeli stabilization of 1986, with Israel's receipt of $4.5 billion of U.S. aid, or about 20 percent of GNP. Some stabilizations have started without foreign support (e.g., Germany in 1923), but have been sustained later through foreign finance (e.g., the Dawes Loan of 1924). Since the Latin American countries do not receive much foreign aid and are unable to float new stabilization loans, there is a good historical and practical case for *debt relief* from the commercial banks and from the bilateral creditors as an important ingredient of fiscal retrenchment. Ideally, the relief should be sanctioned internationally, as in the case of Indonesia at the end of the 1960s. The Fund and the World Bank could play a major role in designing international norms for such relief. But if internationally sanctioned relief is not forthcoming, debtor countries should pursue the path of a unilateral debt moratorium, as have Bolivia and Peru with some success during the past year.

So far, the international institutions have given scant attention to this case for relief. Indeed, even in the midst of Bolivia's 50,000 percent hyperinflation, the Fund mission pressed hard on the government for a resumption of interest servicing on Bolivia's commercial bank debts. This was despite the fact that normal interest servicing of the bank debts on market terms would have required about half of central government expenditures at the time, and a larger share of central government revenues. The Bolivian government refused to come to terms with the commercial banks on normal rescheduling terms, and the Fund threatened to withhold approval of the standby program. Eventually the Fund relented on this threat. Incredibly, after several months of price stability in Bolivia in 1986, and after a 50 percent terms of trade decline (tin and natural gas) in late 1985 and early 1986, the Fund continued to press for a large devaluation. The Fund complained that the Bolivian government could not otherwise close the foreign exchange gap as computed by the Fund, a gap which included significant interest payments to the commercial banks.

In effect, the IMF was proposing to the Bolivian government that it use renewed inflation as a financing instrument for renewed debt servicing. The government declined the offer.

"Shock" Programs for Ending High Inflations

Shock stabilization programs are now underway (or are in an intermediate stage of collapse) in Argentina, Bolivia, Brazil, Israel, and Peru. All these programs hark back to the ends of the European hyperinflations, as well as to the ends of the postwar inflations in Japan, the Republic of Korea, and the Taiwan Province of China, in their attempt to achieve a sudden end to high inflations (see Sargent (1982)), for case studies of the ends of the Central European hyperinflations). Of the group, only Bolivia was suffering from a true hyperinflationary rise in prices, with inflation equalling 20,000 percent in the twelve months (August 1985 over August 1984) preceding stabilization. In the other cases, the pre-shock rise in prices was much less: Argentina, 3,000 percent; Brazil, 300 percent; Israel, 700 percent; Peru, 200 percent.

All the programs share the feature of pegging the exchange rate to the U.S. dollar as a device for bringing the inflation down suddenly to the world dollar inflation rate. The central idea is to make this new pegged rate viable by bringing the government budget deficit under control in a decisive manner. In Argentina, Brazil, Israel, and Peru, the exchange rate pegging and the accompanying fiscal actions are complemented with a wage and price freeze that aims to make sure that domestic wages and prices stop rising at the same time that the exchange rate is pegged. Finally, in Argentina, Brazil, and Peru, a new currency was introduced at the time of pegging, which served in Argentina at least as a brilliant technical device to overcome the legacy of pre-existing financial contracts.

Pegging the exchange rate to end a high inflation is familiar from the end of most hyperinflations in history. A controversial aspect of the current programs, with the exception of Bolivia, is the use of wage and price controls in conjunction with the exchange rate peg. The theoretical argument for such ancillary policies is clear. The key point is a distinction between hyperinflations (as in Bolivia) and merely high inflations. During a true hyperinflation, domestic nominal contracts virtually disappear. Goods prices are generally quoted in a foreign currency. The domestic prices of commodities are calculated according to the world price, converted at the spot exchange rate prevailing at the time of a transaction. Thus, in a true hyperinflation, stabilizing the exchange rate is *sufficient* to stabilize the domestic currency price of goods. At a lower inflation, however, nominal contracts and lagged indexing schemes still exist. Pegging the exchange rate is not sufficient to end the inflation instantaneously, because of the overhang of nominal wage and price contracts written before the stabilization is put into effect. The result of immediate pegging can therefore be a significant and unwarranted real exchange rate appreciation, as in Chile during 1979–81. The wage and price controls are used to override the pre-existing contracts and to make wages and prices conform to the newly pegged exchange rate.

In the case of Bolivia, which reached hyperinflationary rates of price change, pegging the exchange rate was sufficient to stabilize domestic prices, without the use of wage and price controls (indeed, existing controls were dismantled at the start of the stabilization program). As documented in Sachs (1987), domestic prices stopped rising and began falling within 9 days of the new exchange rate peg. In the cases of the other high inflations, the starting conditions were much less severe. Pegging the exchange rate was probably not sufficient to stabilize the exchange rate, and was not perceived to be so by the national authorities. Thus, controls were instituted along with the pegged rate. In all these countries, the initial effect of the combination of a pegged rate and a wage price freeze was sufficient to reduce the measured inflation rate almost to zero. In Brazil and Peru, however, the controls provoked almost immediate shortages of some commodities, with attendant black market increases in prices.

As I have illustrated earlier, a pegged exchange rate without accompanying fiscal actions will have some short-run viability, even if it is widely believed that the peg will break down in the near future. The key to maintaining the new peg for the longer term is, of course, a degree of fiscal adjustment that obviates the need for the inflation tax. While comparable up-to-date data on fiscal positions are not publicly available for the five countries with shock programs, it appears that varying degrees of fiscal correction have been taken. In Bolivia and Israel, the fiscal actions were deep, and probably large enough to maintain low inflation for a sustained period of time (unless political pressures force a reversal of the fiscal austerity). In

Argentina and Peru, the fiscal actions were more moderate and probably only enough to reduce the inflation rates to high double digits (or low triple digits) for the near future. In Brazil, the fiscal actions were probably perverse, in the sense of widening the deficit at the outset of the program. Not only were real public sector salaries raised, but the government deficit widened as well because of increased subsidies that were used to help sustain the price freeze. The absence of corrective fiscal actions in Brazil has been manifest to close observers of the Cruzado Plan, and this is why many expressed widespread skepticism of its success already in the summer of 1986, despite the near euphoria of the Brazilian government and the international commercial banks.

It is noteworthy that a major part of the fiscal action in Bolivia, and perhaps *the* major fiscal action in Peru, was a partial suspension of interest payments on external public sector debts. Quantitatively, this suspension of payments has been a crucial factor in the success of the Bolivian program. Perhaps the greatest threat to the program is that the government will eventually accede to the pressures of the international community to "be responsible," and resume using the inflation tax to finance debt servicing to the international creditors. In Israel, the need for such an action was largely obviated by the extensive foreign aid received from the United States, as well as by the large fiscal actions in other areas undertaken by the Israeli authorities. In Argentina and Brazil, where domestic fiscal actions of the necessary magnitude have not been forthcoming, an eventual turn to a debt-servicing moratorium cannot and should not be ruled out.

A crucial aspect of the shock programs is the matter of timing in the integration of all of the pieces of the program. A problematic fact of life is that the exchange rate and price actions will almost necessarily supercede many of the supporting fiscal actions. It is simply impossible to plan and execute a tax reform in the midst of a very high inflation, for example, so that price increases must be halted before new kinds of tax revenues can be raised. In Bolivia, the tax reform package passed the Bolivian Congress only 9 months after the start of the anti-inflation program, and the beginning of implementation took a full year after the start of the program. The budget cycle might similarly require that certain budget cuts be postponed until after the beginning of the shock program. The lag between the exchange rate (and wage–price) actions and the supporting fiscal actions need not cripple a program, however, as long as expectations are stabilizing during the interim period, since households give the government some fiscal breathing room by rebuilding real money balances (and thereby increasing central bank reserves) at the beginning of the stabilization program. The real risk is that the authorities come to believe during the interim that the program runs on its own, without the need for the supporting and politically painful fiscal actions.

The major unresolved analytical issue in the design of "shock" anti-inflation programs is the question of interest rates and monetary policy in the wake of stabilization. Each of the countries has experienced very high ex post real rates of interest in the wake of stabilization. Dornbusch (1986) has attributed the high real rates to the failure of the monetary authorities to allow the money supply to rise adequately in response to falling inflationary expectations. Sachs (1987) attributes the high rates in Bolivia to a continued lack of confidence in the program for many months after its inception. Blejer and Liviatan (1987) seem to support this latter view for the cases of Argentina and Israel. To the extent that the high rates reflect tight monetary conditions, there may be a case for an initial expansion of domestic credit at the beginning of the program in order to supply the increased money demand. To the extent that the high rates reflect a continuing lack of confidence, however, such a domestic credit expansion will just cause a loss of central bank reserves, and would further undermine confidence.

Income Distributional Aspects of Stabilization

There are always two fundamental ways to reduce a budget deficit: higher taxes or lower expenditures. Their distributional consequences are of course very different. There is an overwhelming presumption these days at both the Fund and World Bank that lower expenditures are the appropriate method of adjustment. Blejer and Liviatan (1987) are typical of this view in claiming blithely that "the basic task of reducing the public sector is, therefore, the main test the [anti-inflation] programs [of Israel and Argentina] must face in the longer term." Ironically, they discuss favorably the 1967 Argentine stabilization program, without ever noting that the program collapsed in an explosion of labor unrest (the so-called Cordobazo) two years after its inception. The problem for Argentina, and the other countries of the region, has long been to find a set of stabilization policies that are both technically sound but also socially sustainable. Programs based mainly on spending cuts will probably not fit these requirements in many Latin American countries.

Here once again we are reminded of a crucial, but unappreciated, lesson of East Asia. The policy freedom of the East Asian economies to undertake adjustments in the name of efficiency exists by virtue of the relatively equal income distributions in these countries. In the absence of such income equality, policies oriented mainly toward efficiency may exacerbate an already very unequal income distribution, and may be enforceable only with heavy repression, as in Chile. Consider, for example, the policy prescription of a deep real exchange rate depreciation for the purpose of export promotion. In Latin American economies characterized by highly unequal land and natural resource holdings, such a policy might have very adverse distributional consequences, and may indeed be politically destabilizing. The same policy in the more egalitarian setting of East Asia might be both economically and politically efficacious.

The distributions of income in the Latin American countries are among the most unequal in the world, and most observers suspect that income inequalities have widened considerably in the 1980s (see, for example, ECLAC (1986)). Upper-income individuals have systematically escaped the brunt of the crisis through capital flight, government takeovers of private external debts on favorable terms, and in some cases, declines in tax burdens, while lower-income individuals have suffered through reduced public sector expenditures, especially in education and health, and sharply lower real wages in the public and private sectors. Table 5 shows that in the midst of cuts in overall public sector expenditure, the cuts in education and health expenditure have been even sharper than average. (Unfortunately, the data are available only through 1983; the situation since has probably become much worse.) Peru provides a remarkable and tragic example of this situation. Between 1981 and 1984, cutbacks in expenditures forced a reduction in food aid to mothers of 54 percent, to nursing mothers and pre-schoolers of 37 percent, and to school age children of 17 percent (ECLAC (1986, p. 53)).

It should be stressed by the World Bank and Fund that increases in taxes, especially on upper incomes and property, rather than cuts

Table 5. Shares of Public Expenditures on Education and Health
(In percent)

Country	1979	1983
Argentina	10.0	9.0
Bolivia	39.2	30.0
Brazil	13.8	11.0
Chile	21.2	19.8
Mexico	22.6	12.2
Peru	19.9	24.7[1]
Uruguay	14.1	9.9
Venezuela	24.8	27.7

Source: European Commission for Latin America and the Caribbean (1986), Table 19, p. 111.
    [1] 1982.

in public expenditures, can often bring about more equitable adjustments to the current crisis. We have seen that when compared with East Asia, the Latin American countries are not overtaxed, and indeed if anything are undertaxed. There is simply no evidence for the proposition that spending cuts, rather than tax increases, are to be vastly preferred on efficiency grounds as the method of adjustment. One can speculate, however, that in the absence of much more vigorous policies to meliorate the extremes in income inequality in Latin America, the likelihood of sustained and durable economic growth in a context of social stability is dim indeed.

Conclusions

This paper takes issue with the urgent priority that the Fund and the World Bank appear to be giving to market liberalization in the debtor countries. I suggest that the more pressing problem in these countries is the prolonged fiscal crisis, which has caused a sharp retrenchment of public sector investment and social welfare expenditures and has led to high inflations in several countries. To a large extent the international debt crisis is a reflection of this fiscal crisis, rather than a reflection of the transfer problem from debtor nations to creditor nations. The experience of the successful countries in East Asia is invoked to suggest three major lessons. First, stabilization should precede any dramatic shift to liberalization. Second, export orientation can be pursued without an across-the-board import liberalization and can be fostered by an activist government. Third, the relatively equal income distributions in East Asia free the hand of governments to focus on issues of efficiency. For this reason, in addition to social equity itself, adjustment programs in Latin America should strive to improve the extremely unequal income distributions in these economies.

The paper also investigates the use of shock treatments to end high inflations. Such programs, as now underway with significant success in Bolivia and Israel, and partial success in Argentina and Peru, combine a pegged exchange rate with fiscal discipline to achieve a rapid disinflation. In the context of hyperinflation, as in Bolivia, pegging the exchange rate is sufficient to end the hyperinflation. For high inflations, but not hyperinflations, it is probably wise to supplement the exchange rate pegging with incomes policies and price freezes. A troubling part of these programs is that almost inevitably some of the fiscal retrenchment will have to proceed after the initial exchange rate pegging, since major tax increases are likely to be achievable only after the high inflation has been brought under control. This means that the initial step of pegging the exchange rate is fraught with the danger that the fiscal actions will not be forthcoming. This danger is increased by the fact that for a short period of time a program based *solely* on exchange rate pegging will appear to be successful, with reserves increasing and inflation decelerating.

Given the centrality of the fiscal crisis in Latin America, and the political and economic limits of rapid fiscal reform, it is likely that a greater measure of debt relief will have to play a role in the stabilization process. Substantial foreign assistance has been a major factor in the ends of most high inflations, including the hyperinflations in Central Europe, the high postwar inflations in Japan, the Republic of Korea, and the Taiwan Province of China, the post-Sukarno hyperinflation in Indonesia, and the end of the high Israeli inflation in 1986. Similarly, a suspension of debt service payments was instrumental in ending the recent hyperinflation in Bolivia. Such actions may become warranted in Argentina, Brazil, and Mexico. The outcomes in such a case would be greatly enhanced if the relief is implemented in a cooperative arrangement, mediated by the World Bank and International Monetary Fund, rather than as a unilateral step by the debtor governments.

References

Allen, G.C., *Japan's Economic Expansion* (London: Oxford University Press, 1965).

Balassa, Bela, and others, *Toward Renewed Economic Growth in Latin America* (Washington: Institute for International Economics, 1986).

Bhagwati, Jagdish, "What We Need to Know," in *International Trade and Finance*, ed. by P. Kenen (Cambridge: Cambridge University Press, 1975).

Blejer, Mario, and Nissan Liviatan, "Fighting Hyperinflation: Stabilization Strategies in Argentina and Israel, 1985–86," *Staff Papers*, International Monetary Fund (Washington), Vol. 34 (September 1987).

Buiter, W., "Borrowing to Defend the Exchange Rate and the Timing and Magnitude of Speculative Attacks," NBER Working Paper No. 1844 (Cambridge, Massachusetts: National Bureau of Economic Research, February 1986).

Calvo, G., "Incredible Reforms," unpublished, presented at the Latin America Econometric Society meetings, Cordoba, Argentina, July 1986.

Choksi, Armeane, and Demetris Papageorgiou (eds.), *Economic Liberalization in Developing Countries* (New York: Basil Blackwell, 1986).

Cole, David C., and Princeton N. Lyman, *Korean Development: The Interplay of Politics and Economics* (Cambridge, Massachusetts: Harvard University Press, 1971).

Dooley, Michael P., "Country-Specific Risk Premiums, Capital Flight, and Net Investment Income Payments in Selected Developing Countries," unpublished, International Monetary Fund, Washington, March 1986.

Dornbusch, R., "Tight Fiscal Policy and Easy Money," unpublished, Massachusetts Institute of Technology, Cambridge, July 1986.

ECLAC (Economic Commission for Latin America and the Caribbean), "The Economic Crisis: Policies for Adjustment, Stabilization, and Growth," 21st Session in Mexico City, April 1986.

Fei, John C. H., G. Ranis, and S. W. Y. Kuo, *Growth with Equity: The Taiwan Case* (Washington: World Bank, 1979).

————, *Formulation of Exchange Rate Policies in Adjustment Programs*, Occasional Paper No. 36 (Washington: International Monetary Fund, August 1985).

International Monetary Fund, *International Capital Markets* (Washington: International Monetary Fund, December 1986).

Johnson, Chalmers, *MITI and the Japanese Miracle* (Stanford: Stanford University Press, 1982).

Krueger, Anne O., *Liberalization Attempts and Consequences* (Cambridge, Massachusetts: National Bureau of Economic Research, 1978).

Kwack, Sung Yeung, "The Economic Development of the Republic of Korea," in *Models of Development*, ed. by L. Lau (San Francisco: Institute for Contemporary Studies, 1986).

Lin, Ching yuan, *Industrialization in the Taiwan Province of China, 1946–72* (New York: Praeger Publishers, 1973).

————, "Latin America and East Asia: A Comparative Development Perspective," unpublished, International Monetary Fund, Washington, 1985.

Lucas, Robert E., Jr., "On the Mechanics of Economic Development," unpublished notes for Marshall Lectures of Cambridge University, University of Chicago, April 1985.

Mason, Edward, and others, *The Economic and Social Modernization of the Republic of Korea* (Cambridge, Massachusetts: Harvard University Press, 1980).

Mizoguchi, T., "Economic Development Policy and Income Distribution: The Experience in East and Southeast Asia," *The Developing Economies* (Tokyo), Vol. 23 (December 1985), pp. 307–24.

Myers, Ramon H., "The Economic Development of the Republic of China on Taiwan, 1965–1981," *Models of Development*, ed. by L. Lau (San Francisco: Institute for Contemporary Studies, 1986).

Pazos, Felipe, "Have Import Substitution Policies Either Precipitated or Aggravated the Debt Crisis?" *Journal of InterAmerican Studies and World Affairs* (Beverly Hills), Vol. 27 (Winter 1985–86), pp. 57–73.

Sachs, J., "External Debt and Macroeconomic Performance in Latin America and East Asia," *Brookings Papers on Economic Activity: 2* (Washington, 1985), pp. 523–64.

————, "Managing the LDC Debt Crisis," *Brookings Papers on Economic Activity: 2* (Washington, 1985), pp. 397–431.

————, "The Bolivian Hyperinflation and Stabilization," *American Economic Review* (Nashville), Papers and Proceedings, May 1987.

Sargent, T., "The Ends of Four Big Inflations," in *Inflation: Causes and Effects*, ed. by R. Hall (Chicago: University of Chicago Press, 1982).

Smith, Thomas C., *Political Change and Industrial Development in Japan: Government Enterprise, 1868–1880* (Stanford: Stanford University Press, 1955).

Tsiang, S.C., "Taiwan's Economic Miracle: Lessons in Economic Development," in *World Economic Growth*, ed. by Arnold Harberger (San Francisco: Institute for Contemporary Studies, 1984).

World Bank, *World Development Report 1986* (Washington: World Bank, 1986).

Discussion

Charles H. Dallara
Executive Director
International Monetary Fund

I see my task as a discussant this morning in three parts: first, to offer a few of my own personal reactions to Professor Sachs's paper; second, to stimulate some further thought and exchange of ideas on this paper; and third, to leave enough time for that exchange to take place.

First, I found the paper very interesting, very thought-provoking. My effort to respond to some of the points this morning might have been made a bit easier if I had perceived in the drafting of the written text the same degree of humility which Professor Sachs stressed this morning in his oral presentation. I think he is correct—we must bring "genuine" humility to these issues in forming our judgments and in reaching what sometimes appear to be rather definitive statements about these issues.

There are a few points in the paper, and a thesis in the paper, with which I can agree. That is that reducing fiscal imbalances, particularly in the Latin American economies, is a matter of the highest priority. The paper says that "without the necessary fiscal actions, no extent of exchange rate devaluations or trade liberalizations can stabilize the economies of Latin America." I have no difficulty with that statement nor with the thesis which runs through the paper that fiscal action is essential. I also can agree that liberalization may well not succeed, or it certainly will not make major progress in many cases, in the midst of substantial macroeconomic instability. I also have no difficulty with the view, which we observe regularly in the Fund, that governments cannot be asked to do everything at once. In addition, I think that we must recognize the validity of his point that the policies of Japan and the Republic of Korea some decades ago, and even in some respects today, are not characterized by the free market orientation that sometimes is associated with those programs.

Aside from those points and theses, however, there are themes in the paper with which I have rather fundamental disagreements, particularly the notion that liberalization and stabilization should not proceed hand in hand, but that macroeconomic stabilization should precede liberalization—particularly trade and exchange rate liberalization.

The following points briefly illustrate why I cannot find much with which to agree in that view.

First, I don't find the experience of the East Asian countries in the 1950s and 1960s particularly relevant for how Latin American economies should respond today. This is due in part to factors similar to those that Professor Sachs himself noted in his paper and in his oral comments yesterday. For example, in commenting on the comparisons drawn between Turkey and Latin America, he noted that the labor market environment in Latin America is very different from that which existed in the early 1980s in Turkey, where labor unions were not a powerful force. The same applies to the Asian economies in the 1950s and 1960s when labor unions were generally not an important factor. Clearly, unions must be reckoned with in any consideration of Latin American stabilization and liberalization today.

More generally, however, it is the change in the world economy that I think makes it particularly difficult to draw relevant conclusions from the East Asian experience and apply it to Latin America today. Not only do we have much slower growth in the world economy and in world trade flows, but we have economies which in Latin America are primarily dependent on international capital markets for their external financing. This certainly was not the case in Japan, the Taiwan Province of China, or the Republic of Korea in the 1950s and 1960s.

That means that the Latin American economies must be concerned with private market creditworthiness, and that in turn means that they must be concerned with competitiveness. These countries must focus on policies which can stimulate confidence in international capital markets. Certainly the international banking community has left little doubt in the last few years, as I suspect we will hear again today, that liberalization of certain aspects of the economies of Latin

America is perceived as critical to maintenance of creditworthiness on the part of many of these economies.

A second general point relates to the need for liberalization to facilitate fiscal adjustment. It seems to me that perhaps inadequate attention was given in the paper to the need for liberalization to help achieve the objectives of a stable and lasting reduction in fiscal imbalances.

It can be difficult to achieve substantial reductions in fiscal imbalances while simultaneously eliminating trade-related sources of revenue. But we have a recent case, Chile, which in the last few years has managed to reduce its trade-related sources of revenue without compromising substantial progress in reducing fiscal imbalances.

This suggests to me that one of the key areas of liberalization that was not addressed in the paper and that may need to accompany redressment of fiscal imbalances is the process of tax reform. At the same time, one cannot hope to create a lasting and legitimate revenue base without a relatively rational investment structure in these economies. And it is difficult for me to see how one can move toward a more rational structure of investment in Latin American economies without a more open trading regime. The history of Latin America, as well as of many other economies, is that investment in the context of substantial protectionism and in the context of substantial government subsidies may well not be the most efficient pattern of investment.

In addition, price liberalization, and liberalization of state enterprises generally, can and must be in many of these economies an important component of fiscal redressment. The need, for example, to improve the management and, in some cases, to privatize must be seen as important components of a long-run move to fiscal stabilization that will have a lasting effect.

Perhaps the fiscal progress that was achieved in the early 1980s in some economies in Latin America, such as Mexico, did not last not only because there were political pressures, but because in some cases fiscal adjustment was not accompanied by major fundamental reforms in parastatal pricing and management techniques. Such reforms might have facilitated a more lasting improvement in the fiscal positions.

I have some difficulty also with the notion that the emphasis on liberalization is part of crisis management and that there is an expectation inherent in the current debt strategy that everything could be accomplished at once. I think we could all agree that in a sense a crisis persists in many of the Latin economies, and yet the emphasis in the Baker Initiative is not to try to liberalize everything at once, but to move forward in a number of complementary areas. In many of the programs that come to the Fund Board, and I believe many that come to the Bank Board, there is a clear sense that the process of liberalization, particularly trade liberalization, must be gradual. I don't recall one case of trade liberalization that the Fund Board has approved that has not been preceded by study after study, by marginal step after marginal step, and I think it is fair to say that in many of the cases one now sees on the part of the authorities themselves some degree of regret that the initial steps toward liberalization might not have been somewhat more aggressive.

Liberalization can provide a more lasting basis in some cases for sustainable growth than can fiscal deficit reductions alone. It is clear that the process of political dynamics in many Latin American economies makes it possible to achieve substantial reductions in fiscal deficits during a period of time. But it is also possible, as we have seen, for the progress in that area to dissipate and for fiscal deficits to return to substantially higher levels.

While there have been numerous instances where trade liberalization has been partially reversed, the degree of reversal that generally occurs with trade liberalization is less than the degree of reversal that has often occurred in fiscal adjustment. Progress in that area might be somewhat more lasting.

There is a notion in the paper, and of course it is one that is widespread, that there is a certain fatigue in the debtor countries with the adjustment process. That, I believe, is an entirely legitimate and valid point. And when I begin to wonder why that fatigue exists, it appears that in part it exists because in some cases there has been a perhaps excessive emphasis on fiscal, credit, and, even in a few cases, exchange rate adjustment. Of course, those adjustments were necessary, and should have received substantial emphasis, but in the absence of appropriate liberalization measures, such as other expenditure-switching policies that might have enhanced the capacity of the economy to move into the tradable goods' sector and might have increased the overall level of productive capacity, these measures were relatively less effective. And too much of the burden of adjustment was carried by reductions in absorption.

It is perhaps, therefore, not surprising that in an environment where the emphasis has been on the reduction of absorption that adjustment fatigue has emerged. And I would hope that an adjustment approach that is more broadly based on liberalization, as well as fiscal and credit adjustment, would reduce the pain of adjustment.

Let me make just a few last points. First, I was somewhat disappointed to see the support for unilateral debt moratoriums, although Professor Sachs did make it clear that he believes that debt relief most appropriately occurs in a cooperative context supported by the Fund and the Bank. What I find puzzling in his position is that substantial—one might consider massive—debt relief has occurred in the context of Fund and World Bank-supported programs. Indeed, I think something in the order of $168 billion in medium- and long-term debt relief has been provided by the private banking community alone in the four-year period 1983–86; $63 billion has been provided by the official creditors.

I think it is a misreading of what Secretary Baker and others say to suggest that he believes, or others believe, that adjustment is simply a matter of countries pulling themselves up by the bootstraps alone. Two critical components of the Baker Initiative were the need for the commercial banks to continue to provide substantial and increased support for growth-oriented economic programs and the need for the multilateral institutions to continue to play important roles. In this connection, it was recognized that the World Bank should play a strengthened role.

In the case of Bolivia, it seems to me that perhaps there are a few facts in the Bolivian case—and I am not the expert that Professor Sachs is here—that need to be stressed. First of all, Bolivians did not entirely stop servicing their debt. They have continued to service multilateral institutions through the entire period, and that is an important distinction between Bolivia and Peru. The Bolivians also continued to service their Paris Club creditors on at least a partial basis, even when the Paris Club was not particularly expecting to receive continued debt service.

C. David Finch

Director, Exchange and Trade Relations Department
International Monetary Fund

In commenting, I am faced with a broad task. The intent in holding the seminar was to see what advice, in a sense, could be given to us and through us to our members on how to get better growth and better results in the current world environment. This particular session was to focus on the degree to which openness in trading and competitiveness in exchange rates were to be a feature of programs that encourage growth.

In that respect, I felt Mr. Bhagwati's paper set out the issues very comprehensively, and I have very little comment to make. I think his remarks are going to be a very useful part of the record and should be closely studied by countries that have the problem of how to grow out of the difficulties which they currently are in.

Professor Sachs's paper, I felt, was more addressed to the Fund staff and to U.S. legislators and was attempting to deal with much broader issues. I have sympathy for many of the points that he makes. I like the emphasis on fiscal adjustment. It is an issue on which the Fund has been way out in front, and it is welcome to see that point made. I felt, though, that his way of putting the issue was muddied and to a degree was, as I remarked to him before the meeting, mischievous. Thus, while as mentioned I like the emphasis on the fiscal issue, that is not all there is to growth, as Mr. Dallara has remarked. It seems to me that growth has to come out of countries' linking themselves more effectively into the world economy.

There are two issues in this regard. One is the exchange rate, and the other is the degree of liberalization—the stance of trade policies. On the exchange rate, I think that Professor Sachs on the whole wants to emphasize much the same issues as we would. I think he believes it is critically important to correct overvalued exchange rates, and not, as it were, to try to force water uphill. Exporters should be adequately rewarded for producing for outside markets. Although I think Professor Sachs is firmly supportive, this is not quite apparent in the way he put it when he talked of Japan having had a 60 percent appreciation, and still achieving an enviable record of exports. This gives an impression that I think is completely wrong for most of the countries that are trying to find ways out of their current problems. We would want to stress very strongly the importance of getting the exchange rate right for effective linking with the rest of the world.

On liberalization he raises the interesting and important point, that government has a responsibility in this area. Linking to the rest of the world is not going to work simply by decreeing an opening up of the economy. It needs supporting government policies and a willingness to accept the transitional costs of creating an environment in which exports will grow.

Professor Sachs notes how helpful it can be to have an efficient government export promotion mechanism. But, of course, for the majority of developing countries, such a mechanism does not exist. There isn't the equivalent in most of these economies of the institutions in Japan that are able and ready to be effective in encouraging the exporters and export sectors with the most growth potential. It is conceivable perhaps that Brazil has had a better focus on this issue than most of the rest of Latin America. But the tendency—as I think Professor Sachs would agree—in most of Latin America has been more to emphasize import substitution, to use the machine in nonconstructive ways.

In such cases, it is unrealistic to say that there is another model. The question is whether the right conditions and the orientation in those countries can be fostered by a government machine. It is our view—and I think that Professor Sachs on the whole would support that—that there is a need in these cases for liberalization so that market forces can create the right incentives for realizing the countries' growth potential.

As I say, the whole purpose of this symposium was for us to receive guidance, but I would want to stress that there are two points on which we in the Fund are constrained. The Fund and the Bank— the Fund perhaps more particularly—have a responsibility to foster open trading, as the Articles state. It is not conceivable that the Japanese model could work for the world if everybody tried to follow it, and I think it's necessary for the Fund and for those gathered together in such international meetings as this to stress that the more we can foster growth by open trading, the better the chance for the world. It is not something that we can be neutral on. I think it is incumbent on us to press for open trading to see that everybody is given a reasonable chance.

A further point that also influences us in this area: we are dealing as trustees of repayable funds. We therefore have to be thinking of the export possibilities, of countries finding ways of earning the money to repay, to keep the funds revolving. It is not, as I felt Mr. Helleiner was saying yesterday, that we are operating with public funds that can be given away. In providing resources to promote world welfare the Fund does have to worry particularly about the recovery of countries' external accounts, and that means that we have to stress the importance of export-led policies in promoting growth.

Attila Karaosmanoglu

Vice President, East Asia and Pacific Region
World Bank

Professor Bhagwati has given us a fine and provocative paper. Broadly, he has defined a measure of outward orientation; presented the empirical evidence that links rapid export growth with rapid economic growth; presented the theoretical justification for believing this link can be explained by economic behavior; asked whether recent protection represents a reason for retreating from an outward-oriented strategy; explained why developing country governments should take an activist negotiating stance on trade barriers.

For a "practitioner" like me, Professor Bhagwati's approach facilitates comment in two key respects. First, the paper recognizes that theory, not correlations, defines policy options. It shows great concern to find a sound microeconomic foundation for the correlation we observe between export growth and economic growth. For us practitioners, the theoretical basis is crucial. The weaker our understanding of the microeconomic forces at work, the weaker will be our policy advice. Indeed, outward orientation could be misunderstood to mean export maximization, that is, countries might hope to grow by giving their exports away (not, unfortunately, a contrived example).

Second, the paper recognizes that policymakers must act even when faced with imperfect economic models and incomplete information. Those not responsible for policy can speculate and investigate until they are satisfied; then they can recommend action. Those responsible for policy, though, are held as accountable for not acting as they are for acting—a tax is either lowered or not lowered, a quota is either removed or not removed. So it is immensely important that investigators like Professor Bhagwati are willing to say essentially, "Look, we don't know everything and we are even missing some important things, but we probably know enough to go more safely in this direction than in other directions." It is, perhaps, unacademic for him to take this risk, but it marks the difference between a paper valuable to a practitioner and an intriguing but abstract exercise.

Professor Bhagwati moves us ahead of a naive adoption of a simple neoclassical, laissez-faire, no-externality interpretation of openness. He introduces the possibility of success of an "ultra-EP" strategy, the possibility that differentiated incentives may be useful (he advises watching the average incentive, not the dispersion around the average). He permits some unequal treatment of foreign investment, and, broadly, allows a larger constructive role for government.

I will first make a few remarks about where my own emphasis lies in trying to link outward orientation and growth. Then I will turn to a lengthier treatment of government policy, because despite Professor Bhagwati's expansion of the appropriate scope for government, government policy still remains too small and insufficiently spelled out operationally. Finally, I will touch on what we do not know— the unsettled questions that represent the weak links between our economic logic and the advice we give.

Potential That Outward Orientation Creates for Growth

As Professor Bhagwati and others have noted, current economic theories can explain why an outward-oriented strategy can produce a jump in output, a rise in efficiency. These same theories do not, though, adequately explain why outward orientation increases growth rates. For my part, much of the reason outward orientation seems to increase growth lies not in the part of trade theory that explains efficiency. Rather, I think it lies in the gray areas that Professor Bhagwati describes, where perhaps art dominates theory, and intuition dominates induction.

First, the industrial export sector is modern in all the vague and broad sense of that word. When a developing country competes against an industrial country outside the developing country's home market, it can only succeed by "being like them." A traditional agriculture exists; a traditional semiconductor industry does not. With an import-substituting strategy, though, the developing country takes on the industrial country on its home territory; the pressures to continue modernization decline. Second, an outward-oriented export sector creates an interest group within the country with a stake in sound macroeconomic and development policies. In an open economy, private actors clearly and quickly feel the costs of delaying response to changing international environment. Governments of such countries respond more promptly.

What Government Policies Help Realize That Potential?

Outward orientation works when private decisionmakers face relative prices that reflect the true costs and returns to society of their activities. Outward orientation works even better when governments also align their expenditure and investment decisions with the same set of prices. Then the social overhead capital installed by the government backs up the private capital, conforming to the social price signals really facing the economy.

Professor Bhagwati's paper takes some important steps forward in spelling out the appropriate role of government in an outward-oriented strategy. It gets us away from laissez-faire prescriptions that these countries ignore anyway. It begins to lay the groundwork for permitting us to advise countries on their policy choices. I would add other policies to his list though.

We should see what outward orientation is and what it is not. It is not a strategy where the government makes production decisions, nor is it a strategy of picking winners. Rather, it is a strategy of making sure that the public policy and investment decisions back the winners chosen by the market.

What does this mean for the advice we give? First, it means get the exchange rate right. Exchange rates need to reflect the likely evolution of export revenues and capital inflows over the private investor's investment planning horizon. How often have we seen major projects undertaken at overvalued exchange rates, only to prove economically nonviable later at any realistic exchange rate an economy might hope to sustain?

Second, get macroeconomic policy right at the right speed. Make sure that macroeconomic policies aimed at controlling inflation and bringing down external deficits rest on monetary and fiscal policies that do not produce unnecessarily high rates of unemployment and increases in the incidence of poverty. Design adjustment periods over sufficiently long periods in order to minimize short-term losses from adjustment; make sure that some safety net exists to cushion the losses to those least fortunate who are bound to lose during the adjustment period. Without such care, the finer policy adjustments called for in developing an outward-oriented strategy will be sacrificed to the political necessities of dealing with the larger unemployment crisis.

Moreover, as Professor Sachs reminds us, an outward-oriented strategy and such liberalization as produces it are longer-term development strategies. They rarely by themselves constitute an adequate response to an immediate set of problems revolving around current account deficits, debt payments, and unemployment.

Eliminate rules and regulations that impede responses to market signals. We can often redesign regulations to achieve the same equity ends at a much lower efficiency cost. Other regulations serve no equity end; rather they reflect a motley assortment of interest groups, often a hangover from past macroeconomic decisions that may or may not have a correct historical basis, as, for example, the import licensing cliques that flower in the wake of overvalued exchange rates. Elimination and modification of such rules and regulations are often fit subjects for loan conditions.

Fourth, line up public investment and expenditures with the private economic activities that are profitable when the exchange rate is right.

Fifth, promote technology transfer by providing hospitable surroundings to direct foreign investment that aims at exports, not at jumping tariff walls.

Sixth, back up industrial exports with sophisticated government trade negotiations, as Professor Bhagwati points out.

Seventh, and critically, tailor advice to the maturity of the government. Some governments can execute some strategies well; others cannot. The Bank must keep its policy advice in line with the abilities of the government.

What We Do Not Know

In offering up all these guidelines that, for us, define the operations necessary to further an outward-oriented strategy, we need to keep sight of the important point raised at the outset.

We still do not have a good account of how openness produces high growth rates. Without that account, the policy dialogue remains difficult. The world does not conform well to the model that Professor Bhagwati describes. And policymakers in our client countries know this. For policymakers in many countries, what others have done often sounds more convincing than what theory claims.

Countries that have combined high rates of manufactured export growth with high rates of economic growth, as is well known, highly protect their domestic markets. They also subsidize their exports, particularly by providing services, especially finance, priced at rates below the market. Oligopoly, not perfect competition, characterizes their domestic markets. They exploit their home markets and they follow practices that may be interpreted as dumping. Their consumers have, by static economic measures, paid far more for commodities than was necessary. Yet, some grow rapidly. Others emulate what appear to be the same policies and stagnate, just as we would predict.

When we advise the winners, we may assert that they would do even better if they were to adopt policies closer to our idealized outward-oriented strategy. But it is precisely when we assert this counterfactual proposition that we are limited by the tenuousness of the underlying logic linking trade and growth—as Professors Bhagwati and Sachs remind us.

Moreover, even where policymakers share a common model, they might still rationally pursue different policies. Countries assign different costs to different outcomes and to different errors in policy choices—they will have different "loss functions." Rational policymakers in those countries will make different decisions in the face of different anxieties about the "second type" export pessimism, or dumping, or of differing political costs of unemployment and declines in living standards when they design adjustment programs.

The advice we give about the policies they follow must show sensitivity to these differing concerns. We cannot force countries into common policy molds and still give them useful policy advice. Failing to take account of these legitimate differences in policy choices is not just bad politics; it is bad economics as well.

For the countries of the East Asia and Pacific Region, these issues are not academic. These countries see policies that they think work and they want to practice them. They think they see them practiced by the successful developing countries, and by some major industrial countries—preeminently, though not exclusively, by Japan. Improving our analysis of these issues is the next major item of business.

Mario Draghi
Executive Director
World Bank

The main message of the paper before us is that for the highly indebted developing countries the route to stability with growth is a combination of fiscal balance and of trade protectionism. This message is based on lessons the author draws from the experience of three successful Asian countries: first, stabilization should come before any extensive trade liberalization takes place; second, export growth does not necessarily require import liberalization but can be successfully promoted through other non-laissez-faire means; third, a balanced income distribution makes any stabilization easier to achieve.

The author criticizes the World Bank and the Fund for an excessive insistence that their adjustment programs be based on across-the-board tariff liberalization accompanied by massive real exchange rate depreciations and for their lack of emphasis on effective and lasting measures of fiscal retrenchment.

It would be hard to disagree with Professor Sachs's main message or with the three lessons he draws from the Asian experience. All these are sensible per se; they do not need any direct reference to reality to prove that they are right. Practical experience sometimes may show that policies, beside being right in the abstract, even can work in the real world. I just doubt that Professor Sachs's references to the economic history of three Asian countries in the 1960s demonstrate the "workability" of the same policies in Latin America today.

Furthermore, Professor Sachs's criticism of the World Bank, though perceptive, is somewhat unbalanced and, being based on a very limited set of country experiences and of policy statements made by Bank staff, it cannot be addressed to the general strategy of the World Bank.

Professor Sachs rightly shows how wrong it is to claim that the growth of Japan, The Republic of Korea, and The Taiwan Province of China was the result of laissez-faire policies, and he criticizes policy recommendations to Latin America based on such a wrong claim. But then he seems to transpose mechanically the Asian experience to different contexts in order to suggest policy recommendations of an opposite nature.

First, the differences between Latin America and the success stories of Southeast Asia are so extensive as to make most comparisons unusable for the purpose of drawing applicable lessons.

Second, his criticisms of the policy advice supplied by the World Bank and by the Fund make the point that the monkey-like repetition of routine recipes can be lip service to ideology and a bad joke for the country concerned. But I do not think that the two institutions are guilty of this error. In general, the prescriptions emerging from the dialogue between the countries and the World Bank or the Fund are the product of a pragmatic assessment of real conditions that are unsatisfactory at the time these prescriptions are formulated. Consider for example the issue of trade liberalization. I would unconditionally agree with the author's view that real exchange rate depreciation and trade liberalization are by no means the only instruments for promoting net export growth. In fact, once we recognize that the world is quite imperfect, we may be more attracted by instruments that are less blind and more selectively efficient in their outcomes, provided there is enough confidence in the country's ability to administer the complex bureaucratic machine required by the vast array of controls, areas in which the Asian countries have shown an absolute advantage with respect to any other countries in the postwar period.

Like the Asian countries that he mentions, many Latin American countries were, until the end of the 1960s, fiscally balanced, and they had a high rate of trade protection. Still, their GNP and export growth rates were not remotely comparable with those of Japan, the Republic of Korea, and the Taiwan Province of China in subsequent years. Like Japan, they had for some periods of time overvalued their exchange rates, but differently from Japan and, notwithstanding their trade protection, the effect on their trade balance was disastrous. The Bank's policy advice may have been exaggerated at times, but it was always based on an existing situation that was profoundly unsatisfactory, often so because of policies that on the surface looked like the ones yielding the Asian successes.

The same considerations apply to Professor Sachs's remarks concerning privatization. He quite correctly points out that one should not refer to the successful Asian countries as examples of small government, since they are even larger than in Latin America. But as there is no reason for a blind support of privatization at all costs, nor is there any reason to keep alive at all costs state corporations that are inefficient and wasteful. Common sense suggests restructuring of public enterprises whenever there is a good case for government intervention, privatization whenever such a case is not there. The World Bank for its part has never rejected, and sometimes even proposed, restructuring of a public enterprise as preferable to privatization.

It goes without saying that land reform and more equal income distribution would be desirable in Latin America, even because, as Professor Sachs points out, they would make more acceptable any macroeconomic stabilization, but the issue is how to enact these reforms. Again, the Asian experience is not helpful. As Professor Sachs notes, most of the land reforms and the related improvements in income distribution were either imposed by military occupation or they were a direct consequence of the war, so that these experiences are not transferable to Latin America in which the main factor of change in income distribution has always been growth itself.

Professor Sachs observes that the timing suggested by the World Bank policy advice may be too tight, threatening the stability of the economy and jeopardizing reforms, and again he refers to the experience of Japan, the Republic of Korea, and the Taiwan Province of China, countries that waited quite a time after full stabilization was achieved before introducing structural reforms.

I would agree that the hundreds of conditions specified in the structural adjustment lending operations often produce an image in their overly broad scope of a big brother descending upon a poor country and laying the grounds for great confusion. In principle we all agree that stabilization should come before trade liberalization and that contradictory policy conditions should be avoided, but it is not at all clear how even these minimal requirements can work in practice. Whether some parts of the structural adjustment turn out to be in conflict with the stabilization program depends on the speed of the country's response to the measures envisaged and on the development of its fiscal structure. The only generalization that can be advanced relates to the second point: the more developed a country's fiscal system, the less likely, in order to achieve fiscal balance, the recourse to budget measures that are in conflict with trade liberalization. When such a fiscal system is not in place and, in order to avoid prolonged stagnation, the transition will have to be financed by means other than cuts in public investments and trade taxes. But this is precisely where I do not find the Asian experience particularly useful in today's context. Its peculiarities are partly brought out by Professor Sachs when he points out the extraordinarily high private savings rates of these countries and the large foreign aid from which they benefited during their transition to export-led growth. Other crucial factors were the sustained world growth and the different international trade situation of those years.

Even the requirement of continued financial assistance, which is rightly included as one of the crucial ingredients in the Asian stabilizations, will have to be rethought so as to adapt it to the quite different Latin American context. Some of the countries that he mentions as examples, way up to the late 1960s, had per capita incomes comparable with those of the poorest countries of the world, so much so that the Republic of Korea was eligible for IDA assistance until 1973, which, with the exception only of Bolivia, is not the case of Latin America. This fact implied that the financial assistance to these Asian countries was mostly official and had motivations different from the ones that could be proposed in the case of Latin America.

One main difference with Japan and other Asian countries lies in the absence in most of Latin America of a well-structured tax system that could make the correction of fiscal imbalances more acceptable socially. I agree with the author that this is indeed a case where the Asian experience, like that of postwar Europe, is useful.

It is not true, however, that the World Bank has not asked for changes in tax structure as a way of correcting fiscal imbalances. Most of the SAL operations that I know of have the implementation of components of a modern fiscal system as an important part of the policy dialogue with the country. (Nevertheless, the Bank could do much more in terms of technical assistance in designing such systems and in improving the process of tax collection.)

The point is that this is a much harder condition to comply with than simply cutting expenditure, so much so that Professor Sachs mentions as the main budget reform undertaken in some Latin American countries the interruption of interest payments on foreign debt. Obviously, this constitutes short-term relief for the government budget, but by itself it doesn't show any serious commitment to a permanent reduction of the deficit. All countries sooner or later abandon the state of fiscal chaos and give themselves a structured tax system. Then, the question to ask is what are the historical circumstances that brought those countries to such a fundamental decision? The answer would not necessarily single out the experience of Asian countries as more telling than others. Furthermore it might not be related to the current debt crisis in any particular fashion, except for the fact that the loss of private foreign credit, which is going to last for several years for the Latin American countries, could turn out to be an incentive to build the tax base necessary for badly needed investments.

The debt crisis is primarily a fiscal crisis, claims Professor Sachs, and I quite agree, though I am not so sure that the link between domestic government deficits and foreign debt is as direct as suggested in his paper. The overall deficit as a percentage of GDP for all the countries of the Western Hemisphere decreases from the maximum level of 6.7 percent in 1982 to 4.5 in 1984 and even lower in 1985, without a corresponding improvement in the debt-servicing capacity. One gets a roughly similar indication looking at individual countries. The fact that most Latin American currencies are not convertible implies that a lower domestic government deficit does not necessarily translate itself into a greater capability to service foreign debt.

The most effective way of securing the proceeds coming from trade surpluses, so that they can be channeled into servicing debt or into other productive uses, is the implementation of a set of capital controls, not dissimilar from the ones that were so common in some parts of Europe not long ago.

The fact that the "(Mexican) government owes the debt, but it does not own the net exports," as Professor Sachs notes, should not constitute a problem. If a government so decides, it can exercise its authority mandating that part of exports remittances be deposited with the central bank, which would change them into an equivalent amount of local currency.

On this point, there is one further lesson that can be drawn from the countries cited by the author. All of them and many others that today are not in financial trouble had rigorous controls on capital movements and on the foreign borrowing that could be undertaken by the public and private sectors.

My final remark concerns a point of Professor Sachs's paper that I like very much—its emphasis on maintaining or achieving an equitable income distribution as a prerequisite for sustainable adjustment. Policy advice is rarely wrong in its prescriptions, but it is often mistaken in its judgment of the social, institutional, and political constraints that ultimately determine its feasibility and its timing. Most of the countries that are of concern to us today need to accomplish or to maintain radical modifications in the structure of their economies so as to generate sizable net export surpluses. As we have seen, this can be achieved, in principle, either through a massive real depreciation of the exchange rate associated with trade liberalization, or through the pursuit of a more stable exchange rate policy, combined with the usually complex array of export subsidies and import tariffs. Sometimes the choice is presented as if it were between "good or bad" governments, the first being based on laissez-faire, the second on a set of active and protectionist policies.

The main merit of Professor Sachs's paper is that it draws our attention to how superficial this way of reasoning is. Let's not delude ourselves into thinking that the first route is better because it doesn't require government intervention. To avoid inflation stemming from depreciations, monetary policy will have to be tight. To avoid unemployment at levels that are socially unacceptable in a democracy, the necessary decline in real wages will have to be negotiated through some social pact or income policy. Such bargaining is implicit in the second route, where one could look at the set of trade subsidies as the outcome of a negotiation among all the interested parties.

In both cases, the object of such negotiations, with different modalities in the various countries, is the change in income distribution necessary to generate the net export surpluses. One may venture to say that democracies choose the route where a social pact is easiest to achieve and to maintain. In general, the World Bank and the Fund have the responsibility only of pointing out the possible contradictions and mistakes within the socially agreed framework. The existence of an agreement bears witness that the adjustment is the outcome of a collective effort of the whole society—this is the main lesson of Professor Sachs's paper—the kind of collective effort that we admire so much in the Asian countries to which he refers. In its absence, we know from the start that any adjustment, no matter which route is chosen, is not sustainable through time.

Comment

Pedro S. Malan
Executive Director
World Bank

We have before us one important topic, two good papers, and four thoughtful comments. What is left for an "initial discussant," as I am defined in the program, is to raise some points which might be taken up by the next speakers.

The first point is related to the dichotomy between import substitution and export promotion. I have always been uncomfortable with simple dichotomic views, which try to reduce a rather complex set of issues to "two schools of thought," or in this case, into a conflict between import substitution diehards and export promotion triumphalists.

Most sensible people both in academia and in policymaking circles in developing and developed countries alike always interpreted this issue in terms of the best policies to increase an economy's tradability, which comprises both exportable production and efficient import-competing activities. This requires, of course, getting prices right, particularly the exchange rate, which can be seen as the relative price of tradables vis-à-vis nontradables.

We should know—and I am glad to hear that Professors Sachs and Bhagwati recognized it—that export promotion does not exclude import substitution in selected sectors, neither should it be equated with the absence of government intervention.

I think the relevant policy discussion should center on how tradability can be increased. This could hardly be achieved solely through reliance on relative price changes. It is important to give appropriate market signals to the relevant economic agents, and often, during an adjustment program the price of tradables is to be increased relative to the price of nontradables. This should, in principle, shift demand, both domestic and foreign, in the direction of domestically produced goods and services. Nevertheless, there is a need for some broader governmental policies and interventions to give further indications that the change is sustainable and that a nominal devaluation will not be eroded very quickly by inflation, rising prices of nontradables, or by some wage reaction which it might generate. This is Mr. Karaosmanoglu's point of view with which I fully agree: the importance of having a companion macro-economic policy that allows for, among other things, a sustained shift in relative prices.

It is too easy to overdraw the distinction between inward- and outward-looking policies. I think pragmatism in policymaking has been and should continue to be the response, and Professor Sachs's advice and appeal for humility and nondoctrinaire positions when it comes to conditionalities should be carefully considered by our organizations as well.

Although I don't have time to go into history here, I just want to point out that so-called theoretical criticism often comes after the event. In the 1930s import substitution was a response to the prevailing beggar-your-neighbor situation. In the late 1940s and early 1950s it was a response to the significant share of trade undertaken with nonconvertible currency areas. In the 1960s it was easy to advise outward-looking policies when international trade was growing at nearly 9 percent a year in real terms and there was a remarkable resurgence of private international capital flows, which had been dormant for 30 years.

We must understand that we are dealing with pragmatic policy-makers in both developed and developing countries who have their own perceptions about the current situation and future scenarios and are responding to the best of their knowledge using "theory," but are also very mindful of the political constraints under which they operate.

I would have preferred that Professor Bhagwati would have started where Professor Sachs began. As a general matter, there is much to be said in favor of outward-oriented development strategies relative to inward-oriented development strategies. But—and I would like to quote Professor Sachs—"General observations such as these do not really justify the equation of outward orientation with market liberalization, nor the emphasis on liberalization as an instrument of crisis management into debtor countries, or even a lasting solution to the debt problem."

It is in this sense that, despite the indisputable merits and insights of Professor Bhagwati's paper, Professor Sachs's paper and presentation are more relevant to the policy discussions now taking place within the Boards of our institutions and to the enhanced policy dialogue that the Fund and the World Bank are carrying on with member countries.

Mr. Chairman, you suggested to us in your initial intervention today that this discussion should ideally lead to some policy advice for both the International Monetary Fund and the World Bank. In the light of the concerns expressed yesterday so candidly by both Mr. Conable and Mr. Camdessus, I would like to reemphasize a statement made by Mr. de Larosière six months ago while addressing the U.N. Economic and Social Council and repeated yesterday by Mr. Camdessus: "Programs of adjustment cannot be effective unless they command the support of governments and of public opinion. Yet, the support will be progressively harder to maintain the longer adjustment continues without some pay-off in terms of growth and while human conditions are deteriorating." This is an important point. It echoes Mr. Karaosmanoglu's comments on the need to tailor policy advice to the level of institutional development and to the particular political and social experience of member countries. It also recognizes something that developed countries' analysts take for granted, namely, that in industrial countries you have to make your point via political persuasion, through the domestic political process, congresses and all that.

We should not regard this as a luxury that only rich countries can afford. Developing countries' governments also have to make their cases through political persuasion. Therefore, policy advice, even when it seems absolutely right from a theoretical point of view, has to be sold, so to speak, through the domestic political process. A better understanding of these issues involving persuasion will help considerably to enhance the two-way policy dialogue between governments and the Bretton Woods Institutions.

The papers by Professors Bhagwati and Sachs represent a useful contribution to this dialogue and fit very well into the general theme of this symposium, which is some years overdue. I hope it turns out to be the first of many to come.

SESSION 5

Structural Policies

Agricultural Structural Policies

D. Gale Johnson

Professor of Economics
University of Chicago

For the 36 low-income economies with per capita incomes of $380 in 1984 and with a total population of 2.4 billion or 46 percent of the world's population as of 1984, 36 percent of the gross domestic product (GDP) came from agriculture. Owing to the difficulties of accurately estimating the incomes of poor farm people, a more appropriate measure of the relative importance of agriculture in these economies was that 70 percent of the labor force was engaged in agriculture. The remaining labor force was equally divided between industry and services (World Bank (1986)). Another indication of the importance of the farm sector, which includes farmers and the locally supporting population, was that 77 percent of the population of these countries lived in rural communities.

As economic growth occurs in the low-income economies, the relative importance of agriculture must and will decline. How fast the decline will be is primarily a function of how rapid is the rate of economic growth, as measured by increases in per capita real incomes. In the lower middle-income countries (per capita incomes from $450 to $1,620) the agricultural labor force constitutes 56 percent of the total and in the upper middle-income countries ($1,700 to $7,260 per capita) 29 percent of the total (World Bank (1986)). Several upper middle-income countries that have about the same share of employment in agriculture as the average of the group include Brazil (31 percent), Panama (32 percent), and Algeria (31 percent).

These data indicate the remarkable transformation in the structure of economies as economic growth occurs, but perhaps the point can be made more strikingly by considering changes in employment in economies that have exhibited sharp falls in the relative importance of farm employment and other economies that have not (Table 1).

Table 1. Agricultural Labor Force as Percentage of Total Labor Force, 1960 and 1984, and Annual Growth Rates of Per Capita Income, Selected Developing Countries

	Agricultural Employment as Percent of Total		Compound Annual Growth Rates in Per Capita GNP, 1965–84 (percent)
	1960	1984	
Countries with rapid declines in farm labor force			
Republic of Korea	66	36	6.6
Taiwan Province of China	50	18	6.7
Brazil	52	31	4.6
Countries with slow declines in farm labor force			
India	74	70	1.6
People's Rep. of China	79	72	4.5
Bangladesh	87	75	0.6
Mali	94	86	1.1
Tanzania	89	86	0.6
Kenya	86	81	2.1
Philippines	61	52	2.6
Thailand	84	70	4.2

Sources: World Bank, World Development Reports, 1984 and 1986, and estimates for China made by author based on data published by State Statistical Bureau, People's Republic of China.

The average annual growth rates in per capita gross national product (GNP) are also given for the two groups, and while there is a high positive relationship between labor force decline and high per capita income growth rates, the relationship is not perfect. The People's Republic of China has had a relatively high income growth rate, but with only a modest drop in the relative importance of farm employment. The Republic of Korea and the Taiwan Province of China both had sharp falls in farm employment and very rapid income growth rates. India had a small decrease in relative agricultural employment, similar to that in the People's Republic of China, and a relatively slow income growth rate. Thus factors other than income growth influence the rate at which agriculture declines, even though income growth may well be the single most important influence. Economic and social policies can influence the structural changes in economies, but more on that later.

In the low-income countries agriculture remains as a major source of exports, though a rapidly declining one in most areas. In 1982–84 agricultural exports accounted for nearly a third of all exports from low-income countries, down from nearly three fifths in 1964–66 (World Bank (1986), p. 3). In low-income Africa farm exports still accounted for 68 percent of all exports in 1982–84. These percentages may be compared with agriculture's 14 percent share of total exports in the industrial countries. Based on the importance of agriculture in the economies and farm people in the populations of developing countries, agriculture and rural people should have a significant priority in development policies. But it has not always been so nor is it so in many—I fear one must say, most—developing countries today. However, there does appear to be a shift in policies in several developing countries toward being more even-handed toward agriculture and farm people. There have emerged a number of rapidly growing developing economies that have turned from negative protection (exploitation) of agriculture to high rates of positive protection, all within two decades or less.

Obviously some economies that have followed policies that exploit agriculture through taxation, price controls, low government procurement prices, and neglect of investment have achieved reasonable rates of growth. China was such an example for most of the two decades 1958–77 during which it had a reasonable rate of national income growth of 3 to 3.5 percent while some other countries, which will remain unnamed but not unknown, have neglected or exploited agriculture and rural people and suffered the appropriate consequences. Unfortunately the latter outcomes did not result in the achievement of justice since the exploited always suffered much more than the exploiters. But China also shows very clearly that good deeds have their rewards. With the drastic revision of agricultural and rural policies in 1978–79, agriculture became the cornerstone of economic reform policy and a highly dynamic component of an economy with a growth rate at least twice what it was the previous two decades.

There is often a tendency in discussions of economic development to stress the negative aspects of the relative decline of agriculture. One of these negative aspects includes the transfer of workers from farm to city. Large numbers of farm people find themselves in urban slums or favellas, and this is considered by many to be highly undesirable, both for the migrants and the cities to which they have migrated. In reaching this conclusion most of the critics fail to realize that the migrants generally had even worse living conditions in rural areas with access to even fewer governmental and social services, with equally poor housing with no better sanitary conditions. The decline in the relative importance of agriculture as economic growth occurs is evidence of a striking and important fact: the share of the nation's resources required to produce food has declined. If the share of resources required to produce food did not fall over time, economic growth would occur at a very slow rate, if at all.

Distortions in Rural and Agricultural Sectors

Governments seem to have an almost infinite capacity to create distortions in their rural and agricultural sectors. Not only is there a wide variety of such distortionary interventions, but the severity of the extortions imposed by some of the distortions has reached amazing levels, as will be illustrated later. Compared with some governments the famous American frontier bandit, Jesse James, was a saint.

In a single paper it is not possible to deal with all the existing distortions created by output pricing policies, input availabilities and prices, credit misallocations and the existence of marketing boards that are both monopsonist and monopolist as well as an arm of the finance minister responsible for collecting part of the national revenue. But I want to first emphasize what is a generally neglected set of distortions that have a major negative impact upon rural people in the present and will result in substantial economic and social costs in succeeding generations, not only for farm people but also for city dwellers.

Neglect of Rural Education and Infrastructure

The neglect of rural infrastructure and public services has been a universal phenomenon in the industrial market economies, the centrally planned industrial economies, and today's developing economies. The industrial countries have had to pay a relatively high economic, social, and political price for such neglect, as do the developing countries today with few exceptions. No one of the now industrial countries provided the equivalent of the urban level of per capita investment in rural infrastructure and services until the farm population became a very small percentage of the total population. Even today some industrial countries do not provide the same educational opportunities in rural as in urban areas. In the Soviet Union, as of 1983, 15 million of its rural population lived in officially designated "future-less villages." These villages are to receive no governmental investment for new social, cultural, and educational structures, nor for roads or public services, such as water and sewerage disposal (Mezhberg (1978)). The objective is apparently to induce these farm people to move to more populous centers by making their present living conditions most harsh and unattractive.

To some considerable degree, the huge expenditures industrial countries now make on price and income policies that distort domestic incentives, that result in excess productive capacity, depress world market prices, and restrict export opportunities for many developing countries have their origins in the failure to provide farm people with the same educational and cultural opportunities provided urban people before World War II and the years immediately after. The fact that farm people, until rather recently, in most industrial countries had less and poorer education than their urban counterparts created a rural-urban income disparity. Failure to provide farm people with the same amount and quality of education available to city dwellers makes it inevitable that human effort devoted to agriculture receives lower rewards than does the average urban person of the same age and sex. Thus the failure to invest in rural education and other aspects of rural life in one generation becomes part of the rationale for governmental price and income supports for agriculture.

In fact, farm people suffer a double income disability. First, there is the lower income that results from more limited human capital and, second, there is the fact that a labor-earnings differential is required to induce farm people to transfer from farm to nonfarm jobs, most often by actually making a physical move. If only a few persons had to make this adjustment each year, the differential could be quite small. But in many instances, 3 to 4 percent of the farm population migrates annually, year after year for several decades. This is in addition to those who transfer partially or wholly to nonfarm employment without a change of residence. In the United States today in three out of four farm families at least one member has a nonfarm job; in Japan approximately four out of five farm families have at least one member with a part-time or full-time nonfarm job.

Policymakers know—or should know—that once per capita incomes reach $500–750 and national income grows at 4 or 5 percent annually, at least one out of two children born on farms will spend their working lives at nonfarm jobs. This raises serious questions about the universal failure of governments to provide farm people with the same access to education that is available to urban people and the unwillingness of governments to assist rural-urban migration and thus narrow the differential required to induce the high rates of migration necessary if farm people are to share fully in the benefits of economic growth and rising real incomes. Governments do not assist effective rural-nonfarm migration even while they give enormous subsidies to urban people through providing urban transport, housing, or food at much below cost. This latter approach results in rapid urban population growth but generates few new productive opportunities in either rural or urban areas. Moreover, because of the high governmental cost of the subsidies, this subsidy actually reduces employment possibilities by adversely affecting investment owing to the competition of the subsidies for available financial and real resources.

But even at per capita income levels below $500 there will be migration from farms to cities if there is freedom of movement. In part this results from population growth rates higher in rural than in urban areas. Consequently even when the percentage of the population engaged in agriculture declines slowly or not at all, a significant percentage of farm youth move to nonfarm areas if permitted to do so. As real per capita incomes increase, the percentage who leave becomes larger. Policymakers have almost everywhere at all times ignored this consequence of economic growth and development.

Output Pricing: Direct and Indirect Distortions

The nature and extent of governmental interventions in farm output prices is explored in considerable detail in the World Bank's *World Development Report* (1986). My few remarks draw upon that useful document. The general tendency in low-income developing countries is to tax agriculture as part of a strategy of promoting industrialization and urban growth. Some of the taxation is quite direct, such as export taxes, while in other cases farm products are procured in a compulsory manner at low prices, and the product sold to urban consumers at a low price, or the excess comes to a marketing board and is retained by it.

Examples of extreme exploitation of farm producers are unfortunately easy to find. In around 1980 a producer of maize in Tanzania received a price less than 25 percent of the border price, while coffee producers in Togo received less than 30 percent (*World Development Report* (1986), pp. 64–65). In India tea producers received half the border price as was also true of groundnut producers in Mali and cotton producers in Egypt. Export crops are particularly subject to heavy taxation because it provides the government with convertible foreign currency, and such taxes are relatively easy to collect unless they become too onerous. Domestic food crops also may have a low ratio of farm to border prices, as illustrated by a ratio of about 0.4 for rice in Egypt or 0.55 in Ghana.

These are illustrations of direct interventions by which governments openly transfer income from farm people to nonfarm people or to the government. There are other forms of intervention that reduce incentives to produce agricultural products. The first, namely that of protecting domestic producers of farm inputs, will be considered later. There are two other approaches that, taken together, may well be more adverse to agriculture than most of the direct interventions. These include protection of manufactured products as a part of an import substitution policy and the overvaluation of the national currency. In low-income developing countries agriculture is often the major exporting sector. Import duties on manufactured imports act like a tax on agricultural exports, and domestic prices of farm products are low relative to the prices of the protected manufactures (*World Development Report* (1986), p. 63).

The overvaluation of currencies can be the most onerous tax on tradable agricultural products. Currency overvaluation can reach remarkable proportions in some cases. In Ghana in the early 1980s the currency may have been overvalued by a factor of more than ten. Overvaluations of 100 percent are not uncommon and existed in both Nigeria and Tanzania in the early 1980s (*World Development Report* (1986), p. 67). Often what appears to be positive protection for farm products when border prices are calculated at the official exchange rate turns out to be negative protection when a realistic value is used for the exchange rate. For example, a positive protection coefficient of 50 percent will be fully offset if the currency is overvalued by 50 percent and becomes negative protection if the overvaluation is greater than 50 percent—a not uncommon occurrence.

Not all interventions in developing countries result in negative protection. In a number of rapidly growing middle-income developing countries the negative protection of agriculture that prevailed during the 1950s and 1960s turned to substantial rates of positive protection by the mid-1970s. This was the path taken by Japan somewhat earlier and followed by the Republic of Korea and the Taiwan Province of China to a lesser extent.

Input Supply and Pricing

There have been numerous instances in which import substitution policies have resulted in the development of high cost farm input industries, such as fertilizer, insecticide and herbicides, seeds, and farm machinery. But there have been many cases in which subsidies are used to lower the costs of these inputs to farmers to offset in part or in whole the high cost of the domestic product. While subsidy rates on fertilizer may seem to be very high—often 50 to 70 percent (*World Development Report* (1986), p. 95)—the net effect may be little more than bringing farm prices of fertilizer down to world market levels. We have, however, limited information on the net effect of the combined distortions—low output prices, high domestic cost of inputs, and input price subsidies. It is hoped that the current World Bank study of agricultural price and income policies will provide such information for developing countries.

We have evidence that there have been many cases of subsidies for machinery in low-income developing countries. Such subsidies are attributable to relatively low tariff rates and an overvalued currency combined with credit subsidies. The benefits of mechanization subsidies accrue exclusively to the larger and better-off farms. At least in the short run, mechanization subsidies reduce the return to farm labor. This means that the relatively well-to-do have benefited at the expense of the much poorer.

Credit Subsidies

Credit subsidies have great potential for resource misallocation and for windfalls for those who are politically well connected. Brazil may represent the extreme example of agricultural credit subsidies run amuck when it provided loans at nominal rates of interest often less than half the rates of inflation then reaching 100 percent or more a year. At one point in the late 1970s the cost of credit subsidies exceeded 5 percent of GDP (*World Development Report* (1986), p. 99). Fortunately the subsidies were sharply reduced after 1980 and are now relatively unimportant. What was supposed to be a credit program turned out to be largely a transfer program, and transfers went not to low-income farmers but to the better educated, more sophisticated, and higher-income farmers.

Subsidized low interest rates discourage lending to small or low-income farmers, presumably the group the subsidies are supposed to help. This need not occur out of malice or indifference. A low-income farmer has a modest credit demand. Many of the costs involved in making loans are independent of the size of the loan. The costs of making a loan for 200 rupees for four months may well exceed the interest collected at a rate of 6 percent, or a total of 4 rupees. From the standpoint of the credit institution under pressure to minimize its losses, it makes better sense to make one loan of 4,000 rupees rather than 20 loans of 200 rupees each.

Marketing Boards

Marketing boards must have been an invention of the devil. Why do I say this? Because the motives in establishing them seemingly represented the best of intentions—to provide price stability, to lower the cost of marketing, and to protect farmers and consumers from the avarice of traders and speculators. But like all inventions of the devil, the good intentions only masked the true outcomes. The true outcomes were that the marketing boards became instruments for the exploitation of farmers, a sinecure for the friends and relatives of the politically powerful, and a source of great inflexibility and inefficiency in carrying out their functions. These outcomes should have been anticipated. Whenever a grant of monopoly power is made to either a private or public body, one must anticipate that such power will be used to further the interests of those who hold that power.

Policy Guidelines for a Productive and Efficient Agriculture[1]

Often the appropriate objective of agricultural policy in developing countries is said to be the achievement of a more rapid growth of output. While increased rate of output growth has some desirable features, by itself it is not the most reasonable objective unless other criteria are also met. These other criteria include achieving output growth at reasonable cost and in a setting that provides farm people with the opportunity to share fully in the fruits of economic growth.

In what follows I emphasize a number of guidelines that I believe will contribute to an agricultural economy that is efficient and provides reasonable returns to farm people. The guidelines, it may be noted, follow rather closely from the discussion of distortions.

The first general guideline is that an efficient and productive agriculture can best prosper if there is a balanced policy approach. A balanced approach emphasizes incentives to produce, through appropriate prices for outputs and inputs, the development or adaptation of new and improved production techniques, and the encouragement of factor markets for labor and capital that will over time result in near equality of returns to comparable resources in agriculture and in other sectors.

In recent years a number of agricultural economists have fallen into the trap of arguing that since productivity change has larger effects upon agricultural output than changes in farm prices, getting prices right is relatively unimportant. Consider the following: "Technological change is an instrument of far greater consequences than the relative price of fertilizer in accelerating the use of this input" or "In the short run, a higher price accompanied by the introduction of new technology may encourage the use of fertilizer and other cash inputs and move output towards a higher production possibilities frontier. But in the long run, to what degree do higher prices

---

[1] The next few pages draw heavily upon my paper "Policy Issues in Rainfed Agriculture," presented at a World Bank Symposium, January 10, 1986.

encourage investment in irrigation, even more superior technology, etc., thereby including a further shift of the frontier?" One wonders why such views are maintained after the work of Schultz, Hayami and Ruttan, Griliches, and others on the role of profitability on the adoption of new technology and the responsiveness of research institutions to potential profitability of innovations upon their allocation of resources.

Agriculture and farm people should receive equitable treatment compared to urban sectors and people—there should be no special subsidies or privileges available to nonfarm people that are not also available to farm people. In many developing economies and some of the more advanced centrally planned economies, there are large food price subsidies, as well as subsidies for transportation, energy and housing, from which farm people are wholly or largely excluded. But these may well not be the only disadvantages suffered by rural communities. At least equally important are the differences in infrastructure between the countryside and the cities—roads, schools, communication, electricity, cultural activities, and the availability and variety of goods and services for sale.

The second guideline, which follows from the previous paragraph, is that farm people should have the same opportunity to acquire human capital as nonfarm people. Unfortunately, that was not achieved in the industrial countries until the farm population had declined to a tenth or less of the total population, and it is not now being provided for in any developing country. Failure to meet this guideline will add greatly to the adjustment costs imposed upon both rural and urban areas as economic growth dictates migration out of agriculture into nonfarm communities.

The third guideline is that the patterns of production should be those that contribute most to the income of the nation, taking advantage where possible of the opportunities provided by international trade. There is a body of opinion that regards as sinful or criminal an export crop that impairs food self-sufficiency. This seems to be accepted even though the export crop results in higher incomes for both labor and land. But this guideline applies not only to taking advantage of the opportunities provided by international trade. Many countries follow discriminatory pricing and subsidy policies with respect to products that are primarily domestically produced and consumed. In particular, countries in Asia discriminate against rice relative to wheat. Both India and China have farm prices for (paddy) rice that are at or below wheat prices, yet international market price relationships would suggest a paddy price significantly higher than the farm price of wheat. The difference in relative prices is not insignificant—domestic milled rice prices are approximately a third lower than domestic wheat prices, using relative international prices as the guideline. The rationale for this pricing behavior seems reasonably straightforward—it is believed that the price elasticity of supply of rice is significantly lower than for wheat. It is not obvious that this conclusion has ever been put to a reasonable scientific test. What may be true is that in developing countries wheat farmers have greater political influence than rice farmers.

I have observed the developments of agricultural policies in a considerable number of countries for the past four decades. One of the most discouraging lessons I have learned is that the failure of a policy measure is almost never followed by the abandonment of that measure. Instead, an effort is made to fix the measure, often in a way that exacerbates its already bad record, or a new measure is introduced designed to offset some of the worst effects of the first measure. If low farm prices inhibit output growth and the adoption of new production techniques, the simple alternative of freeing the price is seldom given more than a moment's consideration; the alternative adopted is to introduce a subsidy on some input such as fertilizer, whose benefits will go primarily to the larger and more well-to-do farmers.

Fortunately one can point to an important exception to the general rule that policy failures are never recognized. The exception is the remarkable series of reforms undertaken by China since 1978. It is hard to believe that there has ever been such a systematic dismantling of failed farm policies as has occurred in China. The consequences have been very positive. In just six years agricultural production increased by 50 percent and agricultural plus industrial activities at the village level increased by more than 60 percent. This was achieved with at most a 25 percent increase in inputs in agriculture.

There is some evidence of change, admittedly at modest pace, in some of the African countries that have had such disastrous agricultural performance in recent years. But in all too many countries failed policies are continued with little or no change.

Let me conclude this part of my discussion by stating a final guideline: Governmental intervention in agricultural markets should occur only when there is a strong affirmative case for so doing. For many of the interventions that we see in the world today, an affirmative case cannot be made. One argument against most of the interventions is that they are both ineffective in achieving their stated objectives and impose substantial costs upon taxpayers and consumers or, in too many cases, are made possible by economic exploitation of farm people.

I do not argue against every market intervention. But such interventions should only be introduced after thought and study. It is clear that once an intervention is introduced, such as a price support, a price subsidy for consumers, or an input price subsidy, it is difficult to eliminate. Thus the expected gain from an intervention should be substantial because it is very evident that the potential economic and social losses can be very large if the intervention becomes a political ploy used in an effort to maintain a group in power or to get into power.

Market Price Interventions That Do Less Harm Than Good

The discussion of the past few pages is not an argument against all forms of governmental intervention in agriculture in the developing countries. The major argument was that farm people should not be discriminated against in the provision of public services and infrastructure such as transport, communication, and cultural facilities. Nor should farmers be expected to pay for a disproportionate share of the costs of modernizing the economy. In this scenario, there is a large role for government in the provision of education, medical facilities, research, and an efficient and extensive rural infrastructure. But governments go beyond these areas and engage in market interventions. What guidelines can be provided for developing countries that wish to use market interventions in a constructive way, not as a means of exploiting farmers or providing jobs for someone's relatives, but in an effort to improve the functioning of the market? Unfortunately, this is not a question for which there is a generally acceptable set of recipes. I shall make a few general comments.

In establishing the general structure of farm prices when governments intervene there are three important considerations that should be borne in mind. This discussion represents primarily an amplification of the guidelines referred to earlier. The first is that of relative farm or producer prices for the various farm products. I can see no rational basis for departing significantly from the relative international market prices for the same products, after appropriate adjustments for quality and location. The second is that of the relationship of farm prices, on the average, to the prices of tradable nonfarm products or to the prices of products that farmers purchase. The third is that where there is direct governmental intervention through procurement and control of marketing, seasonal price differentials should be permitted that encourage storage by producers and consumers. As a corollary, there should also be regional price differences that reflect differences in transport and marketing costs.

What is the particular merit of relative farm product prices that reflect relative international market prices? Relative international prices, averaged over a period of three to five years, are measures of the alternatives available to a nation and thus provide a guide for its own use of resources. If wheat sells in world markets for less than half the price of milled rice, what does any country gain from maintaining the prices of the two grains at substantially different relative prices? This is not a hypothetical statement since a number of developing countries maintain such a price relationship between rice and wheat.

There is nothing in the merit of international price relationships that implies that international market prices are "fair" or "equitable" or that they always accurately reflect world supply and demand conditions. At times international market prices for farm products are significantly distorted, as they are in 1987. But such prices do reflect the terms on which most farm products can be exchanged and thus have an important implication for what resources can profitably be devoted to the production of a particular product relative to acquiring the product by trade.

The second consideration relates, of course, to whether farm people receive a share of the national output commensurate to their contribution to it, based upon relative international values. The question relates to whether or not there is an urban bias expressed through the relative prices of the farm and nonfarm sectors of the economy. Obviously farm people can realize increased incomes over time when the ratio of domestic farm prices to domestic nonfarm prices is less than the similar ratio in international markets. But given the extent that international market prices of major farm products are depressed by the excess agricultural resources in the industrial countries owing to these countries' protection of agriculture, even approximate equality in the farm nonfarm price ratios results in some urban bias in the developing countries. To have a lower ratio of farm to nonfarm prices is to clearly and significantly discriminate against farm people.

Governmental market interventions all too often fail to reflect even a tiny percentage of the subtlety and differentiation with respect to quality, time, and location displayed even by markets that function under what most of us would consider to be primitive conditions under less than ideal conditions. Studies, such as Uma Lele's study of grain marketing in India, show very clearly that the private marketing systems that have emerged in developing countries operate at low cost and with a degree of effectiveness in reflecting underlying demand and supply conditions that one does not find in governmental marketing institutions. It may well be that it is more difficult to carry out various procurement and price stabilizing activities by working with the private market instead of displacing it. But when all costs are taken into account, these difficulties are not large compared with the costs of the alternative approach of creating a governmental bureaucracy to carry out, quite ineffectively, the functions performed by the private market.

It is quite obvious that most governments intervene in agricultural product markets. In most cases the adverse consequences of such interventions to the efficiency and costs of carrying out marketing functions could be reduced. This is as true of the industrial as of the developing countries. The market interventions in the European Community and the United States generally fail to reflect adequately quality, location, and seasonal differentials. Thus it should not be altogether unexpected that in the developing countries the distortions resulting from market interventions are often quite substantial.

Since governments do intervene, it would seem that rather more attention should be given to how such interventions can be carried out with less adverse consequences. To the best of my knowledge, there has been little research on this topic. True, the case against the majority of the parastatal marketing agencies has been made in numerous instances. But since governments are going to intervene for a variety of reasons, it would seem appropriate to seek approaches that are more cost effective and achieve most of the objectives sought by the government.

Concluding Comments

It is not too difficult to specify what constitutes appropriate structural policies for agriculture. What is far more difficult is to explain why actual structural policies for agriculture in the developing countries are so different from the appropriate policies. I have not attempted this in the present paper. Yet it seems to be a topic that merits far more attention than it has so far received. If governments nearly universally extract large rents from agriculture even though eventually it is obvious that they will kill or badly maim the goose that lays the golden egg, inducing a change in such policies should be facilitated by a better understanding of why so many countries have followed policies that have significantly reduced the productive capacity of agriculture. Industrial countries, of course, follow opposite policies, namely ones that result in the creation of excess productive capacity.

I fear that we have not advanced our understanding very much from what Adam Smith wrote in 1776:

> The laws concerning corn may every where be compared to the laws concerning religion. The people feel themselves so much interested in what relates either to their subsistence in this life, or to their happiness in a life to come, that government must yield to their prejudices, and in order to preserve the public tranquility, establish that system which they approve of. It is upon this account, perhaps, that we do seldom find a reasonable system established with regard to either of those two capital objects.

References

Lele, Uma J., *Food Grain Marketing in India: Private Performance and Public Policy* (Ithaca: Cornell University Press, 1971).

Mezhberg, Yu A., "Present-Day Problems of Restructuring the Countryside," *Voprosy Ekonomiki*, No. 5 (May 1978), pp. 78–88. Translated in *The Current Digest of the Soviet Press*, No. 30 (1978), p. 6.

Smith, Adam, *The Wealth of Nations* (New York: Modern Library Edition, 1937).

World Bank, *World Development Report 1986* (New York: Oxford University Press, 1986).

Growth-Oriented Adjustment Programs: Fiscal Policy Issues

R. J. Chelliah
Member
Indian Planning Commission

If the external payments problem facing a country is considered a short-run phenomenon, attributable, say, to a temporary fall in agricultural output or generation of excess demand through the budget, the remedy might be sought in a stabilization program which emphasizes contraction of demand or reduction in "absorption." In the short run, productive capacity is taken to be fixed and while the degree of utilization of the existing capacity could be increased to an extent, the demand side may be said to offer greater scope for manipulation. Since the 1973 oil shock, however, several events have aggravated the balance of payments problems of developing countries, and it has become more and more clear that the restoration of equilibrium would require longer term measures leading to structural changes. In the context of fundamental disequilibrium owing to structural deficiencies, a large reduction in absorption, while often imposing an unacceptably severe cut in real income or welfare, would leave the fundamental causes of low growth, underutilization of capacity and the tendency for balance of payments deficits unattended. It is now recognized more clearly—by the Bretton Woods Institutions as well as by the member countries—that a more comprehensive set of policy prescriptions are called for, including supply-side measures, and that a longer period of adjustment is often needed during which the inflow of external capital is to be maintained at the required minimum level. If the criterion of growth is explicitly brought

---

Note: The views expressed here are those of the author and do not reflect the views of the Indian Planning Commission.

into the analysis, there is less danger that whatever demand-contracting measures are recommended would be such as to slow economic growth.

In the simple financial programing framework employed by the Fund, say, during the 1960s, fiscal policy played the role of restricting government demand for credit. In other words, fiscal policy was considered an aspect of monetary policy; by itself, it was supposed to have no independent effects on aggregate demand and balance of payments. Such a view was taken partly as a result of the concentration on the size of the unweighted budget deficit to the neglect of the composition of revenues and expenditures and any favorable supply-side effects that could be expected from fiscal policy changes would require a fairly long gestation period. In the context of medium-term programing such as that under the extended fund facility or the structural adjustment lending program, fiscal policy could be effectively used not merely for demand restraint but also for effecting structural changes. This paper discusses the role that fiscal measures could play in a medium-term adjustment program.

Before the role of fiscal policy is discussed, it is necessary to specify the basic objectives that a country has set for itself and the institutional structure that it has adopted. I shall assume the institutional structure of a mixed economy in which the public sector is to play an important, if not a dominant, role. This role will be played through the operation of public enterprises in certain core areas thereby determining the broad directions of development. At the same time, public ownership would act as a counterforce to concentration of wealth in private hands. Such an institutional structure has been consciously adopted in several developing countries to promote growth along with social justice. Growth with social justice also means that while growth is emphasized, the government should strive to change the composition of output so as to benefit the poorer sections of society and to ensure for all the minimum of essential goods and services. While in a mixed economy a very large part of the economy would be operated by private enterprises guided by market forces (which could, however, be influenced by indirect means of control, such as taxes), a part of the economy would be planned on the basis of needs. This would comprise the core sector as well as those segments that produce essential consumer goods. The government must take steps, insofar as it is possible, to ensure that sufficient resources will go into the production of these essential goods and they are within the reach of the poorer sections of the population.

It is also widely recognized that certain services, such as primary education and rudimentary health facilities, should be provided free of charge or at subsidized rates. It may also be necessary to provide a certain minimum of food grains and cheap cloth at subsidized prices to people below the poverty line. The core objectives of Fund-supported adjustment programs are the achievement of external and internal balance and of adequate economic growth. I would add the qualification "with due attention being paid to the aspect of social justice."

The Bank works out its program and the magnitudes of the variables needed for it in a medium-term framework. It appears that a variant of the two-gap model is generally used for this purpose. The rate of growth in the medium term is naturally brought in. The theoretical framework employed by the Fund as underpinning for its financial programing exercise, however, remains basically short term in character but can be recast in a medium-term framework. For example, instead of using the expected short-term increase in real output, the maximum feasible increase in output to be targeted in the medium term could be used. The desired rates of growth of government revenues and expenditures could only be worked out against the background of the assumed or targeted rate of growth of the economy.

In the context of the medium term, fiscal policy can come into its own and play an independent role, particularly on the supply side, while in the short run, the impact of fiscal policy is transmitted mainly through the budget deficit. This occurs because significant changes in the composition of revenues and expenditures and in the structures of different taxes cannot be brought about instantaneously or in the short run, and the effects of such changes take time to work themselves out.

The objective of a medium-term adjustment program is to create conditions, through policy measures, which would enable the country to attain an adequate rate of economic growth with social justice, internal price stability (or a fairly low rate of inflation), and a sustainable external payment position. Several measures are called for to achieve these objectives. I confine myself to fiscal policy measures that could be used to help regulate absorption, increase domestic savings and investment, promote the more efficient use of resources, and channel an adequate share of the benefits of growth to the poorer sections of society.

Fiscal Deficit

In many developing countries suffering from balance of payments disequilibrium, the major cause of the problem is often excess demand emanating from the public sector. In these circumstances, a reduction in the budget or fiscal deficit is made part of the adjustment program. Once the size of the budget deficit is brought down to the "correct" level, one needs to plan the subsequent increase in its size in relation to the growth of real output and other relevant factors.

In this context, it is necessary to consider carefully the definition of budget deficit. The Fund and the World Bank make use of the concept of fiscal deficit, which can be taken to correspond to the "overall deficit" used in public finance literature. The overall deficit is defined as the difference between government's total expenditures[1] and current revenues; thus it becomes equal to total net borrowing by the government that finances the deficit.

Limitations to the use of the fiscal deficit as an indicator of stimulus to aggregate demand are well known. The use of the unweighted budget deficit ignores the differential impact of different types of revenues and expenditures; the impact of the deficit depends also on the source of financing it; and insofar as tax revenues are endogenous, the size of the deficit is not fully under the control of the government. In spite of these limitations, the size of the deficit, properly defined, could be taken as a rough indicator of the impact on demand, even though it cannot be wholly attributed to government action. Besides, the budget deficit is an important variable from other points of view, such as the growth of public debt and of interest burden on the budget.

The figure of the government's net borrowing is of significance because it reflects the absolute increase in public debt. Also, to the extent the government is borrowing from abroad, the external liabilities of the country are increased, and domestic borrowing by the government would have implications for the availability of credit to

---

[1] For the present purpose, we can take total expenditure (current plus capital) as excluding net lending.

the private sector. Obviously the government's borrowing program must be carefully regulated. Hence, the figure of overall fiscal deficit is of significance, particularly if it is taken net of net lending. However, in countries in which the government owns and runs important public enterprises, such as electricity undertakings, railways, and telecommunications, whether government borrowing undertaken on behalf of such enterprises and invested in them is to be excluded from the measurement of overall deficit (because that part of the credit is strictly not for government purposes) must be considered. In fact, one of the reforms suggested for countries in which the government borrows on behalf of public enterprises is that such borrowing be transferred to an independent financial agency that can be enjoined to act on commercial principles.

As pointed out earlier, the impact of the budget deficit on aggregate demand depends on the source of financing. It could be legitimately argued that government expenditure financed by borrowing from the non-bank private sector will not result in any significant net expansion because the diversion of private savings will result in the reduction of purchasing power in private hands. In this view, the amount of overall deficit cannot be used as a correct indicator of the expansionary impulse emanating from the budget. In India, a prominent committee has recently suggested that the total net Central Bank credit to the government sector (which leads to an increase in high-powered money) should be taken as the proper measure of budget deficit for measuring the expansionary impact of the budget.[2] Others would argue that total bank credit to the government should be used instead. In any case, the overall deficit generally used by the Fund is not a satisfactory indicator of the expansionary impact of the budget.

In standard Fund programs, the performance criteria include ceilings on total bank credit and often sub-ceilings on net bank credit to the government. One sometimes hears statements about the need to eliminate the fiscal deficit, and the figure of fiscal deficit is presented as a percentage of GDP to show how large it is. Often, this gives an unduly alarmist picture because, for one thing, it includes government borrowing to finance government investment in public enterprises.

---

[2] Reserve Bank of India, *Report of the Committee to Review the Working of the Monetary System* (Bombay: Reserve Bank of India, 1985), p. 152.

(If government *lends* to public enterprises, such borrowing would get excluded if net lending is excluded from total expenditure.) Although, as I said earlier, it is useful to see how public debt is growing, it is necessary to look at the magnitudes of borrowing from different sources for an analysis of the impact of the budget. Just as total bank credit is allocated between the government and the private sector when a sub-ceiling on net bank credit is prescribed, so also a proper allocation of the financial savings of the household sector flowing through non-bank channels should be worked out.

Public borrowing can be looked at from the point of view of demand impact and of growth. For measuring impact on aggregate demand, one should take net central bank credit and net bank credit to the government. (For measuring the budget impact on demand for domestic output, one should consider the excess of domestic budgetary expenditures over all domestic receipts other than borrowing from the banking system.) For considering the impact on growth, one should take the balance on current budget account that reflects government sector's contribution to domestic savings. Government sector saving can be taken to equal government current revenues minus current expenditures.[3] To the extent that current revenues exceed current expenditures, the government is saving a part of the purchasing power it is transferring from private hands through taxes and other means. If there is a current account deficit, it would mean that the government is using a part of the savings of the private sector to finance a portion of its current expenditures.[4] Where savings are falling short of needs, as in most developing countries, government's dissaving affects growth adversely. Hence, I would urge that in any adjustment program a stipulation that the current account deficit of the government would be speedily eliminated.

In terms of Keynesian fiscal policy prescription, it would not matter if the proceeds of government borrowing are spent on capital formation or on public consumption. If there is widespread unemployment and underutilization of capacity owing to a deficiency of effective demand, deficit financed spending by government would,

---

[3] Public sector saving can be defined as government sector saving plus the saving of public enterprises.

[4] If the deficit is financed through foreign borrowing, then there would be an addition to deadweight debt and that much of resources obtained from abroad would not be available for investment.

so it is argued, lead to significant growth in output and employment, thereby increasing government revenues. So long as such increases continue, the interest burden in terms of ratios to government revenue and GDP may not rise. But the Keynesian type of underemployment resulting from deficiency of demand is not typical in most developing countries. Deficit-financed public consumption will not lead directly to any significant increase in real output through the operation of the multiplier.

When one argues that current expenditures should be met through current revenues, one is not saying that current expenditures are unimportant. In the longer term, in which the promotion of the growth of the economy is a major goal, the population has to limit its total current consumption—private and public consumption taken together. It is not that more public consumption may not be desirable, but if it is, private consumption should be correspondingly curtailed and for this higher current revenues should be raised.

In brief, in my view, where public finances have gone off track and the government is incurring deficit both on its current account and on the total of current and capital accounts, as much attention should be given to eliminating the current account deficit as to bringing down government borrowing from the banking system.

The question arises as to how the deficits should be brought down. Obviously, circumstances differ from country to country and the same measures cannot be applied everywhere; however, a few generalizations could be made. To begin with, a distinction has to be made between short-run and medium- or long-term measures. Taking expenditures first, in the longer term, it should be possible to regulate the growth of particular items of expenditure in relation to GDP making the ratio of those items to GDP remain constant or fall; in the short run, the actual level of expenditures would have to be brought down. This would be difficult because, in the short run, several items of expenditures are likely to suffer from rigidity, for example, total employment in the government sector. However, there is some room for maneuver even in the short run. First, expenditure increases could be prevented in regard to government sector employment through a short-term freeze on recruitment and on wages for government employees. Second, action could be taken to reduce subsidies other than those on exports and on essential goods for the poorer sections of society. Third, the introduction of zero-base budgeting in all areas other than key developmental areas would enable savings in current expenditure and re-deployment of staff from nondevelopmental to developmental departments. Fourth, there could be some pruning of capital expenditure of lower priority.

As regards revenues, tax rates are high in a number of developing countries (the tax ratios ranging between 25 and 30 percent of GDP). In these cases, it will be difficult to increase revenues further in the short run. There are other cases where tax ratios are much lower. Short-term increases in revenues would be more possible in those countries, although even there the low level of revenues in relation to GDP may not be attributable to low rates but to an inadequate structure and loose administration.

The problem about raising tax rates in the short run is that higher direct tax rates might induce further evasion and might not result in higher revenue, because rates are already high in many countries; on the other hand, increasing the rates of indirect taxes also might not give any significant addition to revenue in real terms, if there is indexation of wages and salaries and if many prices are administered on a cost plus basis. In fact, often the addition to revenue from rate increases is overestimated.

Net Marginal Product of Additional Taxation

In traditional theory, an increase in tax revenue is taken to be deflationary, that is, it is considered to reduce private demand. In this connection, no distinction is made between increase in the yield owing to a rise in tax rates (including imposition of a new tax) and that owing to an increase in the base because of either improvement in administration or growth. An increase in the rate of a tax (or in the rates of taxes) will normally produce a direct effect in the form of an increase in nominal revenue.[5] But how much of net increase in real revenue there will be depends on several factors.

In many countries, several prices are administered on a cost plus basis. Also, wages in the organized sector of industry and government are indexed to inflation. Hence, an increase in the rates of indirect taxes, which increases prices of inputs or directly affects consumer

---

[5] The exceptions are where a rate increase is accompanied by at least a proportionate increase in evasion or a similar decrease in demand.

goods prices, leads to a further round of increases in prices affecting several goods as well as wages. To maintain government expenditure on goods and wages in real terms, government expenditure in money terms will have to rise. This means that the real value of each dollar of revenue falls. This must be set off against the original increase in tax revenue owing to the hike in tax rates. But at the same time, the secondary rise in prices may bring in some extra revenue. Even allowing for that, taking the original increase in revenue would generally overestimate the net accretion to the budget.

There is another reason why the marginal product of additional taxation may be less than the yield of the additional tax measures. Where several bases are subject to tax, and these bases are interrelated, an extra tax on one base has the effect of reducing the size of other tax bases. Thus, when a number of commodities is subject to tax, an increase in the rate of tax on some commodities subject to inelastic demand would divert purchasing power away from commodities with more elastic demand and would thus cause a fall in the yield of taxes on the latter group of commodities. Similarly, a rise in income tax yield owing to an increase in income tax rates would reduce private consumption and saving. Decrease in private consumption would effect a corresponding reduction in revenue from taxes on consumer goods. And again, taxes that raise prices of inputs would have the effect of reducing the profits of public enterprises. For example, an increase in the tax on diesel, ceteris paribus, reduces the profits of public road transport corporations.

So, one can conclude that the marginal product of additional taxation will generally be less than the nominal yield of the measures introduced and further that the net contribution of such measures to the reduction of budget deficit would be even lower than the marginal product in the case of increases in indirect taxes.

An increase in direct tax rates has a greater chance of bringing about a net reduction in private demand than an equivalent increase in indirect tax rates. Direct taxes, however, generally account for a relatively small proportion of total tax revenue in developing countries. Hence, in the short run, particularly when there are inflationary pressures, reduction in government expenditure would be a more effective way of bringing down the budget deficit and aggregate demand. In the longer run, however, tax revenues can be made to increase faster through a rationalization of the tax structure and

improvement in administration. Tax increases that arise from growth
and improved administration do not lead to price increases or to any
significant disincentives.

If some increase in revenues in the short run becomes imperative
in order to reduce the budget deficit, the best way of doing so would
perhaps be to levy a uniform surcharge on all taxes other than the
corporate tax. That way, the basic structure will not get altered in a
hasty manner, and the extent of rate increase will be the minimum
needed since all taxes but one will be covered by the increase.

Long-Term Fiscal Policy

As generally agreed, in the longer-term perspective, the fiscal
system could be employed for producing the desired supply-side
effects. The most important of these is the increase in the efficiency
of resource use and in the rate of growth of productive capacity. For
achieving the first, there should only be the minimum of undesired
distortions in relative prices of factors of production and of producer
choices; for achieving the second, savings and investment must be
increased, and investment should be redirected to more productive
channels. At the same time, the fiscal system must mobilize sufficient
resources to be used for development purposes.

Revenue Side

Taxes form an overwhelming proportion of current revenues in
most developing countries and are capable of being altered to suit
particular objectives. Therefore, only tax revenues will be considered
here.

In terms of the basic objective of a medium-term adjustment
program, tax revenues must rise substantially to bring the budget
deficits, appropriately defined, under control and, at the same time,
the tax structure must exert a favorable influence on the economy.
This favorable influence leading to higher growth would, in turn, be
reflected in higher revenues. Thus, the level of revenues and the
structure of the tax system are both important. The design of the
structure would be partly influenced also by administrative
considerations.

In most developing countries, the pattern of taxation has been evolved mainly on the criterion of ease of securing revenues rather than on the basis of well-accepted economic principles. Moreover, there has been too much imitation of western models without sufficient adaptation to the different conditions and requirements of developing countries. Often the structures are at variance with the capacity to administer, and the effects are contrary to what is desirable. Take, for example, two countries in many respects very different from each other but both members of the Commonwealth, namely, India and Zimbabwe. Both had developed their personal income tax and the corporate profits tax in imitation of models in the advanced industrial nations. The high progressivity of the personal income tax, the high rates of the corporate profits tax, and the complicated legislation needed to plug loopholes for avoidance induced by high rates—all these were unsuited to the requirements of the two economies as well as to their capacity for administration. The high nominal rates did not lead, at least in India, to progressivity because of substantial tax evasion.

The governments of developing countries depend predominantly on indirect taxes for obtaining their revenues. It is important therefore that indirect taxes levied in these countries do not lead to distortions in the relative prices of factors of production or to any significant degree of cascading. For economic reasons as well as for ease of administration, there must be a general tax with only one or two rates. This could be supplemented by a selective consumption tax levied at higher rates so that the indirect tax structure, taken as a whole, would be progressive with respect to consumption expenditure. (The selective tax should also be applied to petroleum products.) In countries that have built up sufficient administrative capacity the general tax could take the form of value added tax, but it would not be prudent to make it very comprehensive on the European pattern. Most services, for example, would have to be excluded. (A separate tax could be levied on entertainment.) In smaller countries, it might be preferable to have a retail sales tax instead of a value-added tax. Where a retail sales tax is found to lead to a great deal of evasion, the sales tax could be introduced at manufacturing and import levels with provision for setoff for tax paid on inputs by manufacturers. The sales tax and the consumption tax would apply to domestically produced goods as well as to imports. Imports may be subject, in addition, to protective tariff.

In suggesting the adoption of a noncascading general sales tax, I am saying nothing new. What I wish to stress, however, is that the available administrative capacity should decide which of the three kinds of sales taxes I have mentioned should be imposed, in place of whatever exists. In many cases, a sales tax with relief for taxation of inputs might be the best proposition.

If it is desired that the indirect tax system should be biased toward investment, it could be stipulated that the tax paid on machinery would also be eligible for setoff. In most developing countries, however, it might be considered desirable not to encourage capital-intensive methods of production. If so, setoff for tax paid on machinery may not be allowed, but capital goods themselves may be taxed at the lower of the two rates.

An attempt can be made to promote savings and investment through direct taxes that fall on corporations and on the richer sections of the community. Ideally, given the limitations of an income tax, which contains a bias against savings and which can only be levied on a realization basis, direct taxation should take the form of a tax on personal expenditure supplemented by some variant of a cash flow tax on corporations. Nevertheless, neither a universal expenditure tax nor a two-tier expenditure tax (as defined by the Meade Committee)[6] can be administered satisfactorily in a typical developing country. My own study of the way in which income taxes are administered in many developing countries leads me to conclude that these countries are not equipped to administer even a progressive personal income tax. I would suggest that many of them opt for a single-rate income tax—say, levied at 30 percent—which would be mildly progressive because of the exemption limit. Tax theorists would concede that a single-rate or nominally proportional income tax would enable one to get rid of several problems encountered in the administration of a progressive income tax.

A single-rate income tax would not only enable a broadening of the base and a more equitable treatment of income from different sources but also make it easier to check avoidance and considerably ease the task of administration. With a moderate rate of tax, several exemptions and concessions could be done away with; this would

---

[6] The Institute for Fiscal Studies, *The Structure and Reform of Direct Taxation* (London: Institute for Financial Studies, 1978).

broaden the tax base as well as simplify administration. Second, it could be specified that while the individual would be the unit of assessment, there would be a fixed amount of tax-free allowance for each family consisting of husband, wife, and minor children. This amount would have to be divided among the taxpayers in the family. The same amount of tax-free allowance would be granted to partnerships (one individual would be allowed to claim only one allowance either as a partner or as an individual in his own right). Such provisions would effectively prevent any attempts to split incomes that may be made even after a single rate of tax has been introduced. Third, the taxation of capital gains would be much simplified and could be made more equitable: after adequate indexation, capital gains can be included as part of income and there would be no need to make any distinction between short-term and long-term gains. Fourth, the profits of corporations could be taxed at the same rate as personal income; with the exemption of dividends paid to residential holders, there would be proper integration of taxation of individuals and corporations. Fifth, a progressive income tax can only make sense if it can be ensured that full aggregation of income from all sources is reflected in the returns submitted. Unfortunately, it has not been possible to ensure this to a satisfactory extent in most developing countries, with the result that there is higher taxation of income subject to withholding tax than of other types of income. Tax administration in developing countries is also not in a position to check and verify numerous returns. Under the single-rate income tax, individuals whose incomes are from salaries, interest, or rent (dividends may be exempted from tax in the hands of residents) need not be asked to file returns. This would enable tax administration to concentrate on business and professionals whose proclivity for tax evasion could be expected to be reduced considerably because of the moderate single rate.

I recognize, however, that for political reasons it may not be possible to switch over to the single-rate personal income tax. It could also be argued by some that the mere fact that the rate of income tax is moderated would not ensure that savings would be encouraged. They would prefer higher rates of tax that could be moderated through exemptions for savings or particular forms of financial investments. If a progressive income tax is to be retained, it is highly desirable that the rates should be moderate and that the number of rates should not exceed three or four. In this respect, the present Indian system can be taken as a model. The Indian personal income tax falls on each individual taxpayer separately and contains no allowances other than the personal allowance. There are only four rates with the maximum rate being 50 percent. As in the Indian case, introduction of various types of allowances and abetments should be avoided so as not to complicate the administration and to erode the base. If the progressive income tax is retained, it would be necessary to provide for incentives for savings under the tax. Income tax laws in most countries already contain such incentive provisions. But most of these provisions are not such as to reward net savings and often result in widely differing after-tax rates of return to different forms of investment because of variations in the degree of tax concessions. They need to be modified and rationalized. Under the rationalized scheme, deductions from taxable income should be granted in respect of investments in specified accounts up to a monetary limit, while withdrawals from the accounts should be added to taxable income. Funds in these accounts would get invested in the public and private sectors. The eligible investments could include insurance premia and provident/pension fund contributions.

As far as business taxation is concerned, it would be necessary to provide for accelerated depreciation so as to encourage and facilitiate capital formation. The tax on corporate profits is also in need of radical reform in several developing countries. There is no justification or rationale for a high tax on corporate profits except in the case of multinationals engaged in the exploitation of natural resources, such as minerals. I tend to believe that high rates on corporate profits have been introduced in developing countries because such rates exist in a number of developed countries. Even if a progressive income tax is retained for equity reasons, the corporate income tax rate must be kept low for companies in general. A fairly low rate of tax on corporations would induce greater risk taking and investment and leave enough resources for financing the increased investment. Along with the lowering of the rate of corporation tax, many of the exemptions eroding the tax base should be removed.

It has been reported that "changes in direct taxation have not played as important a role in Fund-supported programs as revisions of indirect taxation."[7] Out of the 94 programs surveyed by the Fiscal

---

[7] Fiscal Affairs Department, *Fund-Supported Programs, Fiscal Policy, and Income Distribution*, IMF Occasional Paper No. 46 (Washington: International Monetary Fund, 1986).

Affairs Department of the Fund, direct taxes were proposed to be changed in only 44 and the personal income tax in only 20 programs. It also appears from the report that major revisions of the current tax system were not contemplated. I would urge that in the context of a medium-term adjustment program such as the extended Fund facility or the structural adjustment lending program of the Bank, direct tax reform should be given high priority.

The simplification of the tax structure and the introduction of moderate rates would not only strengthen incentives but also make the tax system more administrable. As things are, the quality of the tax administrators and the logistic and statistical support they receive are far from adequate to administer satisfactorily the complicated systems which have been set up in the developing countries partly on the advice of visiting experts from the developed countries. Improving tax administration will take time but is indispensable for achieving any degree of success through tax reform. Tax structure simplification and reform and improvement in tax administration are mutually reinforcing, and one will not succeed without the other. A Country Policy Department discussion paper of the World Bank points out that work on country adjustment programs has indicated considerable scope for improving tax administration even in such middle-income countries as Argentina, Brazil, Chile, Colombia, and Mexico.[8] The need for improving, rather than entirely revamping, tax administration is far greater in several countries of Africa and Asia.

It is heartening to learn that "there is an emerging consensus (including apparently the Fund and the Bank) that lower marginal tax rates are desirable as a way to preserve the incentives for work and savings and as a pre-condition for further changes that will improve equity among taxpayers."[9] It may be useful to point out how the kind of tax system that I have outlined would increase savings and investment and promote the growth of the economy. I have no doubt that the income elasticity of the tax system would go up considerably after the simplification of the tax structure and with improvement in tax administration. At the same time, the low rate of tax on corporate profits (with the exceptions mentioned above)

---

[8] Armeane M. Choksi, *Adjustment With Growth in the Highly Indebted Middle-Income Countries*, World Bank, Country Policy Discussion Paper, Washington, October 1986.

[9] Chad Leechor, *Tax Policy and Tax Reform in Semi-Industrial Countries* (Washington: World Bank, 1986).

and accelerated depreciation would give a fillip to corporate savings and investment. The single-rate personal income tax would enable much better collection and also increase compliance. With the reduction in the proportion of black income generation, there would be a considerable increase in savings brought into official accounts. Apart from the fact of the low rate itself, the elimination of double taxation of dividends and the removal of the bias in favor of capital gains in the tax system would also serve to promote savings and investment in the right direction. If a single-rate income tax is not acceptable, specific provision for rewarding savings must be introduced into the income tax. Indian experience shows that such provisions can help mobilize savings and draw them into the formal financial sector.

As regards progressivity, I doubt that the overall system recommended here would be any less progressive than the existing systems in their actual operation in most developing countries. If the reforms could succeed in taking far more away from the income taxpayers and corporations than they are paying now, the capacity of the government to use money taken from the richer sections for the benefit of the poorer sections would increase. But it must be admitted that the lack of progressivity in the income tax or the blunting of the degree of progression in it, while enabling greater savings and accumulation by individuals, would accentuate inequalities of wealth. In order to counteract this, an inheritance tax with moderate rates could be introduced, if it is not already being levied. Here again, I would prefer a single-rate tax. Another instrument that may be used to tax the well-to-do and raise revenue, particularly for local authorities, is the property tax. In many developing countries, the structure of this tax has to be rationalized and its administration vastly improved.

In the medium-term adjustment program, revenue increase has to play an important part in bringing down the budget deficit, in particular the current account deficit, and in enabling the government to finance essential services on an increasing scale. If tax ratios are already fairly high, however, it would not be desirable to attempt to raise them any further. In a number of developing countries, the informal and non-monetary sectors constitute a substantial part of the economy. Taxes fall mainly on the formal monetized sector. Hence, a 25 percent tax to GDP ratio would mean a much higher tax ratio with respect to the formal sector that is to spearhead development. The "limit to taxation" has to be decided with reference to the conditions prevailing in each country. Clearly if taxation proceeds beyond a limit in relation to GDP, growth is likely to be retarded. Hence the importance to be attached to the control of expenditure.

Expenditures

In several developing countries suffering from macroeconomic disequilibrium and external payments problems, government expenditures, particularly recurrent expenditures, are seen to have clearly gone out of hand. Strenuous attempts have therefore to be made in the medium term to bring the growth of expenditures in line with that of revenues. In a growth-oriented program, obviously, priority should be given to the objective of eliminating dissaving by the government sector. We therefore concentrate on current expenditures. Four components of current expenditure could be distinguished and considered: interest payments, current development expenditure, current nondevelopment expenditure (on goods and services), and subsidies.

The ratio of interest payments to current revenues (and to GDP) has continued to grow in several countries because government has borrowed money to meet current expenditures, government investment has not been productive enough to raise commensurately GDP and current revenues, and public enterprises in which borrowed money has been invested by the government have been making insufficient profits or are incurring losses. The first and the third causes may be dealt with here.

Although it could be argued that certain types of current expenditures would lead to human capital formation and therefore should be treated on a par with expenditure on material capital formation, as a rule it is safe to proceed on the basis that all current expenditures should be covered by current revenues. This means that the growth of the other three components of current expenditure mentioned above (other than interest payments) should be regulated to bring down the level of total current expenditures to the level of total current revenues within a reasonable period of time. Thereafter the rate of growth of current expenditures must be made to keep pace with that of revenues. As regards loss-making public enterprises, it is necessary to divide them into enterprises in the core sectors such as the infrastructure sectors and those in non-core sectors. In the medium term, enterprises in the latter category that are continuously making losses must be closed down or sold off to the private sector. Public enterprises in the former category must be asked to work out time-bound programs for making their operations profitable; and provided they are working efficiently and wages are not rising faster than labor productivity, they must be allowed price increases justified by increases in the costs of inputs.

In most countries, the size and the composition of capital expenditures during a plan period are decided upon without any reference to the capacity to meet, out of the current budget, increased maintenance or committed expenditure in the subsequent period. Inevitably, in course of time, current expenditures tend to grow faster than current revenues. This then leads governments to put restrictions or squeezes on recurrent expenditures creating the so-called "recurrent cost problems." A recent examination of the situation in 18 African countries identified all but 3 as being affected by this problem. "The problem arises because, faced with a need to restrain recurrent spending, it is difficult to reduce the size of the civil service or to cut wages and salaries. It is the non-wage recurrent items which tend to be cut: transport allowances, supplies of materials and spare parts, sometimes even the use of electricity and telephones."[10] This kind of restraint obviously leads to wastage and inefficiency and reduces the productivity of previous investments. It should therefore become an important element in public investment strategy that in formulating public investment schemes and in determining the total size of the capital budget, the consequential rise in maintenance and running expenditure in the subsequent periods must be kept in view and the composition and the size of the investment plan must be tailored to the expected availability of revenues at the end of the plan period. In the long run there is no other way of averting a fundamental imbalance arising between revenues and expenditures.

Given that the ratio of tax to GDP in many developing countries is under 25 percent, and in some cases below 20 percent, these countries cannot afford to divert a large proportion of GDP to defense and other nondevelopmental expenditures. Nevertheless, countries

---

[10] *Report of the Commission of Inquiry into Taxation* (Harare, Zimbabwe: Government Printer, 1986), p. 302.

have to decide for themselves the fraction of resources that they wish to, and can afford to, spend on general administration, law and order, and defense. In the interest of economic development, the rate of growth of such expenditures must be limited to the rate of growth of GDP, after their relative level has been suitably adjusted.

Expenditure on subsidies is also a significant component of public expenditure in a number of countries. We may consider four kinds of subsidies: subsidies to cover losses of public enterprises, subsidies to encourage the use of a particular input in the interest of the national economy, export subsidies, and subsidies to lower the prices of particular consumer goods for the benefit of all consumers or particular groups of consumers.

One sometimes gets the impression that the Fund and the Bank consider that subsidies, as a rule, are a "bad thing." I am sure that this impression is wrong, because it can be shown that a positive or negative tax intervention in the price system can often be justified just as intervention through the public expenditure side, such as the provision of free education or free highways.[11] Subsidies can, of course, be objected to if they are growing too fast in relation to revenues and in the context of other more urgent demands on revenue. They could also be objected to if they tend to distort resource allocation or incentives for producers. But if incentives for producers are maintained and if the price to consumers or to a targeted group of consumers is lowered in respect of goods that are not subject to a high price elasticity of demand, there could be no objection on economic or efficiency grounds. Take, for example, a public distribution system such as the one operating in India. The provision of wheat, rice, and kerosene through the fair price shops at subsidized rates does not mean any disincentive to producers. In the case of rice and wheat, the cost of the subsidy is borne by the State, and in the case of kerosene, the production and supply is through a State monopoly. The quantities supplied are limited to fortnightly rations. Although this set of arrangements cannot be criticized on grounds of efficiency, it could be argued that given the scarcity of resources and the demands on them for various developmental purposes, the

---

[11] In this connection, note the examples mentioned in Michael Bruno, "Comments," in *IMF Conditionality*, ed. by John Williamson (Washington: Institute for International Economics, 1983), p. 127.

food subsidy must be targeted toward only the poorer sections of the society.[12] Moreover, food subsidies could get out of hand if the degree of subsidization is increased over time. This can happen (it has already happened, to some extent, in India) if the price at which foodgrains are bought from the farmers is adjusted upward in line with the increase in costs of production, but the price at which it is sold to the targeted group of consumers is not raised correspondingly.

It is clear that subsidies that involve disincentives to producers or that lead to significant distortions in the allocation of resources should be eliminated. Also, subsidies on unlimited amounts of consumption, particularly in respect of noninferior consumer items (such as meat in Zimbabwe and general higher education in India), should be avoided because they would lead to artificial inflation of demand.

Equally objectionable are subsidies to cover losses of inefficiently run public enterprises. As already suggested, all those in non-core sectors should be closed down or sold off, and it must be one of the objectives of the adjustment program to improve the efficiency of public enterprises in the core sectors. In the case of even efficiently run enterprises, losses would occur if administered prices are kept below costs and these losses would then have to be covered by budgetary subsidies. Such subsidies also tend to militate against efficient allocation.

This leaves export subsidies, subsidies in favor of the poor, and subsidies on the use of particular inputs that would further public interest. Even assuming that these subsidies are justifiable under particular circumstances, the total of these subsidies in the budget cannot be allowed to grow out of proportion to the growth in national income and government revenues. Depending upon the targeted tax ratio, the permissible ratio of such subsidies to GDP should be determined in the light of other government commitments of higher priority.

We may conclude that government subsidies that tend to distort allocation of resources or worsen income distribution through unjustified lowering of the prices of goods and services consumed by

---

[12] The Fiscal Affairs Department of the Fund has argued that food subsidies are not of much value because foods even at subsidy prices are likely to be beyond the reach of the "ultra poor." It is difficult to accept this argument because there is no justification to deny a benefit to the poor just because the ultra poor cannot avail themselves of it. In any case, for the ultra poor, food for work programs can be started, as in India.

politically powerful groups or other favored sections are harmful or wrong in principle and must be eliminated. Other subsidies, such as those favoring the poor in a limited way and those encouraging particular activities or methods of production, as part of promotional effort, could be justified, but care must always be taken to keep them under control. In a growth-oriented adjustment program, reduction in subsidies should figure as an element but it is important to ensure that the poorer sections are not unduly hurt, or that desirable promotional efforts are not prematurely terminated.

Concluding Remarks

In a growth-oriented adjustment program, fiscal policy has to play an important role both in the short term and in the medium term: in the short term because often increasing budgetary imbalance is one of the major causes of macroeconomic disequilibrium, and in the medium term because the structures of government revenues and expenditures affect savings and investment and the efficiency with which resources are used.

In the short term, the main task of fiscal policy is to reduce budget deficit, thereby bringing down government borrowing from the banking system and government dissaving, if any. In general, however, it is difficult to increase revenues in the short run without fueling inflation or creating other problems. Unless direct tax rates happen to be low, which may be true of some countries, raising direct tax rates significantly may only lead to greater evasion and further disincentives. Since there is generally indexation of wages and salaries and administrative fixing of several prices on a cost plus basis, raising indirect tax rates so as to obtain a significant increase in revenues will lead to a chain cost-push reaction. On the whole, in the short term, a cut in government expenditure other than essential developmental expenditure is preferable and would be more effective in reducing the demand for real resources. In a very difficult budgetary situation, however, it may become necessary to raise tax revenues and at least some public enterprises' prices. Then one may resort to a general surcharge on all taxes so as not to change the differential rates structure without proper study. Also, in regard to public enterprise prices, preference may be given in the short run to raising, where needed, prices of enterprises not producing vital inputs (their turn can come later with resumed growth).

In the medium or longer term, unless the tax ratio is quite high in a country, it would be possible to increase revenues through the reform of the tax structure and improvement in administration. The four guiding considerations should be: simple structures with only limited exemptions and concessions, broad bases, moderate rates, and efficient and strict administration. Moderate rates themselves would increase incentives; but specific incentives to savings and investment could be incorporated, if they do not already exist under the personal income tax, such as accelerated depreciation, low tax on machinery, and exemptions for net savings, at least to a limited extent.

Over time, the growth of current expenditures should be regulated (and in respect of some items reduction should be effected) so that, given the growth in revenues, the current account deficit of the budget can be eliminated and growth of expenditures kept in line with the expected growth in revenues. In this exercise, attention should be paid to the elimination of subsidies that are unjustifiable or that lead to inefficiency in resource use. On the capital account, government expenditure should be restructured so that public investment increases the productivity of private investment through the strengthening of the infrastructure.

When a country has got into serious balance of payments and inflation problems, the process of adjustment is hard and long. The population will undoubtedly be subjected to hardship in the initial stages. Under such circumstances, it is important that the poorer sections of society are not made to suffer equally with others. Hence, some elements of the program must be directed to safeguarding their interests. Fiscal policy may be fashioned accordingly.

Discussion

Miguel Urrutia

Manager, Economic and Social Development Department
Inter-American Development Bank

The paper by Professor D. Gale Johnson attempts to find some generalizations that apply to the problems of adjustment in the agricultural sector of most developing countries. Although some common problems are indeed identified, the solutions are of such a general nature that they might only, with difficulty, be translated into concrete programs of actions and quantifiable targets that might trigger the disbursement of agricultural sector loans by the multilateral financial institutions.

It is one thing to say that most agricultural sectors are discriminated against, and quite another to design specific adjustment policies. Effective devaluation may not lead, in the short run, to greater agricultural exports in a country producing commodities that have high protection in the industrial nations. Special measures may have to be taken to facilitate export diversification, in addition to the more common adjustment measures.

The first obvious conclusion is, then, that there cannot be a general program of agricultural adjustment. In what follows I would like to bring out some specific questions that may require further discussion.

First, Professor Johnson acknowledges that international market prices for farm products are significantly distorted. If that is the case, should distorted international prices determine national policies? Probably not. In the present international trading system, the exports of meat of the United Kingdom have been increasing, and those of Argentina decreasing. Something is seriously wrong with the incentive systems. Should Brazil set internal sugar prices at the international price, which clearly does not cover the costs of the most efficient producers? Again, the answer is probably no. Most nations with limited foreign exchange will have to manage agricultural imports, taking into account the undesirable price distortions of agricultural products in the international market and compensating for them through specific import and export policies.

Second, agricultural sectoral adjustment cannot be looked at in isolation. Such adjustment must be inserted within the general macroeconomic adjustment taking place in most developing economies. In many economies, exchange rates are being adjusted and fiscal deficits reduced. The exchange rate adjustments will produce an export supply response in agriculture. Will industrial countries absorb those exports? The balance of payment surplus countries, Germany and Japan, certainly will not accept much larger imports of agricultural goods. Are agricultural adjustment programs taking this into account? There may be possibilities for increased south-south trade. Mechanisms for increasing such trade might be necessary complements to the recommended adjustments in relative prices being carried out in most developing countries at present. Financing mechanisms for such south-south trade could increase the viability of agricultural adjustment programs that favor the production of exportables.

Third, the paper rightly emphasizes the bad record of marketing boards. Nevertheless, these institutions were originally established to try to integrate farmers into the market. Unfortunately, many marketing boards developed into monsters that exploited these farmers, but their excess should not blind us to the role the state can have in the promotion and growth of markets. There is a need to create institutions that facilitate the functioning of markets in rural areas. Markets sometimes do not develop without some support. Many agricultural production projects have failed owing to imperfections of distribution channels. In developing and industrialized countries, cooperatives and producer associations have integrated many small farmers into national markets. Investment in the infrastructure needed for the growth of markets is a valid development activity. Markets are also fragile. Sudden import or price liberalization may in fact destroy fledging markets. Financial liberalization may fatally weaken some financial institutions that in fact have served poor farmers, unless special measures are taken to avoid such an outcome.

Fourth, macroeconomic adjustment is in all cases making it difficult to maintain food subsidies that affect the government budget. It is likely that better targeting can contribute to fiscal health, but some food entitlements must be assured to the poor. Given the combination of barriers to exports of agricultural goods and the existence of malnutrition in most developing countries, there is a need to design food entitlement systems that will, at the same time, promote agricultural production by increasing demand and diminish poverty. The macroeconomic adjustment programs should contemplate such programs.

In summary, I do not agree with Professor Johnson when he says that it is not too difficult to specify what constitutes appropriate structural policies for agriculture. It *is* quite difficult. The problem must be looked at in the general framework of the macroeconomic program for an individual country, and the policies must be adapted to the particular agricultural production structure.

Professor Johnson states that farm people should not be discriminated against in the provision of public services and infrastructure, such as transport, communication, and cultural facilities. This is true, but it ignores the fact that the provision of services is more expensive in rural areas, particularly when settlement is dispersed. Given the higher costs, it appears more efficient to provide such services first in urban areas, and that may be rational. In Latin America, in areas of dispersed settlement, rural investments are very expensive and may have to be postponed if adjustment programs create serious budget constraints.

On the other hand, it is clear that urban subsidies through user charges are probably unwarranted and excessively encourage rapid urbanization. The whole issue of user charges and income transfers to the poor, particularly those in rural areas through user charges, is a most interesting policy area in a world in fiscal crisis.

Unfortunately, then, the multilateral banks will not be able to use a general formula for agricultural adjustment. The design of agricultural adjustment programs will have to emerge from a complete analysis of each economy and the specific characteristics of each agricultural sector.

Many lessons have been learned, as Professor Johnson well points out. It is hard to justify subsidies for modern inputs or price controls that exploit poor farmers. There are also few convincing arguments justifying subsidized interest rates on loans to small farmers. On the contrary, any agricultural adjustment policy should contemplate the strengthening of credit institutions that serve these farmers, and subsidized interest rates never strengthen such institutions.

But, except for these very general policy recommendations, the design of an agricultural adjustment policy will require much analysis by the country authorities, and much technical assistance and understanding from the international community.

G. Edward Schuh

Director, Department of Agriculture and Rural Development
World Bank

Gale Johnson (in his paper Agricultural Structural Policies) has given us an excellent discussion of the nature of structural adjustments faced by agriculture in economies experiencing economic growth, of the way policies designed to deal with these adjustments often go astray, and of the kinds of policies needed to facilitate structural adjustment. At the same time he focused on the way that agriculture is often plundered to meet misguided policy goals.

Professor Johnson makes four points that I would like to single out for emphasis because they are not generally recognized or given sufficient attention in discussions of agricultural sector policy.

First, as an economy grows from low levels of per capita income, the relative importance of agriculture must and will decline. This means that labor needs to shift from farm to nonfarm employment and that eventually the agricultural labor force declines in absolute terms.

Second, governments universally neglect to provide adequate infrastructure and public services for the rural sector, while at the same time they underinvest in the education and schooling of their rural population. They do this while they simultaneously provide a wide variety of subsidies to their urban population.

Third, the failure to have adequate adjustment policies as development proceeds eventually leads to highly distortionary agricultural policies, but this tends to occur only at fairly advanced stages of development.

Fourth, output growth is not the most important goal of sectoral policy; obtaining efficient output growth and dealing with the wide disparity in per capita incomes between the farm and nonfarm sectors should generally receive higher priority than they do.

I would like to build on Professor Johnson's main analysis by addressing four points.

The Rural-Urban Labor Market, the Migratory Process, and the Inter-Sectoral Income Differential

Professor Johnson fails to address a number of points in his discussion of the persistent need for sectoral reallocation of labor from agriculture to the nonfarm sectors. These are important in designing policies to facilitate the needed adjustment, so I would like to fill in the gaps.

First, the sectoral shift of labor from agriculture to nonfarm employment typically requires the geographic dislocation of labor as well, a phenomenon that is not nearly so important in intersectoral shifts of labor among nonfarm sectors of the economy. This makes the costs to the migrant, both pecuniary and nonpecuniary, a great deal larger and helps explain why the agriculture-to-nonagriculture adjustment process is so difficult and why rural-urban sectoral income differentials often grow so large.

Second, we know the process of geographic migration is highly selective. Those who migrate tend to be the more highly educated, those with more skills, the young and vigorous, and the risk takers and entrepreneurs. That means that the process of migration from agriculture and rural areas drains away the very human capital that could help agriculture and the rural sector to be more productive. This human capital is often financed with local resources and taxes and is in effect given to the higher-income urban sector as a gift. This further exacerbates the consequences of the tendency of governments to underinvest in their rural people in the first place, which Professor Johnson correctly calls to our attention. This explains in large part why problems of regional poverty, such as in the northeast of Brazil, the south of Italy and the United States, and certain parts of Mexico, persist for so long. In effect the migratory process involves significant negative externalities.

Third, this problem can be alleviated by decentralizing the process of industrialization, thus taking employment to the labor force rather than the reverse. More emphasis on strengthening rural infrastructure and public services in rural areas, which Professor Johnson emphasizes, would help facilitate this process, as would raising the level of educational attainment and training among the rural population to levels of the nonfarm sector.

Fourth, investing in the education and training of rural people not only helps narrow directly the income differential between the farm and nonfarm sectors but facilitates the labor adjustment process as well. Education raises the earnings of labor in agriculture by being highly complementary to the introduction and diffusion of new technology in the sector. It also has been found to facilitate the process of labor migration. Hence, investment in the education and schooling of the rural population is a powerful sectoral adjustment policy.

Fifth, fostering migration out of agriculture can also be a powerful growth policy. The large sectoral differentials in per capita incomes between the farm and nonfarm sector mean that the reallocation of labor can contribute importantly to a more rapid rate of economic growth, since labor is taken from low-productive, low-income employment to high-productive, high-income employment.

The So-Called Diversification Problem

The successful introduction and widespread diffusion of high-yielding varieties of rice in south and southeast Asia have given rise to what is widely referred to as a diversification problem. Although the solution to this problem is generally sought in terms of diversification *within* agriculture, the problem is inherently a problem of diversification *out of agriculture* and hence is a classic sectoral adjustment problem. Moreover, such diversification as there is within agriculture will probably take place by means of regional and inter-farm specialization, not by intra-farm diversification.

Rice production is a labor-intensive commodity and, when produced under irrigated conditions, involves significant externalities. As farmers shift out of this activity, the opportunities in other labor-intensive commodities, such as fruits, vegetables, and livestock, are fairly limited. Hence, they will eventually be forced to shift into commodities that are of less value and less labor intensive. This will require the enlargement of farms so as to provide incomes comparable with those in the nonfarm sector, and the shift of labor out of the sector. Considerable upward pressure in the land market will be generated in the process, but this will depend on how rapidly labor adjusts. This structural adjustment problem is likely to be increasingly important in the decade ahead, especially in Asia, and one that policymakers will need to deal with successfully if they want to realize the full benefits of the new production technology.

Wide Swings in Exchange Rates Give Rise to Special Adjustment Problems

In today's configuration of the international economy we are experiencing wide and sustained swings in the value of national currencies, induced in large part by large international flows of capital. Given that the exchange rate system is one of bloc floating, the effects of these realignments in exchange rates extend far beyond the country whose currency is changing in value. Such realignments bring about the need for sectoral reallocations of resources, especially of labor. To date this problem is seldom recognized as the significant adjustment problem it is.

The problem is further exacerbated by the tendency of these capital market-driven realignments in exchange rates to mask and distort underlying comparative advantage for significant periods of time. It is not clear just what policies should be to deal with this problem, other than to note that more generalized floating would probably reduce the size of the realignments, thus reducing the need for adjustment, and that the policies referred to above to facilitate intersectoral mobility would help a great deal.

The Predatory Trade Policies of the European Community, the United States, and Japan Create Serious Adjustment Problems for the International Community

These developed countries are taking virtually no longer-term adjustments in their agricultural sectors in response to changing conditions in international markets, although U.S. agriculture has experienced a collapse in asset values and some restructuring. Instead, the European Community and the United States are engaged in a noisy and expensive export subsidy war, using the power of their national treasuries to dump their adjustment problems on other developed-country exporters and on the developing countries as a whole. Exporting developing countries, such as Thailand and Argentina, clearly lose from these policies, as do producers and landless workers in importing countries.

Professor Johnson finesses this problem somewhat in his paper, although he agrees to the second-best policy of establishing the ratio of domestic farm prices to domestic nonfarm prices at the same ratio as exists in international markets. The classic prescription, of course, is that a country should accept the subsidies of other countries only if they are expected to continue in the future.

This is one adjustment I don't believe developing countries in particular should take, and for two reasons. First, I believe there is ample evidence that the United States will change its policies in the near future, and its policies have been largely responsible for the large decline in commodity prices in 1986 and 1987. Because of the burgeoning budget costs of the deficiency payment scheme, the United States is very likely to shift increasingly to expanded production controls and set asides, and to reduce the expenditures on deficiency payments. In the case of the European Community, there is also growing evidence that the budget costs of its policies are recognized as excessive.

The second reason I believe the developing countries should not accept these subsidies and bear the adjustment costs is that by taking counteractive measures they will make dumping more expensive and thus hasten the day the United States and the European Community will change their policies. The GATT provides for the use of countervailing duties and dumping penalties in such circumstances. I believe the developing countries should take advantage of these provisions and not impose premature and costly adjustments on their own agricultural sectors because of developed-country policies.

Let me conclude by once again complimenting Professor Johnson on his perceptive and well-done paper. If we could only induce policymakers to follow the guidelines he lays out in the last part of his paper, we would rapidly move to a more rational use of the world's agricultural resources, to the benefit of developed and developing countries alike.

Chu S. P. Okongwu
Federal Minister of Finance
Nigeria

Mr. Chelliah's paper has achieved much in clarifying issues and illuminating the surrounding darkness in some of the uncertain areas of the role of fiscal policy in growth-oriented adjustment efforts. The distinction between the short-run and the medium- to long-run impact of fiscal measures sheds much light on the limitations of fiscal policy, depending upon the time frame and considering the relative stages of economic development. It is also useful to note the issue raised in the paper regarding the concept of budget deficit as defined by both the Fund and the World Bank, which the paper considers unsatisfactory as an indicator of the expansionary impact of the budget. In its main thrust, an important role is clearly assigned to fiscal policy in the effort to effect structural adjustment through growth-oriented programs. However, some trade-offs are required in the choice and implementation of various fiscal measures.

From the standpoint of developing economies, the basic assumptions of Mr. Chelliah need be stressed, namely, a mixed economy framework with a dominant public sector with some services provided free of charge or subsidized. These characteristic features, particularly the issue of subsidies and the dominance of government, have been seriously frowned at and indeed considered objectionable by both the Fund and the World Bank programs, as they are largely held responsible for budget deficit and inefficient allocation of resources. Notwithstanding the realities of some negative impact which the dominance of government can foster, the fact is that given the weak private sector in many developing countries, especially in Africa, as Mr. O. Aboyade puts it, "the only feasible institution left for articulating, inspiring, guiding, and managing the development process in socially desirable directions is the machinery of state power." Because private initiative is not always forthcoming in vital areas of long-run economic development owing to inherent difference between the way potential investors read the cost-benefit signals of the future and the way in which public authorities may read the same signals, the public sector may maintain its dominance over time. Many governments from developing as well as industrial countries perceive some industries and other economic activities to be of strategic importance for both economic and non-economic reasons, and, therefore, fiscal policy design and analysis must take account of these realities. This, of course, is not to detract from the fundamental role of the government to direct resources to the productive sectors of the economy and encourage their efficient utilization. Nor should the pursuit of social justice and equity be unduly sacrificed in the operation of fiscal policy for purposes of structural adjustment with growth. This means that fiscal policy must constantly seek to synchronize and optimize sometimes an apparently conflicting set of needs and objectives of efficient resource use, growth, and social justice.

Issues that must be carefully noted in the treatment of fiscal deficit relate to definition and the relevance of assumptions. Mr. Chelliah has seriously called to question both the Fund and World Bank concept of fiscal deficit defined as "the difference between government's total expenditures and current revenues; thus it becomes equal to total net borrowing by the government which finances the deficit." The basic problems are the apparent limitations imposed by the use of budget deficit so broadly defined as "an indicator of stimulus to aggregate demand." Because of the central role of budget deficit in Fund/Bank programs, the need to re-examine its definition and composition cannot be overemphasized. Since the source of financing influences the impact of the budget on aggregate demand, any figure that represents budget deficit should have taken *fully* into account only the *net* effect of that source of finance. For the various reasons and illustrations given by Mr. Chelliah, there appears to be strong evidence in support of his views.

The Fund's model program assumes excessive growth of demand as the basic cause of balance of payments disequilibrium and the reduction of that demand as the basic cure. Evidence abounds to prove that that is not always the case. Mr. R. H. Green notes, "In cases of economies in long-term structural crises (e.g., Ghana and, for different reasons, Uganda) suffering from sustained export purchasing power weakness (e.g., Zambia) or ravaged by international economic depression, the causal factor behind imbalances is clearly not excessive expansion of demand. Rather, it is contraction of the capacity to import to maintain capital stock and sustain agricultural production growth equal to that of population." In circumstances such as these, where supply-side measures are warranted, fiscal measures should be careful not to make aggregate demand the whipping dog. The point has been made that in financing budget deficits, circumstances differ from country to country and therefore the same measures cannot be applied across the board. This should be a universally accepted position. It is consistent with the Fund's principle of a case-by-case approach in dealing with members. Specifically, although the macroeconomic approach to stabilization assumes that the fiscal deficit could be reduced by raising taxes or cutting spending, the question regarding which tax rates should be changed, which new revenues should be adopted, and which expenditures should be reduced or expanded depends on individual countries' relevant economic and socio-political circumstances. The characteristics of an economy affect the tax system through their influence on the demand for goods and government services in general and through their effect on tax bases. A largely agricultural economy has less demand for public services and provides limited tax bases compared with an urban economy that relies substantially on imports and has a large manufacturing sector. All these, including the political and cultural factors, must be taken into account in working out a tax system and structure for growth purposes. Nothing could be so politically frustrating and economically destabilizing as the imposition of imported and irrelevant tax systems and structures.

Taxation for revenue purposes has been broadly effective in developing countries, although it must be stressed that the level of effectiveness varies from country to country and on average is very much below that for developed countries. For most of Africa, according to Mr. Tanzi, the ratio of tax revenue to gross domestic product (GDP) ranges from about 10 to 25 percent. For the underdeveloped countries as a whole, the proportion ranges between 8 to 15 percent, and the bulk of it is accounted for by import and export duties while income taxes remain relatively unimportant. Because of the dominant role of taxes in current revenue, Mr. Chelliah is right in stressing that tax revenue must rise significantly if deficits are to be brought under control. But since substantial increase in tax revenue cannot be achieved without faster economic growth, the fiscal policymaker is locked up in a vicious circle whose exit is to be found only in the medium to long term. This underscores the difficulty of substantially reducing fiscal deficit in the short run. A resort to growth-retarding taxes for purely short-run solution to the problem of the fiscal deficit might make no economic sense in the long run. In certain circumstances, it might even be necessary as part of tax reforms, to encourage changes that could produce less impact on the fiscal deficit in the short run but would have desirable supply-side effects on the economy over the medium term. Essentially, the implication suggests the need for some limited compromise on reduction of fiscal deficit in the short run if the program is to lead to structural changes and growth in the longer run.

The discussion of the relevance or otherwise of various fiscal instruments, particularly with regard to developing countries, is comprehensive and offers useful elements that should be taken into consideration in effecting tax changes for revenue and growth purposes. Mr. Chelliah would advocate taxes on selective consumption, value-added tax, retail sales tax in small countries, and tariffs on imports as well as direct taxes on corporations. Considering the relevant caveats to some of the tax prescriptions, there would easily be a general consensus on the position taken by Mr. Chelliah. The choice of specific fiscal instruments, however, affect work effort, exports, productive investment, savings, capital flight, foreign investment, and so on. In this connection, and in order to realize the potential taxable capacity of its economy, the government of any developing country would need to thoroughly examine the various forms of taxation open to it, subject each kind of tax to its probable effects on the propensity to save, the administrative costs of collecting it, the incentive to work or continue to perform the same service, the foreign exchange implications, the impact on the stability of prices, and the extent to which it facilitates distributive equity.

For growth purposes, shifting resources from consumption to capital formation could be effected through customs duties, which play a strategic role in reducing luxury consumption of imported goods. This, coupled with a selective system of manufacturers' excises, could stimulate domestic output. In the agricultural sector, careful attention must be given to the tax instruments used since this sector constitutes a large share of GDP in many developing countries, especially in Africa. Because of the many inherent constraints—administrative, land tenure systems—it may be unrealistic to expect much in terms of directly enhancing agricultural productivity through taxation. Implicit taxation through the pricing policy of the marketing boards has been found to be unworkable and indeed in some cases counterproductive. Nigeria has since scrapped this system, having learnt from experience, although we still have to put in place an implementor of sensible guaranteed minimum prices.

With regard to Mr. Chelliah's position that direct tax reform should be given a high priority role in Fund-supported programs, on balance there is skepticism about the beneficial impact of such an exercise. There is a consensus on the fact that direct income taxes are generally relatively high in developing countries, even though the proportion of population that pays income taxes in Africa, for instance, is about only 2 percent compared with some 35 to 40 percent in Western Europe. There are the overwhelming problems of defining income, the difficulties of assessing any one individual income, even after overcoming the definitional problem and the obstacles in fixing a rational system of rates and the operational problems of collections and effective compliance. In the case of individual incomes, tax problems also arise with respect to selecting the appropriate adjustment for the family unit, the appropriate level of initial exemption, and deciding whether foreign-source income should be taxed. In view of these problems, and considering the fact that greater possibility exists for achieving growth and balance of payments objectives through indirect taxes, there may be justification for the Fund's action in giving less emphasis to revisions of direct taxation in Fund-supported programs.

Obviously, under direct taxation, important attractive sources of revenue in many developing countries are taxes on business and corporate income. In this case, there is relative ease of collection, and it appears administratively and politically painless, although the sophistication of the large multinational corporations are often reflected in their devices to avoid or evade taxes. However, as Mr. Chelliah has noted, it is necessary to encourage savings and investment and thus promote growth by providing for a low rate of tax on corporate profits and accelerated depreciation. In sum, it is relevant to remind ourselves of Herberger's commandments on tax policy in developing countries:

— If tariffs are used, keep effective rates reasonably uniform.
— If tariffs become excessive, use export incentives.
— Make tax systems as simple and neutral as possible.
— Avoid excessive income tax rates.
— Avoid excessive tax incentives.

Because of the theoretical underpinnings of Fund-supported programs, largely rooted in the Keynesian aggregate demand hypothesis, reduction in current expenditure is considered the cure for balance of payments disequilibrium. Of course, from cases cited earlier, it would appear that that was not a settled issue. Nevertheless, fiscal policy measures taken to influence the aggregate level or rate of growth of domestic demand and absorption would, as in the case of revenue measures, have to be based on country-specific factors. Differences regarding individual countries' expenditure decisions must take into account changes in demographic factors, sociological concerns, sectoral structure of the economy, technological and environmental factors. And this probably explains "the tendency for Latin Americans, Asians and industrial countries to spend *less* than would be expected on general public services and for African countries to spend *more* than would be expected."

However, the desirable goal which is to match current expenditure with current revenues necessarily demands expenditure restraints which involve, inter alia, cessation of government activity in the loss-making non-core public enterprises and the removal of subsidies. The distinction drawn by Mr. Chelliah between core and non-core sectors is important because it would be extremely difficult for any program to justify total elimination of all subsidies or privatization of all public enterprises, given the hard fact that in many developing countries with a very weak private sector, government is the prime mover of the economy. This relatively dominant position of government in overall economic activity must, of course, be gradually made to diminish as the development process accelerates.

The lessons of experience with the design and implementation of Fund and World Bank programs in developing countries clearly reveal that socio-political sensitivities impose limitations on rapid reduction in fiscal deficits, particularly on the removal of subsidies. Mr. Chelliah's cautious approach to the matter is relevant. Only on grounds of disincentives to producers and significant distortions in the allocation of resources would removal of subsidies be clearly justified. Appropriate levels of export subsidies, subsidies in favor of the poor, and subsidies on the use of particular inputs in furtherance of the public interest should be maintained.

It is, perhaps, not surprising that empirical investigation has so far failed to establish a clear-cut link between fiscal policy and savings, investment and growth rate. The well-known proposition of the standard Keynesian models that has largely influenced the design of Fund-supported stabilization and growth-oriented programs is that reduction in government expenditure or an increase in taxation would have a multiplier effect on the level of real income, at least in the short run. The difficulty of establishing clearly this relationship arises because of the existence of close linkage between fiscal policy and monetary policy, which is generally much tighter in developing countries than in industrial countries. This link between fiscal deficit and money supply changes imposes severe limitations on the use of monetary and fiscal policies as independent policy instruments in developing countries. This probably explains the inclusion in Fund-supported programs of ceilings on credit to government or public sector for the purpose of controlling public sector deficit and the growth of total domestic credit.

Thus, although in theory the growth role of fiscal policy is explicitly articulated, in practice, especially in developing countries, its independent impact is not impressive. For instance, in her study that focused on the specific issue of fiscal adjustment in Fund programs comparing the three-year average of the rates of growth beginning with the program year with the three-year average prior to that year, Margaret Kelly of the Fund found that for the 48 upper credit tranche stand-by arrangements implemented over 1971–79, 25 cases showed a decline in the average growth rate while the other 23 showed an increase. As has been noted, the relative unimpressive impact of fiscal policy on growth could, in addition to reasons given earlier, be traceable to the lack of mobilization of the society. Experience and the development process underscore the need for mobilization of the society and its entire resources to the task of economic transformation as the basis for effectiveness of growth-oriented economic policies.

Given available evidence, fiscal policy has an important role to play in the process of economic growth. Therefore, growth-oriented programs must continue to accord it priority. Although empirical investigation has so far revealed the limitations of fiscal policy which makes it difficult to establish a clear-cut linkage between it and growth, the quality and efficiency of fiscal instruments remain important for growth. Largely because of the problem of structural adjustment and the rigidities that prevent the play of market-induced adjustments in many developing countries, the short-run impact of fiscal policy on growth is uncertain, if not negative in some cases. But in the long run, with the removal of serious structural constraints, fiscal policy comes into its own.

In order to enhance the growth-promoting role of fiscal policy, the design of adjustment programs should adequately address the appropriate determination of fiscal deficit, the proper choice of fiscal instruments that takes account of socio-political sensitivities, and the factor of social mobilization, as well as flexibility in the fiscal ceilings.

Vito Tanzi

Director, Fiscal Affairs Department
International Monetary Fund

There are two realities with which the majority of developing countries must deal today. The first is the debt crisis, which has sharply reduced these countries' access to external resources and which, because of the large foreign debts, has made it highly desirable for them to grow at a sustained pace so as to reduce over time the debt burden. The second reality, clearly recognized in Mr. Chelliah's contribution, is that excess demand originating from the public sector has been, at least in part, responsible for the balance of payment difficulties that many of these countries have encountered. These two realities require that the public sector's claims on the economy be reduced while at the same time the productive capacity of the economy is stimulated.

Mr. Chelliah's paper deals with the fiscal policy that would be desirable in an economy that includes some planning to meet basic needs and where, by necessity, there is a wide scope for public enterprises and that wishes to achieve stability with growth *and* social justice. Mr. Chelliah addresses two fundamental questions: how does one measure this excess demand originating from the public sector? And, assuming that that excess demand can be measured in a meaningful way, how should it be eliminated to achieve stability with growth and social justice?

The Measurement of the Fiscal Deficit

As to the question of measuring the excess demand, Mr. Chelliah discusses some limitations of the common or conventional measure of the fiscal deficit that, he says, the Fund uses. He calls this measure the overall deficit defined as the difference between total government expenditure and government's current revenue. He mentions three limitations of this measure: (a) the differential impact on demand associated with different tax and expenditure categories; (b) the endogeneity of tax revenue; and (c) the impact of different sources of deficit financing.

The first of these limitations has a long history. In fact, Haavelmo's balanced budget theorem which recognized a different demand impact of a dollar change in taxes and in real government expenditure is an early version of it. Bator's later argument that transfer payments and real expenditures of the government have dollar per dollar different demand impacts is another. In the 1960s this argument was very popular. It perhaps received the most explicit expression in a book written by Bent Hansen dealing with fiscal policy in seven OECD countries. The problem is that while one should recognize that different taxes may have different demand effects and that different types of expenditures are also likely to have different demand effects, it is difficult to agree on specific and objective weights to be assigned to these differences. It is perhaps because of this reason that the early enthusiasm in this approach quickly vanished and today hardly any attention is paid to these differences, except, perhaps, in traditional and large econometric models of the economy. Another reason is that by putting the emphasis on demand effects this approach reflects an essentially Keynesian view of the role of fiscal policy.

The second limitation mentioned by Mr. Chelliah (the endogeneity of tax revenues) has also a long history; it goes back at least to work done in the 1950s by Cary Brown and others. The question here is the following: should one take as the index of the needed fiscal adjustment of the country the deficit that the country actually has in a given period; or should one adjust that deficit for the effect of the business cycle on revenue and expenditure? Obviously, as economic activity declines in a recession, tax revenues are likely to be lower than in a full-employment situation, ceteris paribus. Some expenditures, unemployment compensation for example, are also sensitive to the cycle.

This point raised by Mr. Chelliah is certainly potentially important. Behind it there is the assumption that, since a recession increases the size of the unused capacity in the economy, a larger public sector demand can be accommodated or may even be desirable to achieve full employment. It is a point that has been at the center of an ongoing debate for guiding fiscal policy in industrial countries. The full-employment budget surplus, a concept introduced in the 1962 *Economic Report* of the President of the United States and one that played a large role in determining economic policy in the Kennedy and Johnson era, was an expression of this aspect. The problem is that in today's world the concept of a full capacity level of output has lost much of its precise meaning for a variety of reasons but mainly because of the greater openness of many economies. Certainly, this concept is suspect for developing countries where capacity utilization and full employment are ambiguous concepts. In these economies and, perhaps, also in many industrial countries, the major constraint on output is not the labor supply or even the productive capacity of the capital stock, but foreign currency availability. A government that attempted to push aggregate demand because of unutilized domestic resources would soon run into a foreign exchange constraint. Thus, again, although Mr. Chelliah's point is an important one, its relevance for developing countries is likely to be limited.

Mr. Chelliah is certainly right in arguing that different sources of financing have different demand effects. Clearly, central bank financing, commercial bank financing, bond financing, foreign financing, domestic suppliers' financing, and so on, will affect aggregate demand differently. This is an aspect that has not received the attention that it deserves. Most observers have not recognized the variety of ways in which the fiscal deficit can be financed in developing countries. I have some difficulty, however, in accepting Mr. Chelliah's conclusion that one should focus only on bank-financed deficit. There are certainly lots of other reasons to focus on different measures. Most important among these is to prevent public debt, both domestic and foreign, from growing at too fast a pace. Another is the need to limit the crowding out of the private sector.

Mr. Chelliah also argues that the borrowing by the government on behalf of the public enterprises should be excluded from the deficit. The reason that he gives is that ". . . that part of the credit is strictly not for government purposes." This is certainly an interesting argument which merits serious consideration. One could argue that if those public enterprises had been private, and if they had done the same amount of borrowing in the capital market, the fiscal deficit would have been lower while the total demand for loanable funds would be the same. This is an argument that has attracted a lot of attention in Italy where the image of the "government as a banker" that just intermediates between the financial market and the public enterprises has been discussed. Several Italian authors have argued, just as Mr. Chelliah does, that this particular part of the deficit should be excluded.

The problem with the above argument is that it implicitly assumes that the public enterprises would do exactly the same amount of borrowing and presumably would produce the same output at similar costs, if they were private enterprises. It also assumes that they would borrow, at presumably identical conditions, regardless of the losses that they might be making. This is unlikely to be so. Many of these enterprises survive because the government is there to provide funds, and one can add that what they produce and the way they produce it is certainly influenced by their "publicness." A study by the Fiscal Affairs Department has shown that these enterprises have contributed significantly to total fiscal deficits and to credit expansion. If the government were not there, many of those enterprises would disappear, or at least they would borrow much less since they would have to pay considerably higher interest rates on loans that they obtained from the capital market. Thus, although Mr. Chelliah's argument has some validity for those public enterprises which are run on efficiency criteria and which may be as efficient as the private enterprises, it certainly has its limitation when it is generalized to all enterprises. In fact, Mr. Chelliah himself, later in the paper, calls for the elimination of loss-making public enterprises.

Mr. Chelliah attaches particular importance to what he calls the current account fiscal deficit. This is the difference between government revenue and "current" government expenditure. It is argued that this difference measures the government contribution to the total saving of the economy and, thus, to growth. On the surface this deficit concept appears very attractive and has thus many supporters. After all governments are supposed to mobilize resources and to contribute to growth and many assume that the government's contribution to growth is measured predominantly through its effect on total investment. This assumption is, of course, a direct outcome of the Harrod-Domar type of literature that was so popular in the 1950s and the 1960s. On closer scrutiny, however, this concept quickly loses much of its magic at least in practice if not in theory. There are several reasons for this.

First, whether the government spends on current expenditure or on what is conventionally classified as investment, the short-run impact of that expenditure on the balance of payment disequilibrium will be the same. In fact, one could go further than that and argue that, at least in the short run, investment spending by the government may have a larger negative impact on the balance of payment than other kinds of spending. The main reason for this is that the import content of investment spending is likely to be higher on the average than the import content of current spending.

Second, investment may be as wasteful as current spending. One could even argue that an unproductive investment which relies much on *imported* capital equipment is likely to contribute far less to both the welfare of the citizen and the growth of the economy than much current spending. The economic history of many countries is full of horror stories of highly wasteful public investment projects which after getting a country into foreign debt became useless white elephants.

As economic development economists have often argued, some current spending on health, education, administration, and so on, can have important effects on growth at least over the longer run. More recently a lot of emphasis had been placed on the need to spend on recurrent costs so that the existing infrastructure of developing countries can provide or continue to provide badly needed services. If a country favors investment over these highly desirable recurrent expenditures, it may badly misallocate available resources and reduce the rate of growth. There are too many examples of new roads being built at very high cost while the existing roads are allowed to deteriorate to such an extent that they become impassable, and of hospitals that cannot provide the services for which they were built because of lack of nurses or equipment. And there are examples of vehicles being unutilized because of lack of spare parts or gasoline. Some of these problems are recognized by Mr. Chelliah. Finally, the dividing line between what is classified as current and what is classified as capital is, in the real world, an arbitrary one that can be moved up and down depending on the picture that policymakers may wish to present to the world. (The rules that determine which expenditures should be classified as capital expenditure vary from country to country and, apparently, even in the same country over time. Even the comparison of capital expenditure by, say, the governments of Germany and the United States is difficult to make because of these reasons.)

Thus, in conclusion, I am skeptical that current account deficits may tell us as much as Mr. Chelliah argues they do although I would certainly be as concerned as he is about a country that is running a fiscal deficit even when investment expenditure, however defined, is netted out. For sure the current account deficit will tell us nothing about the impact of fiscal policy on the balance of payment and perhaps not much on the impact of fiscal policy on growth.

There are many other issues that arise with the conventional measures of fiscal deficit. Some of them are of particular relevance within the context of an adjustment program. While I cannot fully discuss them here, I would like to at least mention a few. Should one adjust the conventional measure for the impact of inflation? Several participants at this conference argued that one should. However, when the rate of inflation is high, there are considerable problems with both deficit measures that include a correction for inflation and those that exclude that correction.

Another big problem encountered in the use of fiscal deficit measures is in the treatment of arrears. Normal cash measures do not show these arrears; therefore, a country could increase its public expenditure but delay payments thus showing no change in the "overall deficit" while it would in fact be increasing aggregate demand. Arrears have become particularly relevant in connection with foreign debt. One should always specify in a measure of the deficit whether unpaid interest payments on foreign debt are being registered as deficit or not. For example, what happens to a deficit measure when interest on foreign debt is rescheduled?

Other problems arise from the fact that very often one measures the fiscal deficit only for the central government. However, other parts of the public sector may show large fiscal deficit. One such part that has attracted considerable recent attention, but still very little analysis, is the fiscal deficit of central banks. In some Latin American countries, central banks have become important fiscal agents. Through their operations governments promote domestic spending without having the budget reflect this contribution to aggregate demand. The fiscal deficit may appear also in public enterprises, in local governments, in social security institutions, or in stabilization funds or marketing boards. If these various components of the public sector were not interconnected, as is, for example, the case in the United States, where the Federal government, the Federal Reserve, and the local governments are essentially independent and where public enterprises are virtually nonexistent, one could perhaps still emphasize the deficit of the central government and attribute to it a central role. The trouble is that when these various components are interconnected, as they are often in many developing countries, one may find that when the deficit is squeezed out of the central government it may reappear in the central bank or in the public enterprises or even possibly in the local governments or in some other public institutions. In these circumstances an adjustment program that focuses on the deficit of the central government may not bring about the necessary adjustment if the reduction in the central government deficit is fully or partly compensated by an increase in the deficit in other parts of the government.

One final problem worth mentioning is the following. Fiscal deficits may be reduced through once-and-for-all changes. For example, a country may sell public assets; or it may introduce once-and-for-all measures such as tax amnesties; or public sector wages may be squeezed well below their long-term political and economic equilibrium; or temporary taxes are levied. These various measures achieve the objective of reducing the size of the deficit in the short run but they do little or nothing toward a permanent improvement of the fiscal situation. For this reason, in some cases, it would be desirable to present a measure of the fiscal deficit that would remove the impact of these short-term measures. This adjustment would give an underlying or core deficit which would better reflect the fiscal situation of the country over the longer run. Such a correction would be desirable although in many cases it might be difficult to do in practice.

A deficit may be like an elephant: one always recognizes it when he sees it even though it may be difficult to measure or describe it in a way that is satisfactory to everybody and for every purpose. Recently, I started writing a paper on fiscal deficit concepts. So far I have already identified about 15 different measures, each of which could be justified for some use and the list is still growing. The conclusion of this is that it is difficult to measure precisely the impact of fiscal policy on aggregate demand, inflation, and other macroeconomic variables. The use of just one number to assess that impact should be de-emphasized and a much closer scrutiny of the fiscal situation should be made. It is for this reason that much more attention needs to be paid to the structural aspects of fiscal policy. I was very pleased to listen to various speakers, such as Michael Bruno, Jeffrey Sachs, Jacob Frenkel, as well as Raja Chelliah, argue that the structural aspect of fiscal policy may be as important as the short-run demand management effect.

This takes me to the second question raised by Mr. Chelliah—how to eliminate excess demand originating in the public sector while still pursuing growth and social justice.

How to Reduce Fiscal Imbalances

About half of Mr. Chelliah's paper deals with ways in which fiscal imbalances can be reduced. He assumes that in the short run fiscal policy can only influence demand while in the medium run it can also be oriented toward increasing efficiency. Although this is the prevalent view, I have always had some problems with this distinction. This distinction between the short run and the medium run should not be carried too far for several reasons.

First, it is difficult to tell where the short run should end and the medium run should begin; economic policy often becomes just a series of short-run programs whereby the preoccupation with the next few months distracts policymakers from basic adjustment. Second, many fiscal measures have long-run implications especially because of their impact on expectation. Here again it is perhaps useful to point out that the Keynesian treatment of expectations continues to prevail in this area. The effect of a tax increase is assumed to be a reduction in demand in the immediate period; in other words, consumption depends mainly on current income. The tax increase is supposed to have no implications for the future. Short-run measures may increase the difficulties of achieving adjustment over the medium run, however, especially in the absence of liquidity constraints and, of course, they may not have the expected effect on current consumption. Third, some tax changes may have short-run supply-side effects on the economy. For example, the introduction of an export tax is likely to reduce exports and the foreign exchange available to the country.

Much of Mr. Chelliah's paper, however, deals with ways to bring down the deficit over the medium run. I am in broad agreement with a good deal of what he says although I have some difficulty with some aspects of it.

Mr. Chelliah deals separately with the revenue side and the expenditure side of public sector finances. He argues that in a country with a large fiscal deficit the level of taxation must rise substantially over the medium run while the tax structure must exert a favorable influence on the economy. He recognizes that in the majority of developing countries the tax structure leaves much to be desired and he favors indirect taxes over direct taxes but warns that indirect taxes should not distort the relative prices of the factors of production and should not lead to cascading. He suggests that a general sales tax, especially a value-added tax, would be a desirable feature for these countries but he makes what to me is a strange recommendation: that smaller countries should introduce a retail sales tax. In our work, in the Fiscal Affairs Department of the Fund, we have found that it is very unlikely that a developing country, be it large or small, can administer a retail sales tax in a satisfactory manner.

Another suggestion with which I have some difficulty is the idea that these countries should introduce an inheritance tax, if it is not already being levied. Again, our experience indicates that these taxes never play much of a role in these countries and, if they did, they would have effects, such as to stimulate consumption and to induce capital flight, which would be most unwelcome for developing countries. Mr. Chelliah favors an income tax with a single rate on the assumption that a single rate would be easier to administer than highly progressive income taxes. While I agree that a single rate would be easier to administer, I find the level of that rate that he suggests—30 percent—to be very high. In general, developing countries should aim at broadening the base of the income tax in order to be able to raise revenue while applying relatively low rates.

One aspect of his paper that I find puzzling is the total absence of reference to foreign trade taxes. These taxes are not even mentioned when in fact they account for about a third of all revenue of the developing countries and they probably are more guilty of distortions than any other group of taxes. If countries are truly concerned about growth, it is the foreign trade taxes that they must first reform. In many cases the export taxes must be reformed out of existence.

Mr. Chelliah recognizes that when the level of taxation is high, one must inevitably look at the expenditure side to reduce the fiscal imbalance. The higher the level of taxation, however, the more important it is that its structure have desirable features. Thus, fiscal adjustment must always include an improvement in the structure of taxation if the economy is to perform efficiently and if the rate of growth is to be kept at a high level.

Mr. Chelliah suggests that fiscal adjustment over the medium run, on the expenditure side, must involve: (1) a freeze on employment and wages in the public sector; (2) a reduction of subsidies; (3) introduction of zero-base budgeting to analyze the various items of the budget; and (4) some pruning of inefficient capital expenditure. I do not have difficulty with the last three of these suggestions, but I would worry about public sector wage freezes since these are often reversed in the future so that they may bring about a short-run fiscal adjustment that is not sustainable. When these freezes are not reversed, they lead to inefficiency and corruption in the public sectors.

Mr. Chelliah focuses much of his attention on current expenditure, in line with his belief that the current account deficit is the one to worry about. But, again, some of his discussion indicates that he may not be as convinced on that point as he seemed to be in the earlier part of the paper. For example, (a) he accepts the need to prune some capital expenditure; he recognizes that (b) some current expenditure leads to higher return on capital expenditure; (c) some loss-making enterprises should be closed down; and (d) transport allowances, supplies and materials, spare parts, use of telephone, and electricity may have been cut excessively in some countries; in other words, he recognizes the need for some increase in current expenditure.

Mr. Chelliah criticizes the Fund for having tried to reduce subsidies in some countries and states that one gets the impression that the Fund is always against subsidies. He argues that subsidies may be efficiently provided and may help the poor and he mentions an Indian example to justify his belief. In contrast to his example, however, one could use many other examples from other countries to show that subsidies have not only increased the fiscal deficit but have also, in many cases, led to serious misallocation of resources without helping the really poor. In any case, I feel that he overstates his case by saying that the Fund is always against subsidies. The

Fund has definitely been against *inefficient* subsidies and it has taken a position against subsidies when this seemed to be the most efficient way of reducing an unsustainable fiscal deficit. It has remained neutral in other cases.

Comment

Gerhard Boehmer
Executive Director
World Bank

In view of the short time, I will confine my remarks to only two points. One remark has been prompted by the support that Mr. Okongwu gave to Mr. Chelliah's argument for a mixed economy. Mr. Chelliah in his paper argues that the involvement of the public sector in productive enterprises should be necessary in order to provide essential goods to the poorest sections of the society. Yesterday Mr. Saracoglu also mentioned another reason for the involvement of the public sector in productive enterprises, as he called it, the locomotive function. That was certainly a deliberate political intention of the Turkish Government when, in the early 1930s, Turkey decided to go the path of modernization and industrialization. I have some doubt if either of these two purposes can be served well through public institutions.

For income distribution and services to the poorer segments of the population, there are, I think, other more efficient mechanisms available. If a country lacks private entrepreneurship, as was the case in Turkey in the early 1930s, I doubt if that lack can effectively be replaced by the public sector.

In most low-income countries another important constraint on the government's involvement in productive enterprises is, in my view, the scarcity of managerial and technical skills. If the public sector is constrained by lack of human capital, then the state should concentrate on the most important public services, which are to maintain public order and to provide the physical and social infrastructure on which the economy can build. If the public sector can perform these core functions effectively, it already makes a critical contribution to development.

My second point is on the revenue side of financial policies and on taxation. For the purposes of a stabilization program that needs to be executed in a comparatively short time, I think restructuring the tax system cannot contribute very much because it takes too much time to produce its effect. But for a program of structural change that aims at liberalization of an economic system, one must look at the tax system in order to remove distortions and possible disincentives to savings and investment.

I am not quite sure whether the liberalization of an economy requires a higher or lower total level of taxation. On the one hand, a reduction in the size of the public service sector, the withdrawal of the government from economic activities, or the shift to user fees for public services may allow a lower level of taxation. On the other hand, an increased reliance on markets may result in a more uneven distribution of income and the need for more redistribution through public budgets in order to protect the lower-income groups. Whatever the answer may be to this question, it will be important to remove from the tax system any bias against private and corporate savings.

The other issue is that of indirect taxation. Highly selective commodity taxes tend to create inefficiencies in the allocation of resources both on the consumption side and on the production side. So I would agree that it is necessary not to overburden a tax structure with distributional objectives, but rather aim at a uniform structure of indirect taxation.

This is not only advisable on grounds of economic efficiency but also because of administrative simplicity and, most of all in my view, for political reasons. Any attempt to differentiate tax rates either for reasons of income distribution or in order to exploit elasticities of demand and supply is bound to be subject to political power play among interest groups in a country, and the result may very well reflect the strengths of pressure groups but not necessarily economic wisdom.

SESSION 6

External Financing

The Role of External Private Capital Flows

John S. Reed
Chairman
Citicorp/Citibank

This symposium on growth-oriented adjustment programs addresses the right issue at the right time, for the real challenge facing developing countries is how to reestablish long-term sustainable growth. This paper provides background information on the role that private capital from abroad can play in helping countries meet this challenge. In particular, it focuses on the role that commercial banks can play in the process.

During the ten years prior to 1982, commercial banks provided a significant portion of the total external capital supplied to developing countries. Since the debt problem emerged in 1982, banks have continued to provide normal financing to many developing countries, but they have limited their financing of countries with severe balance of payments problems to lending packages arranged in connection with rescheduling agreements.

The current system for managing the debt problem is based on unparalleled cooperation among private banks, debtor countries, creditor country governments, and the Bretton Woods Institutions. It is, however, widely agreed that this system is coming under increasing stress owing to the discrepancy between the climate for investment created by certain countries and the conditions for investment required by the world capital markets.

This stress can be resolved in one of two ways. First, countries can succeed in improving the climate for investment and compete for capital on the terms established in the global capital markets. Over the long run—and sustained growth requires a long-run view—we believe this can result in a large, steady flow of funds to developing nations. Alternatively, countries can seek to force providers of private capital to make special off-market concessions. This may give some short-term relief, but it will not attract funds in the global capital markets. This approach will force troubled countries to depend almost entirely on official flows of capital (which are in short supply) to supplement their own savings in financing economic development. Ultimately, official flows come from taxes paid by households and businesses in industrial countries. In this situation, debtor countries will be required to compete for resources in the political arenas of the industrial countries.

The choice between these approaches will be made largely by the developing countries themselves, since they make the policies that determine the path they will follow. The thrust of this paper is to show that it is in the best interests of all parties, particularly the capital-short countries, to take the measures necessary to maintain a creditworthy status in the global financial markets.

History

Starting in the early 1970s, just as the Bretton Woods system of fixed exchange rates was breaking apart, developing countries began to attract significant amounts of private foreign capital. Although the bulk of investment capital in developing countries continued to come from domestic savings, large external capital inflows added a significant boost to investment programs and permitted these countries to accelerate their economic growth in both aggregate and per capita terms.

Most of the external capital came from the world's private capital markets through loans syndicated by commercial banks in the major industrial countries. By the late 1970s, net external borrowing from these intermediaries accounted for over three fourths of the total net inflow of funds from abroad into capital importing developing countries, while inflows from official creditors accounted for less than one third of the total.[1]

---

[1] International Monetary Fund, *World Economic Outlook* (Washington: International Monetary Fund, October 1986), p. 87. These figures refer to the net external borrowing of capital importing developing countries from official and nonofficial sources, as derived from the borrowing country's current account balance. The data cover the period 1978–80. The total borrowing from official and nonofficial sources adds to more than 100 percent since countries built up reserves during these years.

Several factors accounted for this large increase in private external lending. The banks were willing to lend because developing countries appeared to be good risks in the 1970s. The prices for commodity exports were buoyant, and the outlook for continued growth in export earnings looked excellent. In effect, the developing countries appeared to have the capacity to carry larger amounts of external debt. From these countries' point of view, borrowing dollars was cheap with interest rates often less than inflation.

Another reason why developing countries turned to the private capital markets for funds during the 1970s was that the resources of the Bretton Woods Institutions were not keeping up with world trade and the financing needs of these countries. As late as 1970, the resources of the World Bank and the Fund were equivalent to over 15 percent of world imports and to over 70 percent of the external debt of the developing countries. During the course of the 1970s, however, these two percentages fell to approximately 6 percent of world imports and to less than 30 percent of external debt. As a result, when the world economic environment started to change in 1979 because of the second oil price shock and the anti-inflation policies adopted in the United States and other leading industrial countries, the financing requirements of the developing countries had grown out of proportion to the resources of the Bretton Woods Institutions. Consequently, the resolution of the debt problem required a great deal of cooperation among the Bretton Woods Institutions, the private lenders, and the developing countries.

As is well known, the debt problem emerged in August 1982, when Mexico declared itself unable to service its debt in a timely fashion. Since then some 65 capital-importing developing countries have had trouble servicing their external debt, while 60 have not.[2] A comparison of countries in these two categories gives many clues as to why this is the case. By and large countries that had difficulty servicing their debt went into the debt crisis with higher ratios of debt to income and higher barriers to trade and investment.[3] Also

---

[2] International Monetary Fund, *World Economic Outlook*, April 1987, p. 110. Figures in this paper and the tables have been updated following the publication of the April 1987 *World Economic Outlook*.

[3] Much of this can be traced to import substitution policies that were started decades earlier. These policies led to protected markets that stymied domestic competition and encouraged the rise of large, inefficient, government-dominated industrial sectors that could not compete on world markets.

they had higher rates of money growth and inflation, which in turn frequently led to overvalued currencies and depressed export receipts (see Table 1).[4] In combination, these policies meant that countries with debt-servicing problems went into the debt crisis with much *higher* ratios of external debt and debt service to exports—a situation that left the countries more vulnerable to a world recession.

When that recession came in 1979–82, these countries in many cases compounded their difficulties by clinging to the inward focus of their old policies. They tried to postpone adjustments by borrowing more. They further increased their rates of money growth and inflation. In many cases (e.g., Argentina, Chile, Mexico, Venezuela), they allowed their currencies to become enormously overvalued, which had disastrous effects on their current accounts. Coupled with the rise in short-term dollar interest rates, the lack of adjustment caused the ratio of interest payments to exports to jump 2½ times to 24.0 percent between 1978 and 1982.[5] At the same time, foreign exchange reserves plummeted from 25 percent to 10 percent of imports (see Table 1). This decline in reserves relative to financing requirements was the final blow that closed countries' access to the voluntary capital markets and brought about the debt crisis of 1982.

Since then, there have been two phases in resolving the debt problem. The first, which began in 1982, involved reestablishing cash flow equilibrium, or balance in the current account, through short-term adjustment programs under the aegis of the Fund. The second phase may be said to have started in October 1985, when Secretary Baker launched a new growth-oriented adjustment concept designed to help countries get back on the path to long-term sustainable growth.

The first phase of resolving the debt problem occurred in relatively favorable economic circumstances. Industrial countries, led by the United States, recovered rapidly from the severe 1980–82 recession,

---

[4] In other relevant categories, however, the two sets of countries were not significantly different. Their rates of real economic growth were about the same; the prices of their non-oil commodity exports grew at about the same rate; and the gross rate of capital formation was only slightly lower in the countries with debt-servicing problems (see Table 1).

[5] In contrast, countries that did not subsequently have debt-servicing problems went into the global recession in a stronger position and reacted quickly to the changed international environment. They allowed their ratio of debt to income to rise only modestly, so that their interest burden remained relatively manageable (see Table 1).

and this helped reverse the decline in exports that the troubled debtors had experienced in 1981–82. Interest rates declined significantly from their peak in 1981, although they remained relatively high in real terms. Initially at least, commodity prices rebounded (before falling again in 1985).

Within this favorable economic environment, troubled countries and their creditors began to work out a resolution to the debt problem. The approach was country by country, since the problems and the solutions were also largely dependent on the economic policies that each country chose to adopt. By and large, countries that rescheduled their debts took policy measures needed to improve their balance of payments. Often these policy changes were a precondition for the country to receive a Fund loan and to receive new money or restructured maturities from private lenders and governments. The policy changes usually included a devaluation of the currency, a reduction in money growth, a decline in the government budget deficit, and the elimination of wage and price controls. Each country negotiated the timing and content of its particular program with the Fund and then negotiated rescheduling and new money agreements with the banks.

These policies were effective in reducing the aggregate current account deficit of the problem countries from $66.7 billion in 1982 to $21.1 billion in 1986 and in bringing about a slight reduction in the average ratio of interest to exports of goods and services, from 24.0 percent in 1982 to 21.3 percent in 1986 (see Table 1). Essentially, the adjustment programs stabilized the debt situation.

This inevitable adjustment in the balance of payments was not always carried out smoothly and at minimum cost. In many cases payments arrears developed, essential imports were not available, and the nature of the cutbacks in expenditures was influenced by the political constraints in each country. Unfortunately, from the standpoint of long-term growth, there was a marked decline in the rate of gross capital formation in the troubled debtor nations from 24.3 percent (1979–82) to 18.0 percent (1983–86). Real economic activity stagnated or declined. Total gross domestic product (GDP) rose by only 4.6 percent from 1983 to 1986, and real GDP per capita actually fell by 2.1 percent.

Although the external accounts of most developing countries were

Table 1.   Major Economic Indicators
(In percent)

	Countries with Debt-Servicing Problems	Countries without Debt-Servicing Problems
Real growth		
Total GDP		
1969–78	5.5	5.9
1979–82	2.7	4.5
1983–86	1.5	5.9
Per capita		
1969–78	3.1	3.7
1979–82	0.3	2.6
1983–86	− 0.7	4.1
Gross capital formation		
1978	27.2	29.0
1979–82	24.3	27.7
1983–86	18.0	26.5
Terms of trade		
1969–78	1.5	0.7
1979–82	1.0	0.6
1983–86	− 3.6	− 2.0
Non-oil commodity prices		
1969–78	8.9	10.0
1979–82	− 0.4	0.2
1983–86	− 0.3	− 1.4
Debt/GDP		
1978	31.4	19.9
1982	45.5	24.9
1986	54.8	32.5
Interest/exports of goods and services		
1978	9.6	4.6
1982	24.0	7.7
1986	21.3	7.3
Reserves/imports		
1978	25.2	26.3
1982	9.9	21.9
1986	16.0	32.0
Growth in export volume		
1969–78	2.3	8.4
1979–82	− 0.2	5.3
1983–86	3.1	10.5

(Continued)

Table 1. (concluded).   Major Economic Indicators
(In percent)

	Countries with Debt-Servicing Problems	Countries without Debt-Servicing Problems
Exports of goods and services/GDP		
1978	17.5	21.2
1982	18.8	26.0
1986	18.1	28.5
Money growth		
1978	38.8	20.7
1979–82	50.2	27.1
1983–86	79.5	22.5
Inflation		
1969–78	22.9	10.5
1979–82	41.7	14.6
1983–86	80.6	10.9

Source: International Monetary Fund, *World Economic Outlook*, April 1987.

brought into reasonable balance by 1984, the problem remained how to renew a process of sustained economic growth.

This need is at the heart of the Baker Initiative. As originally presented, the Baker Initiative is a three-pronged program involving the debtor countries, the Bretton Woods Institutions (and other multilateral development banks), and the private commercial banks. The scheme is simple: if debtor countries adopt growth-oriented, market-driven economic policies, both the multilateral institutions and the commercial banks are to provide the largest troubled debtor nations with a sustained injection of external capital.[6]

According to Secretary Baker's speech in Seoul announcing the Initiative, the growth-oriented, market-related policies that countries should adopt in order to qualify for new money include:

- maintenance of market exchange rates, interest rates, wages and prices
- the adoption of sound monetary and fiscal policies
- the implementation of growth-oriented structural reforms.

---

[6] Countries included in the Baker Initiative are Argentina, Bolivia, Brazil, Chile, Colombia, Côte d'Ivoire, Ecuador, Mexico, Morocco, Nigeria, Peru, Philippines, Uruguay, Venezuela, and Yugoslavia. Together, these countries account for over 70 percent of the debt of the 65 countries with recent debt-servicing problems.

To obtain new money, countries are to correct the economic policies that caused the debt problem in the first place. In return for adopting these growth-oriented, market-driven policies, countries are to receive additional loans from official and private sources. Specifically, both the Fund and the World Bank are to provide additional credit, provided these countries adopt the necessary structural policy changes. Indeed, Fund and World Bank loans are to contain conditionality clauses to that effect, and the World Bank is to shift its emphasis from project finance to adjustment lending to help assure that countries do adopt the needed reforms. Finally, commercial banks are to supply $20 billion in new financing to the largest troubled debtor nations, again provided that the countries adopt the necessary structural reforms. The Baker Initiative is clear: new money to support new policies.

Like many new initiatives, the Baker Initiative has been slow getting off the ground. Despite these delays, in some countries it is bringing about important changes in attitudes and policies. As the title of this symposium implies, the emphasis is now increasingly on growth, and that is all to the good. In fact, many countries (including Chile, Côte d'Ivoire, Ecuador, Morocco, Nigeria, and Turkey) are now moving toward implementing the initial reforms required to produce sustained growth. In most cases, the reforms fall short of the ideal, but the willingness of countries to change deeply ingrained policies is certainly a step in the right direction.

The Current Situation

Logically, then, the current situation should represent a transition from the stabilization programs begun in 1982 to the growth phase announced with the Baker Initiative in October 1985. In practice, however, a debate has arisen concerning whether countries should proceed along these lines at all or whether instead they should seek to "resolve" the debt problem through some form of debt relief. This latter approach calls for concessions from the banks and could lead to a breakdown of the bank restructuring committee process. This is an important turning point in the resolution of the debt problem and the long-term growth prospects for the countries.

Before turning to the debate, it is useful to review the debt situation as it now stands. Total external debt of the developing countries amounts to just over $1 trillion (see Table 2). More than half of this amount ($624 billion) is owed by countries that are experiencing problems in servicing their external debt in a timely fashion. These countries owe approximately $400 billion to private creditors, principally commercial banks from the industrial countries.

Debt owed by countries with debt-servicing problems is concentrated in 15 large, heavily indebted nations, and it is precisely on these nations that the Baker Initiative focuses. These 15 nations account for over two thirds of the total debt owed by all countries with debt-servicing problems and for over four fifths of the debt owed by such countries to private creditors (see Table 2).

By any modern standard, the debt burden is high for these problem countries. At year-end 1986, their interest payment requirements averaged 21 percent of export revenues, and for the largest troubled debtors, the figure was 27 percent, or approximately four times the level of interest service due from countries without debt-servicing problems (see Table 3). It should be noted, however, that countries with debt-servicing problems have rebuilt their foreign reserves from the extraordinarily low levels reached in 1982, and in some cases

Table 2. Developing Country Debt Profile, Year-End 1986
(In billions of U.S. dollars)

	Countries with Debt-Servicing Problems	Countries without Debt-Servicing Problems	Total
Total debt	623.5	408.1	1,031.6
Due to official creditors	213.9	170.2	384.1
Due to private creditors[1]	409.6	237.9	647.5
Of which: Fifteen heavily indebted countries[2]			
Total debt	434.4		
Due to official creditors	92.4		
Due to private creditors	342.0		

Source: International Monetary Fund, World Economic Outlook, April 1987.
[1] Includes all short-term debt.
[2] Includes Colombia, which has not had debt-servicing problems.

Table 3. Developing Country Debt Profile, Year-End 1986
(In percent)

	Fifteen Heavily Indebted Countries[1]	Countries with Debt-Servicing Problems	Countries without Debt-Servicing Problems
Debt/GDP	48.4	54.8	32.5
Interest/exports of goods and services	27.3	21.3	7.3
Reserves/imports	22.3	16.0	32.0
Annual rate of growth in real debt:[2]			
Total debt			
1978–82	9.9	8.7	4.1
1983–86	0.4	1.4	7.0
Debt due to private creditors			
1978–82	11.5	9.5	6.1
1983–86	−2.1	−2.2	6.5

Source: International Monetary Fund, World Economic Outlook, April 1987.
[1] Includes Colombia, which has not had debt-servicing problems.
[2] Nominal debt deflated by U.S. GNP deflator.

(e.g., Venezuela) reserves amount to a significant percentage of the outstanding debt.

Also, it should be noted that countries without debt-servicing problems continue to enjoy normal access to the world capital markets. In other words, for countries that continue to meet the standards of the market, lenders are willing and able to supply new money (see Table 3). We feel this also can be the case for countries with debt-servicing problems if they take the measures necessary to make themselves creditworthy again.

Indeed, many banks are now in a much stronger financial position to extend new credit to troubled countries than they were when the debt problem started in 1982. Through building up their reserves and capital, U.S. banks' exposure to troubled debtor nations now accounts for a much smaller portion of capital and earnings than it did in 1982. Also, the debt problem has largely been discounted in the price of U.S. bank stocks. In the case of the German, Japanese, and Swiss banks, the decline of the dollar relative to their currencies has effectively reduced the portion of problem country exposure in their balance sheets by 30 percent or more. Furthermore, it is widely believed that many of these banks have reserves that fully cover this exposure.

Ironically, the financial cost suffered by the banking system increases the strength of the banks and is putting a great strain on the bank restructuring process. Banks are now more able to lend new money, but they are also more able to "walk away" from the process entirely. Demands for concessional terms by debtor countries will

Table 4. Members of Bank Advisory Committees
(Percentage Share of Committee in Total Bank Exposure)

Argentina	Brazil	Chile
Bank of America	Arab Banking Corp.	Bank of America
Bank of Tokyo	Bank of America	Bank of Nova Scotia
Chase Manhattan	Bank of Montreal	Bank of Tokyo
Citibank[1]	Bank of Tokyo	Bankers Trust
Credit Lyonnais	Bankers Trust	Chase Manhattan
Credit Suisse	Chase Manhattan	Chemical Bank
Dresdner Bank	Chemical Bank	Citibank
Lloyds Bank	Citibank[1]	Credit Suisse
Manufacturers Hanover	Credit Lyonnais	Dresdner Bank
Morgan Guaranty	Deutsche Bank	Manufacturers Hanover[1]
Royal Bank of Canada	Lloyds Bank[1]	Marine Midland
	Manufacturers Hanover	Morgan Guaranty
(24 percent)	Morgan Guaranty[1]	
	UBS	(35 percent)
	(30 percent)	

Mexico	Philippines	Venezuela
Bank of America[1]	Bank of America	Banca Nazionale del Lavoro
Bank of Montreal	Bank of Montreal	Bank of America[1]
Bank of Tokyo	Bank of Tokyo[1]	Bank of Tokyo[1]
Bankers Trust	Banque Nationale de Paris	Chase Manhattan[1]
Chase Manhattan[1]	Barclays	Chemical Bank
Chemical Bank	Citibank	Citibank
Citibank[1]	Chase Manhattan	Commerzbank[1]
Deutsche Bank	Chemical Bank	Lloyds Bank
Lloyds Bank	Dresdner Bank	Manufacturers Hanover
Manufacturers Hanover	The Fuji Bank	Morgan Guaranty
Morgan Guaranty	Manufacturers Hanover[1]	Banque Paribas
Societe Generale	Morgan Guaranty	Royal Bank of Canada
Swiss Bank		Swiss Bank
(26 percent)	(36 percent)	(27 percent)

[1] Chairman, Deputy Chairman, or Co-Chairman.

drive many banks away from the restructuring and new money agreements. There is a great concern that more pressure for concessions will cause a breakdown of the bank restructuring process, especially if creditor governments should join in advocating such concessions.

Typically, a committee of 10 to 14 banks represents the hundreds of banks around the world that are creditors to a country, and separate committees exist to conduct negotiations with each problem country. Members of the committee come from many different nations. They are chosen by the debtor government on the basis of their exposure and geographical representation and are to represent the views of the banks of their country or region in the negotiations. Although banks on a committee are usually the largest bank lenders to the country in question, the committee members in aggregate generally represent only 25 percent to 35 percent of a country's total external debt to commercial banks. Thus, the committee itself cannot finalize a deal; it must "sell" it to hundreds of banks, small and large, in many countries (Table 4).

For this reason, much of a committee's function involves communicating with all other participants in the rescheduling process. In effect, a committee serves as a go-between for the debtor country and the hundreds of banks that have extended it credit, and a committee must seek to negotiate terms and conditions that are acceptable to the debtor country and that will encourage other banks to participate in the new financing. In addition, a committee is responsible for coordinating the efforts of the commercial banks with those of the Bretton Woods Institutions and with those of the creditor country governments.[7]

---

[7] Much of this work is done by subcommittees that focus on particular aspects of a deal. For example, the economic subcommittees evaluate the economic data supplied by the debtor government to the banks, brief the banks on developments in the country's economy and on changes proposed for the country's economic policies, and work closely with economists from the Bretton Woods Institutions, the debtor country government, and the creditor country governments to provide input into policy decisions by the debtor country government. Depending on the individual country and negotiation, there are also subcommittees that focus on trade financing, cofinancing (with the World Bank), interbank lines, and other matters. These subcommittees have worked to maintain critical short-term financing and to develop a wider menu of financing options. As are the committees themselves, the subcommittees of each committee are comprised of many different banks from a number of different countries.

The ability to sell a particular deal to banks around the world depends on the economic policies the country is following and on the terms and conditions of the deal itself. Structural adjustments along the lines proposed under the Baker Initiative and appropriate macroeconomic policies are essential, since they establish the fundamental conditions that determine the outlook for economic growth and the ability to service debt; however, structural adjustments and good policies are not sufficient in themselves to attract new money. They must be accompanied by market-related pricing and terms in order to be sold to banks around the world. After all, the commercial banks are intermediaries between the world's capital markets and the debtors. Since banks fund themselves at market rates, anything less than market rates represents a loss for them, and they are reluctant to go along.

The difficulty experienced in placing the recent Mexican debt restructuring is a clear example of this. Even more important than the low spread, the package includes concessions in the form of contingency financing and does not offer a menu of options, including on-lending to the private sector. Certain banks around the world have been reluctant to participate in the package and placing it is exhausting goodwill in some areas of the banking community. We now see countries with relatively good economic performance and policies having difficulty in their negotiations because they are demanding on-market features that in their novelty raise substantive and accounting issues. Citibank has been vocal about this because we feel further demands for concessions and unusual arrangements will damage the bank support system and curtail the early momentum of the Baker Initiative.

Turning Point

Currently there appears to be general acceptance of the principles espoused in the Baker Initiative, that is, that the problem is how to get the troubled debtor nations back on the road to long-term sustainable growth, and that the solution invariably entails adopting growth-oriented, market-related economic policies. But what should those policies be, how fast should they be adopted, and should they be accompanied by market terms and conditions on the new funds that troubled debtor nations seek to obtain from abroad? Those are the open questions, and how they are resolved will determine the amount of external financing that developing nations can expect to receive from commercial banks and other private sources of capital during the coming years.

Two schools of thought prevail on how to resolve these open questions. One school argues that lending should be on concessional terms and that countries should be given a longer period of time in which to phase in the new market-oriented economic policies. Some would go so far as to say that the concessions should take the form of debt relief or debt forgiveness.

The other school of thought says that if countries want to return to the market, they should adapt to the conditions of the market. If they meet these conditions, they will restore their creditworthiness and attract new private capital for economic growth. If they do not, investors, be they commercial banks or other sources of private capital, will direct their capital into other uses, and the problem countries will not be able to obtain the external capital they need for economic growth.

Each school of thought bases its recommendation, to some extent, on a calculation of the funds that troubled debtor countries can expect to receive. Those who argue for concessional terms focus on the short term, on the easing of the debt burden that troubled debtor nations can expect to achieve during the next two to three years. Those who argue for market-related terms focus on the funds that countries can expect to receive over the longer term and on the contribution that such funds can make to help countries achieve long-term sustainable growth.

The concessional school of thought implicitly assumes that the major source of funds to the troubled debtor nations are those funds that can be "extracted" in the form of concessions from existing lenders. Proposals for concessions range from not-so-freely negotiated reductions in the spreads on new or existing money to mandatory forgiveness of interest and principal. Virtually all proposals envision that the problem countries must adopt market-oriented structural reforms along the lines of those outlined in the Baker Initiative in order to qualify for debt relief. But even the most far-reaching of these proposals offers relatively little in the way of additional resources to the countries concerned. For the 15 heavily indebted countries, the debt relief envisioned under these proposals amounts to less than

4 percent of the country's exports of goods and services and less than 1 percent of the country's GDP, and for no country would the proposed relief exceed 6 percent of the country's exports of goods and services. It is therefore hard to see that debt relief, by itself, will put countries back on the path to long-term sustainable growth.

If countries are, in any event, to take the market-oriented policy measures envisioned under the Baker Initiative (and under the proposals for debt relief), countries will also find it in their long-term interest to agree to market-related terms and conditions on any new money that they receive from the world capital market. This will assure that these countries have sustained access to the world capital markets, just as the developing countries without debt-servicing difficulties continue to have (see Table 3).

Pricing is only one part of what is meant by market terms and conditions. In fact, this concept represents a broad menu of possible programs. Some are designed to improve the balance sheet of the troubled debtor nation by bringing more equity investment into the country, either from foreigners or domestic residents repatriating capital held abroad. Others are designed to channel credit to the private sector and to support structural reform efforts. The mechanisms by which these programs are implemented can be as varied as the programs themselves. Debt-equity swaps, the creation of mutual funds, and on-lending to private enterprises can be valuable tools in promoting a market-related environment.

As countries adopt market-driven strategies, there will be clear improvements in the investment climate. More investors, both domestic and foreign, will be attracted by investment opportunities, and greater investment flows will be channeled into the economy. This will ease the country's debt burden by reducing its dependence on debt finance today and by improving its income-producing potential in the years to come. Both of these developments would make it possible, in our opinion, to conclude debt reschedulings and new money packages at lower spreads.

Some examples of the gains from market-driven programs are striking. Canada, for example, has traditionally relied on external capital to supplement its domestic savings. In fact, Canada has about the same reliance on external capital relative to GDP as Argentina, Brazil, and Mexico. However, Canada's policies have created an environment more conducive to investment and capital inflow throughout most of its modern history. As a result, Canada has funded its external balance sheet primarily through equity and securities, while Argentina, Brazil, and Mexico have relied heavily on bank debt.

If countries opt for the concessional school of thought, and the associated confrontational attitudes, it is safe to say that they can expect little or no new capital from private sources, especially commercial banks. The little they may attract from private sources would be very expensive. Private investors have a full range of investment opportunities; they have no reason to put their funds where they cannot expect to receive a market rate of return and where repayment is in serious question. That is particularly true for commercial banks, which are only intermediaries between borrowers and depositors from whom the banks themselves borrow money.

Furthermore, if countries opt for the concessional school, it is likely that they will have to depend, at least for a number of years, to a significant degree on official sources of foreign capital to supplement whatever internal savings their economies may generate. How large are such flows likely to be? It is worth noting that during the last four years (1982–86) the large troubled debtors almost doubled their share of net new official credit, and they received over half of the increase in net new official credit supplied to developing countries (see Table 5). Even so, this much larger share of official capital has been meager. During the height of the debt problem (1982–86), large troubled debtor nations received official credits amounting on average to 1.1 percent of their GDP. Earlier (1978–81), these countries had received annual credit inflows amounting to 6 percent of their GDP. Even today countries without debt-servicing difficulties receive total annual credit inflows amounting on average to 2.8 percent of their GDP, or two and one-half times as much as the large troubled debtor nations have been receiving from official sources (see Table 5). Clearly, returning to the world capital markets holds out prospects for greater inflows of resources from abroad and for faster economic growth.

Furthermore, there is no guarantee that the large troubled debtor nations will be able to continue to secure such a large share of the official credit given to developing countries, or that official credit will continue to expand at the same rate it has in the past. There is considerable political competition for the resources of official organizations. For example, there are many contenders for the official

Table 5. Analysis of Official Credit to Developing Countries, 1978–86

	Fifteen Heavily Indebted Countries[1]	All Countries with Debt-Servicing Problems	Countries without Debt-Servicing Problems
Net new official credit[2] *(in billions of U.S. dollars)*			
1978–82	15.8	48.0	41.2
1982–86	46.2	89.5	56.3
Share of net new official credit *(in percent)*			
1978–82	17.7	53.8	46.2
1982–86	30.4	58.8	37.0
Net change in long-term borrowing from official creditors as percent of GDP			
1978–81	0.7	1.4	1.2
1982–86	1.1	1.8	1.1
Total net external borrowing as percent of GDP			
1978–81	6.0	5.7	2.8
1982–86	2.3	5.9	2.8

Source: International Monetary Fund, *World Economic Outlook,* October 1986.

[1] Includes Colombia, which has not had debt-servicing problems.

[2] Net change in long-term debt to official creditors from year-end to year-end.

credit currently available, and a strong case has been made that a greater share of official credit and aid should be given to the truly needy African countries rather than to the relatively well-to-do problem debtor nations.

There is also considerable internal political competition for funds that provide the source of official credit—that is, taxes in industrial countries. In most industrial countries the capital contributions for the entities that grant official credit must be appropriated by the legislature. That puts the Fund, the World Bank, and other multilateral development banks into direct competition with domestic constituencies for health care, unemployment benefits, military expenditures, farm aid, and industrial programs, particularly programs for declining industries that might be harmed by greater exports from the countries to which official credit often is granted. That battle has proven to be a losing one for the proponents of more official credit to developing countries.

Thus, staking one's economic future on the ability to attract official inflows of capital seems a hazardous proposition. If countries are to take the market-oriented policy measures needed to qualify for debt concessions under the proposals made to date, then it would seem in their long-term self-interest to incorporate market-related terms and conditions into their debt reschedulings and new money packages. That is the way back to the world capital market, and that is the way toward long-term sustainable growth.

Conclusion

We are at an important turning point in the resolution of the debt problem with developing countries. We must choose whether we are going to permit the financial disciplines transmitted by the banking system to run their course and restore corrective action or whether these disciplines are to be temporarily avoided by support for concessional lending and slow progress on fundamental economic reforms.

In our view, banks are intermediaries between savers and debtors. Banks borrow from savers and relend to debtors. Savers provide funds to banks, but on terms and conditions that are beyond the control of banks. The reality is that savers will not provide significant amounts of funds to banks, unless borrowers from banks also meet market terms and conditions. Consequently, it is the role of the world capital market to bring pressure to bear on any borrower—be it a domestic manufacturer or a troubled debtor nation—when the borrower takes steps that will jeopardize its ability to service its debt in a timely fashion. This pressure usually takes the form of refusing to lend, unless and until the borrower takes the steps necessary to restore its creditworthiness. Thus, the pressures transmitted by the world capital market should be viewed as part of the recovery process that will induce countries to take the steps necessary to get back on the path to long-term sustainable growth. In this sense, the role banks play by not lending when conditions are wrong is as important as the role that banks play by lending when conditions are right.

We believe the principles set forth in the Baker Initiative are sound.

We also believe that banks and other private sources will provide capital to troubled debtor nations as long as countries adopt market-oriented policies and as long as countries adapt to the conditions imposed by the world financial markets. Banks stand ready, willing, and able to help debtor countries cultivate access to these markets, but banks cannot change the fundamental conditions demanded by these markets, for banks themselves are ultimately subject to the discipline of these same markets. Debtor countries must recognize this, if they wish to enlist bank support in restoring and sustaining the high rates of economic growth they need and deserve.

Official Financing and Growth-Oriented Structural Adjustment

R.H. Carey
Deputy Director, Development Cooperation Directorate
Organization for Economic Cooperation and Development

This paper considers the relationships between official financing (both bilateral and multilateral, concessional and nonconcessional) and growth-oriented structural adjustment programs. It is organized as follows. The first section offers some broad perspectives on the nature and significance of the financial and institutional challenges. There follows a section on the financing/adjustment and growth position of three groups of developing countries identified in current Fund tabulations: 15 highly indebted countries, sub-Saharan Africa, and (as a point of reference) countries without recent debt-servicing problems. This section attempts to place the role of official financing in the context of the current problems of the main groups of developing countries undertaking growth-oriented structural adjustment programs. Next are two sections on the supply of official finance, the first offering some general macroeconomic observations, the second a "flow by flow" analysis of issues and prospects by source of finance. The final section deals with policy and operational improvements that might enhance the role of official financing in contributing to growth-oriented structural adjustment. Some questions about longer-term directions are also raised.

Note: This paper is written and presented on the author's own responsibility and does not necessarily reflect the views of the OECD. Factual data and analysis draw upon the on-going work of the OECD's Development Cooperation Directorate.

436

Introduction: Perspectives on Official Finance and Development in the Mid-1980s

In the mid-1980s, official development finance—bilateral and multilateral aid and nonconcessional lending—is providing no less than 70 percent of the net financial resource flows to developing countries (Table 1). This proportion has leapt from 35 percent at the beginning of the 1980s, and from 45 percent in the early 1970s. Indeed, one has to go all the way back to the early 1960s, before the postwar revival of the international capital markets, to find official development finance playing a comparable role in the financing of developing countries.

The 1980s have brought other notable shifts in the pattern of financial flows to developing countries. Multilateral flows, concessional and nonconcessional, now constitute 24 percent of total flows,

Table 1. Pattern of Total Net Financial Flows to Developing Countries: Main Components, 1960–86[1]

(In percentage shares)

	1960–61	1970	1975	1980	1985	1986[2]
Official development finance of which:	59	46	45	35	60	72
DAC bilateral aid	48	28	17	14	27	33
OPEC bilateral aid	—	2	10	7	3	3
Multilateral aid	2	5	7	6	10	12
Multilateral nonconcessional lending	2	3	4	4	10	12
Export credits	14	13	10	13	2	2
Private flows of which:	27	41	45	51	38	26
Direct investment	19	18	20	9	9	12
Bank sector	6	15	21	38	16	4
Bonds	—	2	1	1	6	2

Source: OECD data bank.

[1] Financial flows as measured in DAC statistics include some technical assistance items which, in principle, should be included in balance of payments records of financial flows, but sometimes are not. They also include administrative costs of aid agencies, as approved by the DAC. These items cause DAC figures on financial flows to exceed by a margin, balance of payments measures. Figures may not add up due to rounding and omission of minor components.

[2] Estimated.

up from 10 percent in 1980 (and only 4 percent in 1960). Officially provided or supported export credits, which accounted for some 10–14 percent of flows throughout the 1960s and 1970s, have tumbled in the 1980s, on a net basis, to around 2 percent of the total.

The background to these shifts in the pattern of development financing in the 1980s is of course the dramatic rise in private bank lending to developing countries, beginning in the late 1960s, to a high (and unsustainable) peak in the early 1980s, and its subsequent dramatic decline. Current evidence suggests that the private international bank sector is now barely maintaining a net flow of new lending to developing countries as a group. Net lending to some 20 creditworthy developing countries, mainly in Asia, is continuing; the aggregate picture is dominated however by the reduced bank flows to "problem" countries.[1]

Private direct investment has played, on the whole, an apparently passive role in this saga, providing about the same volume of flows (i.e., at constant prices and exchange rates) in the mid-1980s as in the early 1970s, thus losing relative position in the overall financing pattern. Episodic increases in direct investment throughout this period indicated the continuing potential of this form of external financing, however, and there was significant use of bank loans and export credits in association with direct investment.

These changes in the pattern of financial flows to developing countries are intimately related to recent economic trends and events in both developed and developing countries, in ways with which we are all only too familiar. The current relative dominance of official development finance is explained, of course, by the fact that a significant number of developing countries have lost their creditworthiness vis-à-vis the private capital markets (and often vis-à-vis official export credit agencies as well). This situation is itself only an indication of the more fundamental reality—that financing and development processes have gone seriously astray in an important range of developing countries, including both more advanced and less advanced countries.

Against this background, what we are witnessing is not just a

---

[1] The Republic of Korea has announced an intention of reducing its net indebtedness over the next few years. Thus bank flows to this creditworthy country may also be negative in the near future.

rearrangement of the pattern of financial flows, but an important new phase in the 40-year record of development cooperation and official financing.

What, fundamentally, is new?

First, a diverse range of actors is being called upon to respond to a large number of specific country situations with a degree of rapidity, flexibility, and coherence not previously a notable feature of development financing processes. Second, the nature of current development problems demands a program approach to the delivery of development assistance and finance, rather than a project approach. In more technical economic terms, there is a general equilibrium problem involving the use of all resources in the recipient economy, and development assistance and other financing agencies cannot divorce themselves from that overall context.

Flexibility and program approaches have by no means been absent from the development cooperation scene. Major changes in the allocation of aid, both geographically and sectorally, have taken place, while program aid has a long history. It would nevertheless not be inaccurate to characterize the development assistance process, both bilateral and multilateral, as having evolved mainly along incremental and project lines. It is also fair to say that the concept of policy-based lending, in any broad, concerted form at least, has not been a part of the "culture" of development cooperation. Even the World Bank has, in the past, kept the policy dialogue with its borrowers on a discreet, partial equilibrium basis. On the whole, the development cooperation industry has been prepared to leave it to the Fund to take the general equilibrium approach, focused on key macroeconomic prices and other variables, having itself neither the orientation nor the competence to handle this difficult task.

To this background must be added a further complication in the case of assistance to the poorer aid-dependent developing countries. Institutionally, the "common aid effort" has become enormously complex, with some 24 donor governments, 10 multilateral development banks and funds, 19 United Nations agencies, and several hundred nongovernmental organizations all interacting at different points and levels with recipient country authorities and employing different terms, operating techniques, and procurement conditions.

In the Organization for Economic Development (OECD), the Development Assistance Committee (DAC) has devoted much effort over the last three years to confronting the need for change in established practices and philosophies to meet the demands of the new development challenges. A set of conclusions released publicly by DAC Aid Ministers and Head of Agencies following their annual High Level Meeting in December 1986, under the title "Aid for Improved Development Policies and Programs and Implications for Aid Coordination"[2] sum up the results of three years of discussion and constitute, in a sense, an extraordinary mea culpa on the part of developed country donors. Two major self-criticisms are implicit:

- the complexity of the aid process has overwhelmed the administrative capacities of the smaller, poorer recipient countries, weakening their central accounting and control functions and thus contributing to a lack of coherence in resource allocation and public budgetary processes;
- lack of attention to the policy environment, far from enhancing the autonomy of the recipient governments, has helped to undermine it.

When the situation is expressed bluntly in these terms, it becomes more evident that the measured rationalism of the DAC's prescription for rectifying these damaging faults amounts to a truly radical and important manifesto for the reform of the aid process. The "firm resolve by aid leaders to work with other donors and recipient countries to relate their individual aid activities more closely to carefully appraised and jointly reviewed programs and policies" involves, as becomes apparent from a reading of the agreed aid coordination principles, a demanding agenda for changes in organizational orientation and practices.

In other words, growth-oriented adjustment in aid-dependent countries is not simply a question of financial and economic issues. Even more fundamentally, it requires solving complex problems of public administration and political cooperation, both domestic and international in scope.

It has thus become clearer than ever that the effective delivery of development assistance is inherently an immensely difficult undertaking. Contemplating the inherent problems of the aid process, Charles Kindleberger, nearly 20 years ago, asked the question whether

---

[2] OECD, Press Release A(86)61, Paris, December 2, 1986.

the resurrection of the international capital market might provide a better medium than aid for the provision of foreign capital needed for developing country growth.[3] His review of this question provides a useful transition in this introductory overview to the role of official financing in meeting the current problems of the more advanced overindebted countries. Kindleberger took the view that in the long run it was desirable that private lending, in debt form, should replace some or most aid and official lending, and that it conceivably could. The case he made provides interesting reading today:

> The allocation of a portion of internationally available capital would be made by a market process—the "invisible," rather than the "visible hand"—thereby relieving the political process of a disagreeable task. Conditions for borrowing would be determined by neither projects nor programs that were imposed by the lenders and that interfered with the sovereignty of the borrowing country. These conditions would be volunteered by the borrower, and they would be in accord with the market's requirements as determined by the borrower and the investment bankers underwriting its loans. Where the market misjudged the creditworthiness of a borrower and default occurred, private negotiations of the Council-of-Foreign-Bondholders type would ensue without the external diseconomy implied by a single cohesive set of lenders whose condoning of one default implied license for all. (A reference to multilateral development banks.)

> More significant, perhaps, the sensible fiscal management needed to restore creditworthiness in the international capital market is the same management needed for effective economic growth. Applied impersonally, rather than by paternalistic officials of international institutions, such management and governmental borrowing from the private international capital market raise a prospect of enlisting local capital in national growth efforts, initially in roundabout, and ultimately in direct, fashion. (The last phrase refers to resident-owned capital held abroad.)

Subsequent history in the 1970s seemed to bear out Kindleberger's judgment. (A wave of developing country lending funded from the

---

[3] See "Less Developed Countries and the International Capital Market," printed as Chapter 17 of Charles Kindleberger, *International Money* (London: Allen and Unwin, 1981).

emerging Euromarkets was indeed underway as he wrote in the late 1960s.) And it is a fact today that a number of developing countries have successfully graduated from being aid financed to being debt financed, with the benefits of greater autonomy as described by Kindleberger. But the existence of the debt problem indicates that the Kindleberger system did not entirely work out in the real world. The restoration of creditworthiness in the heavily indebted countries, that is, growth-oriented adjustment, requires, as this symposium bears witness, a considerable and sustained effort of international cooperation, to support domestic policy efforts. The Kindleberger system, as clearly described in the quoted text, dealt with debt problems and recovery in a different way, through a default mechanism. What has been missing to date in the current situation is a workable default mechanism for bank debt with benefits that outweigh the costs in a way which makes a creditor/debtor deal possible. The absence of such a mechanism not only makes it difficult to clear away past mistakes, but is obviously complicating the "sensible fiscal management" in the debtor countries that Kindleberger cites as the route back to both creditworthiness and growth.

The purpose of this digression is not to argue the merits of writing down bank debt to market values. The facts are, simply, that there is no consensus at present as to how this could be done without causing unacceptable damage to the financing process. Rather the point to be made is that policy-based lending by official institutions to support growth-oriented adjustment in overindebted countries is, to a degree, a response to the absence of a workable default mechanism as part of an orderly restoration of creditworthiness. If at the same time, "sensible fiscal management" and a return to creditworthiness are rendered more difficult by the absence of a default mechanism, as may be the case when debtor governments are unable to solve the fiscal problem presented by interest payment obligations amounting to a significant slice of GDP, then there are reasons for believing that policy-based lending to highly indebted countries could be a somewhat frustrating business in the short run.[4]

---

[4] For an analysis which, based on a "transfer-problem" framework, places the emphasis on fiscal adjustment rather than balance of payments adjustment as the central issue in current debt crisis situations, see Helmut Reisen, "On the Transfer Problem of Major Developing Country Borrowers," OECD Development Centre (Paris), forthcoming.

In other words, while policy-based lending may be a necessary condition for the resumption of voluntary private lending, it may not by itself be sufficient to bring this about. This is the quandary for policy at this point.

It would not, however, be appropriate to judge the merits of policy-based lending by official agencies to support growth-oriented adjustment strategies only on these grounds. While a question mark may still rest over the proximate objective of restoring creditworthiness, there is little doubt that the concept of policy-based lending is bringing a much improved focus to long-run development policies and development cooperation. This is both necessary and likely to be of lasting significance.

Drawing together the various strands of this introduction, the underlying message is that institutional problems and the functioning of capital transfer processes lie close to the heart of the development financing challenges of the 1980s. The analysis which follows in this paper needs to be seen in this light.

Adjustment, Growth, and Official Financing

Before considering issues and prospects in relation to the supply of official finance for growth-oriented structural adjustment it will be useful to look at the situation of the main target groups, in the aggregate, in order to develop an idea of the financial magnitudes and "needs" involved. A range of adjustment, growth, and financial indicators for the period 1978–87 is presented in Tables 2–4 for three country categories—15 heavily indebted countries, sub-Saharan Africa, and "countries without recent debt-servicing problems." (The latter serves to throw into relief the scenes that emerge from Tables 2 and 3.) It is essential, of course, to acknowledge the diversity, indeed the specificity, of individual country situations within the groups and hence the inevitability of a case-by-case approach for substantive, not simply operational, reasons. But some general analysis is possible.

What the statistics show about the recent history and current situation of the heavily indebted countries (the original Baker Group) and sub-Saharan Africa is mostly already familiar. The following points stand out:

i. Striking adjustments have taken place in all three country groups.

Table 2. Adjustment and the Financing Mix, Fifteen Highly Indebted Countries, 1968–87[1]
(In billions of U.S. dollars)

	Average 1969–78	1978	1979	1980	1981	1982	1983	1984	1985	1986	1987
Adjustment											
Exports		68.6	94.2	127.1	126.1	111.5	111.1	123.4	119.2	98.6	101.5
Imports		76.9	96.1	122.7	133.6	108.3	82.8	80.2	78.4	75.7	83.3
Trade balance		−8.3	−1.9	4.4	−7.5	3.2	28.3	43.2	40.8	22.9	18.8
Net interest payments		−11.0	−17.1	−25.1	−37.0	−45.5	−41.5	−46.0	−44.0	−38.2	−35.8
Current account		−24.6	−24.6	−29.5	−50.3	−50.6	−15.2	−0.6	−0.1	−11.8	−14.0
Oil trade balance			21.9	36.8	34.3	29.5	27.6	33.3	32.2	23.6	26.3
Current account as percent of exports of goods and services	−16.1	−28.1	−20.5	−18.3	−30.6	−35.6	−11.2	−0.4	−0.1	−9.2	−10.6
Gross capital formation as percent of GDP		27.0	24.9	24.7	24.5	22.3	18.2	17.4	16.5	17.8	17.6
Real GDP growth	6.1	3.4	6.1	5.0	0.5	−0.4	−3.4	2.2	3.1	3.5	3.2
Real GDP growth (per capita)	3.6	0.6	3.1	2.6	−1.6	−2.7	−5.5	−0.1	0.9	1.4	1.2
Financing											
Non-debt-creating flows		5.3	7.8	6.2	7.4	7.5	4.3	4.2	5.5	4.3	5.1
Net external borrowing		32.5	34.8	49.1	65.2	48.6	24.6	15.1	3.7	3.0	16.3
Long-term official		3.6	3.0	4.5	6.5	3.7	11.3	8.1	8.0	9.5	10.0
Other borrowing		29.4	31.7	43.2	57.3	30.7	−2.4	4.2	−2.7	−7.2	8.9
Reserve related		−0.5	0.2	1.3	1.4	14.2	15.7	2.8	−1.6	0.7	−2.6
Use of reserves		−6.6	−13.1	−8.8	8.3	23.0	−0.5	−12.9	−3.0	6.8	−4.8
Memo Items											
Use of Fund credit[2]		−0.6	0.1	0.5	1.2	2.2	6.3	3.3	1.8	−0.1	0.4
Fund charges and repurchases from the Fund as percent of exports of goods and services[3]		−0.6	0.9	0.4	0.4	0.5	0.9	1.2	1.5	3.0	3.8

Source: International Monetary Fund, *World Economic Outlook, April 1987.*
[1] Fifteen countries accounting for 33 percent of the GDP, 21 percent of the exports, and 47 percent of the debt of developing countries.
[2] Including prospective programs.
[3] Not including prospective programs.

- Current account deficits as a proportion of GDP more than halved in sub-Saharan Africa and the "non-problem" countries between 1981 and 1984, with remarkably little impact on ensuing growth rates, except for a two-year transition in sub-Saharan Africa. (The growth rate in sub-Saharan Africa was and remains, however, unacceptably low.) Gross capital formation has fallen in both of these groups, but not too drastically.

- In the heavily indebted countries the current account deficit, a massive 30 percent of exports of goods and services in 1981, was eliminated by 1984. Gross capital formation fell from 25–27 percent of GDP before 1981 to 17–18 percent after 1983. Real GDP growth resumed after 1984, but remains distinctly lower than pre-1981 performance and well below long-run potential and social requirements.

- Between 1978 and 1982, as debt built up rapidly and interest rates rose, interest payments climbed very sharply in all the groups, multiplying by three in sub-Saharan Africa and the "non-problem" countries, and by four in the heavily indebted countries. In sub-Saharan Africa and the heavily indebted countries this provoked subsequently a virtual cessation in private lending ("other borrowing") and had to be accommodated by fairly drastic import compression, especially in the heavily indebted countries dependent on capital market finance. In the "non-problem" countries, private lending continued (1984 representing a fall in demand rather than supply), and the significance of non-debt creating flows and official lending provided further stability. Import compression was not therefore necessary to accommodate the much higher interest bill. Consumption could continue to rise, whereas it had to fall in sub-Saharan Africa and in the heavily indebted countries.

- All groups had large gains in export revenues from the commodity and oil price boom of 1979–80; all suffered revenue losses in the recession of 1982 and all benefited from the recovery of 1984. But the "non-problem" group clearly gains from its capacity to generate non-commodity export income while the "flat" export revenues since 1982 of the sub-Saharan and heavily indebted groups reflect their dependence on commodity and oil exports.

Table 3. Adjustment and Financing Mix in Sub-Saharan Africa, 1968–87[1]
(In billions of U.S. dollars)

	Average 1968–77	1978	1979	1980	1981	1982	1983	1984	1985	1986	1987
Adjustment											
Exports		16.8	20.5	23.8	21.3	20.0	19.7	21.3	20.6	21.2	22.4
Imports		19.2	22.0	27.5	26.6	24.3	21.4	20.4	19.9	21.1	24.4
Trade balance		−2.4	−1.5	−3.7	−5.3	−4.2	−1.8	1.0	0.7	−1.9	−1.9
Net interest payments		−1.2	−1.8	−2.7	−3.0	−3.3	−3.1	−3.7	−3.8	−4.3	−4.8
Current account balance		−5.6	−5.5	−8.4	−9.9	−8.6	−5.9	−3.5	−3.3	−5.9	−6.3
Oil trade balance		0.5	−0.9	−1.1	−0.5	0.1	0.9	1.6	1.5	0.4	0.4
Current account as percent of exports of goods and services	−14.3	−27.0	−21.8	−28.4	−36.8	−34.2	−23.8	−13.5	−13.1	−21.9	−21.9
Gross capital formation as percent of GDP		21.1	17.3	17.6	17.7	16.7	14.7	14.7	15.1	17.1	18.9
Real GDP growth	3.4	1.9	2.1	3.0	2.4	0.6	−0.7	2.0	3.0	4.8	3.2
Real GDP growth (per capita)	0.6	−0.7	−0.9	−0.2	−0.5	−2.2	−3.6	−0.8	0.1	0.9	0.2

Financing

Non-debt-creating flows	2.8	3.4	4.1	4.0	3.7	3.9	3.9	4.0	4.7	5.9
Net external borrowing	4.8	5.6	8.4	9.2	8.1	6.9	3.6	4.2	6.8	5.7
Long term official	2.2	4.9	4.0	4.8	5.1	3.9	5.4	3.7	4.2	4.9
Other borrowing	2.0	0.2	4.4	2.0	0.7	1.3	-2.5	-1.4	3.2	1.1
Reserve related	0.7	0.5	—	2.4	2.2	1.7	0.7	1.9	-0.6	-0.3
Use of reserves	0.1	-0.2	-0.1	0.4	0.5	-0.3	-0.1	-0.6	-0.7	-0.3

Memo Items

Use of Fund credit[2]	0.2	0.4	0.3	1.6	0.7	1.3	0.4	0.2	-0.3	-0.7
Fund charges and repurchases from the Fund as percent of exports of goods and services[3]	0.7	0.9	0.9	1.2	1.4	2.0	3.1	4.2	5.4	6.3

Source: International Monetary Fund, *World Economic Outlook*, April 1987.

[1] Comprises 43 countries accounting for 6 percent of the GNP, 4 percent of the exports, and 7 percent of the debt of developing countries. Excludes Nigeria and South Africa.

[2] Including prospective programs.

[3] Not including prospective programs.

Table 4. Adjustment and Financing Mix in Countries without Recent Debt-Servicing Problems, 1968–87[1]
(In billions of U.S. dollars)

	Average 1968–77	1978	1979	1980	1981	1982	1983	1984	1985	1986	1987
Adjustment											
Exports		130.4	169.6	214.5	229.9	223.0	230.4	261.4	260.7	280.9	312.8
Imports		155.0	196.7	253.3	275.5	265.7	268.9	280.3	284.8	297.4	329.1
Trade balance		−24.6	−27.0	−38.7	−45.6	−42.7	−38.4	−18.7	−24.1	−16.5	−16.0
Net interest payments		−8.8	−13.3	−18.2	−23.8	−26.0	−24.3	−27.6	−29.3	−29.4	−28.9
Current account		−16.4	−14.8	−21.0	−30.8	−27.9	−27.4	−13.4	−17.0	−5.4	−5.9
Oil trade balance		2.2	1.5	−1.3	−3.4	−3.8	−2.3	2.1	1.7	−0.3	−0.4
Current account as percent of exports of goods and services	−7.8	−9.8	−6.8	−7.6	−10.2	−9.4	−9.1	−4.0	−5.1	−1.5	−1.5
Gross capital formation as percent of GDP		29.0	28.6	28.1	27.1	26.8	26.3	26.4	26.8	26.5	26.2
Real GDP growth	5.9	8.0	4.1	4.8	4.9	4.2	6.2	6.9	5.3	5.1	4.4
Real GDP growth (per capita)	3.7	5.8	2.2	2.8	3.1	2.2	4.3	5.0	3.6	3.3	2.6

Financing

Non-debt-creating flows	10.2	12.7	14.2	14.8	13.6	15.7	14.6	20.3	18.9	18.0
Net external borrowing	19.4	28.3	38.4	48.6	34.4	33.3	23.5	26.2	21.6	15.5
Long term official	7.3	8.4	10.6	15.2	15.6	12.2	14.0	6.4	11.6	11.9
Other borrowing	12.1	20.8	27.4	30.3	15.7	18.2	9.3	20.8	10.6	4.6
Reserve related	0.1	−0.9	0.4	3.3	2.8	3.1	0.6	−1.4	0.1	0.6
Use of reserves	−7.2	−9.6	−10.4	−6.5	−4.9	−6.7	−5.2	−5.4	−2.3	−4.7

Memo Items

Use of Fund credit[2]	0.1	−0.1	0.9	3.1	2.7	3.3	1.0	−1.3	−0.9	1.4
Fund charges and repurchases from the Fund as percent of exports of goods and services[3]	0.5	0.4	0.4	0.4	0.4	0.5	0.7	0.8	0.9	1.0

Source: International Monetary Fund, *World Economic Outlook*, April 1987.

[1] Sixty-three countries accounting for 42 percent of the GDP, 36 percent of the exports, and 39 percent of the debt of developing countries.

[2] Incuding prospective programs.

[3] Not including prospective programs.

ii. Indications for financing and capital imports differ sharply between the three groups.

- The "non-problem" countries retain the capacity to sustain a significant trade deficit and hence maintain import growth while meeting the rising interest bill, which is the corollary of continued capital importing. (The income-generating debt accumulation process is alive and well in a major part of the developing world!) Capital imports are not, however, as important as they were in the 1968–77 period in relation to GDP, reflecting both improved domestic savings capacity and a rational response to higher real world interest rates.

- The heavily indebted countries have ceased to be net capital importers. Their aggregate current account is in balance. A large trade surplus has had to be generated through reduced domestic consumption and investment in order to meet interest obligations. Following the marked fall in international interest rates in recent years, interest payments in 1986 are still expected to represent about 6 percent of their collective GDP in 1986. (This figure varies from 9 percent in the case of Chile to 3 percent in the case of Nigeria.) The interest bill is being paid for by an historically large transfer of real resources in the form of reduced absorption of imports rather than increased exports.

- Sub-Saharan Africa remains a major capital importer, financed now almost exclusively by official development assistance. In fact the region is now much more dependent on external finance than in the 1968–77 period, reflecting the greatly increased focus of the development community on this region over the last decade.

- The Fund lending cycle of the first half of the decade seems now to have run its course. The repayment phase is beginning and is assuming some significance in the heavily indebted countries, but more particularly in sub-Saharan Africa, where the current level of Fund charges and repurchases from the Fund, at 7 percent of export earnings, indicates a problem area.

What conclusions might be drawn from this analysis for the two target developing country groups regarding the role of official finance in restoring the growth process? Something might perhaps be said along the following lines, again, not entirely unfamiliar.

In the *heavily indebted countries*, growth will generally require a restoration of gross capital formation, and a reduction of the huge non-oil trade surplus. (The reduction of the trade surplus in 1986 and 1987, indicated in Table 2, largely reflects the fall in oil prices, as indicated by the oil trade balance.) It is obviously unreasonable for this group of countries to have moved so far away from its 1968–77 profile as a capital importer. At the same time, even the falling level of interest payments (owing to interest rate declines and a halt to the buildup of debt) is proving a strain. From this point of view there is still little capacity for further debt accumulation. One part of the answer would appear to be a quantum leap in the productivity of investment. Large scope certainly exists here, and policy reforms are going in this direction. But they would need to go much further. And how much extra growth can be squeezed out of existing investment levels? Another part of the answer would be a reflow of flight capital. But until internal equilibrium and growth are clearly restored in a sustainable manner this is unlikely.

These considerations no doubt contribute to the continuing reticence of voluntary (and involuntary) lenders. Expansion of official lending then comes into view as a ray of hope. But in the absence of a fairly rapid restoration of debt-servicing capacity and more normal private flows, an official lender intending to operate on any significant scale would quickly become exposed. In essence, the policy quandary identified at the conclusion of the previous section of this paper seems to be confirmed by the numbers in Table 2. A cautious approach to the expansion of official lending, on a case-by-case basis, in step with domestic policy reforms, seems not only prudent, but essential, in these circumstances. And as suggested in the previous section, it unlikely to be a sufficient condition for the return to financial and economic health.

The case of *sub-Saharan Africa* produces a different analysis but perhaps not very different conclusions. This region is importing capital at a rate well above the 1968–77 profile, and is producing less growth with it. Different commodity prices then and now provide some explanation, but not a complete explanation. Even given the need for higher capital formation, is it desirable for the region to become even more aid dependent than it already is? While a few countries have reached the limit and beyond of their debt-servicing capacity, many still have manageable interest bills. But there is a lack of ability to attract new commercial finance. These considerations suggest that the overriding priority in sub-Saharan Africa must be to improve the productivity of these economies and to start restructuring away from the trap of commodity dependence. The record suggests that there is considerable scope for retargeting existing aid and investment activities. Higher aid flows may also be necessary. But the undesirability of moving even more in the direction of aid dependence suggests that this should be carefully restrained. Reforming the aid process along the lines of the DAC Guiding Principles is of high importance, in association with domestic policy reform.

Close consideration of the actual situations in the heavily indebted countries and in sub-Saharan Africa indicates therefore not only the necessity for policy-based official financing in support of growth-oriented structural adjustment, but also the limits to the amount of financial commitment that can be justified on the part of official agencies, in the absence of success in relaunching growth and private financing on a sustainable basis. On the other hand, official financial support will need to reach certain critical minimal levels if medium- and long-term growth-oriented adjustment strategies are to be feasible, politically or economically. The development financing community must somehow find its way along this narrow path.

Supply of Official Finance I: A Macroeconomic Perspective

Institutional Factors, Policy Concepts, and the Allocation of Aid

In considering the possible availability of official financing for growth-oriented adjustment programs, some basic factors need to be taken into account. First, in contrast to market-driven financial flows to developing countries, official finance has a high degree of stability. This derives partly from its long-term orientation, but, and this is important to the present discussion, more central is the fact that decisionmaking occurs through relatively slow-moving political processes. On the mutlilateral level, decisionmaking can be particularly prolonged and subject to limits imposed by negotiating dynamics and burden-sharing issues.

The problem then is how to get the official development finance "industry" to respond quickly and sufficiently to new requirements such as supporting growth-oriented structural adjustment, not just at the level of rhetoric, but at the level of funding and operations. The two years following the emergence of the debt problem in 1982, before the World Bank and the bilateral donors began to formulate a real response, have been viewed by some as an unfortunately long lag. Obviously there is likely to be more public impulse for fast reactions by donors when humanitarian concerns, such as the famine in Africa, are involved than when complex economic and financial problems arise. The two-year lag in any case could partly be explained by the original diagnosis that the debt crisis was mainly a liquidity problem. On this basis, the Fund, which is designed to move quickly on liquidity problems, was much faster off the mark in low-income Africa than was the Bank. While the availability of Fund finance made an important contribution to African economies at a critical time, in retrospect, the terms of Fund finance were inappropriate to many of these cases and now constitute a burden that will have to be absorbed somewhere in the development finance system (though a part will be met through the Fund's new Structural Adjustment Facility).

The redefinition of the debt strategy in late 1985, introducing growth-oriented structural adjustment with a medium-term horizon, provided a concept around which the development community could build a solid and coherent response. This concept holds the promise of being one of those basic ideas that alter the direction of the development effort. Infrastructure development, integrated rural development, and basic human needs are among the ideas that have had such influence in the past. Growth-oriented structural adjustment has the particular merit not only of being appropriate to the times but of being considerably more comprehensive than previous "ruling concepts" and capable of bringing to the aid effort flexibility and economic coherence in a degree missing in the past. This goes back to the points emphasized earlier in the paper. There needs to be a continued effort to develop the concept into a set of operational principles that reach deeply into the orientations and programs of development agencies.

More effort will also be needed to demonstrate how growth-oriented structural adjustment connects with basic long-term development goals. A danger presently exists that donor agencies anxious to establish clearer long-term "development" goals for aid could set up too sharp a dichotomy between development and structural adjustment. Studies that show the relationships between structural adjustment and improvement of income distribution and prospects for the poor might be particularly important in demonstrating that adjustment can be a potent form of development, especially as long-standing policy distortions are unwound.

Changing the orientation of development agency approaches and operations is thus an important supply-side response. Another response is the use of special multilateral funds, such as the Bank's Special Facility for Africa and the Fund's Structural Adjustment Facility. This technique can marginally shift the allocation of aid but not increase overall aid volume. It is a way of concentrating funds on a particular problem, with appropriate delivery techniques and terms. There is likely to be a case for renewing the Special Facility for Africa on these grounds, and it is probable that some donors will make such a proposal. Nevertheless, there is also a certain reserve among donors about special funds in principle (problems have arisen in the U.N. system with the impact of voluntary funds that can undermine collectively agreed priorities). And there is also the possibility of a reaction at a certain point to the degree of priority accorded to countries with growth-oriented structural adjustment programs in the allocation of scarce aid resources and to a lesser extent perhaps (because they are more readily expandable), the lending limits of multilateral development banks. The point is being made with increasing frequency by some donors that the majority of the world's poor live in Asia and that South Asia in particular is a region that should not be allowed to fall into relative neglect. It will need to be recognized therefore that, with relatively fixed financial resource constraints, a limit will exist on the priority that can be given to adjustment programs.

Against this background it should be noted that a major shift in the geographical allocation of aid toward sub-Saharan Africa had already taken place before the "adjustment" crisis arrived. The proportion of aid going to sub-Saharan Africa had risen from 10 percent in 1960 to 20 percent by 1970 and 30 percent by 1983. This share is likely to represent a plateau for some time, especially given the degree of aid dependence it has generated. (On average about 10 percent of sub-Saharan GDP is provided by aid, and some countries have hit a ratio of 20 percent.) Reorientation of aid use in sub-Saharan Africa will therefore be all the more important.

Macroeconomic Considerations: Resource Transfers and Financial Intermediation by Official Agencies

A particular concern in the present context is the phenomenon referred to as the "reverse transfer of resources" from the developing countries to the developed. This phenomenon arises from the fact that swollen interest bills have overtaken shrunken new net lending in the heavily indebted countries. A normal debt accumulation process eventually will generate annual interest payments in excess of new lending. The problem arises when income generated by the capital inflow is not sufficient to pay the interest and also allow rising consumption. A reverse transfer of resources of an "abnormal" character then takes place as consumption and investment are squeezed in order to pay, by forgoing real resources, interest obligations that cannot be financed by net capital inflows.

There is unfortunately much loose talk now about the reverse transfer of resources from developing countries to developed countries. It is a phenomenon concentrated almost entirely on the heavily indebted countries as Tables 5–8 show. All other developing countries, including those in sub-Saharan Africa, continue to have a strongly positive net financial transfer in the aggregate (although a few individual countries, including in Africa, may have negative financial transfers).

What, if anything, can or should official agencies do about this problem? It is essentially a macroeconomic phenomenon caused, on the one hand, by previous waste of capital and by capital flight resulting in loss of creditworthiness and, on the other hand, by high real world interest rates. Insofar as it is an institutional problem, it reflects the lack of a viable default mechanism as argued earlier in this paper.

Clearly, it is important that official agencies should maintain and where feasible increase net disbursements of aid and loan finance. It is not conceivable, however, that they can much affect the net

Table 5.   Net Financial Transfers, All Developing Countries, 1980–86[1]
(In billions of U.S. dollars)

	1980	1981	1982	1983	1984	1985	1986
1. Net inflow[2]	109	125	106	83	79	75	80
2. Investment income, debits	−54	−71	−84	−74	−78	−73	−62
Balance A (1 + 2)	*55*	*54*	*22*	*9*	*1*	*2*	*18*
Of which: Banks	9	—	−13	−16	−31	−31	−31
Other sources	46	54	35	25	32	33	49
3. Net outflow[3]	−3	−12	−10	−7	−10	−8	−10
4. Investment income, credits	20	26	25	19	21	18	13
Balance B (3 + 4)	*17*	*14*	*15*	*12*	*11*	*10*	*3*
Balance C (A + B)	*72*	*68*	*37*	*21*	*12*	*12*	*21*
5. Capital flight, net[4]	−31	−36	−31	−23	−19	−16	−13
Balance D (Balance C + 5)	*41*	*32*	*6*	*−2*	*−7*	*−4*	*8*
Memo item:							
Net flows (1 + 3)	106	113	96	76	69	67	70
Net investment income (2 + 4)	−34	−45	−59	−55	−57	−55	−49
Balance C (net financial transfer)	*72*	*68*	*37*	*21*	*12*	*12*	*21*

Source: OECD data bank.

[1] Excludes Europe and Oceania.

[2] Net inflows include both capital flows and official transfers (which appear "above the line" in current transactions in balance of payments accounting).

[3] Principally export credits and bank loans by LDCs; excludes Persian Gulf surplus countries.

[4] Excludes North Africa/Middle East. Estimates of flight capital are in general conformity with estimates made by other institutions.

financial transfer situation that obtains today in the heavily indebted countries. Neither is it fundamentally relevant to the functions of official development agencies, whether they are individually providing a net financial transfer to developing countries, in the sense that their new lending exceeds their receipts of both amortization and interest payments. The World Bank provides such calculations on a regional basis in its Annual Reports and makes use of the concept in other contexts as well. It is very doubtful, in the view of this author, whether such considerations should play a role in the analysis of the Bank's contribution to development financing. It is a partial equilibrium approach to what is very much a general equilibrium question. An attempt by the Bank to maximize its net financial transfer to developing countries would carry undue financial risks before very long.

Overall resource transfers to developing countries are determined by macroeconomic conditions—growth prospects in developing countries and savings balances in developed countries. The present situation therefore owes something, not neglible, to the imbalances within the OECD area. In addition budgetary policies, insofar as they determine the rate of expansion of grant aid, help to determine the rate at which real resources can flow to developing countries. There is rather clear evidence that the relatively fast expansion of DAC aid flows in the late 1970s and early 1980s, in real terms, owed much to the general expansion of public expenditures in OECD countries in the 1970s. Conversely, present efforts to contain public expenditures

Table 6.   Net Financial Transfers, Sub-Saharan Africa, 1980–86
(In billions of U.S. dollars)

	1980	1981	1982	1983	1984	1985	1986
1. Net inflow[1]	16	17	17	14	13	16	19
2. Investment income, debits	−5	−5	−5	−4	−5	−3	−3
Balance A (1 + 2)	*11*	*12*	*12*	*10*	*8*	*13*	*16*
Of which: Banks		−1	−1	−2	−3	−1	−1
Other sources	11	13	13	12	11	14	17
3. Net outflow	—	−1	—	—	—	—	−1
4. Investment income, credits	1	1	1	—	—	—	—
Balance B (3 + 4)	*1*	*—*	*1*	*—*	*—*	*—*	*−1*
Balance C (A + B)	*12*	*12*	*13*	*10*	*8*	*13*	*15*
5. Capital flight, net[2]	−4	−4	−3	−2	−2	−1	−1
Balance D (Balance C + 5)	*8*	*8*	*10*	*8*	*6*	*12*	*14*
Memo item:							
Net flows (1 + 3)	16	16	17	14	13	16	18
Net investment income (2 + 4)	−4	−4	−4	−4	−5	−3	−3
Balance C (net financial transfer)	*12*	*12*	*13*	*10*	*8*	*13*	*15*

Source: OECD data bank.

[1] Net inflows include both capital flows and official transfers (which appear "above the line" in current transactions in balance of payments accounting).

[2] Estimates of flight capital are in general conformity with estimates made by other institutions.

Table 7.   Net Financial Transfers, Baker Group Countries, 1980–86[1]
(In billions of U.S. dollars)

	1980	1981	1982	1983	1984	1985	1986
1. Net inflow[2]	55	64	52	26	27	19	17
2. Investment income, debits	−30	−42	−52	−44	−46	−44	−37
Balance A (1+2)	25	22	—	−18	−19	−25	−20
Of which: Banks	18	11	−2	−16	−23	−26	−23
Other Sources	7	11	2	−2	4	1	3
3. Net outflow	−4	−12	−10	−7	−8	−4	−5
4. Investment income, credits	8	10	8	5	7	6	5
Balance B (3+4)	4	−2	−2	−2	−1	2	—
Balance C (A+B)	29	20	−2	−20	−20	−23	−20
5. Capital flight, net[3]	−22	−25	−22	−16	−14	−12	−8
Balance D (Balance C+5)	7	−5	−24	−36	−34	−35	−28
Memo item:							
Net flows (1+3)	51	52	42	19	19	15	12
Net investment income (2+4)	−22	−32	−44	−39	−39	−38	−32
Balance C (net financial transfer)	29	20	−2	−20	−20	−23	−20

Source: OECD data bank.

[1] Argentina, Bolivia, Brazil, Chile, Colombia, Côte d' Ivoire, Ecuador, Mexico, Morocco, Nigeria, Peru, Philippines, Uruguay, Venezuela, Yugoslavia.

[2] Net inflows include both capital flows and official transfers (which appear "above the line" in current transactions in balance of payments accounting).

[3] Estimates of flight capital are in general conformity with estimates made by other institutions.

as a proportion of GDP are a major reason why the growth of official development assistance (ODA) volume from the DAC is perceptibly slowing down in the mid-1980s.

It is in this macroeconomic context that the special situation of Japan as a source of development finance can best be considered. This is a relevant issue because the huge size of the Japanese savings surplus has given rise to proposals that part of it could be directed toward the developing countries, and particularly the heavily indebted countries. There is even a view that Japan could remain indefinitely as a structural surplus country, with the role of supplier of capital to the developing countries. The problem with this view is that what use is made of Japanese savings depends on macroeconomic policies in other OECD countries as well. We know that at present it is helping to finance the U.S. current account deficit. Should the U.S. deficit decrease significantly, it might be expected that world interest rates would decline. That in itself might curtail the capital outflow from Japan to a certain extent. With world interest rates lower, developing countries would be able to absorb more of the remaining Japanese surplus. This could be part of the answer to restarting the lending process to heavily indebted countries. But it could happen through world capital markets and would not in principle require a particular decision by the Japanese authorities. The recent offer by Japan to the World Bank of further access to the Japanese capital

Table 8. Net Financial Transfers, Total Developing Countries (Excluding Baker Group Countries), 1980–86[1]
(In billions of U.S. dollars)

	1980	1981	1982	1983	1984	1985	1986
1. Net inflow[2]	54	61	54	57	52	56	63
2. Investment income, debits	−24	−29	−32	−30	−32	−29	−25
Balance A (1+2)	*30*	*32*	*22*	*27*	*20*	*27*	*38*
Of which: Banks	14	7	−6	−13	−24	−25	−27
Other sources	16	25	28	40	44	52	65
3. Net outflow[3]	1	—	—	—	−2	−4	−5
4. Investment income, credits	12	16	17	14	14	12	8
Balance B (3+4)	*13*	*16*	*17*	*14*	*12*	*8*	*3*
Balance C (A+B)	*43*	*48*	*39*	*41*	*32*	*35*	*41*
5. Capital flight, net[4]	−9	−11	−9	−7	−5	−4	−5
Balance D (Balance C+5)	*34*	*37*	*30*	*34*	*27*	*31*	*36*
Memo item:							
Net flows (1+3)	55	61	54	57	50	52	58
Net investment income (2+4)	−12	−13	−15	−16	−18	−17	−17
Balance C (net financial transfer)	*43*	*48*	*39*	*41*	*32*	*35*	*41*

Source: OECD data bank.

[1] Excludes Europe and Oceania.

[2] Net inflows include both capital flows and official transfers (which appear "above the line" in current transactions in balance of payments accounting).

[3] Principally export credits and bank loans by developing countries; excludes Persian Gulf surplus countries.

[4] Estimates of flight capital are in general conformity with estimates made by other institutions. Excludes North Africa/Middle East.

market may have more an optical than a real significance in an integrated world capital market, if it is assumed that there is no impact on the Bank's lending levels. (The offer of an accompanying grant equal to 10 percent of the capital raised is, of course, a different matter.) A slightly different question arises over the Japanese loan of 3.6 billion SDRs to the Fund. This may enable the Fund to raise its lending to developing countries, but this is difficult to judge on present information.

A more meaningful decision by the Japanese government would be to make a major increase in the budgetary allocation for grant aid. A new target for increased aid has indeed been decided, but the grant portion has been limited by the general stance of Japanese public expenditure policy. As a result it is not clear that Japanese aid performance in relation to GDP (relevant not just in terms of aid targetry but in terms of disposal of the Japanese surplus) will increase by very much in the years ahead, especially since Japanese aid planning is conducted in terms of objectives expressed in U.S. dollars.

In sum, therefore, the key issue is the future size of the Japanese current account surplus in relation to the current account position of other OECD countries. It is this, rather than any explicit decisions by the Japanese authorities about intermediation, which will most influence the price and availability of capital to the developing countries. If, however, circumstances develop in which a Japanese surplus was to persist in the context of recessionary conditions in the world economy and deepening financial crisis in developing countries, then some kind of special multilateral facility, funded directly or indirectly on the Japanese capital market, might have a role to play.

Supply of Official Finance II: Prospects and Issues by Category of Finance

This section sets out the various forms in which official financing is made available to developing countries and provides some comments on prospects and issues in relation to the financing of growth-oriented structural adjustment programs. This can be done relatively briefly since many of the issues have already been raised in earlier parts of the paper. Tables 9–11 contain data on the magnitude and

Table 9. Total Net Resource Flows to Developing Countries, 1978–86
(In billions of current U.S. dollars)

	1978	1979	1980	1981	1982	1983	1984	1985	1986
I. Official development finance (ODF)	32.8	37.3	45.7	46.5	44.9	42.3	47.5	48.9	60.0
Official development assistance (ODA)	27.5	31.6	37.7	37.3	34.1	33.7	34.8	37.0	44.4
Bilateral	22.1	25.4	29.9	29.4	26.6	26.1	27.0	28.6	34.4
OECD	13.3	16.5	18.2	18.4	18.6	18.7	19.8	21.9	27.8
OPEC	6.7	6.5	8.7	7.5	4.5	3.9	3.7	2.9	6.6
CMEA	1.6	2.1	2.7	3.2	3.2	3.2	3.2	3.5	
Other countries	0.5	0.3	0.3	0.3	0.3	0.3	0.3	0.3	
Multilateral	5.4	6.2	7.8	7.9	7.5	7.6	7.8	8.4	10.0
Other ODF	5.3	5.7	8.0	9.2	10.8	8.6	12.7	11.9	15.5
Multilateral	3.1	4.1	4.8	5.7	6.6	7.2	8.2	7.9	
Bilateral	2.2	1.6	3.2	3.5	4.2	1.4	4.5	4.0	
II. Total export credits	15.2	13.7	17.5	18.0	14.4	8.3	5.4	1.5	1.6
OECD countries (including short term)	15.0	13.4	16.7	17.0	13.7	7.8	5.0	1.0	1.0
	2.6	2.0	2.4	2.6	3.0	-0.3	-0.8	..	..
Other countries	0.2	0.3	0.8	1.0	0.7	0.5	0.4	0.5	0.6
III. Private flows	60.1	55.8	66.1	74.3	58.4	46.9	32.7	31.2	21.5
Direct investment (OECD)	11.9	13.4	11.2	17.2	12.8	9.3	11.7	7.7	10.0
International banking sector	39.9	35.7	49.0	52.0	41.0	34.1	17.4	13.5	3.0
(including short term)	17.0	16.0	26.0	22.0	15.0	-13.0	-6.0	-10.0	..
Total bond lending	4.1	2.0	1.6	1.3	1.6	0.7	0.6	4.5	2.0
Other private [1]	4.2	4.7	4.3	3.8	3.0	2.8	3.0	5.5	6.5
Total resource flows (I + II + III)	108.1	106.8	129.3	138.8	117.7	97.5	85.7	81.6	83.1
For information:									
ODA grants	15.1	18.7	22.2	21.2	20.3	20.8	22.8	22.9	28.5
Private grants by NGOs	1.6	2.0	2.3	2.0	2.3	2.3	2.6	3.1	3.8
Fund purchases, net	-1.0	0.5	2.6	6.2	6.4	12.5	5.4	0.7	-1.0

Source: OECD data bank.

[1] Including grants by non-governmental organizations (NGOs).

Table 10. Net Resource Flows to Sub-Saharan Africa, 1978–86
(In billions of current U.S. dollars)

	1978	1979	1980	1981	1982	1983	1984	1985	1986
I. Official development finance (ODF)	7.2	8.9	11.1	10.8	11.5	11.2	12.5	12.9	16.0
Official development assistance (ODA)	6.3	7.9	9.2	9.3	9.4	9.4	9.7	11.1	—
Bilateral	4.4	5.7	6.7	6.7	7.0	6.9	6.8	7.8	—
OECD	3.7	4.8	5.8	5.8	5.8	5.6	6.1	6.8	—
OPEC	0.5	0.7	0.6	0.6	0.8	0.9	0.4	0.5	—
CMEA	—	—	0.1	0.1	0.2	0.2	0.2	0.3	—
Other countries	0.2	0.2	0.2	0.2	0.2	0.2	0.2	0.2	—
Multilateral	1.9	2.2	2.5	2.6	2.5	2.6	2.9	3.3	—
Other ODF	0.9	1.0	1.9	1.5	2.1	1.8	2.8	1.8	—
Multilateral	0.4	0.4	0.5	0.5	0.6	0.7	0.8	0.8	—
Bilateral	0.5	0.6	1.4	1.0	1.5	1.1	2.0	1.0	—
II. Total export credits	1.4	2.0	1.9	1.9	1.9	1.1	0.2	0.5	0.6
OECD countries (including short term)	1.4	2.0	1.8	1.8	1.8	1.0	0.2	0.5	—
Other countries	—	—	0.1	0.1	0.1	0.1	—	0.1	—
III. Private flows	3.4	4.3	2.9	4.2	3.8	2.2	0.2	2.0	2.3
Direct investment (OECD)	1.0	1.5	0.1	1.5	1.0	0.9	0.4	0.3	0.4
International bank sector (including short term)	1.5	2.0	2.0	2.0	2.0	0.5	-1.0	0.8	1.0
Total bond lending	0.3	0.1	—	—	—	—	—	—	—
Other private [1]	0.6	0.7	0.8	0.7	0.8	0.8	0.8	0.9	0.9
Total resource flows (I + II + III)	12.0	15.2	15.9	16.9	17.2	14.5	12.9	15.5	18.9

Source: OECD data bank.
[1] Including grants by non-governmental organizations (NGOs).

Table 11. Net Resource Flows to Western Hemisphere, 1978–86
(In billions of current U.S. dollars)

	1978	1979	1980	1981	1982	1983	1984	1985	1986
I. Official development finance (ODF)	3.8	4.8	6.3	7.0	8.1	6.7	9.7	10.5	13.0
Official development assistance (ODA)	2.7	3.3	3.8	4.0	4.2	4.4	4.7	5.2	—
Bilateral	2.0	2.6	2.9	3.1	3.4	3.5	3.7	4.2	—
OECD	1.6	2.0	2.3	2.4	2.7	2.8	3.0	3.4	—
OPEC	—	0.1	—	—	—	—	—	—	—
CMEA	0.4	0.5	0.6	0.7	0.7	0.7	0.7	0.8	—
Other countries									
Multilateral	0.7	0.7	0.9	0.9	0.8	0.9	1.0	1.0	—
Other ODF	1.1	1.5	2.5	3.0	3.9	2.3	5.0	5.3	—
Multilateral	0.9	1.3	2.0	2.2	2.3	2.6	3.6	3.2	—
Bilateral	0.2	0.2	0.5	0.8	1.6	-0.3	1.4	2.1	—
II. Total export credits	2.0	2.8	5.5	5.3	3.1	1.9	0.1	—	0.3
OECD countries (including short term)	1.9	2.6	5.2	5.0	2.8	1.7	0.1	—	—
Other countries	0.1	0.2	0.3	0.3	0.3	0.2	—	—	—
III. Private flows	35.9	33.8	44.5	52.4	39.2	17.9	17.0	8.1	4.8
Direct investment (OECD)	6.6	7.0	6.8	9.3	6.3	3.3	3.6	2.5	3.6
International bank sector (including short term)	25.0	25.0	36.0	41.0	31.5	15.1	14.0	5.0	0.5
Total bond lending	3.2	1.3	0.8	1.2	0.6	-0.8	-1.1	-1.1	-1.3
Other private[1]	1.1	0.5	0.9	0.9	0.8	0.3	0.5	1.7	2.0
Total resource flows (I + II + III)	41.7	41.4	56.3	64.7	50.4	26.5	26.8	18.6	18.4

Source: OECD data bank.
[1] Including grants by non-governmental organizations (NGOs) and debt equity swaps.

composition of financial flows to developing countries, distinguishing among official development finance, officially supported export credits, and private financial flows.

Official Development Assistance

In the first half of the 1980s, DAC aggregate ODA has increased at 3.6 percent a year in real terms. However, as OPEC aid fell significantly over this period, global ODA stagnated. As far as prospects are concerned, a recent survey conducted by the DAC Secretariat suggests that aid growth may fall to about 2 percent a year or less in the next few years. This is in spite of the fact that about a dozen DAC countries are planning to increase their ODA/GNP ratios, in some cases quite markedly and in terms of a pre-set timetable. The 0.7 percent aid target is still proving to be a potent political force. Despite this continuing thrust on aid volume in many DAC countries, the overall outcome will be determined by aid flows from the largest donors, including the United States in particular.

The multilateral share in aggregate aid increased rapidly in the 1970s to reach about one third of the total. This appears to be relatively stable, perhaps indicating that an equilibrium has been reached for the time being in donors' bilateral/multilateral preferences. Recent replenishments have generally met expectations and there is little reason to expect a further advance in the multilateral share in the foreseeable future.

If it can be assumed that the decline in OPEC ODA has nearly run its course, the overall outlook is that global ODA will increase at about 2 percent a year in the next few years, as compared with the zero increase in the last five years, if the indications regarding the supply of DAC ODA are borne out.

The picture suggests therefore that, as emphasized earlier, the most important contribution of aid to growth-oriented structural adjustment will come from reorientation of aid objectives and operations, improved aid coordination and faster disbursement, including the cancellation of no longer appropriate capital projects, which would free resources from often large aid pipelines. Hence the significance of the DAC principles in the attached text. Some operational issues in this regard are raised in the final section of this paper.

Multilateral Nonconcessional Lending

Multilateral nonconcessional lending through the World Bank and the three regional development banks has been the most dynamic sector of official development financing in the 1980s. Disbursements grew by $3 billion a year between 1980 and 1985, an amount which equalled in absolute terms the increase in disbursements of DAC bilateral aid over the same period. By contrast, disbursements of multilateral aid increased very little; multilateral nonconcessional disbursements are now of approximately the same magnitude as disbursements of multilateral aid. (See Table 10.) Of the $3 billion increase, $1.2 billion went to Latin America and $0.3 billion to sub-Saharan Africa. Currently the World Bank represents about 70 percent of multilateral development bank activity, the Inter-American Development Bank about 15 percent, the Asian Development Bank 7 percent and the African Development Bank 5 percent. (These shares include concessional as well as nonconcessional lending.)

The expansion of multilateral development bank nonconcessional lending in the 1980s probably owes much to the renewed bouyancy of world bond markets, part of the trend towards securitization of world financial markets. Multilateral development banks have evolved into the role of intermediator between world bond markets and the developing countries, direct bond issues by developing countries remaining rather limited in scale and restricted to a small number of issuers. The World Bank in particular has exploited financial markets with considerable skill and obtained fine borrowing terms, as well as building up healthy reserves through retained earnings derived from management of its stocks of liquidity.

If the bond sector of international financial markets continues its relative expansion, while developing country direct access to the bond market remains relatively resticted, then clearly the role of the multilateral development banks is likely to become even more important in terms of the incremental financing available to developing countries. The key question is to what extent and for how long the multilateral development banks can increase their exposure to countries to whom international capital markets remain closed. Beyond a certain point, lending in such circumstances would be bound to have an impact on the Bank's own standing in the credit markets. In other words, significant multilateral development bank lending to the current problem countries could only continue in the medium term in the context of a general return to voluntary lending by the private sector. What would constitute significant lending and how long is the medium term? Obviously there is no clear-cut answer. The strategy enunciated at last autumn's meeting of the Development Committee put the emphasis on "quality lending," that is, the World Bank's shareholders are prepared at present to push ahead, and to subscribe more capital as necessary, so long as there is reason to believe that the borrowers are making good progress in improving the productivity of their economies.

There can be little doubt that this stance, and the increased activity and leadership being provided by the World Bank in particular, is critical at this juncture to the management of the financial and development problems of the heavily indebted countries. Policy-based lending may be a little disguised form of balance of payments lending, but its development significance may be just as great, or even greater, than slower-disbursing project finance. After all, crucial policy changes have the potential to raise rates of return widely throughout the economy over the medium and long term. On the other hand what look like sound projects can be undermined, and have been undermined in numerous instances, by a general deteri-oration in the policy environment. The present buildup in the portion of the World Bank's lending accounted for by policy-based loans seems to this author to be thoroughly justified from a development point of view. Apart from this longer-term rationale, there is of course the not unimportant consideration that if quick disbursing loans were not forthcoming, the World Bank's net disbursements would be difficult to sustain in a situation where so many countries are cancelling or postponing projects.

The question nevertheless remains: for how long is this posture by the World Bank sustainable? While no precision is possible, it may not be unreasonable to think that if voluntary lending to the problem countries shows little signs of reviving in two to three years time, the present momentum in activity will have to be slowed, especially if the preferred creditor status of the World Bank and the other multilateral development banks shows signs of coming under strain.

International Monetary Fund

Fund financing has traditionally been regarded as something apart from development financing. The concept of growth-oriented struc-

tural adjustment programs has, however, brought a certain constructive fuzziness to the boundaries between adjustment finance and
development finance. Given that Fund lending in the 1980s has been
almost exclusively concentrated on the developing countries and
given the leadership role of the Fund in the management of major
debt problems, the Fund has become inextricably intertwined in the
issues of development financing.

Important adaptations in Fund rules, before the onset of the debt
crisis, have made this possible, namely the extended facility and
enlarged access, and to a certain extent, liberalized access to the
compensatory financing facility. On the basis of these provisions,
developing countries drew around $30 billion from the Fund between
1980 and 1986 and currently have outstanding drawings amounting
to some $37 billion. In principle, this amount is repayable over the
medium term, and if the Fund's rules regarding continued use are
to be respected, there is not too much scope for avoiding the situation
in which the Fund is withdrawing finance from the developing
countries. This consideration makes the Fund's position of importance
to the overall financing picture in the next few years, and conversely
the availability of other sources of financing becomes of interest to
the Fund. The position in Africa has already been alluded to, and
similar questions must be not far below the surface in the Latin
American region. Obviously the "continued use" provisions should
be stretched as far as possible while normal financing is not available
and countries are maintaining an adjustment effort.

Another question, perhaps more serious, is whether the Fund is
in a position to assist developing countries with significant further
financing in the event of a serious slowdown in world economic
growth in the next few years, or in the event of a rise in the interest
rates of more than a point or so, or in the worst case, a combination
of the two. The question may not revolve around the extent of the
Fund's resources, which can always be augumented by a quota
increase or by borrowing, so much as around the scope for a further
significant increase in developing countries' obligations to the Fund.
The starting point, with $37 billion already outstanding, is quite
different from that obtaining at the beginning of the Fund's recent
lending cycle. What amount would be regarded as tolerable within
the Fund's roles on continued use, given that beyond a certain limit
repayment schedules may begin to be viewed with some skepticism?
It is probably impossible to answer this question. This would be the

first time in the Fund's history that such an issue would have arisen. It occurs as worth raising in the present context, nevertheless, since it is relevant to ask what would be the implications for the financing of growth-oriented structural adjustment programs, should the unfortunate event of a world recession emerge in the near future.

The possibility of a further issue of SDRs as a useful contribution to easing the financial difficulties of developing countries has been on the international agenda for some time. A proposal has even been made for "conditional SDRs" directed towards countries with adjustment programs. There is not space here to examine the arguments surrounding this general question, except to say that proposals aimed at concentrating SDRs on the developing countries considerably modify the intended character of this instrument. In addition, in bearing a market rate of interest, SDRs are not an attractive form of financing for the poorer developing countries.

Export Credits

Official or officially supported export credits from OECD countries have been an important financing flow for developing countries since the 1960s. There was a boom in such lending, following the first oil shock and continuing until the debt crisis erupted in 1982, a period when OECD suppliers faced weak OECD demand while developing country markets strengthened. In the latter part of this period there was fierce competition among OECD governments through the medium of interest rate subsidies, the value of which may have averaged about $5 billion annually on credits amounting to about $23 billion a year in the 1980–82 period. This extreme degree of subsidization was virtually eliminated after an agreement among OECD countries to adopt a system which automatically required export credit rates to follow market rates of interest. Nevertheless an element of competition remains through the practice of providing "mixed credits," that is, the association of an aid grant or concessional loan with a loan at commercial rates. Negotiations on rules to contain this practice are presently at an advanced stage in the OECD.

One of the most dramatic changes in the financing picture for developing countries currently is the sharp fall in net export credit lending to virtually negligible levels. This is partly explained by reduced demand, with developing country investment programs, especially large projects, pared back by falling oil revenues (oil exporters were major users of export credits) and debt problems. It is also partly explained by reduced supply, as export credit agencies have taken countries off cover because of debt problems. But a third reason is that the wave of export credit lending of the late 1970s is now producing a wave of repayments, so that while new export credits remain significant, the net flow is much lower. This situation can be expected to unwind eventually.

There are currently two important policy initiatives in the export credit field, the first relating to the cover policies of export credit agencies, the second to the developmental quality of projects financed by export credits. These initiatives stem from concerns raised by the Fund and the Bank and involve greater cohesion among export credit agencies.

Regarding cover policies, the objective is to achieve greater harmony among the separate agencies on decisions both to withdraw cover in cases in which the financial position of a country is deteriorating rapidly and to restore cover when action has been taken by the country to stabilize its financial situation and adopt an effective adjustment program. Informal consultations are now being conducted between export credit agencies on problem cases, with briefing from the Fund and the Bank, in the margins of OECD Export Credit Group meetings. This is a loose process, with no binding agreements or even recommendations, the main objective being to ensure more mutual information on the stance of export credit agencies in relation to individual problem countries.

In the same framework, a further significant move is the initiative by the Fund and the Bank to encourage export credit agencies not to provide support for projects which fall outside public investment programs established following formal investment review processes by developing country governments in the context of structural adjustment programs. These investment programs are increasingly part of Fund- and Bank-supported adjustment efforts.

This represents an important change in the frame of reference for export credit agencies, who have traditionally seen their role as simply commercial and have resisted the idea that development criteria should influence their decisions. The experience of the 1970s, however, is that a significant proportion of projects financed by export credits have been ill-considered, not very productive, and in the final analysis have contributed, sometimes in a major way, to the emergence of debt problems. In retrospect it is clear that highly subsidized over-guaranteed lending of the kind made possible by OECD government policies in the late 1970s had a damaging impact on developing country decisionmaking and resource allocation, reducing incentives on both sides for proper project appraisal, and encouraging a bias towards capital-intensive investment. The current effort to bring more discipline on the suppliers' side, to match the disciplines being introduced by developing countries, must surely be welcomed.

A further effort to apply development criteria to the export credit process is being undertaken in the framework of the DAC, aimed at preventing the use of mixed credits from distorting the allocation of aid and undermining the developmental quality of investment. A set of guidelines has been drawn up which recommends that highly concessional packages of export finance should be available only to the lower-income developing countries and that projects so financed should be carefully appraised from a developmental point of view.

These various efforts to improve the functioning of the export credit process should help to ensure that export credits become a "cleaner," healthier form of finance for development in the future, with a constructive role to play in growth-oriented structural adjustment.

Official Debt Rescheduling—The Paris Club

The Paris Club process for rescheduling official debt has been working overtime in recent years, proving to be an indispensable piece of machinery in the international system. In a situation where repayment obligations are mounting (the point just made about export credit obligations is relevant here), rescheduling makes an important contribution to net financial flows.

Three major issues currently face the Paris Club process. First, the problem of serial rescheduling, that is, the consequences of repeated rescheduling agreements on the debt profile of the debtor country; second, the question of if and when to make exceptional settlements, that is, beyond the roughly established norm; and third, how settlements relate to other decisions made elsewhere in the financing system in the context of country adjustment programs, that is, the interface with the Consultative Group process and Fund programs.

Serial rescheduling poses the potential problem of the snowball effect. As interest payments are included in the rescheduled amounts, the debt outstanding is continually increased. If this happens several times in succession the process can begin to create more of a problem than it solves, as in the case of the Sudan, for example.

On the question of exceptional treatment, there is a degree of latitude exhibited in Paris Club decisions, reflecting individual circumstances. But truly exceptional agreements, such as those accorded to Indonesia in 1970 and Turkey in 1980, are by definition rare and require exceptional policy changes by the debtor country. In addition, multi-year rescheduling, though endorsed in principle by the industrial countries' London Summit meeting in 1985, has been extended in only a small number of cases since.

Relationships between Paris Club and Consultative Group discussions do not appear to have become any closer despite the evident real need for a more coherent approach to country financial programing for the poorer developing countries. There is nothing like the approach adopted for the heavily indebted middle-income countries where a target for rescheduling and new finance to be met by the London Club is part of the conditions for Fund financing to proceed. Any attempt in consultative groups to establish a broad medium-term financial and policy framework must be based on normative assumptions about official debt relief, which may not be accepted in Paris Club deliberations where other considerations are brought to bear. The question is whether more communication between these two fora might facilitate more satisfactory financial packages for aid-financed countries.

The Paris Club process should in principle be flexible enough to produce modified approaches in all three areas in cases where imaginative solutions could make a large contribution toward restoring financial stability. Is the relative absence of such decisions a sign that there are few such cases? Or is it a sign that Paris Club decisions have become caught in too narrow a frame of reference?

A more general point arises from the previous discussion of the record of export credit lending. If it is conceded that supplier countries contributed to the poor performance of export credit financed projects on a fairly wide scale, is it reasonable for creditor countries to seek to recover this lending at book values? Is this also a case where the Kindleberger critique quoted at the beginning of the paper, of the "external diseconomy implied by a single cohesive set of lenders whose condoning of one default implied license for all" might be seen to apply? Is there not a way in which creditor governments can share with debtor governments the cost of bad decisions made in the past, clearing the way for resumed normal activity?

Conclusions:
Operational Problems and Looking to the Future

It is clear that, at the present stage, official finance is the thread on which growth-oriented structural adjustment programs hang, both in the more advanced and the less advanced developing countries. A principal argument developed in this paper is that while there are limits to the extent to which official sources can expand the volume of financing, both in the concessional and nonconcessional area, growth-oriented structural adjustment programs are bringing distinct and important improvements to the development financing process, correcting some of the faults that had become apparent in a development cooperation "industry" that had become increasingly complex and diffuse in the 1970s. The main improvements, which have the potential to increase considerably the positive impact of development finance, are the increased policy focus and the movement towards more coordination and discipline. On the developing country side, improvements in economic policies and administration are also working in this direction. At the same time it was suggested that official financing cannot by itself be expected to restore the conditions necessary for resumed voluntary lending, and that both private and official creditors may have to play a bigger role in opening up such a prospect. Another point emerging is that in the absence of restored "normal" financing, and especially if a world recession were to be visited upon us in the near future, neither the Fund nor the Bank may be as well placed to extend further help as they have been in the recent past. (That private financial flows might be needed to assist the proper functioning of the international financial institutions is an illustration of the degree of interdependence that now exists between official and private institutions.)

These large questions may not be susceptible to clear-cut responses at least for the present time. There are, however, two areas where there is scope for consensus and action, which deserve attention in the immediate future.

The first is aid coordination, or more particularly, the marshalling of quick-disbursing finance to support adjustment programs in poorer developing countries. The number and scope of such programs in Africa is surely an amazing phenomenon, judged in terms of prevailing attitudes in these countries only a few years ago. Donors have been waiting for this wave of change in African policy directions for some considerable time. Now that it is with us, is the donor community able to respond adequately? It is true that the DAC and the World Bank have put much effort into setting out the requirements for a coherent, effective response. But the changes required in donor practices are considerable; there is a "cultural" factor as well as a policy factor, with strongly embedded interests and staffing geared to different needs.

Donors have, in the United Nations context, undertaken to ensure that the financing needs of individual country adjustment programs are met. (They have been reticent, however, about meeting any global estimate of African financing needs.) But according to the World Bank, donors are lagging behind the pace of policy reform in Africa, so that courageous country programs are underfinanced. In addition, there are complaints from African governments that the policy dialogue is becoming impossibly burdensome with too many actors and procedures and too little coordination in the construction of financing programs.

What, if anything, can be done to cut through such problems? There is unlikely to be an easy answer. Clearly there is a monitoring problem. At the risk of adding yet another actor to the scene, is there a role for a monitoring agent, perhaps a "friend of the Consultative Group," who might keep track of the financial situation and make contact with individual members when performance appears to be falling short of what is needed? One thinks, in this regard, of agents who might parallel the role which the then OECD Secretary General, in cooperation with a German Minister, took in coordinating bilateral support for the Turkish adjustment program in 1979-80.

Finally, in looking to the future, the present heavy weight of official financing in total financial flows to developing countries is hardly desirable in the longer run. For one thing, a significant expansion of capital flows to developing countries will only come from private sources. For another, the development of diversified, pluralistic economies which should be the ultimate objective of growth-oriented structural adjustment, even in poorer countries, requires an enterprise economy with private financing playing a key role. Hence positive action to assist movement in this direction should be an important element in development cooperation. The extension of International Finance Corporation programs, the policy role of the Multilateral Investment Guarantee Agency (MIGA), and targeted activities by bilateral agencies will all be helpful in this regard and should be seen as laying the basis for a different financing pattern than those of the past or the situation we have at present.

Discussion

Guillermo Ortiz
Executive Director
International Monetary Fund

Mr. Reed's presentation has been clear and concise, and his main argument is quite straightforward. He has dealt only in an indirect manner with the subject at hand, which is the role of external private capital flows in the context of growth-oriented adjustment programs. That is, Mr. Reed has not really addressed the question of how private capital flows may contribute to the reestablishment of growth prospects in indebted countries or in what amounts, except to the extent that it cites some elements of the Baker proposal. He has focused instead on the question of how the direction taken by the debt strategy may affect the future flows of bank finance to developing countries and the prospects for normalization of debtor/creditor relations.

Mr. Reed notes that, despite the success of the "first phase" of the debt strategy in avoiding a systemic collapse and in facilitating a dramatic adjustment of external imbalances, the approach followed thus far is coming under stress—as he puts it—"due to the discrepancy between the climate for investment created by certain countries and the conditions for investment required by the world capital markets." We are at a turning point, and Mr. Reed foresees two distinct paths which may be followed.

First, countries may opt for implementing the necessary policies for the reestablishment of an appropriate investment climate, accepting the "discipline of the market," and thus regaining a status of creditworthiness. Countries that follow this route will find it in their own interest in the long run to accept the terms and conditions set by the market. Second, they may opt for another option, following the "concessionalist school" and attempt to force creditors to grant offmarket concessions.

Countries that follow the "market way" will eventually be rewarded with a resumption of private capital flows on a voluntary basis. In contrast, the "concessionalists" will be cut off from international capital markets and will have to settle for the morsels of official finance. In substance, Mr. Reed has made a political statement; but, since this is not a political forum, I will resist the temptation to make a similar type of statement and limit my intervention to two brief remarks.

The argument that countries should accept the market discipline is fundamentally asymmetric if it is not extended to private creditors, and to commercial banks in particular. For some time now, the market has been discounting the debtor countries' debt, which trades in the secondary market at values considerably below those originally contracted. Yet commercial banks insist that the servicing of this debt be done with reference to the contractual value rather than to the market value. If banks, as Mr. Reed puts it, ". . . play an important role in transmitting this discipline (the market's) to all borrowers, including banks themselves, not just the problem countries," why is it that they refuse to accept the market's realities, which should tell them something about the soundness of their lending decisions? In other words, if the disciplinarian does not discipline himself, why expect others to accept it quietly? I will not extend my remarks about discipline to cover the lending boom of the 1970s. It appears that banks did not talk much about discipline in those years.

The significance of the above considerations certainly goes beyond the search for symmetry in the outlook for the future path of the debt strategy. It is becoming increasingly evident that the observed wedge between the contractual and the market valuation of existing debt is an important inhibiting factor for the generation of new investment, both in physical and financial assets. The reason is that potential takers of new debt fear that it would fall into the same category as the old debt, so that the market would value it at a discount. Let me illustrate this point with the same example used by Mr. Reed to show the recent difficulties encountered by "steering committees" to sell concerted financial packages to commercial banks: the Mexican debt restructuring.

Throughout the process of "selling" the package, the reluctance to participate shown by several smaller regional banks has, in my view, more to do with the fact that Mexican debt is selling at a discount in the secondary market than with the so-called concessions included in the package. The worst offender among these seems to be, in the view of Mr. Reed, the inclusion of contingent finance facilities. It is doubtful, however, that these can, first of all, be called concessions, and that they have been an overriding concern to the banks. Let us recall that the so-called oil facility is built around a symmetrical band and that, at least until a few days ago, the prospects were that less money would be required from banks on account of this facility.

Some smaller banks have actually sold debt at a discount in the secondary market. Naturally, the prospect of adding to their portfolios—in the form of new credits—an asset that is being traded at a discount is not very attractive.

An ostensibly positive aspect of decreased cohesiveness of the banking community is that it would allow for a wider range of financial arrangements, such as, for example, the automatic capitalization of interest (which, incidentally, was one of the original proposals of Mexico to the banks). In trying to broaden the range of financing modalities, however, the banks not only find difficulty in reaching agreements with their country customers on the terms and conditions of new financing, but increasingly have problems reaching agreement among themselves as well. This phenomenom, which is typical of the decisionmaking process in cartel-type organizations, has to some extent been fostered by the approach adopted by the governments of creditor countries and multilateral organizations.

It is alleged that, in order to preserve the stability of the international financial system and be able to respond "systematically," a system of "rewards and penalties" has been set up whereby the indebted countries must individually negotiate with groups of creditors, thereby institutionalizing a banks' cartel.

The system of rewards and penalties, however, has become increasingly lopsided. Clearly the "reward" to be received by the indebted countries that have pursued intensive adjustment programs would be the restoration of economic growth and normal relationships with creditors factors, which in turn should lead to recovery of their debt-servicing capacity.

I will return to this point in a minute, since this is my second comment. As is well known, however, the anticipated growth did not materialize, and the chance of restoring "normal" relationships with creditors—a return to spontaneous or voluntary lending—is still very remote for most of the indebted countries. Indeed, some of the contradictions inherent in the strategy pursued so far have become more obvious, particularly following negotiation of the Mexican financing package.

On the one hand, as noted, banks that have already withdrawn from voluntary financing are more and more reluctant to participate in concerted financing schemes. When they do so, they use various means to minimize their participation as much as possible. Economic subcommittees seek to reduce the financing requirements derived from balance of payments projections agreed with the multilateral organizations. Similarly, the banks try to obtain guarantees from the latter for at least part of the financing to be committed.

Perhaps the most obvious paradox is that, although creditor governments, banks, and multilateral institutions have defended the implementation of a case-by-case strategy from the start, the fear of setting a precedent seems to be a decisive factor in the course of negotiations. This is clearly a contradiction in terms with the so-called case-by-case approach.

The banks' reluctance to provide an increased flow of financing to the indebted countries and their inflexibility in granting concessions raise serious doubts as to the viability of the current strategy. First of all, it is clear that no genuine system has actually been adopted for considering each case individually, adjusting the amount and terms of the financing to individual requirements. In fact, the strategy has been one of uniform treatment, in which a series of ritual steps or states must be adhered to by the indebted countries (with one or two exceptions) beginning with a Fund adjustment program and followed by agreements with the World Bank, and so forth, if they wish to obtain from the banks any arrangement on a rescheduling of debt principal or—perhaps—a reduction in surcharges.

Let me now turn very briefly to my second comment, which refers to Mr. Reed's proposition that countries that accept the market's discipline and do not ask for concessions—and, incidentally, one must be careful in specifying what this word really means—can aspire to a prompt return to a creditworthy status and the resumption of spontaneous lending. Countries of the "concessionalist persuasion," on the other hand, will be permanently cut off from capital markets.

While this may be the case, neither history nor present experience provide evidence to support this view.

Debtor countries have so far—or until very recently—maintained normal interest payments to commercial banks, and what we observe is a steady and pronounced decline in the granting of new credits. According to the most recent information compiled by the Fund, bank lending to Latin America has declined from $15 billion in 1983 to $5.6 billion in 1984 and to $1 billion in 1985, increasing to $4 billion in the period January–September 1986.

It would appear that the eventual resumption of spontaneous lending to indebted countries will depend more on improved prospects for the region than on the fact that these countries may be asking for concessions today. Banks will lend again on a voluntary basis when they consider that it is good business to do so, and this in turn will depend to a large extent on how effectively the debt overhang can be reduced to levels that will help the restoration of confidence.

D. Joseph Wood
Vice President, Financial Policy, Planning and Budgeting
World Bank

I find myself responding to a presentation by Mr. Reed that I found in many respects more attractive than the paper. I understood Mr. Reed's presentation as suggesting that there is nothing inherently flawed in the current arrangements, that they need to be applied perhaps with better manners, and that the developing countries must resist the temptation and blandishments of those who would have them go down the concessions path. But given that, one can look forward to satisfactory outcomes in the arranging of external financing packages.

I have to say my own sense is a little less sanguine than that. My sense is that the arrangements for putting together external financing packages for the middle-income countries are under strain (the tension that Mr. Reed referred to) and that it is important to try to understand the sources of that strain so that we can address them effectively.

I understood Mr. Reed's background paper as pointing to the tendency on the part of developing countries to seek more attractive terms as a particularly important source of strain. He was at pains in his oral presentation to indicate that that wasn't simply a matter of interest rates, it was more generally a question, he said, of the texture of the agreements.

Nevertheless, I think one can use the interest rates as a proxy or symbol of the kind of distress that arises in putting together these packages, but I find that that way of looking at the problem distracts attention from what is an important weakness.

In saying this, I don't mean to question the assertion that the lack of overall attractiveness of these packages, including the possibility of narrower-than-desired spreads, makes it harder for the advisory committee to sell these packages—that is obviously the case—but that is really a normal feature of the negotiating process. Each side stresses the difficulties it faces in delivering on any deal that involves terms less favorable than those they entered the negotiations with. Just as the advisory committee members will stress the difficulties of selling the deal to the banks that aren't at the table, so governments can be expected to stress the difficulties they will have in selling the deals to their populations if they can't show some visible signs of progress.

It is tempting, therefore, to take these references to the lack of attractiveness of the packages as simply an extension of the good hard negotiating tactics that one would expect in these negotiations. I don't think anyone really would judge the acceptability of these restructurings or the new money packages in terms of the normal risk/return calculations. What I would assume the banks have in mind is not the alternative of placing their funds at some more attractive risk/return combination, but rather the alternative of losing the servicing of the outstanding debt, that is, a default of interest. Banks are prepared to pay something either through increased financing or in other ways to avert such a situation, and it is natural that they want to pay as little as possible.

Many observers, among whom I include myself, thought that the Baker Initiative, which suggested that the increase in commercial bank exposure only needed to be a small fraction of the interest due, was in fact a pretty good deal from the perspective of the commercial banks. What has happened in practice is that the scale of the new money packages has proven—with Mexico a notable exception—to be, if anything, a little smaller than what Secretary Baker suggested.

But the borrowing countries have conditioned their agreement to these smaller packages on some narrowing of spreads and on provisions for contingency financing. It seems to me a little disingenuous to argue, as the background paper does, that the problem is with the demands for narrower spreads and contingency financing without at the same time acknowledging that the exposure growth has in fact been negligible or even negative in many of these countries.

But if I am right about the collective interest of the banks in securing the contingent servicing of the interest, then why is it that the system for arranging these packages is under strain? Is it simply a matter, as a newspaper has recently suggested, of excessive brinksmanship on both sides? Or are there structural problems?

My own view is it is some of each. There is a degree of brinksmanship in these negotiations that would be regarded as just good tough bargaining in ordinary bank/client negotiations, but as applied in the current arrangements, it is worrisome. It is a little bit like playing with fire in a forest that is becoming increasingly parched. Our prevailing conventional wisdom insists that those with matches have to decide where and when to build their fires since, if the forest ranger instructs them and something subsequently goes wrong, the fire builders could seek redress from the ranger. Surely, however, there is a point, and we may be approaching it now, at which the costs of maintaining this conventional wisdom may become too high.

Apart from this, there are structural weaknesses, and this is really the point I wanted to make, and I think I am here agreeing with Mr. Ortiz. Mr. Carey refers to the absence of any default mechanism that has acceptable long-term costs. I would phrase the problem somewhat differently. While I think the banks have a clear collective interest in closing deals and averting default on interest, I don't think they have in place any very effective decisionmaking machinery. The advisory committees have no power to bind the banks they represent and hence the agreements that they reach have to be kept very simple; some would even say simplistic.

One example is the lack of a threshold for excluding banks that have miniscule exposure, which tends to lead to a prolonged approval process. Another is the continued use of historical base, even when some banks, as Mr. Ortiz mentioned, have managed to dispose completely of the claims that they held on the date of that historical base.

The continued viability of the arrangements for putting together external financing packages depends, in my view, not on ever more labored attempts to maintain the cohesion among a group of lenders with increasingly disparate interests, but rather on devising modifications in the arrangements which will permit some recognition of very real differences in interest. This is already happening to some extent via the use of debt conversions. And I would agree with Mr. Reed that this area deserves the increased attention it is now getting.

In addition, I sense that we may not be too far away from the time when banks will be able to accept actions in a country such as Bolivia that they could not accept in a country such as Brazil; in other words, they will find a way to make distinctions among countries that will be consistent with the rhetoric in favor of case-by-case approach.

Thus, to conclude, Mr. Chairman, my diagnosis is that the problem in arranging external financing packages is not simply a matter of unattractive texture of the deals or a lack of good manners on the part of the Bretton Woods Institutions and the chief U.S. regulator. I think also a part of the problem is a flawed mechanism for reaching and enforcing decisions that reflect the collective but not the monolithic interest of the commercial banks.

Hence, one place to look for improvements is not in trying to shore up an eroding cohesion via avoidance of lower spreads or other things which are unattractive to the banks, but rather in trying to devise ways to ease some of the pressures through new arrangements that permit distinctions to be made among banks and among borrowing countries.

Alassane D. Ouattara

Director, African Department
International Monetary Fund

Mr. Carey's paper raises a number of difficult questions to which there are no easy answers. I find myself in agreement with Mr. Carey that there is a need to strengthen the process of coordinating foreign aid to support the attainment of a sustainable rate of growth under conditions of financial stability in developing countries. In my remarks, I shall confine myself to some key issues that arise from Mr. Carey's paper, drawing on our experience in the African countries.

First, Fund-supported adjustment programs have indeed been

designed to reduce financial imbalances and restore the conditions for sustained economic growth. These programs have, inter alia, helped countries to reduce their financing needs and to mobilize the needed resources on appropriate terms. Thus, these programs have enabled countries to progress faster toward the achievement of a viable external position and sustainable growth rates. In view of experience in Africa, Mr. Carey's assertion that "in restrospect, the terms of Fund finance were inappropriate to many of these cases and now constitute a burden . . ." is not totally correct. While financing on more favorable terms might have been desirable, one has to consider what the alternatives would have been. In the absence of other resources, had the Fund not reacted quickly in the early 1980s to the requests for assistance by these countries, would not the total cost of disorderly adjustment have been higher?

Second, a point not fully brought out in the paper is that, once external financial assistance has been committed to support a country's adjustment program, the *timely flow* of such assistance is critical to the success of the adjustment program. In our experience, shortfalls or delays in the disbursement of committed financial assistance have often hindered the adjustment efforts of a number of countries. In some cases the momentum for adjustment was lost, and its resumption took considerable time.

Third, the impression that the Fund is withdrawing finance from developing countries needs to be qualified. As mentioned before, the Fund reacted quickly to assist the African countries facing major imbalances in the early 1980s. During 1981–84, purchases from the Fund averaged annually SDR 1.7 billion, while repurchases averaged annually only SDR 420 million. During 1985, purchases amounted to almost SDR 1.0 billion, while repurchases were close to SDR 800 million. In 1986, purchases dropped to SDR 800 million, while repurchases rose to SDR 1.1 billion. However, during 1986, efforts to mobilize resources at concessional terms were intensified, as the Fund stepped up its efforts to play a catalytic role. At the end of 1986, the Fund had 20 stand-by arrangements and 6 arrangements under the Structural Adjustment Facility in Africa. Thus, while the involvement of the Fund remains substantial, the emphasis has been increasingly on ensuring that the mix of resources utilized by member countries is conducive to achieving an improvement in their external position and does not overstretch their debt-servicing capacity.

Fourth, I cannot share Mr. Carey's view that Professor Kindleberger's "default mechanism" would have somehow been a positive factor, forcing adjustment. Such a "default mechanism" would have disrupted the working of financial markets and brought about disorderly adjustment, with the attendant costs. The recent debt crisis illustrates well the point. In this regard, the Fund has worked to promote financial stability and orderly adjustment, taking into account economic externalities—both costs and benefits—that are not fully reflected in the workings of financial markets.

Fifth, like Mr. Carey, I am concerned about the impact on the developing countries of a recession in the industrial countries. While clearly the adjustment process would become even more difficult for the developing countries in such an environment, the international community, including the Fund and the World Bank, will need to react promptly to assist the affected countries. I therefore welcome the thrust of Mr. Carey's paper on the urgent need to strengthen the joint effort between the developing countries and the international donor community to ensure that growth-oriented adjustment programs receive adequate financial support in a timely and coordinated manner on appropriate terms. This seems essential given the spread and depth of the adjustment effort in Africa.

In this regard, the Fund has already taken an important further step in facilitating the coordination of financial flows to countries adopting appropriate adjustment programs by setting up the Structural Adjustment Facility (SAF). The Fund has so far approved ten SAF-supported programs, six of which are for African countries (Burundi, The Gambia, Mauritania, Niger, Senegal, and Sierra Leone). Many more are in the pipeline. A key element of this facility has involved the provision of joint assistance by the Fund and World Bank staffs to IDA countries to prepare a policy framework paper that defines the medium-term policy strategy of the country and the financing requirements. While it was envisaged that the document would provide a focal point to coordinate the flow of financial resources to support growth-oriented adjustment programs the document has not yet become as important in this regard as envisaged. As the international community becomes more familiar with this new facility, the policy framework paper could well start to play the role originally envisaged for it.

XU Naijiong

Executive Director
World Bank

I share Mr. Carey's analysis of the trend of slow growth in official development assistance (ODA) over the next few years. Commercial banks will not resume their normal lending to the two country groups during this period. As a result, there will be an enormous gap between the supply of and the demand for development finance in these countries. The point has been raised in Mr. Carey's report, but the solution to this serious mismatch has not been found. I will try to bring your attention to two aspects that I believe might be helpful in addressing this issue.

As Mr. Carey pointed out, there have been significant and notable shifts in the pattern of financial flows to developing countries. One shift is that multilateral flows now constitute 24 percent of total, up from 10 percent in 1980. This shift reflects not only recent economic realities but also a fundamental change in the philosophy of aid policy among donor countries.

As we all know, the current dominance of ODA in the provision of financing to developing countries will continue. This means that ODA is going to play a crucial role in assisting the two country groups to implement their growth-oriented adjustment programs. Therefore, the effectiveness of ODA is more critical than ever at this juncture.

Mr. Carey's report has rightly pointed out that two new and fundamental changes have emerged in today's development financing. First, ODA providers need to respond to a diverse range of country situations rapidly, flexibly, and coherently. Second, the nature of current development problems demands a program rather than project approach to the delivery of development assistance and finance. Both developments indicate that the efficiency and effectiveness of ODA have an important bearing in the success of the bold adjustment program undertaken by developing countries.

I fully share the OECD's conclusion or self-criticism with regard to the deficiencies in ODA and, more specifically, in bilateral aid. The slow-moving political decision-making process and complicated aid procedure have made bilateral aid inflexible, irresponsive, and ineffective. Furthermore, we know all too well that political and commercial considerations are being weighed heavily in determining bilateral aid allocation.

Despite the recognition of these deficiencies in the donor community, we all appreciate how difficult it is to make improvements. While anticipating some minor changes, such as better coordination and less complexity in the aid process, we have to admit no fundamental solution is in sight. Therefore, if we expect ODA to play an effective role in development finance, we should rely more on multilateral institutions.

Multilateral flows are now on a rising trend. We consider this a healthy trend and welcome it. We feel, however, that the role of multilateral development institutions can and should be further strengthened. They are not only more flexible and more effective but can play more roles than bilateral agencies.

Let me take the World Bank as an example to illustrate what a multilateral institution can do. We all agree policy environment holds the key to a sustainable growth. ODA can be effective only if it is tailored to the specific development needs of individual countries. The Bank has a wide range of experience in different countries with diverse political, economic, cultural, and social structures. In addition, the Bank is served by a large international staff representing a number of ways of thinking and considerable collective wisdom. Therefore, the Bank is in a good position to help countries design their development planning and program. Moreover, since political and commercial factors play less a role in allocating Bank's resources, the Bank can be neutral and objective in formulating each country's lending program with the result that resources can be efficiently put to productive and effective use. The Bank enjoys a comfortable edge over bilateral agencies in this respect.

Exactly for this reason, the Bank has stood as a reputable and major player in the cause of development over the past 40 years. Of course, some shortfalls do exist in the Bank's operations. We always caution the Bank management not to be overconfident. The Bank should avoid imposition of its policy prescriptions on member countries. A one-way track in policy dialogue is bound to fail.

Another strength of the Bank lies in its technical assistance. For each country, the Bank makes long-term planning including institutional building and human resource development. The Bank can help countries to strengthen weak links so as to enhance the efficiency of use of resources. We think this assistance is as valuable to recipient countries as is financial assistance. For example, recently the Bank has launched programs providing debt- and financial-management assistance to member countries. If we had had this assistance in the 1970s, debt problems for some countries might have been less serious than they are today.

At this time, I believe multilateral development institutions should play a larger role in helping countries to return to a sustainable growth path. I hope to see more resources shifted from bilateral to multilateral channels. In this connection, I disagree with Mr. Carey on one point. I believe that net transfers are a key factor in measuring the World Bank's contribution to development. As long as the resources are being put to effective use, the Bank should aim at maximizing its net transfer to developing countries.

In my view, the credit standing of the Bank can be strengthened by stronger support from all governments, such as by injecting large amounts of capital in the Bank's capital base and maintaining adequate reserves.

I would also like to comment on the recycling of Japanese or other countries' capital surplus. I agree with Mr. Carey's analysis in the paper. I think, however, we need some innovative ideas in this respect. The recycling mechanism in the 1970s is no longer working in the 1980s. If we do nothing and just wait for things to happen, we are going nowhere. Even if the market eventually goes back to normal, the help this brings will come too late and too little. In my view, we have to act to accelerate the process. For one thing, the commercial banks are not going to be the key players in recycling in the 1980s. Perhaps the surplus could be intermediated through multilateral institutions. Greater access to Japan's market by the World Bank and direct loans to the Fund are ways to achieve this intermediation. These, however, are sporadic measures, lacking a long-term framework. Probably, the time has come for us to take a serious look at an old idea—the Bank's Bank.

Comment

Fawzi Hamad Al-Sultan
Executive Director
World Bank

Mr. Carey makes two extremely important points that have also come up in various comments by other speakers. First, the nature of the problems in developing countries demands both a change in approach and response capacity from institutions involved in development assistance. This no doubt applies as well to nonconcessional flows from the commercial banking institutions and the international capital markets. Second, the adjustment process, because of the severity of the problems and the increasing volatility of commodity prices, interest rates, and other variables has tested the administrative abilities of both the smaller and larger developing countries, but particularly in smaller and poorer ones.

I feel, as do many other speakers, that the Bank has adjusted its approach more adequately than has the Fund, but both institutions still need to emphasize much more institution building, particularly among the poorer countries, if these countries are to achieve the basic fundamentals for growth. In terms of response capacity I think the Bank needs to develop more speed. In fact, the Bank has shown itself capable of reacting very fast in certain situations, but the overall process is still much too slow. Also, in terms of response, both the Bank and the Fund need to be able to respond with more funds. Mr. Reed makes the point well in his paper, showing a relative diminishing role for both the Bank and the Fund in developing countries. An increase in developmental assistance would enable countries to lengthen the adjustment process and make it more politically feasible.

Before going into some financing aspects, I want to emphasize one point, made earlier by some speakers, which is the need to separate the debt problem from the adjustment problem. If one can draw the parallel between countries and companies, then the adjustment process involves changes in the companies' strategy, management, productive machinery, and so forth, while its debt problem would involve financial restructuring. If we concentrate on the debt problem,

Mr. Carey, among others, argues for a workable default mechanism, and Mr. Reed feels that a larger equity component, through developing countries' opening up their capital markets, should be part of the long-term solution. I don't think that there is any question that there should be relief; the question is how much and how should this relief be structured so as to safeguard the soundness of the financial institutions and maintain the developing countries' access to these capital markets.

A fundamental requirement when we are talking about relief is the change in attitude required from both ODA institutions and commercial banks in addition to the "culture" change to meet new needs proposed by Mr. Carey. As to ODA, other speakers have spoken of the real transfer of resources from the developing countries to the OECD as being close to $100–120 billion annually as a result of the decline of oil and commodity prices. To offset this, there has been tangible real increase in the level of ODA from the OECD countries. Some form of concessional mechanism for recycling such flows could be part of the relief package, and achieving the 0.7 percent aid targets should be pursued seriously. Also, their attitude toward increasing the World Bank's resources, in particular, should allow a more liberal use of the guarantee mechanism. The combination of both can be used to negotiate lower margins and rescheduling fees for the middle-income indebted countries. Concessions can also be made within the present framework particularly since much of this aid was tied to procurement. As to the commercial bank role, I found Mr. Reed short on self-criticism on the efficiency of capital markets and the banks in particular. From the 1970s, capital markets have become increasingly international, and over the past year there has been even more deregulation and more globalization. Not only has this led to a much larger number of offshore and consortium banks, but it has also fostered a larger syndication of loans. However, there are two crucial aspects to this expansion. First, this led to such intense competition that quality was sacrificed. Funds were being made available to borrowers at levels and rates that even the borrowers were surprised at. Second, the extranationalization went beyond national regulatory authorities' control, which led to higher multiplier effects and greater liquidity, which have contributed to greater volatility.

The point I want to make is not one of blame, but that more prudent banking could have eroded the size of the debt problem, and that the banks too need to make an adjustment to the changed circumstances. I don't think that the approach should be "either the countries adjust or the banks would walk away." The banks have a fundamental interest in the development of the "problem" economies, particularly since that is where the growth and an increasing part of their business is expected to come.

I agree with Mr. Reed that banks should be part of the recovery process. The traditional rescheduling exercises work if, as Mr. Carey mentions, the problem is seen as one of liquidity. However, if the problem, as we know it, is more fundamental—then the need is to restructure the debt and so inject new funds so that the debt-ridden countries are given sufficient medium-term relief to make further funds available for growth and a resumption of creditworthiness. It would be up to the capital markets and the commercial banks to be more creative in finding new ways of carrying long-term debt and increasing its transfer into equity instruments. In the case of the poorer developing countries, some debt forgiveness would have to be contemplated. I understand that this might have to involve changes in regulations in the major financial markets, particularly those regulating commercial banks, and changes in the attitudes of developing countries toward the role of the private sector and equity investment, so that the transfers into equity are not expected to be substantial over the next three to five years. This makes us look the debt burden straight in the face. If the Banks are willing to change their attitude and approach, however, I am confident that the market will too.

Round Table Discussion

Ernest Stern

Senior Vice President, Operational Staff
World Bank

I have been struck, both in this conference and in similar discussions of this topic, by the amazing consensus today about the importance of having an adjustment process that also takes into account the need for growth, both current and prospective, and by the wide range of definitions that people who write about this subject take as a starting point from which their conclusions follow without too much difficulty. Much of the debate then revolves around those conclusions, whereas in fact quite often there exists a different set of starting points and starting assumptions.

We have heard in the course of the discussion implicit or explicit definitions of development and the contention that adjustment is about the same as development or that development is about the same as adjustment. It is true that all growth and development require adjustment to changing circumstances, different technologies, and the evolution of the economic structure of a country.

Too much adjustment is the antithesis of growth—and here the word isn't really adjustment but more properly austerity. But even appropriate adjustment does not provide much assurance in the short term that you end up with a basis for sustainable growth. It is important in thinking about how we in the Bank and the Fund can help countries view their problems to consider what kind of advice we can give. By doing so we will have perhaps a clearer understanding of what is intended by these phrases.

It is clear that we are looking at adjustment programs in countries that are in great difficulty. Whether development is the same as adjustment or adjustment is an integral part of development is not too germane. Countries that by definition failed to adjust adequately in the past are facing particularly acute problems; whether these problems are of internal or external balances or both is not germane.

There is a sense of urgency to the adjustment process, which is different from the normal development process. Normal relationships are different. Future prospects cannot be based on present practices because what is going on has led to the problem. The relationships between debtor and creditor are changed; the relationships between domestic institutions and the public have to be changed; government strategy needs to be reexamined not only as regards quality and implementation but also as regards long-term effectiveness. And this needs to be done quickly because normally a country in this position is running out of the resources to grow and the capacity to adjust.

The adjustment process is multifaceted. There are basic issues of macroeconomic adjustment, since ultimately resource use must equal the resource envelope. But the real adjustment process goes well beyond that. It involves, particularly if you are looking at adjustment with sustainable growth, it seems to me, the philosophy of the country and its government and whether that philosophy is consistent with sustainable growth in a current or prospective resource environment. It involves administrative ability, managerial skills, and the capacity of public institutions to adapt. Without such skills, measures to restore macroeconomic balances often fall apart. If the country has not dealt with the underlying problems, even when times get better, the country will run into very much the same set of problems again.

Structural changes supporting these macroeconomic aggregates are as important, if not more important in the long term, to the success of a program and to the resumption of sustainable growth, thus the initial austerity program. Middle-income and lower-income countries that are going through the adjustment process provide good examples of how difficult change is and how slow progress often is.

Adjustment involves many difficult political choices in open or democratic countries. Even in nonparliamentary countries there are still political processes at work, and it is rare that a single person can decree these choices without undermining his support.

It is clear that many countries, even with the best of will at the top and a clear desire to change the basic strategy, have great difficulty persuading their bureaucracy to accept change. Even when the ministers are all abroad, political leaders have great difficulty in breaking with tradition.

Even if they can do so, the results are not instantaneous and can sometimes be a bit perverse. With all the knowledge accumulated in the Bank about how this process works, and if I may add, with all respect, in the Fund, when a country starts on this process, unexpected developments occur and unexpected results emerge. Once begun, the process is ongoing and another barrier arises because few countries are well endowed with indigenous advisory capacity. Moreover, there is generally inadequate analytical capacity that feeds back to the government allowing it to make necessary mid-term corrections.

Adjustment with growth will not be achieved in a short time and is not an emphemeral issue awaiting the magic solution to the debt overhang. It is a process that needs to continue in many countries for a good number of years to achieve sustainable growth in an external environment where resources will generally be available for some time only in modest amounts, modest not because resources are absent but because the investment opportunities in these countries are less attractive owing to high risk or to low returns.

The weariness that the world seems to have about solving the debt problem is going to continue and probably increase because of the political difficulty and uncertainty of the process and the changing external environment, which, as a number of discussants have pointed out, isn't getting any better. There are going to be lots of setbacks. Countries making the effort will come back for a second or third or fourth time, and this will lead the impatient, often including our commercial banker friends, to question whether anybody knows what they are doing and why don't they do it right the first time. That contributes to their unwillingness to continue to raise resources and to their sense of frustration.

It has been suggested on the one hand that the Bank is still at an early stage of formulating an integrated model of how development and adjustment can proceed and, on the other, that the Bank employs excessively simplistic, rigid, and universal models.

I favor the former suggestion because I myself am skeptical about the capacity of a central model to analyze this highly diversified set of issues in different countries. Clearly, that is not to say that there aren't some well-known basic elements which can be analyzed. But beyond the basics, the real contribution that the Bank can make is not to deal only with those basics, but to go beyond this, to help the country deal with the medium- and longer-term structural issues in their administration, in the operation of public enterprises, and in the incentives not only for the private sector, but for the actual operations of the central bank and financial sector.

Overall, the Bank's role focuses on how the policy framework and the incentive programs affect the behavior of private individuals, firms, and public enterprises, and whether our expectations at the policy level can, in fact, be translated into reality, and if not, in identifying the remaining barriers to policy implementation and how these can be overcome.

Richard D. Erb

Deputy Managing Director
International Monetary Fund

I thought I might address a number of issues that came up during the symposium. The interesting exchange during the discussion of the country studies brought out a wide variety of country experiences, including not only Turkey, which was the subject of the main presentation, but also countries in Latin America, some elaboration of the experience of Thailand, and mention of developments in Morocco. I was struck by the effort to link in a systematic way these experiences and to draw from one set of countries conclusions and implications for policies that other countries might follow. This is not easy. Cross-country comparisons may be useful in developing insights on individual countries, but there are definite limitations on the practical transfer of cross-country experience.

Given the way that Fund missions work with individual countries, I thought not so much about cross-country comparisons, but rather about the evolution of economic developments and policies in each of those countries.

Despite a tendency to think of the Fund as having a short-run orientation toward individual countries and being involved in crisis situations, the reality is—and this was the case in each of the countries just discussed—the Fund has a long working relationship with each of its member countries. At times, that working relationship involves a formal Fund arrangement. This is true of all the countries mentioned. Discussions within the staff regarding a formal arrangement of each of those countries focused on individual circumstances of each country and the trade-offs that each had to make and did so not within a short-run context but in a longer-term consideration.

Looking at the past experience of these countries and looking forward to their future leads me to the broader subject of adjustment versus growth. I know there was during the staff discussions considerable reflection: Is there a trade-off between adjustment and growth? Is there not a trade-off?

Adjustment is a word that means a lot of different things. Adjustment is not a concrete concept; growth is. If I may be critical for a moment, the question is not of adjustment versus growth. Nonetheless, most countries do not think about adjustment in the abstract, nor does the Fund staff. They think of more concrete policy objectives, of which growth is one. Other objectives include external payments sustainability, integration with the rest of the world, employment, and distribution. Each country has a wide range of policy objectives.

In working with a country the Fund staff looks at these policy objectives, analyzes and examines some of the trade-offs that may be involved not only in the short run, but also over the medium term, and assesses the policy instruments that the government will employ to achieve those objectives. These instruments represent a long list, including monetary policy, pricing policies, expenditure policies, and tax policies. Taking into account the domestic and external environment and the unique circumstances of each country, the staff faces a challenge in providing analysis and advice on the trade-offs that may exist among objectives and in setting policy instruments with a view to achieving those objectives not just within a year or two ahead, but over a longer period of time.

This leads me to a second general observation on the question of the short run versus the long run, which I think is an artificial distinction. One must look at the objectives and the trade-offs of objectives within a multiyear context in the same way that the policy instruments need to be examined and analyzed within a multiyear context.

There have been particularly difficult discussions of the use of Fund resources in which objectives differ and may conflict: external adjustment comes in conflict with growth, or immediate growth comes in conflict with longer-term growth. I think that the most difficult discussions occur when the staff feels that the economic policies that the government is putting in place for the present may encourage growth in the very short run but discourage it in the longer run. Of course, most governments have a short time horizon and would like to maximize economic growth in the short run. They consequently give less attention to the implications of the policy mix on the longer-term growth prospects.

Regarding the debt strategy, about which there was considerable discussion, I would make a couple of observations. A lot of progress has been made since 1982, but at the same time there is no doubt— as is clear from many comments, including those of Mr. Reed—that serious problems remain. In the early days of the debt strategy there was a debate over whether debt was a liquidity problem or a structural problem. Over time, it has become clearer that is it not simply a liquidity problem but a fundamental structural problem. There exists what some call a debt overhang. I personally do not like the term "debt overhang" because it is as imprecise as the word "adjustment." I like the more specific formulation that the market value of the debt for many countries is well below the par or contract value of the debt.

I recall Mr. Reed saying that, yes, that is true, and indeed commercial bank investors and equity markets have discounted the difference between the market value of the underlying debt and its equity value. A return to more normal creditor relationships requires a closing-up of the market value and par value relationships. One key to solving the debt problem lies in identifying additional ways to reduce the gap between the two.

Another key is not to interfere with the normal market relationship between creditors and debtor countries with less serious debt problems.

Certainly, the management of economic policies within the debtor countries will contribute to the elimination over time of the gap between the market value and the contractual value of debt, but just as certainly other means must be developed. As I think many of those means need to be market oriented, I think that is the current challenge facing the official international community as well as the commercial bank community in closing the gap. For example, an exit bond may be viewed narrowly as a means of freeing smaller banks from the debt problem. It could also be viewed as a more general means of dealing with the debt overhang.

But with just those few comments, I would like to close.

Lal Jayawardena

Director
World Institute of Development Economics Research

I should like to focus my remarks on an issue that grew out of the debate, on the paper on the adjustment process in Latin America by Mr. Bianchi and his colleagues. Mr. Bianchi's introductory presentation emphasized the current mood of "adjustment weariness" in Latin America, where after a great deal of effort to improve the trade balance, a substantial *additional* effort is now required, which is, in fact, *greater* than the effort expended over the last five years in all countries except Brazil, Colombia, and Uruguay. He tended to rule out a significant additional *domestic* effort essentially on political grounds because of the import compression and expenditure cutbacks that had already taken place, which had driven per capita income generally well below 1980 levels; the only available solution, therefore, was to look to the procurement of additional external resources. Additional resources might be raised in several ways: lower interest rates, reversing capital flight, and new lending—and all of these were found wanting in the Latin American context. I had the feeling that Mr. Bianchi then rather reluctantly raised the issue of debt forgiveness in some form or another as being the last option available.

This promptly elicited a reaction from Mr. Kashiwagi, who asked how one could possibly entertain the thought of debt forgiveness at a time when one was seeking new lending from banks on the substantial scale that the situation warranted. We couldn't get to grips with that crucial issue at that session, but I would like to address it at this point.

The question is really whether we can have a form of debt forgiveness—noncommercial interest rates or partial cancellation of principal which will avoid, so to speak, a bankers' strike. Some of us have been working on a set of ideas, which Richard Carey alluded to in his presentation, namely, for redirecting a portion of Japan's current surplus away from financing the U.S. deficit to financing developing countries. The team that worked on these ideas comprised Dr. Arjun Sengupta, Dr. Saburo Okita, Chairman of The Board of The World Institute of Development Economics Research (WIDER) and a former Foreign Minister of Japan, and myself. I would like to offer this for consideration as an alternative to debt forgiveness together with a proposal developed by Mr. Hattori, a former comptroller of the World Bank and also a former Governor of the Bank of Rwanda.

As outlined personally to us, Mr. Hattori's approach was to wipe the slate clean, so to speak, of present debt, so that banks would then have a clear way ahead to resume lending. This proposal has obvious affinities with the well-known Kenen and Rohatyn proposals, but in my view has some particular attractions that justify a restatement at this stage.

The idea is very simple. One takes as a starting point the discount at which bank debt is currently trading and reckons that this would be equivalent to nonconcessional lending by banks at 4 percent interest over a 22-year maturity, including a 2-year grace period, with the difference that this discount is not now passed on to the debtor developing countries but is enjoyed by the purchasers of bank debt in the market. Supposing a facility were to be set up that would take over bank debt on just these terms and developing countries offered slightly harder terms at 4.5 percent over 20 years; this would provide a margin for meeting default up to 10 percent of all loans. Taking over developing country debt in this manner would be conditional on the adoption of an appropriate policy package; but the terms could be altogether attractive to both debtor and creditor and could clear the decks in a nondiscriminatory way to enable banks to resume lending.

As Dr. Sengupta and I were really in no position to react immediately to this proposal, we simply listed it as an example of something that might be considered at an appropriate time. But what struck me about that proposal, as I heard the discussion yesterday, was that it was the kind of *general* proposal that would make it difficult for the banking system to penalize any particular country seeking debt forgiveness in an ad hoc way.

I did some homework last night on Professor Sachs's ideas, which I think we all found extremely interesting. He had presented an earlier version of his paper in Helsinki to a conference held at WIDER in memory of Carlos Diaz-Alejandro, a well-known Latin American economist. Now what is interesting about that set of ideas is the following: The key to granting debt relief, he says, is to make it selective so that not every debtor country feels a need to suspend its international payments and so that the contractual basis for future international lending is not fundamentally undermined.

I think these ideas are important because all of us are now looking at selective debt relief as a way of keeping the process of new lending going. I think Professor Sachs's way has much to commend it, because his plan separates the heavily indebted Latin American countries from the less indebted ones. For the list of countries Professor Sachs read out very hurriedly at the end of his presentation, his plan would imply a loss of 15 percent of bank capital for the major U.S. banks and 5 percent of bank capital for all other U.S. banks. The proposal relates to the suspension of interest payment for only a five-year period to give the countries concerned the necessary breathing space to adjust, with the missed payments forgiven rather than capitalized.

I did some calculations according to Professor Sachs's formula, and the absolute magnitudes corresponding to these percentages turn out to be surprisingly low. Debt forgiveness à la Sachs means US$ 6.5 billion in the case of the major U.S. banks and rising to US$ 9.5 billion if all other U.S. banks are additionally brought in. As the proposal is couched in terms of a claim on bank capital, commercial banks are bound to share my worries about the precedent this might set. The crucial question is whether we are left with any other option.

If one looks at the problem in terms of recycling part of the Japanese surplus to developing countries, I suspect resource availability ought not, if the issue is imaginatively handled, to be too much of a problem.

I will not go into the WIDER proposal in detail, but what I simply want to note for the moment is that the Wharton Econometric Forecasting Associates' January 1987 report, entitled "Status Report: The Debtor Countries after the Debt Crisis," picks up the idea. Let me just say a word about their comments. They say, "A new opportunity for securing a net flow of funds back to the debtor countries may be on the horizon. Just as the need to recycle the petrodollar surplus in the 1970s led to a dramatic increase in lending, the Japanese current account surplus may now be the source of the next wave of new finance for the debtor countries."

Regarding the WIDER proposal which they christen, after the Chairman of the WIDER Board, the Okita plan, Wharton Econometric Forecasting Associates say that "in late December 1986 Japan appeared to be moving in the direction suggested by the Okita plan," and that the Japanese Government has "announced a program to recycle US$ 9 billion of their current account surplus to developing countries."

On this point, I have to take issue with Mr. Carey's way of describing the proposal. He sees no necessity for the structural current account surplus of Japan to persist. But if looked at in terms of Japanese savings behaviour, which is as high as 27 percent of GDP, there is doubt as to whether any reasonable degree of domestic expansion will absorb the greater part of these savings domestically. Given the level of savings, there are bound to be substantial amounts available for investment abroad in the form of current account surpluses despite domestic expansion.

The question is whether these surpluses can be diverted away from financing the U.S. deficit to financing the deficits of other nations. What has to be worked upon are the terms, conditions, and guarantees that will make that happen. One element of such a scheme might involve the use of part of Japan's official development assistance as an interest subsidy to provide annual lending that is a significant multiple of the subsidy. For example, an interest subsidy of only 4 percentage points would cost no more than US$ 400 million of official development assistance monies to generate lending of US$ 10 billion in the first year of an annual program of loans on this scale to developing countries; subsequent annual subsidy requirements would depend on the terms of lending.

Mamadou Touré

Minister of Economy and Finance
Senegal

Like Mr. de Groote, I would like to make remarks on the whole symposium, not only on the discussion yesterday when I was in the chair.

My first remark concerns the broad and unanimous consent on the propriety of the title of the symposium, Growth-Oriented Adjustment. Nobody questions that growth adjustment is the right thing to do now. This therefore constitutes an important step because it was not well recognized years ago. In his opening address, the Managing

Director indicated two extreme positions that have to be rejected in dealing with the subject. First, there is no inherent conflict between growth and adjustment. Second, growth does not automatically follow adjustment. The tone was set for our discussion by the papers presented by Mr. Michalopoulos and Mr. Guitián and the suggestion that we are confronted with a series of trade-offs or, according to some, with a false dilemma. I can cite some of the trade-offs.

Besides the one already mentioned and rejected by the Managing Director, the dilemma or the trade-off between adjustment and growth is the temporary use of Fund resources versus the medium-term loan needs of financing adjustment. Some see no distinction between the work of the Fund and that of the Bank in making short-term as opposed to long-term loans. I think this is broadly correct, although the resources of the Bank and the Fund are different. The Fund has short-term or medium-term resources at best, while the World Bank has long-term resources. Therefore, countries that are contemplating programs with the Fund and the Bank should know what is involved in use of Fund resources.

The Fund has a principle of revolving its resources over a period of time, which is sometimes short-term, sometimes medium-term. Is it advisable for a country to take on a Fund program to finance structural adjustment whose benefits will be derived only after a long period of time? This problem has arisen recently when, after the cycle of the Fund programs, some African countries were hard pressed to repurchase from the Fund. The distinction between short-term and long-term policies in the Fund and the Bank has to be taken into consideration when we are putting adjustment programs together.

Another dilemma or trade-off was signaled by several speakers: the trade-off between inflation and balance of payments growth. There is yet another. Can Turkey or Japan or Korea be considered a general model for other developing countries or are there as many models as there are developing countries? Some of the speakers seem to think so: Nations have just to take measures and to liberalize and then everything will be all right.

The address of Mr. Saracoglu gave hopes for solving situations that are desperate but not serious, as people used to say. In his country a bold package of important financial responses in support of a comprehensive structural adjustment program has led to success.

This may be so, but we have to take into consideration the environment and adapt to it the general scheme. The strategy of straitjacket cannot work. All of us in this room cannot wear the same jacket. In sum, though basic principles may be retained, we have to tailor programs to the particular environment of a country to achieve lasting progress.

Another false dilemma or trade-off lies in the sequence of action: stabilization first, then adjustment and growth, or together. Perhaps we should try to develop guidelines in this matter.

It is not right to expect growth in a destabilized economy. Therefore, in an economy that has been destabilized by fiscal and external imbalances, the first thing is to stabilize. One cannot build a building on unstable foundations. The same is true for economic management. Therefore, stabilization programs are essential, though the words to express such a program have changed over time: stabilization program, financial program, adjustment program. I believe the difference has to be made very clearly between stabilization, on one hand, and the other programs, on the other.

What do adjustment and growth mean? We don't have a definition of adjustment, but fortunately we have a definition of what structural adjustment is, in the *Manual of Operations* of the Bank, in Mr. Michalopoulos's paper. He defines structural adjustment lending as non-project lending to support programs of policy and essential change necessary to modify the structure of an economy so that it can maintain both its growth rate and the viability of its balance of payments in the medium term. Adjustment programs should aim at these objectives. I define the programs by their objectives. For the least-developed countries what is at stake is not only growth but development. If we are to speak about development-oriented adjustment, we would see the structural problems, the structural bottlenecks, and the necessary investment that has to be made in human resources and in infrastructure. Indeed, there can be growth without development. What we need is development and growth together.

I need just to say two words about the debt problem, which constitutes the most serious constraint on developing countries at this time. Here again, I would like to single out the IDA countries that negotiate with the Paris Club rather than with other creditors, that is, commercial banks. There are two categories of debt: debt that can be rescheduled, and debt that cannot and is mainly owed to multilateral institutions.

As to the first type, many countries have reached a level where there is no longer a possibility to reschedule. About 50 or 60 percent of the debt is not eligible for Paris Club rescheduling because it has already been rescheduled. Therefore, a certain limit has been reached.

As to the second type, much could be said about the shared responsibility between the parties concerned: the Bretton Woods Institutions, the private sector, and the governments. Each one has a role to play.

On the Bretton Woods side, we have to be very careful about how to enter programs. I wish to refer you to a quotation from an open letter to the President of the World Bank by Mr. Richard E. Feinberg in *Between Two Worlds, the World Bank's Next Decade*, "A long list of requirements either holds an entire program hostage to a secondary issue or is open to highly subjective assessment." I feel that the Bretton Woods Institutions should concentrate on the basic program, do some monitoring, and then leave to the countries the flexibility to attain their objectives.

One last point I only want to mention. For developing countries like ours, even if we make efforts to liberalize and to be outward oriented, we are confronted with low commodity prices. If the swings in the price of commodities make changes in our programs, they can offset the programs within one year and lengthen to three or four years the times required to adjust the economy.

T.P. Lankester

Executive Director
International Monetary Fund/World Bank

I would like to comment on some themes recurring at the session on external financing.

If there is one point on which practically everyone is agreed, it is that growth-oriented adjustment programs are a lot more likely to succeed if the countries concerned can obtain a reasonable flow of external finance. The form this should take for countries in different circumstances is becoming a matter of increasing debate: I will come back to it later in my remarks.

I am not going to try to say what would be a reasonable flow of finance. What one can say is that, for the major indebted countries, if the experience of the last two or three years—at least as regards commercial bank flows—were to be repeated for very much longer, those countries' growth and debt-servicing prospects would be fairly bleak.

In the case of the low-income sub-Saharan African countries, external financing has been reasonably maintained. In an ideal world, it would be desirable for it to be substantially increased. But since we are talking here largely about official financing, the prospects for such an increase are frankly not very great. The priority therefore has to be for donors and recipients to get better value—in developing terms—from the financing that is available.

With the greater emphasis now on institution building and on policy-based lending, my guess is that aid effectiveness is on an improving trend. But much needs to be done. It may sound tautologous, but aid to Africa will not be effective unless adjustment programs are well designed *and* determinedly implemented. An issue from the donors' side that must be addressed is the need to reduce the great burden that often-competing aid agencies place on fragile administrations. There may be a need to look at some aspects of Paris Club procedures, which also place a heavy burden on African administrations.

For the highly indebted middle-income countries, the central question is how to restore the flow of private external capital. The principles laid out by Secretary Baker, I believe, remain valid in the sense that growth-oriented policies and stepped-up lending by the multilateral development banks are necessary conditions for the resumption of private lending. But questions are beginning to be raised whether these conditions are sufficient.

John Reed has sought to identify one constraint when he argued that new lending is being held back by countries' insistence on non-market-related terms. It seems to me that there may be an element of truth in this. But there is a real question as to what market-related terms mean in a situation of nonspontaneous lending.

If we were back in the spontaneous lending phase with banks competing with each other for lending business, it would be possible to talk of "market terms." But as long as we are in the present concerted lending phase, the terms of any package seem bound to involve a certain amount of non-market- related or political bargaining. It may be that a particular package would be more easily put together with a higher spread. But what if the borrower walks away and decides instead to limit its debt-service payments?

But I do think that new bank lending might be better facilitated if borrowing countries were more sensitive to the requirements of the banks in other ways. The banking community might be more willing to provide new money if, for example, ways could be found to channel more of it directly to the private sector—though unless there are appropriate exchange rate and monetary policies in place, the relevant foreign exchange will not become available to the monetary authorities to help the governments in question meet their obligations. (This is another aspect of the fact that the private sector already has considerable net foreign exchange assets in many countries while governments are net debtors.) Debt equity conversion schemes and more encouragement for private direct investment, besides bringing in capital from non-bank sources, would also be welcomed by the banks without imposing necessarily undue costs on the borrowing country.

Maybe, too, the Bank and the Fund have to be more sensitive to the commerical banks' requirements. Instead of offering them financing packages almost fait accompli, perhaps the size and type of financing required in connection with Fund/Bank supported programs ought to be discussed at an earlier stage with the banks. The country concerned should be a party to these discussions.

There are some other questions. First, will the banks differentiate between "good" and "bad" debtors? Or will the good debtors be tainted in their relations with the banks by their bad neighbors? I suspect the answer at present is partly yes and no. It seems to me that it would be very much in their own interests if the banks were fully to recognize the good performers in Latin America.

Second, do the banks have adequate machinery and mechanisms? The problem of how to bring in, or take out, banks with small exposures is posing greater difficulties than ever. This is something the banks need to address. It has, for example, been suggested that some form of de minimis rule would enormously simplify new money negotiations and be bearable for the banks with large exposures.

It seems to me also that, with the different preferences and prejudices of individual banks, banks will need to be given (or give themselves) a range of options as to the form in which they offer new financing. For example, banks in some countries have expressed a preference for interest capitalization.

This brings us to the question of the form of finance that debtor countries would prefer. There are two major categories or forms of finance: those that add to debt (and debt servicing) and those that reduce the present value of existing debt such as write-offs and thereby provide savings on interest payments. The latter, as John Reed has stressed, could have major implications for access to sources of new finance, and the banking community as a whole seems very unenthusiastic. As well as the question of future access to external finance, there is the related question of whether countries would have as great an incentive to adjust. Nonetheless, some economists think there is scope for going down this road.

Some speakers referred to the absence of a default mechanism that might enable countries with extremely high debt ratios to limit their debt-service payments, at least for a while, without causing lasting damage to themselves or to their creditors. Except for some vague references to the 1930s, I am not clear what such a mechanism might consist of in today's circumstances. But one related concept that was mentioned perhaps needs to be explored further. This is the idea of subordinating old bank debt for new. Is this feasible? Since it may involve write-offs, could it not create great difficulties for the banks?

The Bank and Fund will need to go on playing an active catalytic role in bringing new money packages together. The Bank and the other multilateral development banks will need to be a substantial net provider of funds. But Richard Carey in his paper rightly warned against the Bank's exposure rising too fast relative to other creditors. If the banks are unwilling to lend, and the World Bank lends more instead, sooner or later its credit rating is going to suffer, with possible consequences for other borrowers and shareholders. For the same reason, a massive increase in World Bank guarantees is not the answer.

One final point. There is a tendency these days for people to say that the case-by-case strategy enunciated by Secretary Baker won't work. I believe that is a premature judgment. No doubt there need to be modifications at the edges, some of which I have referred to. But in my view the basic strategy remains the best strategy the debtors and creditors have.

Jacques de Groote

Executive Director
International Monetary Fund/World Bank

Mr. Chairman, when we discussed in the Boards of the Fund and the World Bank the possibility of this symposium, several of my colleagues expressed serious doubts as to the usefulness of such an exercise. But, on the whole, I think these doubts were not founded if we look at the experience of these last hours.

During the brief interludes you left us for social contacts, I tried to gather some reactions of my colleagues in the two Boards and in the staff, and I think it is almost unanimously recognized that the exposure to high-level outside criticism is timely, especially on the topics that are central in growth-oriented adjustment programs, such as export-led outward-looking strategies and exchange rate activism.

I will center my remarks, therefore, not only on what was said during my panel but on what I feel could be the experience of that symposium for those who have to follow Fund and Bank business on an everyday basis.

Let me first say that I am sure I shall not be the only one to feel the need to be more cautious or more humble, to use the word that was used a lot during this meeting, in the day-to-day sort of elaboration and examination of Fund and Bank programs.

For instance, we will be very careful, I think, in examining whether the case we have before us is one of export promotion or one of trade liberalization, and I think it will easily be recognized that there are specific situations in which it might be appropriate to start fresh with a period of export promotion before attempting to liberalize the countries' trade and payments across the board.

Almost all participants here now recognize that it is imperative to assess the results in terms of growth that are expected from trade liberalization by taking into account the budgetary situation and the distribution of income. The Fund and the Bank programs might usefully incorporate those relationships more explicitly. We also will have to make sure that the notions of budgetary deficit used in our different deliberations and documents reflect best the development preoccupations, and it is anyway always useful to have a word with

Mr. Tanzi about it to know whether the notion we deal with is the appropriate one.

The discussions also gave many good reasons for helping us to avoid exchange rate dogmatism and to check even more carefully whether accompanying measures and external circumstances justify the rate adjustments recommended by the staff. Staff is perhaps oversensitive in using this instrument, which is within the Fund's province, because it has witnessed with professional despair the massive appreciation in real terms of the currencies of the poorest countries that remained pegged to the U.S. dollar when the dollar rose during the early 1980s.

I think we also might become in the future a little more cautious in referring candidates for adjustment programs to the model cases. Turkey and Korea no doubt responded to the adopted policies in the expected way, and the financial markets responded to the quality of the programs. But it was probably because of the special circumstances and especially the political will in those countries that those policies were successful.

It is a salutary exercise to keep those good examples in mind as a distant image because in our day-to-day business we almost never have to deal with such ideal cases, which, by the way, appear more ideal when you look at them afterwards.

In many of those countries the philosophy and managerial capabilities are not always conducive to broadly oriented strategy. Therefore, we have to deal with situations that are halfway in between, shadowy, and for which we have to look for approximative solutions that do not perfectly fit ideal models.

I think it is also useful that attention was drawn to the need to look at adjustment programs over a somewhat longer perspective than one year and to try to see how we can build up multi-year approaches, which are already part and parcel of many of the Fund's and, of course, of the Bank's activities. It is also useful that attention be drawn to the sequence of reforms. Should one start first with stabilization? Should a country attempt to start at the same time with stabilization and supply expansion?

The symposium made me also understand better how the representation of Fund and Bank activities is lagging unavoidably behind practices. For instance, the notion of growth-oriented adjustment— and it is useful perhaps to mention this—didn't find its way into

Fund programs on the occasion of the Baker Plan nor is it predominantly embodied in the Structural Adjustment Facility. It was nevertheless already fully recognized many years ago, especially when we implemented the Extended Fund Facility, and Turkey in that respect led the way.

I remember vividly the discussions I had with Mr. Ozal, who was at that time the Chief Economic Adviser of the Turkish Government. He was vividly aware that durable correction of the balance of payments could not be obtained only through action on the supply side. The elimination of price controls and subsidies and the dismantling of state economic enterprises were essential ingredients of a program aimed from the outset at achieving a relatively high rate of growth. Turkey was also the first case for which we developed medium-term balance of payments projections, trying to look beyond the annual segmentation.

And on the Bank side, where growth is obviously a direct preoccupation, the integration of stabilization elements in development programs as a precondition for their success has been a growing concern for the last, say, eight or nine years. I would say that the Bank and even the Bank Board have developed some expertise in that regard, and there is now a general practice of trying to assess development strategies of member countries not only when they propose for approval non-project-related loans but also on the occasion of the discussion of projects. Moreover, in the general discussion of the development strategies of a country, the implementation by a country of a stabilization program is generally taken as one of the basic elements for the success in the medium term of the Bank's own development objectives.

Both Boards have now the benefit of the presence of staff members of the other Board. Consequently, the discussion in the Bank Board of stabilization aspects and the discussion in the Fund Board of growth aspects are now, I would say, day-to-day business. I cannot recall one single program for low-income countries in the Fund during the last two or three years in which the issue of growth was not discussed at length and in great detail, and I think we have tried to consider also more specific subjects, such as sectoral priorities or the development of local savings.

Of course, this is far from an easy exercise in day-to-day business because in many cases countries come indeed very late to the Fund so that the stabilization has to precede growth ambitions. And a long time is often needed, as was pointed out by Mr. Stern, before the growth effects can be perceived.

Another interesting fact relating to the topics that have been discussed during the symposium is the Fund's explicit acceptance that the country's income evolution and export proceeds should explicitly be taken into consideration at least once in a while, and for some countries in the definition of their access to Fund resources. The Mexican case came about not as a result of a discussion of principles but, as is often the case, in a pragmatic way. This case has been already discussed in the Board in a broad way, and several colleagues and myself have examined the possibility of trying to consider more explicitly in Fund programs the evolution of a country's income and export proceeds.

Now trying to reconcile in everyday practice business growth and development preoccupations raises a number of basic problems and difficulties, on which it might be useful to center attention, and which could perhaps be taken as subjects for further reflection in another symposium. I am thinking, first of all, of the problem of the duration and the size of the assistance given by the Fund in combination with the World Bank. Of course, as Mr. Finch pointed out, the Fund is a trustee of repayable money and thus has to be careful that that money is reconstituted in due time. It must never be forgotten that the counterpart of that lending is reserves for the countries whose currency is used, reserves that have to remain liquid. It is an erroneous notion of the Fund's liquidity to consider only the use made of its resources by developing countries. Those countries that provide reserves do so in the full expectation that they are liquid at all times.

How can we reconcile that obvious liquidity preoccupation with the need to assist countries using Fund resources during a time sufficiently long for supply effects to manifest themselves? Do we have to consider lending over longer periods? Is this compatible with the Fund's role? Can we develop closer forms of cooperation with the Bank so that countries would have the certainty that they can count on financial assistance for a certain period? And how far would that also be helpful for the country to develop better relations with the banking community, which also in its turn has to know for how long the country can have the benefit of Fund assistance under appropriate conditions?

Another interesting issue that we might discuss is the adaptation to the circumstances of Fund policies on the use of Fund resources. It was decided that the policy of enlarged access to Fund resources had to be considered as temporary and had to be dismantled over time. And the dismantling or the stabilization of the policy of access to Fund resources had been pursued irrespective of the evolution of countries' export prices and income.

Are there ways for circumventing in that way the distribution of quotas? You have seen Mr. Fekete's proposals in that respect. He thinks of an allocation, the proceeds of which could be used for debt stabilizaton purposes. Others have thought of allocations that could be retransferred by industrial countries to the Fund for assisting programs, either the Fund's general programs or programs of the Mexican type.

Another interesting topic that I might briefly raise is why we haven't referred more to the experience of industrial countries. We gave all the time the impression that the Fund is only concerned with developing countries, and it is true that only developing countries are the Fund's customers now. But many industrial countries follow shadow programs under Fund guidance and monitoring. Belgium is an obvious case where the stabilization program introduced in 1982 continues to be monitored by the Fund and where every year the government reports to the public and to Parliament on the basis of the Fund's report.

For those countries, growth was also an important issue. And the Fund managed to advise an important transfer of resources from households to enterprises and from households to the government. Shouldn't we consider more explicitly the experience of industrial countries as it results from the daily consultation with those countries in the Fund Board?

Another issue is whether we shouldn't think of financing more explicitly countries involved in systemic changes, a country that, for instance, steps over from a dirigiste economy to a market economy. Does that country have a way to use Fund resources, and could it justify that use by the effects of such policy on its balance of payments?

The last issue that I think we might also usefully consider is how to associate better the banking community. I am not too sure that I followed completely Mr. Reed's suggestion at the end of his very stimulating exposé. Is there a way to give to the banks more information than what they have already? He definitely gave the impression that the banks learn at the last minute what is happening. I have some reservations about the interpretation. I think all along the Fund and the World Bank are very careful to inform the banking community. It is a matter of responsibility more for the country to try to maintain appropriate relations with possible lenders.

Jacques J. Polak
Financial Consultant

The title of this symposium, Growth-Oriented Adjustment Programs, was not chosen by accident. It correctly conveys the joint challenge of the Fund and Bank. Certainly the two main aims of the organizers of this conference are to come to a balanced view of the interrelationship between adjustment and growth, and to present evidence of a meeting of minds between the Fund and the Bank on how they should discharge their respective responsibilities in this area.

The presentation during the first session from the side of the institutions was helpful in setting this process in motion. Substantially, the message of the Fund's Managing Director was that adjustment and growth are both attainable and can reinforce one another. He started out by rejecting two simplistic propositions: that adjustment inherently conflicts with growth, and that growth follows automatically from adjustment. The rejection of this second simplistic proposition is not recent. It dates back over 25 years to the 1961 Annual Meeting in Vienna, when the then Managing Director, Per Jacobsson, stressed that "to introduce monetary stability is often only the beginning of the efforts needed to achieve growth. While the subsequent efforts largely fall outside the sphere of Fund activities, the Fund does not underrate their importance and, insofar as it can, is anxious to assist these efforts in every possible way." The Managing Director elaborated on his basic propositions by emphasizing that "the extent to which adjustment is conducive to growth depends in good measure on the quality of adjustment." From my own experience in the Fund and from discussions with former colleagues, I feel able to add that these views (and their elaboration) represent views held by the Fund Board and the Fund staff generally.

The paper by Mr. Michalopoulos conveyed a similar message. It reflected on most issues a highly pragmatic, eclectic approach, with the broad message that a judicious combination of policies (dealing in particular with demand management, exchange rates and other prices, and liberalization), plus a certain amount of foreign financing, can attain over the medium term the objectives of adjustment and growth. Mr. Michalopoulos acknowledges that in the short run a slowdown in growth is almost a prerequisite for successful stabilization.

Mr. Guitián's paper focused on the constraints that adjustment poses on economic policymakers. There is a great deal of empirical validity in many statements in that paper. Thus, there are, unfortunately, far too many examples in the Fund's experience of countries that opt for delayed or mitigated adjustment on the grounds that this is necessary to maintain growth and that usually grow neither now nor later but are forced into harsher adjustment later. Similarly, when growth is maintained by expansionary demand policies financed by foreign borrowing or by using up reserves, the end result is frequently a more painful adjustment later and less growth over the medium term.

These observations from experience suggest that there are limits, indeed rather narrow limits, on the extent to which adjustment can be traded off against growth, even with the best possible use of a wide range of demand and supply policies and a prudent use of foreign savings. But it is going too far to say that there is *no* trade-off between adjustment and growth, or that an accurate short way to describe the role of foreign borrowing, if one wants to put it in a nutshell, is that foreign borrowing "can make it temporarily possible for domestic demand and the rate of growth to reach levels beyond those that the economy can sustain." I am sure that Mr. Guitián would not disagree with these observations.

There has been further widespread support in this conference— and here I quote again from the Managing Director—for country-specific program designs in a medium-term framework and hence against inflexible precooked policy packages. If these are, as I believe, the broad views both of our guests and of the two institutions on the question of adjustment with growth, I think we have a common basis for Fund and Bank work in this area.

Richard N. Cooper

Professor of Economics
Harvard University

I could ease all of your pain, I suppose, by simply thanking you all for coming to this symposium and calling it to a conclusion. I will not try to summarize the conference, but I would like to comment on several themes of the conference and some of the character of the discussion.

First, I am going to begin in an academic way on the tiresome but necessary topics of nomenclature and methodology. We simplify complex matters in order to comprehend them and designate the generalizations with simple labels in order to economize language. But that process runs the risk that the labels may become slogans. Words such as "liberalization" and "privatization" and "adjustment and growth" may become slogans used by both proponents and opponents of particular courses of action. If this happens, the debate can occur without sufficient refinements and therefore without being really joined. We need to remind ourselves that such terms are not well defined and are not monolithic.

One of the nice things about economics is that it rarely dichotomizes cleanly, but rather has continuous gradations and therefore gives rise both to subtle distinctions and to possibilities for compromise. That is especially true of such terms as "liberalization," to which I will return below.

Methodology concerns how we learn. Policymakers are rightly skeptical about acting on the basis of purely theoretical reasoning. They distrust models and the conclusions of models. They want to know what experience has taught us. But when experience contains apparent lessons that they do not like, they have to resort to subterfuge, identifying the experience as valid for only a special period of time, or as a special and unique case not applicable to the circumstances that they are currently interested in. This typically leaves us in a quandary. If we reject models and we reject experience as too special or unique to be relevant to our task at hand, how do we learn? Too often such rejections leave us and the policymakers to wing it or to rely on preconceived notions, which in fact involve implicit models typically far less well developed than the models that have been rejected.

We have to draw a model, as Professor Fischer underlined strongly in his paper, to a consistent framework for looking at the problem at hand. We must also draw on experience, the past experience of our own country or of other countries, which is far richer in detail than any model can be. But both the model and the experience have to be strongly tempered with judgment to bring them to bear on the particular problem. Judgments will legitimately differ as to the precise relevance of models or experience to the problem at hand, which will always have some unique features; but drawing on models and experience helps to isolate the unique features and force an evaluation of their importance. We should listen carefully to the experience of other countries, even when the circumstances seem quite different, because of the lessons they might offer to our particular country and our particular set of circumstances.

I turn now to some of the themes of the symposium, starting with stabilization and liberalization. There was wide consensus that sta-bilization is a necessary condition for growth. Sustained growth year in and year out is not possible if the macroeconomic environment is constantly disrupted. So stabilization is a necessary condition, al-though we did not define precisely what we meant by it and, in particular, whether it encompassed a steady rate of inflation. I suspect opinion would differ quite sharply on the question of whether steady inflation year in and year out would or would not undermine growth. It is noteworthy that formal monetary models all-but-universally have the property that steady, anticipated inflation can have at most negligible impact on economic efficiency and growth. As Professor Sachs noted in his paper, Japan had inflation—the numbers sound small now in comparison with what has happened in the last decade— of 6 to 7 percent a year measured by the consumer price index right through the mid-1960s, a rate far higher than that in other OECD countries. (As was pointed out, there is a serious problem of measurement, and the choice of measure must be guided by the use to which it is to be put: the consumer price index is inappropriate for calculating real exchange rates.) Clearly, however, highly erratic inflation creates all kinds of problems. So I have open the question of exactly what we mean by stabilization, except to note the general consensus that a stable macroeconomic environment is necessary for growth.

I sensed more disagreement on whether liberalization was necessary either for stabilization or for growth. Mr. Finch pointed out that at least one form of liberalization is necessary for stabilization; namely, if you want to reduce absorption without running the economy into a recession, you have to substitute external demand for internal demand. So at least to that extent there is a link between them. One can identify other links between both liberalization and growth, but I did not sense any consensus on this issue.

Even if liberalization is not necessary for either stabilization or growth, it may be thought to be desirable. It is a well-known phenomenon that on difficult matters governments act more decisively in a period of crisis than in a period of calm, perhaps on the principle that if something is not broken, don't fix it. There is therefore a temptation for those who believe that liberalization is desirable for a variety of reasons to use a stabilization crisis to shoe-horn liberalization in. This is quite understandable, but it requires a refined political judgment to decide whether that is merely taking advantage of an opportunity that might not otherwise come, or overloading the system.

As I suggested, it is necessary to distinguish between different types of liberalization to make clear that liberalization can be viewed as a process rather than a state and to disassociate liberalization from laissez-faire. In liberalization, I see two elements. The first is getting prices closer than they were to efficiency prices; the second, equally important, is allowing economic agents to make decisions on the basis of those prices. By emphasizing the first element, one can have a lot of liberalization and still remain far from laissez-faire.

Liberalization has different dimensions, and it is worthwhile for completeness to identify six of them. The first dimension concerns the market for domestic goods and services. Two aspects of that, state enterprises and agriculture, generated considerable discussion in the symposium. A second dimension is external goods and services. That, in turn, has two sub-components: exports (getting export industries focused on world prices) and imports. A third dimension is the domestic financial system (interest rates and credit markets). Fourth is the link with the international financial system (the nature and extent of capital controls). A fifth dimension is the domestic labor market (whether or not there are wage controls). And sixth, for completeness, is the link of labor to the rest of the world—whether there are controls on immigration or emigration. When we talk about liberalization, we do not have to give equal weight to all these dimensions, but to avoid misunderstanding it is necessary to be clear about which kind of liberalization we are talking about in each particular instance.

We did not discuss these dimensions in detail, but two general points of consensus seemed to come out. The first was that, insofar as one can say anything at all, external financial liberalization, the fourth dimension in my list, should follow, perhaps by a long distance, other forms of liberalization. At least there was not dissent from that view. Other distortions elsewhere in the economy will provoke a socially unwarranted outflow of domestic capital, or, conceivably, an inflow of capital that is not in the country's best long-run interests.

Second, whatever is done with the rest of the economy, it is important to get export prices right. Liberalization is this sense is important for growth. That leaves open lots of topics that we either did not discuss at all or on which there seemed to be substantial disagreement, such as, for example, somewhat to my surprise, agricultural prices. There seemed to be disagreement on the propositions that Professor Johnson put forward. One thing we can be sure about is that import substitution as a source of growth for most countries—the United States, the U.S.S.R., China, and India might be exceptions—has distinct quantitative limitations. A country experiences a rapid spurt while it is first substituting domestic production for imports, but once that process is more or less complete, future growth industry by industry is limited to the rate of growth in domestic demand, and that is generally not very high for most industries. Countries that want industrial growth beyond that limitation must rely on export markets. This is a very simple model, but it is quantitatively understandable. Even so populous a country as Indonesia before the first oil shock had a domestic market for manufactured goods about the size of Norway's. That exemplifies how import substitution as a growth strategy is distinctly limited for most countries, and how some kind of export orientation is necessary.

As Professor Bhagwati pointed out, there are semantic ambiguities in the expression "export orientation." Ten years ago it meant reducing bias against exports moving back toward neutrality. As

Professor Sachs and others pointed out, however, in the historical experience of some countries it actually meant much more that that—active and aggressive support for exports, a bias in favor of exports. Again terminology is an issue: we should be clear on what exactly we are talking about.

I will make two other observations on liberalization. One is that while liberalization is not the same as laissez-faire and while everyone seemed to agree that there is an important role for government, we do have one example that we can draw on for what lessons we can learn about laissez-faire, namely Hong Kong. Hong Kong is a minimal state, a law-and-order state with a British sense of rectitude and a Chinese sense of commercial integrity, and it has been enormously successful. Unique, everyone would say. Certainly every country is unique, but nonetheless it is worth noting that laissez-faire is not an obviously absurd strategy, nor a guarantee of failure to develop. At least in certain circumstances it has been notably successful.

The other point I would make is that we have talked mostly about developing countries. Two weeks ago I was in New Zealand, a small, high-income country, which 30 years ago was toward the high end of the range OECD countries in terms of per capita income. Last year it was at the low end of the range in terms of per capita income. This country has been highly dirigiste over the last 30 years, and its per capita income has slipped quite markedly—an example of Professor Fischer's non-convergence. The new Labor government has moved strongly toward liberalization of the whole economic system. Most of that liberalization is focused on domestic markets so far, but it includes some external liberalization as well. It is too early to pronounce a judgment on the outcome of these policies. I mention them because as are talking about not only problems of developing countries but of developed countries as well, and there is considerable experience that can be drawn on.

Where liberalization involves the external sector, especially trade, historical experience suggests that it is a lot easier to liberalize in the context of a major inflow of resources. Professor Sachs pointed to the cases of the Taiwan Province of China and the Republic of Korea in the early 1960s. We heard about the case of Turkey in the early 1980s. I might add the case of Indonesia in the late 1960s and early 1970s. In all these cases a liberalization program was undertaken with a substantial inflow of external resources to tide the country over a difficult transition period in which it might experience a surge of imports. As Governor Bruno pointed out, the surge in imports might not occur, but it is nice to have the funds available in case a surge does occur so as to provide credibility to the program. Chile and Brazil also had heavy injections of funds in the context of liberalization programs in the late 1960s, and these programs unraveled in the course of time. So there is not assurance of success; other elements must have accompanied them. But matters go easier if foreign funds are available to backstop, and that is something for the international community to keep in mind.

On external debt, the issue here is the dead hand of the past, which it would be advantageous to remove, as a number of participants mentioned, but it is difficult to do so without jeopardizing the future. I think I speak for most of us in expressing pleasure and surprise at how flexible at least one leading commercial bank seems to be on the range of issues involved in debt, as reflected in Mr. Reed's remarks yesterday afternoon. He seemed to suggest that the rigidities in the debt renegotiations are not all on the side of the banks; they are elsewhere in the system. That may not be entirely true, but it is worth taking note of to make sure that where the banks are willing to be flexible, others in the system, be they American or European officials, or officials of the Fund, are equally flexible.

We had a brief discussion of the possible parallel between private and sovereign debtors; the point was made that excessive private debts often involve write-downs, although Mr. Kashiwagi said the analogy did not apply to countries. It is another one of those analogies that is suggestive but applies imperfectly to countries. I would suggest that the mechanism that we have established in the Paris and London Clubs linked to a Fund program is the surrogate in the realm of sovereign debt for the court-appointed receiver in the case of a private debt. Where purely private negotiation fails, the old management is literally taken out of the firm before liquidation, before write-down of the debt, and court-appointed management is put into the firm, often as a prelude to both reorganization and to a write-down of debt.

It is hard to push this analogy to its extreme in the case of sovereign debts, but the Fund is in the unhappy but necessary role of being the analog of a court-appointed receiver who tries to work out a viable reorganization of a debtor country's economic policy.

One final substantive point, and it surprised me that it was not given more emphasis, although Mr. Carey addressed it, concerns the problem of aggregation for the world as a whole. Policies that seem sensible and straightforward for one country or three or even ten, may not be perfectly straightforward if applied to 50 or 60 countries, because they form a big enough group to influence the environment in which the adjustment is taking place.

To bring this point into the present, let me remind you of the current U.S. trade deficit of $150 billion, which everyone claims must be reduced substantially. A program is underway to do that. There has been a sharp devaluation of the dollar. The forecast for the U.S. GNP for the coming two years shows a substantial part of the modest growth, 2.5–3 percent, coming from a major turnaround in U.S. net exports. That forecast may, of course, not come to pass; but if it does, that is the environment in which we are asking the developing countries to push their exports very hard. With a sharp reduction in the U.S. trade dificit, and indebted developing countries striving to increase their net exports, there will have to be a large reduction in the net exports of Europe and Japan.

It is especially incumbent on the Bank and the Fund to take the global environment into account when they work out policy packages with individual countries. There is perhaps an implicit assumption that of 20 arrangements with 20 countries, only 2 will really work and the other 18 will fail for various reasons. This seems to be a bad operating assumption on which to base programs.

So much for substantive remarks. Let me close by saying that a common theme has run through the conference, and that is while general principles are all very well they have to be adjusted to the diverse circumstances of individual countries. There was general agreement on that. That raises the question of whether the Fund and the World Bank staffs, and in particular the teams sent out to individual countries, are capable of doing this. Are there enough team leaders who are seasoned, sensible people of sound judgment, able to make a general framework, which must be common framework in institutions such as these, and adapt it subtly and creatively to the circumstances of the individual country? This is of great importance. The team leaders are the equivalent of ambassadors and have to be skillful diplomats we well as first-rate analysts with the flexibility to adapt general principles to local circumstances.

Finally, this conference has relied mainly on generalities. There have been few concrete suggestions. Mr. Cline gave some this morning on debt. Mr. Sengupta gave one that I especially like regarding the Fund's gold. This gold serves no useful purpose sitting there with a market value of over $400 an ounce and book value of $42 an ounce. We should sell some of it, as was done in the 1970s, and use the capital gains for constructive purposes.

Apart from a very few concrete suggestions, we have coasted on generalizations, and in a way it is too bad the conference is not beginning now. We have become used to one another's styles. We have moved the generalizations out of the way, and the really constructive work involves getting down to operational details. What exactly do we do about debt? What exactly do we do in particular circumstances, taking the general environment into account?

I will bring this conference to a close by thanking and congratulating the World Bank and the Fund for holding what I understand to be the first joint conference that they have held since Bretton Woods, and urge them to hold more. So the symposium is adjourned.

Address

Korea's Adjustment Policies and Their Implications for Other Countries

Kim Mahn Je
Deputy Prime Minister
Republic of Korea

I would like to begin by thanking the World Bank and the International Monetary Fund for inviting me as the guest speaker this evening on the occasion of the Bank/Fund Joint Symposium on Growth-Oriented Adjustment Programs. In 1980, I was here in Washington, then as the President of the Korea Development Institute, with a policy proposal package for Korea's first structural adjustment loan. I am both personally honored and proud to be here again some seven years later to tell Korea's success story on structural adjustment.

In these times of rapid technological changes and growing importance of world trade, countries that undergo slow changes in their structures in investment, production, or consumption are bound to face inefficiencies in their economies. When structural adjustment efforts designed to eliminate or minimize these inefficiencies are delayed, a country could experience slow economic growth, widening trade imbalance, or rising inflation.

In recent years, on the one hand, we see developing countries that suffer from balance of payments deficits and a growing debt burden, while on the other hand, there are developed countries concerned about either large trade deficits or surpluses. I do not believe that there is any country that does not know *what* efforts are required for structural adjustment. It is the *how* that poses the problem. This is because structural adjustments in any country involve a process of

---

Note: The text of this address, delivered before an invited audience on February 26, appeared in *Korea's Economy* (Washington), Vol. 3, No. 2 (April 1987), pp. 3–6.

difficult and painful compromise between interests of various groups in society for the good of the nation as a whole.

I would like to spend a few minutes with you discussing Korea's experience with structural adjustment in the 1980s and its implications for the current problems in other developing countries.

Structural adjustment in Korea has, in fact, been a continuous process over the past quarter of a century. Since Korea undertook its First Five-Year Development Plan in 1962, the process has involved a series of policy and institutional reforms aimed at shifting the economy from an inward-looking model of development to an outward orientation. Today, however, I will focus my remarks on Korea's more recent experiences in the 1980s.

During the past six years, Korea has been able to regain its growth momentum, reduce its inflation rate, and improve its balance of payments position significantly. The Korean Government's approach to adjustment had three prongs: stabilization, promotion of market efficiency, and balanced growth.

Stabilization naturally received the greatest attention. In 1980, Korea registered a current account deficit of $5.3 billion, or 9 percent of the GNP, and annual wholesale price increases reached almost 40 percent. Under such circumstances, painful structural adjustment involving a certain amount of belt tightening for everyone was inevitable in order to reduce inflation and improve the balance of payments position.

With inflation soaring, the government concentrated on using macroeconomic tools—a conservative monetary policy and tight fiscal measures—to restrain aggregate demand. In particular, the Government saw fiscal restraint as a key to price stability and concentrated on reducing the public sector deficit.

The fiscal restraint has had greater effect than what textbooks tell us about controlling inflation; it had the important side effect of promoting a spirit of frugality in the whole society. When the Government voluntarily froze the salaries of its civil servants at one point, workers agreed to lower wage increases without serious complaints, and farmers tolerated smaller increases in grain procurement prices.

Nevertheless, as in every country, reductions in government programs entailed significant political risks, meeting strong resistance from groups of people that suffered directly from the cutbacks.

Positive effects, meanwhile, were widespread and indirect. The Korean Government tried to tackle this dilemma through a public information campaign and discussion programs, rather than yielding to political pressures.

Introducing new discipline in monetary management has not been an easy task, either. Excessive monetary growth in the 1970s led the nation's businessmen to take measures to hedge against inflation. They had always tried to increase bank borrowings in order to purchase real assets that would increase in value without inflation. Stable prices and the spirit of social frugality, however, have gradually changed the businessmen's attitude toward and patterns of investment financing, and the Korean Government has been able to contain annual monetary growth from 30 percent in the late 1970s to around a 15 percent level in more recent years.

The success of the stabilization program has been outstanding. The rate of consumer price increase fell dramatically, and it has been in the 2–3 percent range since 1983. The balance of payments also continued to improve, finally turning the nation into a surplus country in 1986 for the first time in history.

Notwithstanding the success of our stabilization program, we were not single minded about stability, for it was clear that drastic measures would have been politically unsustainable. Therefore, at least a 5 percent growth rate was maintained during the recession years, and the average growth rate turned out to be 7–8 percent between 1981 and 1985. Of course, our foreign debt increased substantially as a result during this period. In short, achieving stability was necessarily a step-by-step process, with flexibility built into policy formulation and implementation.

The second major feature of our adjustment strategy was improving efficiency through the promotion of market competition. Externally, the Government reduced barriers to imports and foreign investment; domestically, it fostered competition by introducing anti-monopoly and fair trade legislation, denationalizing commercial banks, and simplifying regulations on private sector activities. In short, the market mechanism was strongly emphasized over government intervention in every facet of economic decision making.

Policymakers in many developing countries, when faced with balance of payments difficulties, are always tempted to increase government intervention either to promote new export industries or to support import-substituting industries. Korea was no exception. During the 1970s, the Korean Government promoted the development of heavy and chemical industries with many tax and financial incentives. The result was gross misallocation of resources and increased dependence on the government by private entrepreneurs.

This valuable lesson led the policymakers in Korea to adopt a market-oriented liberalization program in the early 1980s. As a result, businessmen strengthened their efforts to diversify their products, improve quality, and increase investment in technological development. Consequently, investment in R&D has doubled in the last five years, from 1 percent of GNP to a 2 percent level, and this increase was mostly due to private sector investment. Enhanced competitiveness because of price instability and technological development enabled Korea to increase its exports and finally to achieve a trade surplus last year.

The improvement in the balance of payments position has also enabled Korea to begin reducing its external debt, which stood at $47 billion at the end of 1985. Equally important, the liberalization of imports has had few of the dire effects predicted by its critics. By and large, competition has forced domestic firms to increase their efficiency, in some cases so successfully that they are now ready to begin exporting.

The third major goal of structural adjustment in the early 1980s was more balanced growth of the economy. As the Korean economy was reaping the fruits of structural adjustment, balanced growth became another important task. This is because, if disparities continue to widen between big cities and rural areas, large and small businesses, and income groups, the Government could not expect cooperation from a wide range of people, and structural adjustment efforts would not be sustainable.

The most important task facing the Government was reducing the income gap between urban areas and the countryside. Although the gap was narrowing, further improvements were delayed because stabilization policy necessarily involved limiting agricultural price increases and reducing farm subsidies. In order to promote rural development, the Government introduced the idea of agro-industrial complexes and encouraged small and medium-size businesses to locate their plants in rural areas. This helped create employment opportunities and non-farm income sources for farmers.

Balanced regional growth and income distribution, as well as more even development of large and small firms, are long-term goals. The Korean Government will place top priority on this area in the next several years, now that price stability and the balance of payment improvements have been achieved.

Many lessons may be drawn from the Korean experience of the last seven or eight years, but I will concentrate on those that strike me as most applicable to other developing nations.

The broadest lesson concerns the basic conditions of achieving structural adjustment. The Korean experience shows that, in order to undertake successful adjustment programs, we need flexibility in policy choices, social adaptability to new policies, and strong political commitment to structural reforms.

Flexibility in policy choices, and effective and expeditious policy coordination are very important, because international and domestic environments constantly change. If policies do not adjust effectively and rapidly enough to accommodate changing conditions, structural reforms cannot be sustained. In Korea, a unique institutional setting in which an agency called the Economic Planning Board encompasses planning, budgeting, and coordination functions, turned out to be very effective in coordinating economic policies.

In addition to flexibility, consensus should be established among various economic players in the society with respect to policy direction. If these players constantly resist or are nonconforming to government policies and programs, it is obvious that structural adjustment cannot succeed. Above all, however, strong political leadership is needed to guide the nation in the right direction for structural adjustment. Structural adjustment is, after all, sacrificing specific group interests for national interests or sacrificing short-term for long-term goals. Such programs cannot be pursued satisfying every interest group.

Let me now say a few words about general policy lessons from the Korean experience in the context of the continuing Third World debt problem. Broadly speaking, I believe that the developing debtor nations should focus their adjustment efforts on three areas: stabilization based on monetary and fiscal restraint to achieve price stability, reforms in the public sector to minimize waste and increase efficiency, and industrial policies that stress less government intervention and promote the working of the market mechanism.

Fiscal restraint, in addition to helping stabilize prices, will have the effect of transferring more resources to the private sector and enhancing government credibility. This will also create a favorable environment for implementing income policies. Structural deficits incurred by public corporations, which are among the most vexing problems in many developing countries, should be corrected through reduction of government subsidies and price rationalization. A one-time increase in prices will far outweigh the costs of continuously rising government subsidies in future years, however difficult the political realities may be for such reforms. Above all, private initiatives should be promoted, and government intervention discouraged as much as possible, in all investment decisions. Businessmen should be allowed to make their own decisions according to market signals.

A program that combines stabilization, public sector reforms, and reduced government intervention will definitely achieve positive results, particularly when the basic conditions, which I mentioned earlier, prevail. Among other things, it would greatly increase domestic savings, promote greater investment efficiency, and bring about balance of payment surpluses to repay external debts.

In addition to these internal measures, trade policies of the debtor countries deserve closer inspection. Often, the inclination of developing-country policymakers in the midst of economic crisis is to close markets to competition, in the hopes of protecting domestic industry and reducing the external payments deficit. This is a vain hope, however. In the long run, adding barriers to the domestic market will only lead to deteriorating export competitiveness, thereby worsening the external balance. Instead, developing countries must reduce both domestic and external barriers to competition in the economy.

As for the developed countries, a concerted effort to assist adjustment programs in the debtor nations is essential not only for these countries but also for the developed countries themselves. Most importantly, industrial countries must keep their markets open to exports from the debtor nations, and should allow them to run some trade surpluses. The indebted countries need such access and surplus in order to be able to maintain and improve their debt-servicing capacity.

At the same time, new funds should be made available to debtor countries, in coordination with international commercial banks and multilateral institutions like the Fund and the World Bank. Developing debtor countries need some flexibility to institute long-term structural adjustment, and adjustment policies cannot be sustained without some investment and growth. In this regard, Secretary Baker's initiative seems like a very positive idea.

In addressing the Third World debt problems, we need to adopt a long-term approach, as the Baker Initiative suggests. We should avoid the temptation to apply a "quick fix" and accept the fact that it takes time to achieve results. In Korea, there is a saying that "the more you are in a hurry, the more you should go the roundabout way." The seriousness and immediacy of the debt problem tempts us to find a fast solution, but a less direct and slower method may be more effective.

In addition to providing continued market access and new funds, major industrial countries should cooperate for greater macroeconomic policy coordination among themselves. This is because imbalances among industrial countries have disruptive effects on the orderly growth of world trade and economy, thereby obstructing speedy structural adjustment for developing countries. Special attention should be paid to keeping international interest rates low and stabilizing exchange rate movements.

Much of what I have spoken of and what you've discussed at this conference bears witness to the growing interdependence of the world economy. The international trade network and global financial market make it certain that economic problems in one country will be felt, sooner or later, in others. Therefore, we must all be willing to cooperate and share the burden of adjustment.

In closing, let me note that Korea is still a developing country that faces many tasks for continuous structural adjustment. Korea has been successful so far in growth-oriented adjustment, having become a $100 billion economy and the twelfth largest trading country in the world whose exports now range from automobiles to semiconductors. Still, there is a great deal of work to be done. As a next step, we plan to launch a "growth and distribution-oriented structural adjustment program." If Korea is just as successful in this task, then I may be invited back to Washington for a similar symposium in another ten years, but perhaps not as a representative of a debt-ridden developing country.

Appendix

Other Participants in the Symposium

P. Arlman	*Executive Director, World Bank*
P. Aspe	*Under Secretary, Secretariat of Programing and Budget, Mexico*
M. Benachenhou	*Executive Director, World Bank*
A. Camarasa	*Executive Director, World Bank*
Q. Dai	*Executive Director, International Monetary Fund*
A. Donoso	*Executive Director, International Monetary Fund*
A. El-Kuwaiz	*Assistant Secretary General for Economic Affairs, Cooperation Council for the Arab States of the Gulf*
J. Fekete	*First Deputy President, National Bank of Hungary*
M. Finaish	*Executive Director, International Monetary Fund*
G. Grosche	*Executive Director, International Monetary Fund*
B. Hamdouch	*National Institute of Statistics and Applied Economics, Morocco*
U. Haxthausen	*Executive Director, World Bank*
J.E. Ismael	*Executive Director, International Monetary Fund*
M. Jembere	*Executive Director, World Bank*
A. Kafka	*Executive Director, International Monetary Fund*
Y. Kashiwagi	*Chairman, Bank of Tokyo*
R. Keating	*Executive Director, World Bank*
H. Lundstrom	*Executive Director, International Monetary Fund*
S. Mawakani	*Executive Director, International Monetary Fund*
A. Milongo	*Executive Director, World Bank*
Y.Á. Nimatallah	*Executive Director, International Monetary Fund*
G.A. Posthumus	*Executive Director, International Monetary Fund*
N.F. Potter	*Executive Director, World Bank*
M. Ramli Wajib	*Executive Director, World Bank*
C.R. Krishnaswamy Rao Sahib	*Executive Director, World Bank*
M. Rouge	*Financial Counsellor, Ministry of Economy, Finance and Privatization, France*
M. Rubio	*Executive Director, World Bank*
C.R. Rye	*Executive Director, International Monetary Fund*
G. Salehkhou	*Executive Director, International Monetary Fund*
J.E. Suraisry	*Executive Director, World Bank*
C. Thanachanan	*Deputy Governor, Bank of Thailand*
K. Yamaguchi	*Executive Director, World Bank*
K. Yamazaki	*Executive Director, International Monetary Fund*